Boundless Optimism

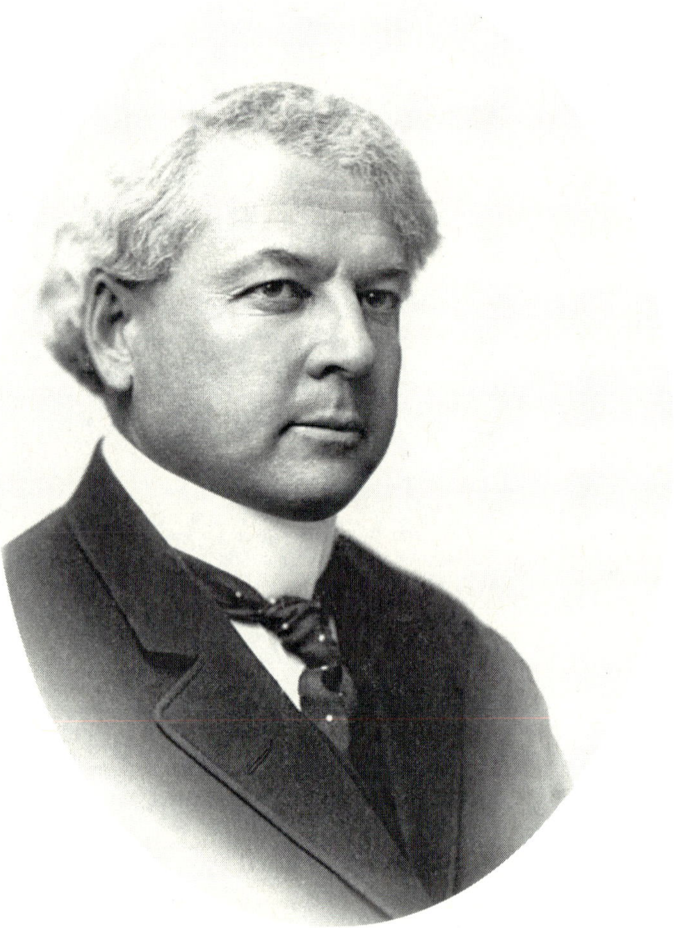

Boundless Optimism

Richard McBride's British Columbia

PATRICIA E. ROY

© UBC Press 2012

All rights reserved. No part of this publication may be reproduced, stored in a retrieval system, or transmitted, in any form or by any means, without prior written permission of the publisher, or, in Canada, in the case of photocopying or other reprographic copying, a licence from Access Copyright, www.accesscopyright.ca.

21 20 19 18 17 16 15 14 13 12   5 4 3 2 1

Printed in Canada on FSC-certified ancient-forest-free paper
(100% post-consumer recycled) that is processed chlorine- and acid-free.

Library and Archives Canada Cataloguing in Publication

Roy, Patricia
    Boundless optimism: Richard McBride's British Columbia / Patricia E. Roy.

Includes bibliographical references and index.
Issued also in electronic formats.
ISBN 978-0-7748-2388-3 (bound); ISBN 978-0-7748-2389-0 (pbk.)

    1. McBride, Richard, Sir, 1870-1917. 2. Prime ministers – British Columbia – Biography. 3. British Columbia – History – 1871-1918. 4. British Columbia – Politics and government – 1903-1916. I. Title.

FC3824.M25R69   2012 971.1'03092   C2012-904165-3

Canadä

UBC Press gratefully acknowledges the financial support for our publishing program of the Government of Canada (through the Canada Book Fund), the Canada Council for the Arts, and the British Columbia Arts Council.

Frontispiece: Richard McBride in his prime, c. 1915. Royal BC Museum, BC Archives, A-01410

UBC Press
The University of British Columbia
2029 West Mall
Vancouver, BC V6T 1Z2
www.ubcpress.ca

Contents

Illustrations / vi

Acknowledgments / xi

Introduction / 1

1 A Young British Columbian in a Young British Columbia / 11
2 "Dewdney Dick": In a Chaotic Legislature, 1898-1903 / 37
3 Establishing a Government, 1903-07 / 75
4 Toward a Wider Stage, 1907-09 / 119
5 Boundless Optimism, 1909-12 / 159
6 The Beginning of the End, 1912-14 / 209
7 Optimism Challenged, 1914-15 / 262
8 Respite in London / 300

Conclusion / 316

Epilogue / 321

Notes / 328

Note on Sources / 392

Index / 395

Illustrations

Map of British Columbia, c. 1915 / viii
"The Belle of Canada" / 3
"Glad-Hand Dick" / 9
New Westminster Provincial Jail / 13
British Columbia Penitentiary / 14
McBride as a small boy / 17
Richard and Margaret McBride / 32
View of Atlin / 42
McBride and acquaintances at Atlin / 44
"Leader of Obstruction" / 63
"The Mortgage on the Brain" / 98
"Not Lost, but Gone Before" / 102
"The Dog in the Manger Logger" / 105
"Piqued" / 116
"A Man Who Does Things" / 131
The home on the Gorge / 132
McBride's daughters / 133
McBride and friends on tour / 154

"The Need of the Hour" / 162

"Bowser is Willin'" / 186

BC dinner at the Savoy Hotel / 188

Margaret McBride in her presentation gown / 189

"Why Didn't He Think of That Before?" / 191

"A White Man's Burden" / 194

"Colossus of Roads" / 201

McBride, Bowser, and Thomas Abriel at Nakusp / 204

"Looted" / 216

"Miners; Lives of Secondary Consideration" / 227

Reception for McBride at Prince Rupert / 236

McBride at Port Alberni / 238

"Too Proud to Speak" / 245

"A Timely Query" / 260

HMS *Shearwater* and *CC1* and *CC2* / 263

"The Crisis in B.C." / 289

"An Edifying Spectacle" / 301

McBride leaving Victoria for the last time / 303

"The Smoke of Our Sacrifice" / 305

Elevation (metres above sea level)
2400
1800
1200
200 km
Lake Bennett
Yukon
Northwest Territories
Atlin
Cassiar
Alaska
Telegraph Creek
British
Columbia
Omineca
Peace River
Alberta
Stewart
Cottonwood Canyon
Portland Canal
Granby (Anyox)
Skeena Crossing
Hazelton
Nass R
Kitselas
Terrace
Smithers
Bulkley R
Grand Trunk Pacific Railway
Port Simpson
Kaien Island
Prince Rupert
Skeena R
Lakelse
Kitimat
Port Essington
Nechako R
Willow River
Queen Charlotte City
Ootsa Valley
Prince George (Fort George)
McBride
Yellowhead Pass
Quesnel
Barkerville
Cariboo
Soda Creek
Pacific Ocean
Quatsino
Vancouver Island
Fraser River
Revelstoke
Kamloops
Kelowna
Nelson
Cranbrook
Crow's Nest Pass
Vancouver
Victoria
Washington
Idaho
Montana

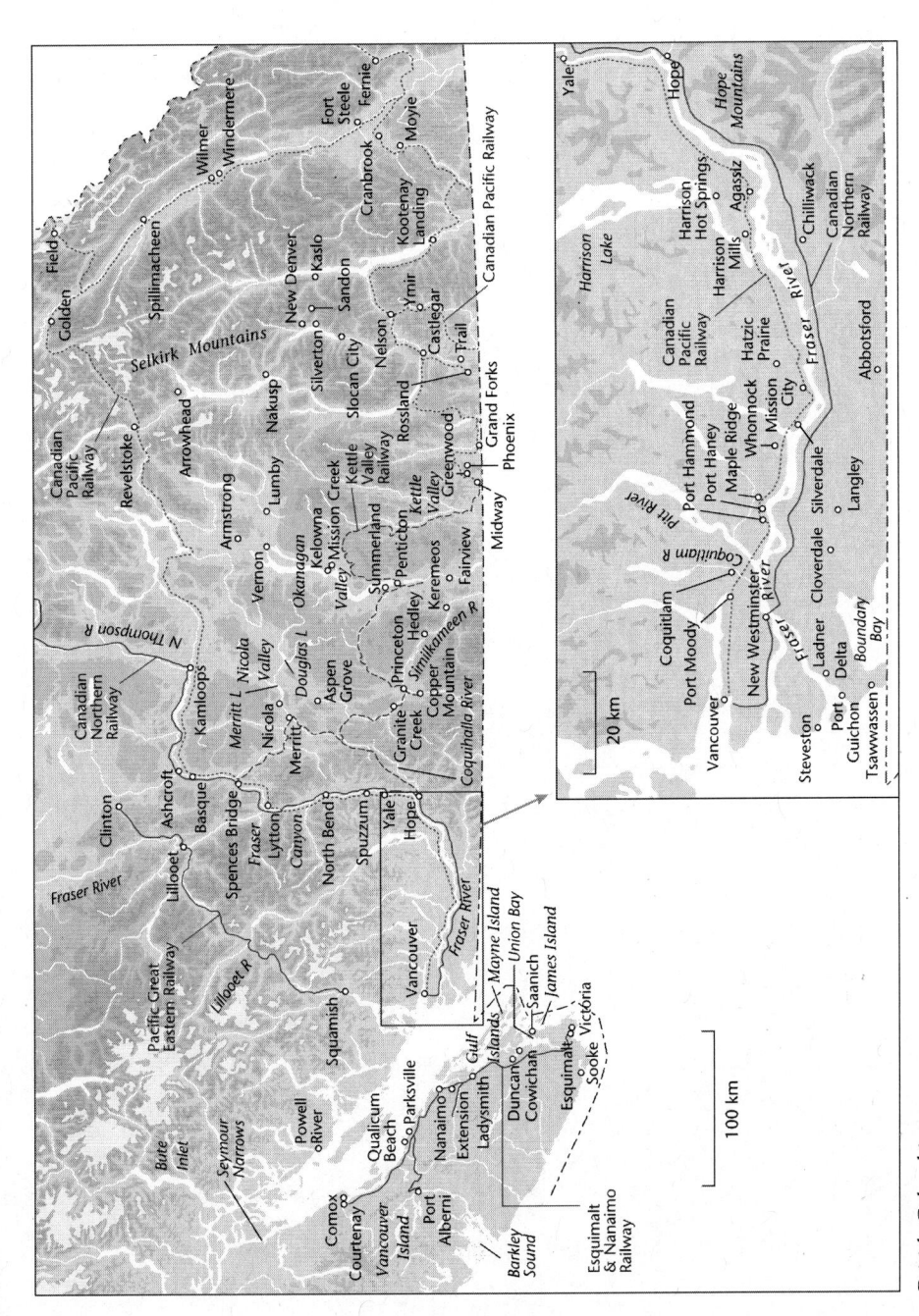

British Columbia, c. 1915

Acknowledgments

This biography began its life in 1958 as a term paper, "Sir Richard McBride as a Provincial Premier," in Margaret Ormsby's course on the history of Canada since 1867. She confirmed my interest in British Columbia history and took me on as both an honours and a PhD student. In 1958, I did not have the benefit of access to her *British Columbia: A History,* which was published a few days after the essay was due. The essay, however, introduced me to primary sources, notably the Charles Hibbert Tupper Papers in what was known as the Howay-Reid Room of the University of British Columbia Library. The essay also had the benefit of extremely thorough marking, although I was disappointed that the grade was only a B+. Several years later, I discovered that the anonymous marker was Brian R.D. Smith, who had been Ormsby's research assistant and was then completing his master's thesis on McBride.

Since then, I have explored many aspects of British Columbia's history, particularly its railways and electrical utilities, its attitudes toward Asians, and its relations with the federal government. In all of those subjects, McBride had a role. Most of my research was done in British Columbia at the Special Collections Division of the University of British Columbia Library, the Library of the University of Victoria, the City of Vancouver Archives, the Legislative Library of British Columbia, and especially at the British Columbia Archives. So many archivists and librarians in the province have assisted me over the years – some of them without knowing it – that I cannot thank them individually. However, I do want to make one exception. Just as I received the readers' reports with requests for more on McBride's private life, Don Bourdon of the British Columbia Archives let me know that McBride's family had just transferred a small but important collection of his papers, including his diaries, to the archives. I am grateful to him for letting me use them before the archives' staff processed them and, of course, to McBride's descendants for preserving them and making them available to historians.

McBride was more than a provincial figure. Thus, I have benefited from the work of Library and Archives Canada for making the records of the leading political figures of his time so very accessible not only in Ottawa but also by a program that some years ago distributed microfilm copies of the Wilfrid Laurier Papers to major depositories across the country. At the Dalhousie University Archives, I learned of McBride's career as a law student, and at the Churchill Library at Cambridge University I found material on his Better Terms fight in London and on Canada's naval debate. To all the archivists and librarians who preserved the documents and made them available, thank you. Thanks are also due to several friends and fellow British Columbia historians who have shared snippets about McBride found in their own research. They will find specific thanks in the notes.

Although we don't agree on all points, I thank Robert A.J. McDonald of the University of British Columbia for kindly reading early drafts of several chapters and sharing with me his vast knowledge of BC political history. My colleagues at the University of Victoria, Hamar Foster and Wendy Wickwire, offered valuable comments on a draft of my article on McBride's Indian policy, a portion of which appears in this volume. Thank you too to the anonymous readers for UBC Press who forced me to think harder about McBride's imperial role. Although this meant extra work, the book is better for it.

Last but certainly not least, thank you to my editor, Darcy Cullen, and to her associates at UBC Press, especially Anna Eberhard Friedlander and Holly Keller, who shepherded the manuscript through the production process. Special thanks also go to Deborah Kerr, the copy editor, whose careful and thoughtful attention helped me to clarify some matters and made the text more readable, and to Dianne Tiefensee, who proofread the text.

Boundless Optimism

Introduction

It is no mere dream of an enthusiast to see, in the not distant future, a province on the Pacific equal in population to the provinces of Ontario and Quebec, and – owing to its situation – a province of paramount importance to the Dominion and the Empire.

– Richard McBride, "Introduction," in
Adam Shortt and Arthur G. Doughty,
Canada and Its Provinces

Richard McBride was born in the colony of British Columbia on 15 December 1870, seven months before it became a Canadian province. He died at age forty-six in London, the heart of the British Empire. Throughout his life, the British connection remained strong – although he was a loyal Canadian, and above all, a British Columbian, he was also a keen imperialist. Ever the optimistic and steadfast believer in the prospects of his province, McBride wrote in 1913 that he believed British Columbia would soon be "a province of paramount importance to the Dominion and the Empire." Through the lens of his biography, one can see how a recent colony and distant part of the empire viewed its relationships with London and with its new political centre, Ottawa. At the same time, his biography sheds light on a formative period of British Columbia's history, when its population grew almost exponentially, much of its modern infrastructure was laid, and the party system was introduced to the provincial Legislature.

McBride, like many Canadians of his time, was a staunch British imperialist and very much a part of what has been called the "British World."[1] Although his parents were Irish immigrants, his father was from Northern Ireland and had served in the militia before emigrating to British North America. No doubt he instilled a respect for all things British in his children as he raised them in the Anglican faith. As a schoolboy and law student, Richard was exposed to British history.

Being a British imperialist at the turn of the twentieth century was a popular stance in English Canada, with the South African war strengthening "Canadian enthusiasm for the Empire."[2] British Columbia was no exception to this inclination. In 1900, when the headlines featured news from South Africa, McBride was among the provincial legislators who unanimously resolved that "British Columbia is British, and we desire the Home Government and the Government of Canada to know that we, as an integral part of the British Empire can be depended upon to assist by men and means, to uphold our Empire."[3] British Columbians boasted of their connection with the mother country. Although the Royal Navy had begun to withdraw from Esquimalt in 1906, its presence there was a visible reminder of the connection with Britain. Not surprisingly, cartoonists represented the province as an attractive young woman clad in a Union Jack skirt. To encourage the loyalty of young British Columbians, the Department of Education provided special lessons for schools on "Imperial Unity on Empire Day."[4]

Massive immigration reinforced British sentiment. As early as 1873, the provincial agent-general in London was promoting immigration by such means as publishing "information for emigrants," but not until McBride's time in public life did Britons pour into British Columbia.[5] Whereas those born in Britain or its possessions numbered 31,982 in 1901, that number had risen to 116,529 by 1911, at which point they formed 34 percent of the province's white population. And they were still coming. In the spring of 1913, the *Vancouver Daily News-Advertiser* reported that large numbers of immigrants from the "old country" were arriving daily and that five hundred from England and Scotland had arrived in Vancouver during a single week.[6] Moreover, many of the Canadian-born, like McBride, were the offspring of British-born parents.[7]

Not only did British Columbia want British immigrants, but like other Canadian provinces, it sought and received British investment. Indeed, Canada was the main beneficiary of British capital exports between 1904

THE BELLE OF CANADA IMPRESSES THE WHOLE WORLD.

British Columbia was proud of its growth, its British heritage, and its Canadian identity. *Saturday Sunset*, 21 September 1907, cartoonist, N.H. Hawkins.

and 1914, much of which came to British Columbia.[8] McBride's era was the epitome of what has been called the "Angloboom" that in many places in the British Empire drove the "Progress Industry" – "the massive activity generated by the process of migration itself, and by the rapid creation of infrastructure, notably transport infrastructure."[9] British investors put money into mining, forestry, and land companies. Bonds sold in London financed most of the new railways, municipal utilities, and the British Columbia Electric Railway Company, which provided the street railway services as well as electricity and gas in Greater Vancouver and Victoria. After the pre-war boom collapsed in 1913, McBride increasingly spent time in London, endeavouring to raise money for the new railways and to negotiate franchises and fares with the BC Electric. British investors, including some who were personally associated with McBride, also speculated in BC real estate.

The Week, a local magazine, was only slightly exaggerating when in 1913 it declared, "There is not in Canada today a more truly British and Imperial statesman than Sir Richard McBride."[10] McBride's annual visits to London – some of them of an extended duration – began in 1907 when he first met such prominent Britons as Winston Churchill and the Canadian ex-patriate Hamar Greenwood. With his bonhomie, he easily formed personal as well as political friendships that strengthened his imperial sentiments. As early as 1902, he had spoken of imperial federation, a scheme that might have led to representation of the colonies in the British Parliament and common imperial tariff and defence policies; later he toyed with the idea of seeking a seat at Westminster. As the Anglo-German naval race accelerated, McBride's initial concern was the defence of British Columbia, but Churchill convinced him that a Canadian cash contribution to Britain's navy would be a more effective means of defence. In Canada, McBride argued so strenuously in favour of this that he was granted a knighthood, that imperial imprimatur so coveted by many colonial politicians. London became his refuge when scandal, failing health, fading popularity, and a declining economy made life in Victoria difficult.

Although he was a keen imperialist, McBride was also a loyal Canadian. In October 1913, he told Toronto's Empire Club that "we are true and loyal Canadians, and that we feel in our heart of hearts – that the best way to reach the superlative degree of loyalty of this kind is to be true and loyal Britishers as well."[11] Like a true colonial, he appealed to London when the federal government sought an amendment to the British North America Act, a British statute, to make an unsatisfactory response to his demand for Better Terms, a more generous federal subsidy, part of a "final and unalterable" settlement of dominion-provincial financial relations and when Ottawa disallowed provincial laws designed to halt Asian immigration. He was not alone among provincial premiers in seeking higher subsidies, but he argued that, because British Columbia's rugged topography scattered settlement and increased the cost of providing transportation facilities and other services, the province had a unique claim on the nation. Yet, he was always a loyal Canadian.

His campaign for Better Terms made him a national figure. Some federal Conservatives urged him to come to Ottawa to succeed Robert L. Borden as leader of the Opposition. Once the federal Conservatives were elected in 1911, Borden invited him to join the cabinet. McBride had campaigned hard for the Conservatives in that election and fought reciprocity, a form of free trade with the United States, because of its possible economic impact on BC industries and his fear that it would endanger Canada's British connection. Paradoxically, he welcomed American investors in the forest industry.

McBride's first loyalty was to British Columbia, whose population was rapidly growing. With the construction and completion of the Canadian Pacific Railway, the population doubled from 50,000 in 1881 to 100,000 in 1891, almost doubled again during the 1890s, and more than doubled to almost 400,000 by 1911.[12] Throughout this time, the size of the Native population changed little, which encouraged McBride and others to seek to reallocate Indian reserves so that reserve land adjacent to cities could be made available for industrial development by the white newcomers. The province, however, was cosmopolitan, with Asians forming 7.8 percent of the population in 1911. Like their contemporaries elsewhere in Canada, in the United States, and in other British dominions, notably Australia and New Zealand, who wanted to keep their countries white, McBride and British Columbians firmly opposed Asian immigration. In addition, British Columbia had a variety of European immigrants, including members of the Russian-speaking Doukhobor sect who settled in the southeastern part of the province. McBride paid little attention to the Europeans, who generally had a low profile, but did have a royal commission investigate the Doukhobors.

As Michael Dawson noted in his study of tourism in the province, whereas much North American literature relating to modernity focuses on "the search for *order*," the evidence from British Columbia suggests that North Americans were equally determined to search for *"opportunity."*[13] McBride had incredibly good luck in the timing of his accession to office. The silver, lead, and zinc mines of the Kootenays and the copper mines of the Boundary District, which had boomed since the late 1890s, drew investors' attention to the province and contributed to provincial coffers. In the case of copper, for example, the province produced $875,000 worth in 1898; by 1907, that figure was $8.2 million.[14] The mining developments inspired demands for a railway to link the coast with the Kootenays.

Responding to them had put McBride's unstable predecessor governments deeply into debt for railway subsidies without providing a railway. Meanwhile, the tripling of the population of the Prairie provinces between 1901 and 1911 created an "almost insatiable" demand for BC lumber and lumber products, creating jobs and, through various lease and licence fees, contributing to the government's revenues.[15] McBride was keen to encourage development in these primary industries and agriculture, although, with some reason, critics accused his government of squandering provincial resources.

McBride would have recoiled at the label of liberal. Yet, his interests fit well into what Ian McKay has defined as the classic liberal order in Canada.[16] He encouraged industrial development and private investment, and he favoured a limited state that concerned itself mainly with preserving law and order, providing education and a few social services, maintaining a strong attachment to the British constitution, and protecting civil and political liberties but excluding some by race or gender from political debate. Nevertheless, as historian Robert McDonald has noted, in the case of British Columbia, working-class liberalism must be taken into account. Certainly, McBride was aware of this, particularly during his first administration when he relied on the support of two Socialist and one Labour member of the Legislature.[17] By 1909, Socialist/Labour members formed the official Opposition but with only two members. Although they traditionally won about 12 percent of the popular vote province-wide, their strength was largely confined to the mining regions of Vancouver Island and the Kootenays and to some areas in Vancouver, but the city was a single multi-member constituency, so left-wing voters had little chance of electing anyone. Although McBride worked with capitalists, notably William Mackenzie and Donald Mann, promoters of the Canadian Northern Railway, he never expected that the province would have to honour the bond guarantees it gave to the Canadian Northern and other railways. Moreover, he was sympathetic to the working man. Much of the limited legislation he introduced while serving as minister of mines in the Dunsmuir government was designed to improve the working conditions of the miners; it also annoyed some mine operators. A decade later, however, he had little sympathy for striking Vancouver Island coal miners.

McBride was fortunate in his mentors. He was the protege of Lieutenant-Governor Sir Henri Joly de Lotbinière, whom Prime Minister Wilfrid Laurier specially selected to impose order on British Columbia's political chaos, which saw a lieutenant-governor dismissed and four different premiers in three years. Sir Henri deliberately chose McBride as premier in 1903, required him to introduce party government, and carefully tutored him in the art of governance. With the help of a growing economy, McBride's first minister of finance, Robert Tatlow, put the provincial financial house in order, kept a tight rein on government projects, and forbade railway subsidies.

Once the province showed a surplus on its annual accounts, it was difficult to resist calls for more railways that would open new regions, keep American railways from draining off the trade of the mining districts, and compete with the Canadian Pacific Railway. That better transportation facilities were necessary was abundantly evident to McBride as his regular tours of the province often fell behind schedule because of gaps in the railway system and poor roads. Those journeys reflected and reinforced his awareness that British Columbia extended beyond its southwest corner. Thus, his railway plans included at least the promise of a railway line for many of its regions. With the benefit of the historian's twenty-twenty hindsight, it is clear that he was overly optimistic in believing that simply guaranteeing the bonds of new railway companies would produce new lines without any cost to provincial taxpayers. Although Tatlow and another cabinet minister, F.J. Fulton, thought his railway plans overly ambitious, and both resigned in 1909, few other British Columbians agreed; they showed their support by giving McBride and his Conservatives overwhelming majorities in the 1909 and 1912 elections. Nevertheless, the railways were eventually completed and still operate today, as do other provincial institutions that were created at the time, such as the University of British Columbia. Prosperity certainly aided McBride politically, but his personal attributes – good looks, a "glad hand," and a genuine interest in people – helped him capture the public imagination in British Columbia. Shortly before he retired, the sometimes sycophantic journal *The Week* commented, "His commanding personality, his magnetism, and his tact, constitute him an ideal leader."[18]

His travels through the province allowed him to exploit these assets. On his provincial tours and journeys abroad, Lawrence Macrae, his secretary, often accompanied him and sent dispatches to Conservative newspapers so that those who could not see McBride could read of his doings. As early as 1902, when McBride was only thirty-one, the *Victoria Times* commented, "Nature has done much to assist Mr. McBride, for it has endowed him with a fair presence and a mane of curly grey hair, which lends him a distinguished appearance. A fine flow of animal spirits, and an urbanity and good nature which nothing can disturb have also assisted him materially." It noted that the chief complaint against him was "that he is very young."[19] Years later, people who had been children or young adults during the McBride era could not remember much detail about him apart from his handsome appearance.[20]

Although his striking physique lent credibility on the hustings, there was more to McBride than good looks. He paid attention to individual people. A legislative reporter observed that he never failed "to give credit to those of his colleagues or of his supporters who are associated with him in matters of public interest or enterprise." It was said that he had a "little black book" in which he jotted down names, so that when he chanced to re-encounter a "Mrs. Jones," he could then ask how her husband, Harry, was. He personally apologized to a Ladysmith widow for the "inconvenience and unpleasantness" caused by the visit of a provincial constable in 1915. The woman, who had suffered a stroke, had not fully paid for her farm. Of her three sons, one was a boy, another was in poor health, and the eldest was serving overseas. Due to a misunderstanding, she had not realized that the constable had come to assist in securing a separation allowance for her. McBride also had an uncanny ability to graciously treat those seeking favours. One story referred to a municipal delegation from South Vancouver who came to Victoria to meet McBride and William J. Bowser, his law school classmate, long-time attorney general, and source of problems at the end of his career. The members of the delegation left happy, but while taking the boat back to Vancouver, they began to write a report on their achievement and realized that they had heard nothing concrete. "Every time Dick would say he would do something, Bowser would turn them off. Dick was a 'glad hander.'"[21] He was always polite. When visitors overstayed their welcome, he pressed a buzzer under his desk, which rang in a nearby office. The official there would telephone and ask "Relief?" McBride would answer, "Yes, I'll be up in just a moment" and would apologize for having to leave to discuss an important matter in cabinet.[22]

As well as showing himself to the electorate and demonstrating his personal interest in it, McBride recognized the importance of patronage in keeping voters happy. Although concrete evidence of party funding is slim, ample material reveals that his government secured the good will of newspapers, the sole means of mass communication, by placing its advertising only with those that supported it. Evidence of the extent of McBride's personal investments in newspapers is scanty, but at times he had shares in the *Revelstoke Mail-Herald* and the *New Westminster British Columbian*.[23]

"Glad Hand Dick" at work. McBride was friendly to all, including women, to whom he denied the right to vote. Royal BC Museum, BC Archives, D-05726.

From time to time, McBride endeavoured to influence editorial policy. When the usually friendly *Nelson Daily News* attacked his government in connection with the suspension of a local teacher, McBride advised its editor "to adopt a more amicable policy." He did not desire "slavish support," since independent support was best, but he did not want attacks either.[24] As for the Liberal press, he declared at the 1914 Conservative convention that "the Grit papers of British Columbia were not fit to send back east because of the lugubrious character of their criticism of the government."[25] Criticisms of his policies were never absent but became sharper and more frequent after the boom waned, funds to complete the railways or build a university campus became scarce, and local financial institutions failed.

McBride's personality remained his strongest asset. As his great friend the *Colonist* newspaper observed in November 1914 near the end of his career, "His personality induces all who come in contact with him with a measure of the optimism that is peculiarly his own."[26] The optimism that served him so well in good times was a major cause of his downfall. McBride was a super-salesman and promoter of his native province, but as his personal finances also demonstrated, he was a prodigal son.

Shortly before he resigned, McBride wrote to S.J. Gothard, a sometime labour activist and long-time friend. As well as illustrating that McBride's friendships cut across political lines, the letter neatly summarized his political philosophy, which was that of a practical politician, not a political theorist: "For my own part, I have tried to do my little best and to serve the Province first and the party next. Possibly I may have attempted too much in the end, however, all of the policies I have espoused are bound to reflect creditably on the country."[27] The pages that follow will assess that claim.

I

A Young British Columbian in a Young British Columbia

British Columbia is the wealthiest and most progressive Province in the whole Dominion and [has] ... a great future before it. From childhood upwards he had noticed, and with great pride, the strides the province was taking.

– Vancouver World, *reporting on a McBride speech given at Mission, BC, 4 June 1898*

In 1859, the Royal Engineers, who had come to help secure the new gold colony of British Columbia for Britain, selected the site that became New Westminster, its capital. From its steep tree-covered slopes on the north side of the Fraser River, they could see the river mouth and its delta, the Strait of Georgia, and Vancouver Island to the west; the surrounding forest and the Coast Mountains to the east; and potential attackers from the United States, which lay about twenty miles to the south. The river was navigable for almost another hundred miles inland to Yale, the main point of entry to the Fraser River gold fields, but was not easily accessible to ocean-going vessels. New Westminster merchants served farmers and fishermen in the lower Fraser Valley but could not compete effectively with their counterparts in Victoria, the capital of the older colony, Vancouver Island, for the business of the gold fields. Thus, Victoria became a transhipment point, where cargoes were unloaded from deep-sea vessels and transferred to shallower draft boats that could navigate the river. Goods shipped through Victoria could enter the Mainland colony duty free. To the dismay of New Westminster residents, their governor and many civil servants preferred to live in Victoria. Not until 1864 did the British government give British Columbia its own governor in the person of Frederick Seymour. By then, the gold rush was fading, and the colony was deeply in debt. Two years later, with the intent of saving money, the British government merged the two colonies under the name British Columbia. The bitter commercial and political rivals, Victoria and New Westminster, briefly shared the title of capital, but in 1868, the islanders, who dominated the Legislative Council, made Victoria the permanent capital. Though Governor Seymour liked New Westminster, he and most of his officials soon moved to Victoria.

In the words of Dr. J.S. Helmcken, a Victorian who campaigned to have his city designated as capital, New Westminster was "a very small place – a village, with virtually one street along the water front, with three or four good buildings." In 1870, the population of the district consisted of 1,291 whites, of whom 891 were males and 401 were females, 37 "coloureds," 27 Chinese, and about 300 Native Indians.[1] Among the buildings were three sawmills, a grist mill, a distillery, the deserted Government House at Sapperton, the original settlement of the Royal Engineers, and a jail serving the entire Mainland.

Although some colonial civil servants moved to Victoria, Arthur Hill McBride reversed the trend. A native of County Down, Ireland, McBride served five years in the Royal South Down Militia before coming to North America in about 1859. After spending time in eastern Canada and California, he reached the Cariboo in 1863 and briefly mined on Williams and Lightning Creeks. In Victoria he joined the colonial police service and acquired a reputation as "a faithful and efficient officer."[2] When Captain Pritchard, the warden of the New Westminster jail, died in 1870, McBride, a Victoria jailer, accepted the position, which meant a promotion and an annual salary of $1,058.[3] The New Westminster jail appeared "to have been built with care," and McBride managed it well, with economy and cleanliness. It usually housed twelve to twenty inmates who were serving sentences of varying terms and a few lunatics as the colony had no insane asylum. McBride joined in the activities of his new home. A good marksman, he was drill sergeant for the Volunteer Rifle Corps, whose members thought so well of him that, on his retirement, they gave him "a handsome present" as "a mark of their esteem."[4] When the colony became a province, McBride became a provincial civil servant.

The people of New Westminster had anticipated that Confederation would bring responsible government, a transcontinental railway, and a

The New Westminster Provincial Jail. McBride's father was warden from 1870, when it was the colonial jail, until he moved to the British Columbia Penitentiary. Royal BC Museum, BC Archives, A-03353.

share of federal institutions. They expected to be "the most important part of the Dominion." Soon after Confederation, Hector Langevin, the federal minister of public works, came to assess the province's needs. He noted overcrowding in the provincial jails. The Terms of Union by which British Columbia had entered Confederation required the federal government to provide penitentiary services, so Ottawa paid the province to look after prisoners serving sentences of two years or more. Without hesitation, Langevin recommended building a penitentiary at New Westminster, where, "at what is called the Camp, some few minutes' walk from the centre of town, and on the bank of the Fraser River, [there is] a considerable piece of land, which is public property." The abandoned governor's residence could become the director's home, and prisoners could be easily transported by steamer from Victoria or from Yale, the start of the Cariboo Road. Construction problems delayed the opening of the penitentiary until 1878.[5]

The Liberal government of Alexander Mackenzie appointed McBride as first warden of the British Columbia Penitentiary at a salary of $1,200

The British Columbia Penitentiary as seen from the Fraser River, c. 1890. The white house on the river bank may be the warden's home. Royal BC Museum, BC Archives, A-03357.

per year, the same amount he had earned as provincial jailer. His appointment upset some of the old colonial establishment, including Senators C.F. Cornwall, R.W.W. Carrall, and W.J. Macdonald, former lieutenant-governor J.W. Trutch, and the judges of the Supreme Court. For three years, they had lobbied for Captain Richard Layton, who had served both lieutenant-governors as private secretary. In the Senate they claimed that McBride was "incompetent" and lacked the capacity and education to serve as warden. The New Westminster press, happy with McBride's "first-class record" as jailer, made no comment.[6]

McBride's task was not easy. An obvious problem, a poorly constructed and inadequately drained building, was largely overcome with the help of convict labour. Managing a federal institution so many miles from Ottawa, however, was made difficult by the inspector of penitentiaries, J.G. Moylan, who rarely visited but who instructed McBride "to do nothing without consulting" Moylan's protege, deputy warden James Fitzsimmons. In short, McBride had the title, the prestige, and the salary of the wardenship but little authority. The situation was problematic, but the amiable McBride survived for almost fifteen years.[7] Moylan's failure to visit and his later actions may have influenced Richard McBride's view of Ottawa.

Among the warden's duties was entertaining national visitors. When the governor general and Princess Louise visited New Westminster in 1882, McBride was part of the reception committee; with the help of uniformed guards, he kept order among the large number of Indians who played a prominent role in the vice-regal reception.[8] On 9 November 1889, he again hosted a visiting governor general, but his real glory had come in August 1886, when Sir John and Lady Macdonald toured the specially decorated buildings and grounds. Flags were hung on telephone poles in front of the grounds, and although the lights on a welcoming arch had dimmed by the time the prime minister arrived, the greetings "Hail to the Chief" and "A Thousand Welcomes" were still clear. By then, McBride and his deputy warden were living in apartments on the penitentiary grounds.[9] In 1890, when the Department of Public Works built a new house for the warden, the McBride family moved to Fraser View Villa.[10]

Their residence in the Villa was relatively brief. On several occasions in the 1880s, following allegations of mismanagement, the federal government investigated but found no evidence of wrongdoing at the penitentiary. However, when Moylan visited in 1892, he told McBride that "owing to his state of health and other causes," he would be superannuated, but this did not occur immediately. So much mud was thrown in the campaign to be McBride's successor as warden that the federal government suspended McBride and Fitzsimmons, appointed an acting warden, and established a royal commission under Mr. Justice Drake to investigate the administration of the penitentiary. The commission, which sat in June 1894, heard of rules and regulations being ignored, of friction between the deputy warden and other officers, and of irregularities in recording the disposition of the penitentiary farm's produce, especially to a neighbouring Roman Catholic orphanage. The commission recognized that McBride was "only the nominal head," and he emerged relatively unscathed. The federal government granted him superannuation (a pension), a decision that even the *British Columbian,* a regular critic of the penitentiary administration, approved.[11]

Arthur McBride was a Presbyterian and a member of the Orange Order, but on 8 November 1865, he had married a Roman Catholic, Mary D'Arcy, who was a month short of her nineteenth birthday.[12] A native of Limerick, Ireland, she had come to British North America in 1862.[13] Her "mixed marriage" to McBride might have created social tensions in eastern Canada, but it had little effect in British Columbia, which may explain why the wedding, conducted by a Catholic priest in Victoria, was not reported in the press.[14] Although Arthur pledged that his children would "be brought up in the Catholic Church," they were baptized as Anglicans.[15] Arthur listed himself as a Presbyterian and Mary as a Roman Catholic in the decennial censuses, but when he died in 1909, an Anglican cleric officiated at the funeral; his obituary noted that he was an "Episcopalian" who often attended the Presbyterian church.[16] Mary remained a Catholic and was buried from St. Peter's Roman Catholic Church in New Westminster in 1931. Richard McBride later told his British friend T.P. O'Connor of his parents' good-natured religious rivalry: on 12 July, his father posted a picture of William of Orange; on 15 August, the feast of the Assumption, his mother posted a picture of the Blessed Virgin Mary![17] On another occasion, Richard "convulsed his audience" as he responded to a heckler by "narrating in the raciest fashion how his father had been a ferocious Orangeman from the North of Ireland and his mother an equally determined Catholic from the South with the result that he had imbibed in equal measure the views of both, and had declined ever since to make a choice between them."[18] As a politician, he pleased both Methodists and Presbyterians in 1914 by chairing in Victoria a mass meeting of the Laymen's Missionary Association, an interdenominational Protestant group, and voicing sympathy for the movement that "presented a united front to

A Young British Columbian in a Young British Columbia 17

A very young Richard McBride. Royal BC Museum, BC Archives, B-01628.

the heathen of the world" and "promoted unity among the branches of the Christian church." He expressed the hope that, one day, "even the Roman Catholic church might line up with others in this work."[19]

By the summer of 1870, when they moved to New Westminster, Arthur and Mary had two children, Gertrude (Gert) aged three and William Leonard (Willie), who was a year and a half. In addition, Mary was pregnant with Richard, who was born on 15 December 1870, a little more than seven months before British Columbia became a province of Canada. Though he was born in mid-December, the weather was so mild and sunny that the pear trees were in full bloom, and at Christmas, some residents decorated their homes with roses from their gardens. A third son, Edward German, was born on 13 April 1875. A fourth son, Thomas Darcy, born on 15 November 1883, died the same day, but a daughter, Mary Dorothea (Dodo), born on 26 August 1885, outlived her siblings.[20]

The McBride children participated fully in community events including the annual May Day, with its maypole dancing, sports, and games. Although Warden McBride refused to let the organizers use the penitentiary grounds lest it have a bad effect on the prisoners, Gertrude was May Queen in 1877, and Dorothea was a maid of honour in 1897. Years later, Dick fondly recalled the British-inspired May Day festivities of his boyhood. According to family lore, as a boy he was fond of music and dancing but went to his first dance only after his father threatened "to have him carried there if he didn't go peaceably."[21]

The boys attended the local public school. Initially, it was "totally inadequate for the health, comfort and convenience of the pupils," but the school moved to a two-story building in August 1882. By then, Dick was in the senior boys' class. At the Christmas closing exercises, he was one of seven boys who were rewarded for perfect attendance. He participated in demonstrations of knowledge of reading, spelling, dictation, grammar, mental and written arithmetic, geography, ancient and modern history, and callisthenics, and, with his classmates, entertained the visitors with "a serpentine march." Buoyed by recent British military successes in Egypt and their sense of patriotism, they accompanied the march with their own parody of an American Civil War song:

Tramp, tramp, tramp, the boys are marching
Cheer up comrades, people smile, people smile
We did drive the Egyptian back
For beneath the Union Jack,
In the region of the mighty, mighty Nile.

Dick was both a good scholar and a mischief maker. Many years later, Judge McInnes recalled that, as boys, he and Dick "were always getting into scrapes together."[22]

In the fall of 1883, Dick was ready for high school, but New Westminster did not have a public one. Many British Columbians believed that high school education should not be free of charge; the only free high school was in Victoria. When New Westminster residents complained of this unfairness, the provincial government considered withdrawing all high school grants. New Westminster did have a private non-sectarian institution, which was opened in January 1881 by Reverend Ebenezer Robson, a Methodist, and others, who appointed H.M. Stramberg, a graduate of Dalhousie University, as principal. The school supported itself with tuition fees of up to sixty dollars per year and donations. In August 1883, a lack of funds forced Stramberg to close the Collegiate and High School, which was replaced with tutoring in high school subjects from 3:00 to 5:00 P.M. daily, except Sunday, "so that pupils, by taking at the public schools in the forenoon, the studies common to both public and high schools, and attending these classes in the afternoon, may receive the full benefit of an ordinary high school course." For this part-time instruction, students paid three dollars per month. It was better than no high school but did not satisfy those who desired a superior education for their children. Some parents sent their children to eastern Canada or to private schools. Gertrude attended Brantford Ladies College for a year; the McBride boys went to Lorne College, an Anglican school on the grounds of St. Mary's Church, which, conveniently, was adjacent to the penitentiary.[23]

Lorne College advertised itself as "a school for the Higher Education of Boys and Young Men"; its curriculum included classical and mercantile courses as preparation for university, medical, law, and military school entrance examinations and for business life. It had a commodious building for its twenty students but was so deficient in maps, globes, and suitable desks that at the end of the 1885 school year, the boys were asked to collect $7.50 each to buy a suitable desk and chair. This was in addition to tuition fees of $1.00 per week, $2.00 per year for fuel, and extra fees for tuition in German and French. The school encouraged academic work. Principal Reverend C.J. Brenton believed in encouraging and rewarding "a spirit of healthful competition" because a boy who won prizes would probably "win some of the prizes of life." Dick thrived. At the end of his first year, he ranked a close second in the Collegiate Department, won a volume of Aesop's Fables as the archdeacon of Columbia's prize for mathematics, and recited from Vergil in Latin at the closing ceremonies. In his second year he stood first in the Collegiate Department and ranked first in sacred studies, Latin, French, algebra, geometry, and grammar; Edward led the junior department; and Leonard was second in Latin and first in bookkeeping.[24]

The Anglican tradition suited the boys well, for they had gone to the Holy Trinity Anglican Sunday School, which Dick attended from ages five to ten. His teacher, the daughter of Archdeacon Woods, remembered him as "a clever boy ... and a good boy" with "strong views and opinions ... on religious and political questions." Although Mary sent Gertrude to St. Ann's Academy, a Roman Catholic school, for singing lessons, she did not insist that her children be educated in her own faith. In fact, her brother, Edward F. D'Arcy, the 1891 census taker, recorded all the children as Presbyterians. As adults, Gertrude, Leonard, and Edward were members of Holy Trinity Anglican Church, whereas Dick followed his wife's Presbyterian faith. Denominational differences were not important for him; his long-time secretary recalled years later that "his real religion ... was true Christianity." If true Christianity meant loving one's neighbour, Dick learned it at home. His mother had a reputation for her hospitality. The three boys so often brought friends home that she baked cakes in a milk pan and offered home baking and milk to delivery boys.[25]

Her sons, who got along well, worked in summer at Holbrook's cannery. A contemporary recalled, "They tallied fish from the boats as they were unloaded, kept time for Indians and Chinese and such jobs." Dick told a friend that the Chinese would mark the cans that contained salmon bellies only, the best part of the fish, so they could retrieve them for their own use after the filled cans had been washed and steamed in the retorts.[26]

Despite this seasonal work, the boys had time for fun. According to their younger sister, Dodo, they were excused from household chores. Dick had little experience with team sports apart from a brief stint with a Sapperton junior cricket team that was badly defeated by a New Westminster rival, but he loved the outdoors, a trait he probably learned from his father. He could "swim like a fish," was "an expert with a boat or canoe," usually owned one or two canoes, and would row twenty miles to Pitt Lake to camp and fish. Sometimes, with his brother and other boys, he left home at 4:00 or 5:00 A.M., tramping several miles up the Fraser River to go fishing. At other times, the boys would poach and secure a bag of ducks. He got "to know the men of the woods and Indians," a friend recalled. As premier, he conversed in Chinook with Fraser Valley Indians, who regarded him as "white chief."[27]

The boys' liking for the outdoors once created a *cause célèbre*. Shortly after their evening dinner on Saturday, 20 June 1885, Leonard, Dick, and Eddie went to nearby Brunette Creek, "a favorite resort of youthful bathers," where ladies were sometimes "confronted unexpectedly by humanity clad in the scanty robe which nature supplies." That day, when an unusually large number of boys and young men partook of the swimming hole, Mrs. A.M. Herring, the wife of a druggist, was hosting an all-day picnic for some female friends and their children. The McBride boys waited for the party to move off, but after a while, Dick said to Mrs. Herring, "Will you please leave the bridge, we want to bathe." She declined to move. As Leonard recounted, "If she had not two or three boys of her own, I should have thought that she was anxious to see what kind of looking animals boys were, with their clothes off." He took off his coat, vest, and two shirts.

Ten minutes after Mrs. Herring left the bridge, he unbuttoned his pants. Unfortunately, Mrs. Clarence DeBeck was still present about twenty feet away. She left in "disgust." Three days later, her husband, a lumber merchant, laid a charge against Leonard for indecently exposing his person "with intent to insult certain females." When DeBeck retained the city's three lawyers, A.J. McColl, Gordon Corbould, and Norman Bole, the McBrides were forced to import Theodore Davie from Victoria to defend themselves. Every justice of the peace in the district was invited to preside in the Police Court, and many spectators gathered long before the court met at 7:00 P.M. Arguing for the plaintiff, Bole accused the eldest McBride boy of committing "at least, a grossly unmanly and improper act," but he failed to impress the bench. As Davie rose for the defence, the justices dismissed the case. Davie tried to keep it going so that Leonard could present his side and perhaps win costs but to no avail. To defend his name, Leonard placed cards in the *British Columbian* and the *Mainland Guardian* with his version of the story. The incident cost a few dollars in legal expenses but did no harm to the boys' reputations.[28] A few weeks later, Lorne College publicized their academic successes.

The boys, however, did not return to the college. The provincial government had relented, and in August 1884, it began to support a New Westminster high school. Forty students enrolled, and the average attendance was twenty-seven. Stramberg, who taught all the subjects, complained to S.D. Pope, the provincial superintendent of education, of the impossibility "in the time at my disposal, to teach according to scientific methods all the subjects embraced in the curriculum ... This attempt to perform, unaided, the multifarious work devolving upon me – such as preparing students for matriculation in arts, medicine and law, as well as giving prospective teachers some knowledge of their profession – was only moderately successful." Nevertheless, the McBride family took advantage of the new school. Gertrude passed the teachers' examinations for a third class grade A certificate and secured an appointment to teach the primary grade in the Boys' School.[29] An accomplished singer, she continued to perform at local concerts even after her marriage to William Allison of the Bank of British Columbia in October 1892.

Under the guidance of Stramberg, his "faithful school master," Dick excelled. He won the governor general's bronze medal for heading the school at the midsummer exams in 1886 and at the following Christmas examinations, a fact that was especially commended because he was also studying for the matriculation exams of McGill University. To complete the high school requirements, he had to demonstrate some mastery of English, "generally the formation of a good English style"; mathematics including arithmetic, algebra, and Euclid; French, through such texts as Voltaire's *Histoire du Charles XII;* ancient and modern geography; bookkeeping; natural science; and Roman, Greek, and English history. In the latter subject, where the emphasis was on recall, he prepared to answer such questions as "Name the three greatest Plantagenets," "Give Historical references to the Bloody Statutes and Bloody Assizes," and "Describe five great battles of the present century." Canadian history did not appear in the curriculum until the year after Dick completed his studies, but there was a nod to Canada in the question "How long has Canada been a British possession?"[30] Young British Columbians were being trained to be proud Britishers.

On 28 August 1887, Dick McBride, age sixteen, boarded the newly completed Canadian Pacific Railway (CPR) and left New Westminster on a five-day trip to Halifax, where four years earlier Dalhousie had established the only university law school in the common law provinces. The school was proud of its September 1887 entering class. With twenty students, it was one of the largest and, for the first time, included students from outside the Maritimes – namely, British Columbia. Among McBride's classmates were Frederic W. Howay, who was three years older and had taught school at Canoe Pass on the lower Fraser River after attending the New Westminster High School, and Nova Scotian Robie L. Reid, who had taught in the Fraser Valley for several years to finance his studies. Tuition for the three-year course was forty dollars per annum plus estimated additional costs of twenty dollars for books and a hundred dollars for board for the school year.[31]

To accommodate Dean R.C. Weldon, the only full-time faculty member and the recently elected Conservative MP for Albert County, New Brunswick, the academic year began in September rather than November, which meant that students would complete twenty-one weeks of study by February, when Weldon left for Ottawa. Although a few "general" students followed the old program of articling and taking classes on the side, regular students were required to attend classes and were not permitted to engage in office work during the session. The curriculum was distinguished by its mix of "political science, cultural or public law ... and professional or strictly legal subjects." First-year students studied real property, crimes, contracts, torts, and constitutional history, which was undoubtedly British constitutional history. Initially, McBride was only moderately successful as a student. Whereas Howay and Reid took firsts in all subjects, he had second-class standing in constitutional history and torts, and passes in crimes and contracts. His name does not appear on the real property pass list, but supplementals were available. His youth – he was the youngest in the class – may explain his lacklustre performance. Moreover, he liked a good time. He was probably the "first year man from the region round about the western terminus of the C.P.R." whom the student magazine portrayed as plucking from his shoulder "a slender silken thread of ominous length and texture." In his second year, McBride passed everything; he won the prize in equity, a course taught by Mr. Justice C.J. Townshend, and garnered a first class in sales, a second in evidence, and passes in constitutional law and conflict of laws. In third year, he won no prizes but got firsts in international law, insurance, and bills and notes, as well as a second in equity.[32]

Dalhousie was proud of its "Little Law School," which "was just like a family." Boarding houses added to this congenial atmosphere. McBride shared accommodation with W.J. Bowser, Aulay Morrison, and H.J. Logan. Bowser and Morrison later came to British Columbia, but Logan became a Liberal MP and a senator from Nova Scotia. Students also got to know each other through social events such as the law school dinner in December 1887 where McBride and a classmate toasted "the men and women who make their own wills – fools rush in where angels fear to tread." Compulsory participation in moot court for second- and third-year students provided practical experience. In second year, McBride and his partner appealed an action for breach of contract; in third year, he acted for the appellant in a case involving the sale of a piece of land and won against Howay and another student.[33]

A well-attended and student-organized mock parliament provided excellent training and gave McBride his greatest success. When the government was defeated over a new Franchise Act, McBride, the "Member for New Westminster," formed the government and became premier and minister of justice. In the words of the student magazine,

> The first sitting under Dicky's regime was exciting in the extreme ... The attendance of members was very large, and ... chaos was only prevented by the coolness and decision of the Speaker. Questions of all sorts ... were plied in quick succession. Points of order were raised. Oppositionists disputed with Government supporters, while the jovial ex-Premier [F.L. Fairweather] persisted in declaring that he had the floor. Finally, when certain inquisitive

members had seemingly satisfied their almost insatiable desire for government knowledge, the honorable Minister of Finance [A.E. Shaw] introduced a resolution tending to unite the local Parliament of the Maritime Provinces.

Despite procedural wrangling, McBride's administration was upheld. The next week, his cheek "grew pale" when the "Oppositionists seemed to be in the majority." The whip rounded up supporters; an Opposition member tried to adjourn debate on a motion for imperial federation; and finally, the leader of the Opposition moved a vote of confidence, but the whip had done his work and "McBride and associates received assurance that they were required to guard the Ship of State a little longer."[34] It was good practice for the real politics he would encounter in Victoria.

A year later, the student magazine recalled that "Dick was Premier of the Mock Parliament during almost the whole of the last session; and, in spite of the efforts of Bowser, Sinclair & Co., he held on to the Treasury benches with a firm, unfearing grasp, till at last his opponents were completely baffled." Although better known as a sportsman than as a scholar, Bowser, a New Brunswicker and McBride's future attorney general, was well versed in the rules of parliamentary procedure including non-confidence votes. No doubt their debates continued in the boarding house. By then, Morrison, McBride's first political foe in the real world, had graduated and obtained "a lucrative position" in New Westminster.[35]

During the seasonal breaks, McBride returned to New Westminster. Between his second and third year, he articled with T.C. Atkinson, and after graduating in the spring of 1890, he completed his articles with the New Westminster firm of Corbould, McColl and Wilson. Because he was too young to vote, he could not be called to the bar. (A decade later, that delay may have inspired him to support a proposal in the Legislature to lower the voting age to eighteen to encourage the young to participate in public affairs.)[36] Although he could not vote, his time with Corbould, McColl and Wilson let him observe politics at first-hand. Gordon Corbould, a Conservative, was New Westminster's MP. In the summer of 1892, McBride passed the bar examinations, and in October, the benchers of the Law Society accepted his application for call and admission. The firm honoured McBride and Reid, another of its successful students, with a dinner. *The Victoria Colonist* predicted that McBride would rise "rapidly in his chosen profession."[37]

McBride was a junior member of the firm until 1893, when he set up his solo practice in an office near the courthouse. At first, his name did not appear in reports of court proceedings, but the press did not always name the lawyers concerned. Moreover, although McBride identified himself as a barrister for political purposes, he advertised himself as a solicitor and notary, and he probably had income from that part of his practice. By 1895, though not the busiest lawyer in the city, he was frequently named on the case dockets in the County and Supreme Courts at the spring and fall assizes. He formed a partnership with W.J. Whiteside. Many civil cases were minor – one client sued to recover twenty dollars – and others dealt with garnishee orders, complaints of false arrest, and nonpayment of debts. The press did not always report the results, so it is impossible to draw up a score sheet for McBride as a litigator.[38]

Once, McBride had to defend himself from a client who launched a suit against the Victoria Canning Company and then failed to appear in court. When the *Vancouver News-Advertiser* alleged that the client, Skee, was "only running a bluff," McBride, "to set himself right in the eyes of the court and to ask for its protection," explained that he and Whiteside had taken the case in good faith. With a cooperative client, McBride could be quite skilful. At the 1895 spring assizes, he acted for Henry Gotfriedson, who had been charged with assault. McBride avoided a jury trial by having Gotfriedson plead guilty, provided a character witness, urged the judge to exercise clemency, and had Gotfriedson give the judge a confidential note, the contents of which were not revealed. In sentencing Gotfriedson to three years, Justice Bole praised McBride's "wisdom and discretion" in having his client plead guilty since a jury would probably have convicted him, and the judge would have imposed a seven-year sentence. In Police Court, McBride acted for hotelkeepers who had violated a city bylaw on liquor sales. He admitted that his clients might have broken the bylaw but claimed that they were unaware of it. The police magistrate accepted his request for leniency and let the hotelkeepers go with a warning of future action if they allowed their employees to violate the law.[39]

Once, McBride broke new legal ground. In April 1896, he appeared in County Court on behalf of John Wirth and Frank Reed to whom two Mission justices of the peace had given a three-month jail term for stealing a coat. McBride claimed that Wirth and Reed had a right to appeal even though the coat was worth less than ten dollars. That point had never been raised in the province's courts, but Mr. Justice Bole agreed and heard the trial *de novo*. McBride argued that his clients had been given neither the time nor the opportunity to secure counsel or to demonstrate their lack of criminal intent. He maintained that a magistrate should have heard the case, referred to his clients' previous good conduct, and contended that they had already suffered more than enough for the alleged crime. Crown counsel did not press the case. The judge bound Wirth and Reed over on their own recognizance for $100 and let them go with the hope that they would never again be in court except as witnesses or jurors.[40] In this relatively minor case, McBride demonstrated his knowledge of the law and his persuasive skills.

Because they formed a significant portion of the local population but were not permitted to practise law, it is not surprising that McBride had Chinese and Native Indian clients. For example, he acted for Wo Lang, who sued Jno. Trembath to recover money for cutting firewood. The County Court judge ordered a payment of $300 and costs in favour of Wo but, in a counterclaim, awarded $200 and costs to Trembath. In a criminal case, McBride defended Ging Gong Ming, who was charged with stealing $300 from a co-partnership organized with three other Chinese people to establish themselves as merchants. Ging claimed that his house was broken into and that property, including a large sum of money, was stolen. McBride "made a forcible defence for the prisoner." Saying that the case was "without parallel," he explained that at the previous assizes two other "Chinamen" had been convicted of robbing Ging's premises. The Chinese community had turned against Ging for prosecuting them and was seeking his imprisonment. The jury found Ging not guilty. In another case, however, two Chinese individuals whom McBride defended against a charge of keeping a common gambling house were fined twenty dollars and costs.[41] In dealing with Chinese clients, McBride acted professionally and betrayed no antipathy to them.

His associations with Native Indians reflected the paternalism of his day. In defending Jimmy Page against the charge of murdering Annie, an Indian woman, McBride rested his defence on the grounds that Page had been drinking. Since Page did not know what he was doing when he fired at Annie, he had not committed murder. In urging leniency, McBride asked the court to consider that Page "was an Indian." The argument succeeded; Page was found guilty of the lesser charge of manslaughter. When Keatney Dan was charged with assaulting his wife, McBride pleaded guilty on his behalf but secured him a discharge since he had already spent eight days in jail.[42]

While developing his practice in a very competitive environment – by 1895, New Westminster had twenty legal firms – McBride participated in a variety of community activities that reflected his outside interests and helped make him better known. He was a charter member of the New Westminster branch of the Sons of Erin Society; one year, he was elected to the executive committee of the Boating and Canoeing Club; during another, he served on a committee for the New Westminster Lacrosse Club. While he was chief ranger of Court Lord Dufferin of the Ancient Order of Foresters, the lodge doubled its membership. McBride also commanded respect from his fellow lawyers. He was best man at W.J. Whiteside's wedding and a pallbearer when J.W. McColl lost his wife from complications of childbirth. By 1895, this recognition was professional too; he was elected to the executive committee of the New Westminster Bar Association and appointed to the City Licensing Board, which approved applications for liquor licences.[43]

Dick was too young to do more than observe the 1890 provincial election or the 1891 federal election, but in 1894 he was on the voters' list, and he participated in the provincial election. Bowser, who had settled in Vancouver, came to New Westminster on several occasions to speak on behalf of the Opposition candidate, J.B. Kennedy, who also had Howay's support. McBride, however, favoured David S. Curtis, an "independent supporter of the Government." Although it supported Kennedy, the *Columbian* admitted that McBride was "an excellent chairman" at Curtis's meetings. Howay recalled, "There was no principle at stake [in the election] – no great issue involved." The government of Theodore Davie was returned, but Kennedy, the oppositionist, won in New Westminster. Nevertheless, McBride had displayed his talent for politics and, with his prematurely grey hair, looked older than he was.[44]

British Columbia was the last province to adopt federal party lines in its legislature.[45] Federally, both the Conservative and Liberal Parties were organized, although local Conservatives often referred to themselves as Liberal-Conservatives, a term officially dropped by the national party in the 1870s. By 1896, McBride was vice-president for Ward V of the New Westminster Conservative Association. Gordon Corbould, the Conservative MP, did not seek re-election. His wife had died in 1894, leaving seven children, the youngest of whom was only three. Great interest prevailed in the nominating convention to select his successor. Despite late winter weather that stopped river traffic, sixty-eight of eighty Liberal-Conservative delegates from the lower Fraser Valley attended the convention. After nine men were nominated, the meeting adjourned so that the Langley and Richmond delegates could leave for home. Two weeks later, it reconvened and chose T.C. Atkinson as its candidate. A month afterward, having discovered that he had "not the hold upon public favor," Atkinson resigned because the campaign was interfering with his work. Early in May, the Conservatives reconvened, and this time, McBride, now the secretary of the New Westminster City Liberal-Conservative Association, was one of nine nominees. He adopted the same themes as several other candidates, opposing interference in the Manitoba Schools Question (which revolved around the withdrawal of provincial government funding for Catholic schools), favouring Chinese restriction, supporting the National Policy of a protective tariff, and calling for improved fisheries regulations and river navigation. On the first ballot, E. Hutcherson, a Ladner farmer, won thirty-seven of the seventy-one votes cast; McBride was a strong second.[46]

Shortly thereafter, Hutcherson became seriously ill with gastric fever and sought to restore his health in the Interior's drier climate. The election campaign was already in full swing. When Aulay Morrison, the Liberal candidate, invited his opponent Hutcherson to participate in his meeting at the New Westminster Opera House, McBride was one of three Conservatives who spoke on Hutcherson's behalf. Before over a thousand people, including several ladies, McBride was a great success. The Liberal *British Columbian* reported that he was greeted by a "hearty round of applause," and the Conservative *News-Advertiser* noted the unanimous approval of his speech and predicted "the impression made by his half hour's address to the electors will not soon be eradicated." Little more than two weeks before election day, Hutcherson withdrew from the race. The Conservatives explained that his health had not improved; the *Columbian* suggested that he was the victim of a "knifing" by "a ring" within the Conservative camp but admitted that McBride had no part of it. Since there was no time for another convention, the executive committee named McBride as the candidate. In a backhanded compliment, the *Columbian* expressed regret that "a young man of good parts and hopeful possibilities [would] thus blight at the outset what might have been a bright political career by allowing himself to be made the tool and victim of a corrupt and moribund political combination." The *Fraser Valley Champion,* a newspaper supported by the New Westminster Liberal-Conservative Association, remarked that many "old settlers will remember 'Dick' as a 'small boy' while in mature years his social and business intercourse has attracted to him whole hosts of friends." The *News-Advertiser* cheerfully foretold that McBride would "put a lot of vim into the fight."[47] Indeed, he did.

Despite his personal popularity, McBride had to campaign hard, pull the party together, and revive interest in it. To provide for voters who were registered in New Westminster but who lived in Vancouver, he established committee rooms in downtown Vancouver. He toured the Fraser Valley, speaking at points as far east as Chilliwack and Agassiz, and as far west as

Steveston and Ladner. Often, he spoke in schoolhouses and usually held two meetings a day. Once, he attended as many as four. Though it was a stereotypical campaign technique, when he stooped to kiss a seven-year-old girl who presented him with flowers at Ladner, he was probably giving a genuine expression of his gentlemanly conduct. His schedule was exhausting. Eight days into the campaign, he apologized to an overflow gathering at the New Westminster Opera House for being "physically unable" to speak at length.[48]

His speeches seldom departed from the themes he had expressed on Hutcherson's behalf. They also set out ideas that would be hallmarks of his political career. He noted Canada's "proud position" within the British Empire, he called himself "a straight supporter" of "the old flag and the old [National] policy," and he argued that British Columbia needed even "higher protection to keep out American produce." True to his belief in provincial rights, he refused to endorse his party's line on the Remedial Bill, which would force Manitoba to restore denominational schools. This stance cost him little locally. Publicly supported denominational schools had never existed in British Columbia, a fact that disturbed few people except for the local Catholic bishops. Since Catholics formed only about 20 percent of the population, and many were Native Indians who had no political voice, McBride felt few worries about religious repercussions and could exploit the provincial rights aspect of the Manitoba Schools Question, even though it caused conflict with the national party. When faced with hard questioning, he conceded that "he would vote against remedial legislation even if it should defeat the Government." He favoured clear party lines but, aware of opposition to party politics provincially, claimed that "he did not intend to be a straight party man but to vote as seemed to him best." He cited Dr. R.C. Weldon, who, though elected as a Conservative, sometimes voted independently. He attacked the Liberals and accused their federal leader, Wilfrid Laurier, of being disloyal to Canada. He repeatedly declared that "Mr. Laurier evidently thought there were chiefly Siwashes [a derogatory term for Native Indians] in B.C.," a comment that drew laughter and let him expound on his thesis that the Liberals lacked knowledge of British Columbia, as shown by Liberal MP Edward Blake's reference to the province as a "sea of mountains."[49]

While exploiting local pride, McBride also dealt with local grievances. British Columbians had been opposed to Asian immigration since the first Chinese labourers arrived with the gold rush in 1858. The complex and varied reasons for this hostility included claims that Chinese workers undercut white labour and could swamp the province through immigration. Many arguments were rooted in "racism." After the province protested, the government of John A. Macdonald appointed a Royal Commission on Chinese Immigration and, effective 1 January 1886, imposed a head tax of $50 on any Chinese person entering Canada.[50] McBride proposed raising the head tax to as much as $5,000 and applying it to the recently arrived Japanese, who were making their presence felt in the fishing industry. As a British Columbian, he preferred complete "Mongolian exclusion," even if it interfered "with Imperial plans and caused international complications." He appealed to fishermen with a dodger in which he promised to include them on a local regulatory board, to deny fishing licences to Japanese, Chinese, and alien individuals, and to forbid fish traps. The Conservative press quoted a telegram from Prime Minister Charles Tupper assuring McBride that Ottawa would prevent BC canners from canning fish caught in traps in American waters. Such ideas reflected the wishes of many potential constituents, but when questioners raised divisive issues such as temperance, he was noncommittal – he favoured "practical legislation, not useless laws." He would repeat many of these arguments as premier.[51]

The *News-Advertiser* contended that many Liberals would vote for McBride "on personal grounds alone, apart from political ties." Confident that he would have an "easy victory," the *Fraser Valley Champion* boasted of him as "the first British Columbia-born candidate who has ever offered for Dominion honors." Always optimistic, McBride expressed his confidence in a letter to his fiancée, "My Darling Girl," Margaret McGillivray, who had complained of being lonely because of his absence: "So things are dull – are they? You know dear I warned you about being lonesome & getting the blues & all that sort of thing – So you must keep up your courage till Sunday next – or there will be a big time when your Dick gets back – Politics are on the boom eh? Well dear girl *we* started them & we're going to keep them booming aren't we? I know Margaret that you are entirely anxious for my success & I am only too happy to tell you that my reception throughout has been most enthusiastic." Two days earlier, he had reported, "Everything indicates my return by a good, sound majority. The electors in the District seem to be almost unanimous for your Dick ... The work is certainly hard & trying but thank Providence I feel quite fit for it." It was not to be.[52]

By boat and train, voters registered in New Westminster came to the city on a fair June day. That most were Liberals was shown by their visits to the Liberal headquarters. At about three o'clock, the results began to arrive from eastern Canada, delivering bad news for the Conservatives. When the local votes were counted, McBride found that he too was a defeated Conservative. The unofficial results gave him 1,460 votes, but Aulay Morrison had won 1,758. In its post-mortem, the *Champion* stated that McBride had been handicapped by a lack of time to campaign. After a more thorough analysis, it suggested that he had had the support of the British-born but that former Americans and other naturalized aliens, mainly Fraser River fishermen, had supported the Liberals. It also admitted that many Conservatives, especially in rural areas, had been apathetic. Some years later, McBride attributed his defeat to the failure of the Conservative government to keep out the Chinese.[53]

McBride was not discouraged. He expanded his civic activities by serving as one of the fifteen vice-chairmen who arranged the celebrations associated with the annual exhibition of the Royal Agricultural and Industrial Society. He resumed his legal career. Again, his cases included minor civil suits or routine applications relating to the administration of estates. His criminal cases were varied. He once appeared in court because a client had had second thoughts about laying charges against an Anglican clergyman who had taken the client's canoe in Port Moody and paddled it to Vancouver. Other cases demonstrated his legal skills. McBride repeated his successful ploy of having a client admit guilt to get a lighter sentence. In District Court, he had "young Byron," who had been charged with aggravated assault against a "Chinaman," plead guilty. In consideration of the youth's family, previous good character, and the fact that the crime had been committed "in a weak moment with no idea of the result," McBride got Byron off with an agreement to keep the peace for a year and a $100 fine to cover the cost of the police chase that occurred after he had broken away from the constable.[54] That the victim was Chinese possibly helped secure a lighter penalty.

McBride still had Chinese clients. At the 1897 spring assizes, he defended Song Moon, who had been charged with attempted rape. According to the prosecutor, Song entered the home of Lee Sing and attempted "to commit an assault" on Lee's wife, Martha. Martha, who said she was twenty years old and a member of the Methodist Church, denied McBride's suggestion that she had once been a prostitute. Song claimed that he went to Martha because she would mend his coat for free, whereas a tailor would charge thirty-five cents. According to his story, Lee came home unexpectedly and shot him. The bullet only grazed him, but Lee had taken a knife and cut off Song's ear while Martha cut his queue, or pigtail. To a Chinese man of that era, the loss of the queue was a serious insult. After Song

Richard and Margaret McBride, c. 1896. This may be their wedding photo. Royal BC Museum, BC Archives, B-01680.

charged Lee with attempted murder, the Lees then charged him with attempted rape. The jury believed Martha and found McBride's client guilty. In another case, where the details were "not of a character for publication," McBride defended a Mr. Robertson against a charge of attempting to rape an Indian woman from Langley. On one occasion, McBride ran afoul of Judge Drake, who scolded him for not being "properly gowned," probably because he refused to wear a wig. That, however, does not seem to have harmed his legal career. He acted as Crown prosecutor at the New Westminster spring assizes of 1898, although the docket was very light.[55]

On 23 September 1896, as his legal career advanced, McBride married Christine Margaret McGillivray, the daughter of Mr. and Mrs. Neil McGillivray. McBride had always been gregarious and cheerful, but without his true love, he was miserable. Some weeks before the wedding, Margaret spent a few days with her brother in Vancouver. Various interruptions prevented McBride from taking the forty-five-minute Interurban ride to visit her, but, lovesick and lonely, he wrote regularly. "There's no use talking darling," he explained. "I can't get along without you, and Westminster without my Margaret is the dullest & most dreary spot on the globe. You have no idea how strange the place seemed without you." In the meantime, he was making arrangements to furnish their new home.[56]

Margaret was born on 23 July 1870 in Ripley, Ontario, of Scottish-born parents. Her brother Donald, who became a prominent railway contractor, came to British Columbia in the 1880s to work for Andrew Onderdonk, who had the contract to build the CPR through the Fraser Canyon; her parents and other siblings followed. Margaret had attended the Annie Wright Seminary in Tacoma, Washington, an exclusive private school for young ladies. Although a newcomer to New Westminster, she had many friends, who decorated St. Andrew's Presbyterian Church with a mass of pink and white flowers, and honoured the newlyweds with a shower of old shoes and rice. The groom gave her a ring made of BC gold. Reverend Thomas Scoular presided, but there were neither attendants nor a breakfast for the many friends who were present at the 8:30 A.M. ceremony as the couple had to catch the CPR train that would take them on their honeymoon to Whatcom (Bellingham), Seattle, Tacoma, and Portland.[57] The wedding took place after the election, so Margaret knew of her husband's political ambitions.

By the spring of 1898, a provincial election was again imminent. Four years had elapsed since the last one, and a controversial redistribution bill, giving more seats to the Mainland to recognize population growth in the Kootenay mining districts and in the city of Vancouver, had decreased the influence of Vancouver Island in the Legislature. A few people talked of introducing federal party lines to provincial politics, but Premier J.H. Turner, a Victoria merchant with investments throughout the province, recommended "that voters, whether Liberal or Conservative, should support or oppose the present government as British Columbians and from no other consideration."[58] Several editors agreed that federal politics had no place in the province. The *Vancouver World*, for example, succinctly declared, "We have not yet arrived at that stage in our history when we should tolerate the political bickering which prevails in the older parts of the Dominion," whereas the *Colonist* warned of the undesirability of having a provincial government that was "avowedly hostile to any federal ministry."[59] Thus, the contest was between those who supported Turner, the Government party, and those who did not, the Oppositionists. These were very loose labels. In the four-member seat of Vancouver, a "citizens' ticket" ran but was friendly to the government. Some candidates labelled "Opposition" may have been Labour supporters or Independents.

Early in June, McBride began his campaign. Because New Westminster already had two strong candidates, he ran in Dewdney. This rural constituency lay along the north side of the Fraser River from the eastern boundary of New Westminster to Harrison Lake in the Coast Mountains. It included such communities as Port Moody, Coquitlam, Port Haney, Mission, Silverdale, Whonnock, and Agassiz. Farming, lumbering, and fishing provided its economic base, and the Fraser and the CPR formed its transportation links with New Westminster. When the campaigners had to cross the Fraser River to get from Mission to Abbotsford, Premier Turner helped them pump a handcar across a railway bridge.[60]

McBride ran as "an out-and-out supporter of the Turner Government." He called Turner a successful pioneer businessman whose policies meant progress but conceded that the Turner administration was "far from perfect."[61] Asserting that his first concern was Dewdney's well-being, he indignantly rejected any suggestion that he was an Independent. He would forget the controversy over the cost of the new Parliament Buildings, since that had been the responsibility of the previous administration of Theodore Davie. He admitted that the redistribution bill had many flaws but thought it "a statesmanlike measure, as nearly perfect as could be expected" given the province's size, newness, and "extreme changes in the way of mining excitements," which made it hard to satisfy everybody. Specifically referring to McBride's speech at Mission, where he dealt with many of those issues, the *Columbian* contemptuously referred to "Our native boy, Dick," whose speech, it said, sounded "very much like a quick young lawyer's appeal to a jury to let a horse thief off, not considering his admitted crimes, but looking forward to a brilliant and virtuous future, on his, 'Our Dick's word of honour, you know."

McBride "believed that British Columbia was the wealthiest and most progressive Province in the whole Dominion and had a great future." Since childhood, he had noticed its strides "with great pride." Under Turner's motto of "Progress and prosperity," he made promises, some of which challenged the government's policies. He claimed that taxes had not been increased since 1894 but proposed that a commission investigate the unpopular mortgage tax; he criticized the requirement that mine labourers must buy a miner's licence; he opposed the timber royalties imposed on settlers clearing their farms; he forecast immense benefits from railways to Yukon and the Kootenays; and he supported Chinese and Japanese exclusion. Late in the campaign, he promised to work for the construction of the Vancouver, Victoria and Eastern Railway, which proposed to link the coast and the Kootenays. Curiously, there is no evidence that he spoke on Turner's claim for Better Terms – a bigger subsidy from Ottawa.

McBride's opponents were the incumbent, C.B. Sword, whom he once described as "an old war horse in Provincial politics," and Charles Whetham. Now a Whonnock farmer, Whetham was the former proprietor of Whetham College, a short-lived matriculation school in Vancouver.[62] Whetham criticized the Turner government and attacked McBride as a lawyer whose experience in the riding was confined to fishing expeditions. McBride, who could give as well as he could take, contended that a city lawyer was well qualified to represent Dewdney. Noting that Sword had rarely visited the riding during his eight years as its MLA, he promised to go to Victoria, first as a representative of Dewdney "and afterwards as a promoter of all that is best for the whole province." Specifically, he would work for what the people wanted in the way of roads, bridges, and trails, especially the Dewdney Trunk Road to link the various sections of the constituency. Despite sometimes bitter personal attacks, McBride graciously commented on "the agreeable personal relations" of the other candidates when Sword withdrew lest he and Whetham divide the Opposition vote. Sword's departure and the strong opposition of the *Columbian*, the main newspaper in the constituency, should have made the campaign difficult for McBride, but he attracted enthusiastic audiences. The *Vancouver World*, a Government supporter, commented that McBride, "an eloquent and fluent speaker at once got the sympathy of the audience," despite "the criminal charge preferred against him in the political contest by his opponents, that of being a young man."[63]

On election day, McBride won every poll except Whonnock, which was Whetham's home, and Agassiz. Nonetheless, given the fluidity of support for Turner, the province-wide results were uncertain. The *World* suggested that the Government had won twenty-one seats and that the Opposition had taken fifteen, but the *Colonist* called the results as seventeen for the Government and sixteen for the Opposition, with several seats in doubt. In contrast, the *News-Advertiser* suggested that nineteen ridings had gone to the Opposition, fifteen to the Government, and two to Independents; the *Columbian* agreed but put two Independents in the Opposition camp. Moreover, the election in the two-member seat of Cassiar had not yet been held, and many defeated candidates had launched protests. The *World* observed that "so evenly balanced are the Government and the Opposition, ... no one having regard to the actual condition of affairs will be found to belittle the gravity of the situation."[64] Amid uncertainty, Richard McBride ended his political apprenticeship.

In the courts and on the hustings, McBride had proven himself a persuasive speaker. In his legal practice, he gained the respect of fellow lawyers; in his civic and social activities, he added to his wide variety of acquaintances and friends. His legal practice renewed his contact with Native Indians and the Chinese, but his experiences in court helped confirm his prejudice that, though entitled to justice, they were not "like us." He demonstrated pride in his native province as a student at Dalhousie. At home on the political stage, he boasted of British Columbia's great potential, campaigned for provincial rights, and admitted intra-provincial grievances. In promising to work for his constituency first and for British Columbia second, he recognized the parochialism of British Columbians, especially in respect to public works. He was a proud supporter of the British Empire and a Canadian Conservative in the National Policy tradition but was willing to work with the personal loyalties that marked provincial politics at the time. As a member of the BC Legislature, Richard McBride would have to call on all his innate talents and acquired skills.

2

"Dewdney Dick"

In a Chaotic Legislature, 1898-1903

British Columbia's politics are "a tangled skein, extremely puzzling to other parts of the Dominion."

– Toronto Globe, *9 May 1902*

The new Parliament Buildings dominated the south side of Victoria's Inner Harbour. Capped with copper-sheathed domes that gradually oxidized to an attractive green and designed by the architect Francis Rattenbury, their walls were built of pearly grey stone from Haddington Island, their roof slates came from Jervis Inlet, and the granite in their steps and landings was from Burrard Inlet and Nelson Island. They cost just under $1 million and were formally opened at the 1898 legislative session. Their construction briefly revived an old Island versus Mainland controversy as mainlanders rightly claimed that the buildings would "anchor" the capital on the island even though the province's economic and population centre had shifted to the Mainland.[1]

The new buildings were stable, but the politics within them was not. One word, instability, describes BC politics between 1898 and 1903. British Columbians fought three provincial elections, saw the federal government fire its lieutenant-governor, and had six premiers: J.H. Turner, Charles Semlin, Joseph Martin, James Dunsmuir, Edward G. Prior, and finally, Richard McBride. Politics centred on personalities, not parties. Occasionally, the lines were clear, as in 1900, when almost everybody was opposed to Martin, but factions frequently shifted. In 1900, one newspaper named ten different parties that had fielded at least one candidate in the election; another, in reporting the results, listed successful Martinite, Cottonite, Turnerite, Wilsonian, and Independent candidates, and included McBride as a supporter of Charles Wilson. Another listed the Tupper, Martin, Provincial, and Conservative Parties, as well as Independents, putting McBride in the Conservative camp. The *Toronto Globe* correctly described BC politics as "a tangled skein, extremely puzzling to other parts of the Dominion, where the cleavages are regular and well understood." Indeed, the other provinces followed federal party lines in their legislatures, although Manitoba had done so only since the 1880s. British Columbia also had regional divisions and conflicts between capital and labour, although the Labour/Socialist vote was concentrated in the mining regions of the Kootenay and Boundary Districts and on Vancouver Island.[2] An eastern observer wrote, "Since the days of the late Hon. John Robson [BC premier 1889-92] that Province has languished under the confusion and uncertainties which must ever exist under, and seem to be inseparable from, non-party government ... Everywhere, non-party government has been a failure ... It was particularly disastrous in British Columbia where, under its wing, the public domain, which should now prove an invaluable asset of the Province, was sacrificed piecemeal to covetous and rapacious political hacks who were in public life evidently for what they could get out of it."[3]

During this political confusion, McBride emerged from the position of relatively inconspicuous backbencher to become a cabinet minister and then leader of the Opposition. A Victoria reporter remarked that his "boyish face, surmounted by a wealth of curly gray hair, gave him an air of distinction which will be a valuable asset should he justify the prediction of his friends and become a force in the politics of the province." Although the results of the 1898 election were unclear, McBride expected that, as a successful candidate for the Government party, he would sit on the Government side at least until the Legislature denied confidence to Turner. However, Lieutenant-Governor Thomas R. McInnes, who would demonstrate even greater ineptitude in 1900, dismissed the Turner government before the Cassiar election was complete or all the election petitions had been heard.[4] After McInnes invited Charles Semlin, a Cariboo rancher, to form a government, supporters of the federal Conservative Party organized the Liberal-Conservative Union of British Columbia. McBride was a delegate from New Westminster. Following considerable debate, they agreed to act as a Conservative Party in the next provincial election. When the session opened in January 1899, McBride was on the Opposition side. Semlin had a precarious hold on power. With the number of his friends and foes in the House almost equally divided, he depended on the support of the mercurial attorney general, Joseph Martin, and his followers. As a reporter neatly put it, the government was "'led' by Mr. Semlin but driven by Mr. Martin."[5]

As a rookie backbencher, McBride spoke little, but when he did, his sharp tongue and sometimes hectoring manner often attracted as much attention as the substance of his speeches. The *British Columbian* described his maiden speech as "decidedly of the style so well-known as 'Dick's generalities.'" The *Vancouver Daily Province* thought him "a decidedly good speaker," who "was listened to most attentively by both sides of the house." When the government introduced a bill to let former premier Turner and J.D. Prentice sit in the House while their elections were being contested, McBride condemned the bill as "monstrous" and an "interference with the courts." So vigorous were his attacks in all-night committee sittings that the chairman had to remind him that the House was neither "a debating club" nor the place for "a stump speech." Toward the end of the session, McBride again used "monstrous," this time to attack a proposal to abandon land subsidies for railways; he claimed that the lack of subsidies would impair commercial development and end "the value of the railway promoter to the country." The Speaker once ruled him out of order for rising to speak after he himself had put the question. Another time, the Speaker ruled that McBride had resorted to unparliamentary language in describing proposed legislation on controverted elections as "an iniquitous measure." McBride substituted "obnoxious."

Nevertheless, he did make some constructive suggestions. He showed concern for provincial rights in contending that "peculiar conditions" made BC fisheries "impossible of intelligent direction from a distance" (namely, Ottawa), and he introduced a bill to ask the federal government for a local fisheries commissioner. Had the importance of the fisheries been foreseen at Confederation, he asserted, the Terms of Union would have put them under provincial control. At Semlin's request, McBride withdrew the motion lest it irritate federal authorities without bringing any benefit. His interest in provincial rights overcame his disdain for Joseph Martin, and he supported his bill reserving to the province the right to appoint queen's counsels "inasmuch as it asserted Provincial Rights."[6]

McBride also served on the standing committee on mining and took a turn chairing the House when it sat in committee. There is no evidence that he referred to the Dewdney Trunk Road and the Pitt River bridge, which were so keenly desired by his constituents, but he did oppose the adoption of the Torrens system of land registration because he felt that the existing method was adequate and that switching systems would be costly for landowners. In addition, he endorsed a request that the Dominion government apply provincial mining and land laws in the railway belt (the ungranted Crown land lying for twenty miles on either side of the BC CPR main line east of Port Moody), since many pioneer settlers found it inconvenient to deal with Ottawa. And he defended a measure to assist the city of New Westminster, which lost most of its business district by fire on 10 September 1898, on the grounds that residents required relief even though the city was not bankrupt.[7] McBride lost his own office in the fire, so he spoke from first-hand experience. Like others, he quickly rebuilt. Within a few days, he attended a citizens' meeting to discuss the forthcoming provincial exhibition, the city's main annual event. The fairgrounds had not been damaged by the fire, but many residents could not contribute to the cost of holding the exhibition, so McBride joined a delegation that solicited subscriptions in Victoria. He cited generous aid to the fire victims as evidence of "no sectionalism in British Columbia."[8]

McBride continued to politic. Sometimes, he brought colleagues to political meetings in New Westminster. These included his friend Robert F. Green, the MLA for Slocan, and A. Lucas, the provincial Conservative organizer.[9] During a by-election campaign in Victoria on behalf of Turner, who had resigned because of a conflict of interest and had to seek the voters' approval before he could sit again in the Legislature, McBride's "short bright" speeches impressed audiences. Criticizing the government's "outrageous" election petitions bill, McBride appealed to young men "to show their mettle" and protect their rights and liberties under the British constitution. He accused the government of doing nothing for the working man, or for railways, trails, and other public works, and of "sneering" at his fisheries proposal. And he described Martin, who had been Manitoba's attorney general, as coming "from Manitoba on a big fat fee from the greatest monopoly of Canada – the C.P.R." Deprecating "the introduction of personalities in politics," he attacked Alex Henderson, the MLA for New Westminster, who had run as a supporter of the Turner government against Semlin and others but later joined Semlin's cabinet. "Deafening" applause greeted him at Turner's victory celebration.[10]

Once the session ended in late February, McBride resumed his activities in New Westminster. He now had two daughters, Donalda Mary (called Mary), who was born on 12 July 1897, and Margaret Sydney (called Peggy), born on 8 September 1898. He helped reorganize the Ancient Order of

Foresters and was installed as a past chief ranger. His father was elected as an honorary member of the order in recognition of his membership in the first court organized on the Mainland in 1877. Building his law practice was more difficult. He appeared in court on several minor civil issues, but New Westminster had a surplus of lawyers.[11] The need for income may have influenced his 1900 decision to support Martin's bill to permit champerty, an agreement between a plaintiff and a lawyer who earns his fee by collecting a percentage of the money won in the lawsuit. In 1899, the benchers of the Law Society had suspended Martin for a week for undertaking a civil suit on the understanding that if he won it, he would receive part of the proceeds. Martin argued that the law against champerty preserved the privileges of the rich against the poor. McBride asserted that miners wanted the law to be changed.[12]

McBride dealt with miners when he sought legal business during a mining boom at Atlin in the extreme northwest of the province. Atlin was so remote that the North West Mounted Police thought it was part of the North-West Territories and recorded mining claims under territorial laws. When it was ascertained that Atlin actually belonged to British Columbia, confusion reigned since the North-West Territories permitted 250-foot placer claims, whereas British Columbia allowed only 100 feet. To resolve the confusion, the provincial government dispatched Mr. Justice Irving as special commissioner to settle disputes. Expecting that many claim holders would need a lawyer, McBride joined Irving and his staff on 9 June 1899 for the week-long steamer trip to Skagway and then to White Pass by rail.

The White Pass and Yukon Railway was still under construction and would not reach Lake Bennett for another few weeks, so McBride had to "hit the trail" and tramp to Bennett City, on Lake Bennett. From there he took the *Gleaner*, a steamer, to Taku City, pausing at Cariboo Crossing, where freight was removed and the passengers including McBride helped drag the steamer over a portage. At Taku City, McBride walked over another portage before catching the *Scotia*, which took him to Atlin, where he found a community with about two thousand people and plenty of gold but with hundreds leaving every week, "the claims being so tied up." This, of course, offered such good business that he took only winnable cases and within a few days of arriving had a proposition "with some of the richest claim owners." He wrote to Margaret that the darkness of night lasted just an hour, the climate was "simply perfection," and "the beauty of the country" was an "everlasting topic of conversation" with his bedmate, Monte Woods. Apart from homesickness, his health was good; the

Atlin, c. 1899. Royal BC Museum, BC Archives, B-09599.

only drawbacks were having to share a bed with Woods and dining on "canned vegetables & meats & worst of all preserved potatoes." Within ten days, he had made about $189 in cash and was working from 9:30 A.M. to 10:30 P.M. If he won all his cases, he expected to earn about $4,000 in sixty days, but, he cautioned, "If I lose, it means another thing."[13]

How much he made is unknown, but on his return, a *Columbian* reporter surmised from his smile, the "general drift of his remarks," and a "big pocketful of large nuggets" that "he had no reason to regret, financially," his sojourn in Atlin. After a visit home, he returned briefly to Atlin to complete some business. Although busy as a lawyer, McBride never forgot politics. At an Atlin banquet honouring Lieutenant-Governor Thomas McInnes, he said that his time in the town had "put him in a better position to judge its needs" and "do what he could to have any mistakes rectified."[14]

While McBride was in Atlin, the province underwent a minor political crisis. During a banquet in the Kootenay mining centre of Rossland, Joe Martin blamed his cabinet colleague Francis Carter-Cotton for some unpopular mining legislation and accused him of sleazy dealings. Premier

Semlin, accusing Martin of neglecting departmental business, asked him to resign. Martin refused, so the caucus expelled him. McBride predicted that the rest of the Semlin-Martin combination would fuse with the Opposition or an election would follow. Two months later, with little having changed, McBride suggested that the government would hang on to power but might be defeated on the first division regarding a policy question. He was pleased that people were looking forward to an election on party lines and the promise "of a good strong provincial Conservative party."[15]

He was back in New Westminster in time for the provincial Conservative convention in October 1899, when former prime minister Sir Mackenzie Bowell spoke. By a large majority, the 130 delegates called for the introduction of Dominion party lines in provincial politics – that is, to get away from the old system of organizing around personalities whose followers, in a parliamentary context, were "loose fish" whose support was unreliable. McBride favoured the introduction of party lines. A few months later, in introducing another former prime minister, Sir Charles Tupper, to a New Westminster audience, he predicted an early provincial election in which

McBride, standing at the right, with four friends at Atlin. Royal BC Museum, BC Archives, A-01414.

"the solidarity of the Conservative party would again manifest itself." He also visited Dewdney. At Mission, he attended a meeting of settlers who wanted the Fraser River railway bridge adapted for traffic.[16]

McBride made a twelve-day trip to San Francisco in the fall of 1899 on unspecified legal business, but most of his work was routine, such as probates and minor civil matters, a few criminal cases, a divorce, and especially, violations of liquor laws. In April 1900, he appeared before a judge and jury in County Court for A. McWhinnie, a Ladner barkeeper, who appealed the fine of twenty dollars and costs imposed by four local justices of the peace for selling liquor to an intoxicated woman. Opposing McBride were his old classmate F.W. Howay and N.F. Hagel, a Vancouver lawyer, retained by the Woman's Christian Temperance Union. According to the *World*, McBride, who "had from the first a hard-pan case to buck," endeavoured "to mix up the story of the prosecution" but admitted that the accused had served the drinks. The *World* described his "forensic wit" as "altogether above the sordid nature of the contest, and worthy of a more exalted cause." Despite McBride's best effort, in "a most decisive victory for the W.C.T.U.," the jury sustained the original decision and assigned the cost of the appeal to his client.[17]

The legislative session that began in January 1900 promised to be exciting because the sides were so evenly matched. At least four distinct groups could be discerned: the government, led by Semlin, and three Opposition factions led by Charles Wilson, J.H. Turner, and Joseph Martin. As the *Nelson Daily Miner* commented, political affairs were "in a condition of confusion. No one can make anything out of them. The situation is simply a squabble of individuals to get uppermost." The even blunter *Kamloops Standard* declared, "One of the most hopeless features of British Columbian politics [is] that many of the politicians are as treacherous as Boers and as contemptible as Chinamen."[18] McBride arrived a day after a meeting of MLAs who had formed the Opposition in the previous session, but he had written that he would "battle by their side for the cause of better government." From the last seat in the back row of the Legislature, in what the *Province* called "the best speech" of the Throne Speech debate, he attacked government MLAs for "acting like marionettes," chastised the government for not carrying out its election promises, and criticized Finance Minister Carter-Cotton for not answering "grave charges" levied by Joe Martin.[19] As well, he "carefully but lightly touched upon" schools and the Liquor Licensing Act, and he warned of "disastrous" consequences if the government did not pay more attention to the needs of working men, specifically the desire of Kootenay miners for an eight-hour day and protection against "a cheaper substitute from China and Japan." He praised Mr. Justice Irving and government officials in Atlin, called for representation in the Legislature for Atlin and nearby Lake Bennett, and observed that by denying mining claims to foreigners, the alien labour law prohibited outside investment. He "crossed swords" over disallowance, the action of the federal government in refusing to approve certain provincial acts, rebuked the government for ignoring agriculture, and "wound up a powerful and able speech" with a strong plea for roads for Dewdney and railways for the whole province.[20]

McBride returned to some of the issues that particularly concerned his constituents. He got an amendment to the Supreme Court Bill to restore the right to file certain documents in the New Westminster Court Registry, thus saving constituents a trip to Vancouver; he moved second reading of an amendment to the Municipal Elections Act to let municipalities use a voting machine invented by a constituent; and he spoke out against the most "serious menace" to the province, the influx of Chinese and Japanese. In a province that had ceased to be a British colony only thirty years earlier, McBride believed that London could do what Ottawa could not and urged the provincial administration to make representations "to the home authorities" – the Colonial Office – for protection against cheap Japanese labour. When the Legislature debated a motion to deny naturalization to anyone of Asian race, McBride urged the government to "leave nothing undone to relieve" competition by "Chinese and Japs," particularly in the fisheries. Rejecting a suggestion that the Legislature was wasting time on a matter over which it had no control, he contended, "At this distance from Ottawa it was difficult to appreciate how little Eastern Canadians knew of the extent to which the Chinese were invading this Province." It was a sentiment he would repeat.[21]

With minor exceptions, McBride retained this antipathy to Asians throughout his career. His was a popular attitude. As on the American Pacific coast and in other parts of the British Empire, notably Australia and New Zealand, the complex and intertwined reasons for the anti-Asian stance had common threads: fears of being "swamped" by massive immigration and concerns about economic competition from people who worked harder for lower wages and had a low standard of living, whose living habits threatened public health and morality, and who gambled and used opium. Underscoring all was racial prejudice. Initially, the arguments were directed at the Chinese and were later applied to the Japanese, who began arriving in the 1890s, though with some variations, notably less concern about morality and public health and more fear of military attack.[22]

McBride realized that circumstances were unique in certain parts of the province. When Semlin brought in a bill to redistribute the seats in the Legislature, McBride argued that there was insufficient data about the population of the new mining areas. Similarly, when C.W.D. Clifford of Cassiar moved want of confidence over a measure to prevent aliens from owning placer mines, McBride "electrified the House and made a deep impression" by explaining that, after seeing the act's "pernicious" effects in Atlin, he had changed his mind. When the Vancouver and Victoria Boards of Trade sought an adjustment in the time period for presenting bills of sale, he noted that because of its remoteness, Cassiar required more time for the presentation of such bills but that otherwise "the House ought to look on the Province as a whole."[23] He had learned a valuable lesson: British Columbia extended beyond Victoria and the Fraser Valley.

He also served on special legislative committees. He was appointed a commissioner under D.W. Higgins, a Victoria MLA, to investigate reports of maladministration at the Provincial Asylum, a mental hospital in New Westminster. The appointment was convenient – the asylum was near the McBride family residence – but the commission visited it only once and issued no report. The *Times* noted that McBride was "coming along nicely" and commended his action as chairman of the Liquor License Amendment Committee in "peremptorily" ordering ex-attorney-general Martin to "sit down."[24]

By the end of the 1900 session, the *Times* assessed McBride as "the peer of any member of the opposition bench." Yet he could be difficult. On one occasion, he was in such "fine form" that even the lenient Speaker had to call him to order. Even so, McBride was one of the better-behaved members. In the midst of a crisis, he joined John Irving of Cassiar in physically separating James Dunsmuir and James Baker of East Kootenay. The two had come to blows after an alliance of Opposition MLAs, including such strange bedfellows as Joseph Martin and McBride, combined to help defeat the Semlin government by a vote of nineteen to eighteen on a redistribution bill. Lieutenant-Governor McInnes was in a quandary about how to proceed. The House was equally divided – on several occasions the Speaker had had to cast the deciding vote – but Semlin claimed that he could control it. Nevertheless, McInnes dismissed him and called on Martin to form an administration. McBride accused the lieutenant-governor of inconsistency and claimed that a coalition could have governed. The next day, he joined other MLAs in unanimously voting no confidence in Martin. The ultimate result was the dismissal of McInnes and yet another provincial election.[25]

The adoption of party lines was an early campaign issue. McBride strongly endorsed the Conservative policy of employing "straight federal party lines for future provincial elections." He stated that he "had been a staunch supporter of Hon. Mr. Turner and his Government, but Turnerism was dead. Semlinism was defunct and Martinism was impossible. If the political affairs of our great Dominion were safe within the lines of parties, British Columbia would not suffer by adopting party lines." Thus, he ran as a straight Conservative candidate. He denied any identification with Turner but was not entirely clear on the nature of traditional party lines as he suggested that Liberal friends could support a Conservative candidate on a purely provincial platform in opposition to Martin.[26]

Although a few BC editors favoured party lines as a means of establishing "quiet, permanent, satisfactory government," most shared the belief of the Liberal *Victoria Times* that British Columbians had "a heavy enough task on their hands to secure a clear, stable, progressive administration" without the complication of mixing Dominion and local matters. Francis Carter-Cotton feared that party lines would be detrimental to the Conservatives. At the request of Semlin's supporters in the Legislature, he accepted the leadership of the new Provincial Party, which believed that provincial interests could be served "by the hearty co-operation of men of both Federal parties." Even Charles Wilson, the nominal Conservative leader, admitted that not all Conservatives would unite on party lines or accept him as leader and that rivalries between Vancouver Island and the Mainland still prevailed. He did not mention the feeling in the Interior that local interests had "too long been made subservient to the manipulations of coast politicians."[27]

Despite his sensitivity to the regions, McBride's only campaign forays outside of Dewdney were in New Westminster and to several centres in the Delta riding on the south side of the Fraser River. He did not accept an invitation to attend a major Conservative rally in Vancouver. In mid-campaign, a major advantage came his way: The formerly hostile *New Westminster British Columbian* changed hands. Its new managing editor, J.D. Taylor, enthusiastically supported both the Conservatives and McBride, an "indefatigable" campaigner who showed "other candidates how to handsomely win an election" and who "effectively" answered his opponents' points. Even the *World*, which supported Martin, admitted McBride's "courage and manliness" in arguing with the premier and his colleagues, and thought him "infinitely the superior of his confreres who are opposing the Government." On the same platform as Martin, McBride expressed "his views with quite refreshing candor" but, the *World* concluded, made no "progress with his arguments."[28]

In Dewdney, McBride's only opponent was Charles Whetham, a Martinite, who had also run in 1898. The constituents were chiefly interested in local matters: the long-delayed Dewdney Trunk Road, fishery regulations, and the control of noxious weeds. Claiming that Martin's obstruction had stopped him from doing more for Dewdney, McBride apparently pledged to resign if the government did not soon make a significant start on the Dewdney Trunk Road, regularly alluded to Martin's unreliability, and hinted that Martin and J.C. Brown had reached some sort of "secret understanding" when Brown joined the cabinet. At almost every meeting, he noted Martin's insincerity in attacking the Canadian Pacific Railway (CPR), since he had come to the province with a "fat retainer" from the company, but was especially critical of Martin's plan to link the coast and the Kootenays via a government railway. McBride questioned neither the desirability of such a link nor the principle of government ownership, but he called Martin's scheme an "absurd proposition in definitely ... pledging to accomplish a public work the cost of which he frankly admitted he did not know" but that would be at least

$15 million of public money. He took credit for suggesting that the provincial government should protest directly to the "Mother Land, where we were bound to get British justice and fair play" as the province sought to restrict immigration from China and Japan.[29]

McBride easily won his seat, leading in almost every poll and securing 340 votes to Whetham's 285. In New Westminster, "stalwart supporters" carried him on their shoulders to the headquarters of his law school classmate, Robie Reid, only to discover that they had crashed a political wake: Reid, the unsuccessful Conservative candidate in New Westminster, was thanking his supporters for their help. In Dewdney, McBride's supporters arranged a celebratory picnic at Mission City on 23 June. About five hundred people came by train, wagon, and steamer. When McBride, accompanied by W.J. Bowser and other politicians, stepped off the CPR's Imperial Limited, the band from St. Mary's Mission School played "Hail to the Chief." Between political speeches, the band and the New Westminster orchestra entertained the picnickers, who also enjoyed sports events, including football games for adults and children. As "the people's Dick" was now a member of the cabinet, holding the portfolio of minister of mines, the *Columbian* remarked that the event was now "a double celebration."[30]

Little more than a week after the election, McBride and twenty-four of the thirty-eight newly elected MLAs convened at the Hotel Vancouver. Indicative of the fluid nature of provincial politics, there was uncertainty about what to call it. Island MLAs described it as a Government convention, their Vancouver counterparts were unsure about what to call it, and Interior MLAs had diverse opinions. James Dunsmuir, who had accepted the lieutenant-governor's invitation to form a government, attended. The muddle over nomenclature – some referred to the meeting as the "Anti-Martin" convention and others as the Opposition convention – reflected continuing political confusion. The press was not admitted but learned that the sometimes stormy meeting unanimously demanded the recall of Lieutenant-Governor McInnes and that some attendees, notably Robert Tatlow of Vancouver, attacked Dunsmuir and his cabinet minister J.H. Turner for accepting office. McBride, who two years earlier had run as an "out-and-out supporter" of Turner, now opposed any "renewal of the former Turner administration" and endorsed the convention's decision to support Dunsmuir for one session so that the government could advance public works and approve the necessary expenditures. Dunsmuir promised not to introduce any contentious legislation and to reorganize the cabinet at the end of the session. After the members sent a telegram to Prime Minister Laurier declaring that "the usefulness" of the lieutenant-governor was "gone," the meeting ended in harmony. Dunsmuir then gave the members a banquet. He could afford to do so, for he and his family owned the major collieries on Vancouver Island as well as the Esquimalt and Nanaimo Railway (E&N).[31]

The press speculated on the likelihood that the convention was a prelude to the introduction of party lines and on the choice of cabinet ministers. One of Dunsmuir's mouthpieces, the *Colonist,* optimistically suggested the birth of a new political party, a "Unionist Party," that would "have a long and useful life." The *Nelson Tribune* predicted "the division of the house upon federal party lines."[32] Uncertainty about party lines persisted, but conjecture about the cabinet ended on 21 June: Dunsmuir, who had earlier named Turner as minister of finance and D.M. Eberts as attorney general, announced that his cabinet was complete with J.D. Prentice as provincial secretary and minister of education, W.C. Wells as chief commissioner of lands and works, and Richard McBride as minister of mines.

Response to McBride's appointment varied. Coastal papers were willing to give him a chance. The *Colonist* expected that he would bring to the office "all the enthusiasm of youth and considerable practical experience in the needs of miners," which he had gleaned during his time at Atlin. The *World* thought his appointment "puzzling," given the "critical state" of mining affairs, but conceded his "undoubted abilities" and urged mining men to give him a trial. The *Inland Sentinel* correctly predicted that a New Westminster lawyer would "not be acceptable to the mining community." Even though one Interior paper described him as "the handsome man" in a group portrait of the cabinet, and some Interior editors admitted his abilities, they wondered if anyone "could have been selected who had less acquaintance among the mining men of the Kootenays and Yale." The unkindest comment came from the *Sandon Paystreak,* which called him "a shyster lawyer" who "didn't know a mine from a gravel pit."[33]

McBride was determined to learn something about the industry, which, though prospering, was troubled. He knew of problems between capital and labour, and though he did not ignore the owners' interests, he was concerned about the well-being of the miners. A major problem in the Kootenay and Boundary Districts concerned legislation that, in 1899, had established the maximum of eight hours of daily work for metalliferous miners. Mine owners had vigorously opposed the measure. When it came into effect, the Slocan mines closed after the owners announced that they would pay only $3.00 a day rather than the $3.50 they had paid for a ten-hour day. This first major strike of the province's hard-rock miners ended after six months when miners and owners reached a compromise of $3.25 a day, but tensions between miners and owners remained high. McBride hoped to resolve that and other problems relating to the industry by having a commission examine the mining acts with a view to amending them at the next session. When a delegation of the Associated Boards of Trade of Eastern British Columbia visited Victoria in August 1900, he told it that a commission would consider its resolutions.[34]

Opinion on the desirability of such a commission was divided. Friends such as the *Nelson Daily Miner* welcomed any measure to end conflict and looked forward to an inquiry on mining taxes. Mine operators were agreeable to the commission. Some opponents claimed that its only purpose was to satisfy those who wanted to repeal the eight-hour law. Miners actively petitioned against a commission. Others argued that the best thing the government could do for the industry, apart from building roads and trails, would be to stop "tinkering" with the law. The Legislature's mining committee also intimated that the industry would be best served by being left alone. Nevertheless, the ministry invited "experienced and reputable mining men" to give their opinions on mining laws, asked gold commissioners, mining recorders, and other provincial bureaucrats to consult mine managers and union officials about a proposed "uniform code of signals" for the mines, and circulated projected amendments to the Placer Mining Act.[35]

When Smith Curtis, the Rossland MLA, introduced a bill to end the eight-hour day, McBride said his proposed commission had nothing to do with hours of work. Apart from introducing minor legislation to deal with specific problems such as a dispute over claims in the Lake Bennett mining division and a measure to relieve British Columbians serving in South Africa from time limits that might affect their claims in their absence, McBride did little in the 1900 session to change mining legislation or to appoint a commission.[36]

In late November and early December 1901, almost three months after the session ended, McBride toured the mining communities of the southeast "to ascertain the requirements of all the men" in the industry. He spent much time with delegations from boards of trade and mining organizations. At Rossland, he apologized for delaying his visit because of the heavy duties of a new government but was impressed by the industry's urgent needs and promised to act as soon as possible. As immediate favours, he announced appropriations for a School of Mines, a wagon road on Sophie Mountain, and a government contribution to the forthcoming Glasgow Exhibition. He promised that after the commission reported, the government would codify and consolidate the mining laws, make titles more secure, and reduce the attendant legislation, but he also promised, "in the most emphatic manner possible," that there was "no fear of constant changes in the mining laws." To gain more knowledge of the industry, McBride toured the Hall Mines smelter at Nelson and the Ymir mine, and went through some of the workings at the Mother Lode copper mine near Greenwood and the Old Ironsides and Knob Hill mines at Phoenix. At Fernie, he inspected the Coal Creek Mines. He also visited Moyie, Kaslo, New Denver, Silverton, Slocan City, Nelson, Cranbrook, and Grand Forks.[37]

Political enemies charged that he used the tour to "stump" for the Conservatives in the federal election then under way, but most meetings were private ones, and at best, they received passing mention in the local press, often after the election. He met leading businessmen and, more importantly, let them meet him and see his interest in their communities. Sometimes, as at Cranbrook, his arrival was unexpected, and many stops were brief. At Phoenix, he had to leave before a lunch with local residents. At public meetings, such as those sponsored by boards of trade at Moyie, Grand Forks, and Greenwood, he heard requests for new bridges, better school buildings, and more mining offices, and for letting claim holders work on roads and trails to help meet the requirement that they complete a certain amount of improvement on their claims.

In the summer of 1901, he spent ten days with Denis Murphy, the local MLA, visiting Princeton, Aspen Grove, the Nicola Valley, and Copper Mountain, travelling mainly by stagecoach, visiting mines, meeting local residents, experiencing rough roads, and listening to "any who have grievances or think they have." From Ashcroft, McBride took the train to Kamloops and Revelstoke, and made a quick visit to Vernon, where MLA Price Ellison drove him to the Coldstream Ranch. He snatched a few moments of leisure, managing to bathe in some creeks and on one occasion to catch "two fine trout in ten minutes."[38] He was working hard to get to know the province and to have the people of the province know him.

The Dominion government saved him from having to appoint the controversial mining commission. During the federal election campaign, Clifford Sifton, the minister of the interior, indicated that Ottawa would investigate the mining industry. Moreover, McBride learned that "persistent tinkering" with the mining laws "at the hands of ignorant legislators has been the curse of the country." Thus, in 1901, he introduced a minimum of new legislation and only after getting advice from others, especially MLAs with particular interests in the industry. He endorsed another time extension for claim holders serving in South Africa but would not give them lifetime licences. He did not change laws relating to hydraulic mining; he asked the Nanaimo MLA for help in amending the Coal Mines Regulation Act to provide competency tests for underground miners; and he got advice from practical miners, mining recorders, and the MLAs for placer mining in Cassiar, Cariboo, and Lillooet to supplement his own observations at Atlin before amending the Placer Mining Act. These amendments, designed "to prevent rich hydraulic companies from getting possession of large areas" and to "do justice to the poor miner and improve his chances of profitable work," allowed larger claims and prevented wholesale staking and claim jumping.[39]

Laws affecting prospectors and coal miners did not concern Kootenay metal mine operators, but measures to improve mine safety did. The *Kaslo Kootenaian* objected to the "remarkable emanations from the brains" of the Legislature's mining committee. The *Rossland Miner* called a law requiring mine engineers to use a code of signals an "asinine act" and complained of the compulsory provincial inspection of steam boilers. It declared that the mining industry was "Sick Unto Death Because of the Operation of Whimsical Legislation Placed Upon Statute Books by Demagogic Legislators ... Useless to Look for Outside Capital Until Drastic Reforms Shall Have Been Inaugurated." At the end of June, the British Columbia Mining Association, representing metal mine owners, passed a petition that they called the Mine Managers' Memorial. Their objections to the Alien Labour Act and American customs duties lay beyond provincial remedy, but they also wanted relief from the "oppressive" provincial legislation of the past four years, including the eight-hour law, the "vexatious fees for boiler inspection," the new code of signals, and taxes. They blamed these laws for declines in investment and production, the closure of some mines, and the suspension of dividends by others. The CPR complained of inadequate returns in the past three or four years in the mining regions. Not everyone agreed with the mine owners. The *Cranbrook Herald* saw the Mine Managers' Memorial as special pleading; the *Rossland Evening World* thought it "hopelessly mixed up." The *Colonist,* Dunsmuir's mouthpiece, suggested that mine owners wanted to keep "the kernel of mining to themselves and leave only the husk for the rest of the people." McBride sought to encourage investment and "co-operate as far as possible" with investors while "endeavouring to hold the balance evenly between the employer and employee." He dismissed the memorial as a "political move mainly directed against the Provincial government" and, to a lesser extent, the federal government.[40]

He was much more concerned about tense relations between capital and labour. The Vancouver Island coal fields were notorious for labour disputes; Fraser River fishermen had only recently settled their second strike in as many years; and what was to become a long, bitter strike by miners at Rossland was under way. Sympathetic to miners, McBride warned that the antagonism and embitterment of class relations caused by any change in the eight-hour law "would do more harm in unsettling stable conditions than its continuance could possibly do injury to the country" and noted that the Miners' Union endorsed the signal codes, which only the manager of the Velvet Mine at Rossland opposed. He claimed the "few" amendments of the last session would make mining investments safer and encourage prospecting; he attributed a depression in the industry to "over booming" (speculation) and shortages of capital resulting from the South African war. Not everyone agreed. The *Rossland Miner* accused the government of breaking its election promises not to tinker with mining laws.[41]

In cabinet, McBride participated in general administration and attended meetings that were normally held at least once a week and sometimes daily. Much of the business was routine, such as appointing road superintendents and notaries public, granting hydraulic leases, issuing land and water records, and regulating hunting seasons. From time to time, especially during the session, the cabinet met delegations with requests for bridges, aid for local hospitals, and the like. After the session, McBride travelled on mining matters and constituency affairs. In the summer of 1901, for example, he discussed a gold assay office with the Vancouver Board of Trade and joined other cabinet members and MLAs on the Canners' Association's overnight excursion to see salmon traps in American waters.[42]

McBride faithfully attended the Legislature, and though he seldom participated in debate, his thrust remained sharp. Although they had been boyhood friends, his relationship with fellow MLA W.W.B. McInnes, the son of the discredited lieutenant-governor, did not prevent him from "giving back blow for blow, and scoring once or twice rather heavily" after McInnes accused the government of being a "partisan, a Conservative combination, which had dismissed Liberals." McBride had no mercy for Liberal leader Martin. When the former premier repeatedly tried to draw

Attorney General D.M. Eberts into debate, McBride, "with unimpassioned words, handled the leader of the opposition so keenly that the latter was fleeing to find shelter under the cry of order." Later that day, when Martin attacked John Irving, McBride "again turned the attack to the amusement of the house."[43]

McBride was most likely to speak on issues of interest to the Fraser Valley. In answering Opposition charges that the government had called out the militia to put down a fishermen's strike at Steveston, he said that the situation there was now "most quiet and orderly," and that the government had tried "to harmonize" relations between fishermen and canners. Although wanting to limit Asian competition, he sympathized with the salmon canners and accused the Opposition of "gallery play" in seeking to prohibit the employment of Chinese and Japanese labour on government land grants or assisted work projects.[44]

McBride knew that the province's scattered population made it impossible "to distribute benefits exactly as the government and the people might wish" but wanted everyone to enjoy as many services as possible. He endorsed an amendment to the Supreme Court Act to allow the court to sit at Nelson and Rossland but "deprecated any further decentralization" such as having the appellate court sit in the Kootenays. Earlier, he had argued that requiring all persons seeking naturalization to appear before a Supreme Court judge would cause hardship in distant places, but he voted for the measure because it would impede the naturalization of Chinese or Japanese immigrants. He supported a population-based graduated fee for liquor licences because a $200 fee was a hardship in sparsely settled areas. He asserted that people in distant locales paid taxes too and that the efficiency of remote schools must not be sacrificed for the benefit of city dwellers. In opposing a controversial redistribution bill, he argued that British Columbia needed a measure to "give justice to every portion of the province."[45]

Cabinet duties required McBride's presence in Victoria, so he moved Margaret, Mary, and Peggy to the city, where they established a home at 39 Victoria Crescent, a few minutes' walk from the Parliament Buildings. Complete with an Irish American nursemaid and a Chinese cook, the large house allowed for visitors and a growing family. "Another girl," Dorothea (called Dolly), was born on 30 September 1901.[46] McBride, who was often away, took trips on departmental business, went to New Westminster and Dewdney, where he examined the need for flood relief, opened fall fairs, attended picnics, and planned the construction of the Dewdney Trunk Road. Once he showed other MLAs the local salmon canneries and the city of New Westminster, which some of them had never seen. He was the lawyer of record in civil cases, but his partner J.D. Kennedy probably handled the courtroom work.[47]

Although McBride stuck to departmental duties during his Kootenay tour, rumours had surfaced in December 1900 that Dunsmuir wanted to get rid of him because his active support of the Conservatives in the federal election had upset the premier's Liberal supporters. McBride thought it no "crime to be a Conservative." As the recently elected president of the Liberal-Conservative Union of British Columbia, the name by which the Conservative Party was officially known, he played a minor role in the federal election by giving a few speeches and regretted that departmental duties prevented him from taking a greater part. Other cabinet ministers may have vetoed his participation in federal politics. At New Westminster, he attacked the federal Liberal candidate, Aulay Morrison, for doing nothing about American fish traps or the loose naturalization laws that let recent Japanese immigrants secure fishing licences and for helping his "alleged friends, the canners secure Japanese labor."[48]

Although the Legislature almost unanimously supported anti-Asian measures, it was divided on railway policy. Rumours persisted of conflict in cabinet and caucus, and of cabinet shuffles. The most divisive issue was the proposed railway to link the coast with the booming Boundary and Kootenay mining districts. The idea was popular, but the questions around it were complex: Should the railway be wholly a government work? If it were a private enterprise, should the CPR or the Vancouver, Victoria and Eastern (VV&E) get the necessary government subsidy? Because it held an effective monopoly, the CPR was not popular, but the VV&E was suspect because of its association with the American Great Northern Railway, whose branches from its main line in the United States were already carrying BC ore to American smelters.[49]

Though he thought Martin's plan to build the Coast-Kootenay railway as a government project was "a whirlwind proposition," McBride was keen for such a railway to be built. In the fall of 1900, he had expected it to be under construction within a year. In the 1901 Throne Speech debate, he attacked the hypocrisy of Martin's argument for a government railway since the Manitoba government, of which Martin had been a part, built the Red River Railway but sold it to private interests because it was a losing proposition. Without referring to the timing of construction or choice of company, McBride stressed that in any bargain with railways, the government's "sacred duty [was] to safeguard the rights and interests" of British

Columbians. As "lobbyists, log rollers and grafters" swarmed around the Parliament Buildings, seeking a subsidy for the new railway, the press reported "a sentiment of distrust and suspicion on both sides of the chamber." Some newspapers referred to "a crisis at Victoria," a split in caucus and cabinet that would defeat Dunsmuir. The cabinet favoured the CPR, but seven or eight backbenchers wanted the line to be independent of it. McBride, "with much desk thumping," told caucus that cabinet would not change its mind about favouring the CPR and that it, not the Legislature, would decide on the railway contract. The next day, the government brought in a Loan Bill authorizing it to borrow $5 million to assist public works including a railway from English Bluff (Tsawwassen) to Midway in the Boundary District, with provision for daily ferry service to Vancouver Island. Symptomatic of political confusion were a split in the Opposition, evidence of "extreme friendliness" between Dunsmuir and Martin, and the government's "coquetting" with some Opposition members. The railway subsidy bill that strained relations between the government and some of its former supporters was a catalyst for general dissatisfaction with the Dunsmuir government among those who had accepted it only as a "tentative" administration. "The game of politics in British Columbia" was indeed "a most exciting pastime."[50]

McBride was the government's only spokesman in the debate on second reading of the Loan Bill. He chastised those who had been "swayed by a few agitators" to clamour for immediate construction at any cost. He supported government ownership of railways but thought it impractical because the railway needed eastern connections, which would mean an arrangement with the CPR. Mass meetings in Vancouver, Victoria, and Rossland had called for a line independent of the CPR, but McBride argued that despite the company's faults, he favoured "our own great national highway instead of adding to the wealth of a foreign monopoly." To get a continental connection, the VV&E would almost certainly link up with another railway, probably the American-based Great Northern Railway, and maintain high passenger and freight rates. McBride promised that, if a company were to receive the subsidy, it must let the province control its rates. Finally, he chided coastal residents who pressed their own interests. He reminded them that the New Westminster Bridge, then under construction, would bring American lines into Vancouver without additional cost and that the Loan Bill provided for ferry service to Vancouver Island. Yet, he argued, "Vast districts [were] almost wholly without proper communication and the government would be false to their trust if they neglected their duty in that respect." The Opposition press did not agree with the terms of the Loan Bill: the *Times* complained that the CPR had more friends in government than the city of Victoria did and that a provision in the Loan Bill to provide $500,000 for the New Westminster Bridge would benefit Vancouver and New Westminster but not Victoria; the *Nelson Daily Miner* called McBride a "political transgressor" and accused the government of engaging "in intrigues to perpetuate a wrong."[51] The government made some concessions and the Loan Bill passed.

Speculation about a cabinet shuffle continued. According to one report, McBride would become provincial secretary, and R.F. Green of Kaslo, one of his best friends, would become minister of mines. While McBride was in the Interior on department business, rumours circulated that Dunsmuir would appoint J.C. Brown of New Westminster as provincial secretary, replacing J.H. Turner, who had resigned to become provincial agent-general in London. That, the *Times* speculated, would "create a most interesting situation" since Brown and McBride were enemies, and Brown's presence in cabinet would "minimize" McBride's "prestige" on the Lower Mainland. It recalled that McBride had earlier threatened to resign if Brown were appointed. On the evening of 2 September, McBride, who had learned of Brown's appointment from a newspaper, returned from the Interior. The next morning Dunsmuir announced that Brown was joining the cabinet. McBride was indignant. After briefly consulting his father, who was visiting and who advised him to "resign everything but your honour," McBride went to a cabinet meeting at 10:30. Within the hour, he had resigned from the cabinet. He told the press, "I have resigned from the government for reasons which the government will surmise." McBride declared that, by putting a Martinite in the cabinet, Dunsmuir had "betrayed his party." He asked, "What's the use of being in a cabinet, when there's a man present for whom politically you have no use?" He turned his resignation into a point of principle.[52]

Press interpretations of his resignation varied. The *Colonist* called it a "surprise," and a confidante of the premier suggested that Dunsmuir "had no idea of the storm which his peculiar action had caused." The *Times* thought McBride "too tender in his political sensitivities" and was shocked that anyone would "throw up a cabinet position" because he objected to a colleague. Friendly journals such as the *British Columbian* described his action as "a noble example ... of standing for the right against political trickery and prostitution." The *Nelson Tribune* put it simply – "McBride did right." Other editors were pleased to see McBride go. The *Kootenay*

Mail of Revelstoke claimed that his "excessive" partisanship had brought considerable trouble to the cabinet and suggested that he had "shown the white feather"; the *Inland Sentinel* stated that McBride had "ignored the Premier's coquetting with the Martin-Brown element" as long as it only voted with the government but, being unable to "stomach having to share with Mr. Brown the dispensation of the government pap," would "now pose as the Tory chieftain who sacrificed a good job for the sake of his party." Trying to make sense of the confusion, the *Vernon News* explained, "We now have virtually three parties in the Province: the Dunsmuir-Martin combination; the faction led by McBride, and that under the leadership of Smith Curtis. Until a count is made when the next session is held it will hardly be possible to know exactly how we stand."[53]

For the McBride family, the resignation meant returning to New Westminster. For McBride himself, it meant living at the Imperial Hotel in Victoria during the 1902 session and making weekend trips to visit the family and attend to constituency business. He often travelled with Thomas Gifford, who won the by-election caused by Brown's appointment to the cabinet. McBride participated in Gifford's campaign and remained active in New Westminster. He served on the Legislative Committee of the New Westminster Board of Trade, and he gave toasts at banquets of the Ancient Order of Foresters and of the Masons and in honour of the Shamrock Lacrosse Club. With Aulay Morrison, the Liberal MP, he opened a bazaar at St. Peter's Roman Catholic Church, and with Margaret, he attended the Bachelor's Ball.[54]

In Dewdney, he helped open the Coquitlam town hall and held public meetings in Maple Ridge, Mission, Port Moody, and Port Hammond. In September 1902, accompanied by Margaret, he spent several days touring the constituency and opening fall fairs in Mission and Coquitlam. He usually mentioned local concerns, mostly roads, and boasted of how, despite scanty appropriations and discrimination against Opposition constituencies, he had secured funds to build the Dewdney Trunk Road, which the *Columbian* called his "hobby, if he has one." He explained his actions in the Legislature, his break with Dunsmuir, and his dissatisfaction with the government's railway and financial policies. When he was not with constituents, he found opportunities for relaxation. During the fall of 1902, with Gifford and other local sportsmen, he made a week-long fishing trip to the Lillooet River, which was in his constituency. Later that fall, he had a good bag of ducks and geese during a hunting trip up the Pitt River.[55]

After resigning from the cabinet and withdrawing his support of the government, McBride emerged as the leader of a recognized faction. He was centre stage at the New Westminster meeting of Oppositionists early in January 1902 but was not yet confirmed as leader of the Opposition. In February, he and Gifford were among those who spoke at a closed meeting of labouring and business men in New Westminster who opposed Martin "and all his works" and who planned to sink "all questions of party lines in an uncompromising opposition to Martinism." McBride and Gifford left almost immediately to catch the *Charmer,* the steamship that would take them to Victoria, where they planned to attend a caucus meeting on the eve of the opening of the Legislature. The *Charmer* was late, so the meeting started at 10 P.M. and went on to 3:00 A.M. The eighteen MLAs present selected McBride as their leader, with R.F. Green, Robert Tatlow, A.W. Neill, C.W. Munro, Denis Murphy, and H.D. Helmcken as an advisory committee. The others were Gifford, Smith Curtis, F.J. Fulton, J.F. Garden, W.H. Hayward, Thomas Kidd, A.E. McPhillips, E.C. Smith, and Thomas Taylor. C.W.D. Clifford and S.A. Rogers left before the meeting ended. McBride told the *Times* that his group was "thoroughly organized" and would take "active and aggressive action" without being a "factious opposition." He expected the defeat of the government, the formation of "a good strong working government ... to carry on the business of the House to the end of its natural political term," and the support of two Liberal-Labour members, J.H. Hawthornthwaite and Smith Curtis. On 20 January, the first day of the session, McBride accepted the congratulations of friends, rose, "threw out his chest," and "on behalf of the members of His Majesty's Loyal Opposition," gave what the *Times* called "a rather clever introduction" of himself as the leader of what the *Province* dubbed "the Dickey birds" as it questioned the cohesiveness of his group.[56]

With the support of McBride and his allies, the government narrowly won the first vote on a routine procedural matter. Martin's loyalties, however, were uncertain; he had told fellow Liberals that he would behave in an "entirely untrammelled" manner in the House, where he acted as the leader of the Opposition by seconding the motion to name an acting Speaker and took over the Opposition caucus room, forcing McBride and his supporters to meet in the Cedar Committee Room. In the meantime, legislative staff moved the desks on the floor of the chamber to indicate that McBride was the Opposition leader. Sitting in the leader's chair, with Smith Curtis and A.E. McPhillips on either side of him, McBride refused Martin's order to move. Saying that it was "a blackguardly, low, dirty thing to put me out of my seat," Martin accused him of being a bully and proposed to take his former seat. Curtis told Martin that he was no longer leader of the Opposition and should move to the government side. The gallery cheered. During the opening prayers, Martin took McBride's seat. Curtis pushed him back. After prayers, Martin and his supporters McInnes and H.B. Gilmour continued their physical fight with Curtis, who had Hawthornthwaite's assistance. At one point, Martin sat in the chair and McBride spoke from the desk! During a three-hour stand-off, no business was done. Eventually, a compromise allowed Martin and his five supporters to sit at the foot of the Opposition row.[57]

A week's break did not cool tempers. In the interval, J.P. Booth, who was elected Speaker in absentia, died after a long illness. In the vote on a new Speaker, both Martin and McBride sought to second a motion calling on C.E. Pooley of Esquimalt to take the chair. Martin caught the clerk's eye and was thus able to second the motion. Seconding such a motion was traditionally an Opposition prerogative, so the symbolism was significant. The next day, however, the new Speaker and Premier Dunsmuir recognized McBride as the leader of the Opposition. As McBride rose to speak, he was applauded. After thanking Opposition members for choosing him as their leader, he said he wanted to refrain from "fractious opposition," explained his resignation from the government, and outlined what could loosely be called a program. It presented many themes to which he would return in future. Recognizing regional differences, he expressed pleasure that the old Island versus Mainland "cry was now buried" and that redistribution had unanimous support. Yet he was surprised by Dunsmuir's plan to have the Toronto-based railway promoters William Mackenzie and Donald Mann build a line from Yellowhead Pass to Bute Inlet. He criticized the failure of the Throne Speech to say much about the Coast-Kootenay railway or about the Cariboo and East Yale (the Okanagan). Noting strong support for Better Terms, he voiced the common argument that British Columbia had had to pay for some public works that, in other provinces, had been funded by Ottawa, but he attacked the Legislature for not making a decided stand on the issue. He opposed the use of fish traps, supported a ban on log exports, referred to the province's "most serious" financial condition, complained that the Throne Speech did not mention the Asian question, and warned that the Japanese were "making inroads into the realm of white labor." In conclusion, expressing his British loyalties, he called the Prince of Wales's recent visit to Canada "a distinct movement in the federation of the British possessions."[58]

In the meantime, McBride actively participated in the Victoria by-election campaign to replace J.H. Turner. At the large public meeting in Victoria that opened the campaign, he was presented with a lavish bouquet as leader of the Opposition. He expressed pleasure at the support of "a solid, united body of earnest, conscientious men," repeated calls for the construction of railways and public works, redistribution, the development of natural resources, and a ban on Oriental immigration. He promised to "preserve the heritage of the people, and discountenance 'grafting'" in government financial dealings.[59]

Provincial politics remained in a fluid state, as indicated by the fact that McBride, a Conservative, spoke at several public meetings on behalf of E.V. Bodwell, a Liberal who opposed the Dunsmuir government and was running for the Opposition against E.G. Prior, the government's Conservative candidate. While emphasizing the need for improved railway communication, McBride attacked the proposed contract with Mackenzie and Mann "as a fake" that authorized them only to put surveyors in the field. He especially criticized the government for going "to the east" to hire J.N. Greenshields, a Montreal lawyer, who allegedly also worked for Mackenzie and Mann, to be its agent in dealing with them. At one meeting, he asked, "Was Mr. Dunsmuir and his business connection going to rule the country, or were the people going to run it?" One of Prior's advertisements asked whether voters wanted "A Business Government or a Lawyers' Government," a reference to the fact that McBride, Bodwell, and several of Bodwell's supporters were lawyers.[60]

By a narrow margin of 1,539 to 1,484, voters chose Prior. The *Columbian* doubted that government could find stability as long as men such as Martin and his followers held the balance of power. The *Vernon News,* however, expected that Prior would strengthen the Dunsmuir government, which was "immeasurably superior to anything" that McBride could form. The *Ladysmith Leader* thought that McBride looked "somewhat subdued" after the by-election, adding that, if Bodwell had won, the legislative chamber would have been too "small for his accession of self-importance." Many issues raised in the by-election reverberated throughout the unusually long session – 121 days on which the Legislature actually sat for 102 – and raised uncertainty about the survival of the Dunsmuir administration. A few days after the by-election, McBride began charging that Prior had won his seat under false pretences and demanded to see the papers relating to the contract with Mackenzie and Mann. Despite Dunsmuir's agreement that a royal commission under Mr. Justice George A. Walkem would investigate the matter, McBride so violently denounced the proposed deal

In a Chaotic Legislature, 1898-1903

LEADER OF OBSTRUCTION.

The *Victoria Colonist* vigorously opposed McBride in 1902. Here, its cartoonist portrays him as using a light to draw attention to himself. Note, too, how the cartoonist emphasized McBride's hair in the caricature. *Victoria Colonist,* 1 June 1902, cartoonist, Gordon Smith.

that the Speaker called him to order. Hawthornthwaite and Curtis accused Dunsmuir of a conflict of interest in proposing to offer an "excessive" subsidy to Mackenzie and Mann in order to sell his E&N to them at a higher price, but McBride did not think that any member of the government was "guilty of a deliberate, dishonest or dishonourable act."[61] He soon changed his tune. Appearing before the Walkem royal commission, he attacked the use of Greenshields and called the proposed subsidy of $4,500 to $4,800 per mile and a generous land grant "exorbitant." In the House, he moved a want of confidence because of the government's "vicious" intent to give away the people's land and money "on a wholesale plan, to fill the pocket of railway promoters." The government survived the motion with a two-vote margin. McBride persisted. Little more than a week later, he moved for the return of papers relating to Greenshields's appointment. He said that Price Ellison, the member for Yale-East, had been "made a tool of by the government." When Ellison demanded that he retract his statement, McBride acceded to the Speaker's request that he apologize for using unparliamentary language, but the Speaker repeatedly called him to order as he accused the government of "bribery, corruption, and malfeasance" in the Greenshields matter. As the session dragged on, McBride returned to the subject of Mackenzie and Mann's railway – the Edmonton, Yukon and Pacific – also known as the Canadian Northern Railway (CNR).[62] Declaring that the Opposition "had a duty to perform," he threatened to fight the issue even if took all summer.[63]

Premier Dunsmuir's position was precarious. His government usually survived with a one- or two-vote margin. When it was finally defeated by one vote on a supply motion to provide funds for government operations, McBride immediately rose, cited British precedents, and moved that, having lost control of the Legislature, it should resign. His motion was defeated by one vote. After Dunsmuir invited him to a private meeting, the Opposition caucus met secretly and allegedly discussed a possible rapprochement with the government. Afterward, McBride and several other MLAs went to the Mainland, supposedly to discuss the situation with friends and constituents. The press speculated that Dunsmuir had offered to resign at the end of the session. One report suggested that if Dunsmuir were defeated, the lieutenant-governor would call on McBride to form a new government. In the meantime, by offering a land subsidy for a railway on the Queen Charlotte Islands, Dunsmuir gained the support of two members and survived a vote on the budget.[64]

In the budget debate, McBride spoke from midnight until nine in the morning, with only a little huskiness in his voice betraying fatigue as his followers provided cooling drinks and throat lozenges. He severely criticized the government's policies, stressed that "he would avail himself of any means" to defeat it, and claimed that he would rather be a humble politician than a minister "in a government in which decency, manliness and honesty were wanting." Yet he called Dunsmuir "an honest man" who had been "led astray and dominated by a coterie of unscrupulous politicians," a reference that particularly applied to Martin. As for the budget, he complained that it did not show confidence, offered no idea of how to consolidate the provincial debt, and did not mention the "most important matter" before the public – railway policy.[65]

Railways remained a divisive topic. Ironically, in light of his subsequent actions as premier, McBride called the CNR "a promoter's company" without financial standing, accused the government of being "dishonest and shameful" in connection with the contract, and argued that because the CNR would be under federal control, a clause in the contract giving the province 2 percent of its gross earnings would be ineffective. He averred that evidence presented to the Walkem royal commission suggested that Dunsmuir's only objective was personal gain through the sale of the E&N and that in making the contract with the CNR, his "sole purpose" was "to deceive the people and enable the government to retain power." Implying that Attorney General Eberts was also guilty of misconduct, he concluded that he himself could never "affiliate again" with members of the government. By two votes the Legislature defeated his amendment that no agreement with the CNR should take effect until the Legislature ratified it. McBride also asserted that plans for railways from Midway to Vernon and from Kitimat to Hazelton were wanting.[66]

Railways were not his only interest. They and many other issues of that time would concern him as premier. He agreed with the government that Better Terms, the demand for a more generous subsidy from Ottawa, was "the most important question" before the province. He joined Martin in condemning Ottawa for citing "imperial reasons" in its most recent disallowance of British Columbia's attempts to halt Asian immigration. He threatened Dunsmuir with a vote of confidence for delaying the tabling of the relevant correspondence with Ottawa and asked the government to educate public opinion in eastern Canada on the matter. Given the special problem of dealing with Japan because of Anglo-Japanese treaties, he proposed using "diplomatic means" to restrict Japanese immigration and employment. He urged the attorney general "to put his foot down and take a firm stand against the encroachment of the aliens on the rights of our own subjects" but observed that a proposed clause in the Fisheries Act to deny fishing licences to Asians might imperil the bill. Instead, he proposed to change the wording of the amendment to declare that licences should be issued only to British subjects. The Legislature agreed with his proposal.[67] However, many Japanese immigrants became naturalized British subjects, so the measure did little to slow their influx into the industry.

He conceded that the government had tried to present a fair redistribution bill but added that Vancouver Island and possibly the city of Vancouver were overrepresented at the expense of the Kootenays and the rural districts. His concern for fair redistribution was sincere, but his attack was so strong that the Speaker twice called him to order. He opposed increasing the number of MLAs and "deprecated entertaining any Island vs. Mainland feeling" since the province "could not afford to entertain sectionalism."[68]

After the Dunsmuir administration narrowly survived the budget vote, the *Nelson Daily News* had suggested that its fate would be decided by the relative "physical endurance" of the government and the Opposition. The *Times* noted that the youthful McBride had the most physical endurance of any MLA. Some newspapers, however, accused McBride of being an obstructionist. The pro-Dunsmuir *Colonist* called some of his long speeches "an endless rehearsal of political generalities," a "purely obstructionist" tactic. In reviving the old Island versus Mainland conflict, it described the Opposition as the "Mainland Conservative Party" and McBride as a "hide-bound lawyer." On a point of privilege, McBride complained about "certain scurrilous passages" in "Premier Dunsmuir's newspaper" and read from it until Speaker Eberts, who was Dunsmuir's solicitor and a director of the *Colonist,* called him to order. That encouraged the *Colonist* to continue its tirades against McBride, though it admitted that he could perhaps "live down" his reputation for obstruction.[69] Similarly, the *Province* accused the Opposition of formulating its discussion of public affairs not for the people at large but for party purposes "in the most restricted sense of the word." The *Ladysmith Leader,* also in Dunsmuir's pocket, alleged that McBride had engaged in nine-hour speeches and obstructionism to keep Dunsmuir from attending the coronation of King Edward VII. Denying this claim, McBride said that the Opposition would vote supply and pass other necessary legislation if the government made a few concessions and agreed to test provincial opinion on its railway policy in a general election.[70]

The *Colonist*'s claim that the Opposition was a "party of sixteen men with sixteen different ideas of policy and at least ten different ideas of who should eventually be leader" was exaggerated but had some basis in truth. The Opposition was not fully united. Neither W.H. Hayward, the member for Esquimalt, nor H.D. Helmcken joined McBride in voting against the controversial CNR contract. When Joseph Hunter taunted him for claiming to have twenty followers, McBride replied that he would have had that many "if members had kept their word." Although Hawthornthwaite did not attend caucus meetings, McBride believed that "he was always ready to vote with the opposition to defeat the government." When, by a two-to-one margin, the government won a vote on second reading of a measure relating to the Coast-Kootenay railway, the *Colonist* predicted that McBride's leadership "was approaching its conclusion." In contrast, as the session finally ended, the *World* observed that "despite predictions to the contrary, the opposition led by Mr. McBride stood well together ... and has the unchallengeable credit of, in many ways, checking a reckless government and safeguarding the interest of the province."[71]

Over the summer, the press printed rumours regarding the future of the government. One story had Eberts as premier; another named Prior. Both suggested that any new administration would include McBride. Given that McBride had attacked Prior for a supposed alliance with Martin, he was unlikely to be chosen for any cabinet that Prior might form. Press friends dismissed as a slur on the Opposition the suggestion that McBride and his allies could be "tempted to political wrong-doing by the offer of a cabinet position."[72]

In New Westminster, on 15 December 1902, which was incidentally his thirty-second birthday, McBride and Thomas Gifford recounted the previous session. Accusing the Dunsmuir administration of being "afraid of the people," McBride called for a general election before the government introduced legislation that would entail "immense concessions of the assets of the province," a reference particularly to the "iniquitous" CNR scheme from which, he said, only the Opposition's firmness had saved the province. Yet he complained that some members who had pledged to support the Opposition were "so closely identified with the Canadian Northern legislation" that they forgot their promise.[73]

As the time of the Liberal-Conservative convention at Revelstoke approached, speculation grew: How would the convention divide on the adoption of party lines? Prior promised to "bend his energies" to bring about a Conservative government, whereas McBride favoured party lines but wanted an election first. With only Semlin dissenting, the convention accepted McBride's view. Several editors expressed the hope that the introduction of party lines would end the political instability.[74]

The convention's other major issue was leadership. Would the new leader be Prior, Eberts, Tatlow, or McBride, or would certain Vancouver and Victoria Conservatives prevail in their desire to postpone the selection of a leader? Fearing "serious dissension and tempestuous controversy" – apparently because of strong opposition to McBride – some provincial Conservatives persuaded the relatively new federal leader Robert L. Borden and several MPs who were touring the West to attend the convention. In his memoirs, Borden, who presided over a federal party that was in a transitional state, recalled that McBride was the "obvious choice."[75] A hundred delegates, including McBride's brother Leonard, who represented Delta, reached a compromise. After listening to McBride, Prior, and Francis Carter-Cotton speak, they refused to accept Charles Wilson's resignation as leader, even though he had not sat in the Legislature since 1886.[76] In quipping "Well if it's not Prior, it shan't be McBride," a *World* correspondent possibly captured the mood of the convention, which ended with a "love feast" of Carter-Cotton, Prior, and McBride united in a common front against Martin. Editorially, the *World* wondered how they could fall into line behind Wilson despite "McBride's unchallengeable leadership at the present." Any harmony that had prevailed at the Revelstoke convention dissipated once it seemed likely that Dunsmuir would resign. According to one report, Wilson believed that he should be premier and that "no Island man should in future be eligible for the premiership." The *Kamloops Standard* grumbled that Vancouver-area Conservatives believed "they are British Columbia." Happily, it added, the Interior "is not consumed with such jealousy" and was friendly with both Prior and McBride. Ever the diplomat, at the opening of new Conservative clubrooms in Vancouver, McBride paid a "graceful tribute" to Wilson, who would certainly lead the party "to victory."[77]

Dunsmuir, who had assumed the premiership solely on an interim basis, resigned on 21 November 1902, a move that surprised no one. Since the province had not yet adopted party lines, the press speculated as to who could command the most support in the Legislature and who might be invited into the cabinet in an effort to solidify the government. There were no party whips, and alliances could shift according to the issue of the moment or personal pique. One report stated that Eberts believed he could form a cabinet, with McBride as minister of mines. Some said that Prior was competing for the premiership but that the "straight party men" on both sides feared a general election. "These political rumors from the coast," mused the *Nelson Daily News*, "show to what a low pass the business of governing this province has fallen." Constitutionally, Dunsmuir had the right to recommend a successor and so advised Lieutenant-Governor Henri Joly de Lotbinière to ask Prior to form an administration. McBride, F.J. Fulton, Gifford, and Thomas Kidd were in Victoria at the time. When McBride was asked about the likelihood of any Opposition members entering the cabinet, he replied, "You may say that I just laughed," a comment echoed by R.F. Green, his "trusty whip." McBride denied having received any messages on the subject from Prior and said that he would not accept them. This may have been correct, but three days later the press quoted Prior as saying that he had offered portfolios to McBride and Tatlow, who had briefly considered them before refusing.[78]

The Opposition caucus was not solid. Denis Murphy left to join the cabinet. That, suggested the *Province*, made McBride less confident of defeating the government, but Murphy soon withdrew from the necessary by-election in Yale West, possibly because of scant support in his home base of Ashcroft. In his place, Charles Semlin accepted the nomination as Opposition candidate. When Prior cancelled the by-election, apparently because he thought Semlin would win, McBride attacked his "high-handed action."[79]

Another by-election was held in North Nanaimo after W.W.B. McInnes was appointed to the cabinet. McBride visited just after the writ was dropped, but the Opposition did not run a candidate and may have supported Parker Williams, the Socialist. In the coal-mining town of Ladysmith, McInnes claimed that McBride "was trying to make a monkey out of the Socialist Party" by supporting Williams. McInnes won easily. At almost the same time, the government finally held a by-election in North Victoria, which included the Gulf Islands, to replace J.P. Booth. On Mayne Island, McBride chaired the annual Christmas tree party at the school and the next day spoke on behalf of T.W. Paterson, the successful Independent candidate.[80]

The government soon found another candidate to run in Yale West; this was George Sanson, who, according to the Opposition, had "unlimited funds" from Dunsmuir. Following the issuing of the writ early in 1903, McBride made several tours on Semlin's behalf. He first concentrated on the Fraser Canyon communities of Lytton, North Bend, and Hope, then visited Ashcroft and the Nicola Valley before going to Hedley, Princeton, and Granite Creek, and returned to Spences Bridge and Yale. From time to time, Tatlow accompanied him, but what attracted attention was the presence of John Oliver, a Liberal, on the platform at several meetings. With the lack of federal party lines provincially, this should not necessarily have been surprising, but Oliver had attacked McBride during the previous legislative session and had been allied with Joseph Martin. The *Colonist* "smiled" as it asked what Oliver and McBride had in common with each other or with Semlin. The meeting at Ashcroft appears to have been typical. Tatlow criticized Prior's recent manifesto and plan to borrow $3.5 million to subsidize a transcontinental railway; Oliver focused on the CNR proposition; and Semlin attacked the public debt. McBride concluded the meeting by suggesting that the CNR agreement would put millions of dollars into the promoters' pockets. He also read a telegram from T.W. Paterson, who had won in North Victoria, as evidence that the Opposition was strong. At Lower Nicola, he said that voting for Sanson, the government's candidate, would "centralize the railway at Victoria." Occasionally, due to the vagaries of the railway timetable, the candidates and their supporters were obliged to hold joint meetings at unusual times. At Yale, where the meeting began at 11:00 P.M., the *Columbian* reported that Prior and Eberts were "heard in silence," whereas McBride and Oliver "were cheered to the echo." The partisan *Colonist* said that McBride and Oliver encountered "cool receptions." The *Kamloops Standard*, which circulated in Yale West, accused McBride of allying "himself with every man and every principle he was elected to oppose" and blamed him and Tatlow for the blunders of the Dunsmuir government. Betraying sectionalism, it concluded its scathing editorial by remarking that "these prominent political failures who come streaming up from Vancouver and its vicinity to induce West Yale to make its interests subservient to those of the coast, only serve to emphasize the helplessness of Mr. Semlin and the selfish aims of the coast."[81]

Semlin won all but three polls, a result that had a province-wide significance. Although the *Colonist* was unsure whether the victory properly belonged to McBride, Martin, or Semlin, it thought a defeat for the government was "an unfortunate thing for the province." The *Province* warned that McBride could not sustain a government since "the joyous 'combination' which stumped West Yale has been dissolved." It predicted the adoption of party lines and a general election, a prognostication echoed by the *Inland Sentinel*, which claimed that many people had voted for Sanson lest the defeat of the government put McBride in power. Similarly, the *Nelson Daily News* suggested that a McBride government "would be a greater menace to the country than the present Prior administration held in check by the Martin faction." This comment would not have surprised its readers; earlier, the paper had referred to McBride and the "little clique of office seekers who constitute his following." Martin's statement that he preferred Prior to McBride led some to conclude that, without the support of the Martinites, McBride could not maintain a government.[82] Given McBride's antipathy to Martin, such support was unlikely.

The session opened on 2 April, but McBride and many other MLAs went to Victoria early in March. According to one rumour, Prior and McBride had negotiated an "emergency coalition" to let Prior survive the session. Other speculation concerned party lines. Some opposed them. The *Province* claimed that adoption of party lines would "inevitably" lead to "a whole train of evils ... corruption at the polls, ballot-stuffing, in filling public offices with incompetent men who have obtained the promise of position as the price of their political freedom." Grudgingly, the *Times* proclaimed, "If party lines are the only means by which these ignoble squabblings can be brought to an end and responsible government made possible in British Columbia, by all means let us have party lines." But, it admonished, party lines would "not change the disposition of our public men." Both the Liberals and the Conservatives had disunited caucuses. Few Liberals would work with Martin; not all Conservatives, including McBride, supported Prior. Moreover, recent history had shown a willingness of some MLAs to ignore party lines. The *Kamloops Standard,* for example, was concerned about F.J. Fulton, the Kamloops MLA, who seemed to belong to what it called "the unholy alliance" of McBride, Oliver, Smith Curtis, and Joseph Martin. In including Martin's name in this list, it was out of touch, for McBride and Martin were certainly not in any alliance. The *Standard* was on firmer ground in wondering whether McBride and Tatlow realized the inconsistency of campaigning for Bodwell in Victoria. It reminded them that under party lines they would have "to come together as soon as possible, instead of fighting as much as possible." The *Times* noted that most Conservatives favoured party lines and that, with McBride and Wilson working together, only Prior stood in the way of forming a Conservative government.[83]

The Throne Speech promised conciliatory legislation to resolve severe labour problems, notably conflict in the coal fields and among CPR workers, which led Ottawa to have a royal commission investigate. The speech pointed to growth in the prairies that would create markets for BC products, voiced such an auspicious outlook for railway construction that little aid would be needed, and promised to make dyking more accessible, improve safety regulations for coal mines, and readjust taxes on metal mines. It hailed Ottawa's plan to raise the Chinese head tax to $500 and promised to re-enact disallowed legislation relating to Oriental immigration in the hope that Ottawa "would recognize the wisdom of such legislation" and let the "rights of the province" prevail. In the subsequent debate on the Throne Speech, McBride cited the recent by-election results as evidence of lack of confidence in the government. Nevertheless, he admitted some good points in the government's plans while chastising it for its failings. He agreed with the need for new labour legislation but thought the government's plan more of a "subterfuge" than a "well thought out and decisive remedy." Strikes, he said, were "terrible things," and he added that, in the recent troubles at the Ladysmith collieries, "the employer and not the employee was to blame." He hoped that Ladysmith's management and labour could soon resolve their differences and end the work stoppage, and he suggested looking at New Zealand's conciliation legislation. He revived old complaints about fish traps and urged negotiations with the United States to replace them with gill nets to preserve "an imperilled industry." He blamed the depressed state of the mining industry not on taxes but on the promoters of fraudulent mining ventures – "floaters of rotten companies" – and urged the province to cooperate with federal and imperial authorities to devise a means of punishing them. He wondered why Natal and New Zealand could exclude Asians, whereas British Columbia could not, and accused the government of not pressing Ottawa hard enough for Japanese exclusion. Introducing a tactic that he would put to good use later in his career, he declared that if Ottawa did not act, the province should appeal "to the throne itself." In another foretelling of his later policies, he asserted that the premier's "first duty" was to see to the construction of the CNR.[84]

McBride's critics were not impressed by his remarks. The *Kamloops Standard* called them "positively inane," "a pitiful exhibition," and a disappointment since McBride, usually a good and interesting speaker, admitted that he had not had time to study the Throne Speech. After accusing him of wandering over a variety of topics for an hour before getting to the speech itself and to the future of the government, the *Colonist* declared that the Opposition might be able to defeat the government but that McBride could not form one. It may have been correct, but the *Columbian* remarked that whenever McBride won a new supporter, Prior's "magnet draws a floater from the opposition caucus." The Throne Speech was accepted without division. Then, on 15 April, Smith Curtis called for dissolution and an appeal to the province. McBride thought the recent redistribution, the by-election results, and the need for settled political conditions were strong arguments for an election. The vote on Curtis's resolution was seventeen to seventeen; the Speaker saved the government.[85]

The Prior administration faced other problems, including a scandal concerning the cancellation of a land grant to the Columbia and Western Railway (C&W), which had become a subsidiary of the CPR. When the company was chartered in 1896, the province had granted it 20,000 acres per mile to build from Trail to Penticton. It built 100 miles from Trail to Midway. Under the subsidy, the company was entitled to select Crown lands contiguous to the right of way. When it requested that the grant encompass two large blocks of land, Blocks 4593 and 4594 in the Crow's Nest Pass, some three hundred miles to the east, which were thought to contain coal and petroleum, the Dunsmuir government had complied, granting the lands to the C&W by Order-in-Council in August 1901. Some months later, it cancelled the grant, a measure that the Legislature ratified in 1903. McBride, who was in the cabinet at the time of the original grant, supported this move. Given the CPR's unpopularity in British Columbia, the cancellation should have been well received and should have proceeded smoothly, but it was rumoured that the lieutenant-governor would not assent to it, presumably because the whole matter was under investigation.[86]

On 7 April 1903, John Oliver moved for the appointment of a select committee to investigate the C&W land grant. Having been involved in the cabinet discussions concerning the original subsidy, McBride was a major witness at the select committee, which held thirty-three sittings, heard twenty-three witnesses, and published an 815-page transcript of the evidence. Though somewhat ambiguous in his recollections and pleading cabinet confidentiality, McBride admitted not paying much attention to the matter, which lay outside the jurisdiction of his department, but he did remember hearing W.C. Wells, the chief commissioner of lands and works, say that transferring the remote Crow's Nest Pass lands to the C&W was a good deal because it would preserve for the government 200,000 more accessible acres elsewhere. Only after he left the cabinet had he learned of the coal and petroleum. The CPR had not approached him for help in getting the grant, and he "had no pecuniary advantage to gain by it."[87]

As a result of the committee report and allegedly because of inefficiencies in their departments, Premier Prior asked Wells and Attorney General Eberts, who had not supported cancelling the C&W grant, to resign. Further weakening the cabinet was W.W.B. McInnes's announcement that he would resign once the supply bill passed in order "to expedite the holding of a general election on party lines." The weakness of Prior's government was obvious; it lost motions to go into supply and had to adjourn for the day. Admitting defeat, Prior said he would seek dissolution. McBride suggested that if the lieutenant-governor acceded without Prior having the support of the House, it would mark "a new departure in constitutional history." Believing that the people favoured him, McBride asked Prior how long he would continue "with no one really in control of the House" and with a government reduced to the premier and one cabinet minister.[88]

As the cabinet almost disappeared, it was learned that Prior's hardware firm had been awarded a government contract for material to build the Chimney Creek bridge in the Cariboo. It was alleged that Prior saw the other tenders before his firm submitted its bid. When a select committee of the Legislature inquired into the matter, Prior denied any involvement with the bid or its acceptance. Moreover, he did not think it inappropriate for his firm to deal with the government.[89] About 10:00 A.M. on the morning of 1 June 1903, Prior received a letter from Lieutenant-Governor Henri Joly de Lotbinière informing him that his views "in explanation and justification of your action, in your answer to the Committee ... are so incompatible with, and so completely at variance with what I have always understood to be the true principles of Parliamentary Independence of members and above all of a Minister of the Crown that ... I am to my sincere regret unable to continue feeling that confidence in your judgment which would justify me in acting, any longer, on your advice." As the *Province* noted, Sir Henri did not "impute actual dishonesty" to Prior but thought he had "improper ideas of ministerial honor." Soon after making the letter public, Sir Henri dismissed Prior and denied him the customary practice of nominating a successor. In exercising his task of establishing political stability, or the "order" needed "for the efficient operation of a 'liberal' form of government," Sir Henri called on McBride to form the new administration. McBride's many critics had often called him the "leader of obstruction" and complained of his "intolerable" verbosity, but as leader of the Opposition he had impressed the lieutenant-governor, who told his son that he "is the youngest member in the House, and I think he is well disposed to do what is right. I treat him as if he were my son, so fas as advice and encouragement can do it, and he trusts me."[90]

3
Establishing a Government, 1903-07

> *[I hope] to establish a strong and honest government under which the magnificent resources of our province may be successfully developed, and an era of permanent prosperity inaugurated.*
>
> – Richard McBride, 7 June 1903

On the evening of Saturday, 30 May 1903, McBride advised the lieutenant-governor that he must consult his supporters to determine whether he could form a government. The consultations succeeded. About 1:30 on the afternoon of Monday, 1 June 1903, Sir Henri summoned McBride to Government House, and within half an hour had sworn in McBride as premier. McBride immediately returned to the Parliament Buildings. Since an MLA who accepted an office carrying emolument under the Crown had to resign and be re-elected in a by-election, McBride could not sit on the floor. R.F. Green read his acceptance letter, which asked for an adjournment until 3:00 P.M. the next day.[1]

Immediately after adjournment, McBride met several Liberals and Conservatives in a "secret conclave," where they discussed forming a composite government. John Oliver later claimed that on 31 May, McBride had said he would ask him and another Liberal, T.W. Paterson, to join the cabinet. McBride told another prominent Liberal, Smith Curtis, that he "was in a quandary as to the line on which to form his government and appeal to the people." Curtis took credit for turning "the scale" to party lines by reminding McBride that both Conservatives and Liberals favoured it. The key to its implementation was the Conservative caucus. A.E. McPhillips and Charles Semlin opposed party lines, but the majority followed McBride's wishes and adopted them. In the Legislature on 2 June, Robert Tatlow, president of the council – a post that carried no salary – read McBride's letter announcing that, in view of the pending dissolution of the Legislature, "the interests of the country would best be served by division on party lines." As soon as possible, McBride stated, he would "appeal to the country on party lines," which he had always favoured and which he believed the electors wanted. His government would be "Conservative in character." Forming "another corporate Government" would continue a "wretched state of affairs." Expressing "appreciation of the valued co-operation of the Liberals" and regretting his inability to recognize their service with cabinet seats, he promised to "take no undue advantage" in preparing for the forthcoming election. Some editors expressed pride in the selection of a young British Columbian as premier. One noted that, though he was only thirty-two, "his appearance would justify one in calling him at least ten years older" and added that he had demonstrated his possession of "many qualities that go to make up a successful leader of men." An eastern magazine reported that he was "commanding in appearance, always faultlessly dressed, invariably engaging in manner ... a striking figure in the house," who was "tall and massively built, an athletic figure. His face is full, but pale; his eyes dark and keen, though kindly, and his hair is quite perceptibly streaked with grey, which is the fashion nowadays; a young face, if it be comely, and grey hair being considered the most attractive combination possible, especially among the women." Another described him as "a hail-fellow-well-met sort of man, good looking, easy-going, both as to industrial and political morals."[2]

Observers expected party government to mean holding someone "responsible for the blunders" that an administration might commit. In extending congratulations, McBride's former classmate W.J. Bowser declared "nothing but a Conservative cabinet will go." Similarly, Charles Hibbert Tupper, son of former prime minister Charles Tupper, himself a former federal cabinet minister and now a Vancouver lawyer, wired, "The Conservative party can now bring order out of chaos and return the good name and fame of our Province." In contrast, the *Colonist* thought that McBride was inspired by a "desire to put himself in office and not the Conservative party"; Liberal editors described the formation of a Conservative government as "treachery," "deceit," or "betrayal." The Liberals had their own problem – Joseph Martin suddenly resigned as their leader.³

To do routine government business, McBride asked five members of the former government and five of the former Opposition to revise the estimates, the government's spending plans, before asking the House to pass supply and private members' bills such as acts incorporating companies. Tatlow presented the estimates as creations of the former government. No one accepted his invitation to propose changes, and the estimates passed quickly. With dissolution imminent, McBride named his cabinet. Despite his misgivings about party government, McPhillips joined as attorney general. Green became minister of mines, and Tatlow took on finance and agriculture. For the time being, McBride kept the post of chief commissioner of lands and works for himself. A few days later, Charles Wilson, who did not have a seat in the Legislature, was sworn in as president of the council. Many Conservatives were dissatisfied because they or their friends were not appointed. John Houston of Nelson was "disgruntled." The *Province* reported that some Vancouver Island party members were disturbed because Prior, Eberts, and other leading Conservatives were not included and because only McPhillips came from the island. The *Colonist* objected to the presence of three lawyers and the absence of Prior. In response to its criticism, McBride commented that "the men who have taken the most prominent and influential part are lawyers," and "if a lawyer is the right kind of a man, his profession is really no drawback." After the provincial election campaign was officially under way, McBride appointed A.S. Goodeve of Rossland as provincial secretary and minister of education to represent the Interior.⁴

The serious business of forming a government temporarily set aside, McBride returned to New Westminster and opened a championship lacrosse match, where the city band greeted him with "For He's a Jolly Good Fellow." He promised to build roads and trails in addition to those under construction in Dewdney and Delta, and he forecast that the new Fraser River Bridge would make the city "the Liverpool of British Columbia." Such promises were part of his political objectives of establishing "a strong and honest government," developing the province's "magnificent resources," and inaugurating "an era of permanent prosperity."⁵

The festivities constituted only a weekend's respite, however. Routine work had to be done and the party had to be organized. Dissolution was delayed until 16 June since an earlier date would have cancelled the voters' lists used to calculate the number of voters in an area before a liquor licence could be issued. McBride also informed the lieutenant-governor that his administration had nominated collectors of votes and other officials required to prepare the new lists. Most of these officials were permanent civil servants, and though they promised to perform their duties in a nonpartisan manner, that did not mean they were independent. After calculating the time required to prepare the lists and the Courts of Revision, which corrected the lists, the *Colonist* expected that the election would take place in mid-September. The voters' lists could be manipulated: for example, expecting that Comox loggers would vote against the government to express their dissatisfaction over log exports, Bowser questioned the wisdom of enumerating them.[6]

Although McBride claimed to eschew patronage, his government was not immune to this common Canadian practice. It was only ten days old when Stuart Livingston, a Conservative, replaced G.F. Cane, a Liberal, as a Crown prosecutor.[7] Supporters expected patronage and some sought to have particular individuals appointed to such traditional plums as foremen of road repair crews or awarded contracts to supply lumber and other goods. Civil servants acted as political advisors: an unsigned letter written on provincial government stationery told McBride that the people of Dewdney wanted "roads, roads, roads" as well as the jobs required to build them. The government agent at Ashcroft informed McBride that announcing the completion of the Highland Valley Road to Merritt Lake would "naturally aid our cause here."[8]

Claiming that politics should not "interfere with the efficiency of our road service," McBride offered to seek money in the Contingency Fund for the Ladner Trunk Road in Oliver's constituency. Yet he knew that roads could be a political issue, and he did not neglect his friends. He told a Nicola Lake supporter that public works there would be furthered without delay; he informed a constituent that the current budget for public works had been spent but that local residents should recommend the most urgent ones; and he advised the Conservative candidate in Greenwood that he would give orders for the immediate construction of the West Fork wagon road, which would also help Conservatives in the adjacent riding of Similkameen.[9]

The Conservative organization was poorly developed. Desiring "a strong central organization with branches in every riding," McBride discouraged the formation of local bodies. When party members reported disputes over nominations, he urged them "as far as possible, [to] sink personal matters for the good of the party." He hoped that candidates would be the unanimous choices of local conventions and thought it unwise "to thrust candidates on local Conservatives against their wishes." Nevertheless, he did intervene in a few cases. He asked C.H. Dickie, the Independent Conservative for Cowichan, not to run as the "Conservative standard bearer." In the Okanagan, Price Ellison, the sitting member, said he could no longer afford to give his time to politics. He had a want list of public works, though, and McBride persuaded him to run by promising to do something for him. While seeking the nomination, Ellison allegedly said that he had been promised a cabinet portfolio, and according to H.W. Raymur, who felt cheated out of the nomination, he "freely distributed liquor." In reflecting on the campaign, however, the *Western Methodist Recorder* suggested that despite the "contemptible effort" of the "liquor interests," the election was "conducted with less resort to questionable methods than usual."[10]

Tatlow was responsible for distributing campaign funds. One rumour stated that the Canadian Pacific Railway (CPR) was financing the Conservatives and that the Grand Trunk Pacific (GTP) was subsidizing the Liberals.[11] Whether the CPR provided funds is unknown, but it did not approve of political involvement by its staff. After its employee Thomas Caven ran unsuccessfully for the Conservatives in Cranbrook, the company dismissed him. McBride lobbied the CPR for Caven's reinstatement, but, having warned Caven not to seek the nomination, the company would not comply. Feeling guilty for encouraging Caven to run, McBride asked R.B. Bennett, the CPR's solicitor in Calgary and a prominent Conservative, to intercede. Eventually, Caven got his job back.[12] The British Columbia Electric Railway Company (BCER), which operated the street railways and the electric and gas systems in Greater Vancouver and Victoria, donated $1,000 to the Conservatives and $200 to the Liberals. "Other local Corporations with large interests" employed a similar ratio in their contributions. The BCER believed that being "on good terms with both parties" was essential in aiding the "lobbying and wire pulling" via which it constantly sought and received favours. Disingenuously, McBride boasted that he preferred defeat to being "tied up to any corporation." He told a party organizer that many "friends" had failed to provide promised funds and that he had "fought the campaign without funds although, had he chosen to do so, he might have had an ample supply."[13]

Usually, McBride heard only of problems, one of which focused on W.J. Bowser, who was at the centre of Vancouver's five-member constituency. Bowser predicted future trouble with Francis Carter-Cotton, the publisher and editor of the *Vancouver Daily News-Advertiser*, who had served in the Legislature during the 1890s but was defeated in 1900 when he ran for the Provincial Party. According to Bowser, Carter-Cotton planned to take over from McBride after the election. Bowser had exaggerated; the same day, Carter-Cotton told McBride that he would urge old Provincial Party members to support him and sought information for use in the *News-Advertiser*, which at times would take "its own course." Carter-Cotton was nominated in the rural suburb of Richmond, but not all Richmond Conservatives were happy with Carter-Cotton. Robert McBride (not a relation) complained that Bowser and the Vancouver machine had "shamefully" sacrificed Richmond by imposing a candidate on them. As a protest, he would vote for the Liberal, and he warned that "the party has got to drop Bowser permanently or they will be beaten everywhere his influence extends." Nevertheless, Carter-Cotton won this suburban constituency. Rank-and-file Conservatives in Vancouver, including members of the Orange Order, challenged Bowser. The primaries in each ward rejected him, and he missed the nomination by "a hair's breadth." Inexplicably, however, he became a Conservative nominee.[14]

Conservatives elsewhere also encountered problems. In Chilliwack, J.L. Atkinson resorted to some "wire pulling" after winning eight of sixteen votes at the nomination meeting and thus became the candidate. Provincial fruit inspector Thomas Cunningham, who was one of McBride's confidantes, warned that if Atkinson's candidacy were "not speedily withdrawn," the situation would become "doubtful." He recommended appointing Atkinson as a constable in "some outlandish place where he can do no harm or make terms with Munro," who was Chilliwack's Liberal candidate. Undeterred, Atkinson ran but C.W. Munro won. Local advisors in Rossland, Nanaimo, and Cranbrook needed candidates who could win the labour vote. At Nelson, John Houston overcame opposition to get the nomination. The situation was entirely different in Victoria, where Conservatives seemed so united that the *Times* described the nominating meeting as "a triumph for the McBride faction," which controlled the party's "purse strings." Because of the late hour, McBride's speech at the Victoria nomination meeting was brief. Given Victoria's resentment at not having one of its own as premier, he promised to keep the campaign free of "that ruinous cry of Mainland against the Island" and added that, always friendly to the island, he had supported Premier J.H. Turner of Victoria.[15]

McBride knew that British Columbia extended beyond Vancouver Island and the Fraser Valley. In July and August, as chief commissioner of lands and works, he made whistle-stop tours as far east as Fernie and as far north as Atlin. In the Interior, he was accompanied by the assistant commissioner, a civil servant, and on the coast, A.E. McPhillips and C.W.D. Clifford, the Conservative candidate in Skeena, joined him. Most issues were local, including questions about transportation and prospecting licences in the Columbia and Western Railway (C&W) lands. He spent a full Sunday at Namu, a cannery village. In honour of the Sabbath, he did not begin his speech, which touched on railway policy and Asian labour, until midnight. When he finished at three in the morning, there was "not a drowsy eye" among the sixty people present.[16]

On 5 September, McBride announced that the election would be on 3 October. Recalling his earlier comment that it would be held "as soon as practicable," he explained that it could now proceed because the voters' lists were in order and few appeals had delayed them. Second, the government wanted the approval of the electorate before initiating various reforms. Anticipating accusations of unfairness in his choice of election date, he said that the cabinet had not considered it until after the Courts of Revision had completed their work on 31 August. He predicted a "short, sharp and decisive" campaign. The Liberals were unhappy with the schedule, particularly in New Westminster, where election day coincided with the annual exhibition. Exhibition officials feared that up-country exhibitors and visitors would stay at home. The New Westminster Liberal candidate, W.H. Keary, who was also the exhibition manager, was especially upset. Although his friend the *Columbian* argued that delaying the election would be a greater loss than anything the fair might suffer, McBride was loyal to his hometown. He promised to establish polling stations near the city for Fraser Valley voters and said that, if the fair lost money, he would consider compensation. Meanwhile, Keary's workers distributed a flyer claiming that members of McBride's family had secured fish trap sites from the government and attacking McBride's opposition to log exports. In defending McBride against this "criminal libel," the *Columbian* asserted that he had "never been under suspicion of profiting privately out of public office."[17]

McBride opened the campaign in New Westminster on Saturday, 12 September. In a ninety-minute speech that outlined "a broad policy for the development of the Province," he called the introduction of the party system the "only way" out of deadlock and noted that Green and Tatlow had already pressed provincial interests in Ottawa. Blaming the CPR's "prohibitive" rates for impeding settlement, he favoured new railways but insisted that "not a yard of British Columbia's soil should be turned" unless the province controlled rates, the GTP began work at the coast, and no Asians were employed on railway construction.[18] As for the Columbia and Western land grant, he conceded that he had participated in negotiations for the grant but maintained that accusing him of any improper action was "monstrous."[19] He took credit for not surrendering a major portion of northern British Columbia to railway promoters and for the new bridge across the Fraser River, which would remain under government ownership.[20]

After a day's delay caused by an inflammation of the bowels, attributed to "overwork and the mental strain incidental to the campaign," he began touring. In accepting the Dewdney nomination at a "monster Conservative convention" in Mission City, he referred to railway policies and said that the province had sufficient revenue so that it could, "with economy," carry on with all its public works. He promised to maintain municipal wagon roads and provide funds to municipalities. His later speeches included variations on these themes and added the need for efficiencies in the civil service, revised labour laws, and a halt to Asian immigration, especially of the Japanese.[21]

On election night in New Westminster, the city band led the carriage carrying McBride and Thomas Gifford, the local winner, to a celebration with music, singing, and cheers. Nonetheless, early returns suggested a Liberal sweep. In Victoria, the Liberals won all four seats, possibly because of anti-Mainland feeling, and the Conservatives took only one seat on Vancouver Island, a result that McBride attributed to a lack of both organization and campaign funds. Delays in receiving results from outlying polls and a few close races caused suspense for several days, but gradually the situation improved for the Conservatives. To their surprise, they had won all five of Vancouver's seats. No matter the outcome, McBride said he would meet the House as premier. The press speculated that he might invite some Liberals to join his cabinet or negotiate the support of the Socialist and Labour members. The final results gave the Conservatives twenty-two of the forty-two seats. The Liberals had taken seventeen, and Socialist or Labour members had won three. After conferring with Tatlow and McPhillips, who had lost in Victoria, McBride concluded that even with a Conservative Speaker, he could safely meet the Legislature.[22]

First, he had to reorganize his cabinet. The necessary by-elections could endanger his slim majority. Tupper provided constitutional advice as did Lieutenant-Governor Henri Joly de Lotbinière, who reminded him that no previous cabinet had consisted of more than five members. Another problem was the surplus of talent. Faced by rumours that he was seeking a cabinet post, Carter-Cotton, however, asked McBride to say that he had declined it because of private business. The *Province* claimed that Charles Wilson was acceptable as attorney general, but Bowser wanted the post as a reward for returning the "Solid Five" in Vancouver.[23]

John Houston of Nelson, the official head of the Conservative organization, was *the* problem of the hour. The *Province* suggested that he might "precipitate a crisis" if he did not become chief commissioner of lands and works. Bowser warned that having the "no good" Houston in the cabinet would "'queer' the party." Wilson warned that "a more discordant element" could not be introduced. An East Kootenay lawyer warned that Houston was "using the Conservative party for business purposes" and that, "if you do not appreciate this now, you will before long." Partly because of "a very bad attack of La Grippe," McBride did little about the cabinet for several weeks. Finally, on 23 October, he informed Houston that the lieutenant-governor would not accept him as a cabinet minister. Houston announced that though he was still a Conservative, he would not support McBride. He complained to Sir Henri that the people of Nelson had been "slapped in the face" and added that if he were unworthy to administer a department, he must be "equally unworthy" to sit in the Legislature. Sir Henri replied that he had rejected Houston "on account of the unfortunate incident of the last Session when you forgot what was due to the Legislative Assembly as well as to yourself, in your responsible position." (This was a reference to an episode in November 1902, when Houston had interrupted a debate and refused to sit down though ordered to do so by the Speaker.)[24] The lieutenant-governor's refusal to accept the premier's advice to name Houston to the cabinet should have set off a constitutional crisis. A public meeting, called by the mayor of Nelson, criticized McBride's failure to resign in protest, but it may have been the other way round. Although the evidence is not firm, McBride may have asked the lieutenant-governor to relieve him of a problem by taking responsibility for not appointing Houston to the cabinet. Sir Henri admitted that he was an "advisor to his advisors" and let Houston direct his anger at him, not McBride.[25] McBride thought the affair gave "our enemies something to talk about" but otherwise "caused absolutely no excitement," and it soon blew over.[26]

With four members plus the premier, the cabinet announced in early November was one member smaller than its predecessor. McBride himself took on the portfolios of provincial secretary and minister of mines, and R.F. Green, who had been minister of mines, became chief commissioner of lands and works. R.G. Tatlow remained as finance minister, and Charles Wilson joined the cabinet as attorney-general. To represent the Interior, McBride invited F.J. Fulton of Kamloops to become president of the council, an office without salary and therefore not requiring a by-election. In the spring of 1904, McBride appointed Fulton provincial secretary despite Fulton's uncertainty regarding his chances in the ensuing by-election. Many farmers had complained of increased taxes and assessments on grazing lands, and the Liberals had gathered "a lot of evidence" against him during the general election. The *Inland Sentinel* had accused him of taking "along with him cases of whiskey and a heeler to pull the corks" when he canvassed the electors. Fulton's worries proved groundless. Claiming that McBride broke faith with them regarding the by-election date, the Liberals decided not to enter a "one-sided contest" since their nominee was on holiday in California. Fulton won by acclamation. Carter-Cotton succeeded him as president of the council. A glaring absence in the cabinet was any minister from Vancouver Island. The *Times* complained that only four cabinet ministers would receive a salary, whereas the constitution authorized five, and it suggested that McBride was unwilling to open a seat except in Vancouver.[27]

Wilson's appointment as attorney general did make a by-election necessary in Vancouver. As a courtesy, the Opposition did not always challenge the incumbent, but young Vancouver Liberals nominated J. Duff Stuart to run against Wilson. In the campaign, McBride said that even if the Liberals won, they could not form a government. He blamed Joseph Martin, who had kept James Dunsmuir in office, for the province's financial problems. Agreeing with demands for railways to the West Kootenay and Yukon, he insisted that provincial aid depended on control of their rates. In short, "eastern millionaires and promoters" would no longer be enriched at the expense of British Columbians. He accused the Liberals of giving the "glad hand" to the Japanese, who were "more dangerous" than the Chinese because they did not confine themselves to menial work.[28] The campaign was successful; Wilson easily won the by-election.

Even before the cabinet was firmly in place, the new government acted swiftly to put its finances in order by cutting expenditures. Lottie Bowron, a stenographer in the premier's office, recalled that "the word that I seem to remember most in doing shorthand, et cetera, was 'retrenchment.'" McBride told F.J. Fulton that "the financial situation" gave him "no choice" but "to shut down practically everything in the country," a phrase repeated in letters to those who lost jobs. Following an election promise to implement stability in government departments as a prelude to civil service reform, a number of temporary civil servants were dismissed for an annual saving of $32,000. Finance Minister Tatlow warned of more cuts. Most of the terminated employees were engaged on public works, but some were provincial constables or staff of departmental offices. The press generally approved of lopping a bloated civil service. A few cuts were cancelled: Seven or eight labourers were briefly rehired after Fulton reported that they required only about ten days to complete their road work and that leaving the work undone would be "a great waste of money" as well as politically embarrassing, given rumours that their termination was an election-time "political dodge." Similarly, after residents of Telegraph Creek complained that it was "absolutely necessary" to have a local constable, McBride personally asked the constable to resume his duties immediately.[29]

A Miss Turnbull of the Boiler Inspector's Office in New Westminster was a less fortunate victim of the "spoils system." McBride instructed David Robson, the government agent, to dismiss her and replace her with Mrs. McColl, the widow of Mr. Justice A.J. McColl, with whom McBride had articled. When Robson said that she did not have the necessary stenographic and typing skills, and that her position in the Land Registry Office paid ten to twelve dollars more per month than Turnbull received, McBride let the women keep their jobs until he could give the matter his "personal attention." After a "careful review," he reiterated his instructions to Robson, with the result that Turnbull was dismissed and McColl was moved to the Boiler Inspector's Office. McBride took care of other friends and family. He arranged for his uncle, Edward F. (Ned) D'Arcy, who had been the chief construction engineer's clerk, to become a toll taker on the new bridge, but Uncle Ned became a "male attendant" at the Provincial Asylum.[30]

McBride did not need A.E. McPhillips's reminder that Conservatives had been promised "that in all appointments, fitness also being considered, the party would have all the appointments." He knew the difficulty in making "these selections satisfactory to all our friends," MLAs, and defeated candidates. He admitted that R.R. Maitland, who sought the post of deputy registrar at New Westminster, had "claims on the party," but "this patronage" was subject to nomination by Gifford, the local MLA.[31] If an opportunity presented itself, McBride would help Maitland secure "some permanent Government position." Future consideration was a stock reply to applicants.[32]

Although it was often heard "at election time that every Government official is a Government campaign agent," McBride theoretically believed that the civil service "should be absolutely free from politics," since its members were "servants of the people," and that nothing should be done to impair its efficiency. He told a government agent at Atlin, who also acted as magistrate, that his position as magistrate "excused" him from participation in politics. This implied that other civil servants could participate in politics, provided they did so on the government side. A fish hatchery employee who engaged in "open and offensive political partisanship" for the Liberals in the Lillooet by-election lost his job. The by-election had become necessary because Lillooet's Conservative MLA, Archie Macdonald, drew a salary as road superintendent. He had been elected by acclamation, and though the Legislature let him retain his seat for the session, it declared his election null and void. McBride persuaded Macdonald, the "strongest man we can get" at Lillooet, to run again. During the campaign, McBride visited the constituency, and according to the *Inland Sentinel,* lavishly distributed patronage.[33] Whether Macdonald won because of patronage or personal popularity was beside the point – his return helped McBride retain his precarious majority.

The Legislature had to deal with the parlous state of provincial finances. For the fiscal year ended 30 June 1903, net revenues were $2,044,630.35 and net expenditures $3,393,192.25 of which $396,127.82 went to interest payments. Within three weeks of taking office, McBride asked to borrow an official of the federal Department of Finance to make an independent "careful and thorough enquiry" into British Columbia's "entire fiscal system." During the Vancouver by-election in November 1903, Finance Minister Tatlow admitted that the government had spent $1.5 million more than it had taken in despite dramatic cuts in public works expenditures. So strained were provincial finances that Byron E. Walker, the general manager of the Canadian Bank of Commerce, publicly spoke of the bank's anxiety that the province should get its financial affairs in order. Reinforcing the bank's concern, the manager in Victoria advised Tatlow that it would honour its agreement to dispose of treasury warrants only if the government did not let its expenditures exceed its income and did not add to existing liabilities by subsidizing enterprises seeking its assistance.[34]

McBride also had personal financial problems. While he was in Opposition, his income had consisted of whatever he earned from his legal practice plus his MLA's sessional indemnity of $800, though this was diminished by $104 in various deductions. As provincial premier, he maintained his legal firm but probably received little or no income from it. Also as premier, he got an extra $1,000 per year, and as minister of mines, the portfolio he took after the election, he received the $4,000 paid to cabinet ministers. His total income from his participation in government was $5,800 per annum, which the Liberal *Nelson Daily News* alleged was "probably the limit of his earning capacity in any other field of industry."[35]

McBride needed every penny of his salary; he was a poor financial manager and his glad-handedness often came from his own pocketbook.

Within weeks of becoming premier, "some private financial matters" forced him to defer planned additions to his New Westminster house. Margaret, who had given birth to their fourth daughter, Ruth, on 31 August 1903, hoped to use the house during the Christmas holidays, so he did not wish to rent it out. Nonetheless, keeping it was a luxury that he could not afford. "For financial reasons," he did not renew a $5,000 accident insurance policy. He also had to cover old debts. Possibly through his legal practice, he had guaranteed a number of modest loans. A month after he became premier, the New Westminster manager of the Bank of Montreal warned that the bank inspector was due to visit, so McBride must attend to three notes, guarantees of loans to acquaintances, one of whom was the proprietor of a failed newspaper in Delta. The total of the loans was $956.40 plus interest. The debt grew; the following summer a new branch manager asked McBride to "kindly attend" to a note for $1,187.95 that had fallen due two weeks earlier. McBride also borrowed from the New Westminster Bank of Commerce. In April 1903, a payment of $551.56 was overdue, and the bank had charged his account with another $75.00. By what McBride called the bank's "oppressive measures," he reduced the debt to $685.00, but by March 1904, it had risen to $1,069.00. The manager, realizing McBride's recent heavy expenses, was prepared to write the debt down to $1,000 if McBride "definitely" promised to have a credit in the account by month's end, to "*not again*" be overdrawn, and to reduce the debt by at least $50 per month. Other dunning letters probably followed; two months later, McBride angrily informed the manager "that having been very frankly advised that my business was not wanted by your people, the only alternative was to go elsewhere." If the local manager had no objection, he proposed to write to the president of the Bank of Commerce. In September, the bank received his note for $870.00 and a cheque for $56.80.[36]

Despite these financial misadventures, McBride continued to guarantee loans. One request came from his father, who needed a guarantee of $450 to purchase a $1,500 property in New Westminster and who did not wish to mortgage anything to raise the balance. Although McBride told some of his friends that he could not accommodate their requests to guarantee bank loans, he offered to put in a "good word" for them with bank managers. He was not always consistent in following this wise policy, with the result that some borrowers continued to drain his finances. In 1908, for example, when a borrower failed to pay off his debt, McBride sent the Royal Bank in Victoria a cheque for $53.50 and agreed to renew a note for $450.00. A few loans had short-term political purposes, such as the $100 that McBride advanced for one month to the proprietor of the *Revelstoke*

Herald "because of the loyalty and decency with which the Herald has always treated me and my friends."[37] A loan of $175, which enabled the proprietor of a Vancouver-based mining magazine to pay a printer's bill, was probably extended due to similar sentiments. Fortunately for McBride's pocketbook, it was promptly repaid.[38]

In one case, McBride proposed to use patronage to get a note repaid. Théodore Théroux of Mission City had borrowed $150 from the Bank of Montreal, with McBride as his guarantor. Théroux was out of work and though McBride was willing to renew the note, the bank manager was not, since only a small portion had been repaid. After Father L. Fouquet told McBride that "the Catholics of this district would feel gratified" if he helped Théroux, McBride recommended giving Théroux a job at the provincial mental hospital. In the meantime, Théroux found work in a sawmill and planned to pay off the debt in three months. On some occasions, McBride did not expect repayment. He gave a $100 cheque to an old friend in Chilliwack who had had "bad luck," though the recipient insisted that it be regarded as a loan.[39]

McBride personally participated in the speculative fever that gripped British Columbia. When the president of B.C. Permanent Loan and Savings reminded him that payment on his stock was overdue, he found $25 to put it in good standing. He subscribed for $200 worth of shares (the total issue was $1,000) in the Transvaal group property that its promoter, former MLA Smith Curtis, promised would not result in any loss and would become "the biggest copper mine opened in the Province." Real estate was another attraction. He bought ten acres at Naramata near Penticton, where he planned to develop a peach orchard. Thomas Cunningham, the provincial fruit inspector, called the site "one of the most promising orchards" in the province and said that planting apples as well could produce an income of $6,000 per annum. To show his faith in another community, McBride bought property in Grand Forks. Closer to home, in a transaction arranged by F.J. Hart, a New Westminster real estate dealer, he purchased a third of a share in 100 acres at Cloverdale for $1,000. Hart predicted that when subdivided into 10-acre plots, the land should yield $8,000 to $10,000. McBride also owned two lots in New Westminster, which he wanted to sell as a package for $3,000. He sold a holding near Port Moody for $75 per acre. The sale was made privately, but the real estate agent who had listed it wanted a commission.[40]

On a rainy day in late November 1903, the lieutenant-governor opened the first session of the tenth Parliament. The Throne Speech emphasized the need to improve provincial finances, and the next day, McBride introduced a number of bills designed to do so. Explaining that during the election campaign, he had not realized the critical state of provincial finances, he blamed much of the problem on Ottawa's failure to listen to the province's request for Better Terms, a point echoed by many MLAs. During a debate that lasted until midnight, he warned of a "disaster" if the Legislature did not authorize borrowing $1 million at 5 percent interest, which was needed to meet obligations in London. The banks had insisted that the Loan Bill and an Assessment Bill must pass before 15 December. He optimistically predicted that one cause of debt, the new bridge at New Westminster, would soon produce revenue through tolls. The *Province* admitted that McBride had inherited a problem because of "the criminally extravagant administration of former Governments" and observed that British Columbia was so deeply in debt that the president of the Bank of Commerce was its de facto finance minister. Some new taxes "surprised" friends, but the government claimed that they were less sweeping than they seemed. The "taxable list" included "all manner of lands, real and personal property," revisions to the graduated income tax, and a reduction in the exemption on personal property from $1,000 to $500. The *Colonist* found the new taxation so complicated that discussing the details "would leave our readers and ourselves in a bewildering fog." Despite rumours of division in the cabinet, the bills carried with the support of the Labour and Socialist MLAs.[41]

Since mining and forestry were major industries, increased imposts on them were a likely source of additional revenue. The Coal Mines Act was amended to allow prospectors to secure leases and options on coal and petroleum lands in return for higher fees and royalties. The government sought to raise taxes on other kinds of mines. McBride admitted that some "mining men" objected to the existing 2 percent tax on ore but could not agree on an alternative, and the government needed revenue. After the Christmas adjournment, saying that upsetting existing conditions would be unwise, McBride asked the Mining Committee to review proposed amendments to the mining acts. The committee was noncommittal about a projected 1 percent tax on the gross value of a mine's output, so the amendment did not go forward. Loggers complained that new licence fees would harm small outfits since the large enterprises held timber limits under old rules. The owner of a Vancouver Island company said that the "unjust and exorbitant" taxes would force him to halt operations. The government made some amendments to the fees.[42]

However, the Assessment Act caused the most controversy. Its intent was to raise the taxes of those "who can well afford to pay, namely, large corporations, holders of immense tracts of wild land, etc." The *Province* described the initial version as proposing "an embargo, almost intolerable, on commercial enterprise" and objected to "the lightness of the assessment" on banks in the final version. The Victoria Board of Trade complained, but the Vancouver board did not. Amendments to the bill relieved some of the burden on merchants. The CPR virulently opposed it. Its president, T.G. Shaughnessy, called a more than threefold increase in the assessment on railway rights of way, rolling stock, and sidings "neither reasonable nor justifiable." He was particularly angry since the taxes would impose on the CPR "the burden" of paying for "the stupendous blunder" of the "expensive and useless" New Westminster Bridge, which let American railways enter Vancouver and compete with it. Shaughnessy's letter of complaint prompted laughter among the legislators when McBride read it aloud and commented that the railways were not "a whit behind" farmers, miners, lumbermen, and others who complained of the new taxes.[43]

Late in 1904, the government appointed an Assessment Commission, which the Liberal *Times* saw as proof "that the Assessment Act was conceived in ignorance and is being enforced with partiality." The *Colonist* concluded that the establishment of the commission showed that both people and corporations regarded taxes as "obnoxious." The commission recommended reducing the unpopular personal property tax, altering exemptions, creating assessment districts, changing taxes on wild lands, and imposing a $100 annual licence fee on commercial travellers. It described the income tax as the "most equitable form of taxation." In 1905, the government adopted many of its recommendations, such as reducing the personal property tax with a view to eliminating it and relying only on property and income taxes. It also required non-resident commercial travellers to buy a licence. That angered outside companies but produced revenue – though it was difficult to collect – and protected local merchants.[44]

As well as imposing new taxes, the 1904 estimates dramatically reduced the public works budget. Knowing the importance of roads and bridges, McBride privately recommended particular expenditures such as flood control on Mission Creek near Kelowna and improvements to the government reserve at New Westminster and to the Lillooet Road. Refusing to grant special favours to Dewdney was useful provincially. When the MLA for The Islands, a constituency comprised of the Gulf Islands, complained that the appropriation for his constituency was only $2,500, McBride said that he was sorry but pointed out that Dewdney, which was fifty times larger, got a tenth of that amount. In the fall, he admitted that, because of the "depleted exchequer," a number of promised small repair and renewal projects would not be undertaken, but he expected the situation to improve. In the spring, despite sparing "no effort to have the necessary public works carried out," he apologized for being unable to secure all that was required. He confided to a political friend that "with an empty Treasury and no patronage the task of Party Government" had "been by no means easy. At times I have felt that some of our friends have overlooked these things." Indeed, some Conservative MLAs privately expressed dissatisfaction at having to vote for the government's bills whether they liked them or not.[45]

Financial problems were not the only inherited difficulties. In its last days, the Prior government had passed Bill 16 to ratify the cancellation of Crown grants in the Crow's Nest Pass, where 625,000 acres in blocks 4593 and 4594 were to have been given to the C&W Railway, a CPR subsidiary. The CPR had duly protested to Ottawa. McBride, who thought the province should retain the lands, proposed to re-enact Bill 16 should Ottawa disallow it. When Sir Henri advised him not to have Charles Wilson and R.F. Green raise the issue during their Ottawa visit in July 1903, McBride concluded that the lieutenant-governor would not countenance any provincial attempt to dispose of the properties, so he moved slowly. He informed Charles Hibbert Tupper, whose client the Western Oil and Coal Company could not renew a mining licence in the affected land, that no orders against renewal had been issued. He told the Legislature that the government would recognize all statutory rights secured by applicants for coal and petroleum licences in the two blocks but would deal with the land only after the time for disallowance had expired. Many had applied for these lands, and their payments would benefit the treasury. In the end, Ottawa did not disallow the legislation. By Order-in-Council in mid-June 1904, the province granted licences to prospectors seeking coal or petroleum in block 4593. Tupper accused the government of trafficking in licences and adopting a policy that would cause "endless confusion and litigation." His interview with the *Vancouver World* was so venomous that McBride did not believe initial reports of it and feared the dispute would reflect badly on the Conservative Party. Tupper concurred and felt that they should try to settle their differences, but the C&W question did not disappear.[46]

McBride was then in the thick of a federal election campaign and in charge of Conservative campaign funds in several constituencies.[47] Late in November, when Robert L. Borden, the federal Conservative leader, sought information about his party's prospects in British Columbia, McBride replied that "the old strife is gradually but surely dying out," although "our little internal troubles have not served to advance matters in the best fashion." Borden asked about the availability of Tatlow as a federal candidate but admitted that McBride would be sorry to lose him. McBride was already promoting the candidacy of J.D. Taylor, editor of the *New Westminster British Columbian*. At meetings on Taylor's behalf, he referred to local issues such as the New Westminster Bridge and Asian labour but, adopting a national outlook, warned Conservatives "to view the campaign from a wide Dominion standpoint" and not "be swayed by local grievances and requirements."[48]

Rifts in the party remained. McBride told Victoria Junior Conservatives to "overlook little personalities and fight for principles" and to organize well. Despite their conflicts, McBride had kind words about Tupper, and he shared a platform with him in Duncan on behalf of Clive Phillipps-Wolley. Tupper, however, complained that neither McBride nor any member of his cabinet attended a meeting in support of E.G. Prior and reported rumours that the government was "secretly assisting the Grits" against Prior. In a major speech in Victoria, Tupper spoke mainly on federal issues, chiefly the Grand Trunk Pacific (GTP), and he mentioned Better Terms but did not refer to McBride. The previous winter McBride had worked with Prior "on the most amicable terms," with "the old time breach having nearly completely healed," and he wanted to see Prior elected but, given the disgrace surrounding Prior's departure from the premiership, did not think it in the party's interest to speak on Prior's behalf. Nevertheless, he and several ministers, especially R.F. Green, spent so much time on the campaign trail that the *Times* complained they neglected departmental responsibilities.[49]

McBride had optimistically believed that the federal election results would not be affected by Prime Minister Laurier's plan to build the GTP through northern British Columbia. In the event, his confidence was misplaced – the Liberals won all seven of the province's seats. The *Colonist* observed British Columbia's "peculiar genius for supporting the side that is in power in Ottawa" but agreed that prosperity, Laurier's prestige, and especially the GTP explained the Liberal success. Without providing details, McBride attributed the Liberal victory to "money and whiskey."[50]

Despite earlier internecine problems, when McBride spoke at a banquet honouring Borden in Toronto in December 1905, he boasted that the BC Conservatives were "a unit for the party" and for Borden. How much of an impression McBride made on the eastern press is uncertain. The *News-Advertiser* claimed that he was "well received." The *Toronto Globe* referred to him as the "Hon. Robt. McBride!" The *Toronto Telegram* reportedly noted that his hair looked "as if it was fresh from the crimping irons of the hairdresser." Betraying its ignorance of western geography, it remarked that "breezy he is as the soft chinook that sweeps the snow from his native mountains, but when you've done shouting, 'Be loyal to the party,' and, 'if you can't boost don't knock,' you have all he said in half an hour."[51]

While McBride made this step onto the national stage, the situation was improving at home. As a result of retrenchment and a strengthening national economy, Tatlow's budget revealed a surplus of $345,087 on the previous year's accounts. A surplus of $424,299 in 1906 was better, although the Liberals attributed it to "taxing people to death and starving the country by withholding needed public works." Privately, the cautious Tatlow feared that, once work on the GTP began, any surplus would disappear because of the need "to supply all the requirements of civilization in the Northern wilderness."[52]

Past grants to railways were a major cause of the government's financial woes. After the Legislature approved the $1 million Loan Act in December 1903 that provided funds to let the government pay its bills, McBride informed the Bank of Commerce that his government did not plan to add to its obligations through railway aid but wanted to assist projects, notably the Coast-Kootenay railway, that had been endorsed by previous legislation. Yet he told Price Ellison, who wanted aid for the Midway and Vernon (M&V), that, given the party's weak hold on the Legislature, a bill to aid that railway could destroy the administration and give a "black eye to the project." Nevertheless, he could not ignore the desire of British Columbians for more railways. In February 1904, McBride hinted of plans to subsidize railways. He did not favour state ownership of railways but discussed buying the Esquimalt and Nanaimo Railway (E&N) from James Dunsmuir in order to resolve the matter of settlers' rights in its land grant; privately, he told Dunsmuir that the province could not raise $3,500,000 in cash but could possibly offer the equivalent in provincial inscribed stock. Dunsmuir agreed to accept the stock but wanted to retain both the coal and the freedom from taxation on his lands, an arrangement that was unacceptable to the province. Eventually, Dunsmuir sold the E&N to the CPR.[53]

As for the long-desired Coast-Kootenay railway, McBride thought that either the CPR or the Great Northern (GNR) could build it and hinted of communications with the GNR about an all-Canadian road. He twice visited Seattle to discuss the prospect with GNR officials and was optimistic about signing a contract when J.J. Hill, the GNR president, visited the coast. After McBride learned that Northern Securities, the company controlling the GNR, had financial problems, he was less sanguine. No other viable firm was interested in building the line. Despite having "patiently, faithfully, earnestly and persistently" negotiated with the GNR, he had nothing to report. T.G. Shaughnessy of the CPR, however, discussed provincial assistance for new lines in southern British Columbia. Meetings with other CPR officials and cabinet ministers followed, but the province's financial problems meant that there could be no cash bonuses. The CPR rejected McBride's offer of a provincial bond guarantee for a line into the Nicola Valley since it could borrow money more cheaply than the province.[54]

McBride's policy was "to secure railways, but not to cumber the statute books with useless railway legislation." He did not publicize his negotiations with railway companies. When Bowser reported "a hell of a lot of talk and criticism" among MLAs about the lack of action on the Coast-Kootenay railway, McBride offered no details but "in strictest confidence" said that negotiations were "well under way." When the Legislature met early in 1905, he was obliged to admit that no company had offered suitable terms for the Coast-Kootenay line. "The history of railway aid in British Columbia," he explained, "did not encourage the belief that it would be good practise to go into the bonusing of railways" without being certain that they required such aid. He would resign rather than support any railway legislation that was beyond the province's financial ability.[55]

While lobbyists for railway promoters "thronged" the corridors of the Parliament Buildings, the caucus became impatient about the lack of a railway policy. Rumours swirled that MLAs were "in a belligerent mood," that McBride had become "a tool" of the "big corporations," that up to eight Conservatives had joined the Opposition, and that MLAs had refused to pass the estimates until the railway question was settled. The Legislature's work dropped off. The *Times* declared that whatever McBride's "strategic purpose" might be in his railway dealings, the situation was such "a scandal and a disgrace" that it required "a complete clean-out of the whole nest of parasites which infests alike the legislative chamber and its lobbies." The next day, the paper reported that an unsmiling McBride had presented a railway policy to caucus, which covered all parts of the province "as with a blanket." Instead of favouring any particular project, he told the caucus to take its pick and try to get it through the House "as he washed his hands of it." Over the next few days, the caucus had several "very lively sessions." At least two MLAs, A.H.B. Macgowan (Vancouver) and L.W. Shatford (Similkameen), boycotted some meetings. Despite lacking a full report on the situation, some editors predicted that the government might fall. The *Province* indicated that the key questions were the route for the Coast-Kootenay railway and whether the line would be built by the CPR or the McLean Brothers, a Vancouver-based railway contracting firm. The questions were moot, as no aid was available. The *Times* suggested that the CPR merely wanted to keep other corporations out and was in no hurry to see railway legislation passed. Caucus remained unhappy. George Fraser (Grand Forks) demanded aid for the Kettle Valley Railway, and at least three other members, Shatford, Robert Grant (Comox), and Macgowan, supported him. Finally, McBride accepted the inevitable and informed the Legislature of the impossibility of devising a "comprehensive" railway scheme that would "protect the people and ensure adequate transportation." Even the *Colonist* called the government's reluctance "to present a straight-cut railway programme" a possibly "fatal devotion to the shibboleth of expediency." McBride, however, was keen to develop railways in the North. When the Pacific Northern and Omineca Railway requested a cash subsidy in order to undertake such a project, he demurred and proposed to its president, Forbes G. Vernon, that the government might offer up to 15,000 acres for each of the 135 miles between Kitimat and Hazelton, and that it might consider a partial cash subsidy. "As the ability of the Province will permit," he added, "nothing will be spared towards attaining that end."[56]

The major railway interest in the North, the GTP, was a federal project. Soon after taking office, the cabinet asked Ottawa to require the GTP to commence its construction at the Pacific coast. In November 1903, McBride asked Charles M. Hays, president of the GTP, about "the probable nature of the work" in the province and reminded him of the desire to have it begin at the coast. The GTP's need for a terminus and a right of way through Crown land gave the province a strong bargaining chip on that particular point and in its insistence that the GTP not employ Asians. It surrendered one chip in May 1904, when it approved a secret Order-in-Council binding it to let the GTP select as its terminus ten thousand acres on Kaien Island, the site of the future Prince Rupert, in return for a payment of $10,000. When rumours of this bargain circulated, the *Colonist* remarked that the government "would be committing suicide" if it were to offer a large "unsolicited" land grant to the GTP.[57]

The 1905 session was difficult. Another controversial matter was a bill to make school districts more responsible for their costs while giving rural school boards greater independence from a very centralized educational administration. McBride admitted that the necessary tax increase was unpopular but expected better management of the schools since the "people would feel more directly their responsibilities" and would encounter fewer inequalities. He believed that his own constituents could meet the added expense. After the government increased grants for teachers' salaries, the bill passed third reading without division. At the next session, the Legislature added unworked mines to assessable property and increased the number of trustees in each school district from five to seven.[58]

Although the School Act somewhat decentralized school finances, Victoria was still vitally involved in the day-to-day problems of education, and teachers with problems often wrote directly to the premier, a fact that reflects the smallness of the government. One case reveals the communication difficulties between Victoria and school boards, many of which administered only one single-room school. When the trustees at Comaplix on the upper Arrow Lakes asked for a new teacher, the Department of Education sent one. When she arrived, after paying her own travel expenses, she found that the trustees had hired another woman. The department ruled that she should receive a salary for August as compensation. When relations between the locally hired teacher and the pupils "were not pleasant," the trustees gave the teacher they had hired her thirty days' notice effective the end of November. On the advice of the superintendent of education, McBride told her that she had no claim to a salary for August or December.[59]

The Legislature passed most of the government's bills in 1905, but McBride could not rely on the support of every Conservative. Liberals alleged that the government depended on the "goodwill of a coterie of legislators who are freakish in their ideas" and was beholden to the two Socialist MLAs – the *Times* called J.H. Hawthornthwaite "the Socialist dictator." Early in the 1905 session, McBride told Opposition leader J.A. Macdonald that the government was not "Socialist-led or Socialist-leading" but was proud of the Socialists' support. Hawthornthwaite told Vancouver Socialists that the McBride government represented "the highest point of capitalistic development, and the Liberals, by standing for the middle class" were "the worse of the two." He added that the Socialists could not bring down the government, did not vote on confidence motions, and were there only to deal with matters affecting working men. McBride supported a Socialist motion to reduce election deposits, but he did not approve of all their suggestions. When Hawthornthwaite proposed an eight-hour day for smelter workers, McBride agreed that twelve hours was too long a day but doubted that conditions were as bad as portrayed and feared that since the mining industry was just recovering from depression, such a law might drive the smelting business south of the border.[60]

When the 1905 session ended, even the *News-Advertiser* was disappointed by the lack of a railway policy or any striking measure but commended the government's honest attempt "to improve the fiscal system and place it on a better and more scientific basis." The *Province* praised Tatlow for putting finances in order but thought it disgraceful that a timid and secretive cabinet had produced "colorless and imperfect" legislation and had "prostituted its own dignity and the interests of the province to the demands of a few members whose public ambition seems to be to hamper or destroy private enterprise." After an extended interview with McBride, the *Province* conceded that he had satisfactorily defended the government's policies.[61]

Stability increased during the summer of 1905, when a Conservative won the Alberni by-election that had resulted after the incumbent, W.W.B. McInnes, a Liberal, resigned to become commissioner of Yukon. McBride and Green toured the constituency on behalf of the Conservative candidate, William Manson. McBride answered complaints about taxes and land policies, and a recent allegation by John Oliver, a Liberal MLA, that the government had connived with the returning officer to "steal" the Fernie seat in the 1903 general election. When a *Times* editorial, in commenting on this and other issues, declared that the McBride government had been "conceived in treachery," McBride sued the *Times* for $10,000 for libel. The unabashed *Times* charged that the government placed polling stations in Alberni at locations where there were Conservative voters but not where the majority were Grits.[62]

Increasing prosperity allowed McBride to do more about railways. During an eastern visit in December 1905, he met the presidents of the CPR and the GTP, William Mackenzie and Donald Mann of the Canadian Northern Railway (CNR), and J.J. Hill of the GNR. En route home he told a public meeting at Cranbrook that he wanted new railways but not with "a policy ruinous to the province." Vancouver reporters thought he had "a railway policy in his pocket," but when asked for details, he merely "smiled – a wistful, faraway sort of smile" since he must report to cabinet first. He did say that the GTP had selected its terminus. A few days later, he denied saying that he had a railway policy. Meanwhile, lobbyists for the GTP and the GNR converged on Victoria. McBride told the Legislature

> **THE MORTGAGE ON THE BRAIN**
>
> HON. R—D MCB—DE: Hope there's nothing serious the matter with the girl, doctor
> FAMILY PHYSICIAN: No; just the old trouble—railroadmania—you know. She wants a change of air and a little cheerful company.
> HON. R—D MCB—DE: That's all right, then; I'll send for her pal, Master Jimmy Hill, to play the Coast-Kootenay game with her.

Emily Carr's cartoon alludes to British Columbia's great desire for railways, especially one that would link the coast and the Kootenays. McBride had already discussed such a railway with J.J. Hill, the president of the Great Northern Railroad. *The Week*, 29 April 1905, cartoonist, Emily Carr.

that the government had considered but rejected twelve to fifteen requests for land and cash grants for railways since all seemed based on a desire for personal gain. There would be no railway legislation during the current session. Without government support, the Vancouver, Victoria and Eastern (VV&E), a GNR subsidiary, was building to the coast, and another railway was about to tap the Nicola Valley. Not every colleague accepted McBride's refusal to introduce railway legislation. Ellison was "agitated" because McBride, without consulting the caucus, had denied a time extension on an old subsidy of $5,000 a mile, which would have enabled the Midway and Vernon (M&V) to extend its line to Kamloops and Penticton. The *Times* reported that several Conservative MLAs favoured assisting the

M&V. McBride devised a "truce" by referring the matter to the courts, which determined that the M&V had begun work before the time prescribed and so was eligible for the subsidy.[63]

Another old issue was the Columbia and Western Railway. The CPR had pressed the government to confirm the 808,872 acres that remained to it under the subsidy. On 26 February 1906, R.F. Green introduced a bill to confirm Orders-in-Council authorizing the government to issue Crown grants once surveys were complete. McBride denied that his government was "the creature of the C.P.R. or any other corporation," but he added that, despite the CPR's unpopularity, it had "honestly earned" the lands, and thus the government must "do right where right should be done."[64] At one point, it seemed likely that the opposition of Ellison and others might cause the government to fall. Thanks apparently to lobbying by Dunsmuir, the bill passed easily. In the midst of the 1906 session, however, Attorney General Charles Wilson resigned because he did not "see eye to eye" with his colleagues on the C&W and had been restrained from making his position clear on the floor of the House.[65]

An even larger railway problem emerged. Other enterprises shared the GTP's interest in Kaien Island. The Vancouver Power Company (a British Columbia Electric Railway subsidiary) applied for timber and water rights there. Its deposit was returned, but McBride and Green, the chief commissioner of lands and works, advised it to wait while McBride did "all in his power" to protect its application. A year later, the Vancouver Power Company complained that it had heard nothing. In the interval, several individuals took up scrip issued to veterans of the South African war and filed for pre-emptions on Kaien Island. When the government rejected their applications, they hired Tupper to represent them. Tupper made common cause with J.A. Macdonald, the provincial Liberal leader. Possibly in an effort to forestall agitation, the government made public the text of its agreement with the GTP regarding Kaien Island.[66]

This move simply encouraged the Opposition. In the Legislature, J.A. Macdonald called the grant an illegal bonus to the GTP "made without sanction of the legislature." Editorially, the *Times* noted that members on both sides of the House seemed to look on the transaction "with the greatest suspicion." At Macdonald's request, a select committee of the Legislature investigated the issue, and McBride testified that he had first heard of the GTP's plans for a townsite at Kaien Island during a "casual" conversation with E.V. Bodwell, possibly in Green's presence. The cabinet had decided that it would only deal directly with the GTP and only if it could reach an advantageous agreement, but it accepted Bodwell's word that he was acting for the GTP. The Opposition press claimed that Bodwell was actually acting for a company of speculators and hinted that some members of the government expected to profit personally from the deal. The government had kept the arrangement for the land transfer with the GTP secret until it was complete lest "all kinds of objections" be made to the terminus site. The land was third class, and without the terminus it "would not be worth twopence." The Opposition press called the whole arrangement "a nasty piece of business" in which the government, or some of its members, "was party to a deliberate scheme to defraud" both the province and the GTP and it accused them of making a deal favouring private speculators, possibly including Bodwell.[67]

When rumours spread that McBride would hasten prorogation to avoid meeting the House, Lieutenant-Governor Joly told him to insist that the committee deliver its report on the Kaien Island transaction and to have a vote on the report before prorogation. A few days later, the committee's majority report effectively exonerated the government by stating that the transaction benefited the province and that no government member or official had received any personal direct or indirect reward. Macdonald's minority report declared that the government knew that it was dealing with a band of speculators, not the GTP, that it had rejected other applications on false grounds, and that it had lacked the power to make the grant without the approval of the Legislature. Secrecy, he added, gave the speculators an advantage in securing other lands in the area. The government printed the majority report in the *Journals* of the Legislature but refused to publish the minority report, a move that sparked a "torrid" fight in the Legislature. When the *Times* printed both reports, McBride claimed that because the committee functioned like a jury, it should reach a unanimous verdict, which would preclude the need for a minority report. He spoke of punishing the newspaper. When called to order in the House, he withdrew his unparliamentary language. Although two Conservative MLAs were out of the province and two others, "in open rebellion," could not be depended upon for support, the Legislature rejected a Liberal resolution to invalidate the secret Order-in-Council of May 1904, which had granted the Kaien Island site to the GTP. When the cabinet rejected Tupper's call for a reference to the court, he commented, "Your Government has one rule for Corporations and another for private citizens." He appealed to public opinion. After Tupper sent McBride a letter that looked "like a threatened bomb which would wreck him [McBride] *and* the Conservative party," McBride asked Clive Phillipps-Wolley to determine what would satisfy Tupper. Tupper insisted that the matter must go to court since there was evidence "proving Green's malfeasance in office."[68]

McBride's hold on the government was tenuous. When Carter-Cotton and Fulton were not present at a debate, the Liberal press interpreted this as a sign of division. Wilson, however, shared the platform with McBride at a Conservative meeting in Vancouver. There, McBride defended the Kaien Island transfer as a simple "business transaction" between the government and the GTP, with no "middle men" taking profits. As for the C&W, he explained that repudiating the contract would damage the province's financial reputation, and given the court decision on the M&V, the government would pay the money. In short, as the trustee of the people, the government's duty was "to see that the money of the country was not given away without good cause."[69]

For some time, reports had circulated that Green would be asked to resign. According to one story early in 1905, Carter-Cotton thought that Green's Department of Lands and Works had "gone to the bow wows" and that Green's alleged inefficiency would give the Opposition plenty of ammunition. A year later, the *Times* discounted a rumour of a caucus "round robin" in which McBride had been asked to dismiss Green, although some Conservative MLAs did favour Green's resignation. The chief complaint revolved around Green's handling of the Kaien Island lands. More rumours surfaced. In June, it was said that Dunsmuir, now lieutenant-governor, would no longer accept Green as an advisor. Scandal dogged Green. The next one concerned the sale of a parcel of waterfront land at Laurel Point in Victoria's harbour. W.J. Pendray, the proprietor of a soap factory there, wanted to purchase an adjacent lot owned by the government, so he offered $2,000 through a public tender. Allegedly, this figure "leaked out" of the Department of Lands and Works, and a Mrs. Logie, who was the government's favoured purchaser, bid $2,100. The Victoria Board of Trade objected to the land falling into private hands. It was also claimed that after Pendray threatened to publicize the leak, Green offered to lease the lot to him for a nominal rent. McBride was touring the North when the issue arose. Under Acting Premier Tatlow, the cabinet quickly appointed Frederick Peters, a Liberal lawyer, to investigate the situation. As Tatlow pointed out, the choice of Peters guaranteed that "they could hardly accuse us of seeking a whitewash." Peters found that none of the charges were true and that neither Green nor his officials had done anything "in the slightest degree worthy of censure." Nevertheless, the taint of scandal persisted. Late in December, Green resigned, citing personal business reasons. He

NOT LOST, BUT GONE BEFORE
The Premier – Alas, poor Bob! He was my soul's Jonathan, Captain.
The Captain [Tatlow] – Be resigned, Dick. He cannot come to us, but we will follow Him on the 2nd.

Robert Tatlow and McBride commiserate with each other on the loss of Robert F. Green, who sets out toward "Oblivion," burdened by the various land scandals that prompted his resignation. Green was McBride's close personal friend. The cartoon in the *Times*, which supported the Liberals, predicted that after the election on 2 February, Tatlow and McBride would join Green in political oblivion. Tatlow and McBride won, but Charles Wilson, who sought a seat in Cariboo, did not. *Victoria Daily Times*, 28 January 1907, cartoonist, C.R. Patterson.

was a scapegoat for Kaien Island and other land issues; his departure helped deflect criticism of land policies.[70]

The Liberal press frequently complained that, through corruption or incompetence, the government was letting natural resources pass into private hands. Forests, the most important resource, produced royalties for the provincial coffers – 17 percent of the provincial revenue in 1905 – and provided much employment.[71] Early in the century, British Columbia's forests drew the attention of American timbermen whose own forests were being depleted. In 1901, the provincial government banned the export of raw logs to preserve both milling jobs and the forests. Coast loggers resented their inability to export logs, especially low-grade cedar logs that had no local market but commanded good prices in the United States. They petitioned the government to remove the export ban, but the cabinet decided that doing so would be "inadvisable in the public interest." To circumvent the ban, many "wealthy organizations" bought hand loggers' licences for their workers because these licences, designed for small loggers, permitted exports. On discovering this "loophole," the government tabled a bill proposing to cancel all exports. Opponents claimed that such a measure would "extirpate" small loggers and waste second-class lumber. The opposition to the proposed cancellation was so strong that in committee some government members, including Macgowan, voted against it. This revealed what the *Inland Sentinel* called "the slender thread by which the Government retains power." After some modifications, the bill passed. As the *Columbian* observed, the ban produced "a great deal of good," and public sentiment was "on the side of the government."[72]

Under the basic timber policy adopted in 1884, timber was allotted in a system of licences that imposed a royalty on wood cut on Crown lands and forbade the sale of Crown lands that were valuable for timber without clearly defining such land. However, the rapid growth of the lumber industry at the turn of the twentieth century, combined with the realization that speculators held a great deal of land, that logging practices were wasteful, and that little revenue was going to the government, made it imperative to revisit the policy. In the Legislature, W.W.B. McInnes accused the government of disposing "of enormous areas of valuable timber lands for purely nominal sums." Conservation was also becoming an issue. Some leases drew particular attention. In the spring of 1905, loggers protested the lease of an immense amount of cedar land on northern Vancouver Island to the Western Canada Pulp and Paper Company, pointing out that the cedar was excellent for lumber but unsuitable for pulp. Not only did the allocation of the lease suggest inadequate knowledge of the forested area in question, but the *World* also drew attention to the fact that McBride's name was included on the company's prospectus. He dismissed as "absolutely untrue" the charges that he had an interest in the company. He had given a letter to Michael King, a friend since boyhood, in which he had recommended him "as an expert timber cruiser." King's report was in the prospectus, and he had listed McBride and several banks as references. McBride was willing to say under oath "that neither directly nor indirectly have I been interested in this or any other pulp or lumber concerns here or anywhere." Conservative editors thought the denial "scarcely necessary," given McBride's well-known "personal integrity" and honesty. In graciously accepting the *World*'s printed apology, McBride handwrote to Victor Odlum, its publisher, "The Session's cruel aspersions I am glad to say are at once removed by your open & candid article."[73]

The government attempted some reforms. In 1905, largely at the behest of independent loggers who wanted better collateral on which to borrow operating capital, the province began replacing older limited non-transferable licences with twenty-one-year transferable licences on specified forest areas. It also adjusted the amount of royalty and rental payments annually. McBride noted that timber could no longer be cut before the land was surveyed and that he expected less speculation. Had the existing system been permitted to continue, he foresaw that in a few years, no timberlands would be left near transportation. Due to the increasing demand for lumber, especially in the Prairie West, the concern in the United States about its own dwindling timber supply, and the amount of lumber needed to rebuild San Francisco after its 1906 earthquake, the number of licences rose dramatically in 1906 and 1907. The government's revenue from timber licences increased from $177,984 in 1904 to $1,339,351 in 1907.[74] When the *Toronto Globe* urged British Columbia to halt alienating large tracts of timberlands to companies, an incensed *Colonist* observed that eastern Canadians "suppose the administration of the affairs of this province is one prolonged potlatch." It told the *Globe* that the policies had changed. Liberal journals warned that the province was "dissipating her capital, her prime source of wealth for the future, at an alarmingly rapid rate." In fact, the new licensing scheme did not eliminate speculators and led to massive American investment. Determining the extent of the holdings of Americans and other outsiders, chiefly from Ontario, is impossible, but as one historian has recounted, the policy produced "chaos," "inefficiency," and an "uneconomic harvest," partly because of the forced twenty-one-year deadline for logging the land. McBride perceived the problems. He informed Henri Joly de Lotbinière that the industry was doing well but that "the timber question seems to demand the first attention of the Government." In September 1906, he told a Canadian Forestry Association meeting in Vancouver that "British Columbia's timber wealth is practically illimitable." Regretting wasteful logging practices that left large quantities of timber to rot, thus increasing the numbers of forest fires, he promised to endeavour to stop poor practices and educate the public but added that the geographic area was great and the province had a "mere handful of ratepayers."[75]

Although forest lands were a source of revenue, the province also used land to attract settlers. The basic problem was its lack of arable land, usually

THE DOG-IN-THE-MANGER LOGGER.

PREMIER McBRIDE – So you won't develop the country yourself, and won't let anyone else come in and do it, eh! We've too many of your sort here, my fine fellow. Out you go, quick, and make room for Capital and Industry.

Although frequently criticized for "giving away" provincial resources, McBride was keen to exploit them and develop the province. *The Week*, 10 June 1905, cartoonist, Emily Carr.

estimated to be about 3 percent of the province's total area. The Opposition criticized the Department of Lands and Works for what the *Nelson Daily News* called its "archaic, confusing and absurd" methods. Some valleys, particularly the Bulkley and the Nechako as well as in the North Thompson, looked promising once transportation became available, but the land had to be surveyed. In the Fraser and Okanagan Valleys, much unsettled land was in the hands of speculators. McBride cautioned J.H. Turner, British Columbia's agent-general in London, that despite a shortage of agricultural labourers, wages were low, and only British emigrants who were "possessed of some means" should be encouraged to come to the province.[76]

Some of the best agricultural land in the Fraser Valley was subject to flooding. As Dewdney's MLA, McBride was acutely conscious of this. A few days after he became premier, a local dairy farm was submerged due to a defective floodgate on the Pitt River. Along with some friends and a dyking expert, he chartered a boat and investigated. When he introduced amendments to the Dyking Act in 1905, the Opposition and some caucus members demanded changes. McBride denied helping absentee speculators who held land in the hope of future gain and paid little or nothing in the way of taxes; those affected were resident taxpayers who would have to pay the bills for maintaining dykes. Repeated flooding had washed away the dykes in the small municipality of Dewdney, leaving residents powerless to pay for new dykes and the municipality unable to pay its bills. In introducing a bill for its relief and disincorporation, McBride warned in 1906 that if the government did not act, "every settler would lose his holding," which would be a disaster for the province's reputation. John Oliver, whose Delta riding had also been flooded, said that his constituents shouldered their burden but that McBride would let Dewdney "get out of business without paying its debts." Referring to "The Dewdney Outrage," the *Times* asked how a municipality in the premier's riding differed from the rest and claimed that the Sun Life Insurance Company, for whom Charles Wilson was a solicitor, held provincial debentures and mortgages on many farms in the district.[77] Despite these complaints, the bill passed.

Through correspondence with constituents, particularly political friends, McBride kept abreast of Dewdney matters but could not grant every wish. Retrenchment meant that he could do little to supply public works, including pumps for flood control at Coquitlam. He made a grant for a resident physician at Mission City but denied a similar one to Maple Ridge. As provincial finances improved and an election loomed, he had a school near Harrison Hot Springs placed in the "Assisted Class" to give it direct provincial funding. He also asked the chief commissioner of lands and works to arrange some small public works and advised a Maple Ridge constituent that a needed road would be built once the estimates were passed. A Coquitlam supporter predicted that McBride would do well in the next general election because "everybody is remarking on the good times with plenty of work and good wages" but admonished, "when the time comes give as much of your time as possible to your own constituents." McBride promised not to neglect them.[78]

His responsibilities as premier made his visits to Dewdney less frequent but demonstrated his mastery of "extending the glad hand," a trait for which he was already well known. Some visits had a specific purpose. In June 1904, he studied dyking needs and held public meetings in a number of communities; a year later, he accepted an invitation to "The Peoples'

Dick" from BCER manager Johannes Buntzen to attend the official opening of the Buntzen Lake Power Tunnel, where he provoked laughter by saying that he had never expected Dewdney to "give to Vancouverites the light to read their morning papers and the power to drive their cars." While in the area he held public meetings at Haney, Mission, Port Moody, and Westminster Junction. The next year he made a similar tour, adding Hatzic Prairie and Agassiz to his itinerary and crossing the Fraser River to Chilliwack. A few visits were purely for pleasure, such as an April weekend of fishing in the Lillooet River, where he caught a "basket of beautiful trout."[79]

He often went to New Westminster for personal or family business, to inspect the Provincial Asylum, where there was allegedly much waste, and for such pleasant events as opening the Provincial Exhibition and attending the banquet of the British Columbia Pioneer Society. In the spring of 1904, he spent two weeks there while his mother was ill. He offered to supply swans if the city extended Queen's Park and created a lake near the McBride family home. His major holiday often began in New Westminster. In 1905, it was a week-long camping and hunting trip to the Coquihalla River about ten miles east of Hope with his brother Leonard, A.E. McPhillips, and New Westminster friends.[80] They bagged plenty of trout and game.

Sadly, Leonard, a merchant at Port Guichon near the mouth of the Fraser River, was not on the next year's ten-day camping trip to Pitt Lake. He had died at St. Joseph's Hospital in Victoria the previous February from complications after surgery for what was believed to be an abscess on the lung. He had just celebrated his thirty-fifth birthday and left a wife and four young children. An overflow crowd attended his funeral at Holy Trinity Anglican Cathedral in New Westminster. McBride, who was at his brother's deathbed, was clearly moved. A member of the press gallery recalled that before Leonard's death, he had "fulminated too much and used far too many words to express few ideas," but that afterward he had "toned down" and became "the master of placating political opponents," even to the point of patting Parker Williams, the Socialist member for Newcastle, on the shoulder and smiling after Williams attacked him. Williams later complained of having been "buncoed!"[81]

McBride did not shun travel to various parts of the province, even though it could entail tiring overnight coach rides or catching trains in the middle of the night, with only rare occasions for recreation, such as his favourite pastime, fishing. As a young man, he possessed a great deal of stamina. During his many travels in his first two years of office, he only once recorded illness, a bout of diarrhoea at Lac La Hache. Bowser urged him to get out of Victoria to deal with a feeling among MLAs that the government was doing nothing about railways. In the summer and fall of 1904, he travelled so widely that he seemed to spend more time on the road than in Victoria. From 22 June until 24 July, he ventured as far east as Cranbrook and Fort Steele, and as far north as Barkerville. In the southern Interior, he discussed local matters, including patronage appointments and requests for roads and other public works. At Greenwood, he stayed with his sister Gertrude and her husband, William Allison, and he investigated a recent local scandal.[82] After arriving at Ashcroft on the CPR at 1:30 A.M., he left at 3:30 A.M. for the Cariboo. He travelled mainly by stagecoach, as far north as Barkerville, where he spent a week. As minister of mines, he visited many mines and claims, and he held political meetings. After another brief visit home, he returned to the Interior to campaign for the Conservative candidate in the Lillooet by-election. Before the year was out, he made quick rail trips to Revelstoke for the Conservative convention in September and to the North Okanagan in December.[83]

Much of the late summer and the fall of 1905 were spent on the road. In August, along with Green, A.E. McPhillips, and C.W.D. Clifford, the MLA for Skeena, he spent over a week touring the Skeena and Bulkley Valleys, especially around Hazelton. He encountered a "feeling of confidence" in "New British Columbia" and its mineral, timber, and agricultural prospects. In November, he and Green made a three-week tour of the West Kootenay, Okanagan, and Boundary Districts, where they were often accompanied by local Conservative MLAs. One report claimed that they worked with "political friends" at Nelson to unseat John Houston, but McBride denied this. Throughout, he met local officials and travelled by train and automobile over Anarchist Mountain from Fairview to Keremeos, Princeton, and Penticton. Back in Victoria, he boasted of prosperity, the growing mining industry, and the presence of many new settlers. He noted lumbermen's complaints of low prices, high freight rates, and a lack of tariff protection. In December, en route home from Ottawa, he spoke in Cranbrook on railway policy, Better Terms, and the government's accomplishments.[84]

The trips continued. After a tour of the Kootenays in June 1906, he told Victoria Conservatives that he and his ministers were trying to "familiarize themselves with local conditions by visiting the different sections" of the province. The Kootenay trip took him as far east as Golden and Fernie, and was more a fact-finding tour than a political cavalcade as he had no public meetings in the larger centres. At Cranbrook, his unexpected arrival sent local Conservatives scrambling to set up a meeting. He was briefly home before making a month-long tour to Hazelton, Atlin, and many points in between. To get to Atlin, he had to go to Whitehorse, where he discussed matters of mutual interest with "Governor" McInnes. As well as performing such functions as opening the first County Court at Hazelton and observing the progress of construction and settlement along the GTP and the development of Prince Rupert, he fished for trout at Lakelse. The *Colonist* praised him for ascertaining local sentiment, but the Opposition press interpreted "the journeyings of Dewdney Dick" as an election tour made at the expense of the provincial treasury. In mid-December, he briefly visited the Okanagan. In Vernon, the fire brigade escorted him in a torchlight procession and about 225 people attended a banquet in his honour. At a public meeting, he praised the attractions of the Okanagan, accused the Liberals of doing little except looking for scandal, explained that he could not subsidize the Midway and Vernon Railway, defended the government against charges concerning the C&W lands in the Crow's Nest Pass and Kaien Island, and presented the case for Better Terms. He was evasive about the timing of a provincial election, but he outlined its campaign themes.[85]

Election rumours persisted. The *Times* concluded that the travels of McBride and Green, "making promises here, appeals there, apportioning road work in this place and distributing or promising patronage in that, jollying and junketing everywhere," were evidence of a pending election. Asserting that McBride's nominal control of his administration was "fast slipping out of his grip," Liberal leader J.A. Macdonald toured the province himself, attacking McBride for entering into an "unholy alliance" with the Socialists and letting the CPR be the "master of the government." Decrying increased taxes and reduced public works, he argued that by managing its natural resources properly and taxing the corporations more, the government could reduce taxes. He agreed that British Columbia deserved Better Terms but called McBride a "sulky boy" who should have stayed at the Inter-Provincial Conference of 1906 that had discussed British Columbia's demand for Better Terms in order to "maintain the struggle for B.C.'s demands."[86]

British Columbia's campaign for Better Terms preceded Confederation. When the colonial delegation negotiated the Terms of Union in 1870, it insisted that the province receive a Dominion subsidy sufficient to let it balance its books. For a time that financial arrangement worked, but as the province's needs for infrastructure and services increased, it usually spent more than it took in. Thus, most BC premiers appealed to Ottawa for what became known as Better Terms. Dunsmuir's government collected extensive documentation for the claim that British Columbia was unique due to its "peculiar geographical configuration," the mountains that made road construction and the provision of schools and services extremely costly, "its remoteness from Eastern trade centres," its high freight rates, and its relatively non-industrial character, which obliged it to import many goods and contribute a disproportionate amount to the federal treasury through the associated tariff. Dunsmuir estimated that Ottawa had spent almost $29 million in British Columbia over the previous thirty years but had collected $42 million. In short, British Columbia, with one fifty-fifth of Canada's population, contributed about a twentieth of its revenue. Dunsmuir claimed that though the "Act of Union" was a binding treaty, or compact, it was subject to "modification" since the Fathers of Confederation could not have foreseen the future. Thus, British Columbia must have extra subsidies, and he cited precedents such as the Better Terms given to Nova Scotia in 1869.[87]

Almost immediately after becoming premier, McBride had sent Green and Wilson to Ottawa to discuss several urgent matters, including the need for bonuses for the lead industry and restrictions on Asian immigration. Publicly he said that the quest was "not so much a matter of politics as the conservation of provincial rights." Liberal Senator William Templeman of Victoria correctly advised Prime Minister Laurier that Green and Wilson had come "to find, if they can, a policy upon which to go before the electors." Green and Wilson had brought so many requests that they could not discuss them all with Laurier, but their main concern was readjusting the financial terms. Their arguments and documentation were almost identical to those of the Dunsmuir government, but they were so confident of "the justness" of their claims that they proposed a new idea: having a commission of "experts" familiarize itself with British Columbia's physical conditions and decide on the amount of the settlement. In a suggestion revealing the province's colonial mentality, they proposed that the province and Dominion would each appoint a commissioner, and the colonial secretary would appoint the final arbiter. McBride's efforts to turn the issue to political advantage were thwarted when Borden, knowing that all provinces had their own versions of Better Terms demands, refused to say that British Columbia could expect "generous terms" if he won the next federal election. This may be why McBride made Better Terms a non-partisan issue and did not include it in his 1903 provincial election platform.[88]

Sometimes, McBride made small specific requests of Ottawa: when the federal government was about to incorporate the Columbia River Improvement Company, he asked it to consider how other lumber operators on the river would be affected by this measure, and he asked Ottawa to do its best to protect the sealers whose industry would be affected by any settlement in a long-standing conflict with the United States. Nevertheless, he regretted that since Ontario premier Oliver Mowat had retired in 1896, the provinces had not made "very much progress" toward provincial rights.[89] Mowat had championed provincial rights, especially during the 1880s, though for him, as premier of the wealthiest province, provincial rights were more constitutional than financial.

McBride also attacked the Laurier government. Complaining that Ottawa had not listened to Green and Wilson, he threatened that if it did not adjust British Columbia's financial terms, the BC MPs "would have to take drastic steps to obtain justice" and that "an agitation" would become a "partisan debate." Because other provinces also sought Better Terms, Laurier wanted "a uniform, systematic and final basis" for all of them. He refused to supply federal assistance for the New Westminster Bridge, and he viewed Indian reserves as "purely departmental" business. As a gesture of conciliation, he said that the federal minister of marine and fisheries would soon visit British Columbia to gain "a better understanding" of its fisheries. The prospect of a visit from a federal minister did not mollify McBride, especially since Laurier opened his reply with an attack on McBride's warning regarding "agitation" and partisan debate. McBride regretted Laurier's "wholly negative" answer, repeated the justice of British Columbia's claim, and attacked the idea of a uniform system of financial relations for all the provinces. Facetiously, he concluded his angry letter to Laurier with "Thank you for the very courteous nature of your letter," adding that it "materially assists in the definition of the issue." McBride told the Legislature that Laurier's letter "took little stock in British Columbia's case" and repeated his warning that if the province did not get satisfaction soon, the question would become acute. The *Columbian* interpreted Laurier's unsatisfactory letter as indicating "little hope" of readjusted terms.[90]

An imminent federal election led provincial Conservatives to seek to have Robert Borden, their federal leader, endorse British Columbia's claims. G.H. Cowan, a Vancouver lawyer who wrote a pamphlet on Better Terms, would not run for the Conservatives unless Borden promised to adjust the Terms of Union if elected. McBride understood Borden's worry that a special arrangement for British Columbia could affect other provinces but reiterated that all he wanted was a commission to investigate the claim. Although the *Times* said that Laurier had promised an investigation, McBride told Borden that a promise to hold a commission "would greatly help the [Conservative] cause in British Columbia."[91] Tupper secured a statement from Borden that British Columbia's claim required "immediate inquiry and investigation." Despite the *Colonist*'s declaration that Better Terms was not a "political" or secession cry but a movement "founded upon right, justice and indisputable facts," the Conservatives made it a campaign issue. At a meeting in Duncan, Tupper reported Borden's pledge to right any wrong that British Columbia had suffered from Confederation, and McBride rehearsed the history of the Better Terms campaign. He argued that the Liberal MPs had done nothing for their province. Furthermore, Ottawa had not helped with the New Westminster Bridge, even though it had spent "hundreds of thousands on a bridge in Quebec." Nor had it maintained navigation devices in BC waters, and the contract with the GTP offered limited benefit for the province since it did not oblige the GTP to build from the west as well as from the east. The *Nelson Tribune* suggested that Better Terms was a live issue only on the coast, but McBride referred to it in Kamloops, and Martin Burrell, the Conservative candidate in Yale-Cariboo, mentioned it in his campaign.[92]

When the Liberals swept British Columbia, McBride remained undeterred. In thanking Cowan for his Better Terms pamphlet, he remarked that Cowan and R.E. Gosnell, the editor of the *Colonist,* were the authorities on the subject and that he would seek Cowan's advice, for "the movement is in its infancy and yours are the efforts upon which the agitation to come must rest its foundations." Early in the 1905 session, McBride declared that Ottawa had ignored British Columbia's claims and violated the Terms of Union, which required the Dominion government to use its influence "to secure the continued maintenance of the Naval Station at Esquimalt," a reference to a report that the Admiralty was leaving Esquimalt. His resolution on Better Terms repeated the traditional plaint that conditions had changed since Confederation and that geography made the cost of government disproportionately high. J.A. Macdonald introduced a friendly amendment, rephrasing the resolution to read that British Columbia's previous representations had not been heeded and that its "peculiar" and "permanent" situation – the exceptionally high cost of governing the province and developing its natural resources, as well as its large contributions "to the Dominion by way of customs duties and otherwise" – entitled it to "distinct and separate relief ... based upon an equitable consideration of conditions." The resolution passed unanimously.[93]

McBride asked Laurier to review British Columbia's claims for "special consideration" before taking "definite action" in creating the provinces of Saskatchewan and Alberta.[94] A fourteen-page printed memorandum, "The Case of British Columbia for Better Terms," offered no new arguments but warned that McBride would "persistently demand" a readjustment of financial relations. An opportunity to press the issue arose when Premier Lomer Gouin of Quebec, complaining that Ottawa had ignored the resolutions of the 1902 Inter-Provincial Conference, invited the other provinces to ask "the Federal Government to consider and recognize their claims for a re-adjustment of the Federal Subsidy." McBride sent a letter of agreement to Gouin but noted British Columbia's "peculiar conditions" and enclosed a letter for Laurier. If Gouin approved of its contents, McBride asked him to forward it. Gouin did so, adding a covering note about British Columbia's desire for special consideration.[95]

On 28 November 1905, along with Tatlow and his new private secretary Lawrence Macrae, a former journalist, McBride left for Ottawa to deal with departmental matters but principally to confer with other premiers on financial terms. Yet he told an Ottawa reporter that his visit had nothing to do with Better Terms. That may well have been true as he and Tatlow had to deal with many "odds and ends," particularly respecting mining and fishing. Managing the fisheries was perennially divisive. The BC and Dominion governments had agreed in 1901 that the latter would fully control the province's fisheries, collect the revenue, and pay the costs. When the federal Department of Marine and Fisheries claimed that its costs exceeded revenues, the province replied that, even so, it was getting off cheaply since, with few exceptions, the province had built wharves on navigable waters, whereas elsewhere, Ottawa paid for such wharves. Canners and Fraser River fishermen favoured Dominion management, although the canners thought that the province deserved some revenue. The *Skeena District News* noted that the provincial treasury could not afford to develop deep-sea and other fisheries, and that the provincial administration of the fisheries had been a disaster. Laurier referred the fisheries question to the premiers' conference, where the subject was lost in the bigger issue of Better Terms.[96]

Press reports of McBride's discussions with Laurier are contradictory. According to the *Colonist,* McBride said that he and Laurier did not discuss Better Terms in view of the forthcoming premiers' conference and British

Columbia's earlier documentation of its case. According to the *Province,* McBride told Laurier that given British Columbia's large contribution to Dominion revenues, "it should receive even better terms than any of our sister provinces." McBride informed the *Toronto Telegram* of his grievances with Ottawa, such as its failure to build wharves in his province. During a trip to Montreal, McBride also met T.G. Shaughnessy and Hugh Allan of the CPR, and he spent a few days visiting Dalhousie friends in Boston and New York, and possibly seeing some financiers. On returning to British Columbia, he complained to Ottawa about its failure to survey and select the Peace River lands that the province had ceded to it in 1884. He did not demand their return but argued that Ottawa's dilatoriness had "virtually locked up" over 100 million acres and prevented settlement in the North, which the GTP was making accessible.[97]

McBride was "much discouraged" by Laurier's failure to deal with Better Terms but did not press the issue. Then, in September 1906, anxious to keep the Liberals in power in Quebec, which wanted a larger federal subsidy, and knowing that the older provinces desired readjustments of their financial relations, Laurier invited the premiers to meet in Ottawa for a Inter-Provincial Conference on 8 October. In anticipation, the provincial press revived discussions of Better Terms, which it treated as a non-partisan issue.[98]

At a banquet hosted by the Canadian Club on the second evening of the conference, McBride boasted of the great things coming to the West because of the transcontinental railways under construction, but in the business sessions, he was less sanguine. The other premiers were generally satisfied with a new subsidy formula and Laurier's insistence that it would be "final and unalterable," but McBride was not. He was "the most striking figure at the Conference," and British Columbia's claim for special treatment "was the chief issue before the meeting." He repeated his arguments for Better Terms and a special commission to investigate, and he added a new argument – that, although the CPR benefited all of Canada, British Columbia had subsidized it by transferring 3.5 million acres of "the best agricultural lands" in the Peace River District to Ottawa.[99]

McBride believed that the main purpose of the conference was to help the Maritime provinces, that Quebec, Ontario, and Manitoba were chiefly interested in extending their borders, and that the new provinces of Alberta and Saskatchewan were "simply on hand to watch proceedings." After a few hours, the only "unfinished business" was British Columbia, and the conference spent seven-eighths of its three days on the BC demand for

Better Terms. At times, the conference seemed in danger of breaking up as McBride insisted on "sticking to his guns." The *Toronto Globe* called him "the disturbing element" at the conference and surmised "that the big clean-shaven chubby-cheeked head of the British Columbia Government" was seeking a "trump card in the forthcoming provincial election." It claimed that the other delegates were so angered by McBride's "obstinacy" that they recommended anything special for British Columbia only after federal officials had "urged patience." A conciliatory McBride, it speculated, might have got double the amount.[100]

Realizing that he had little chance of success, Premier Rodmond Roblin of Manitoba did not raise his own grievances at the conference, but he did support McBride. There were hints that Gouin might follow suit, but Roblin, Gouin, and the other premiers wanted a specific proposal from British Columbia. McBride suggested that British Columbia should receive the subsidy granted to all provinces as well as a dollar per capita per year on a scale that would decline to twenty-five cents per capita when its population reached 2,500,000. Its current population was probably about 200,000. The other premiers did not agree to this suggestion. Their unanimous consent was essential, for, if the revised terms were to be "final and unalterable," the British Parliament would need to amend the BNA Act, a process that would be made easier if all the premiers accepted the new terms. Hoping to win their agreement, Laurier said that if they thought it advisable, he would consider establishing a commission. Conceding that geography entitled British Columbia to a special subsidy, he asked the premiers to set the amount of a special subsidy. The Conservative press in British Columbia headlined this development as a "victory" but soon discovered that such was not the case. After "fully" considering McBride's evidence, the premiers rejected a special commission and said that $100,000 a year for ten years was a "reasonable additional allowance" to British Columbia for "exceptional" treatment. On hearing this, McBride withdrew from the conference, saying that he would go to London as his "final court of appeal," just as George A. Walkem had done in 1874 in connection with the CPR. Some reports had him slamming the door on his way out. McBride himself said that he left "simply and quietly" because of "unfair" treatment and the "simply absurd" sum offered. He complained that Ottawa had unilaterally created two new provinces but now insisted that all provinces must agree on any special claims.[101]

Responses in British Columbia were predictable. The Liberal press accused McBride of sacrificing the province to his "personal spleen," of

> **PIQUED**
>
> **FEDERAL FRUIT STAND**
>
> PREMIER MCBRIDE OF B.C. – "If I can't have the biggest apple in the pile, I don't want nothin'"

Federal greengrocer Wilfrid Laurier distributes various apples of subsidy. The other provincial premiers look on as McBride walks away in a sulk. Eastern Canadians regarded British Columbia as a spoiled child. The *Victoria Daily Times* reprinted this cartoon on 23 October 1906. *Toronto News,* 16 October 1906, cartoonist, Newton McConnell.

preferring a grievance to an increased subsidy, of letting "pique run away with him," and of going "to Ottawa to get, not better terms, but an election cry." The *Times* suggested that he had hoped his claims would be rejected so that he could ignore agitation about Kaien Island. According to the *Inland Sentinel,* many residents believed that the province should not go "begging" at Ottawa since wise administration of its resources could provide adequate revenue. In contrast, the Conservative press praised McBride for "the fight of his life" and his refusal "to barter the right of the province for the mess of the porridge offered to him at Ottawa." The *Province* declared that British Columbia, still "the milch cow of Confederation," had asked for bread and been offered a stone. It extolled him for having the "moral nerve" to take the "one decent, manly, honorable course" of walking out. McBride, it declared, stood out as the only man at the conference "who did the right thing at the right time in the right way," and it suggested honouring him with a banquet. Its Ottawa correspondent reported that McBride was "the most talked-of man in Ottawa last week, and for a few days at least, for the whole of Canada, he enjoyed that distinction." The *Colonist* praised him for being the "big man" of the conference who "secured recognition of British Columbia's special claims." When he went to England to fight the issue, it added, "this recognition will certainly count."[102] Without doubt, McBride's actions drew the attention of eastern Canada to him and his province.

McBride came home via a two-day trip to New York and brief visits to Toronto and Montreal. He had planned to visit Sir Henri at his St. Lawrence River estate but could not find a boat to take him there. At Field, his first stop in British Columbia, he was greeted by a large crowd of Liberals and Conservatives. He turned down an invitation to a banquet in Revelstoke because he needed to get back to Victoria. His train was late, so he stopped in New Westminster rather than proceeding to Vancouver, where Conservatives had planned to meet him. En route to Vancouver the next day, he told the *Columbian* of how much he appreciated the applause and numerous telegrams that had greeted him as he passed through the province. In Victoria, a carriage took him from the *Charmer* past "throngs" that lined the sidewalks. After a packed "enthusiastic" meeting at the Ancient Order of United Workers Hall gave him a "rousing welcome," McBride explained that Laurier and the premiers had recognized the province's entitlement "to special recognition" but had refused to have a board of arbitrators investigate the matter. His hint of a pending provincial election led the *Times* to suggest that he was posing "as the hero who has been ordained to deliver us from the thraldom of the East." It attacked his plan to appeal to the "foot of the throne."[103]

Over the next few weeks, in speeches given at Vancouver Island, the Okanagan, and the Fraser Valley, McBride spoke on Better Terms, his government's accomplishments, and its British heritage. Before a full house of supporters in New Westminster, he would not "cry secession or separation from confederation" but stated that if the case were carried through constitutionally and consistently, the province would win since "it could not be denied its British birth right." He accused eastern Canadians of an "appalling ignorance" of British Columbia and cited the shock of the Prince Edward Island premier upon learning from McBride that his entire province would fit into a BC lake. Yet he was confident that after the rest of Canada became more familiar with the West, the problems could be resolved.[104]

McBride's Christmas gift to British Columbians was the announcement on 24 December that they would be going to the polls on 2 February 1907. Speculation about an election had persisted for months, fired by McBride's provincial tours and the Lands and Works scandals. In September, McBride had denied asking for dissolution with an election set for 1 December. That had cooled speculation. On 2 November, he asked Lieutenant-Governor Dunsmuir for an immediate dissolution, explaining that since 1903 his government had introduced important measures including amendments to the Assessment, School, and Land Acts to increase taxes and royalties as required by the province's financial state. He admitted that his policies had elicited "a certain amount of adverse criticism" but with the "change from a deficit to a surplus," the moment was opportune to seek the electors' approval. Dunsmuir told McBride that he must give "ample time" for the electorate to learn of the election. Dissolution was announced on 24 December, perhaps because Dunsmuir was waiting for Green to resign.[105] Green's resignation late in December cleared the way for a general election in which Better Terms was a major issue, though not the only one.

4
Toward a Wider Stage, 1907-09

*I am always devoted to the interests of British Columbia,
first, last and always and all the time.*
– Richard McBride, 10 October 1908

Although McBride claimed that he had no wish to make Better Terms an issue in the 1907 election and that the Opposition Liberals supported the principle, his handling of the matter ensured that it became one. Because both parties favoured economic development and Oriental exclusion, the Liberals, who launched their campaign before dissolution, concentrated their attacks on the government's treatment of these issues and especially its alleged mismanagement of provincial lands and natural resources. Once the mudslinging and dirty tricks of the election were over, the government had to deal with resource policies, but McBride's immediate concern was taking his Better Terms fight to London. As the province began to enjoy prosperity, he could think of new projects such as a university and more railways.

McBride opened his election campaign at his nomination meeting in Mission City the day before official dissolution. After W.J. Bowser described the province's improved financial situation, extolled the benefits of the School Act, and challenged the Liberals to produce evidence of scandal related to Kaien Island, McBride chided the Liberals for focusing on scandal. He denied any wrongdoing in connection with the Kaien Island lands or the Columbia and Western (C&W) land grant, he defended taxation and retrenchment, and he observed that the federal Liberals had been in power for seven years before British Columbia experienced prosperity. As for Dewdney, he asserted that roads and dykes were built to benefit the riding, not due to patronage.[1]

The *Columbian*'s report of the Mission City meeting made no mention of Better Terms, possibly because neither McBride nor Bowser mentioned it. Following Opposition attacks, McBride soon explained that if British Columbia were to get a "measure of justice from the Dominion Treasury," Better Terms was now a campaign issue. A Conservative manifesto proclaimed that Better Terms was the sole reason for the election; the *Colonist* said that the main issues were Better Terms and "the maintenance of a stable government." The Conservative manifesto also reiterated general promises, defended past actions, and accused the Opposition of dwelling on alleged scandals. Although it conceded that the government was not wholly responsible for the province's prosperity, the manifesto credited its economical administration for such "desirable conditions" as a surplus, lower direct taxes, and new public works, especially to open new areas for settlers. Moreover, the government promised to do more to promote settlement by distributing information on Crown lands, studying irrigation and ditching, and encouraging the immigration of white working people, preferably from the British Isles, in numbers defined by circumstances. It would maintain stability in mining laws and change the licensing system to secure a better return from timber. Despite taxing the railways more and granting them no subsidies, the government was "not unfriendly" to them, for they were coming in any case. In short, the government's aim was "to protect the public interests in the natural resources and opportunities for investors and willing workers."[2]

As McBride toured the province, his speeches had common themes, especially Better Terms. He told voters that if they did not return the Conservatives to power, the eastern provinces would conclude that they were not serious in their arguments. He always addressed topics of local interest. At Rossland, where the eight-hour day was a major issue, he told over a thousand people that he had "always tried to give the working man a square deal in return for their confidence," especially since he too had been a working man, labouring "honestly and continuously" in the Fraser River canneries for seven years. He probably did not add that his cannery work had been a student's summer job! In the lower Fraser Valley, he said that Interior residents accused him of favouring New Westminster. He took credit for the new bridge but denied punishing Liberal ridings such as

Delta. The Liberal candidate for The Islands accused him of "being too good" to Dewdney by relieving its ratepayers of a dyking debt.³

The Liberal leader J.A. Macdonald called for the construction of roads and railways to open the North. He took pride in the Canadian Pacific Railway (CPR) but declared that the people must be its masters, not its slaves, and he accused McBride of not doing enough to restore the Peace River lands to the province or to reduce the size of Indian reserves that tied up some of the best fruit lands in the Similkameen and Okanagan Valleys, and occupied double or triple the area required by the Indians. Macdonald endorsed Better Terms but accused McBride of mishandling it by storming out of the Dominion-Provincial Conference. Liberal policy, he observed, was promoting "the material welfare and development of the province" and offering "government for the people, not for railroads and corporations, and ministerial friends."⁴

The Liberal platform of material development was not much different from that of the Conservatives, so the Liberals focused on mismanagement and the Conservatives on defending themselves against such allegations. When a Rossland Liberal accused McBride of being a creature of the CPR, which had held a train for him at Nelson for forty-five minutes, McBride replied that the CPR had charged $236.95 for a special train to take him from Cranbrook to Kootenay Landing when the westbound train was late. Moreover, his government had raised taxes on railway companies. The Liberals were not convinced. The *Times* accused his "Potlatch Government" of working for the CPR and intimated that R.F. Green had resigned because he had allied himself with the Canadian Northern Railway, which would compete with the CPR.⁵

The Liberals' attempt to benefit from the Kaien Island controversy withered after Green's resignation and his challenge to debate the matter with any Liberal.⁶ But the Liberal press soon found a new scandal and alleged that in return for $37,000 of its stock, Green had leased coal lands to the Transcontinental Exploration Company, whose head, Sir Adolphe Caron, had served in federal Conservative cabinets from 1880 to 1896. McBride immediately denied this accusation. Unconvinced, the *Times* agreed that technically he was correct – the lands had not been leased to Caron's company – but it accused him of attempting "to hoodwink the public" until the election was over. When Green sued the *World* for libel, the matter was removed from the political arena.⁷

The Liberals sang from the same song book throughout the province but also played on local issues. F.W. Howay, McBride's Dalhousie classmate and a Liberal candidate in New Westminster, called its new bridge an "Old Men's Home" because patronage lay behind the appointment of so many of its toll collectors. C.W. Munro complained that Chilliwack had been unfairly treated in dyking matters. And at Kelowna, K.C. MacDonald noted the alleged "theft" of the Fernie riding. In Vancouver, the Liberals fielded some heavyweight candidates – W.W.B. McInnes, who had resigned as commissioner of Yukon, and Alex Henderson, who had left his position as a County Court judge. The choice of McInnes was contentious. A headline for a front-page editorial in the *Cranbrook Prospector* asserted, "No Yukon Carpet bagger for Premier of British Columbia."[8]

Both parties opposed Asian immigration. Without advancing any evidence to back his claim, McInnes took personal credit for raising the Chinese head tax to $500 and asserted that the McBride government "was the first to fall down in the fight to keep this a white man's country" by failing to re-enact the Natal Act (which legislated a language test for would-be immigrants) and to erect "a barrier of legislation ... so high around the province that no Japanese, Chinese or Hindu could ever get over it." J.A. Macdonald repeatedly declared his opposition to "Oriental" and "Hindu" immigration. The Liberal press interpreted a statement made by McBride at Kamloops to intimate that he favoured a scheme to import Chinese labour. In response, articles, editorials, and advertisements in the *Colonist* recalled that the federal Liberals had been responsible for disallowing the Natal Act. The *Columbian* suggested that a Liberal vote equated with admitting Chinese labour to build the Grand Trunk Pacific (GTP) and with favouring fish traps and the Japanese. Bowser suggested that the Liberals would enfranchise Asians. On election eve, when it was too late for the Liberals to publicize a denial, a *Province* headline screamed "Fifty Thousand Japanese for British Columbia." Its associated story stated that the GTP was delaying construction until McBride, whose "anti-Mongolian legislation stood in the way," was out of office and it could employ Asians. It falsely added that the Liberals might "eventually enfranchise the Japanese horde." In contrast, the McBride government would re-enact the Natal Act, and though the Laurier government would disallow it, the local administration would make "a strong fight" and the province would "come to very little harm." The *Columbian* briefly reported the *Province*'s story, which Bowser cited at a final Conservative rally. Outside Greater Vancouver and Greater Victoria, the roorback (last-minute falsehood) had little effect because most electors had already voted before local newspapers could publish the story.[9]

Both parties employed a variety of dirty tricks. The *Cranbrook Herald* objected to provincial civil servant's participating in the election campaign. In Columbia, the provincial mining recorder, who worked on the Conservative campaign, complained that Liberals imported voters and spread "all kinds of dough." In Revelstoke, Fred Fraser, the gold commissioner, was accused of taking "a definitely partisan stand against the interests of the Government."[10] At Telegraph Creek in the Far North, the government agent was a Conservative organizer. McBride accused the Liberals of having federal civil servants speak at campaign meetings. A customs officer and postmaster in the Similkameen apologized for being unable to do "very much open work for the Conservative party." An organizer at Armstrong claimed that whereas the Grits gave out money and champagne, the Conservatives won the vote of naturalized Americans. According to the *Colonist*, Rossland Liberals freely distributed liquor, cigars, and money on behalf of J.A. Macdonald and had Mrs. Macdonald and several other women canvass door to door. When Macdonald won 46 percent of Rossland's popular vote (a Labour candidate took 19 percent), a Conservative organizer attributed it to Italian and French electors.[11]

Antipathy to the French and to Catholics appeared elsewhere. The *Province* claimed that Laurier attacked every province except Quebec. Religion may have been less important in British Columbia than elsewhere in Canada, but it did play a role in some constituencies. Okanagan Conservatives alleged that the Liberals were pledged to create separate schools, a live issue given the action of the Laurier government in 1905, when it had provided support for separate (denominational) schools via the Autonomy Bills that created Alberta and Saskatchewan. Cranbrook Conservatives blamed their candidate's ninety-five-vote defeat partly on approximately 120 Catholic and French voters who thought that Laurier's school policy in the new provinces was right. Although the Conservatives won all five seats in Vancouver, Bowser believed that the Catholics split their votes and opted for Liberals instead of himself and A.H.B. Macgowan. In Cariboo, Charles Wilson and his Conservative running mate blamed their defeat partly on about 50 "half-breed" voters, many of whom were Roman Catholics. As Wilson remarked, they "will vote as they are directed by their spiritual advisers 'for our good friend Laurier.'" Only 327 people voted in Cariboo, so 50 was a significant number. Wilson suggested disfranchising "the whole lot," whom he described as "little if any better than Siwashes and in fact some of them are actually Indian born." Alternatively, he proposed, the constituency boundaries could be changed "to hive nearly all the Liberal vote."[12]

Ensuring that supporters go to the polls is an essential part of election organization. In Vancouver, Conservatives offered a novelty – automobile rides to the polls. In Atlin, where only about 150 individuals voted, the government agent reported that the Opposition brought in 8 voters to Telegraph Creek from points more than a hundred miles away. However, the Conservative, Henry Esson Young, who had a medical practice in Atlin, won easily. Cranbrook Conservatives were disappointed when the CPR reneged on an apparent promise to bring in the outside vote, but Kaslo Liberals attributed their defeat to $10,000 or more of CPR money that was in the possession of the Conservatives. What the CPR contributed to the campaign is unknown. The only clue – an ambiguous one – is a handwritten letter from its president, T.G. Shaughnessy, informing McBride that the CPR would refund the money for a special train to Kaslo that had not been used. The letter also authorized McBride "to say most positively either in respect to train service or tickets or aid of any kind whatsoever you are not under any obligation to the Canadian Pacific directly or indirectly to the extent of one brass farthing."[13]

For some donations, the documentation is better. The $1,000 donation of John McKane, a Rossland mine owner, "was very timely and served a most useful purpose." A Vancouver brewer claimed that the city's liquor businesses "contributed a considerable sum of money to the election fund & besides spent time & money in personal efforts" on behalf of the Conservatives. Yet campaign funds may have been short. When two defeated candidates complained of unsettled accounts, McBride told them of "considerable difficulty in making matters meet in all of the constituencies." He advised them to write to Green.[14]

One of the coldest winters on record made campaigning physically difficult. Wilson, who ran in Cariboo, "a perfect Grit hotbed," complained of "a hell of a life – Not a day has the thermometer risen above zero and then only in the sun." He found that getting around in minus 42°F weather was almost impossible. McBride, who was often accompanied by Bowser, fared little better than Wilson. At Cranbrook, he had a "splendid meeting" even though the temperature was at minus 44°F. Ice on the Fraser River forced him to walk and use a hand car to get to Hammond. In the Similkameen, he travelled by sleigh from Greenwood to Penticton, and ice so slowed the boat on Okanagan Lake that he missed a meeting at Kelowna. Hard winter travel took its toll. At Kamloops, early in the campaign, he complained of a cold. Toward the end, after addressing more than thirty meetings in sixteen constituencies, he was unable to speak at Mission Junction and had to remain there overnight. The doctor feared he was suffering from pneumonia, but his 102°F fever broke, and his illness turned out to be the influenza then sweeping Canada and the northern United States. Speaking at Chilliwack, he lost his temper and was unable to hold the audience, lapses that may be attributable to illness. He recovered sufficiently to defy doctor's orders to attend Conservative rallies in New Westminster, Vancouver, and Victoria, where his paleness, strained voice, and hacking cough were evident, although the *Province* called his Vancouver speech "brilliant and at times eloquent." After his Victoria speech, he took the midnight boat to Vancouver, voted in New Westminster, and returned to Victoria on the afternoon boat. After the election, he was so ill with "la grippe" that he was confined to his room for several days, and his doctors ordered that he see only a few people for brief visits.[15]

As in the past, McBride ran in Dewdney but he also made what the *Colonist* called a "courteous and courageous" decision in accepting an invitation to run in Victoria as well, where the Conservatives had been shut out during the previous election. Due to his province-wide responsibilities, he made only two appearances in Victoria, both of them late in the campaign. The second, on the election eve, was the city's "biggest political rally" in many years. The next evening, despite illness and frosty weather, he joined a victory parade led by a brass band that went from his home to a celebration at the Liberal-Conservative rooms.[16] He led the polls in Victoria, which returned a full slate of four Conservatives, won 61 percent of the votes in Dewdney, and saw his Conservatives win twenty-six of the province's forty-two seats. John Houston, who ran as an Independent in Ymir, was defeated. The Conservatives swept Vancouver, and the Liberals were reduced to thirteen MLAs. The Socialists J.H. Hawthornthwaite and Parker Williams won in Nanaimo and Newcastle respectively and were joined by John McInnis of Grand Forks.

Although William Manson of Alberni, the provincial secretary and minister of education, was defeated, the *Kelowna Courier* observed that the Conservatives "need no longer lean on their Socialist allies, and real government on clear-cut party lines will ensue." The *Province* described the election result as a "good working majority" for the Conservatives that was not so large as to render Opposition criticism ineffective. Indeed, Victor W. Odlum, a prominent Liberal journalist, congratulated McBride for his "good majority" but warned that "we will now be watching you closely to see what you can do when you have a chance." To replace Manson, Henry Esson Young joined the cabinet. As a result of this, Young's Atlin riding was required to hold a by-election, but he won by acclamation and took his seat in the Legislature soon after the session began. McBride delayed choosing a new attorney general. He was under some pressure from the "Conservative machine" in Vancouver to appoint Bowser and had Pinkerton's detectives watch Bowser and his supporters. What the detectives found is unknown, but in the summer, Bowser, nicknamed "the little Corsican" in an allusion to Napoleon, became attorney general. The Opposition press speculated that he had triumphed in a caucus struggle for the position. He, too, was subject to a by-election and was obliged to fight for his seat when the Socialists fielded a candidate. In this easy campaign, McBride spoke at Bowser's meetings and visited Conservative workers by automobile.[17]

On 7 March 1907, Lieutenant-Governor James Dunsmuir opened the first session of the new Parliament with a Throne Speech reporting "general prosperity," "satisfactory" provincial finances, steady and continuously expanding industries, and negotiations with transportation and immigration agencies to promote "a desirable class" of immigrants from the United Kingdom. The speech forecast legislation to reduce taxes on real and personal property, to validate the transfer of the C&W lands in the Crow's Nest Pass, to set aside Crown lands to support a planned provincial university, to investigate irrigation and the water supply in the "dry belt," and to assert the province's rights "in the lands set apart as Indian reserves." In addition, legislators would be asked to consider financial relations resulting from the Dominion government's acknowledgment of "the right of British Columbia to 'better terms.'" The *New Westminster Daily News* opined that the speech offered a "meagre bill of fare," but other Liberal papers, such as the *Nelson Daily News* and the *Times,* found little to criticize except the absence of a railway policy. In what the friendly *Columbian* called a "brilliant and masterly" reply to John Oliver's criticism of the Throne Speech, McBride interpreted the election results as "resentment of Ottawa interference" and of eastern Canada's failure to understand the West. Much of his speech reviewed financial policy and the satisfactory conditions for working men, rising wages, and the absence of strikes and lockouts. He promised to apply part of the government's surplus on its annual accounts to reducing taxes and establishing an applied science program at the new university. He also hoped to resolve long-standing problems concerning coal and oil licences in the southeast Kootenay, the reversionary rights to Indian reserve lands, and jurisdictional problems relating to the fisheries.[18]

Finance Minister Tatlow's budget speech confirmed the rosy financial picture, predicted that this satisfactory condition would "be speedily surpassed," and reported higher than anticipated revenues from timber and other resources due to greater demand and new licence fees. In 1904, licence fees had produced $177,984, whereas in 1907 they garnered $1,339,351. The government was already spending the 1905-06 surplus of $366,767 on public works rather than collecting bank interest. Tatlow's budget was no flash in the pan. Despite a brief depression, he presented a "very favourable statement" a year later, largely because of the Prairies' great demand for lumber. The government also benefited from land sales, particularly around Vancouver. For the fiscal year ending 30 June 1907, the province had a surplus of $1,201,083 despite an over-expenditure of $175,323 on public works. The next year was even better, with a net surplus of $1,388,381. An update for the six months ending 31 December 1908 showed a further surplus of $0.5 million.[19]

Improved finances permitted planning for a university. This idea was not new – a university had been created on paper in 1890 but fell victim to Island versus Mainland rivalries. McBride saw the university as a cultural centre and a training ground for professionals, an optimistic concept at the time. In 1908, the province had only sixteen high schools, whose 1,470 students had passed rigorous entrance exams. To pursue further education, they could join the 48 students at McGill University College in Vancouver, which had evolved from the Vancouver High School, or attend its smaller branch in Victoria. The interest created by these junior colleges united the province's university graduates, who had been debating the merits of affiliation with McGill or Toronto. The province would not aid denominational institutions, but Columbian College in New Westminster, an affiliate of the Methodists' Victoria University of Toronto, and the provincial bodies of the Presbyterians and the Baptists favoured a provincial university in which they could have constituent colleges. When asked about the location of the proposed university, McBride gave a "delightfully indefinite" reply.[20]

Not everyone wanted a university. John Oliver thought that free public school textbooks were more important and that if a university were established, "honorable industrial pursuits" were more urgent than "learned studies." More pointedly, the *Kamloops Standard* thought that a university was needed "as badly as a dog needs two tails" and suggested supporting existing Canadian institutions rather than sacrificing "the true collegiate spirit to provincial or local vanity." A Fernie miners' union opposed using public funds or lands for it. McBride, however, expected that members of the working class would take advantage "of the privileges" of a university and gave their representatives "every opportunity to express their wishes." As a concession to opponents, the government began providing some free textbooks in the elementary schools. For the new university to compete with universities elsewhere, however, McBride declared, "We must see to it that we get the very best." Yet he had considerable sympathy for a university that offered a practical rather than a theoretical education. In an address at the University of California in 1913, he declared, "Our universities ... should aim less to arrive at a uniform standard for their students than to develop individuality; to encourage vocational aspirations; to specialize rather than to generalize; to hold up definite purpose and usefulness in a career as the object of training rather than the sharpening of wits by a theoretical emery process; that finding out and doing things for oneself is infinitely more educative in effect than accepting the conclusions of others." In short, for him, education consisted "in solving problems ... by the exercise of brain power but a curriculum that had students simply accept the conclusions of others was futile."[21]

The government expected a university to produce revenue and to keep students and their money at home. With its forestry and mining schools, it would also attract students from other provinces. McBride named Henry Esson Young as his minister of education and gave him a free hand in creating the university. In February 1908, Young presented a bill to set aside up to 2 million acres in the North and the Interior that should give the university an annual income of about $200,000. On 7 March 1908, the Legislature, with little debate, incorporated the non-sectarian University of British Columbia. To make education widely available, tuition would be free in the arts and women students "would have equality of privilege with men students." UBC received a provincial monopoly of degree-granting powers except in theology. Given the view that education had utilitarian purposes and possibly to assuage organized labour, the act incorporating the university authorized it, to the extent that its resources permitted, to provide instruction to serve "manufacturing, mining, engineering, agricultural and industrial pursuits," as well as "in all branches of liberal education as may enable students to become proficient ... in science, commerce, arts, literature, law, medicine and all other branches of knowledge." The university would prosecute "original research in science, literature, arts, medicine, law and especially the applications of science."[22]

Such goals reflected the popular belief in "experts," which also influenced civil service reform, an idea with currency in Ottawa, where a royal commission was examining the operation of the federal service. In 1908, the province introduced a superannuation fund for civil servants. As the *Colonist* explained, their salaries were not large but they were expected to maintain "a certain standard." A guaranteed pension would encourage competent men to stay in the service and improve its quality. Young drafted a new Civil Service Act to make the growing service a "modern" one, with standardized grades, pay scales, and promotion criteria. The act was revised the following year as the Public Service Act, 1909, and a three-man commission was appointed to manage regrading, hiring, and promotion. The Opposition press welcomed the idea as a means of ending patronage appointments, but the Public Service Act did not eliminate them.[23]

At the same time, the press discussed raising the salaries of cabinet ministers, an idea that found some support. The Opposition press argued that a higher salary would give cabinet ministers no excuse to continue practising law or engaging in private business. This attack was aimed at Bowser, who maintained a law practice in Vancouver and, to a lesser extent, at Francis Carter-Cotton, the managing director of the *Vancouver Daily News-Advertiser*. As president of the council, Carter-Cotton received no extra salary, and the post may even have cost him personally. In anticipation of a cabinet decision on the BCER's request to build a dam on the Coquitlam River, for example, he sold his shares in that prosperous company.[24]

Many Conservatives expected rewards for their loyalty to the party. The government apparatus was so small that they often wrote directly to McBride and mentioned their connection with the party. A teacher whose temporary certificate was not renewed, for example, cited his work for the local Conservative candidate and his contributions to campaign funds when he asked McBride to intervene on his behalf with the Department of Education. McBride was sympathetic but could not override the law. Some appointments reduced the short-term political usefulness of individuals. McBride told the new government agent at Golden, "You will be missed in our [election] campaign, but the Government has in you an official who will 'make good' in any position in which you are placed." In 1907, L. Norris, the government agent at Vernon, advised McBride that had the elections come later, he would have had the appointment of road superintendents "in better shape." One defeated Conservative complained that men on road gangs spent "their whole time abusing the Party from which they receive their pay." The *Times* summarized the Opposition charges: "Seven eighths of the strength of the McBride government lies in its effective distribution of patronage for the purpose of purchasing support. Every job, from the conduct of important or petty legal business in the courts, to repair of the roads in the rural districts is farmed out with a view to bringing advantage to the party."[25]

Oliver also complained that constituencies with Conservative MLAs received larger appropriations than those with Opposition members. Cranbrook was allocated only $5,000, whereas the adjacent Conservative ridings of Columbia and Fernie received $18,000 and $22,950 respectively. The Opposition press criticized the government for choosing to place routine advertising in friendly newspapers. The press was a great political asset; by 1906, every constituency except Revelstoke had a Conservative newspaper. Yet one Interior observer noted that the inferior Conservative papers had smaller circulations than the Opposition journals.[26]

McBride no longer depended on the Socialist MLAs but did not forget the past assistance of J.H. Hawthornthwaite. He consulted him when appointing a new police commissioner at Nanaimo and supported his bill to give smelter workers an eight-hour day. He had opposed such a law when the industry was losing money, but it was now prospering and his recent tour of the Kootenays had opened his eyes to the need for it. McBride was probably sincere in his comment about smelter workers, but he feared that extending the eight-hour day to all workers might harm "economic conditions." Similarly, he did not support all of Hawthornthwaite's initiatives; he helped defeat a bill to amend the Workmen's Compensation Act.[27]

In the election, McBride had run and won in both Victoria and Dewdney. Since he could not effectively represent both, he made the "difficult" decision to sit solely for Victoria. The premier should represent the capital, and visiting constituents would be easier. The *Columbian* was certain that "Dewdney Dick" would not neglect Dewdney. Though not entirely happy with McBride's choice to leave their constituency, Dewdney Conservatives accepted McBride's advice to nominate William Manson as his successor. When McBride travelled home after a trip to England, Manson, who had been elected by acclamation, boarded the train at Kamloops to discuss Dewdney's needs. McBride promised to visit soon and to have planned public works under way in a fortnight. Residents of Agassiz honoured him by naming their new school after him. At its opening, the children expressed their gratitude for "this nice, new school building. Most of us lived so far away from any school before the school started that we were unable to get to school very much."[28]

As MLA for Victoria, McBride was a target of the *Times*. It complained that, due to Bowser's influence, Vancouver "has got everything it asked from the McBride government," and it repeatedly accused McBride of doing nothing to secure a Normal School (a teacher-training college) for the city, to construct more roads on the Saanich Peninsula, or to establish an appeal court in the city. He denied Victoria a grant to help beautify its

Toward a Wider Stage, 1907-09 131

"A MAN WHO DOES THINGS."

The Liberal *Victoria Times* complained bitterly that Vancouver MLA W.J. Bowser *(left)* seemed to be getting an unfair share of provincial investments for his riding while McBride, the MLA for Victoria, looked on complacently. *Victoria Times,* 26 September 1910, cartoonist, Wilson.

harbour as long as parts of the province lacked roads and schools. Two years later, voicing intra-provincial rivalries, the *Fort George Herald* complained that the government was "making daisy beds round the Parliament Buildings," whereas no road linked South Fort George and Fort George. As one of Victoria's four MLAs, McBride shared local responsibilities. He spoke at the openings of an addition to St. Joseph's Hospital, of a Nurses' Home at the Royal Jubilee Hospital, and of a new clubhouse for the Victoria Yacht Club, and he laid the cornerstone at the private University School for boys. On the last two occasions, his wife, Margaret, accompanied him.[29]

In 1908, the McBride family moved to this large waterfront home in Victoria's then fashionable Gorge district. Royal BC Museum, BC Archives, B-01630.

The McBrides now made Victoria their permanent home. Their rented quarters on Victoria Crescent were "half way between the Old Ladies Home and the hospital" and only a short walk from the Parliament Buildings. They were large enough to hold a dinner for the press gallery and an "At Home," probably in honour of Mrs. McBride's niece Tina Mowbray, who made her debut at the Union Club Ball. During the 1908 legislative session, Margaret McBride gave a tea but spread it out over two consecutive days to handle the number of guests. Among them were the wives of the lieutenant-governor and several politicians as well as the premier's personal secretary, Lottie Bowron. In addition, she returned the hospitality she received at many teas and card parties. In June 1908, the McBrides moved to a new home on the fashionable Gorge Road.[30]

A larger house was desirable because the family had grown with the birth of Catherine Anna (called Anna) in October 1905. The oldest girls,

McBride's five eldest daughters – Margaret, Mary, Dolly, Ruth, and Anna – with their adult cousin, Jean McGillivray. This photograph was probably taken in the summer of 1906 at the Victoria Crescent home. Sheila, the sixth daughter, was born in 1913. Royal BC Museum, BC Archives, B-01659.

Mary, Peggy, and Dolly, were among the seventy pupils at Queen's Academy for Girls, a ladies' college founded in 1904 by Dr. S.D. Pope, who had been provincial superintendent of education but had resigned in 1899 over a salary dispute. Located at the corner of Rock Bay and Hillside Avenues, it employed two "lady teachers," including Pope's daughter and a music teacher. Pope himself taught some senior classes. Students could begin in kindergarten and continue until they were "thoroughly instructed in learning in all its branches," including Latin, French, higher mathematics, Roman history, "the Commercial branches," and fine arts, music, drawing and painting.[31]

McBride's family often visited him. During the summer of 1907, McBride's mother, whom he "adored," spent a month in Victoria and shortly after the death of her husband came for two weeks. Tina Mowbray was a frequent guest. McBride's younger sister Dorothea (Dodo), who taught at the New Westminster Girls' School, visited from time to time. The visits were reciprocated. In the summer of 1907, Mary and Peggy visited their grandparents. Two summers later, Mary and her grandmother visited friends at Boundary Bay, a seaside resort south of New Westminster. In August, McBride took Mary, Peggy, and Dolly to Seattle for the unveiling of the J.J. Hill monument at the Alaska-Yukon-Pacific Exposition. Their pregnant mother did not accompany them. On the way back, they were joined by Governor John A. Johnson and Governor Charles Evan Hughes of New York.[32]

McBride, who often referred to himself as "an old New Westminster boy," visited the city regularly for personal reasons, to see family and friends, or en route to the fishing trips that he and old friends made once or twice a year to Pitt Lake. His firm, McBride and Kennedy, was still in business, but Kennedy probably did the work. McBride attended important civic festivities such as the return of the world's championship lacrosse team, the opening of the Provincial Exhibition, and the unveiling of the Simon Fraser Memorial. Margaret visited friends and sometimes accompanied him for such events as the Vancouver Horse Show. While on the Mainland, he usually gave an interview to the press.[33] Increasingly, however, he was away from home, touring the province or representing its interests in Ottawa and London.

Many editorials and congratulatory messages after the 1907 election attributed McBride's success to Better Terms. One correspondent put the sentiment well: "The victory ought to teach this lesson to those in authority at Ottawa that British Columbia will brook no interference with its just & equitable claims for special treatment ... and is prepared to stand by you to the last ditch in our fight for the cause." A Dewdney friend wrote, "Hands off Ottawa was the battle cry and I am proud it found an echo in the hearts of so many true manly Conservatives that rum and money could not influence." McBride told federal Conservative leader Robert L. Borden that "our sweeping victory came as a very hard blow to the Liberals, who, with the aid of Ottawa, had attempted by every means to defeat us. The people of the Province, however, resented this interference in local affairs, and the result was to strengthen our hand."[34]

Although the Liberal press was sympathetic to the principle of Better Terms, it restated election campaign rhetoric in which it blamed McBride's handling of the issue for creating a situation that would probably "work grave injury to provincial interests." If Confederation were to endure, asserted the *Times,* there must be "some form of finality with respect to the relations" between Ottawa and the provinces. On 20 March, McBride gave notice of a resolution to endorse his course at the Inter-Provincial Conference. Its long preamble declared that Ottawa's proposed $100,000 annual subsidy to British Columbia was inadequate and unacceptable as "a final and unalterable settlement." It also reiterated that an independent tribunal should examine British Columbia's claim since the other provinces had a conflict of interest and that the resolution itself should be sent to the governor-general with a request that he forward it to the colonial secretary. The packed galleries of the Legislature were disappointed when McBride accepted Macdonald's request for more time to study the matter. Two days later, McBride remarked that he expected a "fiery" discussion, with "many members having taken considerable pains to prepare for the occasion," but he believed that the people were "determined to have what they consider fair play for the Province." He traced the history of Better Terms and his success in getting the Inter-Provincial Conference to agree that physical conditions justified it, but he regretted that Ottawa proposed "grotesquely inadequate" compensation and would not accept arbitration or a commission of inquiry. Bowser fell asleep during what Liberal reporters called McBride's "tedious" speech! Liberal MLAs agreed with the main principles while attacking McBride's failure to get a better deal at the conference. The motion to endorse McBride's actions at the Inter-Provincial Conference passed but not unanimously. That, the *Columbian* and the *Colonist* suggested, may have weakened British Columbia's position.[35]

The same day that the provincial Legislature debated the matter, the subject arose in the House of Commons. Prime Minister Laurier explained a motion to amend the British North America (BNA) Act to adjust provincial subsidies according to the arrangements made at the Inter-Provincial Conference and to make the terms, including the ten-year grant of $100,000 a year for British Columbia, "final and unalterable." In doing so, he presented such a rosy description of British Columbia's resources and prospects that officials in the provincial Department of Information could not have done a better job themselves. Laurier conceded that British Columbia's unusual problems entitled it to "special treatment," but he observed that the GTP would bring it into contact with eastern markets and that within a decade "it must become one of the most important" provinces, a claim echoed by Finance Minister W.S. Fielding. His remarks did not go over well with McBride, who thought the $100,000 per annum subsidy for ten years inadequate in amount and duration, and who objected to the plan to make the arrangement part of a "final and unalterable" agreement. He told Borden that "people in Eastern Canada have little or no idea of the strong feeling in our Province over Sir Wilfrid's treatment of us." A few days later, McBride told the Legislature that given Laurier's plan to go to London in connection with the proposed amendment to the BNA Act, it was "his duty" to represent British Columbia there so as to counteract Laurier. The Conservative press praised his decision, but its Liberal counterparts dismissed the London trip as "a wild goose chase" and a "pleasure trip at the expense of the people of the province."[36]

Motivated by his feeling "that the case for better terms is so much my own," R.E. Gosnell, a former editor of the *Colonist* who had helped prepare Dunsmuir's arguments for Better Terms, sought the job of formulating the province's case. Gosnell, who was then in England, warned that because the parliamentary session and the Colonial Conference were then under way, seeing British officials would be difficult and that provincial premiers "have no status at Downing Street." Nevertheless, McBride and his secretary Lawrence Macrae, who handled press relations, went to London. Heeding advice from Gosnell and former BC lieutenant-governor Edgar Dewdney, he stopped in Ottawa to secure credentials to present at the Colonial Office. He discussed provincial matters with Allen Aylesworth, the minister of justice, and William Templeman, the BC representative in the cabinet, and he spent most of an evening with Robert Borden. He sailed on the *Empress of Ireland* from Saint John, New Brunswick, on 19 April 1907. Stopping briefly in Halifax, where he visited old friends from Dalhousie, he enjoyed a relatively smooth voyage across the Atlantic, and the *Times* of London reported his arrival on Saturday, 27 April.[37]

After "a good wash & a fairly hearty lunch" at the Hotel Victoria, a "quite reasonably priced hotel," he felt "quite fit for business." In London, he interviewed Lord Elgin, the colonial secretary, and Winston Churchill, who spoke for the colonial secretary in the House of Commons. On 9 May, he cabled Tatlow, expressing optimism about his prospects, but inexplicably Tatlow did not immediately make the cable public. With no word that McBride had gone to the "foot of the throne" or interviewed British cabinet ministers, the Opposition press was disappointed that he had reported nothing definite after almost a month abroad. Finally, in an official dispatch published in British Columbia on 23 May, McBride revealed that Lord Elgin, Churchill, and Sir Francis J. Hopwood of the Colonial Office had listened to his presentation of British Columbia's case for "special consideration from the Dominion government." Conservative papers received this message "with extreme gratification" and suggested that British Columbia had set an "important precedent" – now a province in a self-governing colony could take its grievances directly to the imperial government. The Liberal press complained that the vague reports did not reveal what, if anything, had been accomplished. Privately, McBride told Tatlow of two meetings with Laurier in London and of offering "to withdraw any vicious protest" in return for the elimination of "final and unalterable" from the bill to amend the BNA Act, a proposal to which Laurier quickly retorted, "this could not be & that the whole thing must go." McBride found the fight "novel as well as interesting." Laurier also saw Colonial Office officials and on 20 May asked Churchill and the colonial secretary to let him see the amendment bill in advance.[38]

Though he worked hard, McBride enjoyed his first visit to London. On his arrival, he received an invitation to dine with the Duke of Westminster at Grosvenor House. As a first-time visitor, he was also a tourist. He told Margaret that he could see Nelson's Monument and Trafalgar Square from his hotel window and that "the place looks precisely what we are accustomed to see in pictures." After a walk, he reported that the "people look like the ordinary old country folk we see in the west – only a bit more so – since they are in their native heath. Plenty [of] hats, frock coats, cigarettes galore." He was greatly impressed by the huge double-decker buses. He visited Madame Tussaud's wax museum, ate lunch at the Cheshire Cheese, where he sat in the chairs that Oliver Goldsmith and Dr. Johnson had used in their day, and attended a race meet at Epsom. Although he seldom mentioned venturing into a church at home, he attended services at St. Paul's for three Sundays. He spent the Whitsuntide holiday in Paris and went to the Apollo Theatre. More significantly, he met important people in England and made new friendships. He spoke to the Royal Colonial Institute on 14 May on the loyalty of British Columbia and the greatness of Canada. On 30 April, he dined at Princes Restaurant, where he sat between Sir C. Dilke, whose 1868 book *Greater Britain* had helped revive imperial sentiment in Britain, and Sir George Goldie, who played a major role in adding Nigeria to the British Empire. On 4 June, over sixty local residents with an interest in British Columbia gave him a dinner at Simpson's Divan Tavern on the Strand, where the menu was in Chinook and English, and the dessert was "Better Terms for the Province." The Canadian-born Hamar Greenwood, Churchill's parliamentary secretary, gave him a dinner, and the prominent journalist T.P. O'Connor, who "was most kind," published an article on him. These friendships reinforced McBride's imperial sentiments.[39] When British journalists visited Victoria that summer, McBride told them that almost a third of British Columbians had been born in Britain or one of its possessions other than Canada and were "true Imperialists" and "most intensely loyal" citizens.[40]

McBride claimed to have disabused Elgin, Churchill, and their officials of their belief that in acceding to British Columbia's wishes rather than respecting those of the Dominion and the other provinces, they would appear to be interfering in Canada's domestic affairs. He argued that Confederation could be "regarded as a pact among Provinces as well as with the Dominion," with each province representing "a separate and distinct treaty with Canada," so British Columbia was not required to deal with the others. The Colonial Office was not impressed by this reasoning. On 5 June, Lord Elgin's secretary informed McBride that "in view of the animosity" of the Dominion government and the other provinces, he could neither justify attempting "to override the decision of the Dominion Parliament" nor compel arbitration. Elgin would not express an opinion on the adequacy of the offered settlement. One point was favourable to McBride – the phrase "final and unalterable" was deemed inappropriate in a statute so would not appear.[41]

McBride received a copy of the draft amendment to the BNA Act on 12 June and learned that the bill would be introduced in the House that week. In a letter, handwritten in his room at the Hotel Victoria, he sent comments to Churchill. On 13 June, Churchill introduced the amendment to the BNA Act, which, though "not of great importance" to Britons, had "excited a great deal of interest in Canada." He explained that the BC Legislature, dissatisfied with the outcome of the Inter-Provincial Conference, had protested the settlement "as final and irrevocable." Although his government had no wish to pronounce on the merits of the claim or on Canadian constitutional matters, the phrase "final and unalterable" had been omitted from the bill "in deference" to British Columbia's representations and on the advice of parliamentary draftsmen who said that it was "unusual and unsuitable in an Act of Parliament." Several MPs asked questions, but none objected to the amendment. McBride, who was in the gallery, thanked Churchill and promised to "tell Canadians of the special treatment you have accorded me." In appreciation of Churchill's kindness, he sent him a mounted moose head. The Commons passed the amendment bill on 28 June 1907. McBride had planned to leave for Canada after second reading but waited until the bill passed and confidently set out for home. En route, he spent a few days in Ireland, stopping in Limerick, Dublin, and Belfast. In Dublin, he took a jaunting-car tour of the city and visited the international exhibition, where the Canadian display impressed him.[42]

Response in British Columbia to McBride's work in London was partisan. The Conservative press hailed his "victory," "triumph," and great gain "in personal prestige." The *Colonist* declared that his "name will be associated with a new definition of provincial rights" and that he had "stepped at one stride into the front rank of Canadian public men." The Liberal press called the mission a failure because it had produced no additional subsidy and no commission, and because "final and unalterable" had been omitted from the bill only because it was unparliamentary.[43]

McBride's return was triumphant. Arriving in Quebec City on board the *Empress of Ireland* on 7 July, he proceeded by train to Montreal, where the Lafontaine Club entertained him at dinner. He told reporters that Ottawa had "not heard the last of the provincial subsidies," and he briefly stopped in the capital, where Margaret, who had been visiting friends in Winnipeg, joined him. The *Ottawa Journal* described McBride as a "bold, aggressive and successful" political leader, but the *Toronto Globe* accused him of playing "the demagogic part." Borden congratulated him on his "splendid fight." As McBride travelled westward, Conservatives in Field and Kamloops greeted him. New Westminster Conservatives were pleased that his hometown was his first stop on the coast. On a Saturday night, a large crowd of "non partisans" turned out in spite of the rain to meet him at the CPR station with a parade led by a brass band. McBride, Tatlow, Bowser, several other MLAs, and local dignitaries were taken by carriage to the centre of downtown, where a banner "Welcome home to N.W. Our Dick" greeted him and the May Queen presented him with a bouquet for Mrs. McBride. After McBride told the crowd of his work in London, the entourage boarded four BC Electric Interurban cars for Vancouver. A frustrated reporter complained that during an onboard interview, McBride was more interested in inquiring about friends than in politics. People gathered along the route. At 10:00 P.M., McBride arrived at the Cambie Street grounds, where he received "the grandest, most enthusiastic reception the citizens of Vancouver have ever tendered a public man." The *News-Advertiser* suggested that he arrived as "a Roman conqueror," and the *Province* referred to a "great triumphant march," but the Liberally inclined *World* thought the reception a very ordinary affair, with an audience that was less enthusiastic than that which had greeted Prince Fushimi of Japan the previous week. McBride reviewed the history of Better Terms, which he claimed he had never regarded as a political issue. At midnight, he left for Victoria. The *Times* thought he looked thinner, but he said he was in excellent health and satisfied with the results of his trip, although he had not gotten everything he wanted. At a reception in the Victoria Theatre, local Conservatives presented him with a silver tea service. According to the *Colonist,* the meeting was "packed," but the *Times* saw many empty chairs. McBride described his work in London and praised Churchill's "wide knowledge" of the case. He alluded to rumours that the House of Lords had altered the bill at the behest of Laurier but denied any intention of leading British Columbia out of Confederation – he was "too good a Canadian and too good a Britisher" to do that.[44]

But news from London tempered the joy of the homecoming. Lord Elgin had assured McBride that the Lords would accept the bill as presented to the House of Commons. According to a press report, on hearing of this, Laurier had asked the Lords to restore "final and unalterable" to the bill. Elgin agreed to do so to the extent that was possible. On 1 July, he introduced the bill in the House of Lords. At second reading the next day, he explained that it dealt with "payments from the Dominion Government ... to the provinces" and did not mention British Columbia or the phrase "final and unalterable." In committee he explained that at the Dominion's request, the bill had been changed by the insertion of a schedule as an appendix. The schedule, which he read, described a sliding scale formula for subsidies, the offer to British Columbia of an extra $100,000 a year for ten years, and a clause that "the scale of payments ... shall be a final and unalterable settlement of the amounts to be paid yearly to the several provinces." The Lords approved without debate. When the bill came back to the Commons, Churchill reported the change but made no comment.[45] In short, although the Commons had given McBride something of what he wanted – an inference that the terms were not "final and unalterable" – the Lords took it away.

As soon as he received a preliminary report of the Lords' action, McBride cabled Hamar Greenwood that he understood "final and unalterable" was now to be included in the amendment: "Cannot accept this seriously in view assurance Colonial office letter June fifth and Churchill's statements in Commons. [It] would create serious situation here." If necessary, he proposed to return to London at once. The next day he cabled Churchill in almost identical words but, ever gracious, thanked him for the many courtesies he had received while in London. Greenwood informed Churchill that he had explained to McBride that "final and unalterable" was not in the act but in the schedule. Greenwood urged Churchill to cable McBride "so that he will not feel that he has been badly treated. His friendship for the Government is a mighty influence for our good in Canada and a cable from you will be inestimably valued by him." Churchill himself drafted the cable to "Macbride" [sic], reiterating that "final and unalterable" could not be included in a British statute and that no parliamentary procedure allowed him to resist the request of the Canadian government. In a follow-up cable, Churchill added that the whole affair was a "matter of political controversy in Canada and no authoritative pronouncement on behalf of His Majesty's Government would be possible or proper." Unconvinced, McBride asked Churchill to clarify the effects of the schedule and asked Elgin to ensure that the change would not affect British Columbia's right "to negotiate further" with the Dominion government.[46]

A few weeks later, McBride told his old mentor Sir Henri Joly de Lotbinière that his visit with the Colonial Office was "partially successful," and though it had been gained by "an uphill fight," "the net result will be a great help in the agitation we hope to continue." That fall, when he toured the BC Interior with Borden, he focused on Better Terms. Unexpected help came when W.S. Fielding, the federal finance minister, boasted of having scored a "notable victory" over McBride at the Inter-Provincial Conference. If the entire story of the conference and "the manipulations carried on by some of the Federal ministers with the Liberal Prime Minister present could be told," McBride suggested to Borden, "it would make interesting reading indeed." Publicly, he called Fielding's comments "very unfair."[47]

When the Legislature met in January 1908, McBride tabled the correspondence relating to his trip. The press briefly debated the constitutionality of the imperial government's intervention in Dominion-provincial relations, McBride's sincerity in seeking to eliminate "final and unalterable," and his effectiveness in presenting the case. No editor questioned the province's right to Better Terms, but interest faded. On the last day of the session, the Legislature, without debate, approved McBride's resolution declaring that the ten-year $100,000 grant was insufficient and urging Ottawa "to bring about a fair and adequate settlement of the recognized claim of British Columbia for special treatment at the hands of Canada."[48]

Better Terms re-emerged during the 1908 federal election. The *Times* attacked McBride's idea of having a commission examine the BC case. It suggested that if Ottawa dealt with the provinces separately, the result would be "jealousy and hostility," and that McBride wanted to keep the issue "alive for his own political purposes." In Vancouver, where G.H. Cowan, the author of a pamphlet on Better Terms, was running, McBride deferred to Cowan's "finger-tip familiarity with the subject." Putting his own spin on his visit to London, he boasted of having "final and unalterable" removed from the amendment to the BNA Act. At New Westminster, he recalled sitting in the galleries and hearing with pleasure that, in deference to British Columbia, "final and unalterable" had been struck from the bill. At a smoker in Victoria, where he recalled Churchill's speech on "final and unalterable," he declared, "I am always devoted to the interests of British Columbia, first, last and always and all the time." Yet, though Better Terms received some mention in McBride's speeches, William Templeman, a Liberal cabinet minister who was seeking re-election in Victoria, was probably right when he told a New Westminster audience that the issue "as a political cry is as dead as Julius Caesar." Although McBride believed that Better Terms helped to explain Conservative victories in British Columbia, Martin Burrell, the successful federal Conservative in Yale-Cariboo, told him in the spring of 1909 that raising the Better Terms issue in Parliament would be a "tactical error" as "they have had a good strong dose of B.C. matters and a surfeit is to be deprecated."[49]

Financial arrangements were not McBride's only continuing grievance with Ottawa. He thought that Ottawa was treating the province unfairly in its delay in selecting the Peace River lands that British Columbia had transferred to it in 1884. He complained that Ottawa had neither opposed the withdrawal of the British fleet from Esquimalt in 1906 nor provided a substitute even though the terms of union by which British Columbia joined Confederation required Ottawa to use its influence "to secure the continued maintenance of the Naval Station at Esquimalt." During the 1908 federal election, he appealed to Esquimalt voters by citing their loyalty to Britain and their love of seeing the Union Jack, the British tars, and the "splendid vessels which had done so much to discipline the empire, as well as the world at large." Patriotism was important, but he noted the practical advantage of the Esquimalt base, "a large expenditure of money," as well.[50]

Managing the salmon fishery was another concern. The Judicial Committee of the Privy Council had ruled that the fish belonged to the province, but regulating the fishery was a federal responsibility. From 1901 until 1906, the two governments had operated under a modus vivendi by which the province controlled non-tidal fisheries and the federal government had jurisdiction over their tidal counterparts. Although the Fraser River was both tidal and non-tidal, Ottawa controlled its fisheries, but British Columbia was dissatisfied with its share of the receipts and feared that overfishing was threatening the industry's survival. McBride alleged that Ottawa had not met its obligations and that in framing a Fisheries Act, his government would "keep well within the law" while "very determinedly" exercising its jurisdiction. Ottawa sent S.T. Bastedo, its troubleshooter in such matters, to "feel" out the province about fisheries policies, but Bastedo could not speak for the government and the negotiations got nowhere. In the meantime, the province appointed a commissioner of fisheries, added fisheries to the responsibilities of Attorney General Bowser, and created positions for seven overseers, who would issue licences, collect fees, and generally supervise the fisheries.[51]

In 1908, J.P. Babcock, the provincial fisheries commissioner, limited the duration of the salmon fishery above the New Westminster Bridge. The federal fisheries department also named closing times, but the two schedules did not coincide. When fishermen, mostly at Whonnock, received provincial summonses for fishing without a provincial licence or during a provincially closed time, they were angry at Babcock and indirectly at McBride. Other fishermen ran afoul of federal authorities by fishing with provincial licences during the province's open hours. They pleaded guilty to the federal charges of fishing at a federally closed time, possibly at the behest of the province, in order to create a test case. McBride invited sixty fishermen to meet him and, in the words of the *Columbian,* to display their indignation over the way in which they had been "sandwiched between the Dominion and the Provincial government." He listened to their grievances for over an hour and offered to consider written complaints but could not promise to change the regulations. Speaking "very fast and with conviction," he explained that he had accepted Babcock's advice "to stimulate the fisheries, not harm fishermen," and must enforce the law even if it resulted in his "political extinction." Not surprisingly, he blamed any "inconvenience and annoyance" on Ottawa's refusal to discuss jurisdiction. Unimpressed by this comment and his closing remark that an amicable settlement could be achieved, the fishermen called for the suspension of Babcock and his regulations. J.D. Taylor of the *Columbian* supported the fishermen and called Babcock a "quack." Shortly thereafter, Taylor ran as a Conservative in the 1908 federal election. McBride could not afford to quarrel with fishermen he had known since boyhood and thus endeavoured to mend fences. If Taylor were elected, McBride pointed out, he could apprise Ottawa of the problems. As it happened, Taylor was elected, but that did not solve the fishermen's problems. The *New Westminster Daily News* continued to complain that the province taxed the fishermen but did nothing about their complaints. By then, the matter was before the courts, which, in 1910, ruled the province's fishing regulations ultra vires – beyond the scope of the province's constitutional authority.[52]

Unlike fisheries, which caused conflict with the senior government, natural resources and land were almost entirely provincial responsibilities. Devising policies to increase provincial revenues and encourage development while protecting the province's long-term interests remained difficult. Mining, particularly of lode metals – gold, copper, silver, and lead – and of coal, was a leading industry but had problems. In the summer of 1907, the Kootenay smelters suffered a shortage of coke because of labour disputes and a lack of rail cars. The *Nelson Daily News* claimed that as minister of mines, McBride should have been aware of the problem and done something about it. The Nelson Board of Trade asked him to invoke a clause in the Crow's Nest Company charter imposing penalties if the company did not deliver sufficient coke to the smelters. An official of the provincial mines department investigated the situation, but the crisis had passed. The coal industry was doing well, so in 1908, the government proposed to increase taxes on coal from five cents to ten cents per ton and on coke from nine cents to fifteen cents. It also planned to apply the increase to all mines, including those that had previously been exempt from these taxes. The increased revenue would facilitate other tax reductions. In introducing the measure, Tatlow said that collieries could well afford it, but the Opposition, echoing boards of trade, mining companies, and miners' unions, argued that they would simply pass the increase on to consumers. McBride was not sympathetic to the complaints from the mining industry. He told the Granby Consolidated Mining, Smelting and Power Company, one of the province's largest copper-mining and smelting operations and user of coke, that "the Province should reap some benefit from the natural resources of the country" and that the coal mines should contribute a fair share. There were other problems as well. After consumers complained about coal prices, the Liberals suggested that an inquiry be conducted by a legislative committee, but the government had a Conservative backbencher, Dr. George A. McGuire of Vancouver, ask for a federal investigation of the coal combine. McBride said that trade and commerce were a federal responsibility, which meant that only Ottawa could investigate the matter.[53]

Keen to develop the mining industry, McBride favoured a loan to the Canada Zinc Company, which claimed to have solved the metallurgical problem of smelting zinc from lead ore. It had raised between $55,000 and $60,000 from private investors but needed another $10,000 if it were to develop the zinc-smelting technique. Noting that the federal government had given an outright grant to a similar smelter at Sault Ste. Marie, McBride endorsed a bill to lend the $10,000 to the company, asserting that it applied to a special case that could "revolutionize conditions" in the Kootenays and did not set a precedent. The company built an extensive plant near Nelson, but the system was imperfect and it closed late in 1908.[54]

Regulating the timber industry was a work in progress. The BC Loggers' Association, which happened to meet during the 1907 election, unanimously agreed that the new timber laws "were working out satisfactorily." It especially liked the Timber Measurement Act, under which government scalers measured and graded logs. The *Province* claimed that apart from a few people who did not get the deals they wanted, "every man interested in the timber business" at the coast was "hard at work" for the government because of the ban on log exports. A member of the British Columbia Timber and Forestry Chamber of Commerce asserted that almost all the province's lumbermen had voted for the government. In the 1907 legislative session, McBride said that the government was checking on speculators and could do more "to preserve the forest wealth and increase the revenue," but it backed down from further increases in timber royalties after the "lumber barons" protested.[55]

Despite some claims to the contrary, new timber licence fees did not drive out speculators. When it was reported that an American syndicate had bought timberlands on Vancouver Island for $1.2 million and that the province would get only $12,000 from the sale, Liberal papers remarked that similar deals were being made daily and blamed the "government's timber policy facilitating the quick disposal of British Columbia's timber wealth, with the smallest possible return to the province." In December 1907, an Order-in-Council put a reserve on all unstaked timberlands to conserve forest wealth and prevent speculative staking. McBride explained that the government's chief endeavour was to have the forests "make a proper return to the provincial treasury" but that it "always stood" for the conservation of the province's natural resources for its people.[56]

The 1908 Throne Speech promised legislation that would allow investors "to make a fair return, discourage and prevent waste and destruction, and preserve for all the time to come a source of wealth in which British Columbia is not excelled by any other territory on earth." J.A. Macdonald repeatedly blamed the timber-licensing system for alienating "immense tracts of timber," and the Associated Boards of Trade of Southeastern

British Columbia complained that the forests were "being largely squandered." McBride said that logging companies had taken up only about 6 million of the estimated 132,000,000 acres of timberland in the province, that the government could increase royalties at any time, and that it welcomed "men with money," including "Americans with enterprise and energy who came here to open up our timber and agricultural lands."[57]

Some in the lumber industry thought the existing timber licensing system and the special licences that allowed their holders to cut timber on a particular piece of land were "ideal." Effective in 1905, these licences were good for twenty-one years. Others, however, wanted longer-term leases so they would not have to cut all their timber within twenty-one years, could use the licences as collateral, and be assured of stability in annual rentals. At the time, the industry was experiencing a brief recession. McBride told the Legislature of representations from those who wanted "drastic changes" in the special licences. Confronted with conflicting views and the need to study extensive data, the chief commissioner of lands and works would not "bring down comprehensive legislation" until the next session. Moreover, McBride, who increasingly recognized the value of experts, said that the government would seek advice from "the best authorities" regarding the logging issue.[58]

At the opening of the 1909 session, McBride reminded British Columbians that "timber was a tremendous asset," which had produced 41 percent of the province's revenue during the previous year. He boasted that the holders of timber licences were better protected in British Columbia than in any other province and that by reserving all unalienated timberlands, the government was doing "everything possible to conserve the timber resource." Because of dissatisfaction, it was investigating the twenty-one-year licences but could not promise immediate legislation. When the Liberals persistently attacked the government's timber policy and warned of policies encouraging "cut and run" practices that would rapidly denude the province's "marvellous forest wealth," McBride replied that the government was "overloaded with advice." Nevertheless, he expected a visit from Gifford Pinchot, the chief forester of the United States, and was considering establishing a bureau of forests. The Legislature would be asked to revise the tenure of the licences in light of the advice from a planned royal commission. Duly appointed on 9 July 1909, the Royal Commission on Timber and Forestry was chaired by F.J. Fulton, the chief commissioner of lands, who was assisted by A.S. Goodeve, MLA for Rossland, and A.C. Flumerfelt of Victoria. In late December, it produced an interim report on the tenure of special timber licences, conveniently some weeks after the 1909 election.[59]

The government also wished to increase the province's population. McBride complained that Ottawa wanted to settle the prairies so would not reduce travel costs for immigrants coming to British Columbia. White immigrants were generally welcome. Vancouver City Council, for example, urged the McBride administration to attract desirable white immigrants and provide them with "accurate information" about provincial resources. The government did offer some assistance to immigration. The Bureau of Provincial Information received many requests for white domestic help and farm labourers. As well as advertising in Britain, McBride had boasted during the 1907 election campaign that he was negotiating a subsidy for the Salvation Army to bring in settlers.[60] When organized labour objected to this, he promised that his government would do nothing "injurious to the interests of labour" and assured the Legislature that the Salvation Army brought in only the "best immigrants," not "strikebreakers." The first Salvation Army immigrants arrived in March 1908 and were welcomed as workers and a solution to the Asiatic question. When McBride visited the Okanagan, he was pleased to learn that they had given satisfaction. Through a second arrangement in 1910-11, the Salvation Army brought in 331 women for domestic service in return for a grant of $20,000, half of which was spent on a reception home for them. The *Times,* however, complained that the government had turned its "whole immigration work" over to a religious organization, especially since the Salvation Army immigrants came from towns and cities, and were therefore unacquainted with farming. It complained that the government brought in so few white settlers that "you could put them all into a bob-tailed car and not inconvenience the conductor."[61]

McBride did not favour "indiscriminate immigration," even from the British Isles. Some British immigrants were difficult. In the fall of 1907, the economic depression that struck most of North America reached British Columbia. From Victoria to Moyie in the East Kootenay, white labourers arrived to find that there was no work. In the winter of 1908, unemployment was particularly severe in Nanaimo. McBride promised public works to alleviate the situation, such as clearing the cemetery, but negotiations with city council took time. When a few men were discharged from this work, others quit. It was suspected that not all were destitute. About a hundred men refused to declare their financial circumstances lest they be disfranchised as recipients of relief if they returned to England. Dissidents were rebuffed when they tried to enter the Nanaimo hall where McBride was speaking to a Conservative meeting. At his hotel, McBride said that he would discuss disfranchisement with the cabinet. The men seemed pacified but the *Times* accused him of serving the ends of Hawthornthwaite and thereby antagonizing Nanaimo Conservatives.[62] Fortunately, the depression was relatively short.

British Columbia rejected proposals for colonies of foreigners, since admitting and segregating "people of alien races" would not build up the province or benefit the Dominion. It wanted "skilled agriculturalists, farm labourers, women domestics, and persons possessed of sufficient means to establish themselves as fruit growers, dairymen, poultry breeders and market gardeners." Government immigration publications warned "men without a trade, clerks, and semi-professionals" that they would have problems finding work and "must be prepared to 'rough it,' adapt to new surroundings, and accept whatever occupation may be available."[63]

Several problems explain the apparent lack of British immigrants. The advertising activities, fruit exhibitions, and lectures in Britain had a limited impact because of the inability of the agent-general's office in London to follow up on inquiries or to provide detailed information about the availability of surveyed lands, costs, and ways of reaching them. Liberals, however, blamed land speculation for difficulties in attracting settlers. John Oliver accused the government of letting speculators control "vast acres of land" in northern British Columbia and of not doing enough to colonize farmlands and raise food at home. H.C. Brewster, the Liberal member for Alberni, reported that would-be settlers at Quatsino found that the land they desired was reserved under unused timber and pulp leases. McBride agreed there was a problem; the 1908 Throne Speech announced a large appropriation for surveys.[64] Private and government promoters touted the Okanagan Valley and the Interior dry belt for agricultural settlers. "Dry belt" described the area's major impediment – a lack of water. After a Royal Commission on Irrigation was held, plans to reallocate water rights between mining and agricultural interests became of major importance.

Although British immigrants were welcome for their own sakes, they also helped British Columbia become a "white man's province." There was little sympathy for Asians anywhere in Canada, but the antipathy was strongest in British Columbia, where their numbers were greatest. The province had long denied them the right to vote. When the federal minister of justice proposed to discontinue using provincial voters' lists, McBride complained that this would discriminate "unjustly against British Columbia" since it could give Asians the vote. Following protests, Ottawa dropped the plan.[65]

The voters' lists were a peripheral feature of the Asian question. Asian immigration was a perennial issue, so tiresome politically that, during the 1909 session of Parliament, Burrell advised McBride that raising the matter of Japanese immigration would be unwise, even though McBride had given considerable attention to it in the provincial and federal elections. In 1907, the new Legislature went through the pro forma exercise of passing a bill, introduced by Bowser, designed to halt immigration from Asia. Passing such laws had been an almost annual occurrence since 1900. And each year, with equal regularity, the federal government disallowed them. Because the $500 head tax seemed restricted to Chinese immigration, the 1907 bill was designed to prevent the Japanese "and other Oriental classes" – people from India – "from flooding the country." It could also keep out "ignorant hordes" from Europe. Claiming that the province had the right to pass such legislation and citing Joseph Chamberlain, the former colonial secretary, as his authority, McBride asserted that British Columbia "had to stand up for her rights more than any other province in the Dominion." Despite minor criticisms, the bill passed unanimously, but Lieutenant-Governor James Dunsmuir, whose Vancouver Island coal mines were probably the largest single employer of Asians in the province, reserved it. Dunsmuir explained to R.W. Scott, the secretary of state, that it was only a modified version of previously disallowed bills. As a law, he warned, it "might seriously interfere with our international relations and Federal interests." The Japanese consul had already protested. A few weeks later, the *Times* reported that even if Dunsmuir had approved the bill, it would have been ineffective since a typographical error made the entry of illiterates "lawful" rather than "unlawful." The fact that no one had noticed the error during the bill's three readings shows how pro forma the legislation was.[66]

The matter temporarily faded from the public view, but between January and June 1907, 3,247 Japanese immigrants and over 500 "East Indians" arrived, and more were expected. In Vancouver, the Trades and Labour Council initiated the formation of the Asiatic Exclusion League (AEL), which soon had support from a wide variety of citizens. Bowser sent regrets to the founding meeting, but J.F. Garden, another Vancouver Conservative MLA, did attend. To recruit new members, the AEL organized a parade and a rally at City Hall for the evening of 7 September 1907. That day, under the headline "Bowser's Bill Vetoed on McBride's Advice," the *World* claimed that McBride had asked Dunsmuir to reserve the bill with the intent of embarrassing the federal government for insisting that the BNA Act amendment include the phrase "final and unalterable." Given the timing, this was a plausible suggestion, but disallowance would have been more useful for "Fighting Ottawa." Hostility to Dunsmuir was high. During the AEL parade, he was burned in effigy outside City Hall, and the subsequent rally cheered many motions including ones to condemn the provincial government for allowing Dunsmuir to reserve the act and to ask McBride to explain himself at the next AEL meeting. To accommodate those who could not get inside City Hall, the speakers repeated their speeches outside it. What happened next is not clear, but a mob left City Hall, moved to nearby Chinatown and then to the Japanese quarter, where it inflicted much property damage. News of the riot travelled quickly around the world and embarrassed federal and municipal officials.[67]

McBride learned of the riot and the allegations about the reservation of the bill only when he returned from a two-week fishing trip to Stave Lake, where he had gone to recuperate from the Better Terms fight. In Vancouver, he told reporters that the *World*'s statement regarding the bill was untrue – he had not advised Lieutenant-Governor Dunsmuir to reserve it. Instead, he blamed William Templeman, the BC representative in the federal cabinet, for not apprising Ottawa of the "true situation" and for countenancing repeated disallowances of the Natal Act. As for himself, he had always done his "utmost" to protect white labour and prohibit Oriental immigration, sentiments he repeated at Conservative meetings in Vancouver, Victoria, and Kamloops, where federal Conservative leader Robert Borden was the featured speaker. McBride declined an invitation to speak to the AEL but reiterated his desire to restrain the Asian influx "by proper constitutional means."[68]

No provincial politician questioned limiting immigration from Asia. The January 1908 Throne Speech proposed a measure to restrict "the immigration of undesirable persons." What to do about the Natal Act set off a major debate. In response to a Liberal motion censuring the government for not resigning to protest its reservation, McBride blamed the Dominion government and its agent, the lieutenant-governor, for the problem. He recalled that Laurier had courted BC voters in 1896 by promising to respect their wishes to restrict Chinese immigration and noted that the Lemieux mission, which negotiated the Gentlemen's Agreement whereby Japan limited emigration to Canada, did not satisfy British Columbia. Bowser reintroduced the previous year's bill with only one change, the correction of the typographical error. Subsequently, he withdrew a 1907 clause that had been designed to prevent disallowance by exempting those whose terms of entry had been established by the Canadian Parliament – namely, the Chinese, whose immigration seemed effectively controlled by the head tax. That clause might now cover the Gentlemen's Agreement and so make the Natal Act largely meaningless. When the Opposition press warned that deleting the exemption invited disallowance, McBride admitted that the interests of the imperial and federal governments must be considered but noted that other British colonies "had been permitted to pass Natal Acts as a protection against an influx of cheap, alien labour." Bowser promised that the day after the act became law, he would have the Provincial Police "see that no Japs land in British Columbia."[69]

The Legislature unanimously approved the 1908 version of the Natal Act. Dunsmuir gave his assent and the attorney general's department hired a special officer at Victoria and authorized the Provincial Police elsewhere to administer the language test, as provided for under the Natal Act. A few days later, 233 Japanese immigrants arrived in Victoria, the test was administered, and most failed it. After several challenged the law, Chief Justice Gordon Hunter ruled that the Anglo-Japanese Treaty of Commerce and Navigation made the Natal Act inoperative. The full court sustained his judgment. In another case involving "Hindoos," a government lawyer advised that the act was ultra vires since it was repugnant to existing Dominion laws. Pending an appeal, Bowser suspended the operation of the Natal Act.[70]

Meanwhile, Hawthornthwaite called for an Imperial Royal Commission on Oriental Immigration. To the apparent surprise of the Legislature, McBride asserted that he had abandoned "appealing to Ottawa" and would appeal to London. He believed that an imperial commission "would show the wisdom of prohibiting the immigration of Oriental peoples and encouraging people of the British race." It would also demonstrate that the province did not want "to involve the Empire in any international conflict." He noted Churchill's recent comment that Britain's commercial treaties with Japan had given Canada "utmost freedom" to deal with Japan. Drawing on his experience in London, McBride moved an amendment that since the Colonial Office was unlikely to consider a direct petition, it should be sent via the governor-general. Only the Liberals opposed the amendment.[71]

Outside the Legislature, McBride continued to attack Ottawa for not doing more to halt Asian immigration. He told Esquimalt Conservatives that the Japanese, who were strenuous competitors, especially in the fisheries, "would never become citizens like the white men" and that the province's climate was not suitable for the "Hindus." Privately, he believed that the Gentlemen's Agreement "practically ... handed over to the Japanese Government the control of Japanese immigration to Canada." To prepare for an appeal to the British Parliament, he wrote an article for the *Standard of Empire,* a British publication, in which he quoted a comment from Churchill's *My African Journey* – that "colonies with a white population have a right to forbid the entry of large numbers of Asiatics" – and argued that the immigration question must be taken up imperially. In a clear exposition linking loyalty to the empire with his view of the Asian question, McBride asserted, "Whatever good there may be in the Oriental, his ideas are not those of a white civilisation, nor can East and West ever truly assimilate. The result of an unrestricted immigration of Asiatics could only be gradual extermination of the whites and the absorption of the country by the yellow or brown races, an end which no patriotic citizens of the Empire can view with equanimity."[72]

By 1907, McBride's successes at home and his appearances on the national and imperial stages led the *Colonist* and an unidentified eastern Conservative newspaper to tout him as a future national leader. On returning from his Better Terms mission to London, he told the Toronto press that if the Conservative Party wanted him at Ottawa, he "would have to obey the call to duty." The *Times* intimated that Bowser was plotting to get McBride out of the way so that he himself could become premier. However, when Borden suggested that McBride run for the federal Conservatives in Victoria during the 1908 election, McBride did not think it "advisable" to do so, and he continued to deny any federal ambitions.[73]

Although McBride was involved in federal Conservative politics, he refused Borden's request to help reconcile a division between the supporters of Charles Hibbert Tupper and his own friends in Vancouver. Tupper claimed that McBride had told business people not to deal with the government through him. According to a Liberal paper, McBride had sworn that Tupper should never have political power. Tupper's friends included some of McBride's close associates, notably Finance Minister Robert Tatlow and G.H. Cowan. Cowan asked Tupper to seek the federal nomination in 1908 as did some members of the Orange Order. However, citing opposition from "those enjoying or expecting" provincial patronage as well as "personal abuse" from those in control of the provincial Conservative Party, Tupper withdrew from the nomination fight. McBride did not take sides on the issue. Before the nominating meeting, he dined with the executive, local MLAs, and the candidates. At a standing-room-only audience, he spoke on various issues without indicating whom he preferred as the candidate, although *Saturday Sunset* speculated that he favoured C.E. Tisdall. The Tupper and anti-Bowser faction nominated Cowan. During the subsequent election campaign, McBride shared platforms with Cowan and praised his knowledge of Better Terms. He visited every Mainland constituency, where he focused on Better Terms and Ottawa's use of "imperial reasons" – British concern about Japanese protests against any discriminatory legislation – for disallowing British Columbia's anti-Asian laws, issues that Conservative organizers said would have a significant impact. He also mentioned allegations of extravagance in many federal departments, dissatisfaction with the Department of Marine and Fisheries, and mismanagement of Saskatchewan lands. He decried the "Silent Seven," British Columbia's Liberal MPs, for acquiescing in federal policy.[74]

Liberal candidates boasted that the Gentlemen's Agreement successfully limited immigration from Japan, claimed that the Natal Acts were ineffective, charged that Cowan employed Japanese staff at his Bowen Island summer home, and accused Bowser of acting as solicitor for Saori Gotoh, a Japanese labour contractor. In response to the last charge, McBride pointed out that Bowser had a variety of clients.[75] The Conservatives won five of British Columbia's seven seats, leaving only Nanaimo and Comox-Atlin for the Liberals.

McBride knew the political value of meeting the people. Tours served direct political purposes, as was the case during election campaigns or the 1907 tour with Robert Borden, but were also fact-finding missions and opportunities to demonstrate his charm. He explained that the cabinet "should see as much as possible of the different parts of the country themselves, thus keeping in touch with local needs in a way that would be impossible from mere correspondence." To ensure the maximum benefit, he took "his publicity bureau with him." The Opposition press rightly interpreted his 1908 Kootenay tour as a pre-election junket on behalf of the federal Conservatives at the taxpayer's expense.[76]

His speeches reflected optimism about the province's future and often drew on local examples of progress. During the winter, he confined his tours to Vancouver Island and the Lower Mainland. In January 1908, for example, he toured the Gulf Islands with A.E. McPhillips, the local MLA, asking voters, "Any complaints?" In the spring, along with Provincial Secretary Henry Esson Young and Lawrence Macrae, he toured the Okanagan, the Boundary District, and the Kootenays. The *Nelson Daily News,* which a Conservative had recently bought, was delighted by the prospect of a visit from McBride since only through such meetings could "a wide awake administration ... keep in close touch with the people of a province as large as that of British Columbia." In the Okanagan, the party stopped at Kelowna, where McBride spoke at a non-political smoker under the auspices of city council, and they visited Summerland as the guests of

McBride is seated second left in the front row. His secretary, Lawrence Macrae, with whom he frequently travelled, is second from the right in the second row. McBride easily mingled with British Columbians. This photo was probably taken during one of his tours of the province. Contrast it with the elegance of the dinner at the Savoy on p. 188. Royal BC Museum, BC Archives, H-03005.

J.M. Robinson, a prominent real estate developer. They travelled by automobile from Penticton to Oroville, Washington, took the GNR to Midway, proceeded to Greenwood, drove to Phoenix, and went by train to Grand Forks, where McBride spoke briefly. A washout delayed their arrival in Nelson until after midnight, and they were "very tired." Although McBride was reluctant to give a full interview, he told the *Nelson Daily News* of his pleasure with the "good showing" of the Okanagan fruit industry and the Kootenay and Boundary mines. His speeches at a rally at the Nelson roller rink and at a banquet that lasted to the early hours echoed this boosterism. He expressed satisfaction with the progress of the fruit, mining, and timber industries, and he predicted that Nelson would be "a great city." He asked for support in making British Columbia a white man's country and warned of the need to be cautious with mining legislation because capital "was easily frightened." During the day, he heard various deputations and individuals, visited the new zinc smelter, and met the executive of the Conservative Association. Meanwhile, Young discussed the new university with the University Club, and Bowser, who had joined the tour, visited the provincial jail and the land registry office. McBride and Young attended a banquet and a "large, enthusiastic" meeting at the Conservative Club in Rossland, where McBride attacked the Laurier government's attitude on the Chinese question. He managed to find time to enjoy himself. On Empire Day, he joined people from throughout the region for festivities at Kaslo and watched a baseball game between Trail and Nelson.[77]

From Nelson, McBride, Bowser, and Young went to Cranbrook. At a public smoker sponsored by local Conservatives, he looked "well, healthy, confident, at ease and sure of his ground," and he spoke of "good old Cranbrook, the centre of a most deserving portion of the province." Referring to the fruit industry at Creston, he expressed his determination to make British Columbia "the California of the dominion if not of the whole empire" and reviewed the work of his administration. In Fernie, he noted that the "gratifying" position of the province's finances would permit public works, remarked that hundreds of miles of railway were being built without government aid, and boasted of the new timber dues that were increasing government revenues without discouraging production, which had doubled. In what the *Fernie Free Press* called a "magnificent peroration," he spoke of the province's glowing future.[78]

From Fernie, the travellers returned to Victoria via Spokane, but McBride had little chance for rest, as he spoke at meetings in Duncan and Victoria. At Duncan, the centre of an agricultural region, he found the same sense of "go-ahead" spirit that he had observed in Fernie. As well as reviewing the accomplishments of his administration and its quarrels with Ottawa, he spoke of plans to establish a provincial Department of Agriculture. A few weeks later, he and Young went to Sooke, a community west of Victoria, where he gave his customary overview of his administration's achievements during the previous five years but averred that his intent was to speak on local matters and get an intimate knowledge of local conditions.[79]

On 6 July, McBride, Young, and Bowser left to visit communities along the CPR main line as far east as Golden, with stops in Nicola, Spences Bridge, Ashcroft, Kamloops, Revelstoke, Field, and Golden. He took trips via steamer, railway branch line, private motor launch, or automobile to Spillimacheen, Nakusp, New Denver, Silverton, Wilmer, and Windermere.

After a brief stop at Cranbrook, the party returned home via Spokane, the shortest route to the coast from the Kootenays. The trip was portrayed as non-political in nature, designed to give the government "a better idea of the needs and progress of the different parts of the province." At Ashcroft, the first major stop, residents provided a practical exhibition of local needs by taking their visitors in the Dufferin Coach over the old Barnes Road to demonstrate its precipitous grades.[80] Ashcroft residents also wanted a road from Quesnel to the Nechako in the expectation that, as the nearest rail point to the Cariboo, their community would benefit from the new settlers' trade. Betraying Ashcroft's status as a rural community, they asked that the Legislature pass a Village Act so as to impose regulations to keep cattle off streets and gardens. McBride was sympathetic; Fulton observed that a surveyor was seeking a route for the Quesnel-Nechako road and $12,000 had been set aside for a wagon road. At an evening public meeting, McBride gave "a cheery breezy speech" on British Columbia's "illimitable resources" and, after noting the increase of fruit growing in the Okanagan, suggested that Ashcroft also had a great future in horticulture.[81]

At Kamloops, McBride said that the Department of Lands and Works was taking steps to halt land speculation, predicted that a railway line would run along the North Thompson River, spoke about the new university, and agreed that the local Old Men's Home required a new building. After a day's rest at Emerald Lake, the trio spoke at a crowded evening meeting in Golden, where the *Golden Star* reported that the only complaint about McBride's speech was that it "was all too brief." Immediately afterward, they boarded the steamer. After a brief stop at Spillimacheen the next morning, they proceeded to Firlands and were driven to Wilmer, where McBride spoke for a few minutes. They stopped briefly at Athalmer, reaching Windermere after midnight. Because of the late hour, the planned reception was cancelled, but a large crowd greeted McBride and his ministers. The next morning, they left for Cranbrook by automobile. The *Province* described their cordial welcomes as a response to the government's "resolute policy to encourage and assist in every way possible the development of their district" and to the fact that it focused on the entire province, not just the coast and more accessible parts of the Interior, as previous administrations had done.[82]

McBride visited Fernie again in August for a less auspicious reason – a forest fire had destroyed much of the city. In Victoria, he remarked on the "pluck and enterprise" of Fernie's residents, who had maintained "good order" and were rapidly rebuilding. He authorized the government agent to replace bridges, schools, and other government buildings. This did not satisfy the *Fernie Ledger*, because the province replaced only its own property and denied a grant or loan to the city lest it set a precedent. The denial was particularly galling since two years earlier the province had given $10,000 to San Francisco for relief after its earthquake and fire.[83] He was again in Fernie during early November 1908 as part of his Interior tour on behalf of federal Conservative candidates in Kootenay and Yale-Cariboo, and in June 1909 as part of a two-week tour of the Okanagan, the Boundary District, and the Kootenays.

Distance and limited transportation facilities made travel to the North difficult and time consuming. Moreover, it had so few voters as to make the effort of reaching it seem overly onerous. "Northern British Columbia has too long been represented by proxy," complained the *Port Essington Sun*. The *Omineca Herald* lamented that the province spent less than a third of the money it collected in the constituency but was optimistic when McBride told the Legislature of the government's "tremendous task" to build trails, roads, and schools to meet the needs of the "enormous population" that would probably soon settle there.[84]

In the summer of 1909, McBride went north. Although he did not arrive at Queen Charlotte City until after 10:00 P.M. and remained only while the *Amur* unloaded and loaded cargo, he was enthusiastically greeted at the office of the local newspaper and later sent a thank-you note for the "kind reception." He promised to appoint a gold commissioner for the Queen Charlotte Islands. His stay in Prince Rupert was longer and more elaborate. The Port Simpson Indian band played at the wharf, and the ladies of the city gave him a reception. At an evening smoking concert, McBride spoke of Prince Rupert's prosperous future, the region's resources, and jokingly, of the city's reputation for rain. He announced that steps were under way to provide a water supply as well as health and school facilities. The next day, he inspected part of the townsite, toured the harbour, conferred with the board of trade, and received a delegation from the "Zimshian" tribe, who sought "proper recognition of the rights of our own race." Recalling his many friends among the Indians in the South, he promised "to stand up" for their best interests, noted that the minister of lands was preparing a bill to permit "the Indian to pre-empt the land the same as the white man," and congratulated the bandmaster and his musicians. A trip to Atlin offered some rest as the ship called at several Alaskan ports before reaching Skagway. From there, the party headed to Carcross and Atlin, where McBride spent two days. The journey home was punctuated by brief stops at Prince Rupert, Swanson Bay, and Alert Bay.[85]

During his 1908 tour, McBride celebrated the fifth anniversary of his government and the introduction of party lines. The *Colonist* had already observed his "exceptional qualities as a parliamentary leader" whose "unfailing good humor" meant that he never "wilfully hurts the sensibilities of his opponents, and he is an adept at pouring oil on troubled waters." Its only complaint was that the solidarity of the caucus reduced debate in the Legislature. The *Columbian* congratulated McBride for leading the "most professional" government in British Columbia's history. In an editorial that was quoted elsewhere, the *Province,* though giving some credit to Tatlow and other cabinet ministers, extolled the rehabilitation of provincial finances, noted the expansion of public works, and remarked that when British Columbia was "an object of sinister attack by the Federal authorities," McBride had proved himself "a champion to defend our rights and privileges." A second article noted that though "suavity of manner and prepossessing appearance" as well as a "glad hand" explained McBride's success, now that he had overcome early challenges from his caucus and the corporations, the public recognized that "he could grapple with any hard problem of statecraft."[86] There would be no shortage of problems to test McBride's statecraft.

5
Boundless Optimism, 1909-12

> *[McBride] does not hold the fear of the Little British Columbians that too optimistic a view of the province's future can be held but grasps opportunity by the forelock and is determined in his railway policy to compel the continuance of provincial expansion and prosperity.*
>
> – New Westminster British Columbian,
> *5 November 1909*

By 1909, McBride so dominated BC politics that even the Liberal *Saturday Sunset* observed, "British Columbia expects big things from Dick McBride because he is her own favourite son and because he has been set in a high place and possesses the ability and personality of a leader."[1] Prosperity, well-received tours, and his delivery of the Conservative vote in the 1908 federal election were fine preludes to the 1909 provincial election in which McBride and the Conservatives won a spectacular victory by promising railways to serve most of the settled parts of the southern half of the province. Two and a half years later, with plans for a railway to the North and new branch lines in the South, they won an even greater victory.

All that seemed necessary to bring new railways was for the province to lend its favourable credit rating to railway companies by guaranteeing the interest on the bonds they issued to finance construction. A buoyant international economy, the attractiveness of western Canada to British investors, and the demand for British Columbia's natural resources made such arrangements possible. Liberal MLA H.C. Brewster rightly told the Legislature in 1909 that the McBride government was lucky to have come to office when provincial resources, especially timber, were in great demand. Net provincial revenues rose from $8,874,741.94 in 1909-10 to $10,745,708.82 in 1911-12, and during the same years, expenditures, mainly on public works, grew from $616,965.51 to $11,368,767.04.[2]

One criticism in the 1907 election was that McBride only offered pride in the activities of the Vancouver, Victoria and Eastern Railway (VV&E), the Grand Trunk Pacific (GTP), and the CPR, which were building without provincial subsidies. He maintained this approach: "While we have made every endeavour to encourage the growth and extension of legitimate railway enterprises," he asserted in 1908, "we have given the coldest of cold shoulders to the charter-mongers ... Five years ago we had some 150,000 miles of railway line in view, on paper, but today we have genuine activity in much-needed and important railway construction ... Presently, no doubt, we will have Mackenzie and Mann knocking at our doors. Let us give decent, intelligent encouragement to these undertakings; but let us give nothing more."[3]

He was less sanguine about the GTP, whose construction in British Columbia seemed "a long way off." He complained to F.W. Morse, its general manager, that in the 1907 election, some GTP officials had "created the impression that there was some feud about to be settled between us." He added that his government was "anxious to show every indication of fair play and businesslike dealing with your Company." En route to his Better Terms mission to London, he stopped in Montreal, lunched with senior officials of the GTP, and spent an afternoon with Morse. He was anxious to establish Prince Rupert as the GTP terminus "by any fair & reasonable means," saw no gain in "fighting the Grand Trunk unless for cause," and concluded a preliminary arrangement for the townsite of Prince Rupert after the GTP settled with the Indians. Robert Tatlow, the minister of finance, and F.J. Fulton, chief commissioner of lands and works, warned that "the public will blame us if we do not make the best business deal for the Province." While McBride was in London, the cabinet secured a greater portion of the land on Kaien Island, a higher price per acre, and guarantees that the GTP would immediately begin construction at the western terminal and would purchase supplies in British Columbia. Embarrassed by the actions of his cabinet, McBride explained to a GTP official, "My Colleagues were unable to see eye to eye with me," but he had to abide by the result. Tatlow and Fulton's insistence on getting a better deal foretold their differences with McBride on railway policy. During negotiations for other townsites, a chastened McBride insisted that Fulton set prices and terms. Conservative editors lauded the government for safeguarding provincial interests and promoting trade and development, but the *Times* thought it had "delivered the province, bound hand and foot, to the power of the corporations."[4]

Although he had criticized William Mackenzie and Donald Mann while in Opposition, McBride saw in their Canadian Northern Railway (CNR) a potential transcontinental line. The CNR had a rail network on the prairies and lines in Ontario and Quebec. Soon after the 1907 election, McBride suggested starting discussions with them. As the economy improved, Mann declared that the CNR hoped to build to Vancouver from its main line west of Edmonton but without government subsidies could not say when. In 1908, the CNR put surveyors in the field, secured a federal charter, and began serious negotiations with the province. More than "decent encouragement" was at play, even though Francis Carter-Cotton warned McBride that aiding the CNR would displease the CPR and GTP, and remove "any argument for Better Terms," since it would show that the province had ample financial resources.[5]

On 25 January 1909, McBride announced that he would welcome any "fair and equitable arrangement" with the CNR. After extolling the CNR as "a thoroughly Canadian system, controlled by Canadians" that had done much for Prairie farmers and could do much for British Columbia, he conceded its need for provincial assistance, although he stated that "the interests and rights of the Province will be served." When the GTP inquired about a subsidy for the CNR, McBride admitted that he had listened to a proposal from Mann. He also warned a Conservative gathering of "a momentous question" that could "lead to an appeal to the country." Repeating phrases he had used in the Legislature, he described the need for more railways so the province could "enjoy the benefits of competition and a closer connection with eastern Canada." Noting that the CNR was "knocking at our door" and that the government was negotiating with it, he hoped to go before British Columbians "on the question of railway construction with a policy not unacceptable to them." Election rumours began.[6]

Meanwhile, the CNR continued to conduct surveys, and it secured federal approval of its route. Mann proposed to visit Victoria in mid-October after the surveys were more advanced, but McBride asked him to come earlier since successful negotiations would permit a fall election. In Victoria, Mann publicly said that the CNR would come to the coast and to Vancouver Island. The same day he signed a memo of agreement

THE NEED OF THE HOUR

By 1909, with other provinces assisting railways, British Columbians were clamouring for a railway policy. *Saturday Sunset,* 20 February 1909, cartoonist, W.H.L. Hope.

with McBride whereby the CNR would build from Yellowhead Pass via the North Thompson River Valley to a point at or near Kamloops and onward to New Westminster, Vancouver, and English Bluff (Tsawwassen), with "first class modern passenger, mail, express and car ferry service" to Vancouver Island. On the west coast of the island, it would also lay about a hundred miles of track from Victoria to Barkley Sound. A fair wage clause was included, and no Asians would be employed. On 19 October, the cabinet met until almost midnight to discuss railway policy and an election. In announcing the agreement with the CNR, McBride stated that construction would cost at least $50,000 a mile. He would ask the Legislature to guarantee 4 percent interest on bonds for $35,000 per mile. The province would have a first mortgage on the railroad through British

Columbia and a covenant on the whole system. It would exempt the CNR from taxation during construction and for ten years thereafter, and would provide a free right of way through provincial lands and free access to timber and gravel on government land.[7]

Although it did provide competition for the CPR, the CNR offered little for the southern Interior, which, because of the earlier mining boom, was overrepresented in the Legislature. Complaints that the government had not done enough for the Midway and Vernon (M&V) may have explained the 1907 election of a Liberal in Greenwood. The Kettle Valley Railway (KVR), in which the CPR had acquired an interest, did some preliminary work without a subsidy. In September 1909, President T.G. Shaughnessy of the CPR called on McBride. Shortly thereafter, J.J. Warren of the KVR signed an agreement with McBride whereby the KVR would build from Midway to Penticton without aid if the province subsidized an extension from Penticton to a junction with the Nicola, Kamloops and Similkameen Railway. At the province's option, the subsidy for up to 150 miles would be up to $5,000 per mile in cash or in 3 percent inscribed provincial stock. The government would provide a free right of way, access to building materials, and a ten-year tax exemption for the line between Penticton and Grand Forks. The company would complete the line within four years of ratification, operate it continuously, purchase supplies in British Columbia whenever possible, and pay both fair wages and a five-dollar-per-day fine for every Chinese or Japanese person it employed.[8]

McBride simultaneously announced the arrangements with the railways, the dissolution of the Legislature, and the date for the next provincial election – 25 November 1909. The announcement of the election was no surprise. The Liberals had been calling for a policy that was "big and broad enough to gird British Columbia with a network of trails, roads and railways, north, south, east and west" as well as one that was active, "as opposed to the passive programme of the McBride government."[9] John Oliver, the new Liberal leader, expected that a contract with Mackenzie and Mann would give McBride an overwhelming victory but unveiled a map showing railway lines already subsidized by the federal government, extensions that Ottawa was "certain" to subsidize, and lines that a provincial Liberal government would aid and quickly complete, including a coast to Kootenay railway through the Hope Mountains and a line to Barkley Sound on Vancouver Island.[10] Unfortunately for Oliver, Ottawa would not provide subsidies for his proposed railways, but the provincial Liberals did not reveal this. Conservatives joked that other railways had abandoned the Hope Mountains route as impossible. As for the CNR, Oliver observed that much of its proposed route paralleled that of the CPR, but he would support it "if the terms are acceptable." He suspected that the full story of the railway contract had not been revealed and said that McBride would let him see it only under "a pledge of secrecy," which he had declined to make. McBride promised to provide details of the contract when he opened his campaign but only issued a press statement that was "sufficiently definite to serve the purpose of general information."[11] In addition, Oliver was short of campaign funds, strong candidates, an effective organization, and newspaper support. Apart from the *Vancouver World* and *Saturday Sunset,* most Liberal papers, especially in the Boundary Country, favoured McBride's railway plans. In Kamloops, the *Inland Sentinel* said that "the crying need of the province" was for more railways but expressed reservations about the new railway plans when it learned that the CNR line was unlikely to come into the city.[12]

A few Liberal editors worried about the extent of the province's financial obligations, a feeling shared by three of McBride's ministers – Carter-Cotton, Tatlow, and Fulton. McBride persuaded Carter-Cotton to stay on, but Tatlow resigned on the evening of 20 October, and Fulton followed suit the next day. Tatlow told the press that he was still "best of friends" with McBride and that they agreed on everything except his belief that the assistance offered to the CNR was "too great." Fulton expressed similar sentiments and said that the CNR would come without aid. Both agreed to stay for a few days to prepare departmental work for their successors. Bowser replaced Tatlow, and Price Ellison, the MLA for Okanagan, replaced Fulton. McBride regretted their departures but pledged to adopt "the first feasible and businesslike scheme for railway construction through British Columbia." Privately, he admitted that Tatlow and Fulton had to resign since they could not agree with his railway policy but was pleased that, otherwise, "they are most heartily in accord, and exceedingly friendly." That friendliness included their presence at the burial of McBride's infant son, a fact that he noted in his diary, and Tatlow's later visits to the Parliament Buildings to see how "the boy" (McBride) was doing. This friendliness muted the effect of the resignations. Some Conservatives had feared that the Opposition would cite them as meaning that something was "seriously wrong" within the cabinet. McBride thought they had no effect. W.C. Nichol of the *Vancouver Province* told him that at a Conservative meeting, "they took down Tatlow's picture & hung it up again with its face turned to the wall." Fulton suspected that "irresponsible" Conservatives had circulated the story that he and Tatlow had retired because of CPR influence, a rumour that even Oliver rejected. In retrospect, the *Inland Sentinel* rightly warned that the retirement of Tatlow, "the close-fisted guardian of the treasury," meant that "lavish spending will replace an era of economy."[13]

The only other Conservative defector was McBride's old antagonist, Charles Hibbert Tupper. At Revelstoke, on a platform shared with prominent Liberal F.C. Wade, Tupper argued that an additional transcontinental railway was unnecessary, that the CNR contract, which had "been negotiated with undue haste," had "no redeeming features," and that the guarantee on the CNR bonds could have "far-reaching and disastrous consequences." He claimed to be a loyal Conservative but opposed "this radical and extraordinary departure of a so-called Conservative government." On the eve of the election, his open letter explained that though he had not broken with McBride at the time of the Lillooet by-election in 1904, he had not voted for the provincial Conservatives since the Green episode of 1906. McBride contemptuously dismissed Tupper by suggesting that "our railway policy is too important to justify me in wasting time upon a politician whose day is gone and whose name is no longer considered a decent political quantity." Other Conservatives agreed. The Orangemen's provincial organizer said that they had "no use" for Tupper and that 95 percent of them would vote Conservative. After the election, another Orangeman reported, "Tupper dug his own grave."[14]

Most British Columbians agreed with the Conservative promise that "the McBride railway policy" meant "the beginning of an era of railway construction." To the question "What will it cost the province to get this new main transcontinental line?" a Conservative pamphlet provided an answer – "Not one dollar." It was commonly believed that McBride had "gilt-edged" bona fides and that the aid offered to the CNR was merely "sentimental" – in short, that the aid was only moral as the railway was certain to be profitable. Echoing the *News-Advertiser*, the *Province* declared that British Columbia would have "to pay the guarantee" only if the entire Canadian Northern system went bankrupt, a situation as unlikely as all of Canada falling into the hands of a receiver. When questions arose about CNR rates, McBride advised Mann that provincial control of passenger and freight rates must be included in the legislation. On the hustings, he promised that the province would get the CNR "without the cost of a single dollar and without the grant of a single acre of land."[15]

McBride missed the election campaign opening because of the birth of his son on Thanksgiving Sunday, 23 October. "In all my life," he stated,

"I have not had quite so much to be thankful for. It's a boy." Alas, by Thursday, baby Richard was ill and he died the next afternoon of "infantile debility and colic."[16] McBride had little time to mourn; en route to joining Bowser, who began the campaign in Vancouver, he stopped briefly at Spences Bridge to accept the nomination for Yale and to outline the local benefits of the proposed railways and the CNR contract terms. During a ninety-minute speech made at Revelstoke on 3 November, he put his political career on the line on the basis of his railway policy. The Kootenays would benefit from new lines that would compete with the CPR, a campaign theme, and he would consider aiding a CNR branch from Yellowhead Pass to Golden and Revelstoke. Thomas Taylor, the local member who had joined the cabinet late in 1908 as the first minister of public works, declared that Manitoba had never had to pay any bond interest for the CNR. At McBride's request, Robert Rogers, a Manitoba cabinet minister, had sent a report showing that "Manitoba's widespread prosperity and development" dated from its 1901 agreement with the CNR. The province now enjoyed its highest credit rating, improved railway service, and lower freight and passenger rates. Its CNR agreement had worked so well that Alberta and Saskatchewan had copied the policy.[17]

As McBride and Bowser toured the southern part of the province, venturing as far east as Fernie, their speeches showed little variation, although McBride, or possibly local reporters, emphasized local concerns. He promised that a CNR branch would serve the Okanagan, that construction of the M&V could start in Penticton, and that the KVR would have to pay a predecessor's debts before collecting any of a previously granted subsidy. The *Colonist* still hoped that Victoria would get a link to the Mainland via a bridge at Seymour Narrows but admitted that no one would build it at present. Yet Conservatives advertised that a vote for McBride and his party was a vote for "Victoria's Transcontinental Railway." McBride took a less specific stance but promised that the CNR would make Victoria "a commercial centre of great importance."[18]

Whether they arrived by special train, as at Nelson, where a banner reading "McBride and Immediate Railway Construction" decorated the hall, or spoke from the back of a railway car, as at Nakusp, McBride and Bowser were warmly welcomed. At Moyie, they spoke twice to accommodate the different shifts of miners. At Vernon and Rossland, brass bands and torches greeted the campaigners, a reception that was quiet compared to the dynamite blasts that welcomed them to Kaslo. In Vancouver, a banner read "Welcome to McBride, British Columbia's greatest premier," and they addressed two crowded meetings. At one, the audience sang and cheered McBride for three minutes before he could speak. At a joint meeting in Alberni with H.C. Brewster, the Liberal candidate, he got no more than a "faint cheer." In reporting his Victoria meeting, the *Times* described him as being "in a pettish mood" and remarked that he was not a "polished suave speaker" but "a blatant demagogue."[19] The paper was partisan, but McBride may have been physically exhausted.

All told, McBride and Bowser spoke to about twenty thousand voters in twenty-five towns and cities, most of which would benefit from the new railways. Their travels of over two thousand miles by rail, boat, automobile, and carriage illustrate the province's transportation problems. In parts of the West Kootenay, they travelled by chartered train and from Hedley to Keremeos by private train provided by the Great Northern (GNR). The motor trip from Keremeos stopped five miles short of Penticton when the last spare tire gave out. They reached Penticton by horse and rig. They missed the scheduled meeting, but some supporters joined them on the lake steamer, where McBride gave an impromptu address. When the train that was to take them west from Harrison Mills was late, they went downstream by fish boat until they caught up with a river steamer. The delay was fortunate – the steamer that was to have taken them to Ladner sank. The most frightening part of the trip was a thirteen-minute ride in the dark down the steep hill from Phoenix to Greenwood.[20]

Railways were the centrepiece of the 1909 campaign, but McBride frequently referred to the province's prosperous state. Many sympathetic editors credited him and his colleagues for its wealth and for stable government. Nor did McBride ignore traditional issues. He promised to continue to press for Better Terms, and both he and Bowser reiterated their beliefs in "favor of the white race" and the "exclusion of Asiatics." When, late in the campaign, Liberal F.C. Wade accused McBride of selling "Indian lands" to his friends, McBride admitted that his government had sold such lands, "mostly to Liberals." In Vancouver, Bowser argued that the Indians made little use of 535,000 acres of fertile land that was included in reserves, an idea that found wide support. He extolled what he called the government's "successful fight" to retain reversionary interests in Indian lands, but that battle with Ottawa was still in progress.[21]

McBride usually let Bowser explain the local option plebiscite, a non-binding referendum that had resulted from the efforts of a Prohibition group called the Local Option League. Although Prohibition was never popular in British Columbia, organizations supporting it had been active since 1859, and the province was not immune from the continent-wide Prohibition movement. In 1909, the Local Option League, which had fifty

BC branches, presented the government with a petition bearing 50,000 signatures and asking that local jurisdictions be allowed to ban liquor sales in their communities. Although the government enjoyed the revenue from the sale of liquor licences, and "the McBride-Bowser machine" was "notoriously identified with the liquor interests," a petition of such magnitude could not be ignored. As a sop to the prohibitionists, twenty-five liquor licences were cancelled in rural districts. McBride enjoyed a drink but was ambivalent about accepting liquor as a gift. He thanked the Canadian distributor for a case of Peter Dawson's Old Curio Whiskey sent early in 1909, but a year later, when a dealer gave him a case of "Old Banff" whiskey, he sent his thanks and a cheque for $13.50, the list price, because he "made it a rule not to accept presents."[22] The case of Old Banff was more a "thank you" than a bribe.

In response to the Local Option petition, McBride had announced the plebiscite, which the electorate would vote upon at the same time as it chose the provincial government. Supporters of Local Option, such as the prominent Vancouver Conservative H.H. Stevens, questioned McBride's sincerity in introducing Prohibition if the people voted for it, but McBride promised to carry out "the desire of the people of the Province." Dr. D. Spencer, who spoke at the Local Option Convention of the Kootenays, said he thought that McBride had "dealt very fairly with the local option movement by asking for 50% of the requisite vote." But Spencer was misinformed – the government had said that 50 percent plus one of those who voted in the general election would have to vote for local option before it would legislate, and the Legislature would settle the terms. This stacked the decks against Prohibition since many of those who voted in the general election did not cast a ballot on the plebiscite. Despite the efforts of its advocates, Prohibition attracted limited interest. Bowser mentioned it and Spencer spoke at McBride's campaign meeting in Victoria, but the press rarely reported it. McBride repeated his promise to "be bound by the result." Over 100,000 people voted in the general election, but only 47,926 of them cast ballots on the plebiscite. Of those, 22,414 favoured local option and 19,213 were opposed.[23] Since less than half of the voters had cast ballots on the issue, McBride had no mandate for local option. As a concession to the prohibitionists, the government regulated the sale of liquor in unorganized districts, required hotel operators to improve their premises, and enforced Sunday closing laws. McBride later boasted that his administration had passed "the most stringent liquor law in the British Empire."[24]

If McBride was satisfied with the plebiscite, he deserved to be overjoyed with the general election. He won both his Yale and Victoria seats. In Victoria, where he led the polls, a torchlight procession of automobiles, carriages, and other vehicles transported him to the *Colonist* office and Conservative headquarters. Province-wide, the Conservatives won 52.33 percent of the popular vote and all the seats except for four on Vancouver Island. The Liberals elected Brewster in Alberni and John Jardine in Esquimalt. The Socialists J.H. Hawthornthwaite and Parker Williams won Nanaimo and Newcastle respectively. So thin was the Opposition that both Brewster and the Socialists claimed the status of Opposition leader, and though Jardine denied becoming a Socialist, he represented the party on some standing committees. The press ascribed the "sweeping victory" to McBride's "railway policy, stable government and vigorous personality," but some noted disorganization among the Liberals. That too was McBride's interpretation of his "clean sweep," which came as "no surprise."[25]

Some friends added a note of caution to their congratulations. Carter-Cotton wired, "A wonderful victory almost too complete." C.E. Tisdall, who was elected in Vancouver, suggested "that with practically no opposition your responsibility as leader will now be greater than ever." Fulton, who was in Washington, DC, for the Forestry Commission, graciously admitted that the voters had rejected his views but warned that the lack of a strong Opposition, apart from Hawthornthwaite, would be a severe test. W.C. Nichol of the *Vancouver Province* also cautioned about a weak Opposition and the need for a finance minister who, though sympathetic to McBride's views, would also "command the confidence and respect of the solid people of the province."[26]

The 1909 campaign had had fewer problems than in 1907, although the cantankerous John Houston claimed there were more voters than ballot papers in Fort George. A Conservative organizer boasted of having "redeemed" Rossland despite a door-to-door canvass by the local Roman Catholic priest and the fact that foremen and shift bosses stationed themselves at the polling place, where they instructed miners to vote for the Liberal candidate. In Alberni, where Brewster won, a Conservative organizer said that the Liberals had manipulated pulp mill workers at Quatsino to secure their vote but admitted that the Conservative organizer in Comox had not managed to register all Conservatives or strike known Liberals off the voters' list.[27]

As the *Province* observed, the election results gave the government "a clear and unmistakeable mandate" to pursue its railway policy. McBride agreed. In thanking voters and fellow Conservatives, especially Bowser, he promised that the railway bills, including a final agreement with the CNR, would "have first place in the sessional programme." At a Conservative convention in Kamloops, he declared that British Columbia's finances "were in a condition of unparalleled promise," so the government would continue its "cautious administration" of provincial assets but be "generous" with appropriations for public works. Before signing the final contract with the CNR, he spent several days negotiating with Mackenzie and Mann, who came to Victoria in early January. He insisted that the CNR begin construction simultaneously on Vancouver Island and the Mainland, allow the province to control freight and passenger rates within British Columbia, establish a daily ferry service between Victoria and the main line, and when possible, buy all construction materials in the province. On 1 March, McBride introduced the legislation to ratify the agreement with the CNR and to incorporate its BC section as the Canadian Northern Pacific Railway Company. Provincial incorporation enabled the province to control the freight and passenger rates. According to the *Colonist,* McBride appeared a little nervous as he began a "masterly" speech but soon "found himself" and did "full justice" to the subject. Two hours later almost the entire House stood and cheered. The bill passed easily, with only Brewster and the two Socialists opposed. Even the Liberal *New Westminster Daily News* was gratified that the agreement included safeguards for the province.[28] The arrangement with the Kettle Valley Railway was readily ratified.

Despite overwhelming approval of the railway policy, communities that expected to be bypassed by the CNR were unhappy. A rumour that the CNR would bypass his city upset the mayor of New Westminster until McBride sent him a copy of the act, which stated that the railway must run "through New Westminster." When Kamloops learned that the CNR would build its station and yards about three and a half miles north of town, McBride told its board of trade that the city would nevertheless benefit from the railway. Satisfying residents of Sooke, west of Victoria, was not so easy. During the election campaign, its Conservatives had "constantly mentioned the fact of the railway coming via Sooke." Basing their actions on McBride's repeated mention of a line to Barkley Sound, they had made plans and subdivided properties. A route change, which alarmed them, was part of the larger question of the CNR on Vancouver Island. In the fall of 1910, six months after the CNR had started work on the Mainland, construction had not yet begun on the island, which prompted the *Times* to remind McBride and some Vancouver Island MLAs of their pledge to resign if island work did not begin simultaneously with that on the Mainland. McBride recognized the problem, but Mackenzie explained the need to complete surveys and get financial matters "in shape." The CNR soon announced its route from Sooke to Barkley Sound but made no mention of a fast ferry to the Mainland.[29]

The resignations of Fulton and Tatlow meant that the cabinet was short-handed, but McBride was slow to call the necessary by-elections or reorganize the cabinet, perhaps because he needed a rest after a series of family tragedies. Soon after the election, he took Margaret south for a "thorough change and rest" following the birth and death of baby Richard. Eighteen months earlier, Annie Mowbray, Margaret's sister, had died in Victoria after an operation for cancer. On 4 May 1909, McBride had been awakened at 5:45 A.M. by a long-distance phone call from his sister Dodo, announcing that his father, Arthur, had died that morning at home after a brief illness. Despite the family's request for a "semi-private and flowerless" funeral, many prominent people joined the funeral procession. Flags in New Westminster flew at half-mast. Yet another tragedy occurred in February 1910 when his sixty-year-old uncle, Edward F. D'Arcy, the music instructor at the provincial asylum, drowned after falling from the nearby bridge. He was not, the *Columbian* stated, suicidal.[30]

The family tragedies were well known, but the Liberal press had scant sympathy for delays in reorganizing the cabinet. Rumours circulated that Bowser, "the Napoleon of the administration," was unwilling to relinquish the Finance portfolio, even though McBride wanted to replace him. Bowser continued as attorney general, and Price Ellison became finance minister. W.R. Ross, the member for Fernie, became minister of lands. Subsequently, Carter-Cotton resigned. The *Times* speculated that, as "the ablest and best-informed member" of the Legislature, Carter-Cotton had realized that he was out of place, since McBride could tolerate only "one personality [Bowser] ... of greater strength than his own" in the cabinet. Carter-Cotton publicly explained that weekly cabinet meetings in Victoria interfered with his business interests, but his real reason for resigning was his opposition to Ross. The leading Conservative papers lauded the new cabinet for its strength and geographical diversity.[31]

McBride did not resign his Yale seat until November 1910, when he briefly toured the constituency, speaking at Merritt, Ashcroft, and Lytton on behalf of the Conservative nominee, Alexander Lucas. He thanked constituents for electing him and referred to his government's "generous and judicious expenditures on schools, roads, bridges and other public works," its railway policy, and its determination to keep British Columbia "a white man's country." He asserted that the government had done its best to encourage rural settlement and had appropriated $25,000 for "early construction" in Yale of "a portion of the great trunk road" to link the coast with Alberta.[32] The campaign was unnecessary – Lucas was acclaimed.

Public works and the associated patronage were facts of life. In the 1910 budget debate, Brewster alleged that the Conservative organization "included a great proportion of the civil service of the province." He cited road bosses, the Provincial Police ("a very useful cog" in Alberni), and a provincial land surveyor who had loudly boasted that he had done Brewster "out of every possible vote he could" from Cape Scott to Alberni. The *Times* repeatedly complained, often with specific examples, that "the chief end of the civil service ... is to convince faithful 'workers' that their reward is sure." On the eve of the 1912 election campaign, it described the men who controlled road work as "the digits of the patronage system," which gave settlers in outlying districts an opportunity to earn something to help pay their taxes and improve their lands. So many people were employed on road work just before elections that "they got in each other's way," and most were discharged five days after the election. The *Times* claimed that the government had organized a convention of road superintendents so that it could give them instructions for the campaign. Distributing patronage was fraught with problems. The president of the Nelson Conservative Association, for example, objected that his group's recommendations were "invariably" ignored. In suggesting the appointment of a particular individual as auctioneer at a government land sale, Price Ellison reminded McBride that "the recommendations of the Conservative Association in matters of this kind are always given every consideration." In 1910, after a Grading Commission reported the "detrimental effect of long continued patronage appointments," the government brought in a Public Service Act. McBride claimed that it "was designed to improve the Civil Service" but said that he did not intend to dismiss anyone.[33] In fact, the civil service expanded as a result of population growth and the assumption of new responsibilities such as forest conservation.

Civil service reform was then attracting attention in Ottawa, as was the continent-wide interest in conserving natural resources. McBride was prepared to cooperate "in so far as it is possible" with Ottawa's conservation efforts but questioned the efficacy of submitting disputed matters to the federal government's new Conservation Commission. He wanted to conserve forest resources yet develop the industry. Shortly after the Royal Commission on Timber and Forestry reported, McBride hinted to John

Hendry, a prominent lumberman who, with Fulton, represented British Columbia on the Conservation Commission, that comprehensive legislation on forest conservation and timber tenure was forthcoming. During the 1909 election, while the royal commission was under way, McBride promised legislation to grant timber licences in perpetuity or until the timber was removed. The Liberals repeatedly attacked the government for disposing of timber to American speculators and for alienating 11 to 12 million acres from the Crown. McBride said that he had tried to prevent the export of raw logs to American mills, which denied British Columbians the work of milling them. The final report of the Royal Commission on Timber and Forestry, released late in 1910, revealed that the province had no idea of how much timber it had; its estimate of 3,750,000 acres of timberland under reserve was "pure conjecture." Nevertheless, the report optimistically predicted "that the value of standing timber would rise to incredible heights ... if the resource was properly managed." Not until 1912 did the government introduce legislation to incorporate some of the commission's recommendations.[34]

Forest and land policies were closely related. About 1908, the Opposition began complaining that land policies benefited speculators, not farmers, and demanded that some land held under timber leases be opened for bona fide settlers. A Conservative convention called for a land settlement policy; the Vancouver and Victoria Boards of Trade wanted "a more active colonization policy." This idea was not confined to British Columbia. Quebec and Ontario had promoted back-to-the-land movements for some decades, in part because they believed that a rural society was a stable one. British Columbians, as the historian James Murton has suggested, also saw land settlement as a way to re-create "a version of England," a vision actively encouraged by vendors of orchard lands in the Okanagan and Kootenay Valleys. Critics, however, charged that the government's promotion of settlement was "absolutely futile." Detailed information on areas available for pre-emption was often lacking, settlers had to find their own acreage, and the province had to import food to feed British Columbians.[35]

In response, the government made piecemeal changes to land policies such as providing for the pre-emption of lots of up to forty acres for personal occupation and cultivation, and making more Crown lands available for pre-emption only. Several editors wished that change had come earlier, warned that not all pre-emptors were bona fide settlers, or complained that "sweeping" reservations would retard settlement. McBride boasted of setting aside large areas for pre-emption, constructing roads and trails, and providing stumping powder at cost. He noted that the rural population had doubled between 1906 and 1911, and that "millions" might soon live in rural British Columbia. He denied selling land to colonization companies and asserted that the tax on wild land made speculation prohibitively expensive. Moreover, since his government took office, 1,397,000 acres – more than the area of Prince Edward Island – had been pre-empted, and of the 25 million acres suitable for farming, about 796,000 had been surveyed for pre-emptors. In addition, he defended the policy of selling Crown lands since the revenue paid for roads and schools but added that communities must take some responsibility for clearing land or installing telephone systems.[36]

In the summer of 1911, the province created a new administrative system in the Department of Lands, cancelled some timber licences, reserved all unsurveyed lands along the rights of way of the new railways, and announced that once surveyed, land would be sold by auction rather than at a fixed price. Through these measures, it hoped to benefit from rising land prices and, by concentrating settlement, to reduce the cost of providing such services as roads and schools. To bring in more revenue, effective 3 April 1911, an Order-in-Council doubled the price of Crown lands and enlarged some reserves for pre-emptors. The Conservative *Fort George Herald* attacked this measure as two years too late; because of speculation, most land available for pre-emption was uncleared and distant from the railway. Six weeks later, while McBride and Bowser were en route to the coronation of George V, another Order-in-Council cancelled the higher price for lands on which a deposit had been paid before 3 April. The Fort Fraser Land Company, a British firm, whose local solicitors were Bowser, Reid and Walbridge, paid a deposit before that date. It advertised land for sale adjacent to the GTP and implied that, unlike the government, it had not increased its prices. The *Times* hinted that McBride had refused to reduce the price for the lands on which the deposit had been paid, so cabinet had acted in his absence, and it questioned the propriety of Bowser's law firm doing business with the government. Ralph Smith, a Liberal candidate, was probably referring to this company when in the 1912 election he charged that government surveyors staked land for people who had never been near it.[37]

Stories of wrongdoing persisted. The Liberal press decried the "scandalous" sale of lands in the Bulkley and Ootsa Valleys to the government's "camp followers" before the land was surveyed. This was not always the case; sometimes the government refused to sell lands to colonization companies even though its friends acted for them. Because the government wanted to retain land for individuals, "not dispose of it in large blocks," McBride informed G.H. Barnard, the MP for Victoria, whose client wanted to buy 500,000 acres of agricultural and grazing land in the Nass River Valley, that the government had refused many offers from colonization companies. Some Conservatives, however, suggested that colonization companies probably did better than individuals on land requiring irrigation and that farmers who could afford to buy cleared land were "the very best class of settlers." The *Times* insinuated that McBride had personally profited and that for two years, his friends had acquired powers of attorney from across Canada and the United States, and had bought quarter sections of BC land for speculation. Meanwhile, it said, provincial revenues from land sales were falling. At the same time, it alleged that the government was selling property in the Prince Rupert, Hazelton, and Stewart townsites at "phenomenal" prices. The *Fort George Herald* claimed that the government put a reserve on lands within twenty miles of either side of the Peace River after former cabinet minister R.F. Green, a partner in a Victoria real estate firm, secured "some choice lands" there. When Brewster accused the government of participating in "inside rings" to acquire Crown land, McBride claimed that the provincial Conservatives did "not know what it is to have any inside ring" and that they stood for "favors to none and equal rights for all." He expressed pride in the land laws, and although topography made administering them difficult, the government was trying to end speculation. The Liberals were not satisfied; their 1912 platform condemned the land policy and called for free homesteads for genuine settlers, accelerated surveys, assistance with the cost of land clearing, the removal of reserves, and keeping speculators off public lands.[38] Land policy was a minor issue in the campaign, for McBride's previous claims that the electors were not concerned about it held true, but the Liberals had aroused suspicion regarding conflicts of interest and mismanagement, if not outright graft, in the administration of public lands.

Land lay at the centre of McBride's dealings with the Native Indians and became part of his conflict with the Laurier government. Like many of his contemporaries, he favoured making "hundreds of acres of wonderfully valuable land overgrown with noxious weeds," abandoned by the Indians, available for development. His intent was to remake Indians into white men. In 1912, for example, he suggested that they take advantage of pre-emption laws and find employment on roads and other public works. He proclaimed, "We would not be Britishers if we did not give 'British fair play' to the Indians who had certain rights." His sense of British fair play was limited – the province rarely let Indians pre-empt lands and effectively denied them the opportunity to purchase Crown land.[39]

In dealing with Indian lands, he failed to settle the huge matter of Native title, an issue with which British Columbians are still dealing, but he contributed to the solution of the reversionary lands question and resolved the long-standing problem of the Songhees Reserve to the mutual satisfaction of the Songhees and the province. The Songhees First Nation occupied land in Victoria's Inner Harbour, which the city coveted as a site for a railway terminus and industries. Although the Songhees came under the jurisdiction of the federal Department of Indian Affairs, they were in a strong bargaining position because, unlike most BC bands, they had concluded a treaty with the colonial government. Early in 1910, when the negotiations with Ottawa for their removal were proceeding slowly, McBride hired J.H.S. Matson, the publisher of the *Colonist*, to negotiate with the Songhees through Chief Michael Cooper. Cooper and representatives of his people agreed to move in return for a payment of $10,000 to each of the forty-three heads of families on the reserve, their moving expenses, and a new reserve. Cooper insisted that the Songhees were "quite capable of looking after their own affairs" and wanted to receive the cash directly rather than having the Department of Indian Affairs administer it. McBride warned Laurier that if Ottawa did not agree to these terms, a "public calamity" would ensue, given the importance of the project. Indian Affairs eventually acquiesced but took title to the new reserve on land that the province purchased in Esquimalt. In April 1911, after some delays, McBride went to the reserve to complete the details of the "final surrender." In a "very dignified manner," he declared that "we in British Columbia have always lived side by side, white man and Indian, happily and as friends." Alluding to problems in the Nass and Skeena Valleys, where people promoted "trouble, bad feeling and unhappiness between them [local Indians] and their white friends," he praised the Songhees for their industry and conduct during the negotiations. At the ceremony, the Songhees made McBride an honorary chief. Afterward, Chief Cooper and a number of "boys" went to McBride's home for a late-night dinner. When Cooper complained that the meal was more like a lunch, Matson gave him fifty dollars to take "the boys" to a restaurant. At a second ceremony, the cash was distributed and the land officially passed into provincial hands.[40]

Unlike the Songhees Reserve, some reserves were not actively occupied. The province desired to possess those whose locations made them attractive for development. McBride and his cabinet claimed that the federal government had reneged on an 1870s arrangement that gave the Indians only "a right of use and occupation" of reserve lands and the province a right to any reserve abandoned or surrendered by any "Indian band or Nation." This was the so-called reversionary right. Basing its stance on calculations that the province's Indian population had fallen from 25,616 in 1893 to 24,523 in 1901, whereas the amount of reserve land had risen from 480,505 to 525,846 acres, an Order-in-Council stated that this amount of land was "more than sufficient" for the Indians and that the surplus should be given to the province. Despite intermittent negotiations with the federal government, nothing changed until well after 1911, when the Conservatives came to power federally.[41]

The fundamental question was Native title to the land. As "guardian of the Indians," Laurier knew that they would not be satisfied until the Judicial Committee of the Privy Council, Canada's ultimate court of appeal, determined their claim to ownership of all the unsurrendered land in the province. McBride wanted arbitration and refused to go to court lest an Indian victory affect all the land in the province save for some small areas on Vancouver Island and in the Peace River, and thereby jeopardize investment in the province. McBride assured Laurier that there was no reason for "uneasiness" – the Indians had "no reason ... to believe that they have been treated unjustly."[42] In fact, they had been pressing their claims for landownership since at least the 1880s, and like McBride in other circumstances, they looked to both London and Ottawa for redress. Both coastal and Interior Indians formed organizations to press for their rights and had the support of a non-Native group, the Friends of the B.C. Indians. Representing the Friends, W.W. Perrin, the Anglican bishop of Columbia, met with McBride and his cabinet on 7 December 1910. Referring to recent difficulties between would-be settlers and Indians in the Nass Valley, Perrin warned of "continual trouble" and sought help with the cost of taking the case concerning Native title to the Judicial Committee. Unmoved, McBride claimed that "so far as we know, the Indians are peaceful law-abiding Indians, loyal subjects of the Crown," that white men had stirred up the "little trouble" in the Nass and Skeena Valleys, and that no wrongs had been done to the Indians in the province. Adding insult to injury, he stated that the government was considering cancelling reserves not required by the Indians. He refused to be a party to any court case.[43]

The Indians were not deterred. On behalf of his council, Chief A. Wedildahid of Kitselas wrote to McBride, saying, "We have no land."

McBride denied this and reiterated that the province had always recognized reserves "as being for the use of the Indians." Shortly thereafter, Chief R.P. Kelly and almost a hundred chiefs presented a memorial to McBride and the cabinet declaring that "as the original inhabitants of this land," they held "title to the unsurrendered lands of the Province." They had seen their lands sold to speculators, though many of them had insufficient land to support their families and did not even own title to it. In the words of Chief John Chilahitsa of Douglas Lake, "The Indians say that it is their country and if you claim it they want to go to some big court house and have the matter settled." McBride remained unswayed. His affable but vacuous reply expressed pleasure at meeting the chiefs and other representatives of the "Indian Tribes of British Columbia"; he said that he had known "Indians all his life and they were all his friends," and he hoped that all British Columbians would "live in peace and happiness together," with the Indians having an important role as the province built roads and railways. But he reiterated that they had no title to unsurrendered lands and that the government would not take the matter to the courts. When stories spread that unhappy northern Indians might revolt, McBride asked the Department of Indian Affairs to investigate. Fortunately for him, the Indians were patient. Again, they appealed to the king; the Colonial Office discussed the matter with McBride and Laurier during the coronation festivities. On the advice of the colonial secretary, the Friends of the B.C. Indians met with McBride in January 1912. He had not changed his mind regarding the subject of Native title, and the Colonial Office would not interfere. When asked whether Indians could acquire Crown land without securing an Order-in-Council, McBride said, "It would be very unwise to give to the Indians such an unrestricted right."[44]

Provincial land resources also came into play in funding the University of British Columbia. In 1908, the government set aside land to endow it. McBride knew that many cities wanted the institution. To take politics out of the decision and reduce voter alienation, he had a committee of university professors from across Canada, including R.C. Weldon, his former law professor, visit communities aspiring to host the university. The commissioners recommended locating the university in the Vancouver area, specifically at Point Grey, where the province owned extensive acreage.[45]

Given McBride's political success in British Columbia and the frustration of the Conservatives with the inability of their federal leader, Robert Borden, to become more than the leader of the Opposition in Ottawa, speculation began about McBride's national ambitions. One rumour in

1909 claimed that McBride would fight the provincial election for the benefit of someone else, probably Bowser, and then leave for Ottawa. After the overwhelming victory of the 1909 election, F.R. Glover, an old friend from New Westminster and a lobbyist for the BC Electric Railway (BCER), told McBride that newspapers and the men in the Ottawa lobbies and clubs were saying that Borden would "have to give way if you can be induced to enter the Dominion arena." A number of leading Conservatives, including Hugh John Macdonald, the son of Sir John A. Macdonald, suggested to McBride that "there is room at the top <u>for you</u>."[46]

By 1909, Borden's leadership was under almost constant attack. Because of the growing German challenge to British maritime hegemony and the possible non-renewal of the Anglo-Japanese Alliance, naval matters came to the fore. In March 1909, the Canadian Parliament unanimously supported the principle of creating a Canadian navy and of cooperating with Britain's navy in times of crisis. Initially, McBride favoured this policy. He told Prime Minister Laurier that "irrespective of politics," British Columbians would "applaud prompt action" in assisting naval defence, appropriate to Canada's "important position" in the empire. The Admiralty urged the Dominions to create "fleet units" of large ships that could serve with the Royal Navy in emergencies rather than concentrating on the construction of small ships for coastal defence. Canadian imperialists, such as J.P. Whitney and Rodmond Roblin, the Conservative premiers of Ontario and Manitoba respectively, wished to follow the example of Australia and New Zealand in contributing dreadnoughts – large battleships – to the Royal Navy. In April 1909, the Navy League sponsored a crowded meeting in Victoria, which endorsed the plan for a Canadian navy but urged "an immediate and unconditional gift to the Imperial Navy," presumably sufficient cash for it to purchase a dreadnought. After the Navy League passed this resolution, McBride called the idea of contributing a dreadnought "well and good" but added that, in aiding the mother country, Canada should do nothing "spectacular" and noted the need to protect both shipping and the deep-sea fisheries.[47] This was hardly an enthusiastic endorsement of a direct contribution to the imperial navy.

Within the federal Conservative caucus, naval matters divided Quebec nationalists, who believed that Canada should concentrate on its own defence, and ultra-imperialists, who thought that Canada should do its share for imperial defence. As the naval crisis developed in the fall of 1909, Borden, who believed there was an emergency because of the rapid increase of the German fleet, confidentially asked McBride and other leading Conservatives for their opinions of a "generous emergency contribution to the Imperial Treasury" until a Canadian unit of the Royal Navy could be a reliable and "effective fighting force" as "an integral and constituent part of a great Imperial fleet" under Admiralty control. McBride agreed to this plan and said that the grant must "be large enough to be of real service." But, aware of local needs and benefits, he also called for expanded dry docks, coastal defence, and vessels to train an "efficient naval reserve that would eventually grow into an effective unit of the Imperial Navy." In return for its grant, McBride argued, Canada should have representation in the Admiralty, but he did not explain how.[48] Although he was an imperialist, he was also a British Columbian and a Canadian nationalist.

Laurier, who also had to deal with nationalist sentiment in Quebec, insisted that Canada's contribution must be its own navy to protect its coasts. In January 1910, though admitting that when Britain was at war, Canada was at war, he introduced legislation to create a Canadian navy under Canadian control. Like McBride, Borden argued that if Canada participated in imperial defence, it must have a say in making defence policy and called for an immediate contribution to the Admiralty to purchase a dreadnought. Imperialists in Borden's caucus favoured this; most members from French Canada demanded a plebiscite on naval policy. McBride objected to the slow development of a Canadian navy but told provincial Conservatives that debating a federal issue in the Legislature would not be "in the national interest."[49]

By March 1910, dissent in the federal caucus and doubts regarding Borden's leadership had revived rumours that McBride would replace him.[50] Martin Burrell reported that he, J.D. Reid (MP for Grenville, Ontario), George Perley (Argenteuil, Quebec), and several other caucus members expected that if Borden, who was not looking well, retired, there would "be an overwhelmingly strong call" for McBride as leader. If McBride would consider taking the position, Burrell said, "it might be a great help at a critical moment." Two weeks later, Burrell proposed that McBride take over as leader, with Borden remaining in the House. Borden suggested that McBride should be his chief lieutenant but said that he would step down as leader if McBride would not accept that role.[51] But Burrell had exaggerated the strength of the call for McBride to step in; years later, he told Borden that only a "small handful" had favoured bringing McBride to Ottawa. If McBride replied to the request, his answer was undoubtedly "no."[52] In the end, the subject was moot. Borden temporarily quelled dissent and maintained the "loyalty and friendship" of McBride and Bowser.[53]

Borden recalled that McBride's "gentlemanly instincts prompted him" to offer "an extremely warm and indeed enthusiastic reception" to Laurier, who visited British Columbia in August 1910. McBride's gracious hospitality reverberated to his credit in eastern Canada. He saw Laurier's western Canadian tour as the prelude to a federal election and encouraged local Conservatives to prepare accordingly. Nevertheless, he asked the MLA for Columbia, the riding through which Laurier entered the province, to greet the prime minister and assure him of a hearty welcome. In Victoria, two thousand light bulbs were added to the three thousand that illuminated the exterior of the Parliament Buildings, and ten to twelve thousand people greeted Laurier. When McBride and Laurier prepared to leave after a reception, they found that the front door had been accidentally locked. McBride quipped, "You see, Sir Wilfrid, they don't want to let you go!" McBride thought the reception was a "great Success." A contemporary recalled that he had urged Vancouver Conservatives to give Laurier a good reception when he spoke at the Horse Show Building.[54]

McBride's welcome to Laurier also reflected his realization of the benefits of cooperating with Ottawa. He was unwilling to let the Dominion government take the revenue arising from its development of Yoho and Glacier National Parks but, on Burrell's advice, did not press Better Terms. He worked with the Laurier government on conserving natural resources, investigating industrial training and technical instruction, and appointing game wardens in national parks. He sent Bowser to Ottawa to settle disagreements over the administration of water rights in the railway belt – the ungranted Crown land lying for twenty miles on either side of the BC CPR main line east of Port Moody.[55]

As at the 1906 Inter-Provincial Conference, McBride still believed that British Columbia was unique among the provinces. In the fall of 1910, Premier Whitney of Ontario organized an interprovincial conference to consider a seat redistribution in the House of Commons in which the Maritime provinces would lose four or five seats and Ontario itself would possibly lose a few due to the growth of the West. McBride sent his regrets because of the impending legislative session, but that was probably just an excuse. A few months later, he told Premier F.L. Haszard of Prince Edward Island that British Columbia had no right to participate since it disagreed with the Maritimes claim that Confederation was "an agreement between the Provinces." Instead, British Columbia regarded Confederation as being "in the nature of a union the basis of which was individual treaties." Each province, McBride insisted, "has the right to object to any change in the [British North America] Act that might affect its own value and influence." Earlier, in referring to the demands of Alberta and Saskatchewan for control of their public lands, he advised Borden that including provincial rights in the Conservative platform would strengthen "the whole fabric of Confederation."[56]

Had McBride attended the conference, he might have joined Manitoba in seeking Better Terms. That province had not raised the Better Terms issue at the 1906 conference but now demanded an additional subsidy to help cover the costs of an anticipated extension of its boundaries. Premier Roblin argued that the 1906 terms were inconclusive since British Columbia had not accepted them. The federal finance minister, W.S. Fielding, replied, "We all said that British Columbia was unreasonable." Laurier suggested that if Roblin had a special claim, he should have followed the example of British Columbia and made it known.[57]

Meanwhile, McBride travelled. In the latter half of June 1910, he made a mysterious two-week trip to New York and Chicago but spent only a day in each city.[58] Much better documented was his trip to north central British Columbia. In August, with British friends John Norton-Griffiths, Harry Brittain, and Lord Dunmore, along with Carter-Cotton, his secretary Lawrence Macrae, and C.H. Lugrin, the editor of the *Colonist,* he made his first visit to Fort George. At every stop along the way, Brittain observed the warm welcome for the premier. Most of Ashcroft came out to greet the party, but at 6:15 A.M. on 23 August they left Ashcroft in two "strongly-built 48-h.p. Winton cars." Although it was summer, they encountered snow in one of the higher passes. At Soda Creek, "a village entirely unremarkable," they boarded the ship *B.X.,* which was "radiant with streamers and flags in honour of the premier." After several short stops and a longer one at Quesnel, where many Union Jacks flew, they ran through the Cottonwood Canyon. While the ship was tied up one night, Brittain recalled, they made a visit to two brothers. In response to his question about the difficulty of getting men out to vote, one of the brothers told of a man who "came in thirty-five miles on snow-shoes with the thermometer, Lord knows what below, to put down his vote for the Premier." A mechanical problem delayed McBride and his party, but they arrived at South Fort George at 9:30 A.M. on 26 August and carried on another twenty-five miles to Willow River, where low water halted their journey. The fact that they could not proceed farther prompted McBride to ask the federal government to improve navigation on the Fraser River. The party returned to Fort George and drove over three miles of bumpy road to a rival townsite. By the time they left, it was dark and they took turns holding up a lantern so they would not drive off the road. In the evening, they attended a banquet and public meeting, where McBride made no comment on a local controversy regarding the site of future government buildings but spoke of the country's "great future" and hinted at increased expenditures for roads, trails, and bridges. In their speeches, the visiting Britishers avoided party politics and did their "best on the wider questions affecting the Empire at large." Next morning at 5:00 A.M., the travellers left for Quesnel, where they attended a "good meeting" and a smoker. A muddy road thwarted their plan to visit Barkerville. The trip left Brittain with a knowledge and appreciation of "the affection and regard which the people of British Columbia have for the strong man of Western Canada."[59]

With the construction of the GTP well under way, the North captured McBride's attention. Early in November, he and Margaret sailed to Prince Rupert, where he met local officials, including the school trustees and a delegation from Stewart that was concerned about sanitation, the hospital, and the school. Between six and seven hundred people attended his public meeting. Although the weather during the sail was wet and windy, McBride remarked in his diary, "Thank heavens no telephones & interlopers." His travels continued with a quick trip to Nelson via Spokane for a Conservative convention and into Yale constituency for a by-election campaign. Soon after his return, he commented on 15 December, his birthday, "40 years done. Start 41."[60]

By the fall of 1910, after a respite from the naval debate, federal Conservatives were again restless. A Nationalist victory in a by-election at Laurier's old home riding of Drummond-Arthabaska suggested that he had lost his hold on Quebec. In consultation with Borden, George Perley invited McBride to come to Ottawa, where his "advice & influence would be very helpful." In congratulating McBride on his fortieth birthday, the *Colonist* said that those who thought he had "his eyes on the prime ministership" misjudged him as he preferred to advance British Columbia's welfare. The provincial Conservative convention discussed "the probability" of McBride seeking federal honours, but McBride only spoke on provincial issues.[61]

McBride now had serious doubts about Laurier's naval policy. More emphatically than in 1909, he said that the time was not ripe to construct a navy in Canada, but, aware of local industry, he called for efficient dockyards. To the "prolonged applause" of Navy League members, he declared that Canada could not do too much through "a direct contribution to the old land." He echoed this sentiment in telling the provincial Conservative convention, "We are Britishers to the core – we love the flag, we believe in the Empire, we honor the king." He also used this theme in speeches to non-political groups, telling the Canadian Manufacturers Association, which met in Vancouver in September 1910, "We are all good

Western Canadians here but we are more intensely Britishers." At the general conference of the Methodist Church of British Columbia, he described the province's resources as "a heritage not for Canadians but for humanity although we would specialize the Britisher as the one capable of bearing the responsibility of citizenship."[62]

Though uncertain of how to secure "closer consolidation of the Empire," he made "a small personal contribution" to T.P. O'Connor, who toured Canada during the fall of 1910 to promote home rule for Ireland in some form of British federation.[63] Radicals in Britain embarrassed its government by making "abundant political capital" out of the donations that O'Connor had received from Laurier, McBride, and others. McBride did not recant but explained that, like O'Connor, who was his personal friend, he believed that "provincial home rule for Ireland and other parts of the British Isles" was in the "best interests" of the empire. At a meeting in Victoria, where the attendees adopted an address expressing the loyalty of British Columbians to the new king, McBride said that at the coronation of George V, he expected to see "the first tangible movement for such consolidation of the Empire as will lead in the days near at hand to closer union and, if possible, to a stronger bond among the great nations" of the British Empire. He also noted that British Columbia needed the imperial navy to protect its resources.[64]

In the meantime, another national issue increased speculation about McBride's future. On 26 January 1911, W.S. Fielding, the Canadian finance minister, announced an agreement with the United States for free trade in natural products and a few manufactured goods, and for lower tariffs on other goods, including agricultural implements. Canadians had long flirted with the idea of reciprocity with the United States, but the Americans had always rebuffed them. Prairie farmers complained that the tariff increased the cost of equipment and supplies, yet they had to compete on world markets to sell their grain. In the fall of 1910, the United States came courting. When an American professor asked for McBride's opinion about reciprocity, he noncommittally referred him to Borden. When the agreement with the United States was announced, McBride immediately warned that reciprocity would "inflict very serious injury in this province," particularly for its fruit and dairy farmers, lumber producers, and transportation interests by promoting north-south trade rather than east-west trade. He urged Borden to raise the reciprocity issue federally, "without one hour's unnecessary delay."[65]

During an hour-long speech in the Legislature, McBride condemned reciprocity and repeated his economic concerns. He noted that Canada had never before enjoyed such prosperity, that Britain was a more important customer than the United States, and that if reciprocity yielded any material advantage, "ninety-nine per cent would go to the United States and one percent" to Canada. He did not expect reciprocity to "affect the loyalty of British subjects in Canada" or their desire "to take all constitutional means to make for efficient arrangements for Imperial federation." Earlier, when questioned about imperial federation, he had declared the impossibility of laying "down any cut and dried plan" to achieve "closer consolidation of the Empire," but he favoured one that would "rid" the "Imperial Parliament" of small local matters.[66]

In several letters, Conservative MP Martin Burrell informed McBride that the federal Conservatives were split over reciprocity. Prairie MPs desired it; Maritimers wanted free fish and lumber; and the majority was "dead set against Reciprocity and all its works." Burrell also reported serious dissatisfaction over Borden's "go-as-you-please" approach to reciprocity. If Borden retired as federal leader, Burrell declared, McBride was the only potential leader who "would command practically universal assent." Believing that a "cabal" had been organized against him, Borden wired McBride, "Am convinced that interests of party imperatively demand my retirement. Believe party would unanimously accept you as leader ... Situation urgent." The crisis was no secret, and speculation mounted that McBride might become the federal leader. He replied by endorsing Borden's leadership and offering to discuss matters when he was next in Ottawa. Locally, the *Colonist* denied that McBride had any federal ambitions, whereas the *Times* asserted that the "big money powers of the East," who had much to gain from someone such as McBride, had handled the situation so "clumsily" that he could not accept and was biding his time. The *Columbian* may have been close to the mark when it noted McBride's comment that he would consider an invitation to Ottawa only if it came from the parliamentary party as a whole. Lottie Bowron, his long-time secretary and confidante, recalled, "He never wanted to go to Ottawa."[67]

McBride was loyal to Borden. En route to the coronation, he attended an Ottawa banquet hosted by Borden in honour of Bowser, McBride, J.D. Hazen of New Brunswick, and Robert Rogers of Manitoba. Over a hundred Conservatives, including MPs, were present at the banquet, and some believed that Borden had set up the occasion to show himself as a more impressive leader than McBride or other challengers. In his speech, McBride said that should the occasion arise, "some of the men now administering provincial affairs might be impelled to respond to the nation's call." After describing his banquet speech as "weak," the Liberal press

BOWSER IS WILLIN'

The British Columbia Attorney-General is reported in the Toronto Star as having said at Mr. Borden's dinner that the time had probably arrived when the western province might have to make a "sacrifice" in the interests of the federal party.

Some federal Conservatives were challenging the leadership of Robert Borden (in top hat and mourning veil), and promoting the idea of McBride taking over. The press in British Columbia speculated that Bowser would be happy to see McBride go, since this would open up the premiership for him. McBride, however, had no real ambition to serve in Ottawa. *Victoria Daily Times*, 13 May 1911, cartoonist, Wilson.

reported that Conservatives in Ottawa now doubted the wisdom of pressing McBride to move to federal politics. The *Times* quoted an unnamed Ontario MP who had commented that he now understood the claim that "no man could be as wise as McBride looked." A writer in the *Ottawa Evening Journal* described McBride's "interesting and powerful" speech as riveting the attention of the audience, noted his "wonderful" hair, and quoted an MP as saying that McBride's "appearance and personality" would carry him far. The *Toronto Globe* reported McBride as saying that if a call went out "to any individual yonder in the west to serve under the Canadian leader of our party," he would expect him to be loyally received, but despite urging by cheers, he refused to elaborate. In his diary, he merely noted that he had had dinner with Borden. After leaving Ottawa, he stopped briefly in Montreal, where he saw Shaughnessy and had lunch with Sir Hugh Graham, the imperialist publisher of the *Montreal Star,* before leaving for New York, boarding the *Celtic,* and after a sometimes rough voyage, reaching Liverpool.[68]

Britons also recognized McBride's "personal magnetism, great popularity," and skills as a party manager. His loyalty to the imperial cause led some Britons, who wanted to form "a strong Imperial party from both sides of the House," to invite him to serve in the British Parliament. John Norton-Griffiths, an MP and head of a large construction company with investments in British Columbia, offered him a fund of £100,000 and a safe parliamentary seat if he would move to England, where he would "be Disraeli over again." McBride may have been flattered by this suggestion, but his cabled reply was a simple "No."[69]

Nevertheless, he enjoyed London. Along with the other provincial premiers, he attended the coronation in June 1911, and during the accompanying festivities, he mixed socially with the British elite, especially leaders of the Unionist and Imperial Parties. At a private gathering in his honour, McBride extolled their work for "the maintenance and integrity of the Empire." J.H. Turner, the agent-general, hosted thirty-three tables of twelve each at a dinner at the Savoy Hotel in his honour. Among those at McBride's table were Lords Strathcona and Aberdeen, two admirals, and the bishop of Columbia. At the banquet, Winston Churchill spoke of British Columbia's growth under McBride and elicited much laughter by recounting that, though McBride had invited him to British Columbia to kill a grizzly bear, "it might be a no less popular proposition if he had proposed that a grizzly bear from British Columbia should visit the United Kingdom on a contrary mission." Responding to a toast, McBride noted that the province had set aside 261,000 acres for a park on Vancouver Island to be named in Strathcona's honour and boasted that in 1912, the province would see "development easily unparalleled in her whole history and hardly equalled in any section of the British Empire."[70]

Although the banquet may have been the highlight of the visit, it was not the only important social occasion. Harry Brittain, the founder of the Empire Press Union, gave McBride and Margaret a dinner at the Savoy. Among the twenty-three guests were prominent journalists L.S. Amery and J.L. Garvin, and Sir Robert Baden-Powell, the founder of the Boy Scouts. Lord Strathcona, the Canadian high commissioner, gave a supper party, which McBride attended along with Laurier, several other premiers,

J.H. Turner, BC's agent-general, gave this banquet at the Savoy Hotel in honour of McBride. A photograph of the banquet was published in the *Colonist*, 3 September 1911. Royal BC Museum, BC Archives, G-04150.

and Bowser. He attended the Duke and Duchess of Sutherland's reception for fellows of the Royal Colonial Institute and the Coronation Ball given by the treasurer and masters of the bench of the Honorary Society of Gray's Inn. At Norton-Griffiths's country home, McBride and Margaret spent a weekend with other Canadians, including William and Lady Mackenzie of the CNR, Edmund and Lady Walker of the Canadian Bank of Commerce, and the Bowsers. They also enjoyed a week's holiday motoring through England and Scotland, passing through Oxford and its colleges, Stratford on Avon, St. Anne on Sea near Blackpool, and spending a night at Carlisle when the car broke down. In Scotland, they attended a Harry Lauder concert in Edinburgh, visited Culloden, where they picked heather, and of special interest to Margaret, saw monuments to Chief McGillivray and the clan. From Inverness, they returned to London. After the coronation, they briefly visited Belfast, Dublin, and Paris, where they

Margaret McBride in the gown she wore on being presented to the king. Royal BC Museum, BC Archives, B-01632.

saw the Panthéon, the prison where Marie Antoinette was jailed, the Louvre, and Versailles.[71]

On his last morning in London, McBride had breakfast with Churchill and O'Connor. He had enjoyed a grand holiday; the *Columbian* said he was "looking sunburnt" when he returned. Some British Columbians complained of the trip's $11,000 cost. Yet McBride had done some promotional work while in England: At the Royal Colonial Institute, he boasted of British Columbia's abundant and various natural resources, its prosperity, its fine public school system, and the imminent opening of its university. Hamar Greenwood, who visited Victoria a few months later, told the *Victoria Times* that McBride's work would stimulate investment and immigration. Norton-Griffiths came at the end of the year, seeking dock or railway contracts for his construction company and investment opportunities.[72]

When McBride reached Montreal, Borden and the Conservative hierarchy summoned him to Ottawa to urge him to run in the forthcoming federal election. Citing obligations at home, he deferred a decision. He told the press that all he knew about his candidacy was what he read in the papers, that he had not been offered a seat, but that, if one were offered, he would seriously consider it. In any event, he would go into the campaign with all his "might." As he headed west, he argued against reciprocity, pointing out that British financiers and politicians of both parties opposed it, and that American politicians had expressed annexationist sentiments. Echoing a national Conservative campaign theme, he declared, "We cannot afford to sell our birthright for a mess of pottage."[73] Like other Conservative premiers – Whitney of Ontario and Roblin of Manitoba – he vigorously campaigned for the national party and stressed both economic and imperial considerations.

Although reciprocity overshadowed the naval question in British Columbia, both election issues gave McBride many opportunities to exercise his strengthened enthusiasm for the empire. At a Conservative picnic near Victoria, at least two thousand people "from all walks of life" arrived by special trains and enjoyed games, a queen contest, and a baby show. The band welcomed McBride with a rendition of "Hail to the Chief," an ironic choice, given the theme of his speech for the day.[74] Against a backdrop that featured the word "Which?" flanked by a Union Jack and the Stars and Stripes, McBride gave an hour-long speech that developed campaign themes. He declared that British Columbians "are British to the core and British too in the best sense of worthy imperialism." It was necessary to tell Britain "that we are as Canadians still firm and strong for the empire, that we are going to keep as our flag the good old Union Jack." He charged that Americans did not enjoy the "full meaning of law, of liberty, of true equality in citizenship" experienced by those who lived under the Union Jack. In case an appeal to British patriotism was not sufficient to sway voters, he added that reciprocity would mean "the complete surrender by

WHY DIDN'T HE THINK OF THAT BEFORE?
Mr. McBride (at Conservative picnic) – It should be remembered that there are such things as vested interests with nations as with individuals and corporations, and that the vested interests of nations, real or alleged, are terribly binding upon the weaker party."

During the long 1911 federal election campaign, the *Times,* a Liberal paper, suggested that McBride was two-faced in vigorously campaigning against the Liberals' proposed reciprocity agreement with the United States since his government had assisted American lumbermen to acquire extensive timber and land rights in British Columbia. The tiny figure in the drawing is G.H. Barnard, the Conservative MP for Victoria. *Victoria Daily Times,* 21 August 1911, cartoonist, Wilson.

the free and independent producer of Canada to the combine and the clique and the trusts" of the United States, and that it would result in "the severance of Canada from the motherland and her fusion with the nation to the south."[75]

After speaking at several Conservative rallies on southern Vancouver Island, McBride and W.R. Ross travelled over fifteen hundred miles through the southern part of the province as far east as Fernie, speaking, albeit briefly, in almost every settlement en route. Conservative organizers expected that McBride and Ross would have a difficult time in Fernie and Rossland because reciprocity would benefit coke and lumber producers there. McBride stressed the evils of reciprocity, attacked the Laurier government for not restricting Asian immigration, and suggested that two retiring cabinet ministers were abandoning a "sinking ship." Occasionally, he referred to the naval question and linked it to British patriotism. The Vancouver meeting closed with the singing of "Rule Britannia."[76]

After Borden and the Conservatives won the election, the *Colonist* stated that much of McBride's success in delivering a "Solid Seven" of Conservatives to Ottawa could be attributed to "his thorough going belief in the empire." Elections, of course, are not won on rhetoric or emotion alone. McBride intervened to get out the Conservative vote. At the request of J.D. Taylor, the New Westminster candidate, he advised the manager of the local Bank of Montreal that three Victoria bank employees were registered in New Westminster, and he hinted that the Conservatives would be helped if they came to the Mainland to vote for Taylor. His intervention was probably unnecessary, for Taylor garnered almost twice as many votes as John Oliver, the Liberal candidate. Except in Victoria, where G.H. Barnard narrowly defeated William Templeman, the incumbent cabinet minister, and in Comox-Atlin, the Conservatives won by substantial margins. In the latter constituency, the railway contractors Foley, Welch and Stewart spent money "freely" on behalf of the Liberal candidate. Moreover, many of their workers were French Canadians who were solid for Laurier. In addition, since most of the food in the North was imported, the idea of cheap American food was appealing there, as were the prospects of future trade with Alaska.[77]

On election night in Victoria, a Tally-Ho (a horse-drawn bus), two brass bands, and torch bearers conducted Barnard and McBride through the streets to "tremendous" cheering. Once the celebration was over, McBride went fishing. Thus, when Borden sent him a telegram warmly inviting him to join the federal cabinet, Bowser received it. Borden "fully anticipated" that McBride would accept his offer and requested that he answer as soon as possible. In forwarding Borden's message to McBride, Bowser urged him not to reply until they had discussed the matter since McBride's response would "not only affect your own future but may seriously affect this party in B.C." He added that if McBride refused Borden's offer, "Vancouver will consider its claims should prevail over any other part of the province." This remark presumably meant that the BC cabinet post should go to G.H. Cowan, who had been elected in Vancouver. After a second urgent message, McBride replied that, when he visited Ottawa, he would explain why he could not accept the honour. He told Martin Burrell, who had urged him to join the cabinet, that "owing to the development of the Province and matters demanding my attention here, my place just now must be in B.C." To dispel widespread rumours, he informed the press that he would not be joining the federal cabinet. Burrell, "McBride's man," became British Columbia's representative in what McBride called "one of the strongest aggregations of talent" ever in charge of Canadian affairs.[78]

McBride's election rhetoric epitomized how Canadians of his generation could simultaneously be British imperialists and proud Canadian nationalists. With the election over, the naval issue reappeared in English Canada. At Trafalgar Day celebrations in Victoria, McBride said that people in Britain could not understand what he called "optional neutrality," the idea that one part of the empire could not be involved in an imperial conflict. He called "for an efficient fighting unit," which would sail under the Canadian flag on the Pacific and would also be part of the imperial navy. Catering to local concerns, he called for the rehabilitation of Esquimalt as "a strong naval base," with facilities for shipbuilding and repair, and he urged shipbuilders to recruit workers from "our own environment" to replace Asian labour. Rehabilitating Esquimalt was relevant. The Royal Navy had been gradually withdrawing from the base since 1905 and completed the transfer of the base to Canada in May 1911.[79]

Having delivered the BC vote to Borden in 1911, McBride promised that with "the new conditions" at Ottawa, his government would press its "legitimate claims." He had good grounds for optimism. In 1904, Borden had indicated that British Columbia's claim to Better Terms warranted "immediate inquiry and investigation." The long wish list that McBride and Bowser took to Ottawa included a request for a "competent tribunal" to investigate Better Terms and for legislation on Asian immigration, the Peace River lands, the adjustment of Indian reserves, the Point Grey site for the university, various harbour and navigation improvements, the fisheries, and a variety of public works. With W.R. Ross, who joined them in Ottawa, McBride and Bowser interviewed the governor general and federal cabinet ministers. McBride did not expect the immediate granting of his requests, but the *Colonist* reported that Borden had approved a commission to

A "WHITE MAN'S BURDEN"
Ministerial Press [*Victoria Colonist*] announces that on Wednesday next Hon. Richard McBride will leave for Ottawa for the purpose of presenting the case of the province to the prime minister.

After delivering all seven of BC's seats to Borden and the Conservatives, McBride headed to Ottawa with a long list of BC issues. The small man at the left is G.H. Barnard, who was re-elected as the Conservative MP for Victoria. *Victoria Daily Times,* 27 October 1911, cartoonist, Wilson.

investigate Better Terms, would discuss Asian immigration with the Colonial Office, and was expected to provide "satisfactory" answers on Indian reserves and other lands.[80]

Meanwhile, McBride turned the Ottawa visit into a family holiday. After a day in Montreal, where he saw T.G. Shaughnessy of the CPR, he consulted Mackenzie of the CNR and Hays of the GTP in New York City. There, he was met by Margaret, Mary, and Peggy, who had come to see the show at the Hippodrome. From New York, the family visited the mayor of New Orleans, whom McBride had met at the 1909 Alaska-Yukon-Pacific

Exposition in Seattle. He was much impressed by preparations for the opening of the Panama Canal. From New Orleans the family returned via the Southern Pacific.[81]

McBride told British Columbians that he and his party had been well received by Borden and that many long-standing problems were "on the eve of satisfactory settlement." The Dominion government agreed to refer all requests for concessions, grants, or special privilege, especially relating to foreshore rights, to the provincial cabinet for approval, and Bowser and Ross reached an amicable agreement on water rights in the railway belt. That development concerned the BCER, which concluded that it would be "more necessary" than "ever before to stand well with the Provincial authorities." Sam Hughes, the federal minister of militia, recommended giving British Columbia clear title to the land at Point Grey, the future site of the university, and was amenable to erecting a new drill hall in Victoria to replace one whose location interfered with a proposed expansion of the Parliament Buildings. In return, McBride promised to make provincial Crown lands available for military and naval purposes. Despite these advances, negotiating other land-related matters took a frustratingly long time. Ottawa did put some funds in the supplementary estimates to investigate fishing claims.[82]

Soon afterward, McBride told Conservatives convening in New Westminster that Borden had agreed to "an impartial tribunal of investigation" of Better Terms. Privately, he was frustrated that some federal cabinet ministers seemed suspicious of the province's claims. After he presented the correspondence relating to his mission to Ottawa, the Legislature unanimously endorsed the appointment of a Better Terms Commission. Alberni Liberal MLA H.C. Brewster's only criticism was that the Conservatives were using the commission for political capital and had no guarantee that it would redress grievances. The press was generally satisfied; even the *Sun*, the new Liberal newspaper in Vancouver, grudgingly credited McBride for securing the commission, though it suggested that, had he exercised more tact, he might have got it in 1906. A few days later, McBride, who had warned party members to prepare themselves, announced a provincial election. R.E. Gosnell arranged for the printing of 10,000 copies of a Better Terms pamphlet, which was actually a reprint of McBride's very partisan February 1912 speech to the Legislature in which he traced a history of the campaign, boasted of getting an amendment to the BNA Act to ensure that the province could continue to agitate, recalled Borden's promise of an inquiry into Better Terms, and quoted Churchill as saying "that it was not permissible for the authorities at Ottawa to practically dictate the business of the several provinces or frame an arrangement that was not in accord with the views of the interested provinces." The *News-Advertiser,* which was awarded the printing contract, hailed the McBride government for putting itself in a position "to reap the fruits of this long struggle" for provincial rights now that the government in Ottawa had changed.[83]

Railways, however, were the centrepiece of the 1912 provincial election. McBride had seemingly delivered on his railway promises of 1909. In February 1911, after long delays, he had turned the first sod on the CNR line on Vancouver Island and had predicted its completion within three years. Island residents were enthusiastic and wanted more than a ferry connection to the Mainland. The Victoria City Council and Board of Trade studied the prospect of bridging Seymour Narrows; Port Alberni Conservatives liked the idea of such a bridge but argued that their city, not Victoria, should be the terminus of the railway.[84]

At the same time, McBride was negotiating with the BCER for a more realistic railway project, an Interurban line to serve Victoria and the Saanich Peninsula. In 1910, he had driven the last spike on its electric railway, which ran through the Fraser Valley from Vancouver and New Westminster to Chilliwack. To persuade Victoria ratepayers to pass a bylaw protecting it from municipal competition for its light and power business, the BCER promised, among other things, to spend $250,000 on extending its local operations. The company did not deny a report that if the bylaw passed, it would build the Saanich Interurban even though it was unlikely to pay its way. When a rumour circulated that the line would not be built, McBride warned R.M. Horne-Payne, the British financier behind the BCER and chairman of its board of directors, that this would disastrously affect the BCER's standing in British Columbia. He also hinted at legal action if the line were not constructed. The company capitulated. McBride drove the last spike on 18 June 1913. As minister of railways, and conscious of island resentment of the Mainland, McBride rejected a BCER plan to charge four cents per mile on its Saanich Interurban (it charged only three cents in the Fraser Valley). The company responded with a request to raise its Mainland fares![85]

As in Saanich, the BCER and the provincial government had a symbiotic relationship. The company depended on the good will of the government, whereas the government could not afford to alienate Horne-Payne, who had considerable influence in the London money market, upon which the government, various provincial enterprises, and the new railways depended for funds. The lengthy negotiations over the company's franchises in Hastings Townsite and D.L. 301, two areas immediately adjacent to Vancouver, illustrate this well. The former covered approximately 3,360 acres; the latter, a "squared bit of No Man's land," consisted of about 160 acres. In 1908, in what McBride later told the BCER was an "improvident" act, Finance Minister Robert Tatlow, who was also a member of the BCER's Advisory Board, and F.J. Fulton, the chief commissioner of lands and works, had granted the company a perpetual franchise in both sites. The city was planning to annex the two areas but insisted that the franchises expire in 1919 in tandem with its own franchise. Fearing the establishment of a precedent, the BCER warned that reducing the duration of its franchises would make it difficult for "every enterprise doing business in British Columbia on the strength of provincial acts or franchises" to raise money in London. It also cited Ontario's virtual cancellation of the rights of the Ontario Development Company and the subsequent practical impossibility of raising money for any Ontario enterprise. In a handwritten letter to R.H. Sperling, the manager of the BCER, McBride asserted that the Ontario and BC cases were not similar and that the cabinet had carefully considered its decision to pass an Order-in-Council replacing the perpetual franchise with one that would expire in 1929.[86] Nevertheless, he was anxious to give "every encouragement to the company." When the BCER proposed a compromise – that its franchises be reduced to forty years – the cabinet made no change. The matter lay in abeyance for some months until Vancouver sought provincial legislation to make the franchises conform to its franchise. Bowser then indicated that the government would legislate to curtail the power of the BCER franchises. On the company's behalf, William Mackenzie, whose CNR also depended on Horne-Payne's money-raising skills, informed McBride that any change must be negotiated.[87] With the 1912 provincial election looming, McBride made no plans for immediate legislation. During the campaign, the Liberals attacked the government for failing to shorten the franchises. Bowser promised that they would be reduced to twenty-one years and intimated that if the company would not agree, the government would legislate. At Bowser's suggestion, McBride removed the matter from debate by having it announced that after the election, he would meet the BCER board in London with a view to settling the question on a "stand taken by Government and having in mind preservation [of] provincial credit and stability for investment."[88]

Meanwhile, the CNR was beginning to experience financial woes. By the end of January 1912, it had a line through the Fraser Valley to Chilliwack and had spent nearly $7 million in British Columbia but estimated that it needed about $120,000 per mile to build through the Fraser Canyon.

Although construction was proceeding well, selling bonds in London was difficult, partly because financiers were wary of McBride's talk of additional railways and issues of government guaranteed bonds. Mackenzie asked McBride to defer his railway legislation for a year or seek financial assistance from the federal government. McBride was unwilling to postpone his railway plans but asked Prime Minister Borden for a subsidy of $10,000 per mile, or approximately $6 million.[89] He did not get it.

Despite the CNR's difficulty in raising funds, McBride was keen for more railways, and during the 1912 election, his main railway focus was linking Vancouver with the GTP. The idea of a railway to the North dated from the time of the Klondike gold rush. One of the many railways incorporated at that time, the Vancouver, Westminster and Yukon, had built from Vancouver as far as New Westminster. In 1907, the GTP purchased its charter rights to build to the North and considered constructing the line once its main line was complete. However, on 6 September 1911, it informed McBride that it would not build the north-south link. Vancouver business people feared that the GTP would make northern British Columbia a tributary of Edmonton.[90] D'Arcy Tate, the GTP's solicitor, later claimed that McBride, who wanted the GTP to come to Vancouver, where it would compete with the CPR and the CNR, said he would present the Legislature with a measure to construct a line independent of the GTP. Tate ascertained that if he formed a railway company and worked with Foley, Welch and Stewart (FWS), a large firm of railway contractors, the GTP would make a traffic arrangement with it.[91] McBride told Tate that if the contractors "were responsible he would have no objection," but others, including his British friend John Norton-Griffiths, were interested in building it.[92] In return for a franchise for what became the PGE, Tate offered J.W. Stewart of FWS a quarter of the new company's stock and a $500,000 commission from which he was to cover disbursements. Under questioning in 1917, Tate admitted that "incidental expenses" were actually campaign funds, but he refused to provide any information except that they were for the Conservatives and were paid after he received the franchise and the PGE was incorporated.[93]

According to Tate, McBride told FWS that if the guarantee on its bonds were insufficient, he would try to help. On 24 November 1911, Tate wrote to McBride that FWS would build the line in return for a provincial guarantee of bonds and other terms similar to those in the province's contract with the CNR. That day, McBride informed the Conservative convention in Vancouver that he anticipated announcing comprehensive plans for "miles and miles" of railways and that the opening of the Panama Canal would permit the export of grain from the Peace River District. The usually well-informed *Province* understood that McBride was referring to a Fort George–Vancouver railway, a prospect endorsed by a convention resolution urging the construction of a railway from Vancouver to the Peace River. Through Martin Burrell, McBride initiated discussions with Ottawa about provincial control of freight rates.[94]

Speculation abounded regarding McBride's railway plans. His New Year's message predicted "a year of great development," and the Throne Speech forecast measures "to further encourage the building of railways" to meet "the increased demand for transportation facilities." McBride told Victoria's Canadian Club that seven hundred miles of track would be laid on Vancouver Island within three years, and he informed a Vancouver delegation that a railway to the Peace River would be part of his policy.[95]

Meanwhile, negotiations with the railway companies entered their final stages. On 10 February, the government agreed to guarantee principal and interest for the PGE's bonds to the extent of $35,000 per mile. Construction was to begin within six months, and the PGE would work with the GTP. The only cost estimate was J.W. Stewart's calculation, which was written on the back of an envelope. McBride was also negotiating with the CPR about extending its subsidiary, with the Esquimalt and Nanaimo (E&N), and with the KVR, which had announced plans for new lines in southern British Columbia.[96]

On 20 February, in what the *Province* described as "one of the secrets" of his hold on the party and his friendships "even with political opponents," McBride gave credit to colleagues and supporters, and mentioned the MLAs of the districts that would benefit from his new railway policy. The centrepiece was the PGE, which McBride called the first step toward a line to the Peace River. He insisted that the PGE was an entirely independent company "under the control of the government." Recognizing that other regions of the province also wanted new railways, McBride announced that the government would subsidize the KVR to the extent of $10,000 per mile to build through the Hope Mountains and bridge the Fraser River at Hope. This would complete the link between the railways of the Kootenay and Boundary Districts and the coast. The CNR was promised bond guarantees to extend its Vancouver Island line north to Comox and for a branch from Kamloops to Vernon and Lumby. The E&N would be extended to Courtenay, and the Kaslo and Slocan Railway would become a standard-gauge line. All told, the plan meant 860 new miles of railway.[97]

Response in the provincial press was enthusiastic. According to the *Vernon News,* the plan was "the best of good news for everybody in the province." Even the *Sun,* while complaining that McBride's speech contained too much of his "usual jollying tactics" and that a railway to the Peace River would not be provided immediately, asserted that most of his policies had already been advocated by Liberals. Most editors stressed local benefits while setting them in the context of the policy as a whole. The *Fort George Herald* predicted that the railway policy would "carry the district with a roar of approval." The *Nelson Daily News* was excited about the local benefits of the KVR and praised the other plans and provisions for their fair wages clause and the non-employment of Asians. The *Kamloops Standard* enthusiastically described the policy as "typical of the Province whose only thought is the progress and prosperity of the land." Its competitor the *Inland Sentinel* saw several features of local interest in the plan and admitted that no one was likely to attack it, "not because it is perfect but because railways are essential to development." The *Province* envisioned "an immense future" unfolding for Vancouver, and the *Colonist* predicted that the new Vancouver Island lines would lead to a direct rail connection with the Mainland via Seymour Narrows and proclaimed "the whole Dominion is fortunate in having at the head of affairs in British Columbia, a gentleman who is alive to the needs of the day." The only significant dissent came from Prince Rupert, where the editors of both daily papers thought that the PGE would satisfy "Vancouver's insatiable greed" and give the southern city, not Prince Rupert, the trade of the Peace River. H.C. Brewster, the only Liberal in the Legislature, welcomed the railways but correctly warned that the PGE was over-capitalized and that the agreement delivered "the stockholders over to the promoters." Similarly, the *Victoria Times* complained that the railways would have been built without assistance and that again the government had given "the corporations the big end of the deals while the country is made responsible for the price."[98]

To no one's surprise, McBride asked voters to confirm his policies in a provincial election. So likely was his victory that the Liberals did not run candidates in over half the constituencies and seriously considered doing the same in Vancouver. They simply questioned details in the railway plan, such as its failure to serve the Peace River, its apparent sellout to the "corporations," the size of land and mineral grants given to the PGE, and their concerns about payments to the CNR. They also attacked a careless land policy that let "foreign speculators" gain control of timber resources and the fact that the Public Accounts Committee failed to meet. Brewster

After his arrangements to bring the Canadian Northern Railway to British Columbia and to assist other lines in the southern Interior brought him electoral success in 1909, McBride went back to the people less than two and a half years later with another major railway plan, the construction of the Pacific Great Eastern Railway from Vancouver to Prince George. He was, indeed, a "Colossus of Roads." The cartoonist, however, took some licence with McBride's promises – he did not propose to build a bridge from the Mainland to Vancouver Island. *The Week,* 9 March 1912, unknown cartoonist. Royal BC Museum, BC Archives, B-08199.

promised such measures as women's suffrage, prohibition of the liquor traffic, Local Option, revised land laws, workmen's compensation, and municipal reform. A few days before the election, however, he admitted the "hopelessness" of his position.[99]

When the Liberal press complained of the "unbridled, unrestrained, and unjustifiable abuse of power" demonstrated by an election that McBride had called solely to circumvent public opinion, the *Province* asserted that the election would let citizens satisfy themselves about the railways that would make fertile areas accessible and link the coast with the "distant stretches" of the province. McBride, of course, had long recognized that British Columbia consisted of a number of regions, and part of his political success relied on visiting the settled areas of the province and having all districts share in developmental projects. His new railway plan provided something for most of them and filled in gaps left from the 1909 program. A few communities did feel left out, however. The Revelstoke Board of Trade was disappointed that no provision was made for the link with Yellowhead Pass, which McBride had promised in 1909. McBride counselled patience and promised to give the matter "careful consideration." Residents of Stewart, on the Alaska border, circulated a petition against a policy that favoured the South; they thought their town should be the port for the Peace River. In the northcentral Interior, the PGE was popular. The *Fort George Herald* welcomed it as meeting British Columbia's "most pressing needs," particularly since it would mean "railroad transportation from Vancouver" and increased appropriations for roads, trails, and bridges. The rival *Tribune* was not impressed by the local Conservative candidate but could not "conscientiously" oppose a government that guaranteed the Fort George–Vancouver railway. People along the GTP route expected to benefit from a line to the Peace River and from railway development generally. So too did Vancouver real estate agents, who began promoting Peace River land.[100]

In Victoria, McBride boasted that in a few years, Vancouver Island would have a thousand miles of railway running from Victoria to its northern tip and a ferry service that would be "the best of its kind" as he flattered the "intelligent and energetic" people of the island, who had created "one of the proudest possessions of the whole Empire." Lest Victorians fail to appreciate the new Mainland railways, he reminded them that the KVR and the PGE would bring them closer to the hinterland and give their city "every opportunity side by side with Vancouver for a fair exchange of trade." In an interview he hinted that the Bute Inlet connection (via

Seymour Narrows) was not "far off" and expressed optimism about the future of Victoria and the Mainland cities.[101]

Given the time required to visit the North, McBride and Bowser, who travelled as a team, confined their two-and-a-half-week election tour to the South, although McBride personally donated $250 to party funds to assist in sending an organizer to Prince Rupert. Physically, the 1912 campaign was less exhausting than its predecessors, with almost all travel by rail or steamer. Despite expecting to win some seats by acclamation, McBride insisted that "every exertion will be put forth so that the country will be fully apprised of all the details" of his platform.[102] Though he focused on railways, he did not ignore local issues.

At Kamloops, the first major stop, about a third of his ninety-minute speech dealt with railway policy. He stressed that it was not intended solely to benefit the province but was a Canadian and imperial project, and he assured his audience that the CNR would enter its city. Calling the Liberal platform a joke, he wondered why the Liberals had not promised "free motor cars and perhaps flying machines." He suggested that the Liberals favoured women's suffrage out of "desperation" and that British Columbia, "with its many pressing problems," might let one of the older provinces try the suffrage experiment. From Kamloops, McBride and Bowser headed to Field, the most easterly point on the CPR's BC main line. There, McBride took credit for political stability and said that the railways were being built in anticipation of the boom that would follow the opening of the Panama Canal. He admitted the impossibility of pleasing the Socialists on labour matters but added that a Royal Commission on Labour was seeking practical improvements. Adopting the recommendations of a Royal Commission on Taxation, he announced the abolition of the poll tax. Much of his time in Field was spent trying to resolve a conflict over the Conservative nomination. He shook hands with everyone and suggested that they eat breakfast before discussing the matter, but he could not persuade Harold Forster, a wealthy rancher, to withdraw in favour of Henry Parson, the incumbent, who had won the party's nomination. He told the press that a party could not be "efficiently organized unless there is unanimity," a message he repeated at Golden. Privately, he told Parson that he was the official nominee but that if Forster were elected, he would accept his support.[103] Columbia voters preferred Forster.

At 2:00 A.M., the party left Golden via the CPR, had breakfast in Revelstoke, boarded the train to Arrowhead, and took the steamer to Nakusp, where, from the steamer's deck, they spoke of how the area's mines

Given that railways were the centrepieces of McBride's 1909 and 1912 election platforms, it was appropriate that he should tour the Interior by rail. Flanking McBride are Attorney General Bowser (at left) and Thomas Abriel, a resident of Nakusp. Royal BC Museum, BC Archives, A-01415.

and fruit orchards had benefited from the renewal of the Slocan and Sandon Railway. From Nakusp, they travelled to Rosebery on the Nakusp & Slocan Railway, and then south on Slocan Lake. All along the lake, people gathered to greet them. Speeches were not on the agenda for New Denver, but, responding to the crowd's request, McBride and Bowser gave short ones. From Slocan, the train took them to Nelson, where a brass band and many citizens welcomed them; about two thousand people attended a meeting in the Opera House. Perhaps in light of the day-long journey, which a *Province* reporter described as being fine for tourists but roundabout for business, McBride announced that his railway plans were not complete and that he hoped to introduce CNR competition to the Kootenays and the Okanagan. He bragged of forcing the CPR to build competitive roads. Of course, he pointed to the value of the KVR to the Kootenays. In addition, he mentioned the satisfactory settlement of a conflict over the Conservative nomination, the favourable economic situation, the Asian question, Better Terms, and improved relations with Ottawa. From Nelson, McBride and Bowser took the train to Trail. After lunch and an inspection of a bridge and a school that were under construction, they spoke at the opera house. Trail had a Socialist candidate, so McBride asserted that the Conservatives "ruled for the good of the people regardless of class or creed." There should be no talk of "wage slaves and class consciousness" in a province where "one day you may see a man wielding a pick and shovel and the next day in charge of a business of his own." That, he insisted, "is why the people come to this country because it is a land of opportunity, and so our people do not lean towards the doctrines that only tend to make trouble and ill-advised mischief."[104]

After resting on Sunday, McBride and Bowser spent a day in Kaslo, the home of McBride's "great friend" R.F. Green, and attended a luncheon with about a hundred guests, even though the Conservative candidate was elected by acclamation. The luncheon card featured a picture of Kaslo with the caption "Whose prosperity is ensured by the McBride railway policy." McBride boasted of getting the CPR to take over the Kaslo and Slocan Railway, which the GNR had abandoned after forest fires destroyed many trestles and bridges. That development, he predicted, would increase Kaslo's population fivefold in a few years. As for Tupper's recent attack on his railway policy as "reckless speculation," McBride simply said, "The people will deal with him." At an evening meeting, he spoke of the local benefits of the tourist trade.[105]

From Kaslo he went to the East Kootenay. At Fernie, a coal-mining town, he focused on what the government had done for working men and announced that a royal commission would soon investigate the problems of labour, a point that he repeated elsewhere. From there, the campaigners headed west to Cranbrook, where McBride said that Mackenzie and Mann had discussed extending the CNR into the Kootenays. At Grand Forks and a brief reception with Ernest Miller, who had been elected by acclamation, McBride referred to the benefits brought by the KVR to the city, in which he personally owned real estate. At nearby Greenwood, he refused to let the Socialist candidate speak, because "the people are getting tired of listening to the same old story and putting up monthly dues to support a lot of itinerants filled with Karl Marx and Wilshire."[106] This outburst, said the *Vancouver Sun,* was a "typical illustration of his despotic methods of treating opponents when he believes he has the crowd behind him." The Greenwood audience, however, was keen to ask questions. In response to these questions, McBride dealt with the fortnightly wage bill, which was of concern to working men there, promised to pay off the debts of the M&VR, and said that workmen's compensation should provide for foreign dependents. However, he was not prepared to deal with women's suffrage and had always voted against it.[107]

At Penticton, where L.W. Shatford had been acclaimed, McBride summarized his railway policy – "Instead of paper, now you get the steel." That steel was the KVR. A few weeks earlier, the *Penticton Herald* had been pleased to report that with McBride's help, Shatford, the managing director of the Southern Okanagan Land Company, had persuaded the KVR to build through Princeton, even though it would be expensive. McBride also expected the GNR to build into the city from Oroville, Washington.[108]

Not all Okanagan voters were happy with McBride's railway policy. Price Ellison admitted that the KVR would not directly benefit Kelowna. The *Kelowna Courier and Okanagan Orchardist* regarded the KVR as "a weird kind of road," which was known as the "Hot Air" line because of the "airy schemes" of its promoters. By 1912, the KVR had completed only three disjointed sections totalling eighty-three miles of track. The Kelowna Board of Trade favoured a link with the GNR and access to the coast via Wenatchee in Washington State. As for railways, McBride barely mentioned the KVR while he was in Kelowna, denied having anything against the CPR, and focused on the CNR, which he described as a provincial, national, and imperial project. Noting that people wanted competition and that the Prairies had greatly advanced once the CNR was built, he said that the CNR would soon reach Kelowna. Bowser, who dealt with the women's suffrage issue, thought that in fifty to a hundred years, the government would give women the vote. At a crowded meeting in Vernon,

McBride said that his 1909 promises in respect to the CNR and KVR were being fulfilled, that the two railways would be competitors, and that Vernon would grow five- or sixfold in a few years. As well as offering a "second instalment" of the railway policy, he stressed that the government had spent $400,000 the previous year on irrigation projects in the district, described his success with Better Terms, noted the need for more public works, and expressed his desire to keep the province a "white man's country."[109]

Before returning to the coast via Merritt, McBride stopped briefly at Ashcroft and suggested that Liberal claims of the CNR assuming alarming bonded indebtedness simply showed the desperation of the Liberal campaign. On the Lower Mainland, he made an early stop at Ladner in Delta. There too he concentrated on local issues, in this case the Japanese, since Japanese fishermen were a strong presence in the area. Asserting that "people of our own race should be in charge of our seaboard," he declared that "the little yellow men were in such complete control of the fishing that they know every nook and cranny of our seacoast from the 49th parallel to Alaska." Asserting that "if trouble should arise they know more of conditions than our own people," he demanded stronger defences on the Pacific coast.[110]

The next evening was busy. At the Vancouver Opera House, he described Vancouver as "the nerve centre of provincial politics" and referred to the navy, the Pacific, and a new Anglo-Japanese Treaty of Commerce and Navigation to which Canada had not yet acceded. Afterward, he took what must have been a harrowing fifteen-minute automobile ride to New Westminster, given the twelve-mile distance and the state of the road. There, he forecast prosperity for his hometown as a result of its natural advantages and, of course, new railways. So strong was Conservative sentiment that the traditionally Liberal *New Westminster Daily News* reported that a number of Liberals had attended McBride's meeting; its election eve editorial conceded that the Conservatives would win with a large majority.[111]

On Vancouver Island, McBride dealt with railways, the Asian question, and local issues. At Nanaimo he explained that his government had vetoed a bill to incorporate a tramway there because no tramway had succeeded in a city of Nanaimo's size, and it was "his duty to save Nanaimo from rushing into what must end in bankruptcy for itself." In Nanaimo and other constituencies where organized labour was politically significant, he referred to his support for an eight-hour day and improved workmen's compensation. Declaring that his railway policy was national and imperial as well as provincial, he was willing "at any time" to take up the matter of building railway branches to Nanaimo. In Victoria and at Sidney, he briefly described his tour, from which he had returned "looking somewhat tired and worn out," and he confidently spoke of the industrial future of Vancouver Island, summarized his past accomplishments, and stressed the importance of new railways because of the forthcoming opening of the Panama Canal.[112]

McBride returned to Victoria confident of winning all forty-two seats despite a squabble in Esquimalt, where two Independent Conservatives were running against R.H. Pooley. Apparently, after "free whiskey" had been offered at local saloons on his behalf, Pooley had been nominated at the official Conservative convention, which J.H.S. Matson of the *Colonist* privately called "the worst political farce ever held in the province."[113] Overall, the Conservatives won almost 60 percent of the popular vote, and only the Socialist vote in Nanaimo and Newcastle spoiled a sweep. About 10:00 P.M. on election night, a procession, headed by some members of the Fifth Regiment's band in mufti and followed by torch bearers, hacks, and motor cars, gathered at Conservative headquarters in Victoria. When McBride emerged, the crowd cheered, honked horns and other instruments, and marched down Government Street to the Colonist Building, where, after waiting several minutes for quiet, McBride told them that British Columbia "will forge ahead as she has never done before." The *Times* reluctantly conceded that the celebration was "an eloquent tribute to the genius of the statesman who, nine years ago, when receiving the congratulations of his friends over his first election as Premier said 'the thing is to get in, and when you are in to stay in.'" "If he fails to make good," it added, "the entire responsibility must rest upon himself."[114]

6

The Beginning of the End, 1912-14

I shall go to greater advocacy of British Columbia and to the continuance of the safe and proper lines that have done and are doing so much to upbuild and strengthen this most promising portion of his Majesty's empire.

– *Richard McBride,* Colonist, *12 October 1912*

In 1912, McBride was at the peak of his career. Railway construction was proceeding, and the promise of more railways had produced an overwhelming electoral victory. Provincial revenues for the fiscal year ending in March reached $10,745,708 and were rising. Mineral production recorded an all-time high value of $32,440,800. The presence of a friendly Conservative government in Ottawa improved prospects for Better Terms. Not only was McBride British Columbia's undisputed leader but he was being courted as a potential national leader or imperial statesman. He was knighted in 1912, but happy times soon ended. As domestic problems mounted, McBride spent much of his waning energy on national and imperial matters, though often relating them to provincial interests. Yet he remained optimistic. He told a provincial Conservative convention in January 1914 that "the crying need of the day is more faith and optimism."[1]

In the summer of 1912, the Canadian Pacific Railway (CPR) was double tracking its line west of Winnipeg and building branches in the Kootenays and on Vancouver Island. McBride expected the Great Northern (GNR) to build through the Hope Mountains. Neither company had a government subsidy. He boasted of the "splendid financial status" that enabled the province to assist the Canadian Northern (CNR), Pacific Great Eastern (PGE), and Kettle Valley (KVR) Railways, and predicted an expenditure of over $100 million on railway construction in the next four years. The *Times*' observation that railway policy was "becoming more and more reckless" seemed mere partisanship. During his visit in the summer of 1912, McBride found a "magnificent country" along the CNR line in the North Thompson Valley that could support a "teeming population tilling the rich fields." After a fall tour, he made similar reports about the Kootenays and the Okanagan. The next spring, a special CNR train took him, the lieutenant-governor, and others to the end of steel opposite Spuzzum, in the Fraser Canyon. A few weeks later, he asserted that the province had not put up a single dollar for the CNR and that if "anything happened prejudicial" to the company, "some other company would take it up at once, as it was the best built line in the province" and would compete with the CPR.[2]

But not all was well. When the radical Industrial Workers of the World (IWW) organized a strike among CNR construction workers to protest unsatisfactory wages and unsanitary camps, the province found itself spending about $800 a day to preserve the peace.[3] McBride also had to deal with communities such as Kamloops that were unhappy with the route of the CNR.[4] Impatient Victorians phoned "at all hours" to ask about the CNR route into the city. "If I could settle this question by some process of magic," McBride told the Victoria Real Estate Exchange, "I would have done so long ago." When the CNR announced that its ferry terminal would be at Union Bay (Patricia Bay, approximately twenty-seven kilometres north of Victoria), the *Times* recalled that, in 1909, Victorians had been urged to vote for McBride and "an all-rail connection with the Mainland." It also reminded its readers of McBride's promise to resign if Victorians could not "board a palace car here and never leave it until they find themselves in Montreal."[5]

In the spring of 1912, some Victoria residents presented a memorial to the federal government requesting that it build a rail bridge across Seymour Narrows to give Vancouver Island direct rail connection with the rest of Canada. When McBride mentioned this in passing as he was leaving for England, the *Vancouver Sun*, a Liberal paper, engaged in a bit of civic boasting as it described Victoria as a "charming city" whose lack of harbour facilities precluded any of its hopes of taking trade from Vancouver. Nevertheless, Bowser was sufficiently concerned to advise

McBride that it would not take much to create "a nasty Mainland and Island controversy."[6]

That matter soon blew over, but Vancouver residents did have a grievance that, though minor in significance, also illustrated the persistence of regional rivalries in the province. In 1912, the province had opened a new courthouse in Vancouver (currently the home of the Vancouver Art Gallery). The city wanted the province to give it the site of the old courthouse, which was in the heart of the downtown retail district, as "a breathing space," but McBride refused to transfer this "piece of ground that is worth so much money" to the city and did not reply to its proposal that it might buy the site for $250,000. Even the friendly *News-Advertiser* criticized his assertion that the government spent more in Greater Vancouver than it took in. McBride felt "badly" that his comments had been found offensive but added that the courthouse site did not justify the "slightest crisis." He won no favour for himself in Vancouver, and Liberal papers elsewhere objected to any gift being made to Vancouver at the cost of the whole province.[7]

McBride's railway policies, once his major endeavour to serve most settled parts of the province, were now his chief concern. Financial stringency helped settle one problem but caused major worries. A shortage of funds did end the competition between the Vancouver, Victoria and Eastern (VV&E), a GNR subsidiary, and the KVR, a CPR subsidiary, for a route through the Hope Mountains, where steep hillsides towered above the narrow valley floor. After McBride mediated, the companies agreed to share running rights through the Coquihalla Pass. As the economy declined, they extended the area of shared running rights. Because this route bypassed Aspen Grove, McBride's old nemesis, Charles Hibbert Tupper, protested on behalf of British clients who planned to sell farmlands there. McBride pointedly chastised British investors who bought land on the basis of railway maps. Elevation made Aspen Grove unsuitable for agriculture. McBride was anxious to have the KVR built. On one occasion, he and KVR president J.J. Warren stayed up until 3:00 A.M. to discuss problems with a subcontractor.[8]

All seemed well with the PGE, the feature of the 1912 election campaign; its problems would become apparent later. In the spring and summer of 1912, it had sufficient funds to finance construction at least until year's end. A contract was let to Patrick Welch of the contracting firm Foley, Welch and Stewart (FWS) to build the line from Vancouver to Fort George. Under McBride's "surveillance," the PGE bought out the interests of the Howe Sound and Northern Railway, which had surveyed much of the route. The *Colonist*'s comment about McBride's "surveillance" inspired the *Times* to question the role of the minister of railways, Thomas Taylor, in overseeing the project. It was a telling question. Taylor claimed that he had learned that Welch and FWS were "one and the same" only during the course of an investigation by a legislative committee in 1917. Bowser and F.C. Gamble, chief engineer of the provincial department of railways, recalled that "McBride, not Taylor, seemed to be in charge of the whole situation." Those testifying in 1917 were protecting themselves, and the absent McBride, who was in London, constituted an easy scapegoat. Allegedly, he oversaw the construction of the PGE, but he was frequently absent from the province, cost overruns occurred, government friends received subcontracts, and contractors were paid without evidence of work being done.⁹

Early in 1913, McBride informed the Legislature that the PGE would complete its line from Vancouver to Fort George in two years. Although he would not aid its extension to the Peace River until the line to Fort George was well under way, he believed that "Alaska, the Yukon and northern British Columbia make up a veritable wonderland." He told the governor of Alaska that British Columbia would not hesitate to pledge "the credit of our country to the end" and informed Franklin Lane, the American secretary of state, that he could easily approach Prime Minister Borden, his "close personal friend," about extending the line to Alaska. Lane offered to cooperate "in any practicable way," and he and McBride met in Washington in November 1913. McBride had suggested promoting the railway for defence purposes, but now he proposed that Canada and the United States commemorate the forthcoming centennial of their peace by guaranteeing $40 to $50 million of bonds to build a northern extension of the PGE as part of a line from Alaska to Panama. A delighted *Fort George Herald* described British Columbia's needs as "first, last and all the time, railroads, and then more railroads."¹⁰

McBride was pleased when President Woodrow Wilson told Congress of the need for a railway to Alaska and signed a bill to fund a line from Seward to Fairbanks. In congratulating Lane and the governor of Alaska, McBride suggested linking British Columbia and Alaska. He arranged for J.W. Stewart of the PGE to meet a Tacoma lawyer who represented unnamed Americans who were interested in such a line. The *Colonist* praised McBride's "splendid vision," but the *Province* realistically observed the lack of enthusiasm for increased bond guarantees and national concern about the railway situation, and the *Times* feared that Seattle would benefit at the expense of Vancouver and Victoria. McBride was disappointed by

British Columbians' apparent inability "to grasp the magnitude of the American programme and what it means to us." Early in 1914, however, the Legislature approved the guarantee of 4.5 percent bonds for $35,000 for each of the 330 miles of the line from Fort George to the Peace River in order to forestall Alberta's expansion in the Peace River District. The drying up of financial markets ended that plan.[11]

McBride's northern vision included annexing Yukon to British Columbia. He thought it possible to overcome the difficulties, which included the preference of mining companies for Yukon mining laws, the existence of separate (government-funded denominational) schools in Yukon, and the integration of federal public servants into the provincial service. Because annexation would require an amendment to the BNA Act, Borden advised consultation with British Columbia's senators. In Yukon, a large public meeting in Dawson City protested annexation. Nothing further was heard of annexation in McBride's time.[12]

McBride's promotion of a railway to Alaska may have inspired the University of California at Berkeley to award him an honorary degree to represent the joining of "hands between the two typical states of the Pacific Coast." Despite his comments regarding reciprocity in the 1911 federal election and his criticisms of an American plan to discriminate against British vessels using the Panama Canal, McBride told American conventioneers meeting in Victoria that "the international boundary line is really only an imaginary one ... The latch string is out as far as British Columbia is concerned; come in and help yourselves." He welcomed American settlers and investors but put his greetings in a national and imperial context by saying that the more they came to Canada, "the more they would learn to appreciate the meaning of the British flag and all that it stood for in the way of protection and justice."[13]

Even before the Balkan wars began, the London money markets, the main source of investment in British Columbia and a very tangible part of the British connection, were tightening. In June 1912, R.M. Horne-Payne informed McBride that it was "almost impossible to sell public securities" because of the "enormous demand for money" from every Canadian city. Nonetheless, McBride remained optimistic. In October, he told the Beaver Club, an invitation-only club within the Victoria Conservative Association, that the province had $18 million in "liquid assets." Critics noted that two-thirds of this was money owing on land sales. A week later, at the provincial Conservative convention, he described the province's financial situation "as never better" and forecast the abolition of the personal revenue tax and reductions of other taxes. The 1913 budget echoed his optimism but predicted that expenditures would exceed revenues by $7 million. As for tax reductions, Finance Minister Price Ellison offered the immediate abolition of the poll tax and the eventual abolition of direct taxes once the government could rely completely on revenue from its natural resources. Alas, with financial depression, revenues in 1913 were much lower than expected. The *News-Advertiser* exaggerated in saying that the province had "no net debt, but rather an excess of assets." Despite heavy investments in public works, the net debt, which had fallen to slightly over $8 million in 1912-13, had soared to almost $18 million by 1914-15. Neither amount included guarantees of railway bonds.[14]

R.M. Horne-Payne caused a public stir in June 1913 by warning investors that Canadian municipalities were borrowing more than they could afford. In what the *Colonist* conceded was an extremely sanguine speech, McBride told Vancouver's Progress Club that he "invariably" found Horne-Payne "to be strong in his confidence in British Columbia" and unlikely to say anything that could "impair in the slightest degree the high standing that the municipalities of British Columbia enjoy." In August, just as he was departing for London "to get more money into the country for development," McBride viewed "the municipal situation with an indulgent calm, satisfied that everything is all right." But everything was not all right, and he knew it. In January 1913, he had been obliged to intercede with the Bank of British North America when Victoria had experienced trouble in raising funds for routine activities. And he had had to tell the Burrard Inlet Tunnel and Bridge Company, which wanted to bridge Vancouver's Second Narrows, of the difficulty of raising funds in Britain.[15]

Nevertheless, speculation continued. The weekend editions of the Vancouver newspapers printed pages of investment opportunities in such "coming communities" as Hardy Bay (at the north end of Vancouver Island) and Grand Forks, which would soon be the home of seven railways! So exaggerated were some advertisements that *Toronto Saturday Night* urged the province to supervise them to protect investors. When W.R. Arnold, the managing director of the Dominion Trust Company, reported that *Moody's Magazine,* an American financial paper, would publish an article saying that "the ill-advised railway policy of the Victoria government favours the real estate speculator at the expense of the settler," McBride declined to protest the "exceedingly unfair" article but considered ways of refuting it. Early in 1914, the Dominion Trust issued a handsome pamphlet printed on rich cream-coloured paper, probably designed to attract British investors, which declared, "The protection to shareholders, clients, and depositors of trust companies in British Columbia is very complete and the Government is constantly augmenting those safeguards." Soon afterward, McBride admitted that "wildcatters" had created a poor impression of BC land, timber, and mining properties for British investors.[16] Unfortunately, this realization had come too late.

In the spring of 1913, as his own investments suggest, McBride was still optimistic about the economy. Despite a slowing in real estate sales, he predicted an early turnaround after the current "little check" did "the country good" and enabled real estate to "find its true value." Putting on a good face was necessary to attract British investors. After his extended visit to London in 1913, the province issued £310,000 in six-month treasury notes at 5.5 percent, which he expected to tide the government over while it waited to collect delinquent taxes and built public works to relieve unemployment.[17] He discussed municipal loans with John Burns, the British cabinet minister in charge of local government, and studied the British Local Government Act. After returning home, he told the Vancouver Chamber of Commerce of England's "abounding faith" in the province as "a wonderfully strong and solvent community." He forecast greater prosperity with the new railways and the Panama Canal. Nevertheless, while still in London, he had cabled Acting Premier Henry Esson Young, "In view of finances ... urge strictest economy in all departments."[18]

In response to complaints about the public accounts, the government had passed an Audit Act in 1913 and appointed William Allison as auditor general. After working for the Bank of British Columbia and its successor the Canadian Bank of Commerce as well as briefly for the New Westminster Land Registry Office, Allison had become a government agent at Hazelton. The *Omineca Miner* described him as "a capable administrator, fulfilling the manifold and often difficult duties of his position here in a manner as to gain the respect of all." Liberals admitted his experience but suspected that a major qualification for his appointment to the position of auditor general was his marriage to McBride's sister, Gertrude. His published annual reports tended to deal with minutiae such as small accounts rejected by Treasury Board. Yet, he also offered advice. In December 1913, he warned that "the magnitude in which expenditures are now exceeding the revenues of the Province" made it necessary to curtail expenses. He suggested cancelling the appointments of 300 temporary clerks and rehiring only those whose services were "absolutely essential." McBride ordered government departments to shorten their publications, except technical ones, to save money.[19]

"Looted"

Old Mother Hubbard, she went to the cupboard to get her poor dog a bone; but when she got there the cupboard was bare, and so the poor dog got none.

As the economy collapsed, British Columbians accused McBride of squandering provincial resources on graft, such as the commission paid to J.H.S. Matson of the *Victoria Colonist* for negotiating the Songhees land transfer and the generous guarantee of the bonds that Mackenzie and Mann hoped to sell to pay for the construction of the Canadian Northern Railway. The Cartoonist, John (Jack) Innes, claimed that McBride had denied assistance to "legitimate industry." Meanwhile, echoing one of his favourite phrases, McBride looks over the bare cupboard with "indulgent calm." *Vancouver Sun*, 29 September 1913.

The economic situation deteriorated rapidly. Early in 1914, McBride informed caucus of his intention to raise a loan for such capital expenditures as roads, bridges, and the university until money eased, revenues rose, and delinquent royalties and taxes were paid. Publicly, he said that the province was in "splendid" financial shape and that an issue of treasury notes in December was merely "precautionary" in case of unexpected expenses. He admitted that arrears in land sales amounted to almost $10 million but pointed out that the money was earning 6 percent and that calling it in would inflict unwarranted hardships on investors. He warned that letting the city of Sandon, a fading mining town in the Selkirk Mountains, go bankrupt would imperil the credit of all municipalities. Through the Canadian Bank of Commerce, he negotiated a $10 million loan in London, of which about a quarter was subscribed in New York. The 1914 budget blamed problems on the unexpected worldwide financial stringency. It raised taxes on salmon canners, banks, and mines but reduced some direct taxes and introduced more flexible fees for the lumber industry.[20] The new taxes did not make up the shortfall, however, so the Legislature authorized borrowing up to $10 million for public works and additional aid to the railways.[21]

The railways had serious problems. In the spring of 1912, McBride denied rumours that the CNR had not paid the first instalment of its bond interest. Less than a year later, the Legislature increased the limit on bonds for the CNR's terminal facilities. The province had a first mortgage. McBride also brought in a bill to let the CNR abandon plans to build to English Bluff (Tsawwassen), though the line to Steveston and the ferry to Union Bay on the Saanich Peninsula would still go ahead. The *Colonist* saw "no likelihood" that the province would have to cover the interest and claimed that "the increase in the public liability will be more apparent than real." The *Times* presciently warned British Columbians to "piously hope that they do not have to pay the piper."[22]

Donald Mann complained that the CNR could probably sell an issue of 4.5 percent bonds only with a discount (PGE bonds were selling at 4 percent). McBride discovered that only $3 million remained in the account from which the government transferred funds to the CNR as construction progressed. The CNR did not know whether it would have the funds to complete the line, even though the Borden government gave it a $10,000 per mile cash subsidy in 1912 for the line from Yellowhead Pass to the mouth of the Fraser River. McBride denied that the federal government would acquire the CNR because of its financial difficulties but said that if it did, British Columbia would still have the railway.[23] When stories surfaced that work on the CNR and the PGE would stop, McBride called them "canards," claimed that the province's record of railway construction was "unequalled anywhere in the world," and stated that the railways would fulfill their contracts "to the very letter." A *Sun* reporter thought he was trying to avoid "unpleasant truths and excuse the failures of his recent administration." In reporting that the Legislature would be asked for another $25 million for the CNR and at least $15 million for the PGE, the *Times* warned that "a staggering load of liabilities amounting to $100,000,000" had been incurred in a little over three years.[24]

In December 1913, "dumbfounded" by the cost of building in British Columbia, Donald Mann asked for funds to complete the CNR line, buy rolling stock and steamships, and make the province and the company "much safer in every way." Money was so short that his partner, William Mackenzie, wanted to halt work on Vancouver Island. Should that occur, Mann realized that the Legislature might not approve more funding. He wanted an additional $15,000 per mile guarantee of second mortgage bonds for the main line and for the island and Okanagan branches since without a government guarantee, raising money was almost impossible. McBride introduced a bill in a half-empty House just before its 6:00 P.M. closing. According to one story, he had planned to wait until the dying days of the session before doing so, but the CNR's urgent problems forced his hand. A more likely explanation for the timing of his "thunderbolt" bill was a leak to the press gallery. The bill offered an additional $10,000 per mile for a total guarantee of $45,000 per mile, which meant a provincial obligation of almost $23 million. The reduction from the $15,000 per mile requested by the CNR to $10,000 may have been a compromise to satisfy caucus. The *Times* reported that in introducing the bill, McBride was "quite plainly not himself ... He looked worried and ill at ease." When Dr. George McGuire, a Vancouver MLA, opposed further aid to the CNR, some interpreted this as a sign of caucus discontent. In a meeting that lasted past midnight, a delegation of Conservative Vancouver businessmen, headed by C.M. Woodworth, told McBride to drop the bill to aid the CNR and another to assist the PGE or "face the ruin of the party." McBride, said the *Sun,* had "an absolutely haunted" look but persuaded the delegates, except Woodworth, to support the guarantee. In the Legislature the next day, McBride spoke for over an hour, answering complaints of construction delays, of a standard on the island that was a "joke," and of a "jerry-built" main line that gave "an utterly false impression" of the government's policy and the cost of railway construction. He blamed the impossibility of foreseeing financial stringency and a decision to build the railway to a higher standard. Because the Conservatives had a majority in the House, the bill passed easily but without enthusiasm. Even McGuire voted for the loan, persuaded by McBride's speech to the Vancouver delegation and his promise to seek further aid for the CNR in Ottawa as well as his own realization that opinion in Vancouver was "mercurial."[25]

The sycophantic *Colonist* noted the "high tone of optimism" and inspired delivery of McBride's speech. Citing his railway policy as "an example of courage, foresight, and an abiding faith in the province," it cheerfully observed that without spending "a single dollar out of the Provincial exchequer" or granting "a single acre of Crown domain," the province would have a new transcontinental railway within six months. The Liberal press complained that British Columbia was "hopelessly mortgaged," and even the usually friendly *Province* questioned its ability to afford more liabilities. A stanza by an anonymous versifier read

> Now it's all very well for these paid politicians.
> And affluent holders of party positions;
> From the struggle for bread they're entirely immune;
> While we pay the piper, and they call the tune.
> And it's fine sending up these financial skyrockets
> When the money comes out of the other man's pockets
> If the voters are wise, they'll git rid of the clan
> Of Bowser-McBride-Mackenzie & Mann.[26]

Mann thought that the amount offered was insufficient to complete the line, but McBride was becoming cautious. He wanted an additional security of $10 million worth of CNR stock, and a few days later, he asked Mann to immediately send funds for the False Creek terminal to Vancouver and to employ as many local men as possible to relieve unemployment. When the money did not arrive, McBride warned of his "extreme embarrassment." By July, False Creek property owners complained of having "been crucified to accommodate" the CNR and of being unpaid for their foreshore rights.[27]

In endorsing the CNR's appeal to Ottawa, McBride told Borden that it had built a work of "national importance" to the "finest order" at a cost of approximately $70,000 per mile in British Columbia, and he attributed much of western Canada's great development to the "foresight and energy" of Mackenzie and Mann. As he left for Ottawa, he denied being asked to make representations for the CNR but declared that considering giving it financial assistance when necessary was "sound" policy. Canada should "show to the world ... more faith in herself." McBride argued that to compete with the CPR, the CNR needed access to the seaboard, and that estimating construction costs was difficult. If the railway had been developed with "undue haste," he blamed all the western provinces whose governments and people had encouraged it. In addition, the current economic situation justified "large and expensive national development works." Ottawa's documentation of the CNR's financial woes renewed attacks on McBride for piling up huge liabilities.[28]

After extensive debate, Ottawa, worried about the obligations of several provinces and of the Bank of Commerce for the CNR, agreed to help the CNR if it merged its components into a single entity that would be "a work for the general advantage of Canada." A merger would mean the loss of provincial control of its freight rates, a feature of which McBride often boasted. Borden offered no special recognition in rates or a takeover of provincial guarantees. McBride asked why Borden could not accept the province's position on rates since the Board of Railway Commissioners had recently shown the "reasonableness" of its claims for better treatment. Borden laid the correspondence between himself and McBride concerning the CNR and freight rates before Parliament, but McBride was determined that British Columbia would not relinquish control of rates and called for more aid for the CNR.[29]

To strengthen the appeal for financial aid, McBride and others, including J.H.S. Matson of the *Colonist*, inspected the CNR line as far east as Cisco in the Fraser Canyon. Matson told Borden of "the magnitude of this significant undertaking" and sent a report to several eastern newspapers to "enlighten doubting politicians and the public." In a few years, he predicted, Mackenzie and Mann "will be heroes and looked upon as the most courageous men of the century." Once the federal guarantee was approved, Mackenzie and Mann sold £300,000 of bonds in London but at a lower price than anticipated. Optimistically, McBride told Vancouver Conservatives that temporary financial problems were no cause for alarm and that the completion of the new railways would stimulate growth.[30]

While Ottawa helped the CNR, the PGE, a wholly provincial road, found itself "overwhelmed by conditions that had overtaken the world." Costs of labour and material rose, and after the collapse of the real estate market, the PGE "never sold a foot of land." At the request of the CNR, it had deferred a sale of bonds and lost an opportunity to make "a fairly good sale" in 1912. Although it raised $4.8 million in 1913, it had to offer 4.5 percent rather than 4.0 percent interest on its bonds. McBride objected to this higher interest rate. As the economy deteriorated, he was "as liberal as possible" in releasing funds to continue PGE construction. In January 1914, D'Arcy Tate asked for another $10,000 per mile. By availing itself of the ten thousand men, equipment, and river steamers that would become available once the GTP was completed, the PGE could reach Fort George in 1915 and the Alberta border in 1916. The Legislature approved an additional $7,000 per mile. A few years later, F.C. Gamble recalled that, probably in early 1914, he had told McBride of overpayments to the PGE. McBride had asked for a statement but did no more. Because of "bread lines" in Vancouver as the CNR laid off construction workers, he authorized a "more liberal release" of funds to the PGE, but when construction finally stopped in 1916, the company had laid track only as far north as Quesnel.[31]

With economic decline, the resource industries suffered, although McBride anticipated new mineral discoveries. At the 1914 session, the government legislated to conserve any radium that might be found, to secure half of any radium revenues, and to offer a bounty to encourage prospecting for it. The Vancouver Board of Trade, Vancouver Medical Association, and the Chamber of Mines sought $15,000 to establish a radium institute. McBride was sympathetic to the project but had no funds to support it. Similarly, he offered only moral support to a company wanting to experiment on treating complex zinc ore. When the Victoria and Island Development Association sought help to get information on the island's iron ore, he promised only to bring the matter to Ottawa's attention.[32]

Despite new provincial policies, the forest industry had serious problems. The 1912 Forest Act produced a Department of Forests and more attention to conservation.[33] In introducing the act, McBride justified past policies as being appropriate for their times. Moreover, he claimed that apart from the ventures of a few "poor old timber cruisers, prospectors and pioneers" who made a little money by staking a few limits, there had been no speculation. In condemning the "wholesale disposal of timber lands to speculators," the Liberals asserted that "timber barons," often "alien," owned $214 million worth of the province's best timber, were paying a licence fee of less than 1 percent per annum on their investment, and were not logging areas that could subsequently be opened for settlers.[34]

The government did pander to licence holders. Just before dissolution in 1912, appreciating the "magnitude" of the Powell River Company's pulp and paper operations, McBride informed E.V. Bodwell, the Victoria lawyer who acted for its American developers, that the government would modify regulations on pulp wood exports if such a measure were justified by the "economic situation." The company argued that because of these regulations, it faced a "prohibitive" American duty on paper. In the summer of

1912, an Order-in-Council removed export restrictions on pulp wood. The *Times* wondered how this squared with McBride's opposition to the reciprocity agreement in 1911.[35]

In 1913, McBride announced that revenue from special timber licences would rise with increased royalties. Licence holders successfully protested the higher royalties. By summer, however, the dumping of cheap foreign lumber, the depression, and the slowing of settlement in the major market of the Prairies put many lumbermen on the verge of bankruptcy. The public was interested in the revenue from the licences. Statistician Moses B. Cotsworth, who would later make a more serious attack on the McBride administration, told the Royal Commission on Agriculture that McBride's policy was "disastrous to the country's interest" and that the revenue should have been used to help farmers and settlers. In contrast, McBride boasted of successful timber conservation, stating that the Crown still held the land and had more timber in reserve than that alienated.[36]

Attacking timber and settlement policies gave the Liberals a popular issue. The *Sun* repeatedly charged that fertile land was being made available to speculators but not to settlers, as in the case of the first hundred miles north of the PGE's southern terminus at Newport (Squamish). The *Alberni Advocate* accused the "McBride-Bowser combination" of having the "wild pawn-broking policy" of selling valuable land and timber to meet financial needs. The *News-Advertiser* conceded that the government could have done more to encourage settlement but said that it had discouraged speculation by doubling the price of land not occupied by purchasers, reserving large areas for settlers, helping them find good farms, limiting the amount an individual could buy, and imposing high taxes on unimproved land. The deputy minister of lands, however, admitted that the department had no regular system of checking classifications to determine whether it was alienating timberland at the lower price of agricultural land.[37]

When the Vancouver Board of Trade called for a land settlement policy, McBride replied that his government was doing its "utmost" to promote settlement and food production. Moreover, distinguishing between genuine pre-emptors and speculators was difficult: "I have yet to meet a man in British Columbia, land speculator or pre-emptor, who is not willing to turn his property over at a margin of profit if opportunity offers," he declared. Nevertheless, the Department of Lands reported that, in 1913, its new pre-emption inspection branch satisfied those who tried to comply with the pre-emption law but caused resentment among those who ignored its requirements about residency and improvements.[38]

McBride repeatedly denied having given any land to railway or colonization companies, referred to land for settlement at places such as Point Grey, Prince Rupert, and Songhees, and mentioned the opening of thousands of acres to settlers without charge. Before more than a thousand people in Victoria, he responded to the charge of Liberal leader H.C. Brewster that the government was "corrupt and inefficient" by saying that "extravagant and fanciful" land settlement proposals must not precede railways, roads, and markets.[39] In 1914, he again denied that land had been given away and explained that the government's economic policy "was based on the idea of so pruning and paring down the present taxation that the time would come when all the revenue was derived directly from natural resources."[40]

Early in 1911, Alex Lucas, the MLA for Yale, had warned of "widespread discontent, disappointment and hardship" among farmers and fruit growers. Because the costs of clearing, irrigation, and labour made pre-emption unattractive, he suggested that a royal commission investigate "all questions affecting the settlement and profitable occupation" of land. In the fall of 1912, McBride announced that investigations by a forthcoming royal commission would lead to the "speedy settlement" of rich agricultural areas "with a desirable class of farmers," who would be assisted in making the soil most productive. Observers welcomed the commission as a way of ascertaining why settlement was so slow and why "certain individuals who are about as much interested in agriculture as in Nietzsche's philosophies are permitted to grab vast arable areas" for speculation. McBride congratulated the B.C. Fruit Growers Association on developing its industry, but farmers were not prospering.[41] Some could neither raise loans nor sell their farms. The government had no loan fund, but the commission would investigate cheap money for farmers.[42]

The commissioners, including two Conservative MLAs, investigated most aspects of agriculture in the province, and individual commissioners went to Europe, Australia, New Zealand, the Pacific coast states, and Ontario. A preliminary report in February 1914 revealed that the cost of clearing land was a major problem and suggested a system of agricultural credit along the lines of one in New Zealand. Liberal editors expected little action in response, and even the *News-Advertiser* realistically noted that nothing could be done before the 1915 legislative session. Financial problems and the war made changes impossible. The Liberal government elected in 1916 did implement many of the liberal ideas of the commission's final report, which "called for a scientific, state-directed, centrally organized effort to develop agricultural lands left untouched by the previous laissez-faire land policies."[43]

A flurry of royal commissions was a symptom of increasing problems. Six other commissions between 1911 and 1914 examined the milk supply, the administration of the municipality of South Vancouver, municipal government, labour, the coal industry, and the Doukhobor sect. McBride claimed that they were intended to serve in the place of a Liberal Opposition in the Legislature, a doubtful point given that several of the commissioners were Conservative MLAs or known party supporters. Although royal commissions often did useful research and made helpful recommendations, their immediate purpose was to remove an issue from debate. When the Retail Employees Association sought a statutory holiday, for example, McBride told it to wait for the report of the Royal Commission on Labour.[44]

Several commissions attracted little attention. Although they were important for public health, the findings of the Royal Commission on the Milk Supply were mainly technical, and an investigation of the administration of South Vancouver had only local interest. The inquiry into municipal government examined the idea of commission government, which was then gaining popularity in North America, but concluded that the existing system was working well. It did not deal with Vancouver's desire to annex the adjacent municipalities of Point Grey and South Vancouver, even though McBride told the mayor of Vancouver that the government would "move cautiously and safely," consult all interests, and not legislate annexation.[45]

Four royal commissions did attract attention. The most important focused on labour. Initially, McBride did not seem worried about labour unrest. Early in 1912, he urged Vancouver Island coal miners to settle their disputes with the collieries by legal and constitutional means. MLAs, he said, could not give labour all that it wanted since their duty was "to hold the balance evenly among all classes." As for unemployment, no government could eliminate "all want, all lack of employment, and all grievances and discontent." Vancouver City Council banned the street meetings of the IWW, which was trying to organize the unemployed. Though opposed to the IWW's principle of organizing workers on industrial lines, the Trades and Labour Council (TLC) protested city council's interference with freedom of speech. After getting no satisfaction from Vancouver mayor James Findlay, who had been elected on a "law and order" platform, the TLC saw McBride and the cabinet. A speaker at a free speech meeting the next day said that the police would not interfere with such meetings because, with an election imminent, McBride was trying "to save an awkward situation and bolster up his party." After seeing Findlay, McBride advised the TLC to wait for the mayor to clear up "the whole atmosphere" because "harmonious relations" were important "when there is so much progress in substantial growth and prosperity."[46]

In what the *Times* cynically called "a campaign shot, designed to catch the working-class vote" in the provincial election, McBride announced that the Royal Commission on Labour would seek ways of "providing an adequate supply of workmen with an equally adequate amount of work at all seasons of the year." When he finally established the commission in December, labour was unhappy because its only labour member, R.A. Stoney of New Westminster, was a Conservative. When Socialist MLA Parker Williams suggested that all the commissioners should represent labour, McBride replied, "This was not a labor government and not a capitalist government ... We are here to do the best we can in the interests of the people as a whole, irrespective of class distinction."[47]

The situation at the coal mines deteriorated. In September 1912, miners at Cumberland went on "holiday" to protest the dismissal of union organizer Oscar Mottishaw from a Canadian Collieries (Dunsmuir) mine owned by Mackenzie and Mann of the CNR. When miners at Ladysmith and Extension walked out in solidarity with Cumberland, the company locked them out. A few days later, a strikers' delegation asked McBride, as minister of mines, to inquire particularly into discrimination against "gas men," the miners responsible for warning of dangerous gases. McBride regretted the strike and the hardship to miners, their families, and the companies but would not intervene. He believed that existing laws safeguarded "life and limb" and gave "fair recognition" to the companies. In addition, he had insufficient information to investigate under the Coal Mines Regulation Act. He modestly assisted both sides by lending a report of a miners' meeting (possibly from Pinkerton's Detective Agency) to Canadian Collieries and by donating ten dollars for Christmas gifts for the strikers' children. Meanwhile, protected by Provincial Police and special constables, strikebreakers operated the mines. The strike became an issue of union recognition.[48]

The Royal Commission on Labour did not investigate the coal strike. McBride told the B.C. Federation of Labour that the commission was not "designed for strikes." Recalling his election promises of a "thorough investigation" of their complaints, the miners were upset when he refused to enact labour legislation before the royal commission reported. McBride denied intervening on either side but at least twice asked the company to meet with representatives of the United Mine Workers of America (UMWA), an American-based union. It refused. Lacking a joint request from both union and company, he judged it inadvisable "to force" himself into the role of mediator. Perceiving a need to respect law and order, however, the government sent special constables to Cumberland, though only in response to the mayor's request following demonstrations against strikebreakers.[49]

The situation worsened after 1 May 1913, when the UMWA – one of McBride's correspondents called them the Universal Mischief Workers of America – persuaded Nanaimo miners to join it and strike. A July riot in Cumberland was followed in mid-August by riots in Extension, South Wellington, Ladysmith, and Nanaimo. The mayor of Nanaimo warned that local police could not control the situation and asked the province to take charge. McBride was en route to London at the time, so Acting Premier Bowser called out the militia.[50] In November, soon after McBride returned, the recently formed British Columbia Miners' Liberation League, which included representatives of unions and Socialist organizations, invited him to speak at a mass meeting in Vancouver. It sought freedom for twenty-eight miners who had been sent to jail for their roles in the Ladysmith riot. McBride refused the invitation, endorsed Bowser's actions, defended Judge F.W. Howay, who had sentenced the men, and warned of a "dangerous precedent" if the Legislature tried to interfere with the courts.[51]

Using the militia and incarcerating rioters, some of whom were only tangentially involved, aroused widespread criticism. Bowser received much of the opprobrium, but McBride did not escape it. When Reverend W.W. Fraser of First Presbyterian Church in Vancouver accused him of being "negligent," the large congregation clapped its hands and stamped its feet in agreement. Reverend A.E. Cooke of Vancouver's Kitsilano Congregational Church was also critical, and some Liberal journals attacked McBride and Bowser for refusing to hear the "ill-treated miners," for letting Mackenzie and Mann "ride roughshod over the workers," and for allowing "disorder, desolation and want."[52]

On New Year's Eve, McBride met with labour representatives to discuss the liberation of the jailed miners. He agreed that hazardous working conditions might justify efforts to improve conditions but reiterated his duty "to hold the scales between capital and labor." In mid-January, about sixty wives, mothers, and daughters of the prisoners met him at the Parliament Buildings. One woman asked for the release of her nineteen-year-old son, who had been sentenced to the penitentiary for two years: "He is only a boy, Mr. McBride, and meant no harm." Moved by her

McBride was out of the country during some of the critical moments of the 1912-14 strike of Vancouver Island coal miners, which left Attorney General Bowser with the responsibility for maintaining law and order. As minister of mines, however, McBride was responsible for mine safety. The Vancouver Island mines were notorious for being gassy and dangerous. *Vancouver Sun*, 7 February 1913, cartoonist, Graham Hyde.

words, or perhaps realizing that he was losing political capital, McBride gave twenty dollars to the women's tag day fund. Explaining that clemency was Ottawa's responsibility, he said that if he saw reason to recommend pardons, he would contact the federal minister of justice. Six weeks later, he told another delegation of women that he had written to the minister. According to a reporter, "without exactly saying so definitely," he encouraged them to expect his government to help. He also showed some sympathy for individual prisoners. When Parker Williams reported that prisoner Samuel Guthie was suffering from mental problems and possibly tuberculosis because of his incarceration, McBride asked a New Westminster physician to see Guthie and arranged for Williams to visit him. He was less sympathetic when the president of the Miners' Liberation League presented a petition, signed by every woman with a male relative in jail, blaming him for the disturbances and complaining of unfair trials. The league's vice-president warned of a call for a general strike unless the strikers were released within two weeks. McBride felt that a general strike would be "calamitous" but that no threat would influence a pardon for guilty men, and he reiterated that only Ottawa could grant clemency.[53]

In the Legislature, Parker Williams called for an inquiry into the strike. After repeating that the government would intervene only if all parties requested it, McBride blamed the strike on the UMWA desire to control the Vancouver Island mines, whose better-quality coal was also more conveniently located for export than American coal. In short, the strike was on "behalf of competing coal miners in the U.S." The militia had been called out because of "a veritable reign of terror" verging on anarchy. He denied saying anything "alien to unionism," bragged of labour legislation that was "unequalled in Canada," and promised appropriate legislation after a study of the royal commission report.[54]

Despite having no jurisdiction "to deal with the merits" of the strike, the commissioners found "hardship and suffering" at Ladysmith and Cumberland. They concluded that "no class of worker is ... more entitled to generous pay for a fair day's work than the coal-miner who has to spend many hours of his day far removed from daylight and often in an impure atmosphere." Finding no evidence of American union leaders attempting to injure Canadian interests, they recommended that employers should not be allowed to discriminate against union members and that men who preferred to work during strikes should be protected from intimidation, threats, and offensive names such as "scab" and "blackleg." Without saying that a conflict over a gas committee report had set off the strike, the commissioners recommended that underground miners should elect gas committees by ballot and, to ameliorate some ambiguities in the Coal Mines Regulation Act, that they also elect their checkweighmen.[55]

Most of the commission's recommendations, and especially those regarding working conditions relating to health and safety in railway construction and in logging camps, applied generally to other industries. It favoured the fortnightly payment of wages and a weekly half-holiday for retail employees but opposed a minimum wage and compulsory arbitration of labour disputes. A major recommendation concerned compulsory state insurance for workmen injured on the job. The press agreed that the recommendations would greatly benefit labour, but the commission was only advisory in nature, and no one expected that the government would take prompt action in response to its suggestions.[56]

The strike continued and McBride finally intervened. Perhaps the royal commission influenced him; certainly, he worried about the cost of deploying the militia. An amnesty for many prisoners slightly appeased the strikers and their friends. In mid-March, when McBride called the mine owners to Victoria, they said they were producing more coal than was normally the case but that markets were declining. The strike dragged on. In June, he got the operators of three companies to reinstate strikers "without discrimination" as rapidly as conditions permitted and to hire new employees only after all former ones desiring work had been rehired with due regard "for a proper standard of efficiency." The owners would not recognize the UMWA but would let miners join it. McBride told Frank Farrington, the American UMWA organizer, that he expected the operators to honour their promises. Fearing that working conditions would worsen if the union were not recognized, its members overwhelmingly rejected the proposal. The UMWA, however, could no longer afford to issue strike pay, a development that hastened the end of the strike. When war broke out in Europe, McBride got the operators to drop the phrase respecting "efficiency." The miners accepted an offer submitted through McBride's "good offices," called off the strike on 20 August, and asked him to help arrange the details of resuming work.[57]

According to the *Colonist*, McBride was loath to mention his important role in the settlement of the strike and merely expressed his pleasure in it. His praise was overly generous. The war, declining markets, and the end of strike pay had given the miners no choice but to capitulate. The judgment of historians that McBride was contemptuous of the strikers is unduly harsh. He was slow to intervene, but he may have genuinely believed that the parties could resolve their disagreements themselves. The federal minister of labour, T.W. Crothers, had attempted to intervene early in the dispute through the Industrial Disputes Investigation Act, but since neither the operators nor the union would submit a formal complaint, the act's provision for conciliation could not apply.[58] Without the operators' cooperation, a solution was impossible. Moreover, McBride was absent at the time of the riots, and Bowser called in the militia, whose presence antagonized the strikers but may have prevented greater violence. After the fact, McBride endorsed Bowser's actions; to repudiate him would have caused a major cabinet crisis. In short, external circumstances, not McBride himself, ended the strike, and given the hardened positions on both sides, it is unlikely that it could have ended earlier.

Miners were not alone in their unhappiness with the collieries. Consumers had long believed that a combine set an "excessive price" for coal, a major source of domestic fuel. Shortly before dissolution in 1912, MLA George A. McGuire had asked for a commission to inquire into coal prices. McBride replied that trade and commerce were federal matters, but Borden informed him that this was a local matter. As winter came and the strike reduced supplies of coal, the Liberal press blamed McBride for the strike, for being in the grip of "monopolists," and for letting them water their stock. The *Times* wondered whether, in some mines, "for every ton of coal lifted to the surface a ton of water representing inflation of the value of the stock, must be hoisted." Stories that the coal shortage was contributing to division in the caucus led McBride to appoint William E. Burns, a Conservative Vancouver lawyer, as commissioner to inquire into the cost of production, profits, transportation, and supplies in the industry. Burns reported in January 1914, but little was done in response to his recommendations that coal prices be lower. A year later, McBride reminded colliery managers that the commission found that a combine existed and that Vancouver coal dealers "exacted a tribute of 25¢ a ton on all coal sold in North Vancouver." He proposed a meeting but there was no follow-up.[59]

Whereas McBride's relationship with the Vancouver Island colliers was somewhat distant, his connection with the BCER remained close as he continued to be caught between municipal desires to limit the company's franchises in Hastings Townsite and D.L. 301 and his need to maintain good relations with British financiers. As promised, shortly after the election, he left for London. He told the press that his major business would be the BCER franchises, and he expressed anxiety about avoiding the impression that British Columbians "would do anything to impair the value" of the BCER's investments, which were protected by provincial legislation. If "necessary," and if doing so were not "inconsistent with fair and equitable treatment of the company," he suggested, "the legislature might step in." Over four consultations, McBride and R.M. Horne-Payne of the BCER reached a meeting of minds but did not resolve the conflict. After returning to Victoria, McBride said that he had no wish to mediate or arbitrate between the BCER and the municipalities but would simply be "a mutual friend in an endeavour to have them get together." He told a Greater Vancouver delegation that, according to Horne-Payne, the BCER could make no more concessions, including fare reductions, without harming its investment. He asserted that the "financial atmosphere" in London was very different from that in British Columbia. If the government unilaterally changed the franchises, Horne-Payne would tell his shareholders that its move constituted an act of repudiation, which, McBride argued, would seriously affect the money markets. The municipalities were disappointed, and the Opposition press suggested that the London trip was a social triumph but a humiliating business failure.[60]

When Horne-Payne repeated his threat later in the summer, McBride replied that he still hoped to resolve the matter. The deteriorating economy and his dependence on Horne-Payne's good will made him anxious for a settlement. In the meantime, the BCER's directors considered a compromise. Although they were prepared to make it difficult or impossible for British Columbians to raise capital in London, they offered to accept a modification in the street railway franchise if the government extended the Hastings Townsite and D.L. 301 franchises of its subsidiary the Vancouver Gas Company and cancelled the road allowance in a property it wished to develop. Vancouver City Council would have to approve any change in the gas company franchise. McBride warned the BCER that after redistribution of the seats in the Legislature, the Vancouver area would have more MLAs and that a new leader of the government might be less sympathetic than he was. He urged the BCER to cultivate the favour of Mayor T.S. Baxter of Vancouver and noted that MLAs were very "sore" because the BCER had not given Conservatives special fares to their Chilliwack convention. Concern for "the state of the money market" overrode the opposition of the Vancouver MLAs. McBride did not legislate on the matter in 1913 or 1914. Temporizing let him remain on the company's good side, but his government was not subservient to the BCER. In 1911, the collision of a freight train and an Interurban killed fifteen people. Subsequently, the province enacted a Tramways Inspection Act. A conscientious inspector rejected many cars as unfit for service and limited the number of passengers each car could carry. Bowser, who had seen "men hanging on the windows" of trams and heard of men riding atop the cars, was keen to enforce safety regulations. The BCER thought that the "unnecessarily drastic" regulations had been devised, with McBride's approval, to improve streetcar service and to induce it to agree to alter its franchises. The company improved some cars and honoured the regulations "as fully as physical conditions permit" in order to remain in the government's favour.[61]

The BCER also feared that the government might implement a recommendation of the Royal Commission on Municipal Government – that a Public Service Commission should compel utility companies "to give adequate service at reasonable rates." Manitoba and Ontario had recently established such agencies, and the federal government was considering doing so. Because the BCER had just raised its street railway fares, Vancouver MLAs especially liked the idea of a commission. Bowser spoke of his "trouble" with the BCER management and of its failure to cope with the growth of the Lower Mainland. The BCER local manager complained that Bowser had always been "antagonistic" and remarked that without McBride's "consistent friendship," the company "would have fared badly." As for the establishment of the Public Service Commission (which became known as the Public Utilities Commission), McBride listened to the company's arguments that its revenues were declining and that continued "agitation" against it could stop the flow of British capital to British Columbia. Again, he temporized and advised the BCER of his desire to preserve the province's credit. In June 1914, he told the company that he could "not speak definitively" but would let it see the draft of the legislation establishing the Public Utilities Commission that he expected at the next session. More reassuring to the company was Bowser's comment in September 1914 that the government planned very little legislation at the next session. Money was in short supply, and "too much money" had been spent on past commissions. By 1915, faced with competition from "jitneys" (unlicensed motor vehicles that competed with the streetcars), the BCER favoured the formation of a Public Utilities Commission along lines that it would propose but left the matter in abeyance. At a lunch at the Union Club with the lieutenant-governor, McBride told the BCER general manager that he was thinking of appointing a judge to look into the jitney question. Within a few weeks he had resigned, and others had to resolve the jitney question and establish the Public Utilities Commission.[62]

As well as dealing with corporations, McBride had to cope with unhappy MLAs. Harold Forster would not sit in caucus. The *Times* reported that Michael Manson criticized the Doukhobor inquiry; C.E. Tisdall was on "dangerous ground" with suggestions on the coal supply; R.H. Pooley had called for more stimulus for agriculture; and W.H. Hayward did not like a civil service bill. Hayward said that some government supporters privately challenged their leaders' "autocratic methods and their notorious mismanagement of the affairs of every department." Three members voted against an amendment to the Offensive Weapons Act to forbid the carrying of toy air guns. Few objected to a law forbidding the carrying of revolvers and dangerous knives, because, according to the *Sun,* of the "marked" tendency of the increasing "foreign population" to bear such weapons.

The *Sun*, however, argued that the Criminal Code covered concealed weapons, that the law would give new powers of search to the police, and that requiring a police permit to buy a revolver would prevent "honest men" from purchasing a defence against house breakers or protection in the "wilder parts of the interior," where there were no police. When a legislative committee proposed exempting farmers from the gun licence act, ten members supported it, even though McBride did not think that farmers wanted what he called class legislation. In January 1914, the *Sun* reported that McBride looked "worried" and was not smiling "so genially" as at the start of the session. Francis Mackenzie of Delta, Thomas Gifford of New Westminster, Samuel Cawley of Chilliwack, and Harold Forster voted against an amendment to the Municipal Act, forbidding municipalities to invest sinking funds in farm mortgages.[63]

At several Conservative picnics during the summer of 1912, McBride had asserted that the party was in "a very strong position" but noted the need for organization. Even with that caveat, his observation was too sanguine. The New Westminster industrialist E.H. Heaps reported "a strong feeling being worked up against the Government within the party." In Vancouver, East End Conservatives formed an independent association after the government gave a grant to the New Westminster Exhibition but not its Vancouver counterpart. The Fort George Association objected to the denial of a liquor licence to a local hotel. Patronage had become such a problem that the provincial Conservative Association prepared a circular letter reminding local associations that not checking "jealousies and bickering" would "open a breach which may lead to our defeat." McBride thought this letter, which admitted that "patronage is the cause of most unpleasantness," was "very good."[64]

As the circular letter noted, patronage could cause jealousy. When protesting the hiring of a non-Victoria firm to auction the Songhees lands, a Victoria auctioneer warned McBride, "The Party is in such a condition in this city, that it is *only your own personality* which keeps it together." The Victoria Conservative Association complained that the government made appointments without consulting it. McBride rebuked Dr. F.P. Patterson, president of the Vancouver Conservative Association, for stating that only Conservatives should receive government jobs. He noted that Patterson had "no authority to lay down rules for the disposal of patronage" and that individuals were appointed on the basis of merit as determined by examination.[65]

"The genius of the McBride administration," declared the *Times*, "has been consecrated to the task of building up a political machine." But, it added, the machine was "becoming unmanageable." It alleged that civil servants who showed no enthusiasm for partisan work were "dropped from the pay-roll" and that save for a few specialists, every government employee had to "be a Conservative" and must work in the party's interests. The *Sun* accused the government of subsidizing the incomes of its MLAs by appointing them to commissions at thirty dollars per day and of favouring friends with handsome commissions for the purchase of the Songhees and Kitsilano Indian Reserves. McBride denied that his government engaged in anything "savouring of machine politics" but admitted that he listened to party advice on civil service appointments as it "was the custom everywhere and he saw no fault in it." He warned civil servants not to participate in elections and pointed out that fewer than six of them had been dismissed during his administration, a figure that he cited as proof of the service's integrity. This statistic, however, could also mean that the government tolerated the participation of civil servants in politics. Nevertheless, in speaking on a bill to raise the pay of clerks and initiate grading by skill, competency, and experience, he said that, as much as possible, his administration wanted to follow methods used in the "old country," which showed the desirability of removing the civil service from political influence.[66]

Although some appointments may have been based on merit, public works and administrative jobs lay at the heart of a province-wide patronage system. The *Sun* blamed patronage appointments in the Provincial Police, "a spoke in the wheel" of Bowser's political machine, for recent bank robberies in several small towns. It claimed that "the first duty of constables, fire wardens, game wardens, road superintendents and road bosses [is] ... to see to it that every possible elector is transformed into a 'Tory' voter." It quoted a Yellow Lake Ranch settler who said that, before elections, "the henchmen of the government, the road superintendents, will put men to work whom they know have votes." Hazelton Conservatives were upset when the Department of Public Works spent the district's appropriation "to suit the road superintendent," not to build a high-level bridge. Some farmers' organizations complained that road superintendents hired only political favourites and that patronage doubled the price of labour and prevented people from working their farms. In Cariboo, it was alleged that road foremen were required to be loyal Conservatives and to buy supplies from the store of John Fraser, the local MLA.[67]

As well as providing opportunities for patronage, roads were necessary for transportation. The *Columbian* praised "splendid" improvements to the Pacific Highway to the American border and to the Dewdney Trunk

Road, the strengthening of the Fraser River Bridge to carry heavy truck traffic, and the completion of Kingsway between New Westminster and Vancouver. Lower Mainland residents still wanted a bridge across Burrard Inlet to the North Shore, improvements to the Pitt River Bridge, and a replacement for the Cariboo Road through the Fraser Canyon, which had been destroyed by the construction of the CPR. Even well-settled areas were poorly served by roads. The Nelson Board of Trade was humiliated when the automobile used by the Duke and Duchess of Connaught during their 1912 tour had to "arrive by steamer and leave by train." In the spring of 1913, McBride told Vancouver Conservatives that the government's policy was to develop an efficient system of trunk roads and that Interior roads would eventually link to those at the coast. He boasted of doubling road mileage over the decade, of improving roads to deal with motor traffic, of building or planning a number of bridges, and of having built no roads without tenders. He repeatedly said that roads must precede settlement and that good roads were required to attract tourists.[68]

Patronage, especially in small centres, also took the form of subsidizing friendly newspapers with government advertising, such as lists of properties on which taxes were in arrears, deletions from the voters' lists, and routine notices. The Liberal *Grand Forks Evening Sun,* for example, complained that printing delinquent tax lists for the Rossland assessment district in three newspapers within a radius of twenty miles at a cost of $200 to $300 each illustrated "the lavish expenditures of the public funds by the McBride machine for the purpose of retaining power."[69]

The Conservative organization, which dealt with both federal and provincial affairs, also sought corporate donations to help its activities. The Vancouver Island branch of the BCER gave Victoria Conservatives fifty dollars toward a deficit arising from the "great expense" of getting voters on new lists. Conservatives in Vancouver also sought funds from the BCER. Some donations were in kind. The BCER, at McBride's request, gave a street railway pass to two party organizers.[70]

Although McBride had long curried political favour and exploited his personal popularity by making provincial tours, his overseas interests and failing health made these trips fewer and less strenuous. In the summer of 1912, the *Province* noted that McBride and Bowser were following "the more beaten trail to the points where the voters congregate" rather than "blazing the pathway through the untrodden wilderness." A northern trip by steamer and rail stopped briefly at Alert Bay but bypassed the Queen Charlotte Islands, possibly due to discontent over a lack of government spending there but more likely because of the steamer's schedule. McBride

A coastal steamer delivered McBride and Bowser to the docks at Prince Rupert, where residents warmly welcomed them. Royal BC Museum, BC Archives, B-09723.

and Bowser reached Prince Rupert in mid-July 1912. After most of its residents greeted him, McBride opened the new government dock, noted Canada's need to share in imperial defence, and promised assistance for development but urged the city to proceed cautiously. From there, he went by private GTP car to Skeena Crossing and then by river steamer to Hazelton but did not proceed as far east as Smithers, where there was a great demand for roads. At Terrace, he heard complaints that overlapping surveys made it impossible to distinguish between timberland and land available for pre-emption. At Hazelton, local Indians presented "their old request that all lands in the province be turned over to them." McBride listened patiently and promised fair treatment but called their demands impossible. The board of trade wanted road improvements and a high-level bridge over the Bulkley River. At a public meeting, McBride spoke glowingly of the region's prospects, as "a great empire, of untold wealth which would become the easy prey of a foreign foe in case of trouble," and gave a pitch for naval defence.[71]

From Hazelton, the party took a restful two-day journey by ship to Stewart. The only excitement was a fishing contest at 1:00 A.M., but as McBride, a keen fisherman, warned, fish don't bite before sunrise. At

Stewart there was a general holiday. During a fourteen-mile ride on the Portland Canal railway to the Redcliff mine, citizens asked for a railway to open what they called a rich agricultural, timber, and mineral area near Groundhog Mountain, a wagon road to nearby Mezladin Lake, and an extension of the pack trail beyond. In a request made on behalf of those who were temporarily absent because of "hard times" and that revealed the waning of the boom, residents asked that various utility franchises not be cancelled and for a grant so that their hospital would not have to close. At an open-air meeting after dinner, McBride said he could make no promises about a railway until the government knew more about resources and routes. But, he noted, Donald Mann intended to send a railway expert to Stewart, and the provincial mineralogist was investigating resources around Groundhog Mountain. He mentioned the fifty-two miles of road under construction in the region and acknowledged the hospital's needs. He also stopped at Granby (Anyox), where the Granby Company was developing a copper mine. While sailing home with only a brief stop at Powell River's new paper mill, the party amused itself with a mock debate on women's suffrage. McBride participated only after being reminded that "it could do no harm as the women have no votes anyway." On his return, a well-rested and healthy looking McBride reported that everywhere in "the new north," he had seen evidence of "a great future," "prosperity and the faith of the pioneer."[72]

He occasionally visited the Lower Mainland to see construction work on the PGE, lay the foundation stone for a high school at Chilliwack, open new buildings for the Coquitlam Agricultural Association, and attend the New Westminster Fair. His last venture into the Interior, via a private car attached to a freight train, was to attend the October 1912 Conservative convention at Revelstoke and to make a brief motor tour of the Columbia and Kootenay Valleys.[73]

He made no provincial tour in 1913, but early in 1914, he announced that during the summer or early autumn he would tour most major points in the province, including those along the GTP line. Although Bowser and W.R. Ross did make that trip, and Bowser visited the Cariboo, McBride ventured no farther than a seven-hour motor expedition to Port Alberni and Alberni, with stops at Qualicum, Parksville, Hilliers, and Nanaimo. He told Conservatives in the Albernis that "money tightness" was not peculiar to them and that British Columbia had come through "hard times" as well or better than other provinces. He said nothing concrete about extending the CNR to Alberni. In Victoria he enthusiastically spoke of the prosperity he had seen on his island tour.[74]

McBride frequently drew crowds of men, women, and children on his provincial tours. Note the automobiles in the background during this visit to Alberni. Royal BC Museum, BC Archives, D-07834.

His failure to visit the North in 1913 and 1914 contributed to discontent there. The *Fort George Herald* accused the government of treating the area "with inconsideration," due either to a "lack of understanding" of local conditions or the absence of an Opposition in the Legislature. Fort George protested the rejection of a petition for incorporating South Fort George, delays in issuing liquor licences, the failure of the government, which owned a quarter of the townsite, to provide a water system, sidewalks, and a land registry office, and the inadequate appropriations for roads, bridges, and trails. The *Omineca Herald* complained that, though appropriations had been approved, almost all road work had stopped. It contended that the government's forest rangers prevented farmers from clearing their land by burning but that it did not employ enough police to prevent crime. Nor did it pay police officers sufficiently to cover the high cost of living and the hardships of travel, although they produced considerable revenue through fines under the Liquor Act. Because of staff shortages, the paper said, mineral reports were so late that they were mainly of historical value.[75]

The Beginning of the End, 1912-14

McBride repeatedly promised that, as far as possible, "nothing would be left undone to make British Columbia a white man's country." Yet his critics accused him of making no effort to halt Chinese immigration, because the head tax was a source of revenue. They also noted his employment of a Chinese gardener and his admission that if his white cook left her job, he might have to hire a Chinese replacement. Nevertheless, he sought to build up a British community "inhabited by people of the white race possessed of characteristics and blood that will assimilate with those of descendants of the Anglo-Saxon stock." The issue was not one of "race against race" but of economic and social conditions since Asians could not help "but be interested in regard to the great resources and the potentialities of this land." The Chinese head tax was no longer prohibitive, and despite the Gentlemen's Agreement, Canada's Japanese population was growing through natural increase. "It seems," McBride told Borden, "that our Oriental friends are anxious to assert themselves in British Columbia as they are attempting to do in California." He boasted that no Asians were employed on railway construction. When New Westminster tried to segregate Japanese schoolchildren, he told the Japanese consul that local school boards had the authority to arrange classes as they found "most convenient."[76]

An immediate concern in 1913 was Japan's protest against the Legislature's attempt to curtail the employment of Japanese labour in forestry and fishing. When Canada considered renewing its adherence to the Anglo-Japanese Treaty of Commerce and Navigation, McBride urged H.H. Stevens, the Conservative MP for Vancouver, to get "all the protection that the situation will warrant." Parliament approved the treaty. McBride was in California and was late to tell Borden that its safeguards against immigration were inadequate. He did not want to embarrass Ottawa or London but continued to press. In January 1912, he had asked Ottawa to pass a Natal Act, or if it could not do so, to inform the Colonial Office of British Columbia's need to secure the "right class of settlers." Borden gave little satisfaction on this request, so McBride directly told Sir Edward Grey, the British foreign secretary, that Britain must reconcile its pro-Japanese policies with British Columbia's desire to exclude Asians. Grey's suggestion of a provincial Natal Act was unsatisfactory, given Ottawa's repeated disallowance of such laws and the speed with which the Japanese learned English. McBride claimed that his government's opposition to the Japanese was not based on racial concerns but solely on economic ones – namely, different standards of living. Despite his anglophilia, McBride could not see how Downing Street could justify any action tending "to impair the best local and national interest." Thus, he rejected the imperial government's suggestion that British Columbia modify its law relating to employment on timberlands in order to make it appear that the law was not based on racial grounds. Late in 1913, with unemployment high, a federal Order-in-Council prohibited the entry of artisans and labourers into Canada. McBride welcomed it but did not know whether it would affect the Chinese, "outsiders who come here to fatten on the country and say they have no belief in the Empire."[77]

In May 1914, British Columbians learned that a group of "Hindus," the term they applied to people from India, was approaching Vancouver on board the *Komagata Maru*. The ship had been chartered in an attempt to circumvent a Canadian law forbidding the entry of immigrants who had not come to Canada via a "continuous voyage" from their homeland. McBride saw the importance of the incident in accentuating British Columbia's desire "to prevent the flooding of Canada by Asiatics," who, he thought, were "quite unfit for immigration to Canada" because of "the insuperable difficulties of making them a homogeneous part of our population." He recognized the "larger and more serious aspect" of the *Komagata Maru* situation, but fortunately for him, these would-be immigrants were a problem for Dominion and imperial authorities, not the province.[78]

Looking for a counterweight to Asian immigration, McBride became interested in schemes to have British fishermen replace the Japanese and to bring ex-servicemen to Canada. Neither idea appears to have borne fruit. Some years earlier, to show that it was "quite feasible" to use white rather than Asian labour, the government had given $550 to two Catholic priests to recruit French Canadians for employment at the Canadian Western Lumber Company at Fraser Mills near New Westminster. It also gave the Salvation Army $10,000 annually to assist in bringing British immigrants. Although British Columbia welcomed eastern Canadians and Newfoundlanders as "a splendid class of settlers," McBride informed Wilfred Grenfell, a medical missionary in Labrador, that the province advertised for immigrants only in outside countries. This was an incongruous statement given that Newfoundland was not then part of Canada. Realizing the need to be selective, McBride told Malta's governor that British Columbia would receive Maltese immigrants if they did not arrive in sufficient numbers to be detrimental "to the labour class already here." As unemployment increased, the B.C. Federation of Labour complained that many British immigrants were debtors, "usually drawn from the helpless classes." "Helpless" migrants also came from within Canada. Prairie cities sometimes bought transportation to the coast for people who then became a charge on BC municipalities.[79]

Of the Prairie immigrants, the Doukhobors were the problem. They had fled Russia during the late 1890s to escape persecution for their religious beliefs, particularly pacifism. Keen to settle the Prairie West with experienced farmers, the Laurier government had welcomed them and provided land, mostly in what is now Saskatchewan. Many Doukhobors refused to accept any authority except that of God so would not swear allegiance to the crown to take ownership of homestead land, which they wished to hold communally. Through such means as nude parades, they protested efforts to make them conform to regulations. In 1902, they inquired about moving to British Columbia, but the provincial cabinet would not negotiate with people who would not obey the law. Six years later, their leader, Peter Verigin, purchased land in the West Kootenay and around Grand Forks. The Doukhobors initially settled in an isolated area near Castlegar, where they planned to become largely self-sufficient. The press doubted their desirability, but eighteen months later, the *Nelson Daily News* remarked on their "notable progress." By 1912, however, *The Week,* which was edited by William Blakemore, chair of the Conservative patronage committee in Victoria, reported strong opposition to their "peculiar views," so "utterly irreconcilable with those held by Canadians." It said the sooner the last Doukhobor left Canada, the better. The Liberal press claimed that Blakemore received much advertising to be a "jester at the court of Premier McBride."[80]

After a crisis at Grand Forks, when the Doukhobors buried their dead without acquiring a death certificate because getting one meant accepting temporal authority, the provincial government appointed Blakemore as royal commissioner to investigate "matters relating to the sect of Doukhobors." Blakemore described the Doukhobors as "simple and primitive" people who must be dealt with like children. Verigin suggested that, since they were not British subjects and had bought their land privately, they were not required to obey registration laws. He added that if the government gained their confidence, many would become naturalized. Blakemore recommended postponing any legal action until his inquiry was complete lest prosecutions impede conciliation. McBride stated that the government could not interfere with the administration of the law, but Bowser instructed authorities to discontinue the prosecutions. When two Doukhobors were freed from jail, more than a hundred Grand Forks businessmen and ranchers met to protest. The *Grand Forks Gazette* wondered whether Blakemore realized that the Doukhobors did as they pleased and must "be fed on more than milk and honey if they are going to be made to recognize the law." The meeting appointed a committee to pursue the matter with Bowser and McBride. Blakemore's report, presented at the end of December 1912, advised patience, taking "no drastic steps" to force the Doukhobors to comply with vital statistics and school attendance laws, appointing a Doukhobor as a subregistrar of vital statistics, hiring Russian-speaking teachers, and having the school curriculum cover only the elementary subjects. Blakemore also called for cancelling the Doukhobors' exemption from military service. Blakemore had little sympathy for the complaint, particularly at Grand Forks, that Doukhobors who belonged to the community led by Verigin – not all did – tended to purchase supplies from out-of-town wholesalers rather than from local retailers and, with the advantage of communal labour, undercut the prices of other local vegetable producers.[81]

McBride defended Bowser's directive not to prosecute the Doukhobors but asserted that the law could not be relaxed "on behalf of these eccentric immigrants." The *Grand Forks Gazette* was pleased by his stance. "All we want," it said, "is that Doukhobors be required to live up to the law." McBride's statement pre-empted the plan of Grand Forks MLA Ernest Miller to raise the matter in the Legislature, but when the laws were not enforced, L.A. Campbell, Rossland's MLA, told Grand Forks Conservatives that he would go to Victoria to "thresh" out the whole "burning question" since McBride had promised the region's MLAs that the Doukhobors would be made to obey the law. In the Legislature, W.R. MacLean of Nelson attacked Blakemore's report. He argued that Verigin should be treated as an individual, not as part of the community, and that the communal system was "one of the most dangerous trusts in human history dealing as it did with human lives and perhaps human souls." According to the *Times,* MacLean "made no apology for delivering red-hot statements against a people" whom the premier had cited "as an example of a farming community who would do good to the province." The *Nelson Daily News* thought that MacLean's speech showed loyalty to constituents and independence among members while indicating that the government welcomed criticism.[82]

Interior Conservatives remained unhappy with the Doukhobor issue. At South Slocan, over a hundred residents met to urge the exclusion of Doukhobors from public works jobs and a halt to "their further encroachment." In defending the government, J.H. Scholefield, MLA for Ymir, said that it did not employ Doukhobors or Chinese labourers on public works and that if contractors hired Doukhobor teamsters, he asked local road superintendents to dismiss them. In the longer term, he sympathized with objections regarding Doukhobor competition but asked rhetorically how the government could uproot and deport them. Even the *News-Advertiser* complained that the Doukhobors did not obey the law and that the government seemed to be doing nothing about the problem. The *Colonist* admitted that deciding what to do about the situation was difficult but asserted that the government was "doing all in its power to solve the perplexing problem without resorting to drastic steps" such as "wholesale prosecutions." In response to the complaints, the government sent A.V. Pineo of the attorney general's office to investigate. Concluding that the main difficulties were the non-cooperation of the Doukhobors and their insistence on communal rather than individual responsibility, Pineo suggested imposing fines instead of jail sentences and making the community and its leaders responsible for enforcing the law. Bowser accepted his advice and brought in the Community Regulation Act of 1914. "In short," in the words of legal scholar John McLaren, "for communalists who were proving impervious to notions of individual legal responsibility, the law was entitled to demand collective responsibility and hit them where it would hurt, in the communal coffers." The new law pacified local MLAs such as Miller who wanted "something drastic ... to abate the Doukhobor nuisance." McBride wrote to Verigin, regretting the Doukhobors' "continued indifference" to provincial laws but praising their agricultural successes.[83]

In contrast to his satisfaction with the Doukhobors' use of the land, McBride, like many other British Columbians, deprecated the apparent failure of Native Indians to develop their reserves, many of which lay in areas coveted by white settlers. More worrisome were Indian claims to the whole province except for the parts of southern Vancouver Island and the Peace River that had been ceded by treaty. When, on behalf of the Indians, who were its wards, the federal government discussed Indian land title, McBride thought it absurd to suggest that the lands belonged "to the Indians and not to the white people of this province." Yet, he was not certain of that; he refused to take the matter to court lest such a reference "throw doubt upon the validity of titles to land in the Province." However, he would enfranchise the Indians after they transferred certain reserve lands to the provincial government, would pay "a reasonable amount" for the lands, and would give them the right to own new lands. He agreed that they had "a right to enjoy the good things of the country" but insisted that looking "seriously upon the claim of the Indians" would mean a disastrous "revolution in our economic conditions." McBride always behaved in a friendly manner to Indians, but as Chief Basil of the Bonaparte reserve told the Indian Rights Association, he "greeted them with a smile, shook them by the hand, and said they were good brothers, and treated them very kindly to their faces, then his actions were like a kick in the back."

In the spring of 1913, the federal and provincial governments arranged for a Royal Commission on Indian Affairs (the McKenna-McBride Commission), whose responsibilities were confined to the land question and did not extend to "general Indian policy." Once the commission began its hearings, McBride was no longer directly involved in the issue, and though he retired before the commission reported, he would have been satisfied with its results. He had successfully avoided a court case that might have recognized Indian title, and the commission had generally agreed that lands unused by the Indians should revert to the province, which could use them for white settlers.[84]

The Indians were not alone in their dissatisfaction with McBride. His apparent indifference to moral reforms displeased those Protestants who endorsed the Social Gospel, the idea that society must be remade to create the kingdom of God on earth. In 1904, Presbyterian Reverend R.G. MacBeth of Vancouver wrote that the local Conservative Party was "being called the 'Dupont Street party'" because of its inadequate enforcement of prostitution laws in the city's red light district. McBride sent this "latest infusion" to W.J. Bowser, who was then only an MLA, with a note that he did not intend to reply. In any case, prostitution was a matter for the Criminal Code, but enforcing it was a municipal responsibility. Almost a decade later, when Vancouver's Ministerial Association complained that Bowser would not send prostitutes to jail, McBride replied that until a new prison opened for women, the province's limited jail space must be reserved "for more serious offenders." The clergy were not pleased by this response, and the *Sun* suggested that it proved Bowser's dominance of the cabinet.[85]

A much larger issue affecting women was suffrage, the right to vote. McBride had scant sympathy for enfranchising women. After a delegation of women presented him with a petition in February 1912, he recognized their educational campaign but said that suffrage would "not be a party issue." At a Conservative picnic, he claimed that BC women were "quite content" to let men deal with public policies "and to busy themselves with the domestic duties which appertain to their sex." He praised women's

"Too Proud to Speak"

It is assumed that Premier McBride is not in favour of woman suffrage.

McBride respected women but did not think they should vote. *Vancouver Sun*, 24 February 1913, cartoonist, Graham Hyde.

"great part" with charities and hospitals that gave them "an excellent standing the Empire over." In thanking women in Revelstoke for preparing a Conservative convention banquet, he repeated almost verbatim an earlier statement lauding British Columbian women for making "their influence felt without such unhappy methods as had been followed in the old country." As the suffrage movement gained momentum, the pro-suffrage Political Equality League sent more delegations to Victoria. According to a reporter, McBride's answers to them, which sounded "benign and fatherly," included a promise to refer to the cabinet, which he admitted was divided on the issue, and a suggestion that they attempt to launch a private member's bill. He opposed female enfranchisement, thought it would make no "difference in the laws of the country," and believed that women would experience difficulty in attending to both domestic and political duties. Perhaps facetiously, he told the United Suffrage Societies of British Columbia, "If you got the vote, you would soon sit in parliament and it would be reasonable to suppose that some time you would form a women's party and probably run the entire affairs of the country."[86]

McBride's vision of the ideal woman was his wife, Margaret, a generous hostess and mother of his six daughters, the eldest of whom were entering society by attending teas, dances, and special events such as the formal opening of the new Royal Theatre. Lady McBride's sole political activity was appearing, beautifully gowned, at social events with political overtones. Her own public life was confined to membership in the Women's Canadian Club and service on the executives of the local Red Cross Society and the Friendly Help Society. The latter, a non-denominational group under the auspices of the Local Council of Women, sought to raise women and children who were temporarily "dependent, to the rank of self-respecting, prosperous citizens."[87] In McBride's view, women could perform useful services, but politics was not for them.

Moreover, his public life could take precedence over family. He called the 1909 provincial election at the time of the birth of his son, who may have been a premature baby, and delayed his campaign for only a few days after the boy's death. A trip to California almost coincided with the birth of his youngest child, Sheila, in March 1913. Yet, although he was often in London, where the king could have been invested him in the "Most Distinguished Order of St. Michael and St. George," he agreed to have the investiture at a private ceremony at Government House in Victoria. The governor general, the Duke of Connaught, who was visiting Victoria, especially asked that the family attend, so Lady McBride and four daughters were present. The following week, Victoria Conservatives organized a banquet for eight hundred people to celebrate McBride's honour and their victory in the federal election of the previous year.[88]

The family's lifestyle suggested prosperity. Indeed, McBride believed that living well was required to maintain the dignity of his office, a stance illustrated by an incident during a trip east on government business with his thrifty finance minister Robert Tatlow. When Tatlow went to buy a lower berth for himself, the ticket agent informed him that McBride had already reserved two drawing rooms. Tatlow chastised McBride for this unnecessary expense, only to be told that a premier had to maintain some style. This attitude carried over into McBride's private life. The July 1911 census reveals that he had a Chinese cook, two live-in female domestic servants, and a nurse whose total annual earnings were $2,100. He also employed a gardener and a chauffeur. His car of 1913, a six-passenger Cadillac, had cost $3,083.50 less a $1,500.00 trade-in on a seven-seat McLaughlin Buick. His daughters attended the private St. Margaret's School in Victoria, where tuition for four of them for the 1913 January-to-Easter term amounted to $169.20. In the fall of 1913, Mary began studies at Dana Hall Seminary in Wellesley, Massachusetts, whose 1881 founders believed that women had a right to the same education as men. The seminary prepared young women for entry to Wellesley College. Peggy later joined her. When Mary complained about riding lessons, her "Dad" counselled her "to make the best" of it so that, when they were home, they could "ride together in the mornings."[89] His mother, whom he visited during business trips to the Mainland, also required financial assistance. Early in 1913, she thanked him for his "thoughtful kindness" in providing coal. His younger brother Eddie lived at home, had a checkered employment history, and was then "without an office." Eddie had planned to subdivide an Agnes Street property into five small lots and sell them but "could not give real estate away."[90]

McBride's enemies alleged that he had acquired an "immense" fortune by "mysterious" means, but there is no evidence of this apart from some "perks." As a courtesy, the railways gave passes to many politicians, and a wallet full of them survives in his papers, but McBride also secured free transportation from the CPR for Lady McBride and her daughters to visit Penticton. He personally succumbed to real estate speculation. Until 1913, investments in various parts of British Columbia, usually as a member of a syndicate that had invested in mines or real estate, brought him significant income. His most profitable investment came from Prince Rupert land. By January 1913, it was expected to yield a net profit of $13,556.10. Either as an individual or part of a syndicate, he commonly bought on terms of a quarter down and the remainder over three years and at 7 percent interest. He often dealt with old friends such as F.J. Hart, a New Westminster realtor, and his close friend and former cabinet colleague R.F. Green, of Green and Burdick Brothers, a Victoria real estate, insurance, and financial agency. He joined British syndicates that invested in the province, but these enterprises were not successful. When the B.C. Development Association could not account for some £20,000 to £30,000, a receiver took charge. J.H. Turner warned McBride that there was "not likely to be a penny for present shareholders, if there is anything for creditors." T.P. O'Connor promoted the Colonial Realty Company, which bought a 212-acre farm near Ladner, but its sole revenue came from some rent and the sale of hay. O'Connor was disappointed that money was becoming tight.

By 1913, McBride and others in the group, including Green, owed taxes on three properties in Saanich. Yet, that spring, he was buying shares in the misnamed Prudential Investment Company of Vancouver, whose principal asset appears to have been twenty square miles of land near Hazelton. He was sending good money after bad. Finding itself in financial difficulty, the company amalgamated with another firm. By November, pleading that he was unable to pay the balance on his shares, McBride unsuccessfully sought to get his money out of the company, which ultimately failed.[91]

Similarly, he tried to get his money out of the St. James Club, an enterprise that appealed to his love of hunting and fishing. In 1910, some Victorians, including such political associates as Thomas Taylor, Henry Esson Young, and Price Ellison, were among those who formed a syndicate to buy the nearby James Island, which featured fallow deer, pheasants, game birds, and "unsurpassed" duck shooting and fishing. The property included a sixteen-room residence that could be turned into a clubhouse. The promoters expected to cover expenses by selling fruit, berries, sand, and gravel from the island. McBride began paying for his shares with cheques and promissory notes but in June 1913 "could not come in on the investment" for financial reasons. In December, he sought to sell his shares since he did not have time to take advantage of the recreation offered by the island and needed to make some "heavy payments."[92]

One venture ultimately succeeded, though McBride did not benefit from it. Although he was not a golfer, he joined with prominent Victorians in buying shares in the Royal Colwood Golf Course, which James Dunsmuir and J.A. Sayward, a prominent lumberman, began to develop in 1913. McBride subscribed for $2,500 worth of shares, but when Sayward made the first call on them, he replied that he hoped "to be in a position to send a cheque in a few days." By the end of 1914, he was $1,287.60 in arrears to the Colwood Land Company. Replying to a dunning letter, he explained that "some moneys that are owing to me" had not been paid, so making any payments for the next month or two would be "absolutely impossible."[93]

Although the economic situation was rapidly deteriorating during the summer of 1913, few people, and certainly not McBride, expected the depression to continue, and many retained a positive attitude about the state of the province. In June, New Westminster Conservatives, proud of their native son, organized a grand celebration to commemorate his ten years as premier and the introduction of party government. The printed program included "One Hundred and More Facts" on the record of the

McBride administration that emphasized its "good government on party lines," made the dubious claim that it had been "without a single scandal," and cited its accomplishments. These included Ottawa's recognition of Better Terms, reduced taxation, the introduction of the inspection of factories, electrical energy, insurance companies, legal offices, and tramways. It praised the expansion of education, the complete reorganization of the civil service, the land surveys, and the setting aside of 9 million acres for pre-emption. So many people were expected to attend, including several hundred Conservatives from Vancouver Island, that organizers were concerned that the crowd might tax the arena's 12,000-seat capacity. The BCER and the steam railways put on special trains to carry supporters from Vancouver. Only half or less of the expected number attended, but the *Sun* acknowledged that the event had been "a decided success" as a demonstration of "fealty in a party leader." McBride reviewed his railway policy, outlined his accomplishments and future plans, defended his land policy, and spoke of loyalty to the British Empire, especially relating to the navy. As for the depression, it was "a very wholesome tonic." The *Sun*, however, noted his "extravagance" and the acquisition of "tremendous liabilities." Not surprisingly, the *Columbian* remarked that "optimism was in the air," and other Conservative papers focused on stability, prosperity, and statesmanship.[94]

While the economy was still booming, McBride had boasted of prosperity and rich resources but had revived his campaign for Better Terms to take advantage of the presence of a Conservative government in Ottawa after the election of 1911. Prime Minister Robert Borden agreed to the principle of a Royal Commission on British Columbia's Claim, known as the Better Terms Commission, but did nothing to set it up.[95] In the meantime, McBride had R.E. Gosnell and his assistants collect historical information, mainly in Ottawa, to document British Columbia's claims. At a cost of $3,943.50 for travel and staff, Gosnell's elaborate memorandum repeated that British Columbia's "physical conditions" required "a special and additional allowance for purposes of local administration in perpetuity." It declared that "the treaty between the province and the Dominion is separate and distinct," suggested that a royal commission's findings would be "just and reasonable," and called for the return to the province of the railway and Peace River lands because the CPR was a national project, not one of "special benefit" to British Columbia.[96]

McBride may have taken Gosnell's memo to Ottawa in November 1912, where he discussed Better Terms and other issues, or what the *Manitoba Free Press* called "the old flag and 'an appropriation,' with the accent on the appropriation." Subsequently, Borden and McBride appointed Zebulon A. Lash and E.V. Bodwell respectively as their commissioners. These two Liberal railway lawyers were to choose a third person as chair, but if they could not agree on one, they were to ask the colonial secretary to make the selection, an arrangement indicative of continuing colonial sentiments in Canada. Both McBride and Borden sought nominees from the Colonial Office. Bodwell and Lash eventually asked the colonial secretary to select a chair and suggested that British Columbia bring its claims up to date to account for its "great advances" since 1906. This would allow Ottawa to prepare a reply and would enable the potential chair to study it in advance and save time in Canada. Despite Lash's suggestion that British Columbia's financial position had "so materially changed" that its case would be weaker than in 1906, Acting Prime Minister George Perley feared that the province might submit new claims. As Borden suspected, British Columbia had worked on the case for months, whereas, contrary to his request, the federal Departments of Finance and Justice had not.[97]

With Bodwell's advice, Gosnell argued that imperial authorities and Canada had promoted British Columbia's entry into Confederation, but he twisted history by saying that the province had not been consulted about joining Confederation. He also claimed that "a mental attitude" in the East had been unfavourable to British Columbia, that delays in constructing the CPR had hindered its development, and that it had been penalized by the land subsidy to the CPR. He admitted that proving the latter two claims would be difficult. Acting Premier Bowser sent the brief prepared by Gosnell to Ottawa late in September. Borden promised to "take the matter in hand at once."[98]

British Columbia was not alone in seeking Better Terms. Even Premier James Whitney of Ontario, who had led the campaign to limit the subsidy to British Columbia in 1906, wanted assistance for the Temiskaming and Northern Ontario Railway, agricultural education, and highway construction. He also wanted a general increase in the subsidies for the provinces. Ottawa had augmented the subsidies for Manitoba and Prince Edward Island, and its 1913 estimates enlarged expenditures in British Columbia, a measure that enabled McBride to thank Borden for "adequate estimates," which, "for almost the first time in our history," gave the province "the recognition deserved at the hands of the Federal Treasury." When the premiers of Ontario and Quebec invited their counterparts to meet in Ottawa, ostensibly to discuss the parliamentary representation of the Maritimes, whose population had declined relative to other provinces,

McBride doubted that the conference would serve any "useful purpose" for British Columbia. Borden, however, encouraged him to attend. From London, McBride asked Bowser to prepare the file on Better Terms. Bowser could not attend the conference, but Henry Esson Young joined McBride, who stopped on his way home from London. The premiers met behind closed doors, but word leaked out that they had set aside Maritime representation to discuss their financial dealings with Ottawa and to demand a greater share of federal revenues. The *News-Advertiser* reported that other premiers agreed with McBride that the adjustments of 1906 should not be final and unalterable.[99]

Meanwhile, without a chair, the Better Terms Commission was stalled. Liberals speculated that McBride and Borden had concluded that a costly inquiry would accomplish little. The *Colonist* denied that "a very wide divergence of view" existed between the two men, but they did have their differences, especially regarding the commission's scope. McBride argued that the commission had always been intended to be as "wide as possible" and that only British Columbia had had to subsidize the CPR. Borden agreed with the federal Department of Justice that railway lands lay outside the commission's mandate. In addition, reconsidering the terms of union would be "impossible" without doing so for all the provinces, and cabinet, caucus, and Parliament were unlikely to accept an expanded scope. Without an agreement on scope, the proceedings would "inevitably result in difficulty and misunderstanding." A "keenly disappointed" McBride appreciated Borden's problem but insisted that Canadians should "be fair and broad enough to welcome a judicial investigation" of the claim for compensation for the railway lands. The commission, not Parliament, should deal with the lands. Voicing the compact theory of Confederation, he concluded, "Each province should stand on its own bottom and if other provinces have rights and claims peculiarly their own," they should receive similar consideration. He proposed discussing the matter during a forthcoming visit to Ottawa. McBride and Borden remained at an impasse until Borden suggested withdrawing the railway lands from the agenda without prejudicing future negotiations. McBride agreed to this but Borden did nothing about expediting the appointment of the third commissioner. A somewhat embarrassed McBride twice urged Borden to select the third member so that the commission could work while the weather was suitable for travel. Borden's inaction resulted partly from the advice of the Department of Justice: the provincial brief had devoted eight pages to railway lands, and even though the pages formed part of an appendix, their presence would "provoke discussion of irrelevant claims." Bowser, who took the lead on the issue, refused to delete the material and complained that delay embarrassed the provincial government.[100]

When the colonial secretary sought "definite information" about timing, McBride replied on 25 July 1914 that the provincial counsel was ready and that an investigation would take five or six weeks. A week later, the Great War began. McBride did not believe that the war should postpone the commission indefinitely. He complained that Ottawa had had the provincial case for months but had neither sent a counter-statement nor done anything about appointing the third commissioner. In March 1915, after explaining that pressure of the war had delayed his reply, Borden repeated the Department of Justice's insistence that "certain arguments" be dropped but said he would discuss the matter when McBride was next in Ottawa. Perhaps some accommodation could be made; Gosnell was willing to adjust the brief. After this point, the files contain no further correspondence on the subject. The third commissioner was never appointed. When Bowser was asked about the commission in 1916, he remarked that pursuing the fight in wartime would be "unseemly" and that all the suitable commission chairs were engaged in war work.[101] The commission has been portrayed as yet another casualty of the war, which furnished a convenient excuse for Ottawa to avoid an exercise that might recommend costly subsidies for British Columbia and encourage other provinces to seek similar adjustments. In fact, the delays began well before the war – the commission was the victim of the intransigence of McBride, Bowser, and their federal counterparts.

Despite problems at home, possibly to escape them, McBride spent much energy on matters of national and imperial concern, especially defence. He praised the cadet program for teaching discipline and responsibility, and he endorsed Colonel A.W. Currie's recruiting campaign for the Fifth Regiment, but the navy was his main interest. Whereas Borden tried to downplay the naval question in the 1910 and 1911 debates, McBride had tasted the excitement of national and imperial politics. When the Legislature met in January 1912, H.C. Brewster proposed urging the federal government to create a naval unit on the Pacific coast. McBride thought Laurier's policy of an independent Canadian navy "ridiculously inadequate" and offered an amendment, accepted by Brewster, to add a phrase that any "effective" scheme of naval defence must work in cooperation with the mother country.[102]

Even before Premier Whitney offered advice on naval policy to Borden, McBride sent J.D. Hazen, the federal minister of naval affairs, an extract from a letter from Winston Churchill, the first lord of the Admiralty. After warning that "the years which lie immediately before us are serious and critical," Churchill had promised that the Admiralty would be pleased to consult the Canadian government, to do all in its power "to make their naval policy a brilliant success," and to cooperate in any scheme enabling "Canada to take a real and effective part in the Naval defence of the Empire." In March 1912, Borden suspended the Liberals' naval program and planned to consult the Admiralty and other British experts on a new policy. If Canada joined an imperial defence scheme, he insisted that it have a greater voice in imperial affairs.[103]

Just before going to London in the spring of 1912, McBride told the Vancouver Canadian Club of Canada's responsibility to defend itself, the empire, and the Pacific coast. In London, Churchill was a good host, giving McBride a dinner, taking him on board HMS *Enchantress*, and presenting him to the king. At the Canadian Club in London, McBride described Laurier's naval policy as "inadequate and inept" but had little sympathy for Borden's "do nothing" approach. He denied officially discussing naval questions with the Admiralty, a matter "for the Dominion Government alone," but informally acquired "certain information" to be passed on to Borden. He told the press that Canada must "cooperate in maintaining British naval supremacy." A reporter quoted him as saying, "You expect me to protect Canada on the Pacific and you hesitate to provide the force which I require to give that protection" and as chastising the "people of the east" for not realizing the need for defence against the navies of Japan and other nations. McBride accused the journalist of deliberately rendering his statements "as ridiculous as possible" and of making him appear "bombastic and egotistical" about provincial defence concerns. He reiterated that the naval question was a national matter, not a partisan one, and emphasized that "we will never hesitate to stand up and take our part as loyal Britishers towards the maintenance and strengthening of the Empire." Privately, he expected that Borden would soon announce a naval policy.[104]

In Ottawa, McBride delivered Churchill's message about naval defence to Borden and had a "long and satisfactory interview" with him and several cabinet ministers. He also learned that Borden was going to London. In a handwritten letter marked private and confidential, he advised Churchill that Borden and Hazen would probably conduct the negotiations but that he should chat with cabinet minister Robert Rogers, who had some influence. The naval problem in Canada was "mainly due to misconceptions" among Quebec voters. If the Borden government had "pluck," it would adopt Churchill's plan to have Canada make a cash contribution to the imperial navy, and if Churchill came to Canada, he could persuade Canadians to accept it. Churchill did not come. In London, British officials told Borden that they wanted Canada to make an emergency contribution to the Admiralty and mentioned special arrangements to defend British Columbia. The BC Liberal press expected Borden to consult McBride before announcing a naval policy, but when news from London suggested that Borden would act on his own, it facetiously anticipated that such an eventuality would free McBride to look after local problems. When F.D. Monk, a Quebec cabinet member, resigned over naval policy, Borden asked McBride to ensure that the *News-Advertiser* and the *Colonist* made no "harsh criticisms" of Monk's resignation.[105]

For acting as an intermediary between the Admiralty and the Canadian government, McBride was rewarded. Probably due to Churchill's good offices, his name was included on the king's birthday honours list in June 1912, which meant that he would now be Sir Richard, and Margaret would be Lady McBride. The press set aside party lines to congratulate the premier and "his charming wife," though some editors also saw the honour as recognition of British Columbia's importance, a point that McBride graciously acknowledged. At the official opening of the Calgary Exhibition on 1 July, he argued that the navy was a national issue. And he was confident that Ottawa would soon give Canada "a navy in reality as well as in name" to protect its coasts and to be "a powerful adjunct to the Imperial squadrons." As a British Columbian, he decried as "fantastic and absurd" a *Montreal Star* claim that the Anglo-Japanese Alliance protected British Columbia. "God help Canada," he declared, "If she has to turn to anyone for protection in that quarter." After having a "non-political chat" with McBride, the *Toronto Globe* quoted him as saying that Canada needed an immediate "strong and adequate naval policy on the lines launched by Sir Wilfrid Laurier" but expanded by "the creation of an efficient Pacific unit." In case of emergency, British Columbians would approve of Canada contributing $30 to $50 million to the imperial fleet. The article claimed that, according to McBride, "The Asiatic menace to western Canada is a much more serious and substantial danger than the German peril to England" and that on a recent visit to Germany, he had found a "spirit of friendliness." McBride accused the *Globe* reporter of distorting his words to make it appear that he supported Laurier's naval policy and denied ever having been in Germany or saying that there was no naval emergency.[106]

He told provincial Conservatives that Canadians were living in "a fool's paradise" if they believed there was no need to strengthen the Royal Navy.

At Trafalgar Day celebrations, he quoted Churchill on the emergency and asserted that Canada must show "the old home land" that she would "exert herself to the utmost to stand by flag and empire." On the morning of 7 November, McBride and Bowser had a two-hour interview with Borden. After lunch, while Bowser discussed provincial affairs with Martin Burrell, Borden showed McBride "confidential and secret communications from the Admiralty." McBride suggested that a commission should consider a permanent naval policy but otherwise agreed with the Admiralty's proposals. He told reporters of the need "to act promptly" on naval matters and gave his booster talk on British Columbia's resources as well as its reliance on British investment to develop them and on the British navy to defend them. The eastern press praised his "straight talk," but the *Times* questioned the consistency of his arguments.[107]

Finally, on 5 December 1912, Borden announced his naval policy. Essentially, it revolved around a $35 million contribution to construct three battleships or armoured cruisers in Britain, which would then be placed in the hands of the Admiralty for the defence of the empire. In return, the Admiralty promised that contracts for smaller warships would be awarded to Canadian shipyards. A pleased Churchill sent McBride "hearty congratulations and grateful thanks." McBride publicly expressed great satisfaction with the policy, but privately, he did not like the plan to build the smaller warships in Canada, presumably because Canadian shipyards could not construct them with sufficient speed. He also wanted a non-partisan royal commission to examine "the whole Navy question in Canada" as well as the development of navies in the United States, Australia, and England. In the Legislature in late January, he devoted much of a two-hour speech to naval policy, "the very foremost" issue of the day. He called the Laurier government's purchase of two aging British cruisers, the *Niobe* and the *Rainbow*, as training vessels, "a screaming farce." Despite concern about defences against China or Japan, he proclaimed "every confidence" in Borden's policy. The Liberal press suggested that his "cold and flat" speech reflected embarrassment at having to reconcile Borden's naval aid policy with long-standing arguments for coastal defence.[108] That was probably true; his loyalty to Britain seemingly trumped concern for British Columbia, but a strong imperial navy could protect the province.

After several weeks of acrimonious debate regarding Borden's Naval Aid Bill, the House of Commons finally approved it. McBride praised Borden's "splendid fight," but part two of the battle – getting Senate approval of the bill – was yet to come. As the debate in the Liberal-dominated Senate dragged on, McBride told Sir Francis Hopwood at the Admiralty that if the Senate defeated the bill, he expected Borden to call and win a general election. Hopwood warned of the need for haste and asserted, "Churchill wants the ships, the whole ships, the large ships & nothing but the ships & what he wants he struggles to get." McBride told Vancouver Conservatives that the matter must rise above the "plane of party politics" and that in the emergency, a Canadian contribution of three ships would "be extremely useful." The Opposition press noted his seeming abandonment of concern for local defence. When the Senate finally rejected Borden's Naval Aid Bill on 29 May 1913, McBride described the development as "a national calamity" that might affect the ability to raise money in London. He called for Senate reform though conceding the need to abide with decisions made by constitutional means. He suggested that Canada give three dreadnoughts to the king as a birthday present and claimed that British Columbians "overwhelmingly" favoured Borden's plan to grant $35 million to the Admiralty but admitted the "dismal failure" of a small local effort to provide naval training for boys. At Conservative picnics, he spoke of the impact on investors of inadequate naval protection. At a banquet for the officers of the visiting battle cruiser *New Zealand,* he described seeing it as firing up "the patriotic mind" and declared that "no section of the Empire was more loyal than British Columbia."[109]

During an eight-hour visit to Ottawa in the summer of 1913, he made a courtesy call on Laurier, consulted Donald Mann about the CNR, and, over lunch with Borden, discussed naval defence "from the standpoint of the Pacific seaboard" as well as a number of provincial issues. In a conversation with Churchill in London (Borden asked Churchill to discuss the situation with McBride as "fully and frankly as I have done"), McBride revived the idea of a royal commission on Canadian naval policy. Churchill offered technical and expert assistance, and invited McBride to be his guest during a few days' cruise to Queenstown on the *Enchantress*. McBride, who had an "important appointment" for that time, declined. He told the *London Morning Post* that, "to a man," British Columbians favoured Borden's naval policy. As evidence, he cited the warm reception accorded HMS *New Zealand*. At the Carlton Club, he expressed shame for Canada's inability to contribute to the imperial navy and called for the creation of an Imperial Assembly to deal with defence, foreign affairs, and possibly, questions of postal facilities, trade, and shipping. The *Colonist* cheered McBride's speech, but the *Times* warned that such a federation "might involve the surrender of our control over immigration," a situation incompatible with McBride's demands for a "White British Columbia."[110]

In New York, on his way home, McBride told a *Colonist* correspondent that nothing in Canadian history had done more "to make loyal Canada so misunderstood in Great Britain" than the rejection of the Naval Aid Bill. During the Inter-Provincial Conference in Ottawa, the Canadian Club hosted a banquet for the premiers. There, McBride deplored the defeat of the Naval Aid Bill. British Columbians, he asserted, believed that they "ought to do our share in the defence, not only of Canada, but of the Empire." He called for a "handsome" cash contribution to imperial defence as "the first step towards Imperial Federation." Liberals immediately attacked his speech. Premier Walter Scott of Saskatchewan, which was home to a high proportion of recent European immigrants, mentioned its "braggard spirit" and suggested that it was in "bad taste" since not all Canadians were of British origin. Criticizing McBride's "uncouth" performance and "abuse" of his hosts' hospitality, Liberal editors noted that the lack of applause for his speech had contrasted with the initial warmth of his welcome. Not surprisingly, the *Colonist* observed that despite departing from the precedent of not making political speeches at Canadian Club functions, McBride simply expressed British Columbia's view.[111]

McBride probably repeated his concerns about Pacific defence to Borden. Churchill, however, had already told Borden of his hopes that Canada would not "be forced to fritter away" its strength in coastal defence vessels. McBride may not have been aware of Churchill's advice and was discouraged by his inability to convince Ottawa of the need for haste. He complained to Churchill that Borden had done nothing about forming an expert board of advisers or the "appalling" "indifference" to imperial defence in Quebec and among German Canadians in Ontario. He could not say whether Parliament would include a grant to the imperial navy in its naval estimates, an idea that apparently originated with Hopwood. At home, he reiterated his belief that Canadians lived "in a Fool's Paradise" – boasting of wealth but doing nothing to defend the empire – and he accused Laurier of calling for the "absolute separation of Canada from the Empire." As for himself, he told Vancouver Conservatives that "before he was a Conservative, he was a Canadian, and before Canadian, he was British" and that he was ashamed of Canada's failure to contribute to the imperial navy.[112]

As his visits to London became more frequent and longer, critics suggested that he was enjoying a "holiday" or pursuing his imperial ambitions at the expense of provincial taxpayers, a charge that was not entirely fair. McBride dealt with many provincial matters while in London, and in interviews and speeches, he encouraged investment by boasting, not always with complete accuracy, of his province's resources, its prospects in light of the pending opening of the Panama Canal, its sound financial position, its extensive railway construction, and its opportunities for fruit growers. Replying to questions about failed investments, he urged potential investors to examine property for themselves or to hire "respectable and reliable local men" to do so. He completed plans for a new building for the agent-general and met with financiers. After consulting the colonial secretary, various politicians, and officials about Japanese immigration, he was pleased that Downing Street and Ottawa were recognizing British Columbians' determination "to press for the security of their own territory," both in defence and maintaining "a white man's land."[113]

When he left for London on 12 August 1913, McBride had planned to be away for seven weeks. He told the press that he would attempt "to get more money into the country for development," "to pave the way for a still greater influx of British capital to further what I might term the local development of this section of the Empire," and to take up the matter of municipal finances with financial interests. He did not return to British Columbia until 3 November. About four weeks of his trip were devoted to travel and brief stops in Ottawa, Montreal, Toronto, and New York City. In London, he stayed at the Savoy, one of the city's most prestigious hotels, from his arrival on 26 August until 8 September. His hotel bill was over £128, or approximately $620. It included his room at £5.5 per night, most breakfasts, a few lunches and two dinners, just under £3 for liquor and wines, and just over £1 for cigars and cigarettes. During his sojourn, he was a guest of honour at the Imperial Services Exhibition on Canadian Day, attended the king's "brilliant evening party" in honour of the marriage of Prince Arthur of Connaught and the Duchess of Fife, and had lunch with the Duke of Connaught. One Sunday, he and his friend T.P. O'Connor were guests at the country home of David Lloyd George, the chancellor of the exchequer.[114]

Although his tasks in London should have taken less time, he remained overseas until mid-October. The *Colonist* reported that "circumstances" prolonged his stay but did not explain what they were. The *Sun* speculated that he might be transferring "his large personal holdings of land and timber in British Columbia to an English group," but given McBride's personal financial situation, this was unlikely.[115] In fact, he had not spent his entire time in England. He made a brief trip to Belfast to see "Mrs. Tate & girls."[116] His diary for this period is often blank, but he spent time on the

Continent, including several days in Paris, and he visited Fontainebleau. Perhaps jokingly he told his daughter Mary, "You should hear me speak French. I'm a perfect wonder, Spanish & Portuguese too come very easy. My conclusion is that any person who speaks Chinook can readily master these European languages." He was in Madrid on 20 September and probably returned, at least briefly, to England. His diary does not mention a visit to Berlin, but his letter to Mary began with "I am on my way to Berlin and the channel is nice and smooth." He planned to spend three or four days there and look into girls' schools since he thought Mary "would do well to go there." From Berlin, he expected to return to London for six days before departing for home but did not leave London until 15 October. There is scant evidence regarding what he did on the Continent, but he may have been taking a rest cure, as he told Mary, "I feel so much better for the trip and all such. You will note the change when you see me."[117]

Certainly, his health had become a consideration. He publicly denied that he would have surgery, as some newspapers suggested, but he may have been seeking medical advice in London. Over the previous year or so, he had been less physically active. "La grippe" had often laid him low in the past but recovery now seemed to take longer. Increasingly, he needed rest. After a whirlwind trip to Ottawa in November 1912, he took a holiday in New York and went west to Los Angeles and San Francisco in "easy stages." The following spring, a ten-day trip to California became a month-long sojourn that mysteriously took him to Chicago, "still sick," and to New York. He remarked that he had "had a terrible time with the Grippe" but optimistically added that "the loss of a bit of flesh though will do me no harm." That summer, Borden thought he looked "thinner." His failure to make major provincial tours or to holiday in the wilderness, and his comments that his pleasure came from reading, especially the classics or poetry, also suggest a loss of vigour, as did a report that in the 1914 Throne Speech debate, he was "much more animated than usual." On that occasion, he "used the lid of his desk" to emphasize his points, though he may have been trying to awaken an MLA who had fallen asleep![118]

The press regularly speculated that McBride was seeking a wider stage, perhaps the federal cabinet or the British Parliament, a suggestion apparently endorsed by the governor general, the Duke of Connaught. It also commonly suggested that he would be translated to what the *Times* called "snug security" as Canadian high commissioner in London. The death of Lord Strathcona in January 1914 renewed that speculation, especially given the fading popularity of the Conservative government in British Columbia.

A Timely Query

Miss British Columbia—Is it true sir, that having squandered my fortune and loaded me with debt, you are turning your eyes in the direction of this person?

An incensed British Columbia accuses McBride of dalliance with Miss High Commissionership. Increasingly, speculation was mounting that McBride would escape from his problems in British Columbia and move to London. Innes, the cartoonist, often portrayed British Columbia as a woman in a stereotyped Native Indian costume. *Vancouver Sun,* 27 January 1914, cartoonist, John (Jack) Innes.

The *Sun* thought McBride well suited for the position because he was a "good mixer" and "a glad hand artist of the first rank." Its observation was accurate, but he did not have the necessary wealth for the social obligations of the post. He denied a *London Daily Telegraph* report that he would resign the premiership to become agent-general, a claim that would eventually be refuted.[119]

The outbreak of war in August 1914 not only exacerbated old problems but also created new ones. The remaining fifteen and a half months of McBride's premiership were marred by a decline in his own health and in the economy of the province about whose future he stubbornly remained optimistic.

7
Optimism Challenged, 1914-15

I think the present conditions are of a temporary character and when the pendulum swings back, as swing back it will, we will be more prosperous than ever before.

– Richard McBride to the Vancouver Conservative Association picnic, 26 July 1914

There was little to cheer about in the summer of 1914. The province had suffered depression for almost two years, and the Canadian Northern (CNR) and the Pacific Great Eastern (PGE) Railways were running out of money. Unemployment was widespread. Moreover, tension was rising in Europe. Little more than a week after the Conservative picnic, Canada was at war. McBride moved quickly to protect the coast by purchasing two submarines, but allegations of graft caused much grief. So too did scandals concerning the collapse of the Dominion Trust Company, contracts to build the PGE, and a cabinet minister who bought government cattle for his own ranch. Overriding all was the worldwide economic depression and financial stringency. In addition, McBride's health was failing. Nevertheless, he remained optimistic.

With war imminent, McBride acted swiftly. On 31 July 1914, he wired Prime Minister Borden, "Latest news from Europe indicates Empire is face to face with a great emergency." He suggested a national call for at least 100,000 volunteers. He told British Columbians that demonstrating "our loyal determination" to stand at Britain's side would strengthen its

HMS *Shearwater* dwarfs the submarines *CC1* and *CC2* at anchor in Esquimalt. Royal BC Museum, BC Archives, A-00206.

position. Before several thousand enthusiastic Conservatives at a picnic at Goldstream near Victoria, he said that, "when the time of trial came," the province would "rally to the flag" to defend the empire that was responsible for its liberty and prosperity. This sentiment appeared throughout Canada.[1]

Defending British Columbia was McBride's immediate concern. Rumours of German warships in the North Pacific made Victorians nervous. After learning that a Seattle shipyard had two submarines for sale, McBride consulted Martin Burrell, British Columbia's cabinet member in Ottawa, and Royal Canadian Navy officials at Esquimalt regarding their purchase. The situation was urgent, for once Britain declared war, American neutrality laws would prohibit their sale. The Seattle shipyard took the subs to the edge of Canadian territorial waters, where Lieutenant-Commander Bertram Jones, a retired Royal Navy officer, briefly inspected them before turning over a provincial government cheque for $1,150,000 toward their purchase. Jones and Lieutenant R.H. Wood, the chief engineer at

Esquimalt, sailed them home. On 5 August, Borden recorded in his diary: "Authorized purchase of two submarines ... They got away just ahead of U.S. orders to detain them & were pursued by a U.S. cruiser." Once the subs had arrived, a *Colonist* extra announced that "on behalf of the Dominion Government and with their concurrence," McBride had purchased two submarines, which were now at Esquimalt under the command of Jones, whose "knowledge of submarine warfare is not excelled in the Empire." Borden was pleased by McBride's "splendid patriotic action." The Admiralty approved if crews could be obtained, and it recommended advertising the presence of the submarines but not their exact location. The local Conservative press praised McBride's "patriotism and foresight."[2] This was to be the last highlight of his career, but it too would have sour notes.

McBride took a "hands-on" approach to defence. During the first two weeks of August, he was at the Esquimalt Dockyard almost daily, where, according to Commander Hose of the navy, he rendered "invaluable work and assistance." Hose was absent and only McBride "could have dealt with or handled the situation" under "special circumstances." McBride asked the overworked senior naval officer, who had suffered a nervous breakdown, to step down and put Bertram Jones temporarily in charge. In explaining this to Borden, he kindly asked that nothing be recorded against the officer. After naval officers advised of "a strong possibility of attack by German cruisers," he took full responsibility for authorizing the laying of land mines on the approaches to Vancouver. When naval authorities forbade blasting, McBride intervened to allow municipal projects to continue. Patriotism had a downside, however. McBride had to ask recruiting officers not to enlist Provincial Police officers on a wholesale basis.[3]

Early in October, McBride left Victoria for eastern Canada. Over several weeks, he discussed coastal defence, railway finances, particularly the needs of the PGE, improving trade relations with Australia and New Zealand, and the sale of lumber. From Ottawa he went to London, where the press intimated that he would study the financial situation. His diary entries, however, refer only to defence. He had three meetings with Churchill, including a luncheon, and met other Admiralty officials and Lord Kitchener of the War Office. He lunched with Prime Minister Asquith and with the king and queen, and was present when the royal couple inspected the Canadian contingent at Salisbury Plain. He told the *Canadian Gazette* that with the war, the world would soon "know what the British Empire means. Though it is like some huge machine all of whose parts cannot be put in motion all at once, yet every hour brings forth some new activity in some distant part." On his way home in mid-November, he stopped in Ottawa, where he told the press that he had accomplished "all the financial business he went over for" and that provincial financial affairs were "in excellent condition." Nevertheless, his main message was that the war constituted "a life and death struggle for Canada as a part of the Empire." He repeated these sentiments when he reached Victoria. The Opposition press asserted that if there were a crisis, his place was at home, not in London.[4]

Under the Anglo-Japanese Alliance, the Imperial Japanese Navy was responsible for defending British Columbia's coast. Early in the summer of 1914, the government had arranged a warm reception at the Parliament Buildings for a visiting Japanese squadron "to demonstrate to our Trans-Pacific neighbours that our attitude in respect to Japanese citizenship is not based on any national dislike, but ... purely and simply the outcome of economic and social conditions." Two Japanese naval officers were stationed at Esquimalt. Perhaps embarrassed by this, McBride advised Prime Minister Borden that "owing to the war situation, the least said [about the Asian question] the better."[5] When the Legislature met in January 1915, McBride acknowledged Japan's assistance and hoped to remove the "false impression" of hostility to the Japanese people caused by efforts to restrict immigration. He stressed that the province acted solely for economic reasons and that its actions did not reflect on the Japanese people. In January 1915, in a practical demonstration of this sentiment, he ordered the suspension of the ban on Japanese employment on special timber licences. Although he told Japan's consul that he wanted to retain the suspension, six months later, because of severe unemployment and domestic concerns, he found it necessary to reinstate the ban. Nevertheless, he told the consul that his government wanted "to maintain the most friendly relations" with Japan, whose services as an ally had been "very valuable in the war."[6]

The war made it more difficult to raise money abroad, but at its outbreak, McBride predicted that a "favourable turn" would soon occur and called nervousness in monetary circles "a greater enemy than the Germans." Urging creditors to exercise leniency, he warned that the government would act against any who attempted extortion. People must "hold each other up instead of pulling the unfortunate down." McBride had optimistically told the British press that there was "no cause for concern or undue alarm" about investments in BC, that money advanced to assist cities "to cope with the abnormal civic development" was "absolutely safe," and that British Columbia had "mighty wealth."[7] Such optimism was necessary if money were to be raised – it did not reflect reality.

The war complicated financial problems but did not cause them. The pre-war spirit of optimism had inspired local investors to create financial institutions to free the province from depending on eastern Canadian banks, which accepted deposits in British Columbia but seemed reluctant to loan money to its enterprises. Several local capitalists secured a federal charter for the Bank of Vancouver in 1908. It had an authorized capital of $2,000,000 of which by 1912 $1,169,900 had been subscribed and $830,000 paid up. After reporting $569,500 worth of stock subscriptions, it opened on 30 July 1910 with McBride as its first depositor. He was not an original shareholder but acquired five of the bank's almost six thousand shares at $100 each. The bank soon had twelve branches, mostly on the Lower Mainland but including two in Victoria and one each in Hazelton and Fort George.[8]

Even before the war began, the bank was in serious trouble. The Canadian Bankers Association failed to persuade other banks to assist in its "peaceful liquidation." In January 1914, on behalf of L.W. Shatford, the MLA for Similkameen and vice-president of the bank, McBride wrote to the minister of finance in Ottawa and, ironically, given the bank's raison d'être, to the presidents of several major chartered banks, advising them that "with care" Shatford could adjust matters and "avert resort to any extreme measure." He urged the president of the Bank of Montreal to do everything possible to prevent the bank's collapse, saying that should the bank fail, the effects in London for the credit of Canadian banks and the governments and the many securities associated with Vancouver would be "almost ruinous beyond repair." When Shatford sought support in Ottawa and Montreal, McBride wired him, "Keep up courage do not sell or agree till pressed to wall. Am doing everything possible." He seemingly had good news – Alvo von Alvensleben, a German financier based in Vancouver, had sold bank stock in France. In March, R.P. McLennan, the bank's president, told its annual general meeting of the failure to make arrangements with a larger bank and the "strenuous" objection of many shareholders to selling its charter and losing its identity. Despite the poor economy, McLennan believed that British Columbians, with their rich natural resources, could anticipate "the rapid resumption of normal conditions and the consequent revival of good business." To create a contingent fund against depreciated securities and to provide for bad debts, the bank reduced its capital stock by half, a measure that did not impress the federal Department of Finance. Nonetheless, the bank managed to limp along.[9]

War worsened the situation. In addition, von Alvensleben was stuck in the United States because Canada regarded him as an enemy alien and would not permit him to re-enter the country.[10] In mid-November, Shatford again sought assistance in Ottawa and discussed matters with the Canadian Bankers Association. The provincial government rejected McLennan's request for $100,000 since there was no guarantee that it would be sufficient, and it would set a precedent for other troubled financial institutions. The auditor general advised that the bank's problems arose from "earlier mismanagement," the war, and panic following the collapse of the Dominion Trust Company. McBride's plea to the Canadian Bankers Association for "reasonable assistance" in the "present emergency" was of no avail. On the night of 14 December, the bank announced that it had "been compelled to suspend payment." The directors blamed "widespread and amazing rumors resulting in the loss of public confidence and heavy withdrawals," its inability to collect outstanding loans in the "present unprecedented conditions," and its failure to secure "financial assistance." The directors expected to pay depositors in full, a promise that reflected both unfounded optimism and financial ineptitude. The bank had encouraged small depositors, especially children; about 70 percent of its 7,200 depositors had balances of five dollars or less.[11] Fortunately for McBride, the collapse of the Bank of Vancouver had few political reverberations since the federal government regulated chartered banks.

Trust companies, however, were subject to provincial regulation. The final blow to the Bank of Vancouver was the collapse of the Dominion Trust Company, another locally based financial institution. It had the benefit of legislation, which critics complained had been framed specifically to assist it by making it difficult for most other trust companies to comply with the new regulations. In May 1914, McBride recommended that the company be appointed a trustee to issue CNR bonds. Despite knowing that the boom was over, the Dominion Trust acted aggressively instead of retrenching. On 12 October 1914, the body of its managing director, W.R. Arnold, who had shot himself, was found in his Shaughnessy Heights garage. Depositors immediately gave ten days' notice of withdrawals at the rate of $30,000 per day. Acting Premier Bowser explained to McBride, who was in England, that the company was "not in position to meet run." On 23 October, it went into liquidation. Many depositors blamed McBride for the situation. One wrote, "While you were in England I lost my hard earned money owing to the suspension of the Dominion Trust Company." He had made "many sacrifices" for the Conservative Party and hoped that McBride would keep him in mind for government employment. Many working people had put their money in the Dominion Trust, not to earn 1 percent more interest than was given by the banks, but due to the convenience of its late opening hours on Saturdays.[12]

In mid-December, the provisional liquidator stated that the Dominion Trust had failed because, "in violation of its powers," it kept few if any liquid assets on hand "to meet a possible run," invested in "highly speculative assets," and misappropriated trust and other securities "in a vain attempt to save the situation." The liquidator estimated the company's assets as $970,715.97, with liabilities of approximately $2 million. In short, "the company seems to have done most things that a trust company should not do, and this company had no power to do, and few things that a trust company should do."[13]

Early in January 1915, a delegation of depositors sought relief from McBride because they had believed that a company operating under provincial authority would be secure. J.S. Cowper, a journalist and their spokesman, quoted many "pathetic cases" among 2,700 Vancouver depositors. A delegate from Nanaimo said that only two of its friendly societies had not been affected by the collapse of the Dominion Trust and that the Harewood School Board had lost all its funds. They had some reason to hope for recompense. A few weeks earlier, Bowser had stated that the government might legislate to give the depositors "a measure of relief." McBride sympathetically said that the government had given the matter, which affected "so many in this Province and in the Old Country," its "closest attention." Promising to make an announcement before the Legislature met, he said the government desired to cooperate with the depositors and to keep the Old Country investors apprised of the situation. Several weeks after the session opened, he advised the Depositors' Committee that he could not "admit the responsibility of reimbursing all the depositors," and he told the Legislature of plans to make $250,000 available for Dominion Trust creditors, but there is no evidence that this plan was carried out.[14]

Bowser's involvement with the Dominion Trust debacle constituted a political problem. Not only was he attorney general when the Legislature amended the law to allow trust companies to accept deposits but the Liberals stressed that his firm, Bowser, Reid and Walbridge, had been solicitors for the Dominion Trust, which did considerable business with the government, including speculation in provincial lands. "How could the government have been blind to the nature of the company's operations? Besides, what about the provincial inspection of trust companies?" asked the *Times*. Bowser doubted that anyone had been inspired to deposit money in the Dominion Trust because of its link with his law firm, denied knowing for two years that the company was bankrupt, and noted that as late as July 1914, the bonding companies had thought the Dominion Trust was in a good financial position. He appealed for "fair play" and promised in time to "issue a statement completely exonerating himself from any blame in connection therewith." McBride publicly expressed confidence in Bowser and blamed Liberal attacks for a loss in provincial prestige but washed his hands of the issue. He told a journalist shareholder that the government "assumed no [more] responsibility" for the failure than for any other business.[15]

The government had financial problems of its own. The *Times* proclaimed that the treasury was "as bare as Mother Hubbard's cupboard." As the economy slackened, so too did provincial revenues. Despite severe retrenchment, mainly in the form of halving the public works budget by reducing projects and wages, an annual deficit replaced the surplus of which McBride had once been so proud.[16] War exacerbated the problem. When metal markets collapsed, McBride, citing the importance of lead for munitions, urged the federal government to advance the lead bounty to assist the Kootenay and Boundary mines. Two months later, R.F. Green, the MP for Kootenay, secured an arrangement whereby "every leaden missile fired by the contingents from the Dominion will be the product of a British Columbia mine." Prices for all metals, except silver, began to rise in May and June 1915, but uncertainty meant that no new mines opened. The coastal lumber industry "had been under a cloud" for a year.[17]

Soon after war was declared, to elicit the views of the business community and "allay any apprehensions" about economic stability, McBride had invited the mayors of the coastal cities and the presidents of their boards of trade, their MLAs, and individuals associated with large commercial or financial interests to meet in Victoria on 25 August 1914. He told attendees that nothing in the general conditions justified pessimism; the government would endeavour to continue its public works program and the railways their construction work. Those at the meeting reached a "unanimous consensus" to continue as much work as possible but warned of the likelihood of much unemployment during the winter. Many speakers at the meeting favoured a "back to the land" movement to create employment by clearing land. "If we can keep public confidence 'bucked up,'" McBride later told Prime Minister Borden, "we shall not suffer unduly" and relief works would be unnecessary. Toward that goal, he encouraged employers to keep men at work. When he heard a rumour that the Hudson's Bay Company would halt work on its new Victoria department store, for example, he urged it "to keep our citizens employed." Fortunately, the rumour was unfounded.[18]

Most, but not all, of the local authorities at the meeting of 25 August expected to be able to care for their unemployed, although the tendency of the jobless to gravitate to Vancouver meant that it might have to provide relief work. Nanaimo's situation was dire. With its funds and credit exhausted, it could not proceed with planned public works, and its mayor feared "much suffering" if it did not soon receive relief. When the United Mine Workers, whose strike against the collieries had only recently ended, complained that mine managers were discriminating against its members, McBride refused to intervene but did ask the manager of the Western Fuel Company to help reduce "the charity list" by putting some men to work.[19] The province itself offered no help.

McBride was already learning that his earlier optimism was misplaced. Throughout the fall of 1914, the Victoria and the Vancouver Trades and Labour Councils, the Vancouver Ministerial Association, the Victoria Industrial and Development Association, the mayors of Alberni and Port Alberni, and others asked for the creation of employment, especially through public works. McBride replied that the government was maintaining public works to the limit of its ability but warned that, even if they were "financially feasible," undertaking any works that were not "immediately useful and necessary" would be unwise.[20] Nevertheless, McBride asked several MLAs and mayors for information about problems in their communities, even though he could do little more than encourage employers to maintain employment. The government did not follow his advice; during December, it dismissed sixty to eighty temporary civil servants. School boards also cut back, and for the first time in years, there were more teachers than positions for them.[21]

By September 1915, the government had claimed that the unemployment situation had eased as men enlisted in the armed forces, joined the prairie harvest, or found employment as industry, particularly the new pulp and paper industry, picked up. Nevertheless, many communities still had problems. Just before the war, Port Alberni arranged to sell debentures to finance public works, but when war came, the American investors broke the contract. A mass meeting repeated earlier requests for a resumption of work on the CNR branch line. The *Vancouver Province* complained that public works grants of $10,000 or $15,000 to some cities or municipalities did not help men whose poor health made them unable to do such work. Moreover, it argued, "Public works might far better be called political necessities." It favoured having the unemployed clear and cultivate land.[22]

The "Back-to-the-land" movement, a popular solution to unemployment, stimulated further criticism of the government's land policies.

Reverend A.E. Cooke of Kitsilano Congregational Church attacked the government's failure to make "an honest attempt to put the people in possession of their rightful heritage – the land." He accused McBride of finding millions for railways but no land for settlers. When the Richmond Liberal Association deplored unemployment and an inefficient land policy, McBride replied that the government was planning a policy that was "practically one of agricultural development." He had already promised an important announcement on land settlement when the Legislature considered the report of the Royal Commission on Agriculture.[23]

Alas, agriculture had problems. The Okanagan fruit industry was "in a somewhat critical position." A bumper crop in 1912, competition from the United States, and the lack of a marketing plan translated to low prices. Prices rose in 1913 but the crop was light, and the next year was the "worst year." Big crops in both the Okanagan and the United States reduced prices, and a poor economy meant poor sales. On the advice of his deputy minister of agriculture, McBride urged British Columbia's MPs to seek tariff protection from Washington and Oregon growers, who were overproducing and "slaughtering our market." Immediate action was impossible; the federal budget had already been passed. Moreover, the Liberals had attacked BC fruit and lumber producers for "robbing" prairie farmers. Thomas Cunningham, the provincial fruit inspector, blamed many problems on growers who knew nothing of the industry, lacked the patience to wait until their orchards bore fruit, and did not grow peaches and pears, which had a market.[24]

While praising agricultural production in the Peace River, McBride admitted that it was "very difficult to keep in touch" with the area because it was "so far away." The government had only recently learned of its large number of settlers and of their considerable agricultural production. Liberals charged that the government had let people settle where there was neither road nor railway, or any likelihood of either for many years. "Has not the McBride government treated every section of settlers in the north in the same way?" asked the *Omineca Herald*. Conservatives at McBride, a Grand Trunk Pacific (GTP) station named after the premier, had a railway but complained that John Fraser, the MLA for Cariboo, got the lion's share of the public works grant for the southern section of the constituency "while not a road exists in this part."[25]

Despite manifestations of economic distress, in a New Year's interview, McBride noted the stimulus of the war on the pulp and paper industry and the fishery. He said that unemployment, which was "much less acute than is generally supposed," did not exceed 4 to 5 percent of the total population, with public works and railway construction creating jobs. The provincial financial situation, he declared, "is absolutely sound, but strict economy must be exercised in view of the contingency of a protracted war." The Throne Speech echoed those sentiments, but for the first time, reporters noted an "apologetic tone" as McBride admitted the seriousness of the situation.[26]

McBride's New Year's message promised assistance to municipalities and unorganized territories that were experiencing extreme financial problems, but ten days later he denied New Westminster's request for provincial endorsement of a $110,000 loan to meet interest charges. The only hopeful sign was the decision of New York financiers in January 1915 to exercise their option to buy $2,700,000 of BC bonds at 98.5. At year's end, the option was renewed for ten years through the Toronto firm Wood, Gundy at a net rate of 6.29 percent, which McBride thought was probably as good as could be expected.[27]

Small-business people and homeowners, such as a Vancouver grocer who lost his business because of illness and was in danger of losing his house, wanted a moratorium on mortgage payments. Given the difficult financial situation, Manitoba had implemented a moratorium, and the federal government was considering doing the same. The editor of the *British Columbia Financial Times,* however, reported that over 95 percent of the mortgages in Vancouver were being renewed and that most foreclosures arose from money lent at "ruinous rates of interest that would have also led to defaults in good times." Campbell Sweeney of the Canadian Bankers Association stated that a moratorium was unnecessary. In September 1914, McBride said that he had "carefully" considered a moratorium but feared that it would deprive the province "of a very large portion of its necessary revenue" and harm British investors. Thus, the province would implement a moratorium only in a "grave emergency." Nevertheless, he understood the plight of individuals, for he too was suffering. For example, two notes amounting to slightly over $5,000 that he, R.F. Green, and J.D. Taylor had endorsed and that were payable to the *British Columbian* had, in the words of the Bank of Montreal, "not been attended to." In connection with the provincial situation, he announced a compromise: the government would "protect as far as possible" people in "special cases of hardship" from unnecessary harassment by creditors. In short, retroactively to the outbreak of the war, the government would protect those who wanted to pay but could not. The idea of a moratorium worried British investors. J.H. Turner, the agent-general, had received many "anxious enquiries" from the agents of individuals who had invested a total of about $15 million in First Mortgages. McBride's reply – that any moratorium legislation would be very limited in scope – satisfied the London financiers.[28]

The possibility of a moratorium encouraged timber licensees to seek a suspension of their payments until better times returned. In August 1914, McBride told them they were "asking too much," but here too he would consider postponements on an individual basis. On at least one occasion, that concerning the Swanson Bay Forest and Pulp Company, McBride persuaded creditors to grant a brief extension before foreclosing. As the situation deteriorated, legislation seemed necessary. Given current problems, the government had "to exercise some paternal consideration" in "meritorious" cases. The Socialist MLA Parker Williams attacked the bill to extend the time for paying fees on special licences, claiming that it was a reward to speculators. McBride conceded that there were a few "unscrupulous speculators," but on the whole, "every dollar invested in the industry was on a sound basis." The laws, he asserted, had been designed to invite investors from all over the world, and "our American cousins" had done much to develop the logging industry and draw attention to its "true worth." Despite defending American investment, he rejected the request of some Seattle-based timber owners for a reduction in the royalty from eighty-five cents to fifty cents per 1,000 feet. Changing the system, he replied, would "disturb public confidence" and reduce government revenues. In any case, since little logging was being done, the reduction would give slight relief. Ever the optimist, he predicted that with the opening of the Panama Canal and better freight rates, the timber industry would revive and produce revenues "more than enough to provide for the public needs." Similar legislation postponed payments due under the Coal and Petroleum Act, several mining acts, and any act that might be designated later by proclamation.[29]

The economic depression sharply reduced the domestic demand for lumber, and the export market collapsed because American ships, fearing German attacks, would carry British cargo only at exorbitant rates. In search of new markets, McBride discussed lumber shipments to Australia and New Zealand with Borden and George Foster, the minister of trade and commerce, and proposed that federal trade commissioners cooperate with the Provincial Bureau of Information to share information about markets. Chief Forester H.R. MacMillan suggested that since Britain required timber but was cut off from Baltic supplies, British Columbia should offer some timber as a gift. It would be "a great advertisement," and producing 10 million board feet "would relieve our chief industry and give employment." During the boom years, when BC producers could sell their entire output to the Prairies, they had ignored the British market. MacMillan anticipated that a knowledgeable person could go to Britain and secure orders that "would lead to permanent business." In the spring of 1915, he made a successful sales mission to England.[30] While there, he met McBride, who acted as a salesman at the War Office and Admiralty. McBride told BC producers to do more to sell their product in Britain. Given shipping problems, he investigated building wooden ships to create jobs and carry provincial products overseas, had officials collect data on the project, and sought federal assistance for it.[31]

BC manufacturers were eager for war contracts. In the fall of 1914, with the assistance of McBride, Bowser, and several MPs, the Manufacturers' Association persuaded Ottawa to procure locally most of the equipment, except uniforms and some foodstuffs, required by the Second Contingent, which was being formed in the province. Manufacturers also wanted a share of orders from the British government, and because Alberta and Saskatchewan had limited manufacturing facilities, they believed that they, rather than Winnipeg or Montreal, should get a share of the business from those provinces. The orders did not come. "Considering local conditions and ... magnificent contribution [of] men and money," McBride urged Ottawa to recognize the province's manufacturing capabilities. In August 1915, he complained that war orders given to BC manufacturers were "almost nil." Of the $400 million allocated to war orders, less than $2 million had been placed in the province, mostly in the form of small commissions to machine shops. McBride asserted that the province could produce shells, soup, evaporated and canned vegetables, jams, canned salmon, camp materials, boots, shirts, blankets, and more. A report that recruitment had been halted because of shortages of equipment and clothing added weight to his arguments. Under pressure from manufacturers, he persistently beseeched Ottawa, and when patriotic pleas did not suffice, he informed Borden that "it would be in the interests of the Party" to give more business to the province. He suggested appointing a British Columbian to the War Purchasing Commission. A.E. Kemp, its chairman, replied that the commission had not overlooked BC manufacturers, but few could produce what was needed. Moreover, with the need for promptness and the problems in supplying material such as uniform cloth, he stated that the commission had probably "gone too far in trying to give business" to the province. Noting that McBride's complaints were general, not specific, Kemp suspected that "politics [was] at the bottom of the whole affair."[32]

At Borden's request, Senator J.A. Lougheed investigated the situation and found some basis for the manufacturers' complaints. He recommended appointing Frederick William Jones of Victoria to the War Purchasing Commission and establishing a branch in Vancouver with samples of standardized equipment so that local manufacturers would have the same opportunity as their eastern counterparts to prepare tenders. Because of "intensely strong" feelings, "lamentable" financial conditions, and impending federal and provincial elections, he urged Borden to make concessions. Believing that a branch in Vancouver was "wholly impracticable" and that appointing a British Columbian as commissioner would simply encourage the other provinces to demand one of their own, Borden advised that the commission had done its best to satisfy BC producers and even paid more for the product and transportation. As a consolation, he suggested that an industrialists' delegation might visit the commission in Ottawa. McBride welcomed this "friendly co-operation" and urged the Manufacturers' Association to discontinue its agitation. A week later, Borden received Bowser and the delegates. He later told McBride that he expected the commission would bring a "capable, active businessman" from British Columbia to Ottawa and promised to continue to remind Britain of BC capabilities.[33]

Munitions contracts could not resolve the province's major financial problem – the inability of the CNR and the PGE to raise the funds to complete construction. On 5 August 1914, Donald Mann of the CNR informed McBride that construction would halt if the $15 million recently underwritten in London could not be transferred to Canada but that the company would pay off all its labourers. McBride replied, "Hang on with work long as possible. Winston will make good." "Winston" probably referred to Churchill, whom McBride believed had sufficient influence to permit the transfer. He emphasized the defence advantages of the CNR and urged Mann to complete the line because it might "be quite necessary before war much further advanced in case mishap C.P.R. make use your system." Expecting an early reimbursement of the funds he had advanced to buy the two American submarines, McBride scrambled to bring the government's balance at the Bank of Commerce to "an appreciable sum" so that it would advance funds to the CNR. He also endorsed the CNR's request to Ottawa for "immediate assistance," assured Borden that the company was exercising "every economy," and predicted that barring unforeseen incidents, it would join its tracks in the Fraser Canyon "before many weeks." To hasten construction, he suggested that CNR labourers work double shifts. By December, the engineers were doing "everything possible" to finish, including putting track on temporary structures and working day and night.[34]

Speedy construction did not solve the financial problem. At year's end, the CNR could not meet an interest payment. Ottawa was unable to assist, and the payments included $156,000 guaranteed by the province. The only good news came on 23 January, when William Mackenzie drove the last spike at Basque in the Fraser Canyon. A formal ceremony was planned for 9 February, but McBride recommended that it not be elaborate because of the war. Not even a modest ceremony took place; a tunnel collapse prevented Mackenzie and Mann from reaching the proposed site, and arriving by another railway "would have a bad effect." Mann suggested that McBride take the cabinet to Lytton for a celebration in May, but McBride was overseas then. Finally, on 27 August 1915, McBride wired congratulations to Mackenzie for surmounting the "abnormal conditions" of the last two years and arriving in Vancouver on the first through CNR train. Were it not for the war, he observed, "This would be a gala day for British Columbia." At the end of November, he sent another congratulatory note on the formal opening of through traffic to Vancouver. The CNR had built only as far as the New Westminster Bridge, so McBride acted as an intermediary for it to secure running rights into Vancouver from the Vancouver, Westminster and Yukon, a subsidiary of the Great Northern Railway.[35]

Despite McBride's importuning that it "would be very disastrous to me if Island work shut down. Must insist imperative lay some steel and carry on so as at least keep up appearances," the CNR halted its Vancouver Island work on 7 August 1914. Without offering further explanation, McBride disingenuously said that problems with terminal sites had delayed the work but promised that the line from Victoria would reach Sooke by the winter of 1915-16. It did not. When service began to Vancouver, the *Times* recalled McBride's promise to resign if by the summer of 1914 Victoria did not have a modern terminal, ferry service, and a complete CNR line on the island. British Columbians, the *Times* asserted, had assumed a contingent liability of more than $40 million for the CNR, but the island system was incomplete, and the CNR proposed to construct what was only a makeshift terminal.[36]

The PGE faced similar financial problems and, with the collapse of the real estate market, could not sell land to raise funds. Initially, its management had not expected to be affected by the war, and it had sufficient funds to keep the work going. In September 1914, J.W. Stewart of Foley, Welch and Stewart (FWS) went to the United States with letters of introduction to Secretary of State Franklin Lane, the British ambassador to Washington, and two Wall Street firms. The letters explained that FWS, "easily the largest railway contractor on the continent," was building the PGE from Vancouver to the Peace River and had already spent more than $24 million on the project. McBride told a Portland, Oregon, financial agent who might be interested in the venture that it would be "inadvisable to postpone operations."[37]

By December, the PGE was unable to meet the payroll for its six thousand workers. McBride appealed to Borden for a $6 million advance on PGE bonds to permit the work to continue and to avoid unemployment. On 27 October 1914, while he was en route to England, the province forwarded $750,000 to the PGE, but the respite was only temporary. When he returned, McBride informed Borden that the grade would soon be laid from Squamish to Prince George. To avoid unemployment, it was essential to transfer five thousand men to the Peace River, where the federal government owned much of the land. He asked Ottawa to finance the company's provincially guaranteed bonds. Federal finance minister W.T. White thought it impossible to provide direct assistance but felt that the government might advance funds to the Union Bank on the security of such bonds. However, Stewart informed him that the Peace River work would probably not go ahead.[38]

The PGE remained short of funds. In the spring of 1915, McBride asked Ottawa for a grant of $12,000 for each of the PGE's 489 miles from Vancouver to Fort George to complete that line to a junction with the GTP by year's end. This "begging expedition" had limited success. The federal government agreed to advance up to $5 million on the security of $6 million of guaranteed PGE bonds. Unfortunately, the bank would not loan more than $2.4 million. Finance Minister White encouraged McBride to engage an experienced "financial man" to help find funds in London. McBride accepted the advice but was disappointed by the bank's limited response. Whether in politeness or with a touch of sarcasm, he thanked Borden and White for their "trouble." En route to London, he spent several days in the "frightful heat" of New York, futilely attempting to sell PGE bonds. Once he reached London, discussions "with friends" there proved no more successful. McBride and Bowser contemplated halting construction of the PGE, but F.C. Gamble, the government engineer, warned that the road would deteriorate due to slides, storms, snow, wash-outs, and the like. Consequently, McBride approved granting half of the normal 10 percent holdback to the PGE.[39] This measure, which did not solve the problem, simply added to his political difficulties.

Early in 1915, speculation arose that after the legislative session, McBride would resign in favour of Bowser, and an election would follow. Responding to this rumour, McBride told the Legislature that he was interested only in "the conservation of the general public interest" and that the government had "a secure hold on the affections of the people." Noting that unemployment and depression lay beyond its control, he reiterated that "British Columbia was all right and would come through successfully when the present crisis was over." He predicted that the current legislative session would last for about three weeks, with the moratorium on mortgages and redistribution of Legislature seats the only important issues.[40] Redistribution added five seats to the Legislature and went through easily, but other issues caused considerable debate, and the session extended over six weeks.

The Liberals had had no representation in the Legislature since the 1912 election but were reorganizing and gaining support, especially in Vancouver. H.C. Brewster, who became provincial leader in 1913, accused the government of "throwing away" resources to speculators. In concert with other prominent Liberals, such as John Oliver and M.A. MacDonald, he repeated that theme and drew large audiences during his Interior and northern tours. Macdonald charged the government with seriously impairing provincial credit, taking on a "tremendous liability for railways," spending "millions professedly on roads which never go past the [political] machine," and of doing nothing to increase the population or natural wealth.[41]

The complaints spilled over to the Legislature, where Harold E. Forster, the Independent Conservative for Columbia, attacked the Conservative machine, asserted that legislation was "railroaded" through the House, and expressed the hope that the province had "seen the last of the demands of these hungry railway promoters with their insatiable appetites for government assistance." Six months earlier, the *Sun* had reported stories of discontent in the House, but now it saw Forster's attack as "the first of a disgruntled section of the Conservative party to be heard from" and hinted that it was part of an effort to defeat Bowser because of his Dominion Trust connection. Given the problems of the Dominion Trust and the railways, the *Times* suggested that McBride wanted an election before "the political waters become too turbulent."[42]

But the waters did get stormier. For two years, it had been rumoured that Price Ellison, the minister of finance and agriculture, who was an Okanagan rancher in private life, would leave the cabinet. Early in 1915,

McBride learned that in 1912, Ellison had bought thirteen valuable Holstein Friesian cattle and some horses, including a registered Clydesdale stallion, from Colony Farm, part of the new Provincial Mental Hospital in Coquitlam, and had not paid for them for at least a year.[43] The farm produced food for the patients, provided occupational therapy, and, as a demonstration farm, had top-quality livestock. When McBride questioned him, Ellison complained that he had been "badly treated" by the farm, for he had "never paid so much for horses and got so little in return." Two of the mares were barren and the stallion had had to be castrated. McBride's informant also told Forster, who, along with Parker Williams, attacked Ellison. McBride promised to confer with Ellison later. According to the press, several caucus members insisted that Ellison must resign. Conservative papers suggested that Ellison may not have been dishonest but was careless and thoughtless. On 8 March, he resigned as a cabinet member but vowed to run again.[44]

An election announcement overshadowed Ellison's resignation. According to local gossip, D'Arcy Tate, J.W. Stewart, and Patrick Welch met with McBride at his home on Friday, 5 March. They wanted him to remain as premier because he would treat them better than Bowser would. After the next day's caucus meeting, McBride professed himself "surprised and hurt" when Bowser and the majority of the caucus were "dead set" against further aid to the PGE. He announced that he would seek dissolution on Monday. Bowser, who had not been consulted regarding this move, was incensed. Lottie Bowron, McBride's secretary, recalled McBride saying that he would not run again but that caucus wanted another election. Caucus members said, "He didn't take it as we expected; we weren't turning against him." McBride confided to Borden that his quarrel with Bowser "threatens to be disastrous" but that he expected to "to settle differences."[45]

On 9 March, the *Colonist* reported that, on the previous day, the lieutenant-governor had signed the Order-in-Council for dissolution. The next day it was announced that the election would be on 10 April, to allow the required two-week interval after nominations closed. Publicly, McBride explained that an election was necessary because of the war and the need to consult the people about policies to deal with the situation, especially relating to railways. He noted that some cabinet ministers wished to retire and that new ones should be brought in to strengthen the cabinet. Several MLAs hoped to be called to the cabinet, but the cabinet change was minor. Bowser temporarily took over Ellison's portfolios. It was rumoured that Henry Esson Young would resign.[46] The *Province* frankly admitted that the story was gossip but reported that four Vancouver MLAs and several others who did not agree with McBride remained in Victoria and, along with several members of the Conservative organization in Vancouver who joined them, were "very mysterious and solemn about the cause for their coming together." On their return to Vancouver the next day, the Conservatives told the press that they had consulted with McBride about the election and that he was preparing an election manifesto.[47]

With his usual optimism, McBride declared, "I yield to no one in my great and unimpaired faith in the splendid future of British Columbia, so also I purpose giving the best that is in me to the task of bringing to the speediest fruition those projects for the development which have already so successfully been initiated." McBride stated that halting work on the PGE would be "a disaster," that he was preparing his election manifesto, and that he planned to tour the Kootenays, the Okanagan, the Lower Mainland, and possibly Prince Rupert. With an election under way, Conservatives closed ranks. At several nominating conventions in Vancouver, Bowser spoke of "harmony" in the ranks and of an "undivided front." McBride prepared his manifesto and worked on organization. He urged supporters in Yale to do all they could for Alexander Lucas, the Conservative incumbent, who would be touring the province to explain the Agricultural Credits Act. He asked his friend R.F. Green to come from Ottawa to assist in the campaign and help him fight the "good fight."[48]

Two days after asking Green to come, McBride wired him, "Not necessary for you to come. Have postponed election. Expect see you in Ottawa in few days." McBride privately admitted to "some friction" among government members on railway policy but expected the problem would soon be satisfactorily adjusted. "The delay in elections," he explained, "was not due to any trouble in the ranks" but to problems in getting ballot boxes to remote districts and revising the voters' lists. The election would be held before September. That too was the story in the *Colonist*, which commented that, "fortunately," the lieutenant-governor had not signed the Order-in-Council dissolving the Legislature. There was some truth to the explanation about the voters' lists, particularly in the North, where, for example, the *Omineca Miner* complained that thousands would be disfranchised. The government had cancelled the existing voters' lists in 1913 because, despite some revisions, they were ten years old and "padded with fake names and those of absentees." The Liberal press suspected a political ploy since the government had the advantage in preparing and distributing the lists.[49]

Many stories circulated as to why the election had been cancelled. One suggested that Borden had pressed McBride to do so. Another held that after a "stormy interview," McBride gave in to Bowser and called off both the proposed aid to the PGE and the election. The *Sun* claimed that after fifteen caucus members told McBride that they would run as Independent Conservatives if he put another railway aid policy before the electors, others had joined them, and a majority of the caucus supported Bowser. Editorially, the *Sun* observed that the division between McBride and Bowser had "reached an acute stage" and that Bowser's connection with the Dominion Trust had weakened the government. The *Times* concluded, "Sir Richard, after taking stock of the situation, has regained his wonted composure and suspended the election big stick until the skies clear." Although the Liberal press relished a split between McBride and Bowser, it nonetheless continued to castigate what it called the Bowser-McBride government and claimed that the province was "governed by a diumvirate, composed of the Premier and the Attorney-General."[50]

In the constituencies too, there were problems. The Cowichan organization asked incumbent W.H. Hayward to run as an Independent, and in New Westminster, the party "machine" favoured Thomas Gifford, the incumbent, but younger members wanted to nominate Magistrate H.L. Edmonds. Some Victoria Conservatives, unhappy with the machine, formed the Imperial Conservative Association. Individual Conservatives were also dissatisfied. C.M. Woodworth, a former president of the Conservative Association, told the *Sun* that the party's policies no longer bore any resemblance to those of 1903-09. "When Tatlow the good pilot, left us," he explained, "the ship was taken by a pirate crew and run after the style of Capt. Kidd."[51]

While the parties continued their nominating conventions, McBride undertook one of his regular pilgrimages to Ottawa and London. Despite persistent reports that he would join the federal cabinet, his brief stay in Ottawa was merely his annual visit to discuss provincial matters.[52] He saw Borden for only half an hour but met several friends, including cabinet ministers, at the Rideau Club. Next, he spent several days in New York City; he dined in his hotel room with Jim Carruthers, a prominent Canadian grain merchant and president of the Canada Steamship Lines; consulted with officials of the CPR and the GTP, and with Mann of the CNR; and tried to sell PGE bonds before sailing to London, where he was expected to seek funds for the PGE. He checked into the Savoy Hotel but later moved to a room at 4 Whitehall Court. Unfortunately, he contracted influenza soon after arriving, did little work for a week, and then recuperated at Brighton on the seaside. He told reporters that his business related to railways but that he was not after a loan. He consulted the British government about using captured enemy merchant ships to carry BC lumber to Britain. He spent a few days in Paris, trying to persuade the French government to put BC tinned salmon on its list of army rations. In Europe, he visited hospitalized British Columbia soldiers. Always the optimist, he got close enough to the front to say that the Germans were "demoralized and discouraged," and that the Allied troops were "supremely confident."[53]

The Opposition increasingly criticized McBride's frequent absences and the cost of his journeys. Parker Williams observed that McBride had spent $5,480.40 on railway fares, which, at two cents a mile, would provide him with a round trip to the moon and $1,000 to spend there! His salary of $10,000, said the *Times*, was almost as large as that of the prime minister and was paid for him to attend to the people's business. The press variously suggested that he would take over the naval portfolio in Ottawa, become Canada's high commissioner in London, or succeed Turner as British Columbia's agent-general in London. En route home, McBride told an Ottawa journalist that he had seen reports of being the "prodigal son," but he asserted that "the political situation in British Columbia is all right" and left the impression that he planned to stick to provincial politics.[54]

During McBride's absence, Bowser had strengthened "his position at the expense of the premier." Liberals speculated that he and his friends had failed in their plot to have McBride transferred to London, "ostensibly for imperial purposes" but really to become agent-general. McBride, however, does not seem to have questioned Bowser's loyalty. Bowser spoke to party "faithful" and made political tours but was frustrated by McBride's absence and his own lack of information about the premier's activities. He wanted to set an election date before all the road money was spent and unemployment and enemy aliens had become greater problems. "Matters are so critical here," he wrote to McBride, "that I think you should let me know at once what your plans are so that I can handle things intelligently here." McBride replied that he would be leaving London in two weeks. Four weeks passed before he left.[55]

Bowser's problems mounted. The sinking of the *Lusitania* on 7 May 1915 precipitated anti-German riots in Victoria. The jobless, "most of them British and very loyal," resented the employment of enemy aliens in mines, especially in Nanaimo, where they had been hired during the coal strike. After interned Austrians were released to work in the mines of several communities, Bowser feared that "some pay day when both sides get excited through the use of liquor," there could be violence. He worried that Prince Rupert might default on treasury notes and asked McBride to try to get them renewed. McBride had refused to guarantee the debentures, but the city's default could harm the province's credit.[56]

After several unexplained delays, McBride finally left London. He had raised no money but cheerfully reported many inquiries about post-war settlement in British Columbia. After briefly stopping in New York, he went to Ottawa. A "slim" McBride told Borden that he was pessimistic about the outcome of the war and doubted the competency of some British generals. With R.F. Green and G.H. Barnard, the MP for Victoria, he discussed the lack of ocean shipping and the possibility that British Columbia might form regiments, manufacture munitions, and supply Canadian and Allied forces with foodstuffs.[57]

On 4 July, McBride arrived in Victoria. The *Times* and the *Colonist* agreed that he appeared to be in excellent health and spirits. Due to the sales efforts of H.R. MacMillan, he was optimistic about British markets for lumber, and he reported that a gift of canned salmon and food had "made a profound impression" in London.[58] He praised the bravery of Canadian soldiers and the efficiency of the Red Cross. In London he had seen a Zeppelin, which caused no "undue excitement," and he said that most Canadians did not realize that "the very fate of the Empire ... [and] British liberty were at stake" in the war. He would not speak on provincial affairs, because he had not yet read his correspondence. With depressed money markets, he did not think that a provincial election was urgently needed. At the Victoria Board of Trade, he stressed that he had promoted provincial resources that could help the war effort, and he emphasized the need for ocean transport, primarily a Dominion responsibility.[59]

Throughout 1915, McBride remained optimistic. In addressing the Victoria Conservative Association (to whom he said, "Let everyone wear a smile"), the Canadian Mining Institute, and the Grand Post of the Native Sons of British Columbia, he admitted that the war had seriously hindered the economy but quickly added that, with its new railways, roads, and the university, and its rich natural resources, the province would soon prosper again. When opening a new road in North Vancouver, he remarked that because of the increasing number of automobiles, the province must make highways part of its development policy. Nevertheless, he added, railways remained important and he expected that the PGE would continue to the Peace River. If the money markets were not closed, more would be done. His comments elicited only "indifferent applause." The public was losing confidence in the economy, but he was not. In December, he told a correspondent who had complained of personal financial problems that British Columbia had been the "hardest hit" of the provinces and was now at "rock bottom." But, he added, lumbering and mining were picking up, and with its people and resources, the province would "make a full and complete recovery."[60]

Financial stringency forced the government to postpone some projects begun during the pre-war boom. The creation of Strathcona Park on Vancouver Island, British Columbia's first provincial park, was a highlight of 1911, but the park required development to attract tourists and local campers. Plans for this were made in 1912, but the work was delayed by controversy over the employment of an American civil engineer to supervise the building of roads and trails. In November 1915, when a delegation, including the mayor of Victoria, who wanted to develop the tourist trade, called on McBride, he could offer no appropriation.[61]

Plans for the university were in even worse shape. Its first president, Frank F. Wesbrook, soon learned that the government authorized expenditures only from year to year. McBride had believed that the funds made available in the spring of 1913 would permit "a splendid start" on the university. On the eve of the 1914 legislative session, he said that the high cost of building meant that the university needed a substantial additional sum and suggested that the "moneyed men" of the province might help. A year later, he told the university board of governors to shelve its construction plans "pending the return of happier times." Cuts to the university's operating budget followed. In the summer of 1915, it closed its Victoria branch to save money, a development that threatened to revive the Island versus Mainland controversy, but McBride passed responsibility for the decision to the board of governors. If the government were to make any concession to Victoria, he feared the advent of "similar agitations for preferential treatment all over the Province." Yet he believed in serving the province's many regions with higher education. At the time of the university's first convocation in August 1912, he proclaimed that it was to be "Canadian, with a great big imperial scope and generosity of purpose that will stand out well in keeping with the optimism, confidence and culture of this great western section of the Dominion." He wanted the university to have "the best in every way" but, like many British Columbians, he did not believe in ivory towers. In accepting an honorary degree at Berkeley in 1913, he had opined that "the man who can work intelligently and well, though he never saw the inside of a university, may in the true sense be far better educated than a man with a brilliant college career who has much knowledge in the abstract but can do nothing practical or useful." He assured the Farmers' Institute that the university would offer courses in practical agriculture. However, the parlous financial situation trumped his desire to serve all sections of the province.[62]

The creation of an Agricultural Credits Commission to provide cash assistance for farmers and let them borrow on pre-emptions as well as purchased lands was also delayed by financial problems. Its implementation had been a major recommendation of the Royal Commission on Agriculture. McBride put it on the agenda for the 1915 legislative session but warned farmers and W.H. Hayward MLA, the commission chairman, that the bill for its formation would not be proclaimed until the province could "borrow at a good rock-bottom rate." He suggested that the federal government should provide financial aid to farmers and establish some uniformity across the country. Despite the delay, the *Colonist* described the bill as "An Act to Enable the Industrious Farmer to Make Good." Other Conservative journals lauded it, but the *Sun* damned it with faint praise as "a proposal forced upon the government by public opinion ... to catch votes at the forthcoming election." Among the bodies pressing for the bill was the Victoria Board of Trade. Most tellingly, the *Omineca Herald*, situated in an area where recent settlers could benefit from the credits commission, noted that the minister of lands printed pamphlets on loans to farmers but did not say that the money was unavailable. That summer, when a Citizens' Unemployment Committee asked McBride to implement the act, he reiterated his point about the difficulty of raising money. Not until April 1916, after he had retired, did the act come into effect.[63]

The Liberals still alleged that the government had allowed speculators to hold millions of acres, whereas would-be settlers could not gain access to them, and that it had provided inadequate or misleading information about the land that was available for pre-emption. As the economic situation deteriorated and the war created a demand for foodstuffs, McBride heard many requests to ease unemployment by hiring men to clear land and encouraging agricultural settlement. To a delegation from the Victoria and Island Development Association, an exasperated McBride wrote that he had received so numerous and varied proposals on the land question that they would be "an interesting study in themselves." "The great majority," he said, "though plausible, and in many instances, possibly sound under certain conditions, are either experimental or impractical at the present time when the finances of the world are all upset by war conditions." He agreed that the "Back to the Land" movement that was spreading throughout North America was "one of the most important movements of this century so far" and noted that it had been studied by the Royal Commission on Agriculture, but he warned of the "absurdity" of a "hurried and indiscriminate back-to-the land movement" until transportation was available. Yet he admitted an inability to develop an improved land settlement policy, abuses in the disposal of Crown lands in the area served by the GTP, and about $15 million in arrears from speculators who had bought large blocks of land. He thought it unwise to "swing an axe" on these delinquents since their large investments gave them a stake in the province. The government was giving farmers free farms, schools, and road work. W.R. Ross, the minister of lands, later said that only about $9 million was owed, as McBride had probably included arrears on townsites and interest. There was some sympathy for the government's problem. The *Province* thought it "a waste of time to cry over spilt milk" and endorsed Parker Williams's idea that the government should continue to collect taxes on land held by speculators but allow easy payments.[64]

However, this constituted only a brief break from attacks on land policy. Early in March, Moses B. Cotsworth, a statistician, gave a presentation titled "Cause of B.C.'s Financial Stringency and Its Cure" to Victoria's Metropolitan Church Brotherhood. While McBride was in London, the Ministerial Union of the Lower Mainland released a pamphlet, *The Crisis in B.C.*, which Cotsworth had prepared. A damning critique of the McBride administration's land and resource policies, it charged that the government had allowed syndicates, many of them formed by foreign capitalists, chiefly American but including Germans, to exploit much of the province's land, timber, and mineral resources. The pamphlet was filled with statistics and letters documenting its arguments, including the heart-wrenching story of a would-be settler in the Nechako district who found that land sold by real estate agents as a veritable Eden was useless for agriculture.[65]

Reverend A.E. Cooke, the minister at Kitsilano Congregational Church and spokesman for the Ministerial Union, denied that the Liberals had paid for the pamphlet and said that the "whole Union" was responsible for it. At a mass meeting in Vancouver, the Ministerial Union collected funds to send Cooke on a provincial speaking tour and resolved to ask Prime Minister Borden to investigate the charges in *The Crisis*. On his tour, Cooke attracted large audiences, many of whom were bitter about the government. A poster at one meeting read, "McBride and Bowser: Are They Pro-German?" In 1915, this was a grave insinuation. In sending a copy of *The Crisis* to McBride, Cooke claimed that the union was motivated solely by "the highest interest of the people" and asked him to use his influence to secure an investigation. McBride was abroad, so his cabinet ministers were obliged to answer the charges. Ross dismissed them as "the dissemination of as much calumny as possible." Bowser responded with a two-and-a-half-hour speech to an overflow audience at Vancouver's Orpheum Theatre on 29 July. Much of it – forty-six pages in the printed version – was a defence of himself and an attack on Cotsworth, the Liberal Party, and to a lesser extent the clergy who had sponsored the pamphlet. He said little about McBride, but his speech may have done more harm than good. The *Sun* called it a "vulgar and indefensible attack on the character of the men who published" the pamphlet and wondered why, if its charges were untrue, Bowser feared an investigation. Indeed, the controversy seemed to evolve into a personal feud between Bowser and the Ministerial Union.[66]

The Conservative press defended McBride: It stated that much timberland had already been alienated before his time, and the government needed revenue from land sales to build roads, bridges, trails, and schools. The *Columbian* claimed that despite allegations by "unscrupulous opponents of the government," land and credit were available for farmers. Yet its comment that the McBride administration had sold fewer than 6 million acres, most of which were more than three miles from a railway, appeared to support the argument that the government had not made settlement easy. A few days later, it clarified its comment to suggest that, if speculators had purchased land, it was distant from the railways and that they paid a heavy wild land tax. The *Colonist* accused Cooke of forgetting one of the Ten Commandments or not knowing what he was talking about when he blamed the government for the overcapitalization of companies since the government had nothing to do with that. The editor of the *Western Methodist Recorder*, who had written several editorials over the years in praise of McBride and his administration, suggested that "the attack looks too bitter to be sincere" and wondered whether Cotsworth and possibly certain politicians had "used" the clergymen. Nevertheless, he published a communication from the Ministerial Union, which stated that its committee had carefully checked the accuracy of the facts in the pamphlet and that after several "largely attended" meetings, the union had "unanimously and heartily" endorsed its report on the pamphlet. The Liberal press naturally savoured *The Crisis* as a "strong indictment" of the government and wondered whether more was "to be said along similar lines."[67]

The Ministerial Union distributed the pamphlet widely. The *Toronto Globe* based two articles and five editorials on it, attacking "the reckless and prodigal Government of Sir Richard McBride." Similarly, *Saturday*

Night accused the McBride administration of corruption. The *Christian Science Monitor* reported the charges as truth. McBride did not reply to the allegations until September. As he explained to the editor of the *Toronto Mail and Empire*, a Conservative competitor of the Liberal *Globe*, he had not thought it worthwhile to engage in controversy with newspapers outside his own province, but friends had told him that failing to answer, especially given recent scandals concerning the Roblin government in Manitoba, "left a rather painful impression."[68] In responding to critical editors, McBride enclosed copies of the detailed letters he sent to the *Globe* and to *Saturday Night* as well as memoranda answering the statements of Cotsworth, "a very adroit but unscrupulous man who has his knife in the government because he was not allowed to remain permanently in the service." He added that Cotsworth and the clergy associated with the pamphlet had been "thoroughly discredited." He told the editor of the *Christian Science Monitor* that he was accustomed to being attacked but "as a native son and as Prime Minister of British Columbia," he was "much grieved" that statements "by really irresponsible persons" had gained such publicity outside the province. Explaining that he was concerned not about himself but about "the credit of the province," he attacked the *Globe* and *Saturday Night* for accepting *The Crisis* as "gospel truth" when it was nothing more than a "tissue of lies from cover to cover." He noted that while in the government's employ, Cotsworth had written a pamphlet praising its use of timber revenue to build roads. He asked why the editors had vilified "a province several thousand miles away," whose conditions they could not understand. He wondered how Ontario Liberals, strong supporters of provincial rights, would accept the *Globe*'s suggestion that a federal or imperial commission should investigate BC affairs. British Columbia, he insisted, "is capable of handling its own affairs without outside interference or suggestion." After McBride released his *Globe* letter to the local press, the *Times* asserted that "everybody knows that the province for years has been the exploiters' parade." The *Colonist* denied the *Globe*'s assertion that it was McBride's "mouthpiece, called the *Globe*'s reply "largely perfunctory," and said that it revealed little knowledge of agriculture in the province.[69]

Eventually, *The Crisis in B.C.* became a matter for the courts. MLA Alex Lucas issued a libel writ against the Ministerial Union and Cotsworth for saying that in December 1909 the Civil Service Commission had "compelled" him to resign from his position as a timber assessor "on account of neglect of his duties, and a 'timber deal' by which he pocketed about $10,000." Cotsworth added that despite being repeatedly refused leaves of absence, Lucas had gone to Vancouver to complete the deal. When the

"The Crisis in B. C."

Which would you believe?

In asking readers "Which would you believe?" this *Vancouver Sun* cartoon supplies the answer to its own rhetorical question. The crabbed figure of Bowser, armed with the club of professional politics and motivated by gain, is juxtaposed with the principled members of the clergy who produced *The Crisis in B.C.* Bowser, Reid and Walbridge was Bowser's legal firm. Although Bowser was a major subject of attack and was the chief defender of the government's policies, McBride's reputation also suffered. *Vancouver Sun,* 7 October 1915, unsigned but probably by John (Jack) Innes.

libel case went to court in late November, McBride explained that in June 1909, shortly before the commissioners regrading civil servants arrived in Kaslo, Lucas had announced his intention to resign because of the low salary. At that time, McBride replied that he hoped Lucas would stay as he was "a very efficient public servant," particularly in the work of equalizing assessments. McBride denied having encouraged Lucas "to flout his official superiors" and never gave him a leave without the consent of his departmental chief. The jury awarded Lucas $200 and costs. Although the Ministerial Union suspended the sale of the pamphlet, the *Sun* rightly argued that the libel case concerned only one aspect of the issue and did not refute the other allegations.[70]

Nevertheless, the damage to the government's reputation had been done.[71] In commenting on *The Crisis,* the *Province* observed that the real issue went deeper than the collapse of the boom, which had been a "blessing in disguise" because it made people think of production, not speculation. The true problem was that, regardless of whether the government was Liberal or Conservative, "politics are entirely governed by patronage." The *Omineca Herald* asserted that provincial civil servants participated in Conservative meetings and used inside information "to defeat the Liberals and to injure the private business of anyone opposed to the Conservative machine." It expected that no new work on roads, bridges, and trails would be undertaken until an election was called. Then, it said, "Every man in the province will be offered a job." It facetiously commented, "People are learning to live without the government pap."[72]

The Ministerial Union's interest in bringing down the McBride-Bowser government may have been inspired by McBride and Bowser's lack of enthusiasm for Prohibition, a movement that was gaining wide support throughout North America. In September 1914, Right Reverend D.A. Macdonald, the Roman Catholic bishop of Victoria; Bishop J.C. Roper of the Anglican diocese of British Columbia (Vancouver Island); and Reverend J.G. Inkster of the Presbyterian Church interviewed McBride. McBride explained that municipalities controlled closing hours, but he wrote to the province's mayors, suggesting that they consider measures to reduce the sale of intoxicants so as to conserve "the best interests of the country at this critical time." His letters had little effect. McBride told prohibitionists that "until the country as a whole decided in favor of total prohibition the liquor traffic should be surrounded by all the wholesome restrictions possible." He believed that the licence system "was achieving excellent results." A year later, he told Anglican bishop A.J. Doull of Kootenay that something should quickly be done to shorten the hours during which alcohol was sold, to "prevent people drinking themselves drunk during a time of unprecedented crisis."[73]

Prominent businessmen such as W.H. Malkin, a Vancouver wholesale grocer, favoured Prohibition, but not all businessmen did. A deputation of those engaged in the liquor trade and some others told McBride that Prohibition would "menace" business and financial interests, and that it should not be introduced without a binding referendum. After "serious and deliberate" consideration in cabinet, McBride told a prohibitionist that, because the war might have changed the people's attitude, his government would organize a plebiscite. Like a referendum, a plebiscite would reflect public opinion but would not be binding. McBride opposed direct legislation such as a referendum because it was not British, had had some "unsatisfactory and expensive" results in the United States, and would offer only one way of meeting prohibitionist wishes, whereas if a plebiscite revealed that the people wanted Prohibition, the government could choose the means of introducing it. He believed that the plebiscite's ballot should ask voters directly whether they were for or against total Prohibition and that it should contain other "plain and simple" questions relating to the issue. He endorsed early closing of bars during the war.[74]

The Merchants Protective Association, which represented the liquor business, organized a large delegation of businessmen who presented McBride with a petition signed by 33,947 electors asking that no prohibitory legislation be introduced until after the war and that those in the trade be compensated for the loss of their businesses. McBride had already decided to hold the plebiscite simultaneously with the next general election. After reminding the Merchants Protective Association that the prohibitionists wanted a vote on a straight "wet" or "dry" issue, he asserted that "the government does not stand for the temperance class, the merchant or the labor class, but for all the people." He promised that if the people favoured complete Prohibition, the government would enact it but stated that all efforts should be concentrated on the war. He had a personal interest in the Prohibition issue: his brother Edward had recently become a "Family Wine and Spirit Merchant," and advertised that he ran the "Only Bottle House" in New Westminster. Liberal leader H.C. Brewster, a staunch prohibitionist, complained that a plebiscite bore out McBride's "reputation for indefiniteness and clever evasions." The Liberal press concluded that McBride was simply seeking the prohibitionist vote, whereas the Conservative press thought his reasoning "sound." In replying to the Peoples Prohibition Movement, he indicated that if the people "emphatically" declared for Prohibition, Attorney General Bowser would "carry out their wishes without fear or favor." That comment led to speculation that McBride would soon retire. Dissatisfied prohibitionists approached other political parties.[75]

McBride could not escape scandal, and his heroic moment – his purchase of the two American submarines – eventually became a nightmare. Stories circulated that the submarine deal had been tainted by something "discreditable." In the House of Commons in February 1915, William Pugsley, who had been Laurier's minister of public works, asked that the correspondence relating to the submarine purchase be laid before the House. He alleged that the vessels were "somewhat obsolete," and that Chile, which had initially ordered them, would not accept them because they were not up to its specifications and were over-priced. Moreover, the federal government had been too "secretive," and there was "a feeling" in British Columbia that McBride had probably used a commission on the sale for party purposes. Pugsley stressed that he was simply reporting feelings, not making a charge. Initially, even the *Vancouver Sun,* no friend to McBride, commented that Pugsley made no specific allegations about graft and that it was unfortunate that McBride should be put on the defensive. In replying to Pugsley's charges, J.D. Hazen, the minister of naval affairs, said that naval experts had found the subs satisfactory, that having them at Esquimalt was desirable, and that haste had been essential. If McBride had not acted, Borden explained, Canada would not have enjoyed their protection.[76]

Although McBride suspected that Pugsley had been "fully primed from this end of the country," he made no immediate move to defend himself, choosing to wait until he saw the full report of the parliamentary debate. He then sent a copy with a letter to J.V. Paterson, whose company had built and sold the subs to Canada, and asked for any "observations" that would help his defence. Paterson replied that he had read Pugsley's "misinformed" comments "with amusement and scorn." After receiving this letter, McBride made a long speech in the Legislature, declaring that "not a cent of commission had been paid," that the subs, which were of the "highest and most modern type," had been inspected by an Admiralty representative and had immediately been placed in effective service. Without their presence in Esquimalt, he claimed, "both Vancouver and Victoria would have been subjected to a bombardment by German warships." He argued that Pugsley had been misinformed and that British Columbians had the "right to resent this malicious attempt ... to throw discredit on a public man who has tried to do the Empire an important service at a critical moment." The Conservative press hailed his defence. The *Sun* found no evidence of a commission but charged McBride with seeking political capital by saying that "certain Liberals in Victoria" had hired private detectives in an effort "to wreck his political career." All that was required, said the *Sun,* was a denial of the claim that the vessels were inadequate.[77]

McBride had already asked Borden to give the issue "strictest investigation." Although Borden did not think that Pugsley's insinuations deserved notice, he told McBride that he could have his speech to the Legislature read into Hansard and suggested that he leave matters to his, Borden's, judgment. McBride was "very unwilling" to leave the impression that he feared investigation but agreed to let Borden deal with the issue, possibly because he expected a provincial election. After the election was cancelled,

McBride went to Ottawa, where the press intimated that he sought to clarify the situation. The *Times* suggested that by questioning the good faith of Canada's auditor general, who had said that he could not get proper vouchers from McBride, McBride had harmed his case since he knew "little or nothing of the functions of an Auditor-General or a Public Accounts Committee," a snide reference to Liberal dissatisfaction with the local equivalents. McBride's denial did not end suspicions of scandal, especially after federal Liberals linked the submarines with well-founded stories of corruption and graft in the allocation of munitions contracts elsewhere. McBride claimed that an interview with the *London Advertiser*, reprinted in the *Victoria Times*, was "almost libelous." Unimpressed, the *Times* questioned the military emergency in August 1914 because at that time the German fleet was far from British Columbia. McBride admitted that there had been no immediate danger but said he had thought that Canada should have more subs on the Pacific coast in case the German fleet escaped from the Kiel Canal and sailed to the North Pacific. In such an emergency, he told Hazen, "We should not have to depend upon Japan or the United States."[78]

In Ottawa, McBride testified about the submarine purchase to the Davidson Royal Commission, which was investigating war purchases generally. When he left almost immediately for London to seek funds for the PGE, the Liberal press suggested that he had done so to escape interrogation by the Public Accounts Committee. The Conservative press complained that the Liberals had become interested in the submarines only after McBride left and had raised the issue for partisan purposes. In October, when the Davidson Commission came to Victoria, McBride caused a sensation by asking Davidson to call on prominent Liberals who, having circulated reports of graft, must have the evidence to prove it. Davidson rejected his request. After McBride and J.V. Paterson testified, the Conservative press saw no basis for the allegations, but the *Sun* insisted that McBride remained under "a cloud of suspicion." After McBride retired, it conceded that his motives in buying the subs were wholly patriotic and had done much to restore confidence in Victoria. The Davidson Commission's final report, issued early in 1917, completely exonerated McBride and concluded that the price paid for the submarines was fair and reasonable.[79] For McBride, this was a bittersweet end to a patriotic measure designed to protect his beloved British Columbia.

The purchase of the submarines did not end McBride's concerns about coastal defence. In the fall of 1914, after calling at the War Office, the Admiralty, and the Colonial Office, he expected "adequate steps" to protect

British interests in the Pacific. Late in 1914, he informed Borden that a "competent firm" could fabricate eight submarines, suitable for protecting harbours and the coast, in American yards and assemble them in British Columbia. Although publicly he said he was satisfied with efforts to protect British interests in the Pacific, he continued to remind Ottawa of the need for "adequate" coastal defences, including the "betterment of our forts" and the construction of other installations. When Borden told him early in 1915 that the prospect of an attack on the Pacific coast by "any considerable force" was "exceedingly remote," McBride replied that he trusted that Borden's hope was "well founded" but did not drop his campaign for a better defence of the coast.[80]

When several eastern newspapers, including the *Toronto Globe,* accused him of fomenting rumours of a German raid in order to retain an "unnecessary number of troops" in his province to relieve unemployment, McBride called the story "a wicked fabrication" and decried their failure to realize that "a sea coast is in a very different position from an inland city." He referred to the need to protect railways and the "strong pro-German feeling" in many US Pacific coast cities, including Seattle, where the German community was headed by such men as Alvo von Alvensleben, the former Vancouver financier. Von Alvensleben, he told the press, "would be only too glad to seize an opportunity to make trouble. The coast is practically undefended." Germans were not his only concern. In urging the American government to build a railway to Alaska, he suggested that as Japan grew stronger, the United States should appreciate the "immense strategic value" of such a line.[81]

McBride had a "hands-on" approach to military efforts. He wrote to Colonel Sam Hughes, the minister of militia and defence, on such varied matters as the appointment of officers to a local regiment and the care of returned sick and wounded soldiers. Short notice meant that he could not attend an Ottawa meeting on plans for returning and disabled soldiers, but he asked Bowser to give "hearty co-operation" to efforts to promote the "highest efficiency" of the military hospitals commission.[82]

In London in the fall of 1914, McBride had learned that the main need of the war effort was for "*men* and *then more men.*" He called for 150,000 Canadian troops in Europe by June 1915, suggested that Canada pay travel costs for Canadians who enlisted in Britain, and proposed that troops be sent overseas every week or so rather than in huge convoys because of the danger of German attack (an idea deemed impractical by Borden). He forwarded offers to Borden from about sixty Sikhs who wanted to serve in the imperial forces, partly because he wanted to keep them "in their present satisfactory frame of mind." He sent offers from over-age reservists to guard interned aliens and undertake other duties to free younger men for overseas service. He reported that British Columbia's naval volunteers felt that Ottawa was "rather indifferent to them," when Admiral Kingsmill, the deputy minister of naval service, suggested they enlist with the Canadian Expeditionary Force.[83] McBride proposed recruiting Americans for the British army, but Borden feared disturbing the "excellent sentiment prevailing in the United States." When McBride inspected troops training at Victoria's Willows Camp, he particularly welcomed the Americans among them.[84]

McBride genuinely liked the United States and Americans. He often made his eastern trips via American railroads, a point that his critics noted. When former president Theodore Roosevelt visited Victoria in July 1915, McBride met him at the dock and took him on a sightseeing tour. Although he could not parlay it into a railway to Alaska, he commemorated the centennial of the Treaty of Ghent by telling the Legislature that British Columbians were determined to maintain cordial relations with the United States, a sentiment he repeated in thanking Harry Brittain, the British journalist who promoted good Anglo-American relations, for his speech to Victoria's Canadian Club.[85]

The war had created a problem with enemy aliens. When the *Toronto Globe* reported that McBride visited Germany during the spring of 1912, he vigorously denied ever having been there.[86] At home, he had welcomed Germans, especially von Alvensleben, who invested German money in various provincial enterprises. And he had time for other Germans. For example, at the 1912 Deutsche Verins banquet held in Victoria to celebrate the kaiser's birthday, he graciously declared that "much as British Columbia liked the products of the Fatherland the German people were liked better and their presence sought and welcomed," as he hoped that Britain and Germany "should ever dwell in peace." At a banquet in honour of Emperor William's twenty-fifth anniversary on the German throne, McBride thanked Alvo von Alvensleben for his expressions of friendliness to the British people. Although they were commercial rivals, he said that Britain had no quarrel with Germany. In British Columbia, he added, "We daily illustrate for the benefit of the two home peoples how well Germans and Britons can live together." McBride was so impressed by von Alvensleben's enterprises that he subscribed for $500 worth of shares in the German-Canadian Trust Company, which von Alvensleben had formed to bring German capital to the province. He did not receive the stock, so he could honestly say that he had no interest in any of von Alvensleben's companies.

Privately, he favoured confiscating the property of Germans and Austrians who had gone to take up arms against the Allies.[87]

Suspicions of enemy aliens and spies were common during the war. One of the first local casualties was McBride's secretary Lawrence Macrae, whose body was found in his Parliament Buildings office on the morning of 10 September 1914. Rumours that he had committed suicide after being caught stealing and manipulating defence plans were so persistent that McBride issued a press release in January to state that the story was baseless. Macrae "had been suffering for many months with a nervous ailment."[88] McBride also informed Victoria's police chief of a confidential report that a local German was building suspicious tunnels. He was concerned about unemployed enemy aliens in Victoria and Vancouver, who were a charge on the cities' relief rolls, mainly because he thought the federal government should pay for their relief. As for enemy aliens, he assured a German-born Victoria taxidermist who had been a soldier in the German army that there was no reason to "be disturbed so long as you are carrying on an ordinary peaceable occupation." When the son of the German-born long-time MLA H.F.W. Behnsen wanted to join the Canadian Mounted Rifles, McBride vouched for him. He could do nothing for von Alvensleben in his American exile.[89] Although some enemy aliens were rounded up in the fall of 1914, and employers dismissed others, hostility to them really developed after the sinking of the *Lusitania* on 7 May 1915. A month earlier, McBride had sailed to Britain on the ship. Since he did not return until July, Bowser dealt with problems arising from the presence of enemy aliens.[90]

From the time war was declared, McBride promoted patriotism. He spoke at a recruiting rally for the B.C. Horse and at a meeting sponsored by the Imperial Order Daughters of the Empire to raise funds for a Canadian hospital ship. At the latter meeting, he donated fifteen dollars, a significant amount as some donations were as little as ten cents. In Ottawa, he extolled the province's "tremendous enthusiasm" for the war effort. When he visited the Canadian contingent at Salisbury Plain in the fall of 1914, he saw many men who had enlisted in British Columbia. The "spirit of optimism" in London impressed him, though many people wore "the badge of mourning." He praised Canadian soldiers and told graduates of the Royal Jubilee Hospital School of Nursing of the contributions made by nurses to the war. He advised the Victoria Rotary Club that Canada's "responsibility and duty to England was to take the proportionate share in the task." Similarly, he told forty-five hundred people at a Victoria rally commemorating the first anniversary of the war that those who couldn't bear arms should help the Red Cross. When Borden returned from England in September 1915, McBride sent a telegram welcoming him home and assuring him of British Columbia's pride in his achievements in the cause of empire.[91]

The McBride family also participated in patriotic endeavours. Lady McBride convened a bridge tournament at the Empress Hotel to raise funds for the Red Cross. Dressed in flags, Peggy and Ruth ran errands at a charity garden party, and during a garden party at the McBride home, which was sponsored by the Women's Canadian Club to raise funds for the Red Cross, Dolly helped her mother sell donated packets of tea. At another event, Peggy had charge of a clock golf game. Not all social events related directly to the war. Lady McBride hosted the garden party of the ladies of St. Andrew's Presbyterian Church. Sir Richard greeted the guests, praised Canadian soldiers, described the empire as being on trial, and reiterated that British Columbia would enjoy prosperity after a time of stress. He noted that the party was intended to raise funds to pay taxes on the church property since his government "had not felt justified in freeing church properties from taxation." Despite the war, when the legislative session opened in January 1915, Lady McBride provided entertainment "as usual" at her Gorge Road home for the wives of the MLAs. She remained president of the Friendly Help Society. As well as supplying groceries and fuel to the needy, the society, in her words, took "time and thought and consultation to arrive at the right conclusion to render assistance in the best way."[92]

McBride's return from London in July 1915 revived rumours about dissent in his party and the timing of the next election. The *Times* thought a fall election "practically assured" and wondered whether McBride or Bowser was actually in charge of the province, as it noted that the attorney general, not McBride, would be visiting Ottawa. It asked if the *Colonist*'s coverage of Bowser's business there was made with McBride's approval or whether it reflected a belief of the Conservative press that "their future subsidies" relied on Bowser's good graces. Speculation ended when Bowser told eastern reporters that the election would be held in 1916. He also told Borden that McBride would soon resign and go to London. On 2 November, in a letter written with a less firm hand than usual, McBride informed Borden that he expected to resign soon in favour of Bowser, who would almost completely reorganize the cabinet, have a short session, and go to the people in about May. McBride was optimistic that despite a "keen" campaign, Bowser would do well since the new cabinet should prove "popular and efficient," and the united party had a "splendid organization." For the "next few months," he planned to take over J.H. Turner's work as agent-general in London, which would enable him to "follow conditions" there closely and to obtain the medical treatment recommended by his physicians. Optimistic about improving his health, he told Borden, "If by next fall" he felt "equal to an election," he would "try to arrange a federal constituency here & control it in support of your administration." After acknowledging McBride's "kind support and generous encouragement," and complimenting his "wide vision" even when dealing with purely provincial matters, Borden expressed hope that he would recover his health and run in the next federal election. In the meantime, Borden would be pleased to appoint him to the Senate. To accept such a position would have been embarrassing. In endorsing a resolution to increase the number of BC senators from four to six, he had implied that the Senate was of little use and that London had more attractions than Ottawa.[93]

The correspondence between McBride and Borden was so private and confidential that both men wrote by hand rather than having secretaries type their letters, yet the press reported that McBride would retire to become agent-general and that Bowser would form the government. A few weeks later, when Bowser announced the renewal of a loan that was coming due, H.C. Brewster interpreted this as meaning that "McBride is down and out ... that the government is in the hands of the attorney-general and that he is intending to bring on a general election at an early date." The announcement of the loan, said Brewster, was a reminder to the party "faithful" that the treasury had been "replenished" and that they would soon have an opportunity to profit from public works. The *Sun* suggested that McBride was going to London solely to "relieve the impasse now confronting the faction-rent government." It blamed him for incurring heavy liabilities and for permitting the exploitation of provincial resources, but it carefully noted the absence of charges against his personal record, pointing out that the same could not be said for Bowser, Ellison, and Young. The *Times* less charitably catalogued various criticisms of McBride and Bowser.[94]

The Opposition press continued to speculate that Bowser was driving McBride out of office. In March 1915, at the time of the aborted election and the controversy over railway policy, Bowser had definitely challenged McBride's leadership. Yet he had long been loyal. After 1912, when McBride was increasingly absent from Victoria, Bowser frequently served as acting premier. It is not surprising, then, that he would resent McBride, who often gave him the unpleasant task of saying "no" or of dealing with such difficult subjects as the Vancouver Island coal miners' strike or enemy aliens.

Initially, McBride planned to publicize his retirement early in November but then told Borden that he would make the announcement on 1 December. In the end, he delayed until 15 December 1915, his forty-fifth birthday. Despite the many rumours, the press greeted his news with some surprise. Its comments tended to follow party lines. The *Times* claimed that "never have there been so many unsolved problems of vital moment to this province as there are today," deprecated the Tammany system of the Conservative Party machine, and decried McBride's gross mismanagement of provincial resources.[95] The *Sun* labelled him a "complete failure" who had been "thrown out of government" but conceded that personal attacks against him were few and that he had not profited financially as premier. It later admitted that the departure of this "genial companion and sympathetic listener" would cause "no inconsiderable regret." Conservative editors emphasized McBride's "valuable service by focusing on a definite programme and giving his party a centripetal tendency," his "courageous and well-considered" railway policy, and his work in re-establishing provincial credit and constructing public works. They extolled his "attractive personality, his urbanity, genuine comradeship, good nature and kindness of heart," his "imagination and ambition combined with the faculty of impressing those he met with his own viewpoint," and his intuition – "the secret of his success." The *British Columbian,* his oldest political friend, observed that British Columbians would regret losing an administrator who "so well typified the prosperous, democratic spirit of the new land." The *Western Methodist Recorder* echoed these sentiments but also noted that, because his sympathies had always shown "a strong imperial tendency," London would be congenial and would allow him closer "touch with Empire problems, which so strongly appeal to his imagination."[96]

8
Respite in London

I feel that I am fairly entitled to some respite, although under new conditions the duties of Agent-General for British Columbia will be very responsible and quite onerous. It may not be much of a rest so far as work is concerned, but it will be a change.

– Richard McBride to Robert L. Borden,
24 December 1915

After resigning, McBride recollected that early in his administration, he had set out a "definite programme of development," especially relating to railways and public works. He hinted that he had considered going to Ottawa but felt that, in wartime, moving to London would enable him to best serve British Columbia. In a letter thanking Borden for his past cooperation, he remarked that he was "sorry in many ways to drop out of the political field in British Columbia" but had been continuously in the Legislature since 1898. "In many respects a pleasurable experience," it had also been strenuous, and he believed he was "fairly entitled to some respite" and a "change," although under wartime conditions, the agent-general's job would be "very responsible and quite onerous." He anticipated that his principal work would consist of promoting trade, and he hoped to cooperate with Canada's high commissioner.[1]

But there was a problem. McBride stated that the current agent-general, J.H. Turner, was retiring because of "advancing years" (he was eighty-two).

An Edifying Spectacle

The New Arrival: — "Now, I wonder if Mr. Turner will feel put out."

Lurking in the doorway of his London office, J.H. Turner prepares a surprise welcome for McBride. In actuality, though reluctant to retire, Turner graciously assisted McBride when he arrived in London. *Vancouver Sun,* 22 January 1916, cartoonist, John (Jack) Innes.

Turner did not want to leave except under his own terms. He publicly called it "a brutal thing to kick me out" and declared that he was an "unwilling pawn" in the "exigencies of politics." The new BC premier, W.J. Bowser, told the press that Turner's resignation, dated 12 October, had arrived on the twenty-sixth but that McBride had not given it to him until 15 December. The previous summer, McBride and Bowser had offered Turner a retirement allowance, but Turner would not accept it without being allowed to "retire with honour" and a pension guaranteed by legislation. As the Legislature had not yet met, Turner did not consider that he had resigned.[2] He had little option, however. McBride prepared to go to London.

Before he left, friends in Victoria arranged farewell gatherings. McBride told the 250 attendees at a board of trade luncheon that he had always felt his "first duty" as a public servant was "to serve the people regardless of political differences." He graciously accepted criticism that put public servants "on their mettle" and enabled them to "give more efficient and careful service to the Country." Echoing his theme of optimism, he remarked that "the future is full of hope and the West is possessed of incalculable wealth. Time, bright with its development, will prove British Columbia, the richest province in the Dominion." His evenings were busy with entertainments hosted by members of the Royal Commission on Indian Affairs (McKenna-McBride), MLAs, and Lieutenant-Governor F.S. Barnard. Civil servants in Victoria offered him a golden loving cup but, at his suggestion, used the money to furnish a ward at Royal Jubilee Hospital. Their counterparts in New Westminster presented an illustrated engraved address because he was "for years the fountainhead of the civil service," and the city had not made a presentation to its "famous native son." With Lady McBride and his older daughters, he attended a New Year's Eve Ball at the Empress Hotel. Accompanied by the two eldest girls, who were returning to school in Massachusetts, he left Victoria on 5 January. As they set out, their car drove between lines formed by the Sixty-seventh and Eighty-eighth Battalions. At the CPR wharf, a number of political friends, civil servants, and prominent citizens bade him farewell. Before boarding the train in Vancouver, he thanked British Columbians for their past support, but few people were on hand to see him off at the station. The *Victoria Times* blamed Bowser for "the failure of the Vancouver 'faithful' to observe the usual amenities [that] was studied to the point of insult."[3]

McBride arrived in London late in January, but illness prevented him from attending a farewell dinner given for Turner by the other provincial agents-general. In mid-February, he took over from Turner, who was "most kind and attentive" in helping him learn the details of the work. His first task was completing the construction of the new British Columbia House

On 5 January 1916, McBride left the Canadian Pacific Steamship dock in Victoria. The woman in the checked coat is his long-time secretary, Lottie Bowron. Royal BC Museum, BC Archives, C-00549.

on fashionable Regent Street. During earlier visits, he had helped to choose its site and observed its construction. Although Turner moved into the building on 22 December, when the lease on the former office expired, it was incomplete because of a builders' strike and difficulties in getting materials in wartime. Early in March, McBride reported that it was practically finished and would "rank among the very best in London." Unfortunately, it had cost over $100,000 more than the original estimate, and only one of its offices had been leased, which was a problem since rentals were expected to pay for it. Nevertheless, McBride was confident of finding tenants, and in August, he reported that all but one office had been rented. The building, near a popular shopping area, included an exhibition hall, where McBride proposed to have displays of fresh fruit, natural history including fish and game, and "Indian specimens." Alas, the Department of Agriculture said that though apples would keep and could thus be exhibited, the expense of shipping fresh cherries, plums, or peaches could not be justified. The director of the provincial museum would send skins that could be mounted in London but would not include "anthropological material" as the Provincial Museum had no duplicates, and it was better to illustrate "the life history of the aboriginal races of British Columbia ... here in our own Province."[4]

McBride set out to prove his friends' prediction that he would be "the greatest 'drummer' B.C. has ever had." Not only did he seek customers, especially for timber, but he also proposed to take up the shipping problem with Walter Runciman, the president of the British Board of Trade, a government ministry. Although Bowser told the Legislature that McBride was doing "excellent work" on securing captured enemy vessels for use in British Columbia, the effort did not pay off. When the Cameron Lumber Company of Victoria suggested that it charter the *Grahamland,* a captured German ship, to carry lumber to Britain, the Prize Committee, the British agency responsible for disposing of enemy assets, was unwilling to transfer the vessel to facilitate what it perceived as the company's "private gain." McBride persisted in his efforts but in June reported an exceptional scarcity of ships and the near impossibility of getting charters. He suggested that Bowser seek the assistance of the railways minister to get the transcontinental railways to offer a special rate for shipments from British Columbia to Saint John or Halifax to meet Britain's urgent need for lumber and to overcome the Admiralty's inability to send vessels to the Pacific coast. He asked Borden to raise the possibility of selling lumber to Australia when he saw Prime Minister William Hughes in London. A year later, when Borden was at the Imperial War Conference, McBride complained that the Admiralty preferred to buy timber through San Francisco and that the Munitions Department bought plywood and railway ties mainly from the United States, though it had ordered some box and dimension lumber from British Columbia.[5]

Given the shortage of shipping, McBride congratulated Bowser on his shipbuilding plans, which he expected to be profitable. He conferred with E.H. Heaps, a New Westminster industrialist who proposed to build and operate two or more ships to be owned by BC companies, but he advised

The Smoke of Our Sacrifice!

The Daily Province declares that Sir Richard McBride is British Columbia's idol. As the records of the late government are examined, and the sacrifices we have been called upon to offer brought to light, it appears that that assertion borders upon the truth.

Even after McBride left the province and the Liberals won the provincial election of 1916, his enemies still claimed that his government's policies had squandered BC resources. *Vancouver Sun,* 8 March 1917, cartoonist, John (Jack) Innes.

Heaps to deal directly with Bowser. He also promoted the sale of canned salmon but had difficulty in convincing naval authorities that BC pinks could compete with Alaska reds in price or quality. Because Britain was anxious to keep its own fishery alive, it did not favour using BC salmon for civilians, but he got the salmon put on the ration list for Canadian and Allied troops. He also acted as a provincial purchasing agent by investigating sources for scarce wire rope.[6]

McBride had not forgotten Better Terms. He reminded Bowser that the claim for the return of lands in the railway belt and the Peace River had been dropped from the brief with the understanding that the relevant departments would deal with the matter. In reporting this to Borden, Bowser explained that the province had no intention of taking any action in respect of the Better Terms Commission until the "war is well over," but in a phrase reminiscent of McBride, he asserted that British Columbia was the only province that had "had to subsidize Canada in order to have a railway built which is purely of national purpose."[7] When R.E. Gosnell requested additional compensation for his work in preparing the Better Terms case, the *Times* ascribed British Columbia's financial problems to sources other than inadequate subsidies from Ottawa. Indeed, it stated, "The entire revenue of Canada would not have sufficed for the band of prodigals, led by Sir Richard McBride, who squandered the country's resources, all but wrecked its credit, and fastened a millstone around its neck in the shape of a railroad policy which may yet cost us more than one-half of our present revenue in annual interest payments."[8]

From London, McBride looked forward to the resumption of British emigration and received "countless enquiries" about settlement in the province. He advised Bowser "that interest in British Columbia is not at all flagging" and promised to be "most attentive" to anything connected with it. He thought it possible to devise a pre-emption plan for would-be immigrants. When he read about an Australian scheme to welcome British veterans, he asked the Colonial Office to give "every recognition" to British Columbia in any overseas colonization plan. By then, H.C. Brewster was premier and his government's immediate concern was providing care and jobs for its own returned soldiers.[9]

McBride graciously received visiting soldiers. Those who came from New Westminster praised his "kindness and attention." He endeavoured to arrange for prisoners of war from that city to receive comfort parcels from a local committee and made inquiries for soldiers who sought extraordinary leave, but his main duty was arranging for them to vote in the September 1916 BC election. The military authorities would neither accept responsibility for this task nor allow voting to take place at the front. After considerable pressure from the federal government, Bowser, McBride, and the War Office agreed that voting would be allowed at Bramshott and Shorncliffe camps, and in convalescent hospitals. McBride later secured permission to collect votes at the front. In the meantime, the Legislature passed a law permitting six weeks to elapse between the close of nominations and the election, and it allowed men overseas to vote at any time before the end of the year. Bowser appointed Captain Cox of the 143rd Battalion and F.W. Welsh of Vancouver as superintendent and commissioner of soldiers' voting, with McBride as chief returning officer. The Liberals complained that the procedure was wholly under Conservative control since no provision was made for Liberal scrutineers or agents. After protests arose that Welsh was interfering with the soldiers' vote, McBride ordered him to leave his post.[10]

When the results of the soldiers' vote finally reached British Columbia, no significant problems were noted in connection with either the general election or a referendum on women's suffrage that had accompanied it. But the Prohibition referendum was another matter. Voters in British Columbia clearly supported Prohibition, soldiers stationed in Canada narrowly rejected it, and soldiers overseas overwhelmingly opposed it by 12,719 to 2,893. When the overseas numbers were added to the total, Prohibition was defeated. Stories circulated of irregularities in the soldiers' vote: that men had voted more than once or were not from British Columbia at all, that prisoners and even dead men had cast ballots, and that officers had bought votes with alcohol. The new premier, H.C. Brewster, was a strong prohibitionist. With the "increasing frequency" of "allegations and charges," his government created a commission "to make a thorough investigation" of the Prohibition vote. Brewster also asked the commissioners to examine the affairs of BC House while they were in London, to determine the suitability of the property and the value of its services, and to investigate "other matters in connection with the office of the Agent-General." The three commissioners, all Liberal MLAs, found "grave frauds and irregularities" in the vote and recommended ignoring all ballots cast after 14 September 1916, which was election day in British Columbia. This was done and British Columbia adopted Prohibition.[11] It was a damning indictment of McBride.

Nonetheless, McBride's departure had not helped the Conservative cause. On taking office as premier, Bowser had reorganized the cabinet. His minister of finance was A.C. Flumerfelt, a Victoria businessman with a reputation as "a very sound financial man."[12] C.E. Tisdall became minister of railways, and L.A. Campbell was named minister of mines. Those appointments and the vacancy caused by McBride's retirement made by-elections necessary. As the wise old federal politician G.E. Foster had observed during the cabinet crisis of the previous March, Bowser had "a legacy which is sometimes a very bad thing to fall to one."[13]

The Liberals, who had long spoken disparagingly of the McBride-Bowser government, continued to attack its mismanagement of provincial affairs.

In the Victoria by-election, H.C. Brewster defeated Flumerfelt, Bowser's new minister of finance, winning two-thirds of the vote. The *Times,* which saw no doubt of "the evil effect of the McBride government on the province," did not expect the Bowser government "to do anything for the benefit of British Columbia." It described Brewster's victory as "a sweeping condemnation of the government, McBridism, Bowserism, or whatever it may be called." A week earlier, L.A. Campbell had barely retained his Rossland seat, and in Vancouver M.A. MacDonald, a Liberal, easily defeated Tisdall.[14]

The presence of two Liberals in the House put Bowser on the defensive. In connection with the PGE, a major Liberal target, Brewster charged that excess moneys had been paid to it from trust funds. Bowser admitted the truth of this claim, but explained that McBride had approved the payments to stem the flow of unemployed men into Vancouver. Without the transfers, work would have stopped, the PGE would have gone into bankruptcy, and the province would have had to pay interest on its bonds. His explanation did not satisfy Brewster, who wrote to the lieutenant-governor, declaring that at least $6.7 million and probably over $18 million had been paid to the PGE contrary to the statutes, that there had been "gross improvidence" in spending the proceeds of the bonds, that construction costs were 50 percent higher than for similar work on the Canadian Northern, and that the construction contract had been awarded to Patrick Welch without competition. Suggesting that the transfer of funds may have been a criminal offence, Brewster protested "the burdening of the people of this Province with such large liabilities" as those proposed by a bill to authorize borrowing an additional $6 million for the PGE. He called for "a thorough investigation of all the facts" concerning the construction of the PGE and the "illegal payments" of these moneys. The *Colonist* defended McBride and blamed the public for the railway's problems by "selling town lots to each other" rather than doing as McBride wanted – promoting agricultural and industrial expansion.[15]

Bowser's conflicts of interest and his dealings with the Dominion Trust were not forgotten. When the Supreme Court sought an examination of the bill submitted by the auditors of the Dominion Trust, Bowser told Judge Denis Murphy that William Allison, the provincial auditor general, would do the examination. Allison was "a competent man for such work," and as an independent official of the government, he could only be removed by a vote of the Legislature. Allison undoubtedly had the necessary accounting skills, but he was also McBride's brother-in-law. At its first session, Brewster's Liberal government did away with Allison's position, and he lost his job on 1 August 1917. This was hardly a surprise, for as early as 1915, the *Sun* had complained that the province lacked "an independent supervising official."[16]

During the BC election campaign of fall 1916, Brewster repeatedly attacked the government's land policy, Bowser's conflicts of interest, and the overpayments to the PGE. He was sorry that "Bowser had to reach down into the gutter to get issues. Sir Richard McBride was a bigger man, and would debate the big issues." Bowser, who avoided a direct attack on McBride, told one meeting, "I am not casting any reflection on Sir Richard in connection with his policies which the people unanimously approved ... They are my policies too." One Conservative candidate, A.E. Planta in Nanaimo, observed that "unlike Sir Richard McBride, Mr. Bowser was ... not versed in all those arts of vote getting of which Sir Richard was a past master." The election was a disaster for the Conservative Party, which won only nine of the forty-seven seats.[17]

After the election, the Legislature appointed a select committee to examine all matters relating to the construction of the PGE. Several witnesses indicated that McBride knew of the relationship between the contractors and the railway, of the overpayments, and that D'Arcy Tate, the lawyer who secured the original charter, had contributed to Conservative campaign funds out of his commission. When Tate admitted that he had provided campaign funds, Brewster cabled to McBride for further information. McBride, who was very ill, replied, "No bargain made by Tate or Pacific Great Eastern campaign funds" and offered to appear before the provincial cabinet when he returned to the province.[18] But that was not to be.

McBride's family did not join him in London until the fall of 1916. Mary and Peggy remained at school in Boston, and Mary graduated in 1916. In congratulating Peggy for a speech to the YWCA, which Mary had reported was a "huge success," her "Dad" noted "it is not hard to understand the nervous tension of public speaking & you may believe that one can easily appreciate the strain you are under." He apologized for not being able "to send all the money necessary" and added, "I know you will both understand that I did the very best I could. The war has so disastrously affected things in B.C. as to make it practically impossible to turn around." Ever the optimist, he predicted that, though improvement might take two years, "everything will be back in the old stride and B.C. surely must again enjoy abounding prosperity." In Victoria, Lady McBride continued her philanthropic and social activities. At a garden fete at Government House to raise money for the Returned Soldiers Fund, she took charge of the tables at which visitors played bridge or five hundred. She was also a guest at Government House when the Duke and Duchess of Connaught visited. Just before she left for London, Mrs. J.W. Troup honoured her with an informal tea attended by the wives of leading Conservative politicians and prominent businessmen.[19]

In London, the family lived at 36 Thurloe Square in the fashionable South Kensington district, near the Victoria and Albert Museum, an upscale address that was appropriate for a man in McBride's position who was earning an annual salary of $15,000. His enemies questioned the amount of his salary. The *Times* complained that it was outrageously large, noting that Sir George Perley, the Canadian high commissioner, received only $10,000, and that the prime minister and the chief justice of the Supreme Court were paid less than McBride. The paper claimed that the reason for McBride's exorbitant salary was not the high British income taxes but "the price of Mr. Bowser's translation to power." The new BC government complained that McBride's accounts passed through the auditor general's office only after being paid from advances and that there was no information about the purpose of expenditures or indications of revenue from rentals of BC House. The MLAs called for economy in the agent-general's office and disapproved of his $15,000 salary. According to one story, when the new Liberal government proposed to reduce McBride's salary, he refused to accept this change because of the high cost of living in England.[20]

The same optimism that led McBride to mortgage the province's future influenced his own finances. Friends and relatives were awarded government jobs, but McBride himself never received any financial benefit from his position. In 1916, he struggled to pay his life insurance premiums, which, given the state of his physical and financial health, were essential. His correspondence with Lottie Bowron, his long-time secretary, who acted as his financial agent in Victoria, includes a litany of requests, some "very harsh," from banks and trust companies to pay his debts. He was doing his best to pay interest but wondered how his creditors expected him to find the principal when he could "not dispose of a thing."

Some investments were sold or failed before he died. A few examples must suffice. In 1912, at the peak of the real estate boom, he and D.M. Eberts bought a share in the 150-acre Sol Harrison farm on the Saanich Peninsula. They paid $300 an acre and planned to pay it off in three years. During his 1907 trip to London on behalf of Better Terms, McBride became friendly with T.P. O'Connor, the journalist and Irish Nationalist MP. In May 1912, together with A. Shirley Benn, MP, Hamar Greenwood, William

Willett, and E.P. Gaston, McBride, as a silent partner, and O'Connor organized a syndicate known as the British Columbia Exploration Company to invest in BC real estate. Its name was later changed to the Colonial Realty Company. Their local agent, F.J. Hart, was a New Westminster realtor who specialized in Fraser Valley farmlands. They planned to buy large acreages and subdivide them into ten- and twenty-acre blocks. In August 1912, McBride sent O'Connor a draft for £500 with instructions to take out the stock in O'Connor's name; the two would share the profits. On the basis of information from Hart, he was optimistic that they should "have no difficulty at all in making us an excellent profit." By the following spring, although McBride said that the field for good investments was growing daily, O'Connor was disappointed with the returns. He had anticipated that the company would have capital of £200,000 by then, which would have given him and McBride "all the money we should require for the remainder of our days and leave us free to attend to our politics only." However, they were still paying for the land. McBride paid at least one installment early in 1913, and in June of that year, O'Connor drew on him for a final £250. The syndicate's sole investment was a 212-acre farm in Delta that it bought at $310 an acre at a time when 5-acre blocks in the area were selling for $500 an acre or more. Shortly after buying the Delta farm, the Colonial Realty arranged to sell 40 acres at over $400 an acre, but the deal fell through. In the meantime, the farm was rented. O'Connor seemed to think that McBride was personally wealthy, as he suggested that Harold Harmsworth, a well-heeled newspaper publisher, was "always open for a deal in British Columbia" on condition that it be large and that "only two or three other people shall be in it, and that you should be one of the two or three." McBride was in no position to invest in such a deal. McBride put $250 into a Vancouver-based syndicate that was staking claims before drilling for oil in the valleys of the Peace and Pitt Rivers, even though the promoter of this Coast Development Syndicate warned that economic conditions made it difficult for people to put up the necessary money.[21]

    McBride's "friends" also contributed to his financial woes. "Generous almost to the point of extravagance to anybody in need," he had an uncanny ability to make friends but did not always choose them wisely and was a soft touch for those in financial distress. When an old acquaintance from New Westminster wrote in 1912 of financial problems because of his large family, business reverses, and unemployment, McBride replied, "I am so heavily in debt that I am really obliged by my bankers to desist from endorsing notes" but enclosed twenty-five dollars as a gift. To a Dewdney resident who sought a loan of $600, he sent a cheque for $50. During the boom time, he frequently co-signed loans. When financial stringency became the order of the day, many defaulted. One example was D.W. Higgins, an old-time Victoria journalist for whom he had endorsed a $300 note for three months. Explaining that times "are simply awful," Higgins had asked the bank to renew the note and required McBride's further endorsement. J.H. Hawthornthwaite gave McBride a promissory note for $462.95 but did not pay when it came due early in 1917, even though McBride had said in 1914 that the two had "had a long and favourable acquaintance." As McBride rued, "I have been accommodation endorser for many in British Columbia and it would appear as if they are all coming down on me now. I cannot for the life of me understand so many of these persons who called themselves friends, but who at this time and under such stress would willingly load all their burdens on my shoulders." "The tragedy of the whole business," he lamented, "is that I have never had a dollar's worth of benefit from these notes and that my substance must go towards other people's comfort."[22]

Soon after the 1916 election, rumours surfaced that McBride would be replaced as agent-general. One report said that, in counting the overseas vote, "Dick is not playing the game as a strict neutral" and claimed that F.C. Wade, a lawyer and well-known Liberal, would replace him. The *Province* suggested that the government might reduce McBride's salary but would not dismiss him lest he return to British Columbia, where he was still popular in some quarters. McBride had at least one Liberal friend. On hearing stories of his dismissal, Brigadier General Victor W. Odlum, who in civilian life was an owner of the Liberal *Vancouver World*, wrote to Brewster on 30 April 1917, urging him not to discharge McBride unless there was "something serious against him." Odlum also objected to selling BC House as it was "getting to be well known" and would be "a splendid advertisement."[23]

On 15 May, before Odlum's letter reached Victoria, McBride resigned "on account impaired health." Illness had dogged his time in London. Whereas once he frequently addressed various groups, his public speeches were now rare, although he spoke to the Royal Colonial Institute on British Columbia and the war, and he made a case for imperial federation. In May, the physician who had treated him since January found him unfit to perform official duties and unlikely to be able to resume work for several months, though by August he should be well enough to return to British

Columbia. His health had fluctuated for several months. His main problem was nephritis, a kidney disease. During February and early March, a series of "very severe" colds had kept him "seriously indisposed," and he had attended to urgent matters from his bedside. Prime Minister Borden, who visited him on 1 April, found him looking "thin and pale but seeming quite buoyant." Three weeks later, McBride was well enough to dine with Borden and discuss political and imperial matters. The *Province* reported that his health was much improved, and friends expected him to return to Canada to enter federal politics.[24] Their hopes were destined for disappointment. News of his resignation elicited expressions of regret in British Columbia. Though noting his mistakes as premier, the *Province* praised his work as agent-general. Even the *Sun* was sorry for his illness and remarked that "his personal qualities" had won him many friends in British Columbia and throughout Canada.[25]

On resigning, McBride asked for the equivalent of a year's salary because of the high rent and taxes in London, and the heavy expense of moving his family back to British Columbia, which he expected to do in August. Brewster offered only four months' salary, effective 1 June and payable over the next two months, which McBride hoped would not prejudice his request that he receive full pay until the end of the fiscal year, on 31 March 1918. At Brewster's request, J.H. Turner temporarily took over the work of agent-general. He reported that McBride was no longer capable of reading, because diabetes had damaged his sight but that he hoped to recover sufficiently to return to British Columbia. Turner confirmed the heavy expenses that McBride had outlined, noted that the doctor had visited daily for two or three months, and mentioned expensive consultations with specialists. He urged that McBride be paid his salary until the end of the fiscal year.[26]

Early in July, David Whiteside, who was investigating the overseas vote, and Dr. C.J. Doherty, the federal minister of justice, called on McBride, who was in bed and looked "very, very ill." Whiteside criticized Turner's son and assistant for not informing Brewster of McBride's "true condition instead of leaving everybody under the impression that he was simply 'drunk again.'" This, incidentally, is the only suggestion in the record that McBride ever over-imbibed. Although his physician thought that McBride would be well enough to travel, and Lady McBride hoped for a rally, Whiteside was doubtful. Still upbeat, McBride thought his health was gradually improving and expected to leave for British Columbia in August as he urged Brewster to provide the balance of his salary. Several visitors, including Cyrus Peck and Odlum, reported that he was "very badly off in health and finances." Odlum had been told that McBride's illness was aggravated by worry for his family's financial security.[27]

As McBride sent his last message to Brewster, the press in British Columbia reported "alarming news" about his health and his inability to pursue "his one desire" – to return home. After going into a coma, he died on 6 August 1917. His funeral was held two days later at Golder's Green Crematorium, where Reverend Canon J. McP. Almond, the director of the Canadian Chaplains services, officiated. The mourners included Lady McBride and five of her daughters, the Canadian elite in London led by High Commissioner George Perley and his wife, the agents-general of other provinces, J.H. Turner, and a number of military officers.[28]

McBride's ashes were placed in a bronze casket, which Lady McBride took with her when she and her daughters returned to British Columbia. On 6 September 1917, a host of dignitaries, McBride's brother Edward, his sisters Gertrude (Mrs. Allison) and Dorothea, and his six daughters attended a memorial service at St. Andrew's Presbyterian Church in Victoria. For unexplained reasons, Lady McBride was absent. In his eulogy, Reverend Dr. Clay called "friendship" the word epitomizing McBride's character and spoke of his "manly qualities," especially his "great kindness."[29] His ashes were interred at a graveside ceremony at Ross Bay Cemetery.

The obituaries in the BC press, Conservative and Liberal, reflected both his accomplishments and his failures. Typical was the comment of his great friend, the Victoria-based *The Week*. Recalling "his glad hand, his engaging smile and his open heart," it added that "even when the fact could no longer be disabused that his policies had brought his native province to the brink of bankruptcy, there was a complete absence of anger or bitterness in the attitude of his countrymen. They trusted his judgment less but they loved Sir Richard himself as much as ever. Had the regrettable blunders committed by him been made by ordinary politicians there would have been an angry if not dangerous popular outburst." Most editors praised McBride's "irresistible" and "magnetic" personality, its "warmth and humanity," his "engaging smile" and his "intimate understanding of his constituents." They mentioned his lack of business training and lack of attention to detail, or as his old acquaintance and sometime secretary R.E. Gosnell put it, "If he made a mistake at all it was that he was too hopeful of the immediate future and too trustful of the railway companies." The *Sun* agreed that in his railway policy, "his judgment was captured by his optimism." Another editor noted that at the time, "optimism was the only tolerable cult," and the *Colonist* described him as "essentially optimistic." Overriding all, said the *Province,* was "his supreme faith in his native British Columbia," but his obituaries also described his "broad vision and imperial views." They were generous but fitting epitaphs.[30]

Conclusion

McBride was born in a British colony and grew up in a province that was slowly establishing its links with Canada through such federal institutions as the British Columbia Penitentiary, where his father was the warden. As a teenager, his legal studies in Halifax gave him an appreciation of the vastness of the country and exposed him to its political institutions, especially the party system. As a grown man, he presided over a province that was experiencing rapid modernization not only in its political system but also in developing new infrastructure and seeking the best ways of exploiting its rich resources for the short- and long-term benefit of its people. Although it was very much a part of Canada, immigration enabled it to retain the strong British ties that McBride came to symbolize.

McBride was a *British* Columbian. His pride in the British Empire, undoubtedly instilled in him by his father, was reinforced by a school curriculum that had him singing about tramping through Egypt with British soldiers. It saw him, in light of a lingering colonial mentality, requesting imperial assistance in pursuit of Better Terms or appealing to the Colonial Office when Ottawa rejected BC measures to make itself a white man's province by halting Asian immigration. During the federal reciprocity election of 1911, he spoke of the need to tell Britain "that we are as Canadians still firm and strong for the empire, that we are going to keep as our flag the good old Union Jack."[1] Despite welcoming American investment in the forest industry and promoting the idea of a railway to

Alaska, he wanted to protect the province's industries, particularly forestry and agriculture, from American competition.

Though they were rooted in patriotism, his imperial sentiments, like his dealings with the United States, reflected practical considerations and were a manifestation of what has been called the Angloboom.[2] In October 1913, after the defeat of Borden's Naval Aid Act, McBride told Toronto's Empire Club, "It is simply and purely because of the circumstances of Empire defence, the strong arm of Britain, that the wealth of nations is to be found there, and that the counting house to which the children of Britain has always gone has been able to continue strong and efficient."[3] The provincial government, municipalities, the new railways, and major provincial companies such as the British Columbia Electric Railway all depended on the "counting house" – namely, British investors. During his increasingly frequent trips to London, he promoted British investment generally. As the money markets contracted, he sought to assist the CNR and the PGE in raising funds to complete their work.

He also saw the British Empire as affording protection to the province, as was most evident in the naval question, an issue that put him on the national stage. Friendships with such leading British figures as Winston Churchill strengthened his ties to Britain. Patriotism inspired his support for the Admiralty but his pressing for a Canadian contribution to the imperial navy had economic and defence considerations: the province's reliance on British capital to finance its railways and other infrastructure, and its need for coastal defences as the Anglo-German naval race sped up. As he became aware of the larger picture, McBride downplayed, but never ignored, coastal defence. After the defeat of Borden's Naval Aid Bill, he expressed shame at Canada's failure to contribute to the imperial navy and declared that "before he was a Conservative, he was a Canadian, and before Canadian, he was British." Like many Canadians of his time, he had overlapping and complementary loyalties to the empire, to Canada, and to his province.

Though increasingly part of the British world, McBride was also required to deal with Canadian matters, as in the naval question. His relations with Laurier's Liberal government were testy, as in his fight for Better Terms. Conservatives courted him as a federal party leader, but he declined invitations to come to Ottawa, saying that his place was in British Columbia.

The British Columbia of 1915 was in some ways very similar to that of 1903, when McBride became premier, but it was also very different. The difficult geography, the central argument in the campaign for Better Terms, had not changed, but new railways and improved roads opened remote regions and helped overcome geographic problems. The province also had other new infrastructure, including a university.

In 1903, British Columbia was on the brink of bankruptcy, but with prosperity and the prudent management of Finance Minister Robert Tatlow, it soon showed surpluses on its annual accounts. During the first decade of McBride's government, Canada and the world eagerly purchased the products of BC mines, forests, and fisheries. Those seemingly unlimited resources provided employment and produced the revenue that gave the province the good credit rating it lent to the new railways. In 1915, British Columbia was again in financial difficulty, for war and a worldwide depression restricted the flow of British capital, reduced the demand for the province's products, and made the new railways a financial burden. McBride's critics complained that his government gave away its resources, particularly timber and land, to speculators. His administration did experiment with ways of developing resources for the greatest benefit of the province, and its Forest Act of 1912 appeared to put it in the forefront of progressive forest policy but did not solve the problems of managing a resource.[4]

As in the creation of the forest service and of a University Sites Commission, McBride believed in "experts," a faith that was popular at the time. Not only did he establish a variety of royal commissions, but he also persistently called for a commission to investigate British Columbia's case for Better Terms, suggested that a commission devise a naval policy for Canada, and arranged a joint federal-provincial Royal Commission on Indian Affairs. Believing that the Native peoples had few rights to the land, he ensured that the scope of the royal commission would be limited. Appointments to commissions were often politically inspired; government jobs and contracts were important to the party. Despite introducing civil service reform, he did not eliminate patronage. His approaches to problems reflected political astuteness and an understanding of the wishes and needs of British Columbians.

As the results of the 1909 and 1912 elections revealed, McBride enjoyed great popularity in the province. In 1908, the *Vancouver Daily Province*, British Columbia's leading newspaper, had offered new subscribers a portrait of McBride, on eighteen-by-twenty-four-inch heavy gloss paper, and advertised, "Every man who takes the slightest interest in B.C. politics at all has heard him speaking or knows him personally."[5] From his youth, his personal friendships cut across class lines. During his first term in office, he depended on the Socialist and Labour MLAs to keep his government in power. Once he had gained a secure majority, he reminded British Columbians that the duty of the Legislature was "to hold the balance evenly among all classes."[6] His provincial tours and genial manner demonstrated his interest in the entire province and in its people. During his Atlin sojourn, he had realized that the province extended beyond Victoria and the Fraser Valley. Thus, when he presented the electorate with railway plans in 1909 and 1912, he ensured that they included a concrete plan, or the promise of one, for almost every part of the province. The experienced politician Sir Wilfrid Laurier admitted that McBride knew how to play his political cards successfully.[7]

In 1903, after thirty-two chaotic years of political alliances formed around individuals, McBride, with the help of Lieutenant-Governor Sir Henri Joly de Lotbinière, introduced party lines. He moulded the provincial Conservative Party into such a cohesive whole that the Opposition Liberals effectively conceded the 1912 election to him. Yet, four years later, in what the *Canadian Annual Review* described as "one of the most complete overthrows in political history," the electors rejected all but nine Conservatives.[8]

McBride left a party ridden with scandal and a province burdened with debt. The allegations that he had personally profited were unfounded; the public did not know the poor state of his personal finances. Some cabinet ministers, especially Bowser, the *éminence grise* of the administration, created problems. Bowser sometimes acted on his own, as was the case when he halted the prosecution of Doukhobors or made promises about the duration of BC Electric Railway franchises. Despite embarrassment, public resentment of Bowser's Vancouver "machine," and especially conflicts of interest such as the Dominion Trust fiasco, McBride stood by his attorney general. Bowser was useful. He acted as premier during McBride's increasingly frequent and long absences from Victoria. He often accompanied McBride on provincial tours, where he, not McBride, dealt with controversial issues such as Prohibition. Having Bowser say "no" enabled McBride to retain his reputation for benevolence and overcame his chief weakness, a reluctance to say "no," whether for a personal guarantee of a bank loan or a provincial guarantee of a railway bond. A Pinkerton's agent hired to spy on the Liberal caucus quoted caucus member Harry Jones of Cariboo as saying that McBride was "weak or tender-hearted" and that, rather than anger anyone with a flat refusal, he would "half way promise to do what he is asked, for fear he will hurt the feelings of someone by refusing."[9]

Shortly before resigning as premier, McBride wrote in reference to his provincial role, specifically in light of an apparent caucus revolt led by Bowser, "For my own part, I have tried to do my little best and to serve the Province first and the party next. Possibly I may have attempted too much in the end, however, all of the policies I have espoused are bound to reflect creditably on the country."[10] It was a fair assessment. Undoubtedly, he did try to do his best, and much of what he did was a creditable reflection. He benefited from prosperity but was also both perpetrator and victim of the over-optimism that long pervaded the province. Personal charm helped put Richard McBride, British Columbian, on the provincial, national, and imperial stage but could not surmount the challenges of a severe downturn in his own health and the economy.

Epilogue

After McBride's death, his family almost immediately returned to Victoria. Their lifestyle changed, but they maintained an active social life. Lady McBride briefly returned to her Gorge Road home but moved back to 830 Quadra Street in 1919, a more modest establishment that had been rented out after the family moved to Gorge Road. Sir Richard left her a $10,000 life insurance policy, the balance of his salary for the 1916-17 fiscal year of approximately $8,750, and the money provided by the province for the family's return to Victoria.[1] A few of his investments, such as in the Western Power Company, Government of Canada bonds, and some rental property, also produced some income. In her own name, Lady McBride had an interest in the *British Columbian* and the *Nelson Daily News*. Nevertheless, a provincial government grant of $5,000 in 1919 must have been welcome.[2] In 1931, the Conservative government of Simon Fraser Tolmie granted her an annual pension of $2,500 to be paid monthly, but the Great Depression persisted and the demands on the provincial treasury were heavy. A cheque was sent in April 1931, but no others followed.[3]

Also in 1931, McBride's estate was finally probated. Its liabilities far exceeded its assets, and it owed over $60,000 to six different banks. His law library, valued at $600, was sold to his former partner J.D. Kennedy, a sum that the Bank of Montreal in New Westminster accepted as payment on an outstanding loan. McBride's shares and stocks were mainly in BC mines, oil companies, and financial institutions.[4] His real estate consisted of small parcels of land or shares in syndicates, most of which was heavily mortgaged, in various parts of the province. Some property had been used as security for loans and thus was claimed by the lender. The executors of McBride's will sold some land but usually at less than their valuation, and some parcels went for taxes.[5] The Gorge Road home was valued at $15,000 but had a mortgage of $5,175. The estate was unable to sell it, as, with the opening of the Uplands subdivision, the Gorge ceased to be Victoria's fashionable district. McBride himself had made a downpayment on a $20,000 lot in the new subdivision, which the Uplands Company took back in settlement of its claim against the estate. Eventually, McBride's unsecured creditors accepted 14.5 cents on the dollar.[6]

The house on Quadra Street, which the McBride family had owned for some years, better suited its reduced circumstances. It was also more convenient for schools. Ruth and Anna, aged fourteen and twelve respectively, returned to St. Margaret's School, where they won prizes at the June 1918 sports day. That fall, they transferred to St. Ann's Academy in Victoria. The fact that the daughter of Moses Cotsworth, author of *The Crisis in B.C.*, taught at St. Margaret's may have been a factor in the change of schools. St. Ann's also offered the advantage of being only a short walk from the family home, whereas St. Margaret's was a streetcar ride away. At St. Ann's, Ruth secured a diploma in typewriting, and Anna, who passed the high school entrance exams in 1921, won several academic prizes. In June 1923, she was promoted to the junior matriculation class and received the higher grade certificate of the Royal Academy of Music. She retained her links with St. Margaret's and in May 1925 attended the founding meeting of St. Margaret's Old Girls, which ironically elected Miss Cotsworth, the former gym mistress, as honorary president. Dolly also attended St. Ann's and at the closing ceremonies in June 1920, she won a bronze medal for good conduct. That fall, she moved across the street and entered the School of Nursing at St. Joseph's Hospital, graduating in the spring of 1923. Sheila received part of her education at St. George's School on Rockland Avenue. It closed in 1928 and she may have transferred to St. Margaret's.[7]

The social pages of the two Victoria newspapers and sometimes the Vancouver papers are replete with accounts of Lady McBride and her daughters attending dances, afternoon teas, dinners, bridge and mah jong parties, and various functions in honour of friends who were leaving the city, entertaining out-of-town guests, or getting married. Lady McBride and her daughters were also invited to events at Government House in honour of such visiting dignitaries as Winston Churchill, who recalled that his friend Sir Richard had endeavoured to have him visit the province and said that his only regret was that McBride was not present.[8] The McBrides were also hostesses. Among their social acquaintances were prominent names in local, mainly Conservative, politics and society, such as Mrs. W.J. Bowser, Mrs. C.E. Pooley, Mrs. E.G. Prior, Dola Dunsmuir and her aunt Mrs. Henry Croft, and Mrs. F.M. Rattenbury.

All the McBride daughters married, and though their weddings were socially prominent, the celebrations were modest. In October 1920, Mary married Captain Marshall Beck of Vancouver, who had served in the Sixteenth Battalion of the Canadian Scottish. The ceremony at St. Andrew's Presbyterian Church was "of the simplest character and entirely devoid of ostentation," but a large congregation of family friends attended, including Sir Frank and Lady Barnard, Lottie Bowron, and the W.J. Bowsers. R.F. Green gave the bride away. The ceremony was followed by a luncheon at the family home for a few "intimate friends and relatives."[9] The Becks lived on Lulu Island, but Mary and her son, Richard, often visited her mother, who also went to Lulu Island on occasion. In May 1925, at what was expected to be "one of the most fashionable weddings of the early summer season," Dolly married Dr. J.H. Moore, the chief pathologist and anaesthetist at St. Joseph's Hospital. A large congregation attended the church, which friends had decorated, and the reception was held at the family home.[10] Peggy married Captain MacGregor Macintosh, a professional soldier whom she had known since at least 1923, at "a military wedding" on 1 September 1926, also at St. Andrew's.[11] Brigadier J.A. Clark, MP for Vancouver-Burrard and a nephew of Lady McBride's through marriage, gave the bride away. Ruth was the bridesmaid. A wedding breakfast at the family home followed the ceremony. After retiring from the army, Macintosh served as Conservative MLA for Saanich and the Islands from 1931 to 1933 and again from 1937 to 1941. In April 1928, Ruth married Maurice Carmichael, a silversmith, at a "dignified and simple" ceremony at St. Andrew's. Since Lady McBride had recently been ill, the wedding was quiet, with only a small reception at home for "intimate family friends."[12] Anna, the bridesmaid, was a records clerk in the Provincial Board of Health.[13] At a quiet ceremony at home, with only relatives present and her mother "unavoidably absent," Anna married Francis Basil Hood on 1 December 1934. Hood worked in the office of McLennan, McFeely and Prior, a major hardware firm. His mother was the daughter of E.G. Prior, a founder of the firm and McBride's immediate predecessor as premier.[14] On his father's side, Hood was the grandson of Francis Wheeler Hood, fourth viscount Hood.[15] Sheila had married G. Bruce Forbes on 30 April 1934.

After returning to Victoria, Lady McBride resumed her role as president of the Friendly Help Society. During an unemployment crisis in the winter of 1921, she called for efforts to promote the idea of old age pensions but resigned her presidency early in 1923 though indicating that she would continue to take a "deep interest" in the society's work. She also played a role in the local Conservative Association, seconding the nomination of Canon Joshua Hinchliffe as a Conservative candidate in the 1920 provincial election. It was rumoured that if the Liberal premier John Oliver, who had been elected in both Victoria and Delta, resigned his Victoria seat, she might run as the Conservative candidate in the subsequent by-election. Party organizers believed that she would win the women's vote and "make a sentimental appeal" to men who had voted for Sir Richard. Oliver did not resign his Victoria seat, but Victoria Conservatives chose Lady McBride by acclamation as one of two female members of their executive. Most of her political activities, however, were ceremonial ones, such as joining Bowser in opening a Conservative Club in Victoria and participating in the Women's Conservative Club.[16] She also hosted an "at home" to which she invited the wives of Opposition members, including Mrs. T.D. Pattullo. In the late 1930s, she gave up her Victoria home. After a sojourn in Calgary, where she lived with Peggy, she moved to Vancouver and died on 10 December 1937.[17]

One can only imagine what McBride would have thought of the political activities of his younger sister Dorothea. During the 1940 federal election, she spoke on several occasions on behalf of the National Government (Conservative) candidate. She told female voters that "the feminine vote" would have an important role "as many women who had hitherto taken no active interest in politics are awakened to a sense of national consciousness." But 1940 was not a good year for Conservatives, and the Liberal incumbent easily won. However, she ran for the Conservatives in New Westminster in the October 1941 provincial election. In nominating her, George L. Cassidy spoke of the family's past in politics and of the development of British Columbia. In reporting the nomination, the *Columbian* described her as "a sister of the late Sir Richard McBride, the best premier, British Columbia ever had," and noted that her name would "recall her brilliant brother."[18]

Although the paper's praise did little for Dorothea, who came third, such favourable recollections of McBride were not uncommon. In 1919, Bowser prompted a long cheer when he referred to "the ablest son British Columbia has ever produced, Sir Richard McBride." During the 1924 provincial election, the *Colonist* declared that "this Province never experienced better times than under the regime of Sir Richard McBride, who ... laid the foundations of Conservative policies in British Columbia."[19]

During the 1928 provincial election, R.L. Maitland, a successful Conservative candidate in Vancouver, attributed the well-being of the fruit industry to "the alacrity with which Sir Richard McBride seized the opportunities of a world market and kept B.C. fruit products before the people of other countries." Similarly, he praised McBride's work in promoting sales of salmon and encouraging investment, especially in the pulp industry and shipbuilding, the latter of which had "since fallen away." He told electors that McBride had not revised the Mineral Act to let capitalists know where they stood and that the Conservatives would revive this policy of stability. A Conservative candidate in Revelstoke asserted that the Liberals were taking credit for many policies that had been established by the McBride government, but he could not defeat the Liberal incumbent, a cabinet minister.[20]

Not all the claims were entirely accurate. R.H. Pooley told Sooke Conservatives that McBride's far-sightedness was responsible for "the great benefit" the province was now getting from the Canadian Northern Railway, which "had not cost this Province one cent." His point was correct: the federal taxpayer had paid the price when Ottawa, in part to relieve the various provinces that had assumed obligations on its behalf, took it over and merged it with the Grand Trunk Pacific. But some of those taxpayers were British Columbians. Conservatives continued to refer to McBride's accomplishments, such as his fight for Better Terms, but did not necessarily know its history. In 1926, R.L. Maitland, the president of the Provincial Conservative Association, referred to the $100,000 subsidy that McBride had secured from Ottawa and accused Premier John Oliver of allowing it to lapse. Presumably, he was unaware that the subsidy offered in 1906 was to last for only ten years and that McBride had thought it inadequate.

In a similar vein, during a 1927 by-election campaign, Simon Fraser Tolmie, the provincial Conservative leader, noted that his party had reduced the BC debt between 1903 and 1915, but he did not mention that it had more than doubled in the 1915-16 fiscal year, mainly due to obligations for the PGE.[21] When the PGE could not make interest payments, the province took it over and halted construction north of Quesnel and south of Squamish. In the 1920s, the government seriously considered abandoning it. Known derisively as "Past God's Endurance" or "Prince George

Eventually," the PGE long remained a white elephant as successive premiers contemplated shutting it down, attempted to sell it, and failed to unload it on Ottawa.

In the Legislature, C.F. Davie accused the Liberals of doing less than McBride to halt "the Oriental invasion" of the province. No doubt, McBride would have been pleased by the action of the federal government during the 1920s in effectively halting immigration from China, sharply curtailing immigration from Japan, and continuing to enforce the "continuous voyage" clause against immigrants from India. Today, those measures are generally viewed as embarrassing episodes in Canada's history.

What became the Royal Commission on Indian Affairs, the so-called McKenna-McBride Commission, did transfer some apparently unused reserve land to newcomers who desired it but did not deal with the much greater question of Indian title to the land, an issue not yet resolved.

In Opposition from 1928 to 1933, the Liberals attacked the policies of the McBride government, especially its alienation of public land. A.M. Manson, MLA for Omineca, praised McBride's efforts for Better Terms but criticized his methods. When, in the depths of the Depression, the Tolmie government considered closing the university, the *Times* rued the possibility of shutting down an institution that had been founded "with such high hopes" by the McBride government.[22]

Some of McBride's policies appealed to his successors. T.D. Pattullo, who became Liberal premier in 1933, also proposed to annex Yukon and was keenly interested in improving transportation to the North via a highway to Alaska but was thwarted by the Depression and limited federal and American interest. He said that many of British Columbia's problems could be traced to the McBride-era alienation of lands and natural resources, which had been responsible for the isolated nature of provincial settlement. While discussing amendments to the Land Act in 1940, he "saw no likelihood of return to the wild era of land speculation that existed in the days of the McBride government." Like McBride, Pattullo sought Better Terms. Unlike McBride, he did so in wartime and paid the price at the polls in 1941. A result of that election was the formation of a coalition of Liberals and Conservatives in opposition to the socialist Co-operative Commonwealth Federation. When there was talk of abandoning the party system, the *Columbian* reminded readers that McBride had rescued the province from the "log-rolling and trading" that preceded its introduction.[23]

In 1945, the *Province* remarked that "the vision of Sir Richard McBride is now approaching realization."[24] The Coalition government had resumed work on the PGE and had almost completed the line from Quesnel to Prince George before going out of office. W.A.C. Bennett, who became premier in 1952, got the glory of driving the last spike. He did not stop there and, after extending the PGE southward from Squamish to North Vancouver, built it north to the Peace River and beyond. Unlike McBride, Bennett had the advantages of business experience and of prosperity throughout his tenure, so his creative financing did not return to haunt him.

Notes

Abbreviations in Notes

BCA	British Columbia Archives
BCERR	British Columbia Electric Railway Records, UBCSC
BCLJ	British Columbia, *Legislative Journals*
BCSP	British Columbia, *Sessional Papers* (Victoria: Queen's/King's Printer, various dates)
BofVL	Bank of Vancouver Liquidation, LAC, RG19 E26C
CAR	J. Castell Hopkins, ed., *Canadian Annual Review* (Toronto: Annual Review Publishing, various dates)
CHAR	Winston Churchill Archives in WCA
CHTP	Charles Hibbert Tupper Papers, UBCSC
CSP	Canada, *Sessional Papers* (Ottawa: Queen's/King's Printer, various dates)
CVA	City of Vancouver Archives
GR441	Premiers' Papers, BCA
HCD	House of Commons, *Debates*
Joly Papers	Henri Joly de Lotbinière Papers, LAC
LAC	Library and Archives Canada
LFGM	Letters from the General Manager, BCERR
McBF	Richard McBride Fonds, BCA
MS347	Lottie Bowron Collection, BCA
RLBP	Robert Laird Borden Papers, LAC
UBCSC	University of British Columbia Library, Special Collections
WCA	Winston Churchill Archives, Churchill College, Cambridge University
WLP	Wilfrid Laurier Papers, LAC
WSCP	Winston Spencer Churchill Papers, WCA

Introduction

1. Phillip A. Buckner and R. Douglas Francis, "Introduction," in *Rediscovering the British World*, ed. Buckner and Francis (Calgary: University of Calgary Press, 2005), 13.
2. Phillip A. Buckner, "The Long Goodbye: English Canadians and the British World," in Buckner and Francis, *Rediscovering the British World*, 189.
3. While explaining the motion, John Irving (Cassiar) expressed the province's sometimes ambiguous relationship with the federal government by hoping that it would "stir up Ottawa" and "let other nations know that if they attempted to interfere with the Mother land," the colony of British Columbia was "prepared to stay with Great Britain to the finish." *Victoria Daily Colonist*, 3 February 1900.
4. *The Week*, 20 May 1905.
5. [Gilbert Malcolm Sproat], *British Columbia: Information for Emigrants* (London: William Clowes and Sons, 1873).
6. *Vancouver Daily News-Advertiser*, 22 April and 27 May 1913.
7. Jean Barman, *Growing Up British in British Columbia: Boys in Private School* (Vancouver: UBC Press, 1984), 176.
8. Donald G. Paterson, *British Direct Investment in Canada, 1890-1914* (Toronto: University of Toronto Press, 1976), 4.
9. James Belich, "The Rise of the Angloworld: Settlement in North America and Australasia, 1784-1918," in Buckner and Francis, *Rediscovering the British World*, 44.
10. *The Week*, 31 May 1913.
11. Stenographic report of "Canada and the Empire" (speech to Empire Club, Toronto, 31 October 1913), McBF.
12. John Douglas Belshaw, *Becoming British Columbia: A Population History* (Vancouver: UBC Press, 2009), 32.
13. Michael Dawson, *Selling British Columbia: Tourism and Consumer Culture, 1890-1970* (Vancouver: UBC Press, 2004), 17 (emphasis in original).
14. *The Canada Year Book, 1913* (Ottawa: King's Printer, 1914), 208.
15. Gordon Hak, *Turning Trees into Dollars: The British Columbia Coastal Lumber Industry, 1858-1913* (Toronto: University of Toronto Press, 2000), 24.
16. Ian McKay, "Canada as a Long Liberal Revolution: On Writing the History of Actually Existing Canadian Liberalism, 1840s-1940s," in *Liberalism and Hegemony: Debating the Canadian Liberal Revolution*, ed. Jean-François Constant and Michel Ducharme (Toronto: University of Toronto Press, 2009), 356. McKay's definitions of liberalism and the Liberal Order have been contested by other scholars. See various essays in the same volume.
17. Robert McDonald, "'Variants of Liberalism' and the Liberal Order Framework in British Columbia," in Constant and Ducharme, *Liberalism and Hegemony*, 332-35.
18. *The Week*, 10 July 1915.
19. *Times*, 22 and 24 April 1902.
20. William O'Neill, interviewed by Imbert Orchard, 1961, BCA, Imbert Orchard Collection, T0315-0003; Mrs. A.H. Sovereign (née Ellen Ellison), interviewed by Imbert Orchard, 1964, BCA, T1089-0001 and T1089-0003.
21. McBride to Mrs. McNiven, 12 February 1915, GR441, v.166; *Columbian*, 31 December 1909; *Province*, 22 February 1912; H.N. Lidster, interviewed by Imbert Orchard, 1964, BCA, T0332-0001.
22. H.B. W. [Bruce Hutchison], *Times*, 21 June 1932.

23 R.F. Green to McBride, 26 January 1914, McBF.
24 McBride to W. Garland Foster, 22 February 1913, MS347, v.l/3. The government appointed Judge Peter S. Lampman as royal commissioner to investigate the school trustees, past and present. He examined their financial dealings and the firing and rehiring of Robert Thompson, the principal of the public school.
25 *Times,* 23 January 1914.
26 *Colonist,* 25 November 1914.
27 S.J. Gothard to McBride, 5 October 1915, McBride to Gothard, 22 October 1915, GR441, v.132.

Chapter 1: A Young British Columbian

1 *Mainland Guardian,* 6 May 1871; Dorothy Blakey Smith, ed., *The Reminiscences of Doctor John Sebastian Helmcken* (Vancouver: UBC Press, 1975), 225.
2 J.B. Kerr, *Biographical Dictionary of Well-Known British Columbians* (Vancouver: Kerr and Begg, 1890), 245-46; F.W. Howay, *British Columbia from the Earliest Times to the Present* (Vancouver: S.J. Clarke, 1914), 4:5; *Colonist,* 22 July 1870.
3 The salary was modest. Some clerks in the Colonial Service earned up to $1,550. McBride's assistant, A. Moresby, earned $708. E. Mallandaine, *First Victoria Directory* (Victoria: E. Mallandaine, 1871), 89-90.
4 H.L. Langevin, *British Columbia: Report of the Hon. H.L. Langevin, Minister of Public Works* (Ottawa, 1872), in CSP, 1872, no. 10, 36; *Mainland Guardian,* 16 September, 12 October, and 2 November 1870, 8 April, 16 September, and 25 October 1871.
5 Langevin, *British Columbia: Report,* 36-37; *Mainland Guardian,* 20 June and 21 July 1871. See also Jack David Scott, *Four Walls in the West: The Story of the British Columbia Penitentiary* ([New Westminster]: Retired Federal Prison Officers' Association of British Columbia, 1984), 1-4.
6 "Estimates for the Year Ending 31 December 1878," in BCSP, 1878, 542; Canada, Senate, *Debates,* 4 March 1879, 50-51. See also Scott, *Four Walls in the West,* 5; *Dominion Provincial Herald,* quoted in *Colonist,* 13 June 1878. The *Mainland Guardian,* 14 August 1878, expressed similar sentiments.
7 See report from House of Commons, *Debates,* published in *Dominion Provincial Herald,* 28 June 1879; Inspector of Penitentiaries, *Report,* in CSP, 1880, no. 17, 16-18; *Columbian,* 26 June 1894. For details on A.H. McBride's unhappy career as warden, see Patricia E. Roy, "'The Pirates of the Penitentiary': Religion and Politics in Late 19th Century British Columbia," *Historical Studies: The Journal Published by the Canadian Catholic Historical Association* 74 (2008): 7-27.
8 The terms "First Nations" or "Aboriginal" are preferred today; in McBride's time, the former was unknown and the latter only occasionally used.
9 The old Government House had fallen into disrepair. CPR surveyors had used it, but it was abandoned by 1886. A chimney had fallen in, its gardens were overgrown with weeds, and neighbourhood cows trampled the garden and took over the hall and drawing rooms. Some New Westminster residents thought that it should be preserved for historic purposes and as a picnic ground. CSP, 1886, no. 15, xxxiii.
10 *Mainland Guardian,* 23 September and 4 October 1882; *Columbian,* 17 August 1886, 13 October 1892.

11 Department of Justice, *Annual Report,* in CSP, 1895, no. 18, xiii; Moylan to Thompson, 15 May 1893, LAC, John Thompson Papers, 22592; *Columbian,* 26 June 1894, 4 July 1895.
12 Her brother, Edward D'Arcy, sometimes spelled "Darcy."
13 Canada, Manuscript Census, 1901, New Westminster District, D4, 3. Her obituary noted that she came to British Columbia in 1863. *Columbian,* 31 October 1931.
14 The marriage, conducted by Reverend W. Maloney, is recorded in the marriage registry of St. Andrew's Cathedral in Victoria. Arthur is listed as a member of the Church of England. The couple secured the necessary dispensations from Bishop Modeste Demers. In the 1870s and 1880s, 30 to 40 percent of BC brides and grooms were of differing denominations. John Douglas Belshaw, *Becoming British Columbia: A Population History* (Vancouver: UBC Press, 2009), 150.
15 BCA, Vital Events Index to baptisms. A daughter born to Arthur and Mary McBride on 6 August 1866 was baptized as "Gertrude" at St. John's Anglican Church in Victoria on 9 September 1866; on 15 December, she was baptized as "Agnes" at St. Louis Roman Catholic Church "sans parradins" (without godparents). The dual baptism suggests that Mary McBride may have had scruples about her daughter's baptism in the Anglican faith. The lack of godparents and a baptism in a church other than the Catholic cathedral suggests a private ceremony.
16 *Columbian,* 4 and 6 May 1909.
17 *T.P.'s Weekly,* 2 June 1928.
18 *The Week,* 29 November 1913.
19 *Western Methodist Recorder,* February 1914, 6, and March 1914, 22.
20 *Mainland Guardian,* 14 and 29 December 1870. Birth dates are from Canada, Manuscript Census, 1901, New Westminster District, D4, 3.
21 Barry Mather, *New Westminster: The Royal City* ([Toronto]: J.M. Dent, 1958), 60-61; *Columbian,* 21 May 1897, 1 May 1913; Gerald Thomson, "140 Years of May Day in New Westminster, 1870-2010," *British Columbia History* 44 (Spring 2011): 9-15; "Dodo," [?] handwritten memo in McBF.
22 *Mainland Guardian,* 11 December 1880, 26 August 1882; *Columbian,* 23 December 1882; *Province,* 8 August 1917.
23 *Columbian,* 23 February 1883, 4 and 23 July 1883, 29 December 1883, 5 June 1884; *Mainland Guardian,* 12 July 1884.
24 *Churchman's Gazette,* July 1884, September 1884, July 1885. There was a 25 percent discount in tuition fees for second and younger brothers. *Columbian,* 16 July 1884; *Mainland Guardian,* 11 July 1885.
25 Sister Sara to McBride, 5 July 1911, GR441, v.146; *Mainland Guardian,* 16 October 1880. McBride's siblings were buried from Holy Trinity Anglican Church: Leonard (*Colonist,* 11 February 1906); Edward (*Province,* 26 October 1931); Gertrude (*Vancouver News-Herald,* 26 July 1945). When Gertrude married William Allison in 1892, Reverend Thomas Scoular of St. Andrew's Presbyterian Church officiated. Undated script for speech by Lottie Bowron, MS347, v.2/29; *Columbian,* 31 December 1909.
26 J.W. Bell, "British Columbia Memories," typescript in City of Vancouver Archives (thank you to Jean Barman for the reference); handwritten memo, probably by McBride's younger sister, Dorothea, McBF.
27 In his reminiscences, Nels Nelson recalled meeting McBride and his father on the banks of Brunette Creek in 1887. Evelyn Benson, "In Their Own Words," *New Westminster News,* 18 November 1992; *Columbian,* 17, 18, and 28 July 1888, 14 September 1912; *Colonist,* 14

September 1912, 7 August 1917; Peter Peebles, *Province,* 5 May 1929. A photograph with the Peebles article shows him camping.
28 *Mainland Guardian,* 27 June and 4 July 1885; *Columbian,* 1 July 1885. In Victoria a few weeks later, the magistrate said that bathing without clothing was inexcusable, but a trial would be expensive. He let the accused go but warned that he would not be so lenient in future. *Times,* 23 July 1885.
29 H.M. Stramberg to S.D. Pope, 17 September 1886, in British Columbia, Public Schools, *Annual Report,* 1886, in BCSP, 1887, 148; *Columbian,* 2 August 1888. She failed the teachers' exams in 1887 and 1888. After the first failure, the superintendent gave her a temporary certificate but not after the second one.
30 McBride to F.W. Howay, 11 June 1910, UBCSC, F.W. Howay Papers, v.4/18; British Columbia, Public Schools, *Annual Report,* 1885, in BCSP, 1886, xxxvi-vii; British Columbia, Public Schools, *Annual Report,* 1886, in BCSP, 1887, lx, 147; British Columbia, Public Schools, *Annual Report,* 1887-88, in BCSP, 1889, 195; *Columbian,* 14 December 1886. McBride passed the McGill exams in June 1886. He also passed the preliminary law examinations for British Columbia. *Columbian,* 12 June 1888.
31 John Willis, *A History of Dalhousie Law School* (Toronto: University of Toronto Press, 1979), 10, 65; *Dalhousie Gazette,* 4 November 1887, 7; Calendar of the Law School, 1888-89, 10.
32 Dalhousie University, Calendars of the Law School, 1888-89, 1889-90, 1890-91; *Dalhousie Gazette,* 4 November 1887, 21 January 1888; Willis, *A History of Dalhousie Law School,* 40.
33 Willis, *A History of Dalhousie Law School,* 45; *Colonist,* 14 June 1912; *Dalhousie Gazette,* 30 December 1887, 27 December 1888, 9 January 1890.
34 *Dalhousie Gazette,* 28 November 1889.
35 *Dalhousie Gazette,* 30 January 1890, 5 and 26 November 1890; H.J. Logan, quoted in *Colonist,* 14 June 1912.
36 *Nelson Daily News,* 14 May 1902; *Times,* 24 April and 1 May 1902; *Columbian,* 13 June 1902. The Legislature rejected the proposal.
37 *Columbian,* 8 March 1888, 28 July 1892; *Dalhousie Gazette,* 14 March 1889; *Henderson's British Columbia Gazetteer and Directory* (Vancouver and Victoria: Henderson Publishing, 1889), 388; Minute Book of the Benchers of the Law Society of British Columbia, Meeting, 3 October 1892, BCA, MfA1045; *Colonist,* 28 July 1892.
38 Howay, *British Columbia,* 4:6; Advertisement, *Columbian,* 3 January 1894 and following; *Columbian,* 2 March 1895.
39 *Columbian,* 18 May and 18 October 1895, 21 May 1896.
40 *Vancouver Daily News-Advertiser,* 8 April 1896.
41 *Columbian,* 14 April, 13 May, and 13 August 1896; *News-Advertiser,* 13 May 1896.
42 *Columbian,* 7 and 8 November 1895, 10 April 1896.
43 *Columbian,* 2 and 17 March 1893, 1 November 1893, 8 February and 26 March 1894, 20 and 21 March 1895.
44 *Columbian,* 20 June 1894; Howay, *British Columbia,* 2:493; *Province,* 8 August 1917.
45 Manitobans fought the 1886 provincial election on party lines but had not experienced the same political instability as British Columbia. W.L. Morton, *Manitoba: A History* (Toronto: University of Toronto Press, 1957), ch. 9.
46 *Fraser Valley Champion and Farmers' Advocate,* 8 February, 21 March, 25 April, and 9 May 1896; *Columbian,* 10 March 1896.
47 *Champion,* 16 and 23 May 1896, 6 June 1896; *Columbian,* 20 May and 6 June 1896; *News-Advertiser,* 21 April, 20 May, and 6 June 1896.

48 *News-Advertiser*, 5, 10, 19, and 23 June 1896; *Columbian*, 17 June 1896.
49 *News-Advertiser*, 20 May and 16 June 1896; *Columbian*, 20 May 1896, 9, 13, and 17 June 1896; *Champion*, 23 May and 18 June 1896.
50 See Patricia E. Roy, *A White Man's Province: British Columbia Politicians and Chinese and Japanese Immigrants, 1858-1914* (Vancouver: UBC Press, 1989).
51 *Columbian*, 9, 12, 13, and 15 June 1896; *News-Advertiser*, 19 June 1896.
52 "Dick" to "My Darling Margaret" from Mission City, 1:30 A.M. [9 July 1896] and 11 July 1896, McBF.
53 *News-Advertiser*, 6 June 1896; *Champion*, 20 and 27 June 1896, 11 July 1896; *Columbian*, 23 June 1896; *Colonist*, 14 October 1904.
54 *Columbian*, 18 July and 19 August 1896, 13 November 1897.
55 *Columbian*, 17 and 18 May 1897, 10 May 1898. McBride continued to believe that lawyers should not be required to wear wigs in court. McBride to Jos. Martin, 17 March 1905, McBF.
56 McBride to "My Darling Girl," 9 September 1896, McBF.
57 *Columbian*, 23 September 1896, 5 May 1897; *World*, 22 May 1900; *Times*, 10 December 1937. The poor health of the bride's mother may also explain the lack of a reception. Mrs. McGillivray died on 3 May 1897 of "renal calculus" and heart failure, although the death certificate indicated that she was ill for only one day. BCA, MFB13088, file 22383.
58 Turner to A.J. McLellan, Chairman, Provincial Political Association, Victoria, quoted in *Colonist*, 6 May 1898.
59 *World*, 28 May 1898; *Colonist*, 1 May 1898.
60 *Province*, 18 August 1900.
61 *News-Advertiser*, 14, 18, and 26 June 1898.
62 *British Columbia Directory*, 1889, 333; *World*, 12 May 1900.
63 Unless otherwise noted, the account in the three previous paragraphs draws on *Columbian*, 7, 11, 14, 15, 16, 17, 18, 27, 28, and 29 June 1898, 2 and 4 July 1898; *World*, 6, 12, and 13 June l898; *News-Advertiser*, 20 May 1896, 30 June 1898.
64 *World*, 11 and 13 July 1898; *Colonist*, 12 July 1898; *Columbian*, 14 July 1898; *News-Advertiser*, 12 June 1898.

Chapter 2: "Dewdney Dick"

1 F.W. Howay, *British Columbia from the Earliest Times to the Present* (Vancouver: S.J. Clarke, 1914), 2:491-92.
2 *Vancouver World*, cited in *Nelson Daily Miner*, 3 June 1900; *Fernie Free Press*, 15 June 1900; *Kaslo Kootenaian*, 14 June 1900; *Toronto Globe*, 9 May 1902, reprinted in *Columbian*, 17 May 1902; M.S. Donnelly, *The Government of Manitoba* (Toronto: University of Toronto Press, 1963), 46.
3 T.A. Gregg, "Canadian Celebrities No. 52 Richard McBride," *Canadian Magazine* 23 (July 1904): 209. Gregg stated that J.H. Turner (BC premier 1895-98) tried to run "an upright government," but those around him prevented it.
4 McInnes, a Nova Scotian, went to New Westminster in 1874 to practise medicine, was elected to the House of Commons in 1878, and was called to the Senate in 1881. He resigned from the Senate in 1897 to accept the lieutenant-governorship. See John T. Saywell, *The Office of Lieutenant-Governor: A Study in Canadian Government and Politics* (Toronto: University of Toronto Press, 1957), 131-33.

5 *Times,* 16 April 1901, 22 April 1902; *Columbian,* 2 and 3 September 1899; *World,* 17 January 1899.
6 *Columbian,* 19 and 24 January 1899; *News-Advertiser,* 10 February 1899.
7 *Columbian,* 13, 25, and 28 January 1899, 3 February 1899; *Colonist,* 7 and 10 January 1899, 24 February 1899.
8 *Columbian,* 28 September 1898. McBride was among the first to rebuild. *News-Advertiser,* 13 September 1898; *World,* 16 September 1898; *News-Advertiser,* 18 January 1899.
9 The term "Member of the Provincial Parliament" (MPP) was widely used in the nineteenth century, but "Member of the Legislative Assembly" (MLA) was gradually introduced during the twentieth and is used here.
10 Turner resigned after his agent in Nelson sold blankets to the provincial jail. Such resignations over conflicts of interest were not unusual. A.E. McPhillips did so because of a fee paid to his firm. Hall stepped down for selling coal to Government House. In Vancouver, C.E. Tisdall was re-elected by acclamation after resigning because a clerk in his store sold seventy cents' worth of cartridges to a provincial police constable. In Alberni, A.W. Neill resigned for accepting money for road work after the election. *Columbian,* 18, 23, and 26 January 1899, 1 February 1899; *Colonist,* 12, 14, 17, 26, and 31 January 1899, 3 February 1899; *Times,* 25 November 1898.
11 *Columbian,* 20, 23, and 30 March 1899, 14 April 1899, 5 May 1899.
12 *Colonist,* 4 July and 15 August 1899, 9 February 1900; *Province,* 5 September 1899, 9 February 1900; *Columbian,* 10 February 1900.
13 This account draws on several letters written by McBride to his wife in June and July 1899, located in the McBride Fonds.
14 Howay, *British Columbia,* 2:499; *Columbian,* 9 June, 30 August, and 13 September 1899; *Atlin Claim,* 22 July 1899.
15 Peter Brock, *Fighting Joe Martin: Founder of the Liberal Party in the West* (Toronto: National Press, 1981), 225-26; *World,* 5 July 1899; *Atlin Claim,* 15 July and 23 September 1899.
16 *Columbian,* 6 October and 21 December 1899, 2 January 1900.
17 *Columbian,* 24 November 1899, 30 October 1902; *World,* 4 April 1900.
18 *Nelson Daily Miner,* 4 January 1900; *Kamloops Standard,* 11 January 1900.
19 The newspaper reports do not indicate what these charges were, but two days later, Carter-Cotton replied to Martin's complaints concerning the ownership of Deadman's Island in Vancouver harbour, the Columbia and Western land grant, the provincial deficit, and the floating of the government's most recent loan. *Times,* 19 January 1900.
20 *Province,* 3, 17, and 18 January 1900; *World,* 17 and 18 January 1900.
21 *Columbian,* 9, 10, and 12 February 1900, 22 March 1901; *Times,* 17 and 18 January 1900.
22 See Patricia E. Roy, *A White Man's Province: British Columbia Politicians and Chinese and Japanese Immigrants, 1858-1914* (Vancouver: UBC Press, 1989).
23 *Columbian,* 25 January and 16 February 1900; *World,* 24 and 26 January 1900.
24 *World,* 3 February 1900; *Province,* 27 January 1900; *Times,* 7 February 1900. The next year, an Ontario physician conducted a royal commission inquiry into the administration of the asylum.
25 *Columbian,* 25 January 1900, 24 and 28 February 1900, 1 March 1900; *Colonist,* 28 February 1900; *Times,* 22 June 1900; *Province,* 28 February 1900; Saywell, *The Office of Lieutenant-Governor,* 132-40, 249-54.
26 *World,* 9 March 1900; *Columbian,* 21 March and 27 April 1900. British Columbians have often supported one party provincially and another federally.

27 *Nelson Daily Miner,* 1 April and 2 June 1900; *Times,* 5 March 1900; *Colonist,* 8 March 1900; *Inland Sentinel,* 6, 16, and 30 March 1900; *Nelson Tribune,* 6 March and 19 April 1900; *News-Advertiser,* 1 April 1900; *New Denver Ledge,* 5 April 1900; *Province,* 2 and 17 March 1900; *Kootenay Mail,* 20 March 1900. The provincial Liberal executive opposed party lines. *Inland Sentinel,* 9 March 1900; Francis Carter-Cotton to G.H. Cowan, 22 February 1900, CVA, G.H. Cowan Papers, v.1/1.

28 *Province,* 8 June 1900; *World,* 8 and 9 May 1900. One report was that Premier Dunsmuir, who held a mortgage on the *Columbian,* called it in when J.D. Taylor, its managing editor, attacked his government. Taylor appealed to his readers and received sufficient funds to pay off Dunsmuir. *Nelson Daily News,* 3 May 1902; *Columbian,* 28 May 1900.

29 *World,* 12 May 1900; *Columbian,* 23 April 1900, 11 and 28 May 1900, 4 June 1900; *Province,* 22 April 1900.

30 *Columbian,* 12 and 25 June 1900; *World,* 11 June 1900.

31 *World,* 18 June 1900; *Nanaimo Free Press,* 18, 19, and 20 June 1900; *Columbian,* 19 and 20 June 1900; *Times,* 19 June 1900; Tatlow et al. to Laurier, 18 June 1900, copy with F.M. Chaldecott to McBride, 11 July 1910, BCA, T.W.S. Parsons Papers, AM1134.

32 *Colonist,* 20 June 1900; *Nelson Tribune,* 16 August 1900.

33 *Colonist,* 22 June 1900. The *Columbian* noted McBride's Atlin experience, intelligence, and freedom from entanglement in industry controversies. *Columbian,* 22 and 29 June 1900; *World,* 28 June and 12 July 1900. The *Province* agreed that it would have been "more appropriate to have the mines portfolio in charge of a representative to some part of the mining country." *Province,* 22 June 1900; *Inland Sentinel,* 22 June 1900. The *Phoenix Pioneer* thought that McBride's previous record showed him "totally unfit to be minister of mines." *Phoenix Pioneer,* 30 June 1900, quoted in *Inland Sentinel,* 6 July 1900. The *Vernon News* called him "an inexperienced young lawyer of New Westminster." *Vernon News,* 28 June 1900; *Nelson Daily Miner,* 26 June 1900; *Rossland Miner,* 5 July 1900. The *Fernie Free Press* agreed that McBride was a capable minister but was "miscast" in the mines portfolio. *Fernie Free Press,* 12 July 1900; *Sandon Paystreak,* 7 July 1900.

34 *Columbian,* 20 July 1900; *Rossland Miner,* 21 August 1900. For an account of the strike, see Jeremy Mouat, *Roaring Days: Rossland's Mines and the History of British Columbia* (Vancouver: UBC Press, 1995), 75-87.

35 *Kaslo Kootenaian,* 26 July and 9 August 1900; *Nelson Daily Miner,* 20 July, 22 August, and 31 October 1900. The *Colonist* thought a commission was "very wise." *Colonist,* 20 July and 6 September 1900; *Nelson Tribune,* 20 July 1900; *News-Advertiser,* 1, 22, and 29 August 1900; *Phoenix Pioneer,* 11 August 1900, 9 March 1901; *Lillooet Prospector,* 28 September 1900; *Ashcroft Journal,* 22 September 1900. The *Ashcroft Journal* printed the draft bill and for some weeks was able to fill several columns with letters written in response to it.

36 *Times,* 16 August 1900; *Colonist,* 16 August 1900; *Columbian,* 17 August 1900; *Vernon News,* 23 August 1900.

37 *Nelson Tribune,* 22 November 1900; *Rossland Miner,* 29 November 1900; *Fernie Free Press,* 14 December 1900.

38 *Times,* 5 and 12 December 1900; *Semi-Weekly World,* 27 November 1900. Because of geographic problems, the elections in Yale and Burrard were held several weeks after the general election. *Cranbrook Herald,* 13 December 1900; *Phoenix Pioneer,* 8 December 1900; *Grand Forks Gazette,* 8 December 1900; *News-Advertiser,* 9 December 1900; *Nelson Tribune,* 5 December 1900; *Moyie Leader,* 8 December 1900; *Province,* 24 August 1901; *Ashcroft Journal,* 10 and 24 August 1901; *Vernon News,* 5 September 1901.

39 *Columbian,* 28 February 1901, 6, 7, and 27 March 1901, 27 April 1901; *Lillooet Prospector,* 29 March and 12 April 1901; *Moyie Leader,* 15 December 1900; *Cranbrook Herald,* 13 December 1900, 23 August 1901; *Silvertonian,* quoted in *Lillooet Prospector,* 12 April 1901; *Nelson Miner,* 7 March 1901; *Grand Forks Gazette,* 2 March 1901; *Kamloops Standard,* 21 March 1901; *Kootenay Mail,* 2 March 1901; *Rossland Miner,* 22 February 1901; *Colonist,* 22 February 1901, 5 and 6 March 1901; *News-Advertiser,* 22 February 1901, 25 and 28 April 1901; Executive Council, Minute Book, vol. 25, 13 March 1901, BCA; *Semi-Weekly World,* 8 March 1901. McBride also brought in amendments to the Mineral Act to make it harmonize with changes in placer legislation.

40 *Kootenaian,* 9 May 1901; *Rossland Miner,* 17 and 21 May 1901, 11 June 1901; *CAR,* 1901, 58-59; *Ashcroft Journal,* 3 August 1901; T.G. Shaughnessy to P.H. Ashworth, 18 April 1903, quoted in John A. Eagle, *The Canadian Pacific Railway and the Development of Western Canada* (Montreal and Kingston: McGill-Queen's University Press, 1989), 121; *Cranbrook Herald,* 1 August 1901; *Rossland Evening World,* 27 July and 3 August 1901; *Colonist,* 3 August 1901.

41 *Colonist,* 3 August 1901; *Rossland Miner,* 11 August 1901. See Mouat, *Roaring Days,* 131-33.

42 British Columbia, Executive Council, Minute Book, vol. 25, 21 June 1900 to November 1901, BCA, GR444, v.25; *Province,* 18 July 1901; *Columbian,* 6 August 1901.

43 *Times,* 28 February 1901; *Colonist,* 27 February 1901; *Province,* 26 July 1900.

44 *Columbian,* 27 July 1900; *Colonist,* 3 and 8 August 1900.

45 *Columbian,* 28 February and 26 March 1901; *Colonist,* 24 April and 4 May 1901; *News-Advertiser,* 29 July and 15 August 1900, 16 March 1901.

46 *Colonist,* 24 February 1901. Canada, Manuscript Census, 1901, British Columbia, District 4, Victoria Sub District, D6, 4; *Henderson's British Columbia Directory* (Vancouver and Victoria: Henderson Publishing,1901). Street names have changed since McBride's day. The house was probably where Rupert Terrace blends into Quadra Street. The manuscript census lists three lodgers at 39 Victoria Crescent. Their relation to McBride is unknown. McBride, Diary, 30 September 1901, McBF.

47 *News-Advertiser,* 10 July 1900, 14 February and 4 April 1901; *Colonist,* 24 April and 4 May 1901; *Times,* 4 October 1900; *Columbian,* 23 August, 21 September, and 14 November 1900, 6 February and 21 May 1901; *Province,* 25 May 1901.

48 *Inland Sentinel,* 14 and 18 December 1900; *Columbian,* 2 November 1900, 28 February 1901; *News-Advertiser,* 6 October and 18 November 1900; *Semi-Weekly World,* 2 November 1900; McBride, Diary, 30 September 1901, McBF.

49 *Province,* 21 March 1901.

50 *News-Advertiser,* 16 March 1900, 5 May 1901; *Colonist,* 30 September 1900; *Columbian,* 28 February 1901; *Times,* 19, 22, 24, and 26 April 1901; *Inland Sentinel,* 12 March 1901; *Nelson Daily Miner,* 18, 19, 20, 21, 24, and 25 April 1901.

51 *Columbian,* 9 May 1901; *Times,* 8 May 1901; *Nelson Daily Miner,* 18 July 1901.

52 *Kootenaian,* 25 July 1901; *Fernie Free Press,* 23 August 1901. John Houston of the *Nelson Tribune* proposed transferring McBride "to a department where he would have scope to prove that he has undeveloped abilities." Quoted in *Inland Sentinel,* 6 August 1901; *Times,* 21 and 30 August 1901, 3 and 4 September 1901; *Province,* 6 September 1901; McBride, Diary, 1 and 3 September 1901, McBF.

53 *Colonist,* 4 September 1901; *News-Advertiser,* 4 and 15 September 1901; *Times,* 11 September 1901; *Columbian,* 4 September 1901; *Nelson Economist,* 4 September 1901; *Province,* 9 September 1901; *Vernon News,* 5 September 1901; *Lillooet Prospector,* 21 September 1901;

Nelson Tribune, quoted in *Columbian,* 10 September 1901; *Kootenay Mail,* 6 and 13 September 1901; *Inland Sentinel,* 6 September 1901.

54 *Times,* 28 February 1902; *Province,* 2 and 6 October 1902, 13 December 1902, 13 and 15 January 1903, 13 and 21 February 1903; *News-Advertiser,* 23 October 1902; *Columbian,* 17 December 1902; McBride, Diary, 7 and 11 September 1901, McBF.

55 *Semi-Weekly World,* 7 January and 11 February 1902; *Province,* 16 July 1902, 9, 18, 19, and 20 September 1902, 2 and 6 October 1902, 13 December 1902, 15 January and 13 February 1903; *News-Advertiser,* 23 October 1902; *Columbian,* 22 and 29 September 1902, 17 December 1902, 26 January, 26 March, and 15 September 1903; *Times,* 20 June 1902.

56 Denis Murphy's presence at the caucus meeting was significant; he had attended a Liberal convention in Vancouver but withdrew from that meeting because he opposed Martin and the introduction of party lines. *Columbian,* 7 and 20 February 1902; *Province,* 21 and 22 February 1902; *Times,* 20 and 21 February 1902.

57 *Times,* 21 February 1902; *Province,* 24 and 25 February 1902; *Columbian,* 8 and 24 February 1902.

58 *Times,* 4 March 1902; *Columbian,* 3 and 4 March 1902; *Province,* 5 and 6 March 1902.

59 *Colonist,* 22 February 1902.

60 *Columbian,* 1 and 6 March 1902, 22 May 1902; *Colonist,* 1 and 8 March 1902; *Province,* 5 March 1901; *Times,* 8 March 1902.

61 See Patricia E. Roy, "Railways, Politicians and the Development of the City of Vancouver as a Metropolitan Centre, 1886-1929" (master's thesis, University of Toronto, 1963), 62-63; Elections British Columbia, *Electoral History of British Columbia, 1871-1986* (Victoria: Elections BC and Legislative Library, 1988), 88; *Columbian,* 17, 19, and 21 March 1902; *Vernon News,* 13 March 1902; *Ladysmith Leader,* 15 March 1902; *Nelson Daily News,* 21 June 1902; *Times,* 10 April 1902; *Colonist,* 10 April 1902.

62 Mackenzie and Mann planned to use the charter of their Edmonton, Yukon and Pacific Railway, but some contemporaries referred to the Canadian Northern Railway. For simplicity's sake, I have used the latter name.

63 *Columbian,* 15, 24, and 25 April 1902, 7 May 1902; *News-Advertiser,* 17 April 1902, 13 and 14 May 1902.

64 *Columbian,* 6, 7, 9, and 10 May 1902; *Times,* 6 and 7 May 1902; *Province,* 10 May 1902; *Nelson Daily News,* 11 and 13 May 1902.

65 *Times,* 1 May 1902; *Province,* 30 April 1902; *Columbian,* 30 April and 1 May 1902.

66 *Columbian,* 22 and 23 May 1902, 3 and 4 June 1902; *Times,* 3 June 1902; *News-Advertiser,* 4 June 1902.

67 *Columbian,* 24 April 1902; *News-Advertiser,* 16 March 1902; *Times,* 21 and 24 April 1902, 19 June 1902.

68 *Columbian,* 25 March 1902; *Times,* 9 March 1902. He accused Prior of promoting the Island versus Mainland "sectional feeling." *Colonist,* 7 April 1903.

69 *Colonist,* 1, 25, 29, and 31 May 1902, 1 and 4 June 1902; *Columbian,* 28, 29, and 30 May 1902. A few days later, in an unrelated issue, the courts ruled that Dunsmuir and Pooley did not have a right to sit on the board of the *Colonist,* which then turned editorially against the government. *Columbian,* 18 June 1902.

70 *Province,* 28 May 1902; *Ladysmith Leader,* 7 May 1902; *Columbian,* 15 and 28 May 1902. See also *Nelson Economist,* 17 May 1902. The *Vernon News* complained of the Opposition's "intolerable verbosity" and policy of "obstruction." *Vernon News,* 15 May and 26 June 1902.

71 *Colonist,* 11 April, 7 May, and 5 June 1902; *Province,* 16 April and 21 June 1902; *News-Advertiser,* 5 and 21 June 1902; *Semi-Weekly World,* 24 June 1902.
72 *Semi-Weekly World,* 20 and 24 June 1902; *Columbian,* 1 May and 26 August 1902. The story originally appeared in the *Nelson Daily News,* 22 August 1902.
73 *Columbian,* 16 December 1902.
74 Press coverage of the convention was thin. Carter-Cotton of the *News-Advertiser* may have provided details, but the section that might have included the report was clipped from the volume used for microfilming. *Colonist,* 7 September 1902; *Nelson Daily News,* 8 and 24 September 1902; *Province,* 8, 9, and 18 September 1902; *Columbian,* 15 September 1902; *Kamloops Standard,* 18 September 1902; *Nelson Economist,* 20 September 1902; *Times,* 18 September 1902.
75 John English, *The Decline of Politics: The Conservatives and the Party System, 1901-20* (Toronto: University of Toronto Press, 1977), 33; Henry Borden, ed., *Robert Laird Borden: His Memoirs* (London: Macmillan, 1938), 1:90. When Borden spoke in New Westminster, McBride moved the vote of thanks. *Columbian,* 11 September 1902.
76 Elected in 1882 as a member for Cariboo, Wilson was defeated in 1886. He ran as a Conservative in Vancouver in 1900, missing election by just eight votes.
77 *Columbian,* 29 August 1902, 10 and 15 September 1902; *Nelson Economist,* 6 September 1902; *Nelson Daily News,* 3 September and 1 October 1902; *Province,* 11 September 1902; *Semi-Weekly World,* 16 and 17 September 1902, 28 October 1902; *Vernon News,* 18 September 1902; *Kamloops Standard,* 30 October 1902.
78 *Times,* 15 and 25 November 1902; *Nelson Daily News,* 18 November 1902; *Columbian,* 22 November 1902; *Vernon News,* 27 November 1902.
79 *Province,* 25 November 1902; *Columbian,* 29 November and 11 December 1902.
80 *Ladysmith Leader,* 10 December 1902; *Columbian,* 22 December 1902.
81 *Columbian,* 7 and 25 February 1903; *Colonist,* 11 and 12 February 1903; *Standard,* 19 February 1903. The *Inland Sentinel* gave reasonably objective reports of Opposition meetings. *Inland Sentinel,* 17 February 1903; *Province,* 7 March 1903.
82 *Colonist,* 27 February and 4 March 1903; *Province,* 27 February 1902; *Inland Sentinel,* 3 March 1903; *Nelson Daily News,* 6 December 1902, 1 and 7 March 1903; *Semi-Weekly World,* 3 March 1903.
83 *Times,* 6, 19, 21, and 26 March 1903; *Semi-Weekly World,* 10 March 1903; *Nelson Daily News,* 24 March 1903; *Province,* 24 February 1903; *Columbian,* 10 March 1903; *Kamloops Standard,* 19 and 26 March 1903, 2 April 1903.
84 *Colonist,* 3 April 1903; *CAR,* 1903, 212l; *Times,* 7 April 1903; *Columbian,* 7 April 1903. For examples of rotten mining companies, see Mouat, *Roaring Days,* ch. 3.
85 *Kamloops Standard,* 9 April 1903; *Colonist,* 7 April 1903; *Columbian,* 8 and 16 April 1903.
86 Howay, *British Columbia,* 2:486-87, 521-23; *Columbian,* 21 and 24 April 1903; *Nelson Daily News,* 25 April 1903.
87 The committee report was printed as an appendix in BCLJ, 1903. *Colonist,* 6 May 1903; *Times,* 5 May 1903.
88 *Columbian,* 27 and 28 May 1903: *Times,* 28 May 1903; *Colonist,* 30 May 1903.
89 A brief summary of the affair is in *CAR,* 1903, 214.
90 Sir Henri to Prior, 1 June 1903, Joly Papers, 7763; *Province,* 1 June 1903; *Times,* 1 June 1903; *Vernon News,* 26 June 1903; Joly to Edmond Joly, 12 October 1903, quoted in J.I. Little, "Advancing the Liberal Order in British Columbia: The Role Played by Lieutenant-Governor Sir Hector-Gustave Joly de Lotbinière, 1900-1906," *Journal of the Canadian Historical Association,* n.s., 19, 1 (2008) : 96.

Chapter 3: Establishing a Government

1 *Province*, 1 June 1903.
2 *Colonist*, 2 June 1903; *Columbian*, 3 and 6 June 1903, 2 and 4 July 1903; *Province*, 2, 3, and 23 June 1903; McBride to A.F. Carrington, 10 June 1903, GR441, v.76; McBride to J.A. Harvey, 16 June 1903, GR441, v.76; *Times*, 2 June 1903; *Kamloops Standard*, 4 June 1903; *Vernon News*, 4 June 1903; *Armstrong Advertiser*, 11 June 1903; T.A. Gregg, "Canadian Celebrities No. 52 Richard McBride," *Canadian Magazine* 23 (July 1904): 210, 213.
3 *Phoenix Pioneer*, 6 June 1903; Bowser to McBride, 1 June 1903, GR441, v.76; Charles Hibbert Tupper to McBride, 2 June 1903, CHTP, v.4; *Colonist*, 3 June 1903; *Times*, 2 June 1903; *Nelson Daily News*, 3 and 9 June 1903; *Province*, 3 June 1903.
4 *Columbian*, 3 and 4 June 1903; *Province*, 2 and 10 June 1903, 19 September 1903; *Colonist*, 3 June 1903; McBride to Andrew Haslam, 10 June 1903, GR441, v.406.
5 *Columbian*, 6 and 8 June 1903. The New Westminster lacrosse team defeated Victoria by fourteen to three.
6 McBride to R.B. Powell, 13 June 1903, GR441, v.21/4; *Colonist*, 5 June 1903; Bowser to McBride, 23 July 1903, GR441, v.77/2.
7 *Province*, 11 June 1903. Patronage applied in government contracts. In 1906, a New Westminster firm was asked to make emergency repairs to the asylum roof; a few hours later, it was told that it could not have the job, because it was on the "tabooed" list. *New Westminster Daily News*, 14 October 1906. For some Canadian examples of patronage, see John English, *The Decline of Politics: The Conservatives and the Party System, 1901-20* (Toronto: University of Toronto Press, 1977), 26-27.
8 G.W. Le Feuvre to McBride, 11 July 1903, GR441, v.74; L.A. Lewis to McBride, 5 September 1903, GR441, v.75; Anonymous to McBride, 1 July 1903, GR441, v.78. See also E.W. Beckett to McBride, 18 August 1903, GR441, v.71; H.N. Evans to McBride, 12 September 1903, GR441, v.74.
9 McBride to Wm. Manson, 6 July 1903, McBride to A.E. Howse, 6 July 1903, McBride to J. Chessen, 6 July 1903, McBride to T.G. McMannon, 3 September 1903, GR441, v.406; McBride to John Oliver, 24 June 1903, GR441, v.409; J.E. Spankie to McBride, 7 September 1903, McBride to Spankie, 11 September 1903, GR441, v.75.
10 McBride to G.R. Ashwell, 10 June 1902, GR441, v.406; McBride to A. Haslam, 24 June 1903, McBride to C.H. Dickie, 24 June 1903, GR441, v.409; McBride to J.W. Berry, 30 June 1903, v.406. Similar letters are in GR441, v.76; McBride to A.H. Brown, 28 August 1903, GR441, v.22; Price Ellison to McBride, 18 June 1903, GR441, v.73; W.T. Shatford to McBride, 24 July 1903, McBride to Shatford, 27 July 1903, GR441, v.77; H.W. Raymur to McBride, 2 September 1903, GR441, v.74; McBride, Diary, 18 July 1903, McBF; *Western Methodist Recorder*, October 1903.
11 McBride to J.E. Spankie, 11 September 1903, GR441, v.75; R.F. Green to McBride, 17 June 1903, GR441, v.73; *Nelson Daily News*, 7 June 1903. T.G. Shaughnessy of the CPR was pleased that the government was now headed by McBride. Shaughnessy to C.H. Tupper, 10 June 1903, quoted in John A. Eagle, *The Canadian Pacific Railway and the Development of Western Canada* (Montreal and Kingston: McGill-Queen's University Press, 1989), 121.
12 McBride to Richard Marpole, 15 January 1904, McBride to Shaughnessy, 18 January 1904, McBride to Thomas Cavan, 11 February 1904, McBride to R.B. Bennett, 2 February 1904, GR441, v.407; McBride to Cavan, 5 May 1904, GR441, v.408. A number of people in Kamloops sought to have the CPR dismiss J.R. Sutherland for participating in a Conservative campaign meeting while allegedly under the influence of liquor. McBride doubted

that Sutherland was intoxicated and wrote him that "it is really too bad that some folk way out here in British Columbia are so unfair as to try and injure a neighbour simply because of politics." McBride to J.R. Sutherland, 5 February 1904, GR441, v.407.

13 J. Buntzen to Francis Hope, 29 October 1903, Buntzen to Hope, 12 December 1903, BCERR, LFGM, 1903; *Province*, 5 October 1903; McBride to Thomas Caven, 17 December 1903, GR441, v.79.

14 Bowser to McBride, 16 June 1903, Francis Carter-Cotton to McBride, 15 June 1903, GR441, v.73; Robert McBride to Richard McBride, 1 September 1903, GR441, v.74; *Province*, 16 and 17 September 1903. The Orange Order considered nominating its own candidates but endorsed two Liberals, W.D. Brydone-Jack and T.S. Baxter, and two Conservatives, R.G. Tatlow and Charles Wilson. All four were reputed to be members of the order. The *Province* did not explain how Bowser got the nomination. Before the *News-Advertiser* was microfilmed, a column that may have explained the situation was clipped.

15 Thos. Cunningham to McBride, 5 September 1903, GR441, v.74; C.E. Race to McBride, 18 June 1903, GR441, v.77; A. Haslam to McBride, 19 June 1903, GR441, v.73; J.A. Hutchin to McBride, 27 June 1903, GR441, v.76; McBride to W.A. Macdonald, 29 July 1903, GR441, v.406; *Times*, 19 June 1903; *Colonist*, 19 June 1903; *Columbian*, 21 June 1903.

16 *Phoenix Pioneer*, 18 July 1903; *Colonist*, 25 August 1903; *Columbian*, 13 August 1903.

17 *Colonist*, 6 September 1903; *Columbian*, 8, 9, 11, 12, and 23 September 1903.

18 Cabinet passed an Order-in-Council recommending that the GTP Bill, then before Parliament, should provide that the GTP begin work at the Pacific coast and build toward the Rocky Mountains and that no Asians were to be employed on its construction. McBride to Templeman, 28 August 1903, GR441, v.74. Similar messages were sent to the other BC MPs. Copies in GR441, v.385.

19 The C&W grant was not the only embarrassing old land grant. In 1903, McBride approved the grant of lands at Kitimat, whose purchasers had not strictly complied with time limits laid down by statute. In 1905, the Opposition Liberals used this against him. *Times*, 7 April 1905.

20 *Columbian*, 14 September 1903; *Province*, 14 September 1903. He earlier said that the Coast-Kootenay railway was "indispensable" to the region's development, and he favoured government aid to it if the cabinet could control its rates. McBride to W.C. McDougall, 29 July 1903, GR441, v.407.

21 *Columbian*, 16 and 18 September 1903; *Province*, 16 September 1903; *News-Advertiser*, 17 September 1903; *Kamloops Standard*, 1 October 1903; *Vernon News*, 1 October 1903.

22 *Columbian*, 5 October 1903; *Province*, 5 and 6 October 1903; *Colonist*, 4 October 1903. Bowser and Charles Wilson considered which Liberals might be brought over by the offer of a portfolio or government job. Wilson to McBride, 7 October 1903, GR441, v.75; McBride to Tupper, 13 October 1903, CHTP, v.4.

23 McBride to Tupper, 13 October 193, GR441, v.406; Henri Joly de Lotbinière to McBride, 8 October 1903, F. Carter-Cotton to McBride, 21 October 1903, McBride to Carter-Cotton, 26 October 1903, Fulton to McBride, 29 October 1903, GR441, v.78; *Province*, 12 October 1903.

24 John Houston to Joly, 23 October 1903, Joly to Houston, 24 October 1903, GR441, v.409; Joly Papers, 7816. Houston admitted having had "four or five big journs of Scotch whiskey" before the debate but claimed he was sober at the time. *Nelson Daily News*, 30 October 1903. In June 1903, he referred to the attorney general as a "d–d fool." Patrick Wolfe, "Tramp Printer Extraordinary: British Columbia's John 'Truth' Houston," *BC Studies* 40 (Winter 1978-79): 19-20.

25 McBride to Haslam, 30 December 1903, GR441, v.407; Bowser to McBride, 4 October 1903, Charles Wilson to McBride, 16 October 1903, W.A. Macdonald to Wilson, 18 October 1903, McBride to J.J. Cambridge, 26 October 1903, GR441, v.78; McBride to Bowser, 16 October 1903, GR441, v.406; *Colonist,* 28 October 1903; *Vernon News,* 5 November 1903; *Nelson Daily News,* 20, 25, and 30 October 1903; Joly to Edmond Joly, 22 March 1906, quoted in John T. Saywell, *The Office of Lieutenant-Governor: A Study in Canadian Government and Politics* (Toronto: University of Toronto Press, 1957), 38; *Province,* 25 October 1903; Mayor W.O. Rose to McBride, 7 November 1903, GR441, v.22. According to Liberal editor F.J. Deane, the resolutions adopted at the public meeting called by Nelson's mayor did not necessarily reflect the sentiments of its citizens.

26 McBride to W.A. Macdonald, 3 November 1903, GR441, v.79. Houston did not resign from the party until May 1904. McBride to F.A. Starkey, 10 May 1904, GR441, v.408. By 1905, he was absent from the Legislature so often that McBride threatened to have his seat declared vacant. *Times,* 8 November 1905.

27 Fulton to McBride, 24 March 1904, GR441, v.81; *Inland Sentinel,* 25 September 1903, 31 May 1904; *Province,* 7 and 26 May 1904; *Times,* 6 November 1903.

28 *Province,* 11 and 18 November 1903.

29 Lottie Bowron, interviewed by Imbert Orchard, March 1962, BCA, Acc. 1288, tape 1 transcript; *News-Advertiser,* 6 September 1903; *Colonist,* 14 October 1903; McBride to A. Seymour, 30 October 1903, McBride to Herbert Drummond, 5 February 1904, GR441, v.386; McBride to A.D. Cooper, 26 October 1903, McBride to Wm. Manson, 14 October 1903, Fulton to McBride, 11 October 1903, GR441, v.78; *Columbian,* 14 October 1903; *Inland Sentinel,* 16 October 1903; *Phoenix Pioneer,* 24 October 1903; McBride to Fulton, 13 October 1903, GR441, v.406.

30 See McBride to E.F. D'Arcy, 28 January 1904, and other correspondence in GR441, v.8; McBride to W.C. Fowler, 16 March 1904, GR441, v.23.

31 Maitland's son, Royal L. Maitland, was elected a Conservative MLA in 1928, became the party leader, and was attorney general in the Coalition government from 1941 until his death in 1946.

32 A.E. McPhillips to McBride, 6 June 1904, GR441, v.82; McBride to Martin Burrell, 2 March 1904, GR441, v.407; McBride to R.R. Maitland, 24 June 1905, GR441, v.388. For examples in which applicants were promised future consideration, see McBride to A.L. Edmonds, 24 November 1903, GR441, v.79; McBride to W.S. Moor, 25 July 1905, GR441, v.26.

33 *Skeena District News,* 13 February 1904; McBride to E.M.A. Woods, 5 January 1904, GR441, v.80; McBride to J.P. Babcock, 22 August 1904, GR441, v.387; *Inland Sentinel,* 11 March and 2 August 1904; McBride to A.W. Smith, 7 May 1904, GR441, v.408; *Lillooet Prospector,* 30 January 1904. The *Province* claimed that McDonald won some votes through "methods which cannot be justified by any who are desirous of the purity of elections." *Province,* 17 August 1904. The *Colonist* replied that the local public works in question were not unusual and that Macdonald won because of his personal popularity. *Colonist,* 17 August 1904.

34 British Columbia, *Public Accounts ... 1903,* in BCSP, 1903-04, B23; McBride to W.S. Fielding, 19 June 1903, GR441, v.21; *Colonist,* 19 November 1903; *Columbian,* 10 November 1903; George Gillespie to R.G. Tatlow, 30 November 1903, GR441, v.22.

35 Salary information was printed each year in the *Public Accounts.* These numbers are from 1905-06 but did not change from the previous few years. The deputy provincial secretary, who was the senior civil servant, earned $2,100 per year. When it was suggested in 1907 that the salaries of cabinet ministers should be raised to $6,000 per annum plus an additional $400 as a sessional indemnity, press attacks focused on ministers such as Bowser,

who did not devote full time to their government duties, though the *Province* thought that McBride and Tatlow deserved raises. *Nelson Daily News,* 13 December 1907; *Times,* 17 January 1908; *Province,* 10 December 1907.

36 McBride to E.G.W. Sait, 24 June 1903, GR441, v.409; McBride to Fred Brown, 16 October 1903, GR441, v.78; Canadian Bank of Commerce, New Westminster, to McBride, 22 September 1904, McBride to F.J. Hart, 22 September 1904, A.J. Holroyd to McBride, 25 August 1904, GR441, v.83; McBride to Hart, 1 October 1904, GR441, v.84; E.W. Brymner to McBride, 9 November 1903, GR441, v.79; Canadian Bank of Commerce, New Westminster, to McBride, 2 April 1903, GR441, v.73; F.B. Davidson to McBride, 18 March 1904, GR441, v.82 (underlining in original); McBride to Davidson, 9 May 1904, GR441, v.408.

37 McBride to Thomas Taylor, 16 December 1903, GR441, v.79. The *Revelstoke Herald* operated from 1899 to 1905 and became the *Mail Herald* in 1906. The *Inland Sentinel* said that Revelstoke was the only place in the province that lacked a Conservative paper. *Inland Sentinel,* 20 July 1906. An example of McBride's unwillingness to guarantee loans may be found in his 1905 correspondence with Joseph Page, a Galiano Island merchant. McBF.

38 A.H. McBride to Dick, 10 June 1908, MS347, v.1; Manager, Royal Bank, Victoria, to McBride, 5 November 1908, GR441, v.94; G. Sheldon Williams to McBride, 27 April 1909, McBride to Williams, 27 May 1909, GR441, v.96; Williams to McBride, 26 May 1909, GR441, v.97.

39 A number of letters written in 1903-04 are in GR441, v.79, v.80, and v.82; McBride to J. Burtt Morgan, 6 April 1908, Morgan to McBride, 17 April 1908, GR441, v.91.

40 Thomas Cunningham to McBride, 14 November 1907, GR441, v.88. In 1908, McBride thanked an agent of the Summerland Trust Company for selecting his five-acre lot at Naramata and asked him to arrange to have the peach orchard planted and fenced. McBride to R.C. Lipsett, 8 September 1908, GR441, v.93; T.F. Langlois to McBride, 20 November 1903, G.J. Telfer to McBride, 27 November 1903, GR441, v.79; Smith Curtis to McBride, 22 April 1904, McBride to Curtis, 4 May 1904, GR441, v.81; *Columbian,* 26 March 1906; *Grand Forks Evening Sun,* 13 November 1909; Hart to McBride, 2 April 1907, McBride to R.P. Robertson, 14 August 1907, GR441, v.97; McBride to P. Peebles, 11 March 1909, Peebles to McBride, n.d., GR441, v.95.

41 *Colonist,* 27, 28, and 29 November 1903; *Province,* 28 November 1903, 1, 2, 12, and 14 December 1903. When the New Westminster Bridge opened in June 1904, McBride requested a "special holiday" and officiated at the ceremony. As the *Columbian* admitted, the bridge was "a monument" to Dunsmuir's enterprise, although McBride had aroused Dunsmuir's interest in it. McBride to F.J. Hart, 7 May 1904, GR441, v.408; *Columbian,* 23 June 1904. Joseph Martin was invited to the opening but not to the luncheon. Remarking that this constituted "no invitation at all," he declined to attend. *Province,* 25 July 1904; *Times,* 28 November 1903.

42 *Phoenix Pioneer,* 5 December 1903; *Colonist,* 8 and 9 December 1903; *Columbian,* 23 January 1904; *Province,* 30 November and 28 December 1903, 8 February and 3 September 1904.

43 McBride to H.J. Barber, 6 January 1904, GR441, v.407; *Province,* 28 November 1903, 2 and 8 December 1903, 4 January 1904; *Colonist,* 11 and 12 December 1903; Shaughnessy to McBride, 9 December 1903, GR441, v.22.

44 *Times,* 27 December 1904, 18 January 1905; *Colonist,* 13 January and 22 February 1905. A brief account of the controversy over the Assessment Act, especially as it affected commercial travellers, may be found in *CAR,* 1905, 391-93. James Dunsmuir, the collier, was

concerned that though a proposed tax change would free coal mines from taxes on their land, they would be taxed on their fixtures, machinery, and buildings. James Dunsmuir to McBride, 20 March 1905, McBF.

45 *CAR,* 1904, 347; McBride to Chief Commissioner of Lands and Works, 18 January 1904, GR441, v.407; McBride to A. McDonald, 11 May 1904, GR441, v.408; *Columbian,* 29 January 1904; McBride to R.L. Codd, 20 August 1904, McBride to Codd, 12 April 1905, McBride to J.D. Macnider, 10 October 1904, GR441, v.142; McBride to J.A. McKelvie, 24 October 1904, GR441, v.84; *Victoria Truth,* 26 February 1904.

46 A brief account of this complicated story is in F.W. Howay, *British Columbia from the Earliest Times to the Present* (Vancouver: S.J. Clarke, 1914), 2:486, 521-23; *Province,* 12 December 1903, 18 June 1904. Robert A.J. McDonald, "Sir Charles Hibbert Tupper and the Political Culture of British Columbia, 1903-1924," *BC Studies* 149 (Spring 2006): 66, implies that this issue constituted the first step in Tupper's alienation from McBride. In a letter to Wilfrid Laurier, McBride inquired whether Ottawa intended to disallow the bill. McBride to Laurier, 20 March 1904, GR441, v.386; McBride to Wilson, 1 July 1903, GR441, v.73; Joly to McBride, 30 June 1903, GR441, v.76; McBride to A.B. Grace, 4 July 1903, GR441, v.406; Joly to McBride, 30 November 1903, GR441, v.79; McBride to M. Burrell, 26 March 1904, GR441, v.408; Tupper to McBride et al., 4 November 1903, McBride to Tupper, 6 November 1903, McBride to George Fraser, 2 December 1903, CHTP, v.4. Other correspondence between Tupper and McBride in mid-June 1904 is in CHTP, v.4.

47 An undated entry in McBride's 1904 diary notes that he held money for the federal campaign in Duncan, Vancouver, New Westminster, Kamloops, Revelstoke, Ashcroft, Mayne and Saltspring Islands, and several communities in Dewdney.

48 Borden to McBride, 28 November 1903, GR441, v.79; McBride to Borden, 5 April 1904, GR441, v.408; Borden to McBride, 2 January 1904, GR441, v.80; McBride to Borden, 23 January 1904, McBride to Bowser, 8 January 1904, McBride to J.R. Grant, 18 January 1904, GR441, v.407; *Columbian,* 20, 24, and 27 October 1903, 3 November 1903, 9 January 1904.

49 *Colonist,* 23 September 1904, 14 and 23 October 1904; McDonald, "Sir Charles Hibbert Tupper," 66-67; Tupper to McBride, 20 October 1904, McBride to Tupper, 24 October 1904, GR441, v.84; McBride to Borden, 15 February 1904, GR441, v.407; *Times,* 23 November 1904.

50 *Colonist,* 23 September and 22 December 1904; *Province,* 26 November 1904; McBride to D.L. McPhee, 26 November 1904, GR441, v.84.

51 *Toronto Globe,* 15 December 1905; *News-Advertiser,* 22 December 1905; *Toronto Telegram,* quoted in *Times,* 21 December 1905.

52 *British Columbia in the Canadian Confederation: A Submission Presented to the Royal Commission on Dominion-Provincial Relations by the Government of the Province of British Columbia* (Victoria: King's Printer, 1938), 237-48; *Vancouver World,* quoted in *New Westminster Daily News,* 30 May 1906; Tatlow to Joly, 5 November 1906, Joly Papers, 8089ff.

53 McBride to Gillespie, 16 December 1903, GR441, v.22; McBride to Price Ellison, 24 December 1903, GR441, v.79; McBride to Martin Burrell, 12 February 1904, McBride to G.H. Cowan, 9 February 1904, GR441, v.407; *Province,* 10 February 1904; McBride to James Dunsmuir, 23 January 1904, Dunsmuir to McBride, 26 January 1904, GR441, v.406; Eagle, *The Canadian Pacific Railway,* 141.

54 McBride, Diary, 23 June 1904, McBF; *Columbian,* 11 February 1904; McBride to L.W. Shatford, 3 May 1904, GR441, v.82; McBride to Hugh McLean, 10 May 1904, GR441,

v.387. McBride to Shatford, 5 April 1904, GR441, v.408; McBride to Shatford, 22 August and 24 September 1904, GR441, v.83; Eagle, *The Canadian Pacific Railway*, 123-26.

55 *Columbian*, 5 March 1904; McBride to Martin Burrell, 2 March 1904, GR441, v.80; Bowser to McBride, 19 May 1904, McBride to Bowser, 20 May 1904, GR441, v.82; *Colonist*, 15 February 1905; *Province*, 16 February 1905.

56 *News-Advertiser*, 14 February 1905; *Times*, 3, 14, 15, and 23 March 1905, 8 April 1905; *Province*, 11, 13, 22, and 26 March 1905; *Colonist*, 8 April 1905; McBride to F.G. Vernon, 8 April 1904, GR441, v.386. In July 1904, the GTP acquired the Pacific Northern and Omineca charter and a cash subsidy offered by an earlier provincial government. Frank Leonard, *A Thousand Blunders: The Grand Trunk Pacific Railway and Northern British Columbia* (Vancouver: UBC Press, 1996), 37-38.

57 McBride to C.M. Hays, 28 November 1903 and 3 January 1904, McBride to Laurier, 8 April 1904, GR441, v.386; Leonard, *A Thousand Blunders*, 27-38; *Colonist*, 24 August 1904.

58 *Colonist*, 2 March 1905; *CAR*, 1906, 504.

59 McBride to J.M. Cleveland, 20 January 1906, GR441, v.388.

60 *Times*, 9 and 23 February 1905, 30 March 1905, 7 and 10 April 1905; *Province*, 16 and 23 February 1905, 11 December 1905; *News-Advertiser*, 12 December 1905. The Socialists voted against a grant to the militia because of the standing objection of "wage earners" to the militia.

61 *News-Advertiser*, 9 April 1905; *Phoenix Pioneer*, 22 April 1905; *Province*, 30 March, 8 April, and 7 May 1905; *Columbian*, 21 November 1905; *Cranbrook Prospector*, 25 November 1905.

62 *News-Advertiser*, 18 July 1905. He appears to have dropped the suit. *Colonist*, 8 and 14 July 1905; *Times*, 10, 13, and 22 July 1905; *Province*, 13 July 1905.

63 *News-Advertiser*, 20 December 1905; *Province*, 21 and 27 December 1905; *Colonist*, 23 December 1905; *Times*, 26 December 1905, 16 January, 7 February, and 5 March 1906; *Columbian*, 16 January 1906; *CAR*, 1906, 486-87.

64 The CPR threatened that it could ruin the government if the land grant were not forthcoming. McBride, Diary, 6 April 1905, McBF; McBride to Wilson, 23 February 1906, quoted in Brian Ray Douglas Smith, "Sir Richard McBride: A Study in the Conservative Party of British Columbia, 1903-1916" (master's thesis, Queen's University, 1959), 48-49.

65 *Times*, 1 and 15 March 1906; *CAR*, 1906, 490; Eagle, *The Canadian Pacific Railway*, 253-54. McBride apparently had had Wilson's resignation for some time before accepting it. He also had Pinkerton's agents observe the Liberal and Conservative caucuses. They found little that was startling, but information about Liberal thinking gave McBride a tactical advantage. Peter Roberts Hunt, "The Political Career of Sir Richard McBride" (master's thesis, University of British Columbia, 1953), 92.

66 W.H. Wood to McBride, 28 August 1905, GR441, v.26; Tupper to McBride, 17 April 1906, CHTP, v.4; McDonald, "Sir Charles Hibbert Tupper," 66-67; *Times*, 13 January 1906.

67 *Times*, 16 and 17 January 1906, 1, 22, and 26 February 1906; *Inland Sentinel*, 13 March 1906. An unsigned memo in the McBride fonds notes that in November 1905, he gave a number of deeds for lands deemed "unfit for cultivation" and for sale at one dollar an acre to Green with a request that he have them properly examined to determine their true value.

68 Joly to McBride, 5 March 1906, BCA, E/DJ86. A succinct account of the affair and of the committee's findings is in *CAR*, 1906, 495-500; *Times*, 8 and 9 March 1906; Tupper to McBride, 17 April 1906, McBride to Tupper, 28 April 1906, Tupper to McBride, 1 May 1906, Clive Phillipps-Wolley to Tupper, 30 December 1906, Tupper to Phillipps-Wolley, 31 December 1906, CHTP, v.4. Borden failed to reconcile the differences between McBride and Tupper.

69 *Times*, 21 February and 12 April 1906; *Columbian*, 14 April 1906.
70 *Province*, 11 February 1905; *Times*, 26 February 1906, 18 June and 26 December 1906, 8 January 1907; Tatlow to Joly, 4 August 1906, Joly Papers, 8074ff; *Nelson Daily News*, 11 December 1906; *Colonist*, 25 December 1906; *New Westminster Daily News*, 20 June and 29 December 1906. This paragraph is based mainly on Holmes, *Royal Commissions*, 26, and *Times*, 3 August 1906. One report said that Lieutenant-Governor Dunsmuir insisted that Green must go. *Nelson Daily News*, 17 June 1906.
71 A.C. Flumerfelt, "Forest Resources," in *Canada and Its Provinces: A History of the Canadian People and Their Institutions by One Hundred Associates*, ed. Adam Shortt and Arthur G. Doughty (Toronto: Publishers' Association of Canada, 1914), 22:495.
72 *New Westminster Daily News*, 7 December 1906; *Province*, 18 January and 23 June 1904, 31 January and 1 February 1906; Gordon Hak, *Turning Trees into Dollars: The British Columbia Coastal Lumber Industry, 1858-1913* (Toronto: University of Toronto Press, 2000), 100-1. McBride to C.A. MacKinnon, 29 August 1904, GR441, v.387; *CAR*, 1906, 493; *Inland Sentinel*, 2 February 1906; *Columbian*, 31 May 1906.
73 Robert E. Cail, *Land, Man, and the Law: The Disposal of Crown Lands in British Columbia, 1871-1913* (Vancouver: UBC Press, 1974), ch. 6; F. Elworthy, Victoria Board of Trade, to McBride, c. 16 March 1905, GR441, v.25; *Province*, 22 May and 20 June 1905; *World*, 16 June 1905; *News-Advertiser*, 20 and 21 June 1905; *Columbian*, 21 June 1905; McBride to Victor Odlum, 24 January 1905, LAC, V.W. Odlum Papers, v.28.
74 *News-Advertiser*, 7 May 1905; Hak, *Turning Trees into Dollars*, 105-6; Cail, *Land, Man, and the Law*, 102-3.
75 *Globe*, 15 October 1906; *Colonist*, 16 November 1906; *Times*, 15 December 1906; *Nelson Daily News*, 15 September 1906; *New Westminster Daily News*, 15 September and 12 November 1906; Richard A. Rajala, *Clearcutting the Pacific Rain Forest: Production, Science, and Regulation* (Vancouver: UBC Press, 1998), 99; Hak, *Turning Trees into Dollars*, 107-9; Stephen Gray, "The Government's Timber Business: Forest Policy and Administration in British Columbia, 1912-1928," *BC Studies* 81 (Spring 1989): 25-26; McBride to Joly, 16 August 1906, Joly Papers, 8081ff. The independent *Nelson Tribune*, edited by John Houston, frequently referred to the "Joly-McBride government." See, for example, *Nelson Tribune*, 14 and 20 September 1904; *Province*, 26 September 1906.
76 *Province*, 7 April 1905, 26 September 1906; *Nelson Daily News*, 11 December 1906; *Inland Sentinel*, 21 June 1904; Secretary to J.H. Turner, 24 February 1905, GR441, v.388.
77 *Columbian*, 15 June 1903, 25 January 1906; *Times*, 24 March 1905, 26, 27, and 30 January 1906; *Colonist*, 24 March 1905.
78 McBride to Thos. Mars Jr., 15 May 1905, McBride to Wm. M. Reid, 23 January 1906, McBride to J. Chessen, 13 August 1906, McBride to R.F. Green, 1 October 1906, McBride to R.L. Codd, 21 December 1906, Geo. Mouldey to McBride, 12 December 1906, McBride to Mouldey, 31 December 1906, GR441, v.142; *Columbian*, 29 January 1904. J.R. Morrison, a prominent Liberal, was unhappy because a new road would pass through his garden and because the government gave no notice and offered no compensation while workmen "invaded" his property. When the incensed Morrison vandalized a bridge that was under construction, the government charged him with malicious damage. The *New Westminster Daily News* claimed that he was persecuted because he opposed the government. *New Westminster Daily News*, 11 October 1906.
79 *Times*, 8 May 1906; *Inland Sentinel*, 28 July 1903; *Columbian*, 18 and 21 June 1904, 6 and 9 June 1905, 23 April and 26 June 1906; J. Buntzen to McBride, 2 June 1905, GR441, v.25; *Province*, 12 June 1905.

80 *Columbian,* 4 October 1904, 2, 11, and 12 September 1905, 5 March and 14 June 1906; *Colonist,* 11 December 1904; *New Westminster Daily News,* 3 October 1906; McBride to H.T. Thrift, 3 May 1904, GR441, v.408.
81 *Columbian,* 12 February and 22 September 1906; *Colonist,* 10 and 11 February 1906; James Morton, "McBride 1; Oliver, 2," *Colonist,* 11 September 1960.
82 A municipal "crisis" arose at Phoenix when the police magistrate became involved in a case arising from an assault charge laid against the police chief. McBride advised the magistrate to resign, but the deputy attorney general investigated and found no valid reason to dismiss him. A brief summary of the findings is in Marjorie C. Holmes, *Royal Commissions and Commissions of Inquiry under the "Public Inquiries Act" in British Columbia, 1872-1942: A Checklist* (Victoria: King's Printer, 1945), 24.
83 Bowser to McBride, 19 May 1904, GR441, v.82; *Phoenix Pioneer,* 2 July 1904. McBride's diary for 1904 includes a record of the trips, but most entries are little more than itineraries.
84 *Colonist,* 18 August 1905, 7 and 21 November 1905; *News-Advertiser,* 7, 17, and 21 November 1905; *Cranbrook Prospector,* 23 December 1905.
85 *Nelson Daily News,* 7 and 14 June 1906; *Columbian,* 10 August 1906; *Colonist,* 9 August 1906; *Times,* 16 June and 9 August 1906; *Inland Sentinel,* 20 July 1906; *New Westminster Daily News,* 19 and 22 December 1906; *Vernon News,* 20 December 1906; *Armstrong Advertiser,* 28 December 1906.
86 *Province,* 6, 12, and 13 November 1906; *Times,* 17 June 1905, 18 and 30 May 1906, 8 June and 17 September 1906; *New Westminster Daily News,* 5, 11, and 12 June 1906, 11 and 22 August 1906, 11, 20, and 21 November 1906, 19 December 1906; *Nelson Daily News,* 26 June 1906, 12, 18, and 21 September 1906; *Kelowna Courier,* 1 November 1906.
87 *Report of the Delegates to Ottawa,* 1903, in BCSP, 1903-04, K3-K13. The revenue figures were inflated by including customs duties on goods sold in the east whose consumers ultimately paid them.
88 McBride to Laurier, 30 June 1903, GR441, v.385; McBride to Borden, 24 June 1903, GR441, v.409; *Colonist,* 3 July 1903; W. Templeman to Laurier, 9 July 1903, WLP, 74900; Templeman to Clifford Sifton, 9 July 1903, LAC, Clifford Sifton Papers, 120974-5; Wilson and Green to Laurier, 18 July 1903, RLBP, 129177, reprinted in BCSP, 1903-04, G15-17. Henri Joly de Lotbinière agreed that referring the matter to such a commission "would show that the claims of the Province are reasonable and just." Joly to McBride, 24 August 1903, GR441, v.78; Borden to McBride, 11 July 1903, GR441, v.77; McBride to Laurier, 24 December 1903, in BCSP, 1903-04, G23.
89 McBride to Laurier, 11 June 1904, GR441, v.385; McBride to Laurier, 17 November 1903, GR441, v.386; McBride to A.E. McPhillips, 18 May 1904, GR441, v.408. Mowat, a Liberal, was premier of Ontario from 1872 to 1896.
90 *Province,* 1 December 1903, 27 January 1904; McBride to Laurier, 24 December 1903; McBride to Laurier, 27 January 1904, in BCSP, 1903-04, G23, G28-29; Laurier to McBride, 4 January 1904, GR441, v.23; *Columbian,* 21 January 1904.
91 G.H. Cowan to E. Galbraith, 24 December 1903, Cowan to Borden, 6 May 1904, CVA, G.H. Cowan Papers, v.4. Cowan sent a copy of his Better Terms pamphlet to Borden, who agreed that the province had a strong case. Cowan asked Borden for a letter to that effect to use in Vancouver. McBride to Borden, 23 January 1904, GR441, v.407. Borden discussed the matter with Sir Charles Tupper and his son, Sir Charles Hibbert Tupper. Borden to McBride, 4 March 1904, GR441, v.81.
92 After hearing Frederick Buscombe's "very strong speech" on Better Terms, a committee of the Vancouver Board of Trade drafted a resolution on the subject, sought the endorsement

of other boards, and asked G.H. Cowan to speak to it. *Province,* 7 December 1904; *Colonist,* 14 September and 14 October 1904; Borden to C.H. Tupper, 10 October 1904, RLBP, 128999; *Times,* 14 October 1904; *Nelson Tribune,* 12 November 1904, quoted in *Inland Sentinel,* 14 November 1904; *Vernon News,* 17 November 1904; *Kelowna Clarion,* 10 November 1904. The Conservative *Nelson Economist,* 15 and 29 October 1904, referred to Better Terms, whereas the Liberal *Nelson Daily News* did not. The Conservative *Vernon News* reprinted a *Colonist* editorial, "Better Terms," 17 November 1904.

93 McBride to Cowan, 21 December 1904, Gosnell to Cowan, 11 December 1904, CVA, G.H. Cowan Papers, v.2; *Province,* 16 and 26 February 1905; McBride to Laurier, 21 December 1904, GR441, v.25; *Colonist,* 15 and 25 February 1905; *Columbian,* 25 February 1905. The reference to Esquimalt is in Article 9 of the Terms of Union, 1871.

94 McBride to Laurier, 21 January 1905, GR441, v.25. The Conservative press supported this. The Legislature, without dissent, passed Bowser's resolution complaining that provincial rights were infringed upon by the provisions for separate schools in the Autonomy Bills that created Alberta and Saskatchewan. *Colonist,* 7 and 28 March 1905; *News-Advertiser,* 11 March 1905.

95 McBride to Laurier, 1 February 1905, GR441, v.388; *News-Advertiser,* 7 May 1905; Lomer Gouin to McBride, 8 September 1905, McBride to Gouin, 4 October 1905, McBride to Laurier, 4 October 1905, Gouin to McBride, 11 October 1905, GR441, v.26. The *Times* said that by communicating with Gouin and agreeing to Better Terms for other provinces, McBride would make British Columbia "a consenting party to the perpetration of further injustice against herself." *Times,* 7 November 1907. The *Colonist* argued that if British Columbia's claims were settled uniformly with those of the other provinces, it would be no better off but noted recognition of the argument for "an impartial investigation of all the facts." *Colonist,* 8 November 1905.

96 *Columbian,* 31 October 1905; *Colonist,* 30 November 1905; *Ottawa Evening Journal,* 4 December 1905; Fulton to McBride, 19 June 1904, McBride to Laurier, 21 March 1904, GR441, v.23; *Halifax Herald,* 16 December 1905. There were also problems over the effects of damming certain rivers on fish runs. W.D. Burdis to McBride, 8 June 1904, GR441, v.24; *Province,* 4 December 1905; *Skeena District News,* 25 July 1904; Laurier to McBride, 17 May 1906, GR441, v.27.

97 *Province,* 21 December 1905; *Toronto Telegram,* quoted in *Cranbrook Prospector,* 30 December 1905; McBride, Diary, 6 December 1905, cited in Smith, "Sir Richard McBride," 63; *News-Advertiser,* 22 December 1905; *Times,* 15 December 1905; McBride to Laurier, 27 February and 28 March 1906, 11 and 19 May 1906, GR441, v.388. Sir Henri Joly supported McBride in this fight for Better Terms. Joly to McBride, 22 August 1906, BCA, E/D J68.

98 McBride to Joly, 16 August 1906, Joly Papers, 8080ff. For examples of how the press revived the Better Terms issue, see *Columbian,* 3 April, 9 June, and 21 August 1906; *CAR,* 1906, 512-15; *Times,* 31 August 1906. See also *Nelson Daily News,* 3 August 1906; *New Westminster Daily News,* 18 September 1906.

99 A summary of the conference is in *CAR,* 1906, 515-23. The quoted phrases are from that source.

100 McBride to Joly, [early November 1906], Joly Papers, 7862ff; *Columbian,* 26 October 1906; *Colonist,* 10 October 1906; *Globe,* 13 and 15 October 1906.

101 Gouin to McBride, 17 October 1906, MS347, v.1; *Province,* 15 October 1906. Walkem's concern was the delay in building the CPR. *Times,* 20 February 1912. This paragraph draws on J.A. Maxwell, *Federal Subsidies to the Provincial Governments in Canada* (Cambridge, MA: Harvard University Press, 1937), 101-36.

102 *Nelson Daily News*, 16 October 1906; *Inland Sentinel*, 16 and 23 October 1906; *New Westminster Daily News*, 15 October 1906; *Times*, 16 October 1906; *Columbian*, 15 and 20 October 1906; *Colonist*, 14 and 16 October 1906; *Province*, 16, 23, and 26 October 1906; *Nanaimo Free Press*, 17 October 1906.

103 *Province*, 25 October 1906; *News-Advertiser*, 26 October 1906; *Colonist*, 27 October 1906; *Times*, 27 October 1906. Congratulatory letters and telegrams are in GR441, v.85.

104 McBride to Joly, n.d., c. mid-November 1906, Joly Papers, 7862ff; *Colonist*, 9, 11, and 24 November 1906, 9, 19, and 20 December 1906; *Columbian*, 24 and 26 November 1906.

105 *Province*, 19 September 1906; McBride to Lieutenant-Governor, 2 November 1906, GR441, v.389; Dunsmuir to McBride, 2 November 1906, cited in Smith, "Sir Richard McBride," 74; *New Westminster Daily News*, 25 December 1906.

Chapter 4: Toward a Wider Stage

1 *Columbian*, 24 December 1906. John Oliver of Delta, a Liberal, accused the Conservatives of "lamentably" failing to carry out their 1903 platform promises and attacked "inequitable" taxes, especially for rural schools, timber licences that benefited speculators but not small sawmill owners, and land "steals" at Kaien Island, Kitimat, and by the CPR. *New Westminster Daily News*, 21 November 1906.

2 *Colonist*, 27 December 1906, 23 January 1907. Other examples of early mentions of Better Terms as a major issue are *News-Advertiser*, 29 December 1906; *New Westminster Daily News*, 29 December 1906. *Province*, 4 January 1907; *Columbian*, 3 and 22 January 1907. The *Cranbrook Prospector*, 5 January 1907.

3 *Province*, 17 January and 1 February 1907; *Columbian*, 5 and 25 January 1907. A year later, in introducing a measure to relieve Dewdney of a debt acquired through its dyking bonds, McBride said that municipal bankruptcy must be avoided in order to preserve the province's credit. *Kelowna Courier*, 8 February 1908.

4 *Nelson Daily News*, 29 December 1906.

5 *Province*, 17 January 1907; *Colonist*, 17 January 1907. The allegations regarding the CPR were not forgotten. In January 1908, McBride again had to deny that he had received special favours from the CPR or any other corporation during the election. *News-Advertiser*, 25 January 1908.

6 *Province*, 7 January 1907.

7 *Inland Sentinel*, 4 January 1907. In its pre-election coverage, the *Times* stressed scandals concerning Green, and on 16 January, it published a full page on J.A. Macdonald's Kaien Island minority report. The court did not hear the Green libel suit until the summer. Called as a witness, McBride remembered that cabinet had met with C.H. Tupper and G.H. Cowan in April 1906 but was under oath not to disclose what had taken place. He had had conversations with Green about Caron, but if he censured Green, it was only about departmental matters. He retained every confidence in Green, "a man who would not violate his obligation as a Minister of the Crown." McBride attributed Green's unpopularity to the need of Lands and Works to cut spending. Green denied having received any shares in the Transcontinental Exploration Company but admitted agreeing to have some stock set aside in the name of Neil MacKay, who had been McBride's secretary in 1904-05. *Columbian*, 31 July and 1 August 1907. In his charge to the jury, Mr. Justice Clements commented that Green "was either one of the most innocent of men or really believed

there would be some advantage to him in accepting Caron's offer of the shares." *Nelson Daily News,* 3 August 1907. The jury found for the *World,* with costs. *Columbian,* 1 August 1907. Privately, McBride admitted that Green's conduct was "open to question" but was only "an error in judgment." He was sorry to see him retire. McBride to Joly, 8 August 1907, Joly Papers, 8338ff; *Province,* 24 January 1907; *New Westminster Daily News,* 25 and 28 January 1907; *Times,* 25 January 1907. W.W.B. McInnes, Vancouver's Liberal candidate in the 1908 federal election, mentioned the coal lands scandal in the campaign and accused G.H. Cowan, the Conservative, of using it to force Green to resign as commissioner of lands and works. *Province,* 3 October 1908.

8 *New Westminster Daily News,* 14 January 1907; *Kelowna Courier,* 20 December 1906; *Chilliwack Progress,* 23 January 1907; *Cranbrook Prospector,* 19 January 1907.

9 *Vernon News,* 10 January 1907; *New Westminster Daily News,* 12, 14, and 31 January 1907; *Semi-Weekly World,* 18 January 1907; *Nelson Daily News,* 4 and 13 January 1907; *Revelstoke Mail-Herald,* 16 January 1907; *Colonist,* 17 January and 2 February 1907; *Columbian,* 25 and 29 January 1907, 1 February 1907; *News-Advertiser,* 26, 29, 30, and 31 January 1907; *Province,* 29 January and 1 February 1907. See Patricia E. Roy, *A White Man's Province: British Columbia Politicians and Chinese and Japanese Immigrants, 1858-1914* (Vancouver: UBC Press, 1989), 166-68. During the 1909 provincial election, the *Province* said that it received the information about the GTP hiring Japanese labourers from a prominent Liberal and denied that it "knowingly" published roorbacks. *Province,* 22 November 1909.

10 *Cranbrook Herald,* 3 January 1907; W. Scovil to McBride, 23 January 1907, GR441, v.144. The Conservatives won in Columbia and Revelstoke. Thomas Taylor to McBride, 3 April 1907, F.J. Fulton to McBride, 7 June 1907, GR441, v.29. The charge against Fraser could not be substantiated, although he "acted indiscreetly" in accompanying the Opposition candidate to a meeting.

11 J.A. Porter to McBride, 6 February 1907, Daniel McCurdy to McBride, 15 February 1907, F.A. Macfinch [sp?] to McBride, 4 February 1907, A.S. Goodeve to McBride, 4 February 1907, GR441, v.144; *Colonist,* 27 and 31 January 1907.

12 Jean Barman, *The West beyond the West: A History of British Columbia,* 3rd ed. (Toronto: University of Toronto Press, 2007), 223; *Province,* 7 and 12 January 1907; *Times,* 25 June 1907; J.A. Harvey to McBride, 4 February 1907, Bowser to McBride, 4 February 1907, Charles Wilson to McBride, 13 February 1907, L.F. Champion to McBride, 9 February 1907, G.T. Rogers to McBride, 4 February 1907, GR441, v.86; W.T. Pieper to McBride, 4 February 1907, GR441, v.144. Bowser led the Vancouver poll.

13 *Province,* 2 February 1907; J.A. Porter to McBride, 6 February 1907, GR441, v.144; Harvey to McBride, 4 February 1907, T.G. Shaughnessy to McBride, 22 February 1907, GR441, v.86; J.A. Macdonald to V.W. Odlum, 12 February 1907, LAC, V.W. Odlum Papers, v.13.

14 McBride to A.D. Mackenzie, 5 March 1907, GR411, v.87; Charles Doering to McBride, 23 February 1912, L.F. Champion to McBride, 9 February 1907, McBride to Champion, 7 March 1907, GR441, v.86; M. Manson to McBride, 22 August 1907, McBride to Manson, 27 August 1907, GR441, v.88.

15 Wilson to McBride, 2 and 8 January 1907, GR441, v.86; *Columbian,* 7 and 30 January 1907, 1, 2, 6, and 7 February 1907; *Inland Sentinel,* 8 January 1907; *Province,* 1 and 21 January 1907, 1 February 1907; *Colonist,* 25 and 27 January 1907, 2 February 1907; *New Westminster Daily News,* 30 January 1907. McBride's diary includes a few comments on the trip.

16 *Colonist,* 8 January 1907, 2 and 4 February 1907.

17 *Kelowna Courier,* 13 February 1907; *Province,* 6 February 1907; Odlum to McBride, 5 February 1907, GR441, v.144; Tatlow to McBride, 19 May 1907, GR441, v.87; Brian Ray Douglas Smith, "Sir Richard McBride: A Study in the Conservative Party of British Columbia, 1903-1916" (master's thesis, Queen's University, 1959), 52-53; *Port Essington Sun,* 3 August 1907; *Nelson Daily News,* 25 July 1907; *Columbian,* 2 August 1907.

18 BCLJ, 7 March 1907; *New Westminster Daily News,* 8 March 1907; *Nelson Daily News,* 8 March 1907; *Times,* 7 March 1907; *Columbian,* 13 March 1907; *Colonist,* 12 March 1907.

19 *Colonist,* 5 April 1907; Gordon Hak, *Turning Trees into Dollars: The British Columbia Coastal Lumber Industry, 1858-1913* (Toronto: University of Toronto Press, 2000), 106; *Nelson Daily News,* 5 April 1907, 22 February 1908; *CAR,* 1909, 532, 586.

20 Public Schools, *Annual Report,* 1908, in BCSP, 1909, B8. Most high schools had only one room. Through an affiliation, three graduates of Columbian College had received bachelor's degrees from the University of Toronto by 1906. W.J. Sipprell to McBride, 2 February 1906, McBride to Sipprell, 7 February 1906, GR441, v.27; *Province,* 21 September 1906.

21 *Nelson Daily News,* 12 March 1907; *Standard,* 30 January 1904; Gladstone Miners' Union to McBride, 20 September 1904, GR441, v.24; *Colonist,* 3 April 1907; *Columbian,* 3 October 1907; *Inland Sentinel,* 10 July 1908; *Revelstoke Observer,* quoted in *Inland Sentinel,* 18 January 1909; Richard McBride, "Charter Day Address" (speech at University of California, 23 March 1913), copy in McBF.

22 McBride to Sir Henri, 8 August 1907, Joly Papers, 8338ff; H.T. Logan, *Tuum Est: A History of the University of British Columbia* (Vancouver: University of British Columbia, 1958), 34, 38. Dr. Rosalind Young, Young's wife, may have drafted the act. Sylvie McClean, *A Woman of Influence: Evlyn Fenwick Farris* (Victoria: Sono Nis, 1997), 85; *CAR,* 1908, 529.

23 R. Cole Harris, "Locating the University of British Columbia," *BC Studies* 32 (Winter 1976-77): 115; *Colonist,* 17 January 1908. The *Columbian,* 30 January 1908, expressed similar sentiments about the need for better rewards for civil servants. The federal government amended its Civil Service Act in 1908 in an effort to provide for advancement within the service by revising the classification system. J.E. Hodgetts et al., *The Biography of an Institution: The Civil Service Commission of Canada, 1908-1967* (Montreal and Kingston: McGill-Queen's University Press, 1972), 33; *New Westminster Daily News,* 16 March 1909; Robert A.J. McDonald, "The Quest for 'Modern Administration': British Columbia's Civil Service, 1870s to 1940s," *BC Studies* 161 (Spring 2009): 20.

24 *Nelson Daily Canadian,* 13 December 1907; *Nelson Daily News,* 13 December 1907; *Times,* 18 January 1908; R.H. Sperling to George Kidd, 3 March 1909, BCERR, LFGM, 1909.

25 C.B. Lallemand to McBride, 12 March 1907, McBride to Lallemand, 25 March 1907, GR441, v.71; McBride to Fred Stalker, 30 April 1909, GR441, v.96; L. Norris to McBride, 31 January 1907, Charles Wilson to McBride, 13 February 1907, GR441, v.86; *Times,* 14 December 1908. Accusations regarding patronage became a repeated theme of the *Times.* See, for example, *Times,* 1 February 1910, and 4 August 1911.

26 *Nelson Daily News,* 26 February 1908; *Alberni Pioneer News,* 1 May 1909; *New Westminster Daily News,* 21 April and 6 May 1909, 31 January 1911. The complaint regarding government partiality to certain newspapers was justified. In fiscal year 1909, for example, a number of Conservative papers including the *Columbian,* the *Colonist,* the *Vancouver Daily News-Advertiser,* and the *Kamloops Standard* received contracts for printing voters' lists. Liberal papers such as the *Victoria Daily Times,* the *New Westminster Daily News,* and the *Inland Sentinel* did not. Similarly, the *Colonist* received $1,930.55 in government advertising, whereas the *Times* was allocated only $455.00. British Columbia, *Public Accounts ... 1909,*

in BCSP, 1910, B176; *Inland Sentinel,* 20 July 1906; A.E. Watts to McBride, 11 February 1907, GR441, v.86.
27 Bowser to McBride, 13 May 1908, GR441, v.91; McBride to J.C. Walter, 12 March 1908, GR441, v.31; BCLJ, 21 March 1907.
28 *Colonist,* 7 March 1907; McBride to Joly, 22 March 1907, Joly Papers, 8239ff; McBride to A.P. Thompson, 4 March 1907, James Mars to McBride, 12 March 1907, McBride to F. Fletcher, 23 July 1907, GR441, v.143; *Columbian,* 8 and 11 March 1907, 31 December 1908.
29 *Alberni Pioneer News,* 30 January 1909; *Fort George Herald,* 17 June 1911; *Colonist,* 13 August 1907, 8 August and 4 October 1908; *Times,* 29 May 1907, 16 March and 27 June 1908, 8 and 16 October 1908, 6 January 1909.
30 James Morton, "McBride 1; Oliver, 2," *Colonist,* 11 September 1960; *Province,* 18 February 1908; *Columbian,* 7 March 1908; *Colonist,* 19 January and 23 February 1908; *Times,* 22 February, 6 June, and 16 December 1908. The Gorge Road house had been built at a cost of more than $40,000 by a Winnipeg man. Later, after McBride moved out, it fell into disrepair and was demolished in 1933. *Colonist,* 27 May 1933.
31 Brad R. Morrison, "Queen's Academy, Victoria, B.C.," The Homeroom, n.d., http://www.viu.ca/; *Times,* 12 September 1908.
32 Lottie Bowron, interviewed by Imbert Orchard, March 1962, BCA, Acc. 1288, tape 1 transcript; Peter Peebles, "When the Premier of B.C. Laid Aside His Duties," *Province,* 5 May 1929; *Columbian,* 22 June and 10 August 1907, 7 March 1908, 2 January, 27 March, and 12 June 1909, 12 and 24 July 1909, 3 August 1909; McBride, Diary, 2-4 August 1909, McBF.
33 *Colonist,* 22 March 1908, 26 and 28 April 1908, 31 July 1909; *New Westminster Daily News,* 10 January 1907, 14 August 1908; *Province,* 14 August 1908; *Columbian,* 5 October 1907, 29 and 30 September 1908; *Times,* 5 October 1908.
34 John G. Sproule to McBride, 6 February 1907, GR441, v.144; Amos P. Thompson to McBride, 9 February 1907, GR441, v.143. The "hands off" phrase also appeared in the *Cranbrook Prospector,* 9 February 1907; McBride to Borden, 18 February 1907, GR441, v.86.
35 *Nelson Daily News,* 17 and 26 March 1907; *New Westminster Daily News,* 19 March 1907; *Times,* 18 and 26 March 1907; BCLJ, 25 March 1907; *Columbian,* 22, 27, and 30 March 1907; McBride to Joly, 22 March 1907, Joly Papers, 8239ff; *Colonist,* 26 March and 4 April 1907.
36 HCD, 25 March 1907, 5306-07, 5327; McBride to Borden, 8 April 1907, GR441, v.87; *Times,* 4 and 20 April 1907; *Nelson Daily News,* 4 April 1907; *Inland Sentinel,* 5 April 1907. McBride's modest travelling expenses of $1,774.00 may have included other trips. The *Public Accounts* did not break down expense money. Gosnell received $154.55 for expenses for accompanying McBride to Ottawa. British Columbia, *Public Accounts ... 1906-1907,* in BCSP, 1908, B109-10.
37 For Gosnell, see Terry Eastwood, "R.E. Gosnell, E.O.S. Scholefield and the Founding of the Provincial Archives of British Columbia, 1894-1919," *BC Studies* 54 (Summer 1982): 38-62; Gosnell to McBride, 26 February 1907, McBride to Gosnell, 5 March 1907, GR441, v.86; McBride to Borden, 8 April 1907, Gosnell to McBride, 7 April 1907, Edgar Dewdney to McBride, 5 April 1907, GR441, v.87; *Times,* 4 and 20 April 1907; *Nelson Daily News,* 4 April 1907; *Inland Sentinel,* 5 April 1907; *Colonist,* 17 April 1907; *The Times* (London), 16 and 20 April 1907; *Columbian,* 26 June 1907; McBride, Diary, 1907, passim, McBF.
38 *Colonist* and *Columbian,* 23 May 1907. A week later, the *Cowichan Leader,* 1 June 1907, had a similar report, quoting *The Week;* Tatlow to Joly, 9 May 1907, Joly Papers, 8295-6;

Times, 18 May 1907; *Nelson Daily News*, 25 May 1907; McBride to Tatlow, 11 June 1907, MS347, v.1; Laurier to Churchill, 20 May 1907, WSCP, v.10.

39 In Victoria that summer, Greenwood said that McBride "made a distinct impression upon the public men of all parties and in his public utterances and consultations with the imperial government he was certainly worthy of the great province." *Colonist*, 29 August 1907. McBride remembered O'Connor's kindness and sought to help him launch a British magazine about British Columbia in 1913 but could not guarantee provincial assistance. McBride to T.P. O'Connor, 20 May 1913, GR441, v.120; McBride to Margaret, 27 April 1907, McBF; McBride, Diary, 1907, passim, McBF.

40 *Colonist*, 20 June and 7 August 1907; *Columbian*, 22 June and 22 July 1907; *Port Essington Sun*, 22 June 1907. In 1911, 31.3 percent of British Columbia's non-Aboriginal population had been born in Britain or the empire in places other than Canada. Barman, *The West beyond the West*, 3rd ed., 430.

41 McBride to Lieutenant-Governor Dunsmuir, 28 December 1907, in BCSP, 1907-08, C2.

42 Unfortunately, only the cover letter has survived of McBride to Churchill, 12 June 1907, WSCP, CHAR, v.10/45/6; Great Britain, House of Commons, *Debates*, 13 June 1907, 1616-17; *Times*, 13 June 1907; McBride to Churchill, 14 June 1907, WSCP, v.2/30/67; McBride to Arthur F. Sladen, 8 February 1908, GR441 v.90; McBride to Tatlow, 11 June 1907, MS347, v.1.

43 *Columbian*, 15 June 1907, 8 and 10 July 1907; *Saturday Sunset*, 15 June 1907; *Colonist*, 14 and 15 June 1907; *Times*, 13 and 14 June 1907; *New Westminster Daily News*, 19 June 1907.

44 *Colonist*, 10 and 16 July 1907; *Columbian*, 10 and 15 July 1907; *Ottawa Journal*, quoted in *Columbian*, 23 July 1907; *Toronto Globe*, quoted in *Nelson Daily News*, 17 July 1907; Borden to McBride, 2 August 1907, GR441, v.87; *News-Advertiser*, *Province*, and *World*, quoted in *Saturday Sunset*, 20 July 1907; *Times*, 15 and 16 July 1907.

45 *Columbian*, 10 July 1907; Great Britain, Parliament, House of Lords, *Debates*, 2 July 1907, 496, 16 and 18 July 1907, 891; Great Britain, House of Commons, *Debates*, 2 August 1907, 1456.

46 McBride to Hamar Greenwood, 15 July 1907, WSCP, v.10/45/8; McBride to Winston Churchill, 16 July 1907. The letter of 16 July 1907, confirming the cable of the same date, was addressed to "Dear Mr. Churchill." Greenwood to Churchill, 15 July 1907, Churchill to McBride, 16 July 1907, Churchill to McBride, 17 July 1907, WSCP, v.10; McBride to Churchill, 18 July 1907, McBride to Elgin, 17 July 1907, GR441, v.389.

47 McBride to Joly, 8 August 1907, Joly Papers, 8338ff; *Nelson Daily News*, 28 September 1907; *Columbian*, 16 October and 21 December 1907; McBride to Borden, 11 December 1907, GR441, v.89.

48 McBride's correspondence and papers were printed in BCSP, 1908, C7-C23. *Province*, 16 and 17 January 1908; *Times*, 17 January 1908; *Colonist*, 17 January 1908; *Columbian*, 20 January 1908; *New Westminster Daily News*, 23 and 30 January 1908; BCLJ, 7 March 1908.

49 *Times*, 19 and 21 September 1908, 14 October 1908; *Columbian*, 2 and 3 October 1908; *Colonist*, 2 and 11 October 1908; *Province*, 3 October 1908; McBride to D.L. Leenholm, 28 October 1908, GR441, v.93; M. Burrell to McBride, 4 April 1909, GR441, v.95.

50 McBride to Laurier, 22 March 1907, GR441, v.389; Laurier to McBride, 25 March 1907, GR441, v.29; McBride to Joly, 22 March 1907, Joly Papers, 8239ff; *Colonist*, 1 April 1908.

51 *Colonist*, 12 March 1907, 1 May 1908; *Columbian*, 13 March 1907, 2 May 1908; *New Westminster Daily News*, 18 March 1907; *News-Advertiser*, 16 May 1908; McBride to Laurier, 22 November 1907, GR441, v.389. A brief account of the fisheries issue is in *CAR*, 1908, 526-17.

52 Some federal Liberal MPs had opposed Babcock's appointment. Æmeilius Jarvis to McBride, 17 January 1905, McBF; *New Westminster Daily News,* 15 July 1908, 13 and 15 August 1908, 22 January and 14 May 1909; *Columbian,* 15 August and 3 October 1908; *Chilliwack Progress,* 18 August 1908; *Province,* 15 August 1908. Unless otherwise indicated, this account draws on Frank Millerd, "The Evolution of Management of the Canadian Pacific Salmon Fishery," 2000, http://niche-canada.org/.

53 Department of Mines, *Annual Report, 1907,* in BCSP, 1908, L20; *Nelson Daily News,* 22, 23, 24, and 25 August 1907, 1 September 1907. After first reading, the bill was amended to raise the tax on coke to eighteen cents, since a ton and a half of coal was required to make a ton of coke. *Colonist,* 28 January and 4 February 1908; *Nelson Daily News,* 8 February 1908; McBride to Hodge, 6 February 1908, GR441, v.31; *Times,* 11 February 1908. Protest letters regarding the cost of coal are in GR441, v.31.

54 *Colonist,* 1 March 1908; Jeremy Mouat, *The Business of Power: Hydro-Electricity in Southeastern British Columbia, 1897-1997* (Victoria: Sono Nis, 1997), 77-79.

55 *Colonist,* 15 January 1907; *Province,* 31 January 1907; Wm. Shannon to McBride, 3 March 1908, GR441 v.90; *Columbian,* 10 April 1907; *New Westminster Daily News,* 19 April 1907.

56 For an account of timber licences in this era, see Hak, *Turning Trees into Dollars,* 104-11; *Nelson Daily News,* 22 June 1907, reprinted in *Inland Sentinel,* 25 June 1907; *Nelson Daily News,* 14 January 1908; *Colonist,* 24 December 1907.

57 *Nelson Daily News,* 25 January 1908; *News-Advertiser,* 22 January 1908; *Times,* 3 February 1908.

58 *Times,* 3 February 1908; *Province,* 6 February 1908; *Colonist,* 7 March 1908.

59 A.C. Flumerfelt, "Forest Resources," in *Canada and Its Provinces: A History of the Canadian People and Their Institutions by One Hundred Associates,* ed. Adam Shortt and Arthur G. Doughty (Toronto: Publishers' Association of Canada, 1914), 22:495; *Columbian,* 27 January and 12 March 1909; *New Westminster Daily News,* 26 and 27 January 1909.

60 The plan was to give the Salvation Army $1,000.00 for initial expenses, $3.00 for every migrant settled in British Columbia, assistance with transportation costs, and $2,000.00 for a Salvation Army hospital in Vancouver. The Army later negotiated a larger subsidy.

61 *Columbian,* 7 January and 10 April 1907; Acting premier to Comm. T.B. Coombs, 5 December 1906, GR441, v.389; McBride to Christian Sivertz, 8 March 1907, GR441, v.71; *Times,* 4 April 1907; McBride to G.D. MacFarlane, 5 November 1907, GR441, v.20. With the help of the Salvation Army, Tatlow persuaded the CPR to give immigrants a special rate of $39.75 to travel from Liverpool to Vancouver. Tatlow to Joly, Joly Papers, 8220ff; McBride to Commissioner Coombs, 11 February 1910, GR441, v.38; D.C. Lamb to McBride, 9 November 1910, GR441, v.40; Lamb to McBride, 26 September 1911, GR441, v.43; Wm. McQueen to McBride, 2 November 1907, GR441, v.30; *Kelowna Courier,* 19 April 1906; McBride to J.C. Watters, (vice-president, Trades and Labour Congress), 12 March 1908, GR441, v.31; *News-Advertiser,* 15 March 1908; *Province,* 23 May 1908; *Times,* 22 and 26 October 1908; *New Westminster Daily News,* 29 October 1908.

62 A.G. Morley to McBride, 30 November 1907, T.E. Kelly to McBride, 9 December 1907, GR441, v.30; *Times,* 4 February 1908, 25 and 26 March 1908; McBride to A.E. Planta, 27 February and 3 March 1908, GR441, v.389; Planta to McBride, 2 March 1908, McBride to Planta, 3 March 1908, GR441, v.31.

63 McBride to S.D. Chown, 27 December 1909, GR441, v.390.

64 *Colonist,* 1 and 7 August 1908; *New Westminster Daily News,* 6 January 1908; *Nelson Daily News,* 27 February 1908; *Colonist,* 17 January and 27 February 1908; *Times,* 26 February 1908; *Inland Sentinel,* 10 July 1908.

65 McBride to Laurier, 6 April 1908, GR441, v.389. Ottawa's plan was designed to deal with problems in British Columbia, Manitoba, and remote areas of Ontario and Quebec, where the lists did not always give a precise address for voters, making it difficult to ascertain to which federal constituency they belonged. A summary of this complicated issue may be found in *CAR*, 1908, 48-56.

66 *Colonist*, 18 April 1907; *Semi-Weekly World*, 23 April 1907; *News-Advertiser*, 20 April 1907. An investigation by William Lyon Mackenzie King revealed that in January 1907, Dunsmuir's Wellington Colliery completed a five-year contract to import 500 Japanese coal miners and 39 other workers. Roy, *A White Man's Province*, 205-7; R.W. Scott to Dunsmuir, 23 April 1907, in *Semi-Weekly World*, 24 September 1907; James Dunsmuir to Secretary of State, 29 April 1907, Dunsmuir to Kishiro Morikawa, 11 April 1907, BCA, GR443, Lieutenant-Governors' Records, v.9 (mfB2043); *Times*, 21 May 1907; Bowser to E.L. Newcombe, 11 November 1907, BCA, GR429, Attorney General Correspondence, v.15.

67 Roy, *A White Man's Province*, ch. 8.

68 *Nelson Daily Canadian*, 30 August 1907; *Colonist*, 15 and 26 September 1907; McBride to G.M. Grant, 20 September 1907, Grant to McBride, 24 September 1907, GR441, v.30; *News-Advertiser*, 25 September 1907; *Vernon News*, 3 October 1907; *Nelson Daily News*, 28 September 1907; *Semi-Weekly World*, 27 September 1907.

69 *Times*, 16 January and 1 February 1908; *Province*, 21 January 1908; McBride to Alfred Thompson, 23 January 1908, GR441, v.90; *Nelson Daily News*, 7 February 1908; *Semi-Weekly World*, 4 and 7 February 1908; *Province*, 31 January 1908. Although the government courted disallowance with its immigration laws, McBride rejected the AEL's request to deny tax exemptions to railway companies that employed Asian labour because the legislation would probably be disallowed. McBride to G.M. Grant, 8 February 1908, GR441, v.31. When Stuart Henderson, the Liberal MLA for Yale, made a similar suggestion, McBride told him that employment on railways was a matter for the Dominion Railway Commission and that unemployed Japanese labourers would seek work elsewhere. He argued that Ottawa should halt immigration from Asia. *Nanaimo Free Press*, 12 February 1908.

70 J.A. Macdonald to Wm. Templeman, 24 January 1908, WLP, 135853-7; *Times*, 30 January 1908, 12 and 20 February 1908, 14 and 17 March 1908; *Province*, 6 February 1908; *Columbian*, 3 March 1908; *News-Advertiser*, 27 February 1908; A.D. Taylor to Bowser, 13 March 1908, GR429, Attorney General Records, v.15. Japanese immigrants who came to Canada via Hawaii were not covered by the Gentlemen's Agreement, so the federal government blocked their entry by refusing to accept immigrants who did not come by "continuous voyage" from their country of origin. The measure effectively stopped immigration from India as well because no company offered through fares from India to Canada. Ottawa ordered the "Hindus" deported because they had not come by "continuous voyage" from India. The province made no further attempt to enact a Natal Act.

71 *Province*, 22 and 24 February 1908; *Times*, 22 February 1908.

72 *Colonist*, 1 April 1908; *Columbian*, 2 April 1908; McBride to J.H. Turner, 28 September 1908, GR441, v.93. McBride's article was reprinted in the *News-Advertiser*, 1 October 1908, and quotations from it appeared in the *Cranbrook Prospector*, 3 October 1908.

73 *Colonist*, 9 April 1907. On 29 January 1908, the *Montreal Star* published what the *Times* called a "temperate, very thoughtful, very timely and very statesmanlike view" of McBride's alliance with Borden and the Japanese immigration issue. *Times*, 5 February 1908; *Columbian*, 10 July 1907; *Times*, 11 July 1907; McBride to Borden, 5 May 1908, GR441, v.91; *Saturday Sunset*, 18 April 1908; *Nelson Daily News*, 12 July 1907; *New Westminster Daily News*, 22 July 1908; *News-Advertiser*, 23 July 1908.

74 Borden to McBride, 24 April 1908, McBride to Borden, 5 May 1908, GR441, v.91. See Robert A.J. McDonald, "Sir Charles Hibbert Tupper and the Political Culture of British Columbia, 1903-1924," *BC Studies* 149 (Spring 2006): 63-86; C.H. Tupper to R.L. Borden, 13 December 1907, CHTP, v.4; *Times,* 10 September 1908; *News-Advertiser,* 7 January and 1 February 1908, 2 and 25 October 1908; Tupper to Borden, 4 May 1908, quoted in McDonald, "Sir Charles Hibbert Tupper," 70; *Province,* 12 September and 2 October 1908; *Saturday Sunset,* 5 September 1908; *Columbian,* 2 and 26 October 1908; *Colonist,* 1 May and 13 October 1908; *Nanaimo Free Press,* 17 October 1908; Roy, *A White Man's Province,* 223-26.

75 *Times,* 6, 24, and 26 October 1908; *Nanaimo Herald,* 15 October 1908; *News-Advertiser,* 3 and 4 October 1908.

76 Quoted in *Inland Sentinel,* 25 June 1907; *Columbian,* 3 June 1908; *New Westminster Daily News,* 29 June 1908; *Cranbrook Herald,* 9 July 1908; *Times,* 22 July 1908.

77 *Colonist,* 12 January 1908; *Nelson Daily Canadian,* 2 May 1908 (this was the last issue of this Conservative paper); *Kelowna Courier,* 21 May 1908; *Penticton Press,* 23 May 1908; *Nelson Daily News,* 22, 23, 24, 26, 28, and 29 May 1908.

78 *Nelson Daily News,* 31 May 1908; *Fernie Free Press,* 5 June 1908.

79 *Colonist,* 9 June and 1 July 1908; *Times,* 12 June 1908. He gave a similar speech in early August at Metchosin, a farming community near Victoria. *Colonist,* 7 August 1908.

80 The BX Express Company had the coach built for the visit of Governor General Dufferin in 1876.

81 *Cranbrook Herald,* 9 July 1908; *Ashcroft Journal,* 27 June 1908, 4 and 11 July 1908. The Liberal press cynically suggested that McBride's Kootenay trip was in the interest of A.S. Goodeve, the Conservative candidate in the expected federal election. *Times,* 22 July 1908.

82 *Inland Sentinel,* 10 July 1908; *Golden Star,* 18 July 1908; *Province,* 17 July 1908.

83 *Colonist,* 22 August 1908; *Fernie Ledger,* quoted in *Cranbrook Herald,* 27 August 1908, and *New Westminster Daily News,* 1 September 1908.

84 *Port Essington Sun,* 21 December 1907; *Omineca Herald,* 27 February 1909.

85 *Queen Charlotte News,* 14 August and 18 September 1909; *Prince Rupert Empire,* 21 August 1909; McBride, Diary, 14-30 August 1909, McBF.

86 *Colonist,* 8 March 1908; *Columbian,* 30 May 1908; *Province,* 1 and 30 June 1908, also quoted in *Alberni Pioneer News,* 6 June 1908. The *Nelson Daily News,* 23 June 1908, also quoted the *Province* editorial with approval.

CHAPTER 5: BOUNDLESS OPTIMISM

1 *Saturday Sunset,* 13 March 1909.

2 Donald G. Paterson, *British Direct Investment in Canada, 1890-1914* (Toronto: University of Toronto Press, 1976), 79; *Times,* 24 February 1909; *British Columbia in the Canadian Confederation: A Submission Presented to the Royal Commission on Dominion-Provincial Relations by the Government of the Province of British Columbia* (Victoria: King's Printer, 1938), 239, 245. Comparing these figures with those for earlier years is difficult because the end of the fiscal year changed from 30 June in 1908 to 31 March in 1909.

3 *Colonist,* 9 June 1908.

4 McBride to Joly, 22 March 1907, Joly Papers, 8239ff; McBride to F.W. Morse, 26 March 1907, GR441, v.87; *Columbian,* 15 May 1907; McBride to Tatlow, 11 June 1907, MS347, v.1; Fulton to McBride (Montreal), 19 June 1907, GR441, v.89; McBride to C.M. Hays, 7

August 1907, McBride to Wm. Wainwright, 9 February 1908, GR441, v.389; McBride to Jas. Carruthers (Montreal), 22 August 1907, GR441, v.88; *Province,* 2 March 1908; *News-Advertiser,* 3 and 9 March 1908; *Times,* 2 March 1908; McBride, Diary, 18 April 1907, McBF. Unless otherwise noted, this paragraph draws on Frank Leonard, *A Thousand Blunders: The Grand Trunk Pacific Railway and Northern British Columbia* (Vancouver: UBC Press, 1996), 38-48.

5 McBride to Mann, 13 February 1907, quoted in Brian Ray Douglas Smith, "Sir Richard McBride: A Study in the Conservative Party of British Columbia, 1903-1916" (master's thesis, Queen's University, 1959), 120; Patricia E. Roy, "Railways, Politicians and the Development of the City of Vancouver as a Metropolitan Centre, 1886-1929" (master's thesis, University of Toronto, 1963), 104-5; T.D. Regehr, *The Canadian Northern Railway: Pioneer Road of the Northern Prairies, 1895-1918* (Toronto: Macmillan, 1976), 292; Carter-Cotton to McBride, 17 December 1908, quoted in Smith, "Sir Richard McBride," 120.

6 *Times,* 26 January 1909; Hays to McBride, 17 February 1909, McBride to Hays, 23 February 1909, GR441, v.95; *Columbian,* 15 April 1909; *Inland Sentinel,* 9 February 1909; John Oliver to Laurier, 15 June 1909, WLP, 156999ff.

7 *Province,* 3, 8, and 21 May 1909, 5 June and 20 October 1909; D.D. Mann to McBride, 15 July 1909, McBride to Mann, 14 September 1909, McBride to S.D. Chown, 7 September 1909, GR441, v.98. Chown, of the Methodist Church, was inquiring about the timing of the local option plebiscite, a 1909 issue regarding Prohibition. Memo signed by D.D. Mann, 19 October 1909, GR441, v.140; Executive Minute Book, BCA, MS702, v.1. The next day, 20 October, cabinet authorized spending $25,000 for election expenses. *Colonist,* 20 October 1909; *Times,* 16 October 1909; "Memorandum to Form the Basis of a Contract between the Government of the Province of British Columbia, and the Canadian Northern Railway Company, to Be Authorized by a Bill to Be Introduced and Passed at the Next Session of the Provincial Legislature," copy in GR441, v.140.

8 Duncan Ross to Wilfrid Laurier, c. November 1907, WLP, 131445ff; Agreement between British Columbia and Kettle River Valley Railway [Kettle Valley Railway], 20 October 1909, GR441, v.154. Although federal legislation approving a 999-year lease of the KVR to the CPR was not passed until 1913, the CPR and the KVR had cooperated since at least 1908. John A. Eagle, *The Canadian Pacific Railway and the Development of Western Canada* (Montreal and Kingston: McGill-Queen's University Press, 1989), 131-34.

9 *Province,* 20 October 1909. Many provincial newspapers expressed similar ideas. See, for example, *Ashcroft Journal,* 23 October 1909; *Golden Star,* 30 October 1909; *Saturday Sunset,* reprinted in *Inland Sentinel,* 9 March 1909.

10 Oliver's predecessor, J.A. Macdonald, had been appointed to the bench.

11 According to John Jardine, one of the two Liberals elected in 1909, Oliver produced his map at a party meeting shortly before the election. When someone said that Alberni should be included in the proposed railway lines, Oliver drew it in with a paintbrush. When Jardine asked how the lines could be linked to the transcontinental one, Oliver said, "Dick's got us skinned to death before we start in." *Alberni Pioneer News,* 4 February 1911; Oliver to Laurier, 13 October 1909, WLP, 160871; Laurier to Oliver, 22 October 1909, WLP, 160874; Oliver to Laurier, 15 June 1909, WLP, 156999; Oliver to Laurier, 24 September 1909, WLP, 160203; Laurier to Oliver, 6 November 1909, WLP, 161163; Oliver to Laurier, 25 August 1909, WLP, 159186ff; Laurier to Oliver, 10 September 1909, WLP, 159674ff; Laurier to Oliver, 31 August 1909, WLP, 159188. Oliver continued to favour a railway over the Hope Mountains. Oliver to William Templeman, 17 October 1910, WLP, 176142ff; *Times,* 13 and

20 October 1909; *News-Advertiser*, 28 October 1909; *Province*, 20 October 1909; Oliver to McBride, 21 October 1907, GR441, v.l99; McBride to Oliver, 21 October 1907, GR441, v.154. Oliver complained to Lieutenant-Governor Dunsmuir about delays in preparing the voters' lists. McBride assured the lieutenant-governor that preparing the lists would cause "no hardship whatever." The correspondence with Dunsmuir is in GR441, v.36.

12 Oliver to Laurier, 15 June 1909, WLP, 156999; Oliver to Laurier, 24 September 1909, WLP, 160203; *World*, 22 October 1909; *Saturday Sunset*, 29 February 1909, 23 and 30 October 1909, 6 and 13 November 1909; *Similkameen Star*, 27 October 1909; *Grand Forks Evening Sun*, 6 November 1909; *Inland Sentinel*, 15 October and 12 November 1909.

13 *Times*, 30 October 1909; *Nanaimo Daily Herald*, 31 October 1909; McBride, Diary, 20-30 October 1909, McBF; *Province*, 22 October 1909; McBride to J.H. Turner, 29 October 1909, F.J. Fulton to McBride, 22 November 1909, GR441, v.99; Lottie Bowron interview, quoted in Peter Roberts Hunt, "The Political Career of Sir Richard McBride" (master's thesis, University of British Columbia, 1953), 126. Without providing evidence, T.R.E. McInnes, a Liberal, claimed that the CPR threatened to "smash" McBride's cabinet if he assisted Mackenzie and Mann. Fulton acted as a solicitor for the CPR, and Tatlow was "an old CPR retainer." McInnes to Laurier, 25 October 1909, WLP, 161311ff; A.W. Watts to McBride, 25 October 1909, Francis Carter-Cotton to McBride, 22 October 1909, McBride to Carter-Cotton, 22 October 1909, GR441, v.99. Some Liberals and their press made negative comments about the possible financial obligations the province was taking on. *Nanaimo Daily Herald*, 31 October 1909; *Inland Sentinel*, 29 October and 12 November 1909; *Prince Rupert Evening Empire*, 13 November 1909; W.C. Nichol to McBride, 23 October 1909, MS347, v.1.

14 Tupper, open letter, 22 November 1909, CHTP, v.5. The *Province* did not publish Tupper's letter but denounced his earlier criticisms of the government railway policy. *Province*, 2, 18, 20, 22, and 23 November 1909; J.W. Whitely to McBride, 22 November 1909, Thos. Cunningham to McBride, 26 November 1909, GR441, v.144. Tupper remained so angry with McBride over a number of issues that when federal Conservative leader Robert L. Borden sent McBride a congratulatory telegram, he wrote an "indignant" letter to which Borden replied that he knew of no attack by McBride or Bowser on Tupper or on his father, Sir Charles Tupper, a former prime minister. Years later, Borden commented on Tupper's "remarkable capacity for quarreling with his friends." Borden to C.H. Tupper, 20 December 1909, CHTP, v.5; Borden to G.H. Cowan, 17 October 1933, RLBP, 150218. The extent of the Orange vote in British Columbia is unknown but was probably smaller than Orangemen thought.

15 *The Contract with the Canadian Northern Railway* (n.p.: n.p., 1909, pamphlet), copy in McBF; *Vernon News*, 4 November 1909; *Province*, 22 October 1909, 5, 8, and 12 November 1909; *News-Advertiser*, 30 October 1909; McBride to Mann, 29 October 1909, GR441, v.140.

16 *Columbian*, 27 and 30 October 1909; *Golden Star*, 30 October 1909; Vital Statistics Death Records, BCA, MfB1308a, file 1909-022-22232.

17 *News-Advertiser*, 30 October 1909; *Kamloops Standard*, 5 November 1909; *Colonist*, 3 November 1909; *Ashcroft Journal*, 6 November 1909; *Province*, 4 November 1909; McBride to R.P. Roblin, 28 October 1909, Robert Rogers to McBride, 30 October 1909, GR441, v.140; *Nelson Daily News*, 4 November 1909.

18 *Vernon News*, 11 November 1909; *Penticton Press*, 20 November 1909; *Nelson Daily News*, 13 November 1909; J.J. Warren to McBride, 3 November 1909, GR441, v.154; *Colonist*, 23 October 1909, 21 and 25 November 1909.

19 *Nelson Daily News,* 5 November 1909; *Province,* 15 and 20 November 1909; *Times,* 23 November 1909.

20 *Province,* 20 November 1909.

21 *Colonist,* 6 November 1909; *Trail Daily News,* 6 November 1909; *Omineca Herald,* 20 November 1909; *Grand Forks Gazette,* 19 November 1909; *Ashcroft Journal,* 20 November 1909; *Golden Star,* 20 November 1909; *Province,* 8, 18, and 20 November 1909; *Saturday Sunset,* 15 May 1909. See also Patricia E. Roy, "McBride of McKenna-McBride: Premier Richard McBride and the Indian Question in British Columbia," *BC Studies* 172 (Winter 2011-12): 35-76.

22 Harold Tuttle Allen, *Forty Years' Journey: The Temperance Movement in British Columbia to 1900* (Victoria: privately printed, 1981), 14; Douglas L. Hamilton, *Sobering Dilemma: A History of Prohibition in British Columbia* (Vancouver: Ronsdale, 2004), 65-79; Robert A. Campbell, *Demon Rum or Easy Money: Government Control of Liquor in British Columbia from Prohibition to Privatization* (Ottawa: Carleton University Press, 1991), 16-17, 19; *Inland Sentinel,* 19 January 1909; *Columbian,* 27 January 1909; McBride to A.R. Shewen, 1 March 1909, GR441, v.96; McBride to D.D. Dewar, 17 February 1910, GR441, v.101.

23 Elections British Columbia, *Electoral History of British Columbia, 1871-1986* (Victoria: Elections BC and Legislative Library, 1988), 410-11. Some ballots were left blank, and 2,201 were rejected.

24 *New Westminster Daily News,* 2 March 1909; McBride to Chown, 7 September 1909, GR441, v.98; H.H. Stevens to McBride, 21 October 1909, McBride to Stevens, 25 October 1909, McBride to Chown, 22 December 1909, GR441, v.99; *Province,* 2 and 5 November 1909; *Colonist,* 25 November 1909, 14 February 1912; *Times,* 12 February 1910.

25 *Colonist,* 26 November 1909; Elections British Columbia, *Electoral History of British Columbia,* 109; *Columbian,* 22 and 26 January 1910; *Province,* 29 November 1909; *Inland Sentinel,* 26 November 1909; McBride to J.H. Turner, 1 December 1909, GR441, v.99; McBride, Diary, 25 November 1909, McBF.

26 Carter-Cotton to McBride, 25 November 1909, C.E. Tisdall to McBride, 27 November 1909, F.J. Fulton to McBride, 1 December 1909, W.C. Nichol to McBride, 26 November 1909, GR441, v.144.

27 *Fort George Tribune,* 27 November 1909; W.R. Braden to McBride, 28 November 1909, C.B. Christensen to McBride, 1 December 1909, GR441, v.145.

28 *Province,* 26 and 27 November 1909; *Columbian,* 11 December 1909; *Colonist,* 11 December 1909; McBride, Diary, 6-15 January and 2 March 1910, McBF; *CAR,* 1910, 327-28; *New Westminster Daily News,* 2 March 1910; McBride to Mackenzie and Mann, 22 December 1909, GR441, v.140. The legal name of the CNR in British Columbia was the Canadian Northern Pacific Railway; I have used the shorter form for convenience.

29 John A. Lee to McBride, 9 May 1910, McBride to Lee, 11 May 1910, Kamloops City Council and Board of Trade to McBride, 3 August 1910, Sooke and Otter Conservative Association to McBride, 10 June 1910, McBride to Mackenzie, 13 October 1910, Mackenzie to McBride, c. 12 October 1910, Mackenzie to McBride, c. mid-October 1910, GR441, v.140; *Inland Sentinel,* 5 August 1910; *Times,* 9 September 1910; *New Westminster Daily News,* 15 September 1910; *Times,* 6 and 24 October 1910; *Colonist,* 23 October 1910.

30 Like Annie Mowbray, many Mainland patients often had surgery in Victoria. *Columbian,* 16 April 1908, 4 and 6 May 1909, 4 December 1909, 12 February 1910; McBride, Diary, 4 May 1909, McBF.

31 *Times*, 6 and 16 September 1910, 11 October 1910; *New Westminster Daily News*, 5 October 1910; *Fernie Free Press*, 14 October 1910; *Columbian*, 11 October 1910; *Colonist*, 11 October 1910. One report suggested that Ross won the Roman Catholic vote because J.W. Bennett, the Socialist candidate, alienated Catholics by comments on religion in his newspaper. *Ashcroft Journal*, 22 October 1910. Ross won 58 percent of the popular vote; Bennett was his only opponent. The *Toronto Globe* suggested that the cabinet shuffle indicated a breach between McBride and Bowser – the "beginning of the end" of McBride's government. Quoted in *Columbian*, 17 October 1910. While serving as attorney general in 1907, Bowser maintained his legal practice in Vancouver. When it was proposed to raise the salaries of cabinet ministers, the Opposition press argued that such a measure would give cabinet ministers no excuse to continue practising law or engaging in private business. The press was concerned with Bowser and to a lesser extent with Francis Carter-Cotton, the managing director of the *Vancouver Daily News-Advertiser*. As president of the council, Carter-Cotton received no extra salary, and the post may have cost him personally. In 1909, anticipating a cabinet decision on the BCER's request to dam the Coquitlam River, he sold his shares in that prosperous company, which were worth $2,963.58. R.H. Sperling to George Kidd, 3 March 1909, BCERR, LFGM, 1909; Carter-Cotton to McBride, 7 October 1910, MS347, v.1; *Nelson Daily Canadian*, 13 December 1907; *Nelson Daily News*, 13 December 1907; *Times*, 17 January 1908.

32 *Colonist*, 24 November 1910; *Ashcroft Journal*, 19 November 1910.

33 *Times*, 5 and 7 January 1910, 28 February and 1 March 1910, 22 February 1912, 21 January and 23 February 1913; W.O. Ross to McBride, 12 August 1910, GR441, v.104; Price Ellison to McBride, 15 June 1910, GR441, v.37; Report of Grading Commission, January 1910, copy in GR441, v.106; *Colonist*, 25 January 1911.

34 McBride to Laurier, 31 July 1909, GR441, v.35; McBride to F.L. Haggard, 18 February 1910, GR441, v.390; *Columbian*, 26 February 1910; *Colonist*, 26 January and 17 December 1910; *Province*, 5 November 1909; *New Westminster Daily News*, 27 January 1909; *Inland Sentinel*, 9 March 1909; *Saturday Sunset*, 20 March 1909; Royal Commission of Inquiry into Timber and Forestry, *Report* (Victoria: King's Printer, 1910), D16, D20.

35 *Times*, 26 February 1908, 8 March and 19 November 1910; *New Westminster Daily News*, 29 January 1909; *Alberni Pioneer News*, 18 September 1909; *Saturday Sunset*, quoted in *Inland Sentinel*, 11 February 1910; *Colonist*, 14 January 1911; James Murton, *Creating a Modern Countryside: Liberalism and Land Resettlement in British Columbia* (Vancouver: UBC Press, 2007), 11.

36 *Times*, 29 January and 6 May 1910, 16 March 1911; *Inland Sentinel*, 15 May 1910; *Omineca Herald*, 25 September 1909; *Kelowna Courier*, 5 May 1910; *Colonist*, 10 February 1910; *Columbian*, 29 March 1911; Robert E. Cail, *Land, Man, and the Law: The Disposal of Crown Lands in British Columbia, 1871-1913* (Vancouver: UBC Press, 1974), 50, ch. 9. Dealing with land in the railway belt was complicated. The area was accessible but not necessarily fertile. In rhetoric reminiscent of Better Terms, McBride referred to the province's expense of providing services in this difficult terrain and pointed out that Ottawa got the revenue from land sales. *Colonist*, 18 January 1911.

37 *Colonist*, 4 April, 12 May, and 13 July 1911; *Fort George Herald*, 22 April 1911; *Times*, 12 May 1911, 12, 13, and 28 June 1911; *Sun*, 21 March 1912; Cail, *Land, Man, and the Law*, 51.

38 *New Westminster Daily News*, 20 September 1910; McBride to G.H. Barnard, 16 June 1910, GR441, v.38; *Colonist*, 20 and 21 September 1910, 20 October 1910, 21 August 1911, 16

January 1912; *Fort George Herald,* 17 September 1910, 11 November 1911; *Times,* 30 August 1911, 18 and 29 November 1911, 28 December 1911, 13 and 19 January 1912, 2 February and 6 March 1912; *Province,* 16 January 1912; *Sun,* 15 February 1912; *CAR,* 1912, 613.

39 McBride to John Kennedy (Vernon), 23 August 1907, GR441, v.88; *Colonist,* 9 June 1908; British Columbia, *An Act to amend the Land Act,* 7 Edw. 7, c. 25, s. 9; *Province,* 16 January 1912; *Colonist,* 16 January 1912. The right of Indians to pre-empt lands was cancelled during the colonial period, but they could petition for an Order-in-Council exempting them from this ban. This permission was rarely, if ever, granted.

40 McBride to Laurier, 27 October 1910, WLP, 176196 (confirming telegram of 26 October 1910); Laurier to McBride, 20 October 1910, Pedley to Oliver, 3 January 1911, RG10, v.3690; W.R. Ross to Oliver, 30 December 1910, Ross to Pedley, 2 January 1911, Ross to Frank Oliver, 11 March 1911, GR441, v.41; *Colonist,* 27 October 1910, 5 and 14 April 1911; Jeannie L. Kanakos, "The Negotiations to Relocate the Songhees Indians, 1843-1911" (master's thesis, Simon Fraser University, 1982), 74-75; *Times,* 21 March 1916. In 1916, the Public Accounts Committee investigated the Songhees transaction. Earlier, Matson had defended the $75,000 he received for the Songhees negotiations by explaining that after expenses he got less than $30,000 and could show vouchers for payments to prominent Liberals. *Colonist,* 20 April 1913.

41 Report of Committee of the Executive Council approved by Lieutenant-Governor, 28 February 1907, Fulton and McBride to Lieutenant-Governor, 26 February 1907, GR441, v.149. For details, see Roy, "McBride of McKenna-McBride."

42 Laurier to McBride, 8 October 1910, McBride to Laurier, 7 January 1911, [Bowser] to Laurier, 19 November 1910 [not sent], GR441, v.149.

43 R.M. Galois, "The Indian Rights Association, Native Protest Activity and the 'Land Question' in British Columbia, 1903-1916," *Native Studies Review* 8, 2 (1992): 6-7; Hamar Foster and Benjamin L. Berger, "From Humble Prayers to Legal Demands: The Cowichan Petition of 1909 and the British Columbia Indian Land Question," in *The Grand Experiment: Law and Legal Culture in British Settler Societies,* ed. Hamar Foster, Benjamin L. Berger, and A.R. Buck (Vancouver: UBC Press and the Osgoode Society for Canadian Legal History, 2008), 242; Bishop Perrin to Laurier, 5 January 1911, WLP, 179267; Memo of Meeting of McBride, Bowser and Wm. Ross with Bishop Perrin, Rev. A.E. O'Meara, Rev. J.W. Gladstone, F.C. Wade, and others, 14 December 1910, copies in GR441, v.149 and with Perrin to Laurier, 5 January 1911, WLP, 179268ff; *Colonist,* 15 December 1910.

44 Chief A. Wedildahid to McBride, 18 February 1911, McBride to Wedildahid, 3 March 1911, McBride, H.E. Young, Price Ellison, Thomas Taylor, and A.E. McPhillips interview with Indian Chiefs, 3 March 1911, GR441, v.149; Copy of memorial with McBride to Laurier, 25 March 1911, WLP, 183876ff. In a letter accompanying a copy of the chiefs' memorial, McBride reiterated that "the Government had decided there is no question to submit to the Courts" and asked Laurier to forward a copy of the memorial to the Colonial Office. McBride to Laurier, 9 March 1911, WLP, 189920; McBride to Laurier, 13 June 1911, WLP, 186696; *Sun,* 13 and 14 February 1912.

45 See R. Cole Harris, "Locating the University of British Columbia," *BC Studies* 32 (Winter 1976-77): 106-25. The prosperity that enabled the founding of a university also allowed the establishment of the Provincial Archives. In 1908, to celebrate the centenary of Simon Fraser's exploration of the Fraser River, McBride encouraged his one-time classmate Judge F.W. Howay to prepare articles and speeches on Fraser. Part of the $7,000 set aside for the centennial was earmarked for archival activities. In 1910, the government appointed E.O.S. Scholefield, the provincial librarian, as provincial archivist and gave him an acquisitions

budget. Two years later, the archives and the Provincial Library were given space in a new annex to the Parliament Buildings. Howay returned the favour with a positive account of McBride's administration in his *British Columbia from the Earliest Times to the Present*, published in 1914. Terry Eastwood, "R.E. Gosnell, E.O.S. Scholefield and the Founding of the Provincial Archives of British Columbia, 1894-1919," *BC Studies* 54 (Summer 1982): 38-62; Chad Reimer, *Writing British Columbia History, 1784-1958* (Vancouver: UBC Press, 2009), 50-51, 72-73, 78.

46 *Inland Sentinel*, 29 October 1909. The congratulatory letters are in GR441, v.144 (underlining in original). According to one report, George Foster, a leading federal Conservative, had visited to pave the way for McBride to become the leader of the federal Conservative party. *Golden Star*, 16 October 1909.

47 The literature on the naval debate is extensive. A succinct account is Michael L. Hadley and Roger Sarty, *Tin-Pot and Pirate Ships: Canadian Naval Forces and German Sea Raiders, 1880-1918* (Montreal and Kingston: McGill-Queen's University Press, 1991), 25-29. McBride to Arthur S. Barton, 9 June 1909, GR441, v.390; McBride to Laurier, 9 June 1909, GR441, v.34; *Colonist*, 22 April 1909.

48 Henry Borden, ed., *Robert Laird Borden: His Memoirs* (Toronto: Macmillan, 1938), 1:287; Borden to McBride, 19 November 1909, McBride to Borden, 8 January 1910, MS347, v.1. The *London Times* reported that McBride was being touted as Borden's replacement but that becoming leader at a time of crisis in the Conservative caucus would raise suspicions of a cabal against Borden. *The Times* (London), 4 December 1909.

49 McBride to W.M. McKay, 3 March 1910, McBride to W.J. Dowler, 19 February 1910, GR441, v.101.

50 On Borden's problems, see Robert Craig Brown, *Robert Laird Borden: A Biography* (Toronto: Macmillan, 1980), 1:158-69; *The Times* (London), 4 December 1909; *Times*, 11 March 1910. The wildest rumour appeared in *United Canada*, a weekly Catholic journal published in Ottawa. It stated that the federal Liberals had offered McBride the post of his choice and the right of succession if he would leave the Conservative Party and join Laurier's cabinet. *Columbian*, 6 September 1910.

51 Burrell to McBride, 11 March 1910, MS347, v.1; Burrell to McBride, 10 and 24 March 1910, GR441, v.101. According to John English, William Price, a wealthy industrialist from Quebec, and two eastern Ontario MPs, W.B. Northrup and J.D. Reid, formed a cabal with the idea of having McBride serve temporarily as leader before being replaced by Price. John English, *The Decline of Politics: The Conservatives and the Party System, 1901-20* (Toronto: University of Toronto Press, 1977), 56. Borden's memoirs suggest that the situation was the other way round – that "this gentleman" (Price?) would lead temporarily and that McBride would succeed "in due course." Borden, *Memoirs*, 1:287; Burrell to Borden, 17 October 1932, RLBP, 172620. Borden had asked Burrell for recollections of leadership problems in 1910-11.

52 On the basis of an interview with one of McBride's daughters, John English suggests that McBride declined because he was diagnosed with a terminal illness in 1909. That may be so, but there is no other evidence of serious health problems before 1912. English, *The Decline of Politics*, 57n10.

53 Brown, *Robert Laird Borden*, 1:168-69; R.L. Borden to F.H. Hale, 21 April 1910, RLBP, 71213.

54 Borden, *Memoirs*, 1:293; *Colonist*, 14 and 18 August 1910; *Columbian*, 14 October and 2 November 1910; *New Westminster Daily News*, 18 October 1910; McBride to H.G. Parsons, 18 August 1910, WLP, 173907; Lottie Bowron, interviewed by Imbert Orchard, March 1962,

BCA, Acc. 1288, tape 1 transcript; Harold Daly, Draft Memoirs, LAC, Harold Daly Fonds, v.2; McBride, Diary, 17 August 1910, McBF.

55 McBride to Laurier, 31 July 1909, GR441, v.35; McBride to W.L.M. King, 15 January 1910, GR441, v.30; McBride to Lieutenant-Governor, 12 July 1910, GR441, v.37; McBride to Laurier, 18 April 1911, GR441, v.391.

56 J.P. Whitney to McBride, 17 November 1910, McBride to Whitney, 19 November 1910, GR441, v.402; McBride to F.L. Haszard, 18 March 1911, GR441, v.391; McBride to Borden, 3 March 1910, GR441, v.101.

57 *CAR,* 1910, 548-49; Claim of Manitoba against the Dominion of Canada, Conference Proceedings, 2-3 February 1911, RLBP, 5133ff; J.A. Maxwell, *Federal Subsidies to the Provincial Governments in Canada* (Cambridge, MA: Harvard University Press, 1937), 128-30.

58 His diary reveals the route of the trip via Seattle and American Railways but names only two of his contacts, "Dr. G." and "Joel," in New York City. At another place, the diary gives an address for Joel Rinaldo's Restaurant, a famous eatery in the city.

59 Harry M. Brittain, "To the Heart of the Cariboo," *Pearson's Magazine,* February 1911, 212-18; McBride, Diary, 22-28 August 1910, McBF; *Fort George Herald,* 27 August and 10 September 1910; *Columbian,* 30 and 31 August 1910, 1 September 1910; *Inland Sentinel,* 2 September 1910. Brittain probably first met McBride on a visit to Victoria in September 1907. Harry Brittain, *Canada: There and Back* (London: privately printed, 1908), 125.

60 McBride, Diary, 31 October 1910, 4 and 14 November 1910, 15 December 1910, McBF; *Colonist,* 6 November 1910.

61 G.H. Perley to McBride, 19 November 1910, MS347, v.1; *Colonist,* 18 November and 15 December 1910.

62 *Times,* 11 March 1910; *Colonist,* 11 March 1910; *Columbian,* 24 September and 22 November 1910. His speech to the Canadian Manufacturers Association was later printed as a pamphlet. Copy in McBF; *Western Methodist Recorder,* September 1910, 4.

63 McBride to E. Crawshay-Williams, 27 September 1910, GR441, v.105. McBride was sympathetic but noncommittal regarding Asquith's call for a closer union between Britain and the dominions. *Columbian,* 1 April 1911.

64 McBride to Robert Rogers, 25 November 1910, McBF; McBride to J.L. Russell, 7 December 1910, GR441, v.105. Prime Minister Laurier reportedly also made a contribution. *CAR,* 1910, has several references to O'Connor's Canadian tour. *Colonist,* 29 April 1911.

65 McBride to Borden, 30 January 1911, RLBP, 3407; McBride to Jos. Brody, 19 December 1910, GR441, v.40.

66 *Colonist,* 28 January and 16 February 1911. He repeated these sentiments in reply to requests for comment from the press. See, for example, McBride to *Daily Express* (London), 22 February 1911, McBride to *Toronto News,* 13 March 1911, GR441, v.107; McBride to E. Crawshay-Williams, 27 September 1910, McBride to J.L. Russell, 7 December 1910, GR441, v.105; McBride, *Speech to the Legislature on Reciprocity* (n.p.: n.p., 15 February 1911, pamphlet), copy in McBF.

67 Burrell to McBride, 30 January, 12 February, and 22 March 1911, McBF; Burrell to McBride, 16 March 1911, Borden to McBride, 26 March 1911, MS347, v.1; Borden, *Memoirs,* 1:309. For examples of speculation on McBride taking over from Borden, see *The Times* (London), 28 and 29 March 1911; Toronto *Globe,* 28, 30, and 31 March 1911; McBride to Borden, 27 March 1911, RLBP, 3406; *Colonist,* 30 March 1911; *Times,* 6 April 1911, reprinted in *New Westminster Daily News,* 15 April 1911; *Columbian,* 6 April 1911; Lottie Bowron, interviewed by Imbert Orchard, March 1962, BCA, Acc. 1288, tape 1 transcript.

68 Interviews with R.H. Tupper and Arthur Meighen, cited in Smith, "Sir Richard McBride," 167, 169; *Colonist*, 6 May 1911; *Times*, 9, 10, and 17 May 1911; *Ottawa Evening Journal*, quoted in *Columbian*, 18; *Columbian*, 13 May 1911; *Toronto Globe*, 6 May 1911; McBride, Diary, 5-21 May 1911, McBF.
69 J. Norton-Griffiths to McBride, 3 November 1910, McBride to Norton-Griffiths, 29 November 1910, MS347, v.1.
70 *The Times* (London), 20 April, 10 June, and 21 July 1911; *Columbian*, 12 June 1911; *Colonist*, 15, 16, 20, and 27 June 1911, 21 and 23 July 1911. Among those sending regrets to Turner's Savoy Hotel banquet were Lord Grey, the Duke of Argyll, Asquith, and Balfour. At this banquet, Bowser urged British MPs to remind manufacturers of British Columbia's proximity to the markets of the Far East.
71 McBride, Diary, 17 June to 21 July 1911, McBF.
72 *Columbian*, 3 August 1911; *Times*, 25 September 1911, 22 January 1912; *Sun*, 26 March 1912; *The Times* (London), 11 July 1911; *Colonist*, 2 December 1911.
73 *Times*, 31 July and 1 August 1911; *Colonist*, 2 August 1911; *Columbian*, 4 and 8 August 1911.
74 The original source of "Hail to the Chief" was Sir Walter Scott's *The Lady of the Lake*, but it was soon adapted and became associated with American presidents early in the nineteenth century.
75 *Colonist*, 13, 18, 23, and 24 August 1911; *Times*, 14 August 1911. See also *Columbian*, 18 August 1911.
76 A.S. Goodeve to McBride, 14 August 1911, GR441, v.145; *Colonist*, 29 August 1911, 6 and 20 September 1911; *Columbian*, 14 and 20 September 1911.
77 *Colonist*, 4 October 1911; McBride to J.D. Brymner, 9 September 1911, GR441, v.146; Wm. Manson to McBride, 30 September 1911, GR441, v.110. D'Arcy Tate, the GTP solicitor, lost a $200 election bet with McBride. Tate to "Dick," 22 September 1911, GR441, v.145.
78 Borden, *Memoirs*, 1:332; Borden to McBride, 25 September 1911, Bowser to McBride, 25 September 1911, Borden to McBride, 2 October 1911, McBride to Borden, 3 October 1911, MS347, v.1; Burrell to McBride, 23 September 1911, McBride to Burrell, 7 October 1911, GR441, v.108; *Colonist*, 22 September 1911, 4 and 13 October 1911; Brown, *Robert Laird Borden*, 1:202; English, *The Decline of Politics*, 68.
79 Carl Berger, *The Sense of Power: Studies in the Ideas of Canadian Imperialism, 1867-1914* (Toronto: University of Toronto Press, 1970); *Colonist*, 22 October 1911; *Times*, 23 October 1911; Barry M. Gough, *The Royal Navy and the Northwest Coast of North America, 1810-1914* (Vancouver: UBC Press, 1971), 238-41.
80 *Colonist*, 17 and 29 October 1911, 7 and 16 November 1911; Borden to C.H. Tupper, 10 October 1904, RLBP, 5268; McBride, W.J. Bowser, and W.R. Ross to Borden, 6 November 1911, RLBP, 5352ff, 127003ff; *Times*, 15 November 1911.
81 *Colonist*, 8 and 23 November 1911; *Times*, 23 November 1911.
82 *Colonist*, 23 November 1911; Sperling to H. Williams, 29 November 1911, BCERR, LFGM, 1911; Sam Hughes to Borden, 19 December 1911, RLBP, 129019-20; McBride to Hughes, 7 January 1912, RLBP, 129021; McBride to Hughes, 13 January 1912, MS347, v.1; Borden to McBride, 2 April 1912, RLBP, 129062.
83 *Colonist*, 25 November 1911, 20 February 1912; McBride to Martin Burrell, 4 and 21 January 1912, MS347, v.1/2; McBride to Borden, 11 January 1912, Borden to McBride, 12 January 1912, GR441, v.120; *Sun*, 14 February 1912; Gosnell to McBride, 24 February 1912, GR441, v.117; *News-Advertiser*, quoted in *Columbian*, 1 March 1912.

84 *Colonist,* 19 February 1911; *Times,* 2, 6, and 22 February 1912; *Alberni Pioneer News,* 10 February 1912.
85 McBride to R.M. Horne-Payne, 27 January 1911, Goward to Sperling, 10 June 1913, BCERR, b.57; Sperling to McBride, 3 June 1913, McBride to Sperling, 10 June 1913, Sperling to McBride, 17 June 1913, BCERR, LFGM, 1913; Goward to Sperling, 24 June 1913, BCERR, b.40.
86 McBride to R.H. Sperling, 29 April 1910, BCERR, b.717.
87 In a microcosm of the excessive Canadian railway building of the time, the GNR, the BCER, and the CNR eventually all had unproductive lines serving the sparse population in Saanich. Through Horne-Payne, the BCER and the CNR maintained a close relationship. McBride suggested that the CNR buy the Victoria and Sidney Railway from its parent GNR, which provided poor service, but miscommunications between McBride, Horne-Payne, and the CNR resulted in the CNR wasting money by building its own line in Saanich. R.H. Sperling, the general manager of the BCER, had "no doubt" that, "as an astute politician," McBride would seek to have the line "serve as many districts as possible," with a fast ferry to land transcontinental freight and passengers in Victoria. McBride to R.M. Horne-Payne, 25 March 1911, GR441, v.138. For further details on McBride's dealings with the BC Electric, see Patricia E. Roy, "The British Columbia Electric Railway Company, 1897-1928: A British Company in British Columbia" (PhD thesis, University of British Columbia, 1970), 145-49; Patricia E. Roy, "The Fine Arts of Lobbying and Persuading: The Case of the B.C. Electric Railway, 1897-1917," in *Canadian Business History: Selected Studies,* ed. David S. Macmillan (Toronto: McClelland and Stewart, 1972), 238-54; Sperling to Horne-Payne, 3 March 1913, BCERR, b.40.
88 *News-Advertiser,* 1 January 1911; Sperling to M. Urwin, 10 April 1912, BCERR, b.192; F.R. Glover to Sperling, 25 March 1912, BCERR, b.42A; Sperling to McBride, 31 March 1910, Report of a Committee of the Executive Council Approved by Lieutenant-Governor, 27 April 1910, BCER, Vancouver, to BCER, London, 6 February 1912, H.E. Young to Sperling, 11 February 1911, BCERR, b.23B; McBride to Sperling, 29 April 1910, Sperling to McBride, 23 April 1910, BCERR, b.717; Sperling to W.R. Ross, 3 February 1911, BCERR, LFGM, 1911; William Mackenzie to McBride, 13 February 1912, McBride to Mackenzie, 20 February 1912, GR441, v.138; Bowser to McBride, 22 March 1912, McBride to Bowser, 23 March 1912, GR441, v.117.
89 *Chilliwack Progress,* 7 February 1912; McBride to Borden, 24 February 1912, W. Mackenzie to McBride, 7 February 1912, McBride to Mackenzie, 7 February 1912, McBride to Borden, 24 February 1912, MS347, v.1.
90 See Roy, "Railways, Politicians and the Development of the City of Vancouver," 169-79.
91 British Columbia, *Proceedings and Evidence in re Pacific Great Eastern Railway Company Taken Before a Select Committee of the Legislature Appointed March 14th, 1917* (Victoria: King's Printer, 1917), J94, J514 *(PGE Inquiry).* GTP president Charles Hays informed McBride of the GTP's willingness to make a traffic arrangement with the PGE. C.M. Hays to McBride, 24 November 1911, GR441, v.110. On 23 January 1912, the GTP reached an agreement with Foley, Welch and Stewart, which had incorporated the Pacific Great Eastern Railway Company, and gave it its right to build from Vancouver to Prince George. GTP Directors' Meeting, 24 May 1912, in Grand Trunk Pacific Minute Book, v.3, 346-47, Canadian National Railway Archives, Montreal.
92 Others who were interested were John Hendry, a prominent Vancouver lumberman with interests in the Vancouver, Westminster and Yukon Railway; a company with which

Carter-Cotton was associated, presumably the Burrard Inlet Tunnel and Bridge Company; and the Howe Sound and Northern Railway, which had a charter for the route.
93 See Phyllis Veazey, "John Hendry and the Vancouver, Westminster and Yukon Railway: 'It Would Put Us on Easy Street,'" *BC Studies* 59 (Autumn 1983): 44-63; *PGE Inquiry*, J514-16, J519. When asked about the campaign funds, Bowser refused to comment, and Thomas Taylor denied any knowledge of them. R.H. Pooley, a member of the legislative committee investigating the PGE, said that no evidence was presented of PGE money going into campaign funds. *PGE Inquiry*, J635, J587, J580.
94 *PGE Inquiry*, J100; *Province*, 25 November 1911; McBride to Burrell, 9 January 1912, MS347, v.1.
95 *Province*, 6 and 11 January 1912; *Columbian*, 5 January 1912; *Colonist*, 9 February 1912.
96 GTP Directors' Meeting, 24 May 1912, GTP Minute Book, v.3, 346-47; *PGE Inquiry*, J105; McBride to T.G. Shaughnessy, 8 February 1912, MS347, v.l; *Similkameen Review*, 5 and 31 January 1912.
97 *Province*, 21 and 22 February 1912. See Barrie Sanford, *McCulloch's Wonder: The Story of the Kettle Valley Railway* (Vancouver: Whitecap, 1978).
98 *Vernon News*, 22 February 1912; *Sun*, 22 and 23 February 1912; *Times*, 21 and 23 February 1912; *Fort George Herald*, 17 February 1912; *Nelson Daily News*, 21 and 23 February 1912; *Kamloops Standard*, 23 February 1912; *Inland Sentinel*, 23 February and 5 March 1912; *Province*, 21 February 1912; *Colonist*, 21 and 22 February 1912; *Prince Rupert Evening Empire*, 31 January 1912; *Prince Rupert Daily News*, 21 February 1912. John Jardine, who had been elected as a Liberal in 1909, left the party and ran in 1912 as an Independent Conservative.
99 *Sun*, 28 February 1912, 2, 11, 13, 16, and 20 March 1912; *Times*, 23 February 1912, 11, 12, and 23 March 1912; *Columbian*, 2 March 1912.
100 *Times*, 28 February and 12 March 1912; *New Westminster Daily News*, 28 February 1912; *Sun*, 28 February and 6 March 1912; *Province*, 28 and 29 February 1912, 9 March 1912; C.B. Hume to Thomas Taylor, 20 February 1912, McBride to Hume, 23 February 1912, GR441, v.163; *Nelson Daily News*, 8 March 1912; *Vernon News*, 7 March 1912; *Colonist*, 1 March 1912; *Fort George Herald*, 24 February 1912, 15 and 23 March 1912; *Fort George Tribune*, 16 March 1912; *Prince Rupert Evening Empire*, 2 and 18 March 1912; *Omineca Miner*, 2 March 1912. A Vancouver real estate firm ran a full-page ad in the *Province*, advertising lots at Grouard, Alberta, the "commercial centre of Peace River."
101 *Colonist*, 1 and 6 March 1912.
102 W.M. McKay to McBride, 9 February 1912, GR441, v.11; *Colonist*, 6 March 1912.
103 *Kamloops Standard*, 8 March 1912; *Inland Sentinel*, 7 March 1912; *Province*, 8 March 1912; *Colonist*, 8 and 9 March 1912. Forster won 282 votes, whereas Parson netted 263. McBride to Parson, 15 March 1912, GR441, v.117.
104 *Province*, 11 March 1912; *Fernie Free Press*, 15 March 1912; *Nelson Daily News*, 11 March 1912; *Colonist*, 14 and 16 March 1912; *Rossland Miner*, 20 March 1912; *Trail News*, 16 March 1912.
105 Howard Green, Diary, 11 March 1912, CVA, Howard Green Papers; *Colonist*, 12 March 1912.
106 Henry Gaylord Wilshire was a prominent American socialist.
107 *Grand Forks Gazette*, 23 March 1912; *Sun*, 20 March 1912; *Colonist*, 17 March 1912. McBride first voted against women's suffrage in 1899. The next year he said that if the majority in a plebiscite voted for it, he would give women the right to sit in Parliament. *Columbian*, 25 February 1899, 7 June 1900.

108 Eagle, *The Canadian Pacific Railway,* 136; *Penticton Herald,* 9 March 1912. A few weeks later, J.J. Warren of the KVR said that, at McBride's suggestion, he was negotiating with the GNR for running rights through the Coquihalla. J.J. Warren to McBride, 27 February 1912, Warren to McBride, 18 March 1913, GR441, v.154; *Penticton Herald,* 23 March 1912. En route to the coronation in 1911, McBride met GNR officials in Minneapolis. *Columbian,* 4 May 1911.

109 The three KVR sections ran from Midway to Carmi (forty-six miles), Merritt to Brookmere (thirty miles), and Penticton to Trout Creek (seven miles). Andrew McCulloch, "The Kettle Valley Railway Notes" (Canadian Pacific Railway, Penticton,1962, mimeographed); *Kelowna Courier,* 14 October and 11 November 1909, 21 March 1912; *Vernon News,* 21 March 1912.

110 *Colonist,* 20 March 1912; *Columbian,* 21 March 1912.

111 *Sun,* 23 March 1912. Evidently, the driver disobeyed a new provincial law setting the maximum speed limit at twenty-five miles per hour. A new road, Kingsway, was black-topped later that year. *Columbian,* 22 March 1912; *New Westminster Daily News,* 23 and 28 March 1912.

112 *Colonist,* 22, 26, and 27 March 1912; *Nanaimo Daily Herald,* 23 March 1912.

113 *Western Methodist Recorder,* March 1912; Matson to McBride, 14 March 1912, McBride to Matson, 14 March 1912, GR441, v.117. McBride refused to intervene in the Esquimalt situation. Pooley led the five candidates with 46.5 percent of the popular vote.

114 *Colonist,* 19 and 24 March 1912; *Times,* 29 March 1912.

CHAPTER 6: THE BEGINNING OF THE END

1 British Columbia, *Public Accounts ... 1912,* BCSP, 1913, C23; Department of Mines, *Annual Report, 1912,* in BCSP, 1913, K7. Some good examples of McBride's optimism may be found in his 1914 New Year's message. *Colonist,* 1 January 1914; *News-Advertiser,* 1 January 1914; *Sun,* 2 January 1914; *Columbian,* 2 January 1914.

2 *Columbian,* 17 June 1912, 8 and 12 August 1912, 30 October and 2 November 1912; *Colonist,* 13 July 1912; *Times,* 17 June 1912; *Chilliwack Progress,* 21 May 1913; *News-Advertiser,* 3 June 1913; McBride, Speech to Conservative Convention, 22 January 1914, BCA, M/MK.

3 For details of the strike, see Mark Leier, *Where the Fraser River Flows: The Industrial Workers of the World in British Columbia* (Vancouver: New Star, 1990), especially 49-53. Despite rumours of disorder, only one violent incident occurred during the strike: a special constable employed by a subcontractor shot a striker in the leg. McBride denied that the CNR would hire Asians to replace the strikers and opposed the "wholesale importation" of Italians, Serbs, and Austrians as railway workers. *Colonist,* 2 and 3 April 1912; Bowser to McBride, 23 May 1912, GR441, v.112; McBride to E.J. Chamberlain, 10 September 1912, GR441, v.47. The IWW remained a factor in BC. Early in 1914, McBride dealt with its complaint that two of its members had been arrested in Revelstoke on a charge of vagrancy and "tortured" in the Kamloops jail. After learning that the two men would not work, hung around the Revelstoke bars, and refused to leave town when ordered to do so, McBride told the IWW that he could not interfere with a matter that lay outside his jurisdiction. McBride to Albert Fernet, 25 February 1914, GR441, v.55; Bowser to McBride, 17 May 1912, GR441, v.112.

4 J.T. Robinson to McBride, 4 July 1912, T.G. Holt to McBride, 4 July 1912, GR441, v.140. Although they were prepared to have the maintenance shops at Fruitlands, three miles to

the north, Kamloops residents continued to press to have the CNR enter their city. M.F. Crawford to J.P. Shaw, 13 February 1914, GR441, v.141.
5 McBride to G.H. Barnard, 8 February 1912, Barnard to McBride, 12 February 1912, MS347, v.1; *Times*, 10 June, 12 October, 11 November, and 19 December 1912; *Colonist*, 6, 7, and 28 March 1912, 12 October and 25 December 1912. No ferry depot was built.
6 Bowser to McBride, 17 May 1912, GR441, v.112; *Sun*, 23 and 25 April 1912.
7 After McBride retired, the province leased the old courthouse site to the city, which created Victory Square. *Province*, 25 June 1913; *Sun*, 1 August 1913; *News-Advertiser*, 12 July 1913; McBride to A.H.B. Macgowan, 15 July 1913, MS347, v.1; *New Westminster Daily News*, 12 August 1913; *Nelson Daily News*, 26 June 1913.
8 McBride told Tupper that a branch might be built to Aspen Grove if the area developed. J.J. Warren to McBride, 13 March 1914, McBride to Warren, 14 October 1915, GR441, v.154. See Barrie Sanford, *McCulloch's Wonder: The Story of the Kettle Valley Railway* (Vancouver: Whitecap, 1978), 158-59; McBride to "Jonogrif," London, 7 February 1914, GR441, v.394; *Sun*, 3 March 1914; *News-Advertiser*, 3 March 1914; McBride to C.H. Tupper, 2 March 1914, GR441, v.395; McBride to Bowser, 21 October 1914, GR441, v.126.
9 *Province*, 4 and 24 September 1912; *Colonist*, 10 October 1912; *Times*, 10 October 1912. Bowser knew of Welch's connection with FWS but did not discuss it in cabinet. British Columbia, *Proceedings and Evidence in re Pacific Great Eastern Railway Company Taken Before a Select Committee of the Legislature Appointed March 14th 1917* (Victoria: King's Printer, 1917), J584, J620, J628, J380, J618, J588 *(PGE Inquiry)*. In December 1912, F.C. Gamble told McBride that Welch charged "much in excess" of those who billed for similar work elsewhere, but McBride appeared to have done nothing about this. *PGE Inquiry*, J456, J629. The 1917 PGE inquiry revealed several instances of political patronage in awarding subcontracts. A.H.B. Macgowan, a Conservative MLA, claimed that his share of a contract was a reward for his efforts in settling the IWW strike against the CNR, in 1912. McBride had communicated with Welch on Macgowan's behalf. *PGE Inquiry*, J481, J500-1, J510. One subcontract went to McGillivray Brothers, a firm headed by McBride's brother-in-law. Ibid., J601. McBride may have intervened to give an interest in a subcontract to the brother-in-law of a Conservative Victoria druggist. *PGE Inquiry*, J405, J407. Several witnesses hinted that they knew of Conservatives receiving campaign funds but would not give details. *PGE Inquiry*, J544, J555.
10 *Province*, 14 February 1913; McBride to Walter Moberly, 23 August 1912, GR441, v.392; McBride to H.S. Clements, 10 February 1913, McBride to A.J. Thompson, 12 February 1913, MS347, v.1; J. Strong to McBride, 26 May 1913, McBride to Strong, 12 June and 22 November 1913, Franklin K. Lane to McBride, 10 June 1913, GR441, v.121; McBride to Lane, 5 July 1913, RLBP, 7497; *News-Advertiser*, 3 June 1913; McBride to Borden, 12 July 1913, RLBP, 749ff; *Fort George Herald*, 23 August 1913.
11 Rumours stated that McBride had made an agreement to build the line with the Standard Oil Company, a trust that American authorities broke up in 1911, or with the Chicago, Milwaukee and St. Paul Railway. The Alaska Railroad was completed in 1923. "Alaska Railroad History," Alaska Railroad Corporation, 2012, http://www.akrr.com/; McBride to Borden, 23 August 1913, RLBP, 82012-3; *New Westminster Daily News*, 21 July 1913; *Times*, 22 July and 3 November 1913; *Sun*, 8 August 1913; *Province*, 6 December 1913, 28 February and 6 March 1914; *Columbian*, 3 November 1913; McBride to Lane, 15 March 1914, GR441, v.395; McBride to Governor Strong, 13 March 1914, GR441, v.57; *Colonist*, 14 December

1913, 28 February 1914; J.M. Ashton to McBride, 14 January 1914, Ashton to McBride, 26 January 1914, GR441, v.126. The Legislature agreed to assist the PGE to build the Second Narrows Bridge, linking North Vancouver with Vancouver.
12 *Province*, 29 December 1911; *Nelson Daily News*, 3 January 1912; McBride to Borden, 24 June 1913, Borden to McBride, 30 June 1913, RLBP, 7473-7479; Borden, Diary, 27 October 1913, RLBP, v.449; McBride to A. Thompson, 7 February 1914, MS347, v.1. Thompson, the MP for Yukon, outlined the proposed annexation arrangement for Borden but did not pass judgment on it. Thompson to Borden, 5 January 1914, RLBP, 98433ff; *Times*, 6 March 1914.
13 The University of California gave McBride an honorarium of $500, which he returned as a gift toward an atlas of reproductions of early maps of the Pacific coast. B.I. Wheeler to McBride, 10 December and 21 November 1912, H.M. Stephens to McBride, 12 May 1913, GR441, v.119; *Times*, 5 July 1912; *Province*, 12 February 1913, 13 June 1914.
14 R.M. Horne-Payne to McBride, 18 June 1912, GR441, v.138; *Colonist*, 25 February 1913, 13 February 1914; *Times*, 16 October 1912, 25 February 1913; *Province*, 24 October 1912. In 1913, the tax on banks was increased and that on coke was decreased. *News-Advertiser*, 18 January 1913; *British Columbia in the Canadian Confederation: A Submission Presented to the Royal Commission on Dominion-Provincial Relations by the Government of the Province of British Columbia* (Victoria: King's Printer, 1938), 190. The fiscal year was calculated as running from 1 April to 31 March.
15 *CAR*, 1913, 34-35; *News-Advertiser*, 13 August 1913; *Colonist*, 26 June and 12 August 1913; McBride, "British Columbia Today" (speech to Progress Club, Vancouver, 25 June 1913), copy in McBF; McBride to H.B. Mackenzie, Manager, Bank of British North America, Montreal, 9 January 1913, McBride to F. Carter-Cotton, 18 April 1913, MS347, v.1; *Sun*, 19 December 1913.
16 Advertisement, *Saturday Sunset*, 26 July 1913; *Toronto Saturday Night*, quoted in *Fort George Herald*, 25 January 1913; W.R. Arnold to McBride, 29 May 1913, McBride to Arnold, 31 May 1913, GR441, v.122; Donald M. MacGregor, *British Columbia: The Greatest Field for Investment To-Day* (Vancouver: n.p., 1914); *Province*, 8 May 1914.
17 In the usual exchange rate, £1 was worth $4.85, making the amount borrowed $1,500,350.
18 McBride to Horne-Payne, 22 April 1913, GR441, v.138; *Omineca Miner*, 9 August 1913; *Sun*, 26 June and 6 December 1913; McBride to J.H. Turner, 22 May 1913, McBride to H.E. Young, 28 September 1913, MS347, v.l; *Times*, 4 December 1913; *News-Advertiser*, 5 December 1913; *Colonist*, 6 November 1913.
19 *Sun*, 25 July 1913, 26 and 31 January 1915; British Columbia, *Public Accounts ... 1910*, in BCSP, 1911, C38; *Omineca Miner*, 15 March 1913. When the Liberal government eliminated the office of auditor general on 1 January 1917, Allison was out of a job. *Times*, 27 January 1915; Auditor General to McBride, 8 December 1913, GR441, v.54; McBride to cabinet ministers, 7 May 1914, GR441, v.395.
20 The new royalties were designed to raise revenue, meet the varying needs of timber producers, and ostensibly promote conservation. They would be adjusted every five years depending on the price of lumber. In 1913, the government proposed to increase royalties but reconsidered after the industry protested.
21 *Colonist*, 25 and 28 February 1913, 13 February 1914; *Times*, 16 October 1912, 25 February 1913, 23 January 1914; *Columbian*, 20 and 24 January 1914, 10 February 1914; McBride to Turner, 7 March 1914, MS347, v.1; *CAR*, 1914, 697.
22 McBride to G.A. McGuire, 17 March 1913, GR441, v.138; *Province*, 14 February 1913; *Colonist*, 2 April 1912, 13 February 1913; *Times*, 13 February 1913.

23 William Mann to McBride, 7 March 1913, McBride to Mann, 8 March 1913, GR441, v.119. The PGE was a relatively minor Canadian borrower in London. In 1912, the CNR system, which operated throughout Canada, raised £32 million, the GTP raised £98.9 million, and the CPR raised £91 million. T.D. Regehr, *The Canadian Northern Railway: Pioneer Road of the Northern Prairies, 1895-1918* (Toronto: Macmillan, 1976), 334-42; McBride to T.G. Holt, 6 May 1913, GR441, v.141; *Times*, 4 July 1913.

24 *Colonist*, 13 November 1913; *Province*, 13 November 1913. McBride conferred with CNR officials while in Toronto in November 1913. *Sun*, 13 November 1913; *Times*, 25 November 1913.

25 Mann to McBride, 18 December 1913, Mann to McBride, 12 January 1914, GR441, v.141. The 1911 estimate of the average cost per mile for construction from the New Westminster Bridge to Yellowhead Pass was $50,394.11. By 1914, this had risen to $66,191.00. *Times*, 13, 21, 24, and 25 February 1914; *Province*, 23, 26, and 27 February 1914, 6 March 1914; *Sun*, 13 and 26 February 1914; G. McGuire to H.H. Stevens, 25 February 1914, UBC Archives, Lewis Family Fonds, v.2.

26 *Colonist*, 26 and 27 February 1914; *Sun*, 23 February 1914; *Times*, 25 February 1914; *Province*, 25 February 1914; "Yorick," "Mackenzie & Mann and Their Millions," RLBP, 11437.

27 McBride to Mann, 23 and 26 February 1914, McBride to Mackenzie, 11 March 1914, MS347, v.1; Mann to McBride, 24 February 1914, John J. Banfield to McBride, 22 July 1914, GR441, v.141.

28 McBride to Borden, 16 March 1914, GR441, v.395; McBride to Borden, 25 March 1914, RLBP, 11562ff; *Colonist*, 18 March 1914; Regehr, *Canadian Northern*, 365-84. Mackenzie and Mann incorporated each section of the railway separately. There were thirty-one such companies, including Canadian Northern Ontario, Canadian Northern Saskatchewan, and Canadian Northern Alberta. *CAR*, 1914, 738; *Sun*, 11 May 1914; *Inland Sentinel*, 6 and 13 May 1914.

29 Borden to McBride, 29 April 1914, RLBP, 11669; McBride to Borden, 8 May 1914, MS347, v.l; McBride to Borden, 18 May 1914, McBride to Mackenzie, 26 May 1914, GR441, v.395; McBride to Borden, 2 May 1914, RLBP, 11687; Borden to McBride, 9 May 1914, RLBP, 11786; Borden to McBride, 25 May 1914, RLBP, 11847; McBride to Borden, 20 May 1914, RLBP, 11834. While arguing against the CNR aid bill, Senator Hewitt Bostock read the correspondence into Hansard. Canada, Senate, *Debates*, 5 June 1914, 696-729; *Province*, 27 and 28 May 1914; *Colonist*, 17 May 1914.

30 *Columbian*, 11 and 12 May 1914; *News-Advertiser*, 13 May 1914; Matson to Borden, 20 May 1914, RLBP, 11837ff; *Province*, 27 July 1914. For Mackenzie and Mann's financial woes, see Regehr, *Canadian Northern*, ch. 14.

31 *PGE Inquiry*, J97, J64, J394-95, J618, J374-79, J622; *CAR*, 1913, 28, 675; Mann to McBride, 7 March 1913, McBride to Mann, 8 March 1913, GR441, v.119. Under the initial agreement between the PGE and the province, the proceeds of bond sales were deposited in a government bank account and released to the PGE as the work was done.

32 Radium had recently been isolated chemically and was being promoted as a cancer treatment. *Province*, 26 February and 27 May 1914; *Nelson Daily News*, 11 May 1914; *Times*, 18 July 1914.

33 In congratulating McBride on his 1909 electoral victory, F.J. Fulton had reported from Washington, DC, that the deputy minister of lands in Ottawa thought that the province should be concerned with fire protection only and should not establish a forestry department, but Bernard Fernow, a founder of the forestry profession and dean of forestry at the

University of Toronto, believed that such a department was necessary, a view shared by Fulton. Richard A. Rajala, *Clearcutting the Pacific Rain Forest: Production, Science, and Regulation* (Vancouver: UBC Press, 1998), 54-56; F.J. Fulton to McBride, 1 December 1909, GR441, v.144.

34 *Times*, 7 February 1912, 7 and 8 March 1912, 12 August 1912; *Colonist*, 8 March 1912.
35 E.V. Bodwell to McBride, 24 February 1912, McBride to Bodwell, 24 February 1912, GR441, v.44; Bodwell to McBride, 10 July 1912, GR441, v.45; *Times*, 13 August 1912.
36 *Sun*, 18 January and 17 February 1913; *Province*, 11 and 27 February 1913, 3 March 1913; A.E. Watts to R.L. Borden, 9 June 1913, GR441, v.121.
37 For example, *Sun*, 20 August and 9 November 1912; *Sun*, reprinted in *Inland Sentinel*, 28 November 1913; *Alberni Advocate*, 17 October 1913; *Times*, 4 May 1916; *News-Advertiser*, 12 November 1912.
38 *Sun*, 19 and 20 December 1912; *Times*, 19 and 20 December 1912. McBride gave a similar message to the Farmers' Institute. *Colonist*, 22 January 1913; British Columbia, Department of Lands, *Annual Report ... 1913*, in BCSP, 1914, D8.
39 The occasion of the meeting was a 1913 by-election in The [Gulf] Islands, which was caused by the elevation of A.E. McPhillips to the bench. The Conservative candidate, W.W. Foster, won 62 percent of the vote. Elections British Columbia, *Electoral History of British Columbia, 1871-1986* (Victoria: Elections BC and Legislative Library, 1988), 120.
40 *Colonist*, 22 and 26 November 1913; *Columbian*, 24 January 1914.
41 McBride took a practical interest in agriculture, suggesting, for example, that organizers of agricultural fairs use tents as in England, spend less on splendid buildings employed for only a few weeks each year, and apply the savings to larger prizes. *Columbian*, 27 January 1913.
42 Alex Lucas to McBride, 30 January 1911, McBride to Lucas, 8 February 1911, GR441, v.107; *Columbian*, 25 October 1912; *Times*, 18 December 1912, 7 January 1913; James B. Bruce to McBride, 15 February 1913, McBride to Bruce, 22 February 1913, GR441, v.119.
43 *Sun*, 25 February and 5 March 1914; *Times*, 12 January and 24 February 1914; *Province*, 25 February 1914; *News-Advertiser*, 26 February 1914; James Murton, *Creating a Modern Countryside: Liberalism and Land Resettlement in British Columbia* (Vancouver: UBC Press, 2007), 46.
44 *Sun*, 21 January 1913, 26 January 1914; *Province*, 8 January 1914. The *Alberni Advocate*, 2 May 1913, said that matters should be dealt with by MLAs, not by commissions that cost "a pile of money, and get very little in the way of results."
45 *Colonist*, 27 February 1912, 11 January 1913; McBride to T.S. Baxter, 18 June 1914, GR441, v.395.
46 *Province*, 23 January 1912; *Sun*, 19 February 1912; McBride to J.H. McVety, 22 February 1912, MS347, v.1. Unless otherwise noted, this account draws on Leier, *Where the Fraser River Flows*, 74-83.
47 The commissioners were A.M. Harper, a Vancouver lawyer and Conservative; J.A. McKelvie, a Conservative newspaper editor of Vernon; R.A. Stoney; John Jardine, a former Liberal MLA for Esquimalt; and H.G. Parson of Golden, a Conservative MLA defeated by an Independent Conservative in the recent provincial election. *Times*, 27 February 1912; *Columbian*, 25 October 1912; *Province*, 22 January 1913.
48 Earlier, Mottishaw had been laid off from the company's mine at Extension after reporting gas in the mine. W.L. Coulson, the general manager of the colliery, provided McBride with copies of Secret Service reports on miners' meetings at Cumberland in early May.

McBride to Coulson, 10 May 1913, GR441, v.393. Other Pinkerton's reports are in GR441, v.120; *Colonist,* 18 September 1912; McBride to Thomas Dixon, 5 February 1913, GR441, v.393; *Province,* 6 February 1913; McBride to Robt. Walkinshaw, 26 November 1913, GR441, v.151.

49 *Province,* 15 January 1913; *Sun,* 9 January and 28 February 1913; *Colonist,* 24 March 1912; McBride to Wm. Lakeland, Secretary Western Federation of Miners, Greenwood, 18 June 1913, McBride to Coulson, 24 January and 13 February 1913, GR441, v.393. McBride wrote to the Trail Mill and Smeltermen's Union, the Wood, Wire and Metal Lathers in Vancouver, the barbers in Vancouver, and the Victoria letter carriers, indicating that because his earlier offer to mediate between the colliers and the strikers had been rebuffed, he did not think it advisable that he interfere in the dispute. When the editor of the *Methodist Recorder* reported on the difficult situation in Nanaimo, which he blamed on the United Mine Workers of America, McBride sent him a similar letter. Rev. J.P. Hicks to McBride, 28 June 1913, McBride to Hicks, 3 July 1913, GR441, v.123; *Province,* 15 January and 1 March 1913; *Sun,* 9 January and 28 February 1913; *Colonist,* 24 March 1912; McBride to Coulson, 5 March 1913, H.G. Parson to McBride, 1 March 1913, GR441, v.119; *News-Advertiser,* 21 February 1913.

50 Ernest McGaffey to McBride, 22 August 1913, GR441, v.123; *Province,* 12 August 1913. Bowser hired Pinkerton's Detective Agency to spy on the strikers. David Ricardo Williams, *Call In Pinkerton's: American Detectives at Work for Canada* (Toronto: Dundurn, 1998), 152-61.

51 Other trials followed, but only twelve rioters were jailed. Judge Howay, who imposed what were deemed harsh sentences, was McBride's law school classmate. He ran unsuccessfully as a Liberal in 1907. John Hinde, "'Stout Ladies and Amazons': Women in the British Columbia Coal Mining Community of Cumberland," *BC Studies* 114 (Summer 1997): 33; McBride to C.V. Cook, 4 December 1913, McBride to George Hardy, 17 December 1913, GR441, v.394; *The Week,* 8 November 1913; *Colonist,* 6 November 1913; McBride's Reply to Throne speech [1914], BCA, M/M12 (Miscellaneous Material re McBride).

52 *Times,* 15 December 1913; *Sun,* 16 February 1914; *Inland Sentinel,* 6 January 1914.

53 *Sun,* 1 January 1914; *Times,* 15 January 1914; *Province,* 5 March 1914; *Colonist,* 16 January 1914; Parker Williams to McBride, 26 January 1914, McBF. On tag days, canvassers for charities would stand, usually at street corners, and solicit donations. In return for a donation, the canvasser provided the donor with a "tag," or badge, which indicated that he had already donated so other canvassers would not approach him.

54 *Province,* 17 February 1914; *Colonist,* 17 February 1914; *Times,* 17 February 1914; *News-Advertiser,* 17 February 1914.

55 British Columbia, Royal Commission on Labour, *Report* (Victoria: King's Printer, 1914), passim.

56 *Colonist,* 4 March 1914; *Province,* 5 March 1914; *News-Advertiser,* 5 March 1914; *Times,* 4 March 1914. In 1916, responding to a commission recommendation, the Bowser government revised the Workmen's Compensation Act.

57 McBride to Lt. Col. A.J. Hall, 12 March 1914, GR441, v.395; McBride to Bowser, 28 September 1913, MS347, v.1; Lynne Bowen, *Boss Whistle: The Coal Miners of Vancouver Island Remember* (Lantzville: Oolichan, 1982), 189-92; McBride to Frank Farrington, 10 June 1914, GR441, v.395; *Province,* 24 June 1914; *Sun,* 25 June 1914; McBride to Secretary, UMWA, Nanaimo, 14 August 1914, GR441, v.394; Robert Foster to McBride, 19 August 1914, GR441, v.55.

58 *Colonist*, 21 August 1914. The operators reneged on their agreement to rehire strikers and blacklisted many former employees. Bowen, *Boss Whistle*, 134, 194; John R. Hinde, *When Coal Was King: Ladysmith and the Coal-Mining Industry on Vancouver Island* (Vancouver: UBC Press, 2003), 153. Parliament debated a motion (later defeated) to censure the minister of labour for his conduct in the matter. HCD, 3 March 1914, 1267-1327.

59 In 1911, the Associated Boards of Trade of Eastern British Columbia asked the government to inquire into the price of coal to domestic consumers. A.B. Mackenzie to McBride, 26 January 1911, GR441, v.41; Borden to McBride, 18 October 1912, RLBP, 7355. Dr. McGuire asked for an inquiry in 1908. *Times*, 11 February 1908. The Legislature reaffirmed the request in 1909 and 1911, but McBride put the request off by saying that the issue was a federal matter. His correspondence with Ottawa is in RLBP, 14035off. *Sun*, 25 and 27 January 1913, 8 February 1913; *Times*, 1 February 1912, 27 January 1913, 3 December 1915; McBride to General Managers of Canadian Collieries (Dunsmuir), Western Fuel Company, Nanaimo-Vancouver Coal Company, and Pacific Coal Company, 20 January 1915, GR441, v.397.

60 *Province*, 11 April 1912; R.M. Horne-Payne to McBride, 15 May and 15 August 1912, GR441, v.138; *Colonist*, 19 June 1912; *Sun*, 6 and 19 June 1912.

61 "Memo of Matters to Be Discussed with the Premier on January 21, 1913," BCERR, b.55; Glover to Sperling, 11 February 1913, BCERR, b.199; Glover to Sperling, 24 February 1913, A.T. Goward to Sperling, 21 January 1914, BCERR, b.714; Sperling, Diary, 10 January 1914, Minutes Meeting of Management, 21 January 1914, BCERR, b.23B; BCER (London) to Sperling, 28 January 1914, BCERR, b.43B; McBride to G.A. McGuire, 17 March 1913, GR441, v.138; Bowser to Glover, 17 October 1912, Sperling to G. Urwin, 23 November 1912, BCER (London) to G.R.G. Conway, 25 September 1912, BCER (Vancouver) to BCER (London), 14 November 1912, BCERR, LFGM, 1912. See also Patricia E. Roy, "The British Columbia Electric Railway Company, 1897-1928: A British Company in British Columbia" (PhD thesis, University of British Columbia, 1970), 92-116.

62 British Columbia, Royal Commission on Municipal Government, *Report* (Victoria: King's Printer, 1913), 10; Sperling to George Kidd, 21 January 1911, LFGM, 1911; Bowser to A.S. Goodeve, 15 October 1912, BCA, Attorney-General's Papers, file 6874-2-12; Sperling to McBride, 8 January 1914, F.R. Glover to Kidd, 13 June 1914, BCERR, b.714; "Memo of Conference with McBride, 13 January 1914," BCERR, b.82; Urwin to Kidd, 30 July 1915, BCERR, b.731; Kidd to Urwin, 6 December 1915, BCERR, b.83. See also Patricia E. Roy, "Regulating the British Columbia Electric Railway: The First Public Utilities Commission in British Columbia," *BC Studies* 11 (Fall 1971): 4-6.

63 The *Colonist*, 28 January 1913, wanted to "deter criminally inclined foreigners" from working in the province. The law permitted the deportation of aliens charged with offences under the act. British Columbia, *An Act respecting Offensive Weapons*, S.B.C. 1913, c. 83; Forster to McBride, 27 January 1913, GR441, v.118; *Times*, 29 January 1913, 7 and 25 February 1913; *The Week*, 1 March 1913; *Sun*, 4 and 28 February 1913, 17 March 1913, 30 January and 4 March 1914.

64 *Province*, 8 July 1912; E.H. Heaps to McBride, 20 February 1913, John A. Lee to Conservative Associations, with Lee to McBride, 19 February 1913, McBride to Lee, 24 February 1913, GR441, v.119; *Times*, 14 February 1913; *Fort George Herald*, 22 March 1913.

65 Some executive members of the Victoria Conservative Association resigned in protest because Bowser prosecuted tobacconists for opening on Sundays but made no effort to stop hotels and the CPR from doing so. *Sun*, 19 November 1913; Herbert Cuthbert to McBride, 14 March 1913, GR441, v.119 (underlining in original); Reg. Hayward, N.J.

Hopkins, and Henry Callow to president and executive of the Victoria Conservative Association, 19 July 1913, GR441, v.122; *Times,* 6 May 1913, 19 February 1914; *Sun,* 19 February 1914; *Inland Sentinel,* 23 February 1914.
66 *Times,* 4 July 1912, 28 January and 4 October 1913; *Sun,* 22 January and 11 August 1913, 25 February 1914; *Province,* 25 October 1912, 29 January 1913. The Borden government promised similar reforms. John English, *The Decline of Politics: The Conservatives and the Party System, 1901-20* (Toronto: University of Toronto Press, 1977), 72-74.
67 *Times,* 21 January 1913, 6 April 1914; *Omineca Herald,* 8 May 1914; *Sun,* 16 February, 6 June, and 29 August 1913, 27 January 1914.
68 *Columbian,* 19 December 1913, 2 June 1914; *Province,* 26 May 1913, 19 February 1914; *Colonist,* 26 November 1913. The published reports of the Department of Public Works provide details of the number of roads, trails, and bridges built or improved. E.K. Beeston to McBride, 11 October 1912, GR441, v.115.
69 *Grand Forks Evening Sun,* 13 September 1912.
70 McBride to R.F. Green, 20 May 1914, MS347, v.1; R.H. Sperling, Diary, 22 December 1913, BCERR, b.346. The BCER did not record such donations in its books but reimbursed executives for "personal" donations. Goward to Sperling, 16 May 1913, BCERR, b.714; Jno. B. Williamson to McBride, 13 June 1914, McBride to Glover, 16 June 1914, GR441, v.125.
71 *Colonist,* 16 July 1912; *Smithers Interior News,* 1 June 1912; *Times,* 16, 17, and 30 July 1912; *Province,* 16 and 17 July 1912; *Omineca Miner,* 20 July 1912.
72 *Province,* 19 and 22 July 1912; *Times,* 22 July 1912; *Colonist,* 21 and 24 July 1912.
73 *New Westminster Daily News,* 4 and 13 September 1912; *Columbian,* 4 October 1912; *Colonist,* 27 October 1912, 29 July 1913.
74 *Nelson Daily News,* 31 January 1913; *McBride Journal,* 9 July 1914; *Fort George Herald,* 11 July 1914; *Times,* 10 October 1914; *Port Alberni News,* 13 and 17 June 1914; *Colonist,* 14 June 1914; *Alberni Advocate,* 12 June 1914.
75 *Fort George Herald,* 11 January and 9 August 1913, 11 April 1914; *Omineca Herald,* 22 March, 22 August, and 5 December 1913, 16 January and 22 May 1914; *Omineca Miner,* 24 August and 8 November 1913.
76 *Times,* 22 January and 13 November 1913; *Colonist,* 25 February and 3 August 1913; *Province,* 13 November 1913; *Weekly Columbian,* 28 January 1913; *Sun,* 7 August 1912, 24 May 1913; McBride to Borden, 12 July 1913, RLBP, 7491ff; McBride to C. Yada, 26 January 1912, GR441, v.392.
77 McBride to H.H. Stevens, 22 April 1913, MS347, v.1; McBride to Borden, 24 June 1913, RLBP, 7472-3; McBride to Borden, 12 July 1913, RLBP, 7491ff; McBride to Borden, 13 January 1912, RLBP, 5269; Thomas Mulvey to Lieutenant-Governor, 11 June 1913, LAC, Secretary of State's Records, RG6A, v.172; *Province,* 14 October and 15 December 1913; *Columbian,* 11 December 1913; *Colonist,* 12 December 1913; McBride to Lieutenant-Governor, 7 May 1914, MS347, v.1. See also Patricia E. Roy, *A White Man's Province: British Columbia Politicians and Chinese and Japanese Immigrants, 1858-1914* (Vancouver: UBC Press, 1989), 251-53.
78 *The Times* (London), 23 May 1914; *Province,* 27 May 1914; Hugh Johnston, *The Voyage of the Komagata Maru: The Sikh Challenge to Canada's Colour Bar* (Delhi: Oxford University Press, 1979; repr., Vancouver: UBC Press, 1989); McBride to Dr. Henry M. Ami, at Royal Societies Club, 24 April 1914, McBF.
79 J.D. Hazen to McBride, 15 July 1912, GR441, v.114; *Colonist,* 2 October 1912; McBride to Bowser, 5 March 1913, MS347, v.l; McBride to W.T. Grenfell, 25 April 1913, GR441, v.120;

Sun, 10 March 1913; M.R.J. Reid to McBride, 17 August 1912, GR441, v.47; McBride to Sir Leslie M. Rundle, 13 September 1912, GR441, v.392.

80 *Kamloops Standard*, 30 October 1902; *Nelson Daily News*, 13 May 1908, 11 November 1909; *News-Advertiser*, 30 April 1908; *Province*, 22 April 1908; *The Week*, 22 June 1912; *Grand Forks Evening Sun*, 23 August 1912, quoted in *Times*, 28 August 1912.

81 Blakemore to McBride, 11 June 1912, GR441, v.113; Blakemore to McBride, 31 August 1912, McBride to Blakemore, 11 September 1912, GR441, v.115; *Grand Forks Gazette*, 16 and 23 November 1912. Blakemore also suggested reducing the prison term of Fred Gretchen, a Doukhobor who had not complied with registration laws. The report's sixty-six closely printed pages included a history of the Doukhobors, which was based on information from two American scholars. It also featured a study of their communal system, habits, customs, and practices, their attitudes to observing laws, and their experiences in Saskatchewan, derived mainly from information provided by leading Doukhobors. Half of the report dealt with the Doukhobors in British Columbia, where many witnesses criticized their non-observance of civil laws and their economic competition. British Columbia, Royal Commission on Matters Relating to the Sect of Doukhobors in the Province of British Columbia, *Report* (Victoria: Legislative Assembly of British Columbia, 1913); *Sun*, 26 December 1912; *Times*, 27 December 1912; *News-Advertiser*, 27 December 1912.

82 *Colonist*, 22 January 1913; *Grand Forks Gazette*, 25 January, 1 February, and 3 May 1913; *Times*, 24 January 1913; *Nelson Daily News*, 25 January 1913.

83 *Nelson Daily News*, 9 July 1913; *News-Advertiser*, 25 July 1913; *Colonist*, 30 October 1912; *Province*, 10 November 1913, 29 January 1914; John McLaren, "Creating 'Slaves of Satan' or 'New Canadians'? The Law, Education, and the Socialization of Doukhobor Children, 1911-1935," in *Essays in the History of Canadian Law: British Columbia and the Yukon*, ed. Hamar Foster and John McLaren (Toronto: Osgoode Society, 1995), 356; McBride to P. Verigin, 3 July 1914, GR441, v.395. After the *Sun* claimed that Pineo had said that Blakemore's report had made him sympathetic to the Doukhobors but he now agreed with the people of Grand Forks and so had angered Bowser, Pineo denied the *Sun's* "moonshine" report. *Sun*, 7 and 11 November 1913.

84 The previous two paragraphs draw on Patricia E. Roy, "McBride of McKenna-McBride: Premier Richard McBride and the Indian Question in British Columbia," *BC Studies* 172 (Winter 2011-12): 35-76.

85 Rev. R.G. MacBeth to McBride, 2 March 1904, McBride to Bowser, 4 March 1904, GR441, v.81; *Province*, 10 January 1913; *Sun*, 11 January and 11 February 1913.

86 *Times*, 20 February 1912, 17 and 20 February 1913; McBride to Mrs. G. Grant, 5 March 1913, GR441, v.44; *Colonist*, 20 February and 18 August 1912, 30 April 1914; *Province*, 25 October 1912, 10 December 1913, 31 January and 14 February 1914; McBride to Mrs. Minden Cole, 6 November 1913, GR441, v.53; *Nelson Daily News*, 15 February 1913; *News-Advertiser*, 16 February 1913; McBride to Mrs. Gordon Grant, 20 February and 5 March 1913, GR441, v.393.

87 *Colonist*, 27 March 1912, 2 and 3 November 1912, 24 September 1916; *The Week*, 17 August 1912, 2 and 31 January 1914, 14 February 1914.

88 *The Week*, 29 June 1912; *Colonist*, 1 and 12 October 1912. Mary did not attend; she may have been away at school.

89 Interview with Mrs. Cornwall, quoted in Peter Roberts Hunt, "The Political Career of Sir Richard McBride" (master's thesis, University of British Columbia, 1953), 140. Lady McBride accompanied her daughters to school in the East, and they returned to Victoria for the

summer holidays. *The Week,* 3 October 1914, 5 and 19 June 1915; *Times,* 9 and 22 July 1914, 26 December 1914, 25 May and 18 July 1915; McBride to Mary, 28 September [1913], McBF.

90 By 1913, McBride's salary consisted of the basic MLA's indemnity of $1,200, $3,000 as premier, and $6,000 as minister of mines. The salary attached to the Mines portfolio probably influenced his decision to hold it. Salary figures were published annually in the public accounts. These figures are from *Public Accounts, 1913,* in BCSP, 1914, C32, C34, and C50. *Times,* 12 November 1912. One afternoon, while bringing the girls home from St. Margaret's School, the chauffeur hit a woman and child and was charged with reckless driving. The *Colonist* mentioned the accident but did not link it with McBride. *The Week,* 29 June 1912; *Colonist,* 1 and 12 October 1912. Invoices for his automobiles and school fees are in GR441, v.153. Thank you to Patrick Dunae for the census references. Mother to McBride, 5 February and April 1913, MS347, v.1. Occasionally, McBride's mother and, more often, his sister Dodo came to Victoria; the older McBride girls spent their holidays with their grandmother and aunt.

91 The many documents relating to McBride's personal investments are incomplete. The files on investments and T.P. O'Connor are in GR441, v.120, MS347, and McBF. In 1918, the liquidator reported that almost all of the Prudential Investment Company's assets had been "hypothecated" and that most accounts receivable were uncollectible. Yorkshire & Canadian Trust Co. to creditors and shareholders of National Finance Company in liquidation, 31 July 1918, McBF.

92 McBride to J.E. Smart, 8 and 11 December 1913, McBF. The group later moved its interest from James Island to the small Parker Island, off the west shore of Galiano Island in the Gulf Islands.

93 Agreement to take up stock in "Colwood Land Company," 26 March 1913, McBride to J.A. Sayward, 30 September 1914, McBride to Colwood Land Co., 7 December 1914, McBF.

94 "Celebration of 10th Anniversary of the Establishment of Party Government within the Province of British Columbia, 2 June 1913," copy in McBF. Conservatives called the celebration a "pronounced success." *Columbian,* 3 and 4 June 1913; *Province,* 3 June 1913; *Nelson Daily News,* 14 May 1913; *News-Advertiser,* 22 May 1913; *The Week,* 31 May 1913; *Colonist,* 31 May 1913, 1 and 3 June 1913; *Sun,* 2 and 3 June 1913; *New Westminster Daily News,* 2 June 1913.

95 In 1912, Ottawa proposed that grants to the provinces for highway construction should be made on a per capita basis, a suggestion rejected by the Senate. Thomas Taylor, the BC minister of public works, noted that the scheme would be unfair to his province, where construction costs were high because of its terrain. *Colonist,* 17 May 1912.

96 *Colonist,* 30 May 1912; Gosnell to McBride, 14 September 1912, GR441, v.111. Gosnell hired Fred Cook of the press gallery to do research in the archives and Parliamentary Library. Cook expected British Columbia to refer to alleged losses caused by delays in completing the CPR as part of its case. Liberal railway lawyers Zebulon A. Lash and E.V. Bodwell approved of Cook as commission secretary. The federal government was prepared to hire him if McBride approved. Fred Cook to Borden, 17 July 1913, RLBP, 129103ff; Perley to Borden, 8 July 1913, RLBP, 7488; *Colonist,* 30 May 1912; Gosnell, Memo re Better Terms Brief to Commission, c. November 1912, GR441, v.116.

97 *Globe,* 8 November 1912; *Manitoba Free Press,* 8 November 1912; *Province,* 30 November 1912; *News-Advertiser,* 19 March 1913; McBride to Borden, 18 March 1913, RLBP, 7399; McBride to F.J.S. Hopwood, 28 April 1913, MS347, v.1; Hopwood to McBride, 16 May 1913, GR441, v.122; McBride to Borden, 12 June 1913, RLBP, 129106; Borden to L. Harcourt,

21 June 1913, RLBP, 129108; Lash to Borden, 10 July 1913, RLBP, 129127; Lash and Bodwell to Borden, 22 July 1913, RLBP, 129142ff; Lash to Perley, 2 August 1913, RLBP, 129153; Lash to Perley, 1 August 1913, RLBP, 129154; Perley to Lash, 25 July 1913, RLBP, 129146; Borden to Perley, 7 and 9 July 1913, RLBP, 129124ff.

98 Gosnell to McBride, 8 August 1913, GR441, v.138; Bowser to Borden, 26 September 1913, RLBP, 129158; Borden to Bowser, 6 October 1913, RLBP, 129162.

99 Christopher Armstrong, *The Politics of Federalism: Ontario's Relations with the Federal Government, 1867-1942* (Toronto: University of Toronto Press, 1981), 120-26. Brief accounts of the conference are in *CAR*, 1913, 705-6, and J.A. Maxwell, *Federal Subsidies to the Provincial Governments in Canada* (Cambridge, MA: Harvard University Press, 1937), 133-36. McBride to Borden, 24 June 1913, RLBP, 7472ff; McBride to Bowser, 11 September 1913, GR441, v.52; *News-Advertiser*, 29 October 1913.

100 *Times*, 21 November 1913, 14 January and 3 March 1914; *Sun*, 24 November 1913; *Inland Sentinel*, 26 November 1913; *Colonist*, 1 April 1914; E.L. Newcombe, Department of Justice, Memorandum, 26 December 1913. Most of the extensive correspondence, including a copy of the Department of Justice Memorandum, is in GR441, v.138. See also McBride to Borden, 24 April 1914, MS347, v.1; *Times*, 17 July 1914. Convinced that the arguments regarding the railway were important, Gosnell had simply moved them to an appendix.

101 Borden to McBride, 20 July 1914, McBride to Borden, 25 July 1914, Gosnell to McBride, 24 March 1915, GR441, v.139; McBride to Borden, 22 September 1914, McBride to Borden, 18 January 1915, GR441, v 138; Borden to McBride, 12 March 1915, RLBP, 5378l; Maxwell, *Federal Subsidies*, 128; BCLJ, *Journals*, 29 March 1916, 43.

102 Robert Craig Brown, *Robert Laird Borden: A Biography* (Toronto: Macmillan, 1980), 1:225-26; *Times*, 27 February 1913; *Province*, 10 July 1914; *Colonist*, 25 and 31 January 1912, 13 April 1912, 1 June 1913.

103 Charles W. Humphries, *'Honest Enough to Be Bold': The Life and Times of Sir James Pliny Whitney* (Toronto: University of Toronto Press, 1985), 204-5; Churchill to McBride, [26 December 1911], extract with McBride to Hazen, 31 January 1912, RLBP, 67260; *CAR*, 1912, 49, 21.

104 Macrae to *Colonist*, 11 May 1912, Churchill to McBride, 26 April 1912, McBride to Borden, 12 May 1912, GR441, v.147; *Times*, 22, 27, 28, and 30 May 1912; *Colonist*, 13 April, 31 May, and 12 June 1912; *Sun*, 13 April and 28 May 1912; *The Times* (London), 27 May 1912; McBride to Blakemore, 30 May 1912, McBride to Mayor Worthington, Chilliwack, 28 August 1912, GR441, v.392.

105 McBride to Churchill, 8 and 18 June 1912, Draft Memo for Publication from Admiralty, 20 September 1912, WCA, v.13; *Sun*, 25 July and 3 August 1912; *Times*, 27 July 1912; Borden to McBride, 17 October 1912, GR441, v.116; Brown, *Robert Laird Borden*, 1:238.

106 McBride to Churchill, 18 June 1912, WCA, v.13; *Times*, 30 May 1912, 14 and 15 June 1912; *Columbian*, 14 June and 16 September 1912; *Colonist*, 14 June, 14 September, and 26 October 1912; *Sun*, 14 June 1912; *New Westminster Daily News*, 15 June 1912; *Port Alberni News*, 26 June 1912; *Calgary Herald*, 29 June and 1 July 1912; *Province*, 8 July 1912; *Toronto Globe*, 13 September 1912; *The Times* (London), 14 and 16 September 1912.

107 Borden, Diary, 7 November 1912, RLBP, v.449. The confidential and secret communications from the Admiralty may have been a memo from Churchill that was so sensitive that Borden was not allowed to let it leave his hands. Borden to McBride, 4 October 1912, GR441, v.116; Henry Borden, ed., *Robert Laird Borden: His Memoirs* (Toronto: Macmillan, 1938), 1:402; *Colonist*, 26 and 31 October 1912; *Ottawa Evening Journal*, 8 November 1912;

Montreal Daily Star, 8 November 1912; *Times*, 31 October and 18 November 1912; *Province*, 7 November 1912.

108 Churchill to McBride, 9 December 1912, McBF; McBride to Francis J.S. Hopwood, 24 April 1913, MS347, v.1; Gilbert Norman Tucker, *The Naval Service of Canada* (Ottawa: King's Printer, 1952), 1:190; *Colonist*, 5 December 1912, 22 January 1913; *Province*, 22 January 1913; *Times*, 22 January 1913; *Sun*, 22 January 1913.

109 Hopwood to McBride, 16 March 1913, GR441, v.122; Hopwood to Churchill, 16 May 1913, WCA, v.13/19/103; Hopwood to McBride, 9 July 1913 and 19 December 1914, McBride to Hopwood, 13 June 1912 and 24 April 1913, MS347, v.1. Hopwood initially opposed a commission but later thought that it might have produced a "definite and well considered" policy. The Vancouver branch of the Navy League wanted to buy the *Egeria*, a former Admiralty surveying ship, for training, but neither the provincial nor the federal government would contribute, the public was not "keen" to subscribe, and most of the fewer than forty boys who signed on subsequently left. J.F. Garden to McBride, 8 November 1912, GR441, v.48; T.E. Julian to Strathcona, 10 March 1913, GR441, v.50; Brown, *Robert Laird Borden*, 1:240; *News-Advertiser*, 14 March and 25 May 1913; *The Times* (London), 15 March and 2 August 1913; *Province*, 26 May, 3 June, and 28 July 1913; *Times*, 26 and 29 May 1913; McBride to editor, *Montreal Star*, 30 May 1913, GR441, v.121; *Columbian*, 3 June 1913; *Colonist*, 29 May, 26 July, and 3 August 1913.

110 *The Times* (London), 11 October 1913. Borden asked for a Canadian voice in imperial foreign policy. This was less than McBride had suggested and may reflect his earlier interest in imperial federation. The *Colonist* published the full text of his Carlton Club speech on 23 November 1913. Churchill to McBride, 28 August 1913, McBride to Churchill, 29 August 1913, McBF; *Province*, 18 August and 4 September 1913; Borden to Churchill, 14 August 1913, Churchill to Borden, n.d. [may be a draft], WCA, v.13; *London Morning Post*, quoted in *Sun*, 28 August 1913; *Colonist*, 28 October 1913; *Times*, 14 November 1913.

111 Conservative papers believed that McBride accurately expressed BC opinion. *Colonist*, 28 October 1913; *News-Advertiser*, 28 October 1913. Liberal papers disagreed. *Sun*, 29 October 1913; *Prince Rupert Daily News*, 4 October 1913. McBride also spoke to Toronto's Empire Club on the naval question. *Colonist*, 23 October 1913, 2 and 6 November 1913; *The Times* (London), 28 October 1913; *Columbian*, 28 October 1913; *Times*, 28 October and 7 November 1913; *Sun*, 29 and 30 October 1913, 8 November 1913; *Province*, 29 October 1913; *Alberni Advocate*, 7 November 1913; *Prince Rupert Daily News*, 17 November 1913. The *Times* published extracts from eastern papers.

112 Borden, Diary, 27 October 1913; RLBP, v.449; Churchill to Borden, [19 October 1913], WCA, v.13; McBride to Hopwood, 21 November 1913, Hopwood to McBride, 19 December 1913; McBride to Churchill, 19 November 1913, MS347, v.1; *Sun*, 28 November 1913; *Columbian*, 28 November 1913; *Times*, 4 February 1914; *Province*, 28 November 1913. The Royal Navy complicated McBride's problems by having a ship repaired in Seattle, even though "capable local companies tendered." McBride to Churchill, 15 January 1914, MS347, v.1.

113 *Sun*, 3 April and 19 June 1912; *Colonist*, 23 and 26 May 1912, 19 September and 23 October 1913; *Times*, 19 September and 6 November 1913; *Columbian*, 27 September 1913; *The Times* (London), 3 May 1912; *Province*, 4 September 1913; *The Week*, 25 May 1912.

114 Savoy Hotel bill, GR441, v.153/4; *Province*, 18 August, 10 September, and 14 October 1913; *News-Advertiser*, 13 August 1913; *Colonist*, 12 August 1913; *The Times* (London), 14 October 1913.

115 He appears to have ignored Dalhousie University's request for a "very handsome" donation.

Perhaps still hoping for a donation, Dalhousie offered him an honorary degree a month later, but he declined it because he did not have time to go to Halifax. As premier, he had many local obligations such as donating to party funds and charities, and paying for such things as the McBride Cup for an Interior hockey league. A.S. Mackenzie to McBride, 6 February 1913, GR441, v.120; *Nelson Daily News,* 6 February 1913.
116 This may have been the family of D'Arcy Tate, who was originally from Belfast.
117 McBride, Diary, 1913, passim, McBF; "Dad" to Mary, [28 September 1913], McBF.
118 McBride, Diary, 18 March to 17 April 1913, McBF. The diary has no entries between 28 March and 16 April inclusive. Other entries consist of only a few words each day. *Province,* 18 August 1913; *Sun,* 9 October 1913; *Colonist,* 20 November 1912, 18 September 1913; *Times,* 23 November 1912, 24 January 1914; McBride to R.F. Green, 9 May 1913, MS347, v.l; Borden, Diary, 17 August 1913, RLBP, v.449 ; *The Week,* 29 June 1912.
119 *Times,* 24 August 1912, 13 April 1913; *Sun,* 10 December 1912, 13 and 28 May 1913, 12 and 26 August 1913, 12 November 1913, 26 January and 3 February 1914. The comment about Connaught's approval was at least third-hand. J.H.S. Matson quoted Colonel Davidson as saying that the Connaughts were anxious to see McBride join the British cabinet. J.H.S. Matson to McBride, 8 December 1912, McBF.

CHAPTER 7: OPTIMISM CHALLENGED

1 McBride to Borden, 31 July 1914, GR441, v.395; *Colonist,* 1 and 2 August 1914; *CAR,* 1914, passim; Jeffrey A. Keshen, *Propaganda and Censorship during Canada's Great War* (Edmonton: University of Alberta Press, 1996), ch. 1.
2 McBride to Borden, 4 August 1914, RLBP, 20766; Borden to McBride, 5 August 1914, RLBP, 20770; Harcourt to Governor General, 9 August 1914, RLBP, 20774; Borden, Diary, 5 August 1914, RLBP, v.449; *Colonist,* 5 and 6 August 1914; *News-Advertiser,* 11 August 1914; Borden to McBride, 25 August 1914, GR441, v.601. Unless otherwise noted, this account draws on Gilbert Norman Tucker, *The Naval Service of Canada* (Ottawa: King's Printer, 1952), 1:ch. 13, the fullest account of the submarines. The cheque, signed by William Allison and Price Ellison, was to the order of the premier and endorsed by him payable to Lieutenant H.B. Pilcher, the senior naval officer at Esquimalt (copy in RLBP, 20764-5).
3 *Colonist,* 7 August and 6 October 1915; McBride to Borden, 6 August 1914, McBride to Borden, 26 September 1914, MS347, v.1; "Memorandum on Defence Measures by Capt. and Senior Naval Officer, Esquimalt, 26 September 1914," McBF; McBride to Lt. Col. Flick, 19 August 1914, GR441, v.167.
4 McBride, Diary, 3-15 August 1914, McBF. These are the first entries in his diary for 1914, suggesting that McBride recognized the importance of the events that were unfolding; as usual, they are brief. *Sun,* 10 October 1914; *Province,* 26 October 1914; *Colonist,* 27 October 1914, 6, 18, 24, and 25 November 1914; *Times,* 9 November 1914. The *Province,* 6 November 1914, reported that McBride conferred with Borden at Hot Springs, Virginia. According to Robert Craig Brown, *Robert Laird Borden: A Biography* (Toronto: Macmillan, 1980), 2:20, Borden did not leave Ottawa until 23 October, and McBride sailed from New York on 24 October, so this is unlikely. His diary does not mention such a trip.
5 McBride to Borden, 3 August 1914, GR441, v.121. McBride took a similar stance regarding Indian immigrants. In 1915, when the Colonial Office inquired about immigration from India, McBride told Borden that British Columbians appreciated the contributions of

India to the war effort but that "without in any way suggesting racial prejudice, or anything savouring of ill-will to our Indian brothers, we have in British Columbia and in Canada our own economic existence and social standards to maintain." He feared that "unrestricted immigration from India would literally swamp on in British Columbia without diminishing the population there to any appreciable extent." McBride to Borden, 6 July 1915, RLBP, 17901. See Hugh Johnston, *The Voyage of the* Komagata Maru: *The Sikh Challenge to Canada's Colour Bar* (Delhi: Oxford University Press, 1979; repr., Vancouver: UBC Press, 1989).

6 *Columbian,* 27 January 1915; W.R. Ross to McBride, 29 January 1915, GR441, v.64; McBride to Kahuchi Abe, 21 July and 2 August 1915, GR441, v.64; McBride to Borden, 26 June 1914, MS347, l.

7 McBride to Borden, 14 September 1914, RLBP, 22190; *The Times* (London), 8 September 1914; *Province,* 5 September 1914; *Colonist,* 19 September 1914, 18 and 24 November 1914.

8 Canada, *An Act to incorporate the Bank of Vancouver,* 7-8 Edw. 7, c. 166; *Province,* 30 July 1910; F.W. Howay, *British Columbia from the Earliest Times to the Present* (Vancouver: S.J. Clarke, 1914), 1:650. The founders of the Bank of Vancouver included W.H. Malkin, a wholesale grocer, R.P. McLennan, a hardware merchant, and H.T. Ceperley, a realtor, all of Vancouver, as well as several Victoria associates and J.A. Harvey of Chilliwack.

9 Deputy Minister of Finance to D.H. Wilkie, 21 January 1914, Wilkie to T.C. Boville, 11 February 1914, BofVL; McBride to Wilkie, 27 January 1914, McBride to W.T. White, 9 February 1914, McBride to Frederick Williams Taylor and E.L. Pease, 6 February 1914, McBride to Taylor, 25 February 1914, McBride to Shatford, 25 February 1914, MS347, v.1; Bank of Vancouver, *Fourth Annual Report, at Annual General Meeting, 12 January 1914* (Vancouver: Bank of Vancouver, 1914); Henry F. Ross [?], Memo for the Minister of Finance and Treasury Board, n.d. [c. late March 1914], BofVL.

10 In early July 1914, von Alvensleben wrote from Vienna to Harold Mayne Daly, a sometime Vancouver stock broker and Ottawa lawyer, that the bank's manager, Charles G. Pennock, should be replaced by Shatford. Von Alvensleben believed that McBride wanted "to get rid of Shatford" and that despite "certain obligations" to him, would prefer to see him as a director of the bank rather than as a cabinet minister. However, getting Pennock to resign required a buy-out of $10,000. In return for creating a position for Shatford, von Alvensleben wanted the government to give the Bank of Vancouver a certain percentage of the deposits it placed in banks. Shortly thereafter, Shatford became the manager but did not resign from the Legislature. Von Alvensleben to H.M. Daly, 6 July 1914, LAC, H.M. Daly Papers, v.1.

11 D.R. Wilkie to W.T. White, 12 November 1914, BofVL; W.J. Bowser to R.P. McLennan, 9 November 1914, Auditor General to Minister of Finance, 9 November 1914, GR441, v.61; McBride to Alexander Laird, 9 December 1914, GR441, v.396; *Colonist,* 15 December 1914. When the bank was finally wound up during the 1930s, most depositors received six and a half cents on the dollar. The liquidators paid off $890,000 against liabilities of $1,126,242. A lawyer who had deposited three dollars as a child got twenty-two cents. *Province,* 20 December 1934.

12 *Sun,* 24 February 1914; *CAR,* 1914, 696; *Province,* 2 February 1915; McBride to Borden, 9-10 May 1914, RLBP, 11790; *Ninth Annual Report and Proceedings of the Annual General Meeting, Dominion Trust, 24 February 1914* (Vancouver: Dominion Trust, 1914), 8-9; [Bowser] to [McBride], c. 20 October 1914, GR441, v.396. Most of the 380 outfits in the province that called themselves trust companies were marginal operations, and only a handful were registered under the law. The B.C. Permanent Trust also feared a run, but the Canadian

Bankers Association rescued it. David Deane to McBride, 30 December 1914, GR441, v.63. The file has many similar letters.
13 *Colonist*, 11 December 1914.
14 *Colonist*, 23 December 1914, 6 January 1915; *Inland Sentinel*, 9 January 1915; *Province*, 5 January and 18 February 1915; McBride to J.S. Cowper, 4 February 1915, GR441, v.397.
15 *Sun*, 9 and 21 January 1915, 10 February 1915; *Times*, 11 December 1914, 18 November 1915; *Colonist*, 9 January 1915; McBride to Frank Carell, 18 October 1915, GR441, v.69.
16 Provincial Revenues, Expenditures, and Deficits, 1912-16

Year	Revenues	Expenditures	Deficit
1912-13	$12,284,472.66	$15,301,061.94	$3,116,590.88
1913-14	10,224,864.40	15,550,729.03	5,475,864.81
1914-15	7,758,999.42	11,530,354.39	4,178,613.19
1915-16	6,106,502.43	9,235,084.68	3,791,810.87

Source: British Columbia in the Canadian Confederation: A Submission Presented to the Royal Commission on Dominion-Provincial Relations by the Government of the Province of British Columbia (Victoria: King's Printer, 1938), 178, 240-41, 245-46.

17 *Times*, 9 November 1914; McBride to Borden, 26 August 1914, GR441, v.396; *Nelson Daily News*, 29 October 1914; British Columbia, Minister of Mines, *Annual Report, 1915* (Victoria: King's Printer, 1916), K15.
18 *Colonist*, 20 and 26 August 1914; *The Week*, 29 August 1914; A.T. Goward, Diary, 25 August 1914, BCERR, b.345; McBride to Borden, 14 September 1914, RLBP, 22181; McBride to District Manager, Hudson's Bay Company, 11 September 1914, McBride to R.V. Pratt, 16 September 1914, GR441, v.396.
19 Patricia E. Roy, "Vancouver: 'The Mecca of the Unemployed,' 1907-1929," in *Town and City: Aspects of Western Canadian Urban Development*, ed. Alan F.J. Artibise (Regina: Canadian Plains Research Centre, 1981), 393-413; A.E. Planta to McBride, 29 August 1914, GR441, v.156; McBride to David Irvine, 13 November 1915, GR441, v.69; McBride to T.R. Stockett, 15 December 1914, GR441, v.397.
20 *Colonist*, 28 November 1914; *Times*, 25 September 1914; *Sun*, 10 and 15 October 1914; McBride to Rev. A.E. Cooke, 30 September 1914, GR441, v.166; *Port Alberni News*, 2 December 1914.
21 McBride to Wm. Manson, 11 December 1914, McBride to Robert Gaw, mayor, Grand Forks, 11 December 1914, GR441, v.166; *Times*, 6 November 1914; Alexander Robinson to McBride, 19 March 1915, GR441, v.64.
22 *Colonist*, 4 September 1915; McBride to A.W. Currie, 30 September 1915, MS347, v.1; *Port Alberni News*, 6 January and 6 October 1915; *Province*, 29 October 1915.
23 *Colonist*, 26 August 1914; *Sun*, 16 November 1914; *Province*, 2 December 1914.
24 W.E. Scott to McBride, 16 January 1915, McBride to H.H. Stevens and others, 24 February 1915, GR441, v.66; Stevens to McBride, 2 March 1915, GR441, v.65; Thomas Cunningham to McBride, 25 August 1915, GR441, v.67.
25 McBride to A. Williamson Taylor, 12 March 1915, GR441, v.398; *Omineca Herald*, 22 October 1915; *McBride Journal*, 7 May 1915.
26 *Colonist*, 1 January 1915; *Columbian*, 4 and 27 January 1915; *Times*, 27 January 1913.
27 McBride to Charles Wilson, 11 January 1915, McBride to Bernhard Scholte and Co., 7 and 11 January 1915, GR441, v.397. Mayor A.W. Gray of New Westminster, however, was optimistic about raising funds, since he had discussed the possible issue of treasury bonds.

Columbian, 15 February 1915; *Colonist,* 9 January 1915; McBride to J.H. Turner, 9 December 1915, GR441, v.68; *Times;* 13 December 1915.

28 Bradford W. Heyer to McBride, 19 September 1914, McBride to Thomas Kitchin, 21 September 1914, J.A. Pelkey to McBride, 21 September 1914, McBride to Wm. Maiden, 28 September 1914, McBride to W.J. McMillan, 21 and 23 September 1914, J.H. Turner to McBride, 27 January 1915, GR441, v.156; *Colonist,* 26 August and 22 September 1914; McBride to Stevens, 21 September 1914, GR441, v.396; Bank of Montreal, New Westminster, to McBride, 5 and 13 October 1914, McBF; British Columbia, *An Act to Confer Certain Powers on the Lieutenant-Governor-in-Council respecting Contracts Relating to Land,* 5 Geo. 5, c. 35.

29 *Colonist,* 26 August 1914. In an attempt to ease the industry's problems, and under pressure from the banks, the government lifted the ban on log exports. Stephen Gray, "The Government's Timber Business: Forest Policy and Administration in British Columbia, 1912-1928," *BC Studies* 81 (Spring 1989): 32; McBride to R.L. Reid, 8 October 1915, GR441, v.399; Ernest W. Leberson to W.R. Ross, 21 January 1915, GR441, v.145; *Sun,* 20 and 24 February 1915; *Colonist,* 11 and 20 February 1915; McBride to Manager, Royal Trust, Montreal, 15 March 1915, GR441, v.398.

30 MacMillan also made some sales in South Africa, but he had no success in India. R.H. Sperling, the recently retired general manager of the BCER, asked McBride for letters of introduction to the War Office and the Admiralty in order that he might try to get orders for lumber and other products produced by the companies in which he was interested.

31 McBride to E.W. Falls, 17 August 1915, GR441, v.399; Ken Drushka, *HR: A Biography of H.R. MacMillan* (Madeira Park: Harbour, 1995), 78; *Province,* 25 November 1914; McBride to George Foster, 13 January 1915, GR441, v.397; H.R. MacMillan to Minister of Lands, 27 August 1914, GR441, v.167; MacMillan to McBride, 14 September 1914, GR441, v.61; McBride to Capt. C. Gardner Johnson, 18 August 1915, GR441, v.127; *Colonist,* 13 March and 8 December 1915.

32 *Nelson Daily News,* 24 December 1914; McBride to Borden, 15 December 1914, GR441, v.397; McBride to W.T. White, 5 August 1915, McBride to Senator Lougheed, 5 August 1915, GR441, v.398; McBride to Borden, 1 September 1915, RLBP, 27611; H.H. Stevens to A.E. Kemp, 15 September 1915, RLBP, 27641; McBride to Borden, 20 September 1915, RLBP, 27645; McBride to Sen. Lougheed, 25 August 1915, S. Daily to McBride, 24 August 1915, GR441, v.131; A.E. Kemp to Borden, 14 September 1915, RLBP, 27638; Kemp to Borden, 20 September 1915, RLBP, 27647.

33 McBride to Borden, 16 September 1915, RLBP, 23444ff; Borden to McBride, 8 September 1915, RLBP, 27622; J.A. Lougheed to Borden, 22 September 1915, RLBP, 27654; Lougheed to Borden, 24 September 1915; RLBP, 27681; Borden to McBride, 23 September 1915, RLBP, 27677; Borden to Lougheed, 24 September 1915, RLBP, 27687; McBride to J. Hart, GR441, v.399; Borden, Diary, 10 October 1915, RLBP, v.449; Borden to McBride, 13 October 1915, RLBP, 27706.

34 Mann to McBride, 5 August 1914, GR441, v.156; McBride to Mann, 6, 7, and 18 August 1914, MS347, v.1; McBride to Edmund Walker, 27 August 1914, McBride to White, 16 September 1914, White to McBride, 7 December 1914, GR441, v.141; McBride to Borden, 27 August 1914, GR441, v.396; McBride to Borden, 9 September 1914, RLBP, 11918.

35 Borden to McBride, 16 December 1914, McBride to Mann, 28 January 1915, Mann to McBride, 5 February 1915, McBride to Mackenzie, 22 November 1915, Borden to McBride, 16 December 1914, McBride to Mackenzie, 27 August 1915, McBride to Mann, 28 January

1915, Mann to McBride, 5 February 1915, GR441, v.141; McBride to Mackenzie, 1 November 1915, McBride to L.W. Hill, 1 November 1915, GR441, v.399.

36 McBride to Mann, 7 August 1914, MS347, v.1; *Colonist,* 2 March 1915; *Times,* 24 November 1915.

37 *Province,* 14 August 1914; *Railway and Marine World,* October 1914, 465. Despite his earlier interest in extending the PGE to Alaska, McBride passed on to Borden several long letters from Frank O. Smith, a Maryland member of the US House of Representatives (1913-15) who wanted the United States to surrender the Alaska Panhandle to Canada in exchange for British Honduras. McBride to Borden, 15 September 1915, GR441, v.399, also in RLBP, 101762; Borden to McBride, 22 September 1915, RLBP, 101754. Borden and McBride agreed that neither of them could take the initiative and that the time was not opportune to consider such an exchange. *New York Times,* 31 October 1913; McBride to Wilfred Shore, Portland, Oregon, 7 September 1914, GR441, v.153. McBride enclosed copies of Stewart's letters of introduction.

38 *Colonist,* 25 October 1914; Borden to McBride, n.d., RLBP, 110053; British Columbia, *Proceedings and Evidence in re Pacific Great Eastern Railway Company Taken Before a Select Committee of the Legislature Appointed March 14th 1917* (Victoria: King's Printer, 1917), J83 (hereafter *PGE Inquiry*); McBride to Borden, 5 December 1914, RLBP, 110041; White to Borden, 7 December 1914, RLBP, 110043.

39 McBride to Borden, 11 March 1915, MS347, v.1; Borden to McBride, 10 April 1915, RLBP, 110056; McBride to Borden, 16 April 1915, RLBP, 110058; McBride to Margaret, [April] 1915, McBF; *Province,* 5 April 1915; *PGE Inquiry,* J385-86, J395.

40 *Colonist,* 10 December 1914, 2 March 1915.

41 *Sun,* 26 January and 4 February 1915; *Times,* 3 June 1914; *Inland Sentinel,* 21 June 1914; *Alberni Advocate,* 16 April 1915.

42 *Sun,* 31 July 1914, 30 January and 1 February 1915; *Times,* 26 February 1915.

43 Although he may have been more a victim than a perpetrator, Ellison had already embarrassed the government in a situation involving the Albion Trust Company, a local firm. Printed on the back of its money orders was his endorsement of its officers and directors, its plans, its large capital, and the experience that made "it an enterprise which will benefit the people of Western Canada as well as its stockholders." Remarking that this would probably embarrass the government, McBride asked Ellison to have the company withdraw the material featuring his endorsement. Since Ellison remained in the cabinet, he presumably succeeded in doing so. McBride to Price Ellison, 17 December 1912, 26 February 1913, MS347, v.1.

44 *Sun,* 22 and 28 February 1913, 17 January 1914, 2 and 3 March 1915; *Times,* 24 February 1913; Basil Gardom to McBride, 15 February 1915, Price Ellison to McBride, 25 February 1915, GR441, v.64; *Province,* 6 and 9 March 1915; *News-Advertiser,* 7 March 1915; *Colonist,* 7 March 1915; Price Ellison to McBride, 8 March 1915, GR441, v.66. Ellison ran in the 1916 general election but was defeated.

45 A.T. Goward to George Kidd, 8 March 1915, BCERR, b.131; Lottie Bowron, interviewed by Imbert Orchard, March 1962, BCA, Acc. 1288, tape 1 transcript; Borden, Diary, 11 March 1915, RLBP, v.449; McBride to Borden, 10 March 1915, MS347, v.l. McBride sent similar wires to federal cabinet ministers Frank Cochrane and Robert Rogers. Dissent was not new. In January 1912, without providing details, McBride said that, "as for the trials and troubles of a leader, in a small way I have had some rather exacting experiences here." McBride to Burrell, 21 January 1912, MS347, v.1; *Colonist,* 7, 9, and 10 March 1915.

46 It was later alleged that Young received $105,000 worth of shares in the Pacific Coast Coal Company in connection with its receiving foreshore rights. *Sun,* 22 October 1915; *Times,* 19 and 20 October 1915.
47 *Province,* 8 and 9 March 1915.
48 *Sun,* 8 March 1915; *Province,* 8, 9, 16, and 22 March 1915; McBride to R.J. Clarke and others, 10 March 1915, McBride to R.H. Green, 8 March 1915, MS347, v.l.
49 McBride to Charles Wilson, 16 March 1915, McBride to Green, 10 March 1915, MS347, v.l; *Province,* 16 March 1915; *Nelson Daily News,* 3 March 1913; *Times,* 3 and 6 March 1913; *Colonist,* 11 March 1915; *Omineca Miner,* 12 March 1915.
50 Goward to Kidd, 11 March 1915, BCERR, b.131; *Sun,* 12 March 1915; *Times,* 11 March and 4 October 1915.
51 *Times,* 19 and 30 March 1915; *Sun,* 12 and 18 March 1915.
52 *Colonist,* 26 March 1915; *Sun,* 27 March 1915; *Alberni Advocate,* 2 April 1915. Mackenzie of the CNR urged Borden to have McBride join the federal cabinet and said that he would accept the position. Borden, Diary, 5 March 1915, RLBP, v.449.
53 McBride, Diary, 2-6 November 1914, McBF; *Province,* 26 March, 22 April, and 21 June 1915; *Colonist,* 6 April and 9 May 1915; *Times,* 6 April 1915; *The Times* (London), 14 April 1915; McBride to Margaret McBride [April 1915], McBF; McBride to Frank Smythe, 26 May 1915, GR441, v.130; McBride to George Perley, 20 April 1915, McBride to Earl Grey, 21 April 1915, GR441, v.129; McBride to Edward Marsh, 26 April 1915, WCA, b.13; J.C.C. Davidson to McBride, 7 May 1915, GR441, v.120; McBride to Secretary, Overseas Prize Disposal Committee, 5 June 1915, GR441, v.130.
54 *Omineca Herald,* 23 July 1915; *Alberni Advocate,* 16 July 1915; *Sun,* 26 January and 11 February 1915, 1 and 18 June 1915; *Times,* 2 May 1915; *News-Advertiser,* 21 May 1915; *Columbian,* 25 June 1915; *Province,* 25 June 1915.
55 *Times,* 22 April and 19 June 1915; *Sun,* 7 May 1915; McBride to S.J. Gothard, 22 October 1915, GR441, v.132; Bowser to McBride, 11 May 1915, McBride to Bowser, n.d. [c. 12 May 1915], GR441, v.130.
56 Bowser to C.J. Doherty, 17 May 1915, Bowser to G.H. Barnard, 14 June 1915, Bowser to Borden, 16 June 1915, GR441, v.398; Bowser to Borden, 26 May 1915, RLBP, 80568; Robin Fisher, *Duff Pattullo of British Columbia* (Toronto: University of Toronto Press, 1991), 107.
57 *Province,* 14 June 1915; Borden, Diary, 24 June 1915, RLBP, v.449; *News-Advertiser,* 27 June 1915.
58 He arranged to donate twenty-five thousand cases of canned pink salmon to relieve distress in Britain. Because the pinks, though equally nutritious, were considered inferior to the sockeye that was normally sold in Britain, canners feared a challenge to their reputation for a superior product. McBride hoped that the donation would create a demand for pinks in Britain. McBride to Henry Doyle, 16 September 1914, GR441, v.396; *Colonist,* 4 December 1914. The London borough of Hackney received some of the salmon and was so pleased that it sent a framed address to McBride. R.E. Gosnell to S.S. Johnson, 3 March 1915, GR441, v.398.
59 *Colonist,* 6 and 10 July 1915; *Times,* 5 July 1915; *Province,* 5 July 1915.
60 *Colonist,* 26 February and 12 March 1915; *Nanaimo Free Press,* 28 July 1915; *Columbian,* 12 August 1915; McBride to R.D. Rorison, 10 December 1915, GR441, v.400.
61 *Times,* 11 October 1912; *Sun,* 3 October 1912, 20 January 1913; *Colonist,* 20 November 1915. For the history of Strathcona Park, see Paula Young, "Creating a 'Natural Asset': British Columbia's First Park, Strathcona, 1905-1916," *BC Studies* 170 (Summer 2011): 17-39.

62 *Colonist*, 22 August 1912, 17 April 1913, 27 January 1914, 17 August 1915; *Times,* 17 August 1915; *News-Advertiser,* 23 March 1913; *Province,* 14 January 1914; *Sun,* 18 January 1915; McBride to Francis Carter-Cotton, 26 May 1913, MS347, v.1; William C. Gibson, *Wesbrook and His University* (Vancouver: Library of the University of British Columbia, 1973), 120.

63 McBride to Wm. J. Goodwin, 18 January 1915, GR441, v.63. This file and v.397 include many such letters inquiring about the implementation of recommendations of the Royal Commission on Agriculture. McBride to W.H. Hayward, 23 February 1915, GR441, v.61; *Sun,* 2 March 1915; McBride to Mayor Jones, 17 March 1915, GR441, v.398; *Colonist,* 2 and 4 March 1915, 31 July 1915. A number of editors commented favourably on the Agricultural Credits Commission. For example, *Province,* 12 March 1915; *Fort George Herald,* 12 March 1915; *Sun,* 4 March 1915; *Omineca Herald,* 23 April 1915; W.J. Bowser to R.E. Hemphill, 27 April 1916, GR441, v.400.

64 *Colonist,* 28 November 1914, 6 March 1915; McBride to T.S. Brown, 26 November 1914, GR441, v.396; McBride to Herbert Cuthbert, 12 January 1915, GR441, v.166; *Sun,* 27 January 1915; *Times,* 4 September 1914, 21 and 30 January 1915; *Province,* 7 April 1915.

65 *Times,* 11 March 1915; *The Crisis in B.C.: An Appeal for Investigation* (Vancouver: Ministerial Union of the Lower Mainland of B.C., 1915).

66 *News-Advertiser,* 9 May 1915; *Columbian,* 2 June and 2 October 1915; A.E. Cooke to McBride, 6 May 1915, GR441, v.67; *Times,* 17 May 1915; *Colonist,* 9 May 1915; *Reply of the Hon. W.J. Bowser to the Pamphlet Entitled 'The Crisis in B.C.' Delivered in Orpheum Theatre, Vancouver, B.C. July 29, 1915,* copy in BCA, NWp971.5B788; *Sun,* 1 and 5 October 1915; *Province,* 4 October 1915.

67 *News-Advertiser,* 30 April 1915; *Columbian,* 17 and 19 May 1915; *Colonist,* 1 May 1915; *Sun,* 3 May 1915; *Alberni Advocate,* 7 May 1915; *Western Methodist Recorder,* May 1915, 8, and October 1915, 12.

68 Early in 1915, Manitoba Liberals charged that there had been extensive corruption in the construction of the Manitoba legislative buildings. A royal commission heard so much evidence of fraud that two weeks after its hearings began, Premier Rodmond P. Roblin resigned. The lieutenant-governor called on the Liberals under T.C. Norris to form a government. See W.L. Morton, *Manitoba: A History,* 2nd ed. (Toronto: University of Toronto Press, 1961), 341-56.

69 *Globe,* 18 June and 10 September 1915; *Saturday Night,* 31 July and 18 September 1915; *Colonist,* 19 May, 24 June, and 19 September 1915; *Sun,* 7 and 9 August 1915, 27 September 1915; *Omineca Herald,* 6 August 1915; McBride to editor, *Toronto Mail and Empire,* 1 September 1915, GR441, v.129; McBride to editor, *Christian Science Monitor,* 2 September 1915, GR441, v.399; *Nanaimo Free Press,* 16 September 1915; *Times,* 20 September 1915.

70 *Times,* 23 November 1915; *Province,* 25 November 1915; *Sun,* 27 November 1915; *The Crisis in B.C.,* 6.

71 Some of those involved with *The Crisis in B.C.* suffered for their efforts. Reverend G.R. Welch wrote to Premier H.C. Brewster, a fellow Baptist, that his work on the pamphlet had antagonized several members of his congregation at Vancouver's Central Baptist Church and that he was about to lose his job. Brewster expressed appreciation for his work but could not offer him a position in the government. G.R. Welch to H.C. Brewster, 6 November 1917, Brewster to Welch, 29 November 1917, GR441, v.18. Writing from the YMCA in Seattle, Moses Cotsworth, the author of the pamphlet, sent a plaintive plea to all the cabinet ministers asserting that he and his family had endured "seven strenuous

years of persecution by the tyrannous political machine" and that he had lost his life's savings and his home. There is no record of a reply. Moses Cotsworth to each cabinet minister, 3 January 1917, GR441, v.178.
72 *Province,* 4 October 1915; *Omineca Herald,* 19 March, 2 April, and 29 October 1915.
73 McBride to Mayor Alex Stewart (Victoria) and to other mayors, 17 September 1914, GR441, v.396; McBride to Rev. D. Spencer, 1 December 1914, GR441, v.61; *News-Advertiser,* 17 February 1915; A.J. Doull to McBride, 10 August 1915, McBride to Doull, 14 August 1915, GR441, v.129.
74 *The Week,* 21 August 1915; Meeting of representatives of Financial Interests, Vancouver, 16 August 1915, GR441, v.63. See Douglas L. Hamilton, *Sobering Dilemma: A History of Prohibition in British Columbia* (Vancouver: Ronsdale, 2004); Robert A. Campbell, *Demon Rum or Easy Money: Government Control of Liquor in British Columbia from Prohibition to Privatization* (Ottawa: Carleton University Press, 1991), ch. 1; *Columbian,* 18 August 1915; *Colonist,* 18 August 1915; McBride to Rev. Wm. Stevenson, 23 August 1915, McBride to Jonathan Rogers, 6 November 1915, GR441, v.399. McBride's reply to the People's Prohibition Movement is summarized in *Columbian,* 9 and 12 November 1915; McBride to Rogers, 30 November 1915, GR441, v.400; *Times,* 1 December 1915.
75 M.A. Tuck to McBride, 19 October 1915, GR441, v.63; *Times,* 26 November 1915; *Columbian,* 4 January 1915. Edward McBride advertised on 30 April 1914 and 24 September 1915. "Mother" to Richard McBride, 5 February 1913, MS347, v.1. Some New Westminster Conservatives complained that the Civic League "quashed every bottle license in the city" except for McBride's store. *Sun,* 18 March 1915, 10 and 11 November 1915; *Colonist,* 10 November 1915; *Nanaimo Free Press,* 10 and 13 November 1915; *Times,* 9 November and 2 December 1915.
76 *Colonist,* 13 December 1915; HCD, 11 February 1915, 94-116; *Sun,* 19 February 1915.
77 McBride to J.V. Paterson, 19 February 1915, MS347, v.1; Paterson to McBride, 22 February 1915, GR441, v.65; *Columbian,* 25 February 1915; *Colonist,* 25 February 1915; *News-Advertiser,* 25 February 1915; *Sun,* 26 February 1915.
78 McBride to Paterson, 9 March 1915, McBride to J.D. Hazen, 31 July 1915, GR441, v.127; Borden to McBride, 5 March 1915, McBride to Borden, 6 March 1915, McBride to Borden, 24 February 1915, GR441, v.65; *Sun,* 2 April 1915; *Times,* 14 July 1915; *Columbian,* 14 July 1915; *Colonist,* 14 July 1915.
79 The Liberals asked to be heard by the Davidson Commission. Davidson believed that anyone with information would come forward. The commission promised not to disclose its sources of information, and the auditor general provided ample data about the transaction. *News-Advertiser,* 7 April, 27 June, and 6 October 1915; *Times,* 6 April 1915, 6 January 1917; *Columbian,* 24 April, 5 October, and 13 November 1915; *Colonist,* 1 May and October 1915; *Sun,* 29 November 1914, 10 February 1916.
80 A rumour that the submarines would be taken out of commission briefly upset him. McBride to Borden, 6 January 1915, Borden to McBride, 7 January 1915, GR441, v.127; *The Times* (London), 19 November 1914; McBride to Borden, 5 December 1914, Borden to McBride, 8 December 1914, GR441, v.125; McBride to Borden, 21 December 1914, GR441, v.397; McBride to Borden, 26 January 1915, Borden to McBride, 26 January 1915, McBride to Borden, 3 February 1915, MS347, v.1.
81 *Colonist,* 6 February 1915; *Sun,* 9 February 1915; McBride to Franklin K. Lane, 21 December 1914, GR441, v.397.

82 McBride to Sam Hughes, 16 March 1915, MS347, v.1; McBride to Hughes, 17 September 1915, RLBP, 24229; McBride to Borden, 12 October 1915, RLBP, 25413.

83 Kingsmill, who was short of officers and instructors, thought that "slackers" might enlist as naval volunteers because they knew that doing so would probably exempt them from overseas service.

84 McBride to Borden, 28 January and 3 February 1915, Borden to McBride, 19 January 1915, MS347, v.1; McBride to Borden, 2 February 1915, RLBP, 109544; McBride to Borden, 16 February 1915, RLBP, 109548; McBride to Borden, 20 November 1914, RLBP, 12852ff; *Times*, 3 December 1914; McBride to Borden, 11 February 1915, GR441, v.127; Admiral Kingsmill to McBride, 3 November 1914, McBride to Borden, 25 November 1914, Borden to McBride, 28 November 1914, GR441, v.125; *Colonist*, 16 December 1914, 16 January 1915.

85 *Times*, 15 April 1913, 19 July 1915; *Province*, 25 November 1914; *Colonist*, 19 February and 8 July 1915.

86 He may not have visited Germany in 1912, but in 1913, he told his daughter Mary that he was on his way to Berlin. There is no evidence that actually got to Germany.

87 *Globe*, 12 September 1912; *News-Advertiser*, 14 September 1912; *Colonist*, 27 January 1912; *Province*, 16 June 1913; McBride to C.T.W. Piper, 8 September 1914, GR441, v.167.

88 *Times*, 10 September 1914; McBride to editors of all papers, 7 January 1915, GR441, v.125. The rumour linked Macrae with von Alvensleben, whom a Seattle newspaper purported to be a German spy. McBride considered suing the Seattle paper and calling in Pinkerton's detectives to unearth the author of the story. David Ricardo Williams, *Call In Pinkerton's: American Detectives at Work for Canada* (Toronto: Dundurn, 1998), 204-7.

89 McBride to John Adams, 18 August 1914, GR441, v.126; McBride to Sam Hughes, 5 March 1915, GR441, v.129; McBride to von Alvensleben, 20 August 1914, GR441, v.396; McBride to J.M. Langley, 18 September 1914, MS347, v.1; McBride to Borden, 3 December 1914, GR441, v.61.

90 Bowser's correspondence with federal authorities may be found in GR441, v.398.

91 *Colonist*, 8 August, 25 November, and 16 December 1914, 9 July, 5 August, and 24 October 1915; *Times*, 14 August 1914; *Sun*, 10 October 1914; *Columbian*, 9 October 1914; *Province*, 4 and 6 November 1914; McBride to Borden, 4 September 1915, RLBP, 115681.

92 *Colonist*, 21 March and 18 July 1915; *Times*, 18 July 1915. At its 1913 session, the Legislature had removed the tax exemption from church property. *The Week*, 12 December 1914, 30 January 1915.

93 R.F. Green to Borden, 22 September 1915, RLBP, 27661; *Sun*, 12 July, 12 August, and 1 September 1915; *News-Advertiser*, 12 August 1915; *Times*, 20 and 21 September 1915, 23 October 1915; Borden, Diary, 10 October 1915, RLBP, v.449; McBride to Borden, 2 November 1915, RLBP, 28742ff; Borden to McBride, 10 November 1915, MS347, v.1; *Colonist*, 3 March 1914.

94 *Times*, 6 and 18 November 1915, 13 December 1915; *Sun*, 9 November 1915.

95 "Tammany" was a reference to the Tammany Society, which ran the notoriously corrupt political organization of the New York City Democratic Party during the nineteenth and early twentieth centuries.

96 Borden, Diary, 28 November 1915, RLBP, v.449; *Times*, 15 December 1915, 6 January 1916; *Sun*, 16 and 22 December 1915, 6 January 1916; *Colonist*, 15 December 1915; *News-Advertiser*, 16 December 1915; *Nanaimo Free Press*, 16 December 1915; *Province*, 15 December 1915; *Western Methodist Recorder*, January 1916, 9; *Columbian*, 16 December 1915.

Chapter 8: Respite in London

1 *Colonist*, 15 December 1915; McBride to Borden, 24 December 1915, GR441, v.132.
2 *Colonist*, 15 and 19 December 1915; *Times*, 3 January 1916; *Sun*, 18 December 1915. The details of the negotiations between Turner, McBride, and Bowser may be found in Sheila Keeble, "An Infernal Triangle: How Richard McBride Became Agent-General," *B.C. Historical News* 13 (Spring 1980): 8-10.
3 *Times*, 29 and 30 December 1915, 5 and 24 January 1916; *Colonist*, 30 December 1915; *Columbian*, 4 and 6 January 1915; *The Week*, 8 January 1916; *Sun*, 7 January 1916; Civil Service to McBride, 5 January 1916, McBF.
4 *Times*, 8 February 1916; McBride to Bowser, 18 February 1916, Turner to Bowser, 13 January 1916, McBride to Bowser, 6 and 8 March 1916, McBride to Bowser, 24-25 August 1916, McBride to Bowser, 31 March 1916, W.E. Ross to Bowser, 28 April 1916, F. Kermode, memo, 12 May 1916, GR441, v.168.
5 *Province*, 15 December 1915; *Columbian*, 4 April 1916; McBride to Bowser, 6 March, 10 April, 27 June, and 7-8 July 1916, GR441, v.168; McBride to Borden, 22 March 1916, RLBP, 99340; McBride to Borden, 24 April 1917, GR441, v.183.
6 E.H. Heaps to McBride, 17 and 23 August 1916, McBride to Bowser, 26 August 1916, McBride to Bowser, 8 May 1916, GR441, v.168; Dianne Newell, *The Development of the Pacific Salmon-Canning Industry* (Montreal and Kingston: McGill-Queen's University Press, 1989), 157; Bowser to McBride, 3 August 1916, GR441, v.401; McBride to Brewster, 1 February 1917, GR441, v.176.
7 *Times*, 9 February 1916; Bowser to Borden, 27 April 1916, John Oliver and T.D. Pattullo to Frank Carvell, 19 November 1918, GR441, v.336. After the Liberals came to power provincially, Premier John Oliver and his minister of lands, T.D. Pattullo, took up the argument.
8 R.E. Gosnell to Brewster, 8 January 1917, GR441, v.175; *Times*, 26 January 1917.
9 McBride to Bowser, 14 July 1916, McBride to A. Steel-Maitland, 13 July 1916, GR441, v.168; McBride to Bowser, 6 March 1916, GR441, v.169; Brewster to G.W. Taylor, 7 February 1917, GR441, v.176.
10 *Columbian*, 19 December 1916, 13 March 1917; McBride to Bowser, 14 August 1916, GR441, v.174; H.J. Creedy to McBride, 23 May 1916, McBride to Bowser, 6 July, 28 July, and 5-6 September 1916, Bowser to McBride, 31 May 1916, GR441, v.172; F.C. Wade to Wilfrid Laurier, 17 July 1916, WLP, 192590; *Times*, 22 July 1916; *Sun*, 15 August 1916.
11 Elections British Columbia, *Electoral History of British Columbia, 1871-1986* (Victoria: Elections BC and Legislative Library, 1988), 413-16; H.C. Brewster to V.W. Odlum, 31 May 1917, LAC, V.W. Odlum Papers, v.20. A brief account of the overseas vote and the subsequent inquiry is in Douglas L. Hamilton, *Sobering Dilemma: A History of Prohibition in British Columbia* (Vancouver: Ronsdale, 2004), 110-23.
12 George Kidd to R.H. Sperling, 16 December 1915, BCERR, b.131.
13 G.E. Foster to M. Chisholm, 6 March 1915, LAC, George Foster Papers, v.102.
14 *Times*, 12 February and 6 March 1916. A brief account of the Vancouver and Victoria by-elections is in *CAR*, 1916, 752-58.
15 *Times*, 16 May and 1 August 1916; Brewster to Lieutenant-Governor, 26 May 1916, GR441, v.173; *Colonist*, 7 and 14 January 1917, 8 March 1917.
16 Bowser to Denis Murphy, 14 February 1916, GR441, v.400; *Province*, 18 May 1916; *Colonist*, 1 August 1917; *Sun*, 26 April 1915.

17 *Columbian*, 11 September 1916; *Times*, 7 August 1916; *Province*, 2 September 1916; *Nanaimo Free Press*, 1 April 1916. Parker Williams, the Socialist, retained his seat in Newcastle, and W.H. Hayward, an Independent who supported the Conservatives, won in Cowichan.
18 A summary of the select committee hearings may be found in *CAR*, 1917, 817-20, 833-34; Brewster to McBride, 17 May 1917, McBride to Brewster, 22 May 1917, GR441, v.183.
19 McBride to Peggy, 14 June 1916, McBF; *Times*, 28 June, 27 July, and 19 September 1916; *Columbian*, 8 July and 19 August 1916.
20 *The Times* (London), 7 August 1917; *Sun*, 5 January 1916. Salaries are from the annual *Public Accounts*. As premier and minister of mines, McBride had earned $9,100 per annum plus the sessional indemnity of $1,600. When J.H. Turner was agent-general, he earned $10,000 a year. *Times*, 15 March and 4 April 1916, 3 January and 2 May 1917; *Pacific Canadian*, 24 March 1916; *Province*, 2 March 1917.
21 D.M. Eberts to McBride, 5 May 1912, McBride to Eberts, 5 May 1912, GR441, v.147; T.P. O'Connor to McBride, 5 July 1913, M. Innes Patterson to McBride, 27 June 1913, McBride to Patterson, 30 June 1913, McBride to O'Connor, 15 April 1913, and other correspondence in GR441, v.120.
22 D.W. Higgins to McBride, 6 July 1915, GR441, v.121; Robertson, Heisterman and Tait to Bowron, 5 February 1917, MS347, v.2; McBride to Mann, 18 June 1914, McBF; McBride to Lottie Bowron, 9 December 1916, MS347, v.2; *Colonist*, 7 August 1917.
23 *Kamloops Standard-Sentinel*, 17 November 1916. Wade became agent-general in 1918. *Times*, 3 March 1917, citing *Province*, 2 March 1917; V.W. Odlum to Brewster, 30 April 1917, GR441, v.187.
24 Henry Jackson to Brewster, 19 May 1917, McBride to Brewster, 13 March 1917, GR441, v.183; Turner to Brewster, 3-5 March 1917, GR441, v.176; Borden, Diary, 1 and 24 April 1917, RLBP, v.449; *Province*, 1 May 1917.
25 *Colonist*, 20 May 1917; *Province*, 21 May 1917; *Sun*, 21 May 1917; *Nanaimo Free Press*, 12 May 1917.
26 McBride to Brewster, 15 May 1917, Turner to Brewster, 13 June 1917, McBride to Brewster, 9 June 1917, GR441, v.183; Turner to Brewster, 8 June 1917, GR441, v.189.
27 David Whiteside to Brewster, 8 July 1917, GR441, v.188; R.F. Green to Lottie Bowron, 10 August 1917, MS347, v.2; McBride to Brewster, 14 and 28 July 1917, GR441, v.89; Cyrus Peck to Brewster, 28-29 May 1917, GR441, v.183; Odlum to Brewster, 1 June 1917, GR441, v.187.
28 McBride's daughter Sheila was only four years old when he died so may not have attended his funeral. *Columbian*, 26 July 1917; *The Times* (London), 7 and 9 August 1917; *Colonist*, 7 August 1917.
29 *Columbian*, 6 and 7 September 1917; *Colonist*, 7 September 1917.
30 *The Week*, 11 August 1917; *Province*, 6 and 7 August 1917; *Colonist*, 7 August 1917; *Times*, 7 August 1917; *Omineca Miner*, 11 August 1917; *Sun*, 9 September 1917; *Kamloops Telegram*, 7 August 1917.

Conclusion

1 *Colonist*, 13 August 1911.
2 James Belich, "The Rise of the Angloworld: Settlement in North America and Australasia, 1784-1918," in *Rediscovering the British World*, ed. Phillip A. Buckner and R. Douglas Francis (Calgary: University of Calgary Press, 2005), 44.

3 Stenographic report of "Canada and the Empire" (speech to Empire Club, Toronto, 31 October 1913), McBF. The quoted passage was deleted from the printed speech, probably because it repeated points that had already been made.
4 Richard A. Rajala, *Clearcutting the Pacific Rain Forest: Production, Science, and Regulation* (Vancouver: UBC Press, 1998), 89.
5 *Province*, 12 September 1908. Subscribers could choose between a portrait of McBride or Borden.
6 *Province*, 23 January 1912.
7 Laurier to Bostock, 8 November 1910, WLP, 176336.
8 *CAR*, 1916, 780.
9 Pinkerton's report, 10 February 1906, quoted in Peter Roberts Hunt, "The Political Career of Sir Richard McBride" (master's thesis, University of British Columbia, 1953), 208.
10 S.J. Gothard to McBride, 5 October 1915, McBride to Gothard, 22 October 1915, GR441, v.132.

Epilogue

1 McBride's financial records and those of his estate are incomplete. In 1914, he had $47,000 in various insurance policies. How much this yielded in 1917 is not certain. Lady McBride may have received some funds directly rather than through the estate, or McBride may not have kept up the premiums.
2 At the same time, the Liberal government contributed the same amount to the estate of Premier H.C. Brewster, who had died in office in 1918 and left several young children as orphans.
3 *Columbian*, 27 April 1931. At the same time, the Tolmie administration gave a pension of $1,500 per annum to Mary Ellen Smith, the widow of the Liberal Ralph Smith, who was herself a former MLA. *Colonist*, 26 April 1931; *Times*, 25 June 1931.
4 The estate secured slightly over $2,000 by selling shares in the BC Permanent Loan and Savings Company. The Bank of Vancouver and the National Finance Company, however, were insolvent. McBride's shares in the Pacific Coast Fire Insurance Company had increased in value but had been pledged to the Imperial Bank as security for a loan, and it sold them for $7,500. The Richard McBride Fonds contain scattered references to Lady McBride's income.
5 *Columbian*, 7 August 1917; McBride to Percy Venables, 13 June 1912, GR441, v.112; McBride to Theodore Theroux, 11 September 1912, GR441, v.113; Probate of the Estate of Richard McBride, British Columbia, Probate Records, BCA, MfB08918, file 60-1918, v.210. Some real estate reverted for nonpayment of taxes. A property at Stave Lake sold for more than its inventory value but for less than the amount of the mortgage. By February 1930, the liabilities had been reduced to $44,000.
6 British Columbia, Probate Records, BCA, MfBB8918, file 60-1918.
7 J.K. Nesbitt, "Old Homes and Families," *Colonist*, 12 August 1951; *Colonist*, 26 July 1918, 6 May 1925, 3 June 1928; *Times*, 29 June 1920, 28 June 1921.
8 *Colonist*, 6 September 1929.
9 *Times*, 9 October 1920.
10 *Times*, 19 May 1925; *Province*, 31 May 1925.
11 *Times*, 13 November 1923.

12 *Sun*, 11 April 1928; *Times*, 11 April 1928.
13 British Columbia, *Public Accounts, 1931,* in BCSP,1932, N136. Anna earned $750 in the year ending 31 March 1931. Since her name does not appear earlier in the *Public Accounts,* it is possible that hers was a patronage appointment – the Conservatives had formed the government since 1928.
14 *Province,* 1 December 1934.
15 Darryl Lundy, comp., "Francis Basil Hood," The Peerage, http://thepeerage.com/p8182.htm.
16 *Times,* 10 December 1920, 19 January 1921, 6 February 1923; *Colonist,* 11 November 1920, 4 January 1921, 7 December 1926, 4 October 1929.
17 Sir Richard's mother, Mary McBride, died of senility on 31 October 1931 at Mrs. Bond's private hospital in Vancouver. Six days earlier, her son Edward had died of myocarditis complicated by nephritis. He had suffered from nephritis for ten to fifteen years, which suggests that the family had a genetic disposition to kidney disease.
18 *Columbian,* 14 March 1940, 26 September 1941.
19 Bowser made a similar statement in the 1920 provincial election campaign. *Colonist,* 30 September 1919, 16 November 1920, 10 June 1924.
20 *Colonist,* 8 July 1928; *Sun,* 11 February and 7 July 1928; *Revelstoke Review,* 11 July 1928.
21 *Colonist,* 16 September 1920, 20 February 1926; *Sun,* 18 August 1927.
22 *Sun,* 25 November 1929; *Times,* 8 February 1929, 13 January 1932.
23 *Prince Rupert Daily News,* 17 May 1937; *Province,* 29 November 1940; *Columbian,* 5 March 1946.
24 *Province,* 1 June 1945.

Note on Sources

1 Brian Ray Douglas Smith, "Sir Richard McBride: A Study in the Conservative Party of British Columbia, 1903-1916" (master's thesis, Queen's University, 1959); Peter Roberts Hunt, "The Political Career of Sir Richard McBride" (master's thesis, University of British Columbia, 1953).
2 For general histories, see Jean Barman, *The West beyond the West: A History of British Columbia* (1991; 3rd ed., Toronto: University of Toronto Press, 2007); Hugh M. Johnston, ed., *The Pacific Province: A History of British Columbia* (Vancouver: Douglas and McIntyre, 1996). For a study of politics, see John English, *The Decline of Politics: The Conservatives and the Party System, 1901-20* (Toronto: University of Toronto Press, 1977). For books devoted to transportation, see John A. Eagle, *The Canadian Pacific Railway and the Development of Western Canada* (Montreal and Kingston: McGill-Queen's University Press, 1989); T.D. Regehr, *The Canadian Northern Railway: Pioneer Road of the Northern Prairies, 1895-1918* (Toronto: Macmillan, 1976).
3 Margaret A. Ormsby, *British Columbia: A History* (1958; rev. ed., [Toronto]: Macmillan, 1971); Martin Robin, *The Rush for Spoils: The Company Province, 1871-1933* (Toronto: McClelland and Stewart, 1972).
4 Patricia E. Roy, "Railways, Politicians and the Development of Vancouver as a Metropolitan Centre, 1886-1929" (master's thesis, University of Toronto, 1963); Roy, "The British Columbia Electric Railway: A British Company in British Columbia, 1897-1928" (PhD thesis,

University of British Columbia, 1970); Roy, *A White Man's Province: British Columbia Politicians and Chinese and Japanese Immigration, 1858-1914* (Vancouver: UBC Press, 1989).

5 Patricia E. Roy, "McBride, Richard," in *Dictionary of Canadian Biography,* ed. Ramsay Cook (Toronto: University of Toronto Press, 1998), 14:673-78.

6 *Province,* 1 March 1913.

7 *The Week,* 1 March 1913. *The Week,* a Conservative paper, commented that "there never was a time when a Government was more in need of fair criticism" because of the lack of an Opposition. *Province,* 1 March 1913; *Sun,* 29 January 1914.

Note on Sources

It is surprising that apart from two master's theses written in the 1950s, McBride has not been well served by historians.[1] He typically gets no more than passing mention in general provincial histories or in national studies of politics or transportation.[2] Two exceptions are the relevant chapters in Margaret Ormsby's *British Columbia: A History* and Martin Robin's *The Rush for Spoils*.[3] The former is well researched and, though balanced, is generally laudatory, whereas the latter, whose title captures its thesis, draws extensively on Moses Cotsworth's muck-raking pamphlet *The Crisis in B.C.*

This biography began its life as an undergraduate essay in 1958, and I accumulated material relating to McBride for my master's thesis on railways in British Columbia, a PhD thesis on the BC Electric Railway, and a book on BC politicians and their dealings with the Chinese and the Japanese.[4] Much of the remaining research was done during the 1990s in preparation for the McBride entry in the *Dictionary of Canadian Biography*.[5]

The long gestation of this study has created problems and generated benefits. When I first frequented the British Columbia Archives, there were no finding aids, although a few boxes had labels such as "Canadian Northern Railway." I have tried to find the current volume number to what is now GR441 but have not always succeeded. In addition, some boxes that were once open have since been closed under access to information legislation, and a research agreement could compromise material collected years ago. The GR441 records are supplemented by two boxes, mainly of "private and confidential" correspondence collected by McBride's secretary Lottie Bowron during his final years.

Just as I was revising the manuscript, the McBride family donated a small collection of McBride's personal papers, photographs, and memorabilia to the British Columbia Archives. The centrepiece is a dozen pocket diaries. Although the diaries provided space for little more than a sentence per day, and McBride was not a systematic diarist, they did much to document his travels and occasionally his thoughts. A small collection of personal correspondence reveals him as a loving family man and provides detail on some of his travels, especially to Atlin. The financial records reveal that he was personally caught up and caught by the speculative boom that infected British Columbia in the early years of the twentieth century. I saw them before they were catalogued, so my references are to the Richard McBride Fonds.

The papers of other politicians, notably Prime Ministers Laurier and Borden, were also useful. The papers of Winston Churchill, located at the Churchill Library at Churchill College in Cambridge, throw additional light on the Better Terms campaign and the naval question. When I worked through the British Columbia Electric Railway Records, the only guide was an inventory prepared many years earlier by a company clerk. They have since been reboxed, so some box or file numbers may have changed.

My major sources, as the endnote citations testify, were newspapers. When it came to politics, most papers were clearly partial to one party or the other: the *Victoria Times* and later the *Vancouver Sun* could be relied upon to support the Liberals, whereas the *Victoria Colonist* and the *New Westminster British Columbian,* in which McBride had at least an indirect financial interest, were staunchly Conservative. The *Vancouver Province*, British Columbia's most important daily paper during the years under study, was basically Conservative but seldom blatantly partisan. Given its party's limited presence in the Legislature after 1909, the Liberal press sought to play the role of the Opposition. Biases show up most clearly on the editorial page but also affect news coverage. Mainly because the Liberal dailies and the weekly *Saturday Sunset* regularly carried cartoons, whereas the Conservative press did not, the cartoons that illustrate this volume tend to be critical of McBride. The *Province* sometimes printed a cartoon, but the *Colonist* and *Columbian* rarely did. *The Week,* a short-lived Victoria publication, also published cartoons, including some by Emily Carr.

Until the 1970s, the BC government did not publish Hansard, a full report of the legislative debates. In the McBride era, the Victoria and

Vancouver newspapers had shorthand reporters in the press gallery and printed detailed, though selective, almost verbatim accounts of the debates. For example, when W.H. Hayward, a Conservative, attacked the Department of Agriculture, the *Times* printed his criticism, but the *Colonist* did not. In 1913, when it was suggested that the government should sponsor a Hansard, McBride agreed but believed that "on the whole, the work of the parliament of British Columbia had been freely recognized by the newspapers of the province."[6] He promised to look into the matter but was probably deterred by the expense. A year later, he said that if any MLA wished to have his speech printed verbatim, the chief whips could arrange to have the *Colonist* publish it, to which the *Sun* rightly queried, "Why are only readers of the *Colonist* to see the speech verbatim?"[7]

Except for McBride's early years, when the *New Westminster British Columbian* was the main source, the Vancouver and Victoria newspapers were the most important sources of information about him and his government. For material regarding election campaigns and provincial tours, I consulted the regional press, although, when not dealing with local issues, it often echoed the metropolitan papers and in some cases reprinted their editorials.

Especially in Victoria and New Westminster, the press regularly carried reports on the social activities of McBride's wife, Margaret, and their six daughters. We know what Margaret and her older daughters wore to social events but little of their personalities. Similarly, the record contains relatively little of McBride's private opinions or what his contemporaries thought of him on non-political matters. Fortunately, in the 1960s, Imbert Orchard of the CBC interviewed some of McBride's contemporaries, and the anecdotes he recorded give a glimpse of McBride's personality, as do, of course, the handful of family letters.

Index

Note: "(i)" after a page number indicates an illustration.

Aberdeen, Lord, 187
Abriel, Thomas, 204(i)
Agassiz, B.C., 28, 34, 107, 130
agent-general, London, 2, 58, 148. *See also* McBride, Richard, political career in BC; Turner, J.H.
agriculture, 45, 105, 114, 148, 155, 222, 223-24, 232, 243, 271, 284-86, 317, 370n41; Royal Commission on, 222, 223-24, 271, 285, 286. *See also* fruit industry
agriculture credits, 280, 285, 384n63
Alaska Railway, 212, 294, 295, 326, 367n11, 382n37
Alberni, 125, 167, 169, 172, 237, 238(i), 270
Alberta, 113, 114, 123, 166, 172, 181, 213, 221, 274, 347n94, 365 n100, 369n28, 347n94
Alert Bay, 157, 235
aliens, 31, 46, 282, 295-96, 299, 372n63
Allan, Hugh, 114
Allison, Gertrude. *See* McBride, Gertrude
Allison, William, 21, 108, 215, 308-9, 331n25, 368n19, 378n2
Almond, J. McP., Rev. Canon, 314

American investment, 213, 217, 270, 273, 277, 286. *See also* forest industry
Amery, L.S., 187
Anarchist Mountain, 108
Anglican Church, 16, 19
Angloboom, 3, 317
Anglo-Japanese Alliance, 65, 179, 254, 265
Anglo-Japanese Treaty of Commerce and Navigation, 151, 207, 239
Arnold, W.R., 214, 267
Arrowhead, BC, 203
Ashcroft, BC, 52, 69, 78, 108, 155, 156, 171, 182, 207
Asiatic Exclusion League, 149, 354n69
Aspen Grove, BC, 52, 211, 367n8
Asquith, Prime Minister, 264, 362n63, 363n70
Assessment Act, 90, 342n44
Athalmer, BC, 156
Atkinson, J.L., 80
Atkinson, T.C., 24, 27
Atlin, BC, 41, 42-43(i), 45, 46, 85, 109, 124, 126, 157, 319, 335n33
auditor-general, 215, 267, 293, 310, 368n19
Australia, 5, 46, 223, 264, 273, 306

autonomy bills, 347n94
Aylesworth, Allen, 136

Babcock, J.P., 143, 353n52
"Back to the land," 173, 269, 270-71, 285-86
Baden-Powell, Robert, 187
Baker, James, 47
Balkan wars, 213
Bank of British North America, 214
Bank of Commerce, 86, 87, 89, 93, 217, 220, 275
Bank of Montreal, 87, 192, 266, 272, 321
Bank of Vancouver, 266-67, 379n8, 379n10, 379n11
Barkerville, BC, 108, 183
Barkley Sound, 162, 163, 170, 171
Barnard, Frank S., 302, 323
Barnard, G.H., 175, 191(i), 192, 194(i), 283
Basil, Chief, 244
Bastedo, S.T., 143
Baxter, T.S., 231, 340n14
B.C. Development Association, 247
B.C. House, London, 303-4, 307, 310, 312
B.C. Loggers Association, 105(i), 145
B.C. Permanent Loan and Savings, 88
Beaver Club, 213
Beck, Marshall, 323
Beck, Richard, 323
Behnsen, H.F.W., 296
Benn, A. Shirley, 310
Bennett, J.W., 359n31
Bennett, R.B., 79
Bennett, W.A.C., 327
Better Terms, 4-5, 34, 61, 65, 89, 92, 108, 109-17, 116(i), 119-20, 121, 126, 134-42, 152, 167, 182, 193, 194(i), 195-96, 205, 207, 209, 249-52, 306, 317, 318, 325, 346n88, 346n91, 347n95, 348n2, 375n96, 376. *See also* dominion-provincial relations
Blake, Edward, 29
Blakemore, William, 241-42, 374n81, 374n83
boards of trade: Associated Boards of Trade of Southeastern BC, 51; 145-46, 172n59; Hazelton, 236; Kamloops, 170; Kelowna, 206; Nelson, 144, 235; New Westminster, 59; Prince Rupert, 157; Revelstoke, 202; Vancouver, 46, 54, 90, 221, 222, 346n92; Victoria, 46, 90, 101, 196, 283, 285, 302
Bodwell, E.V., 62, 71, 99-100, 221, 250, 375n90
Bole, Norman, 21, 25
Booth, J.P., 61, 69
Borden, Robert, 5, 67, 91-92, 110, 111, 134-35, 136, 141, 150, 152, 153, 178, 179, 180, 181, 184, 185, 190, 192, 193, 195, 198, 212, 219, 239, 249, 250, 251, 252, 253-54, 255, 257, 259, 281, 283, 286, 292, 294, 295, 297, 298, 299, 300, 304, 313, 317, 338n75, 344n68, 354n73, 357n14, 361n48, 361n51, 377n110, 378n4, 379n5, 382n37, 383n42
Bostock, Hewitt, 369n29
Boundary District, 108, 153, 154, 157, 199, 262, 264, 269, 273, 274, 275, 277, 279, 280
Bowell, Mackenzie, 43
Bowron, Lottie, 84, 132, 185, 279, 303(i), 310, 323
Bowser, Reid and Walbridge, 174, 268, 289(i)
Bowser, Mrs. William J., 323
Bowser, William J., 8, 22, 23, 24, 27, 49, 76, 79-80, 94, 108, 119, 122, 123, 124, 126, 129, 130, 131(i), 139, 143, 149, 152, 153, 155, 164, 166, 167, 168, 170, 171, 174, 179, 181, 185, 186(i), 188, 192-93, 197, 203, 204(i), 206, 210, 212, 226, 227, 229, 231, 232, 234, 235, 236, 237, 241, 242, 243, 244, 250, 251, 252, 255, 267, 268-69, 274, 275, 277, 278, 279, 280, 281, 282, 286, 287, 289, 291, 296, 297, 298-99, 301-2, 304, 306, 307, 323, 324, 340n22, 341n35, 347n94, 357n14, 359n31, 365n93, 367n9, 371n56, 372n65, 379n12, 390n19

Bowser-McBride, 219, 222, 281
Brenton, Rev. C.J., 19
Brewster, H.C., 148, 160, 167, 169, 170, 172, 175, 195, 200, 223, 252, 278, 298, 306, 307, 308, 309, 312, 313, 319, 384n71, 388n2
Britain, 2, 120, 126, 147-48, 194(i), 240, 306, 352n40. See also British investment; McBride, Richard, on the imperial stage
British Columbia, finances, 84-85, 86, 89, 93, 97, 102, 120, 126-27, 146, 160, 209, 213-14, 215, 216(i), 217, 265, 269, 272, 283-84, 298, 318, 346n87, 380n26. See also Retrenchment
British Columbia, population, 1-2, 5, 352n40
British Columbia Archives, 360n45
British Columbia Electric Railway Company (BCER), 4, 79, 99, 107, 129, 178, 195, 196, 197, 230-32, 235, 249, 359n31, 364n87, 373n70
British Columbia Exploration Company, 311
British Columbia Mining Association, 53-54
British Columbia Penitentiary, 13, 14-15(i), 16
British Columbia Timber and Forestry Chamber of Commerce, 145
British investment, 2-4, 174, 190, 196, 197, 198, 211, 214-15, 217, 230-31, 247-48, 256, 258, 265, 268, 272-73, 317, 369n23
British markets, 274, 283, 304-5, 383n58
British North America Act, 4, 115, 135, 137, 138, 142, 181. See also Better Terms; Confederation
Brittain, Harry, 182-83, 187, 295, 362n59
Brown, J.C., 48, 58
Brydone-Jack, W.D., 340n14
Bulkley River, 236
Bulkley Valley, 105, 108, 174
Buntzen, Johannes, 107
Bureau of Provincial Information, 147
Burns, John, 215

Burns, William E., 230
Burrard Inlet, 235
Burrard Inlet Tunnel and Bridge Company, 214
Burrell, Martin, 112, 142, 149, 189, 185, 193, 199, 255, 263, 361n51
Buscombe, Frederick, 346n91

Calgary Exhibition, 254
California, 239, 246
Campbell, L.A., 242, 307, 308
Canada Zinc Company, 144-45
Canadian Bankers Association, 266, 267, 272, 379n10
Canadian Collieries (Dunsmuir) Ltd., 225
Canadian Expeditionary Force, 274, 294-95, 296, 306
Canadian Northern Railway (CNR), 6, 62, 64, 65, 67, 69, 72, 121, 161, 162-63, 164, 165, 166, 170, 196, 197-98, 203, 206-7, 210, 216(i), 217, 218-20, 237, 262, 270, 275-76, 281, 308, 325, 337n62, 358n28, 364n87, 366n3, 366n4, 369n23, 369n24, 369n25, 369n29
Canadian Pacific Railway (CPR), 5, 22, 40, 48, 53, 56, 57, 71, 72, 79, 81, 90, 91, 93, 94, 95, 97, 99, 109, 114, 115, 121, 155, 160, 161, 163, 164-65, 205, 206, 209, 211, 235, 247, 249, 250, 251, 275, 339n12, 344n64, 347n101, 348n5, 356n8, 357n13, 369n23
Canadian Western Lumber Company, 240
Cane, G.F., 78
Cape Scott, BC, 172
capital vs. labour, 5, 38, 50, 54, 205, 225, 226
Carcross, Yukon, 157
Cariboo, 108, 123-24, 156, 234, 237
Cariboo Road, 235
Carmichael, Maurice, 323
Caron, Adolphe, 121, 348n7
Carrall, R.W.W., 14
Carter-Cotton, Francis, 42, 45, 47, 67, 68, 79-80, 82, 84, 101, 129, 161, 164,

171, 182, 334n19, 338n74, 359n31, 365n93
Cassidy, George L., 324
Caven, Thomas, 79
Cawley, Samuel, 233
Ceperley, H.T., 379n8
Chamberlain, Joseph, 149
Chilahitsa, Chief John, 178
Chilliwack, 28, 80, 107, 122, 125, 237
Chimney Creek Bridge, 73-74
China, 20, 26, 30, 31, 71, 84, 122, 150, 239, 240, 243, 255
Chown, S.D., 356n7
churches, 271, 356n7, 386n92. *See also* Anglican Church; Presbyterian Church; Roman Catholics; Salvation Army
Churchill, Winston, 4, 136-37, 140-41, 142, 151, 152, 187, 189, 195-96, 253, 254, 255, 256, 257, 264, 275, 317, 321, 352n46, 376n107
Cisco, BC, 220
civil service, 84-86, 123, 128-29, 172, 232, 234, 249, 270, 290, 302, 341n35, 350n23, 373n66
Clark, J.A., 323
Clements, Mr. Justice, 348n7
Clifford, C.W.D., 46, 60, 80, 108
Cloverdale, BC, 88
coal, royal commission on, 224, 230
Coal and Petroleum Act, 273
coal industry, 224, 225, 230, 270, 342n44, 353n53, 354n53, 372n59; Vancouver Island, labour disputes, 54, 71, 225-30, 227(i), 270, 370n48, 371n49, 371n51, 372n58
Coast-Kootenay Railway, 56-57, 61, 66, 93-95, 163, 340n20
Cochrane, Frank, 382n45
Colonial Office, 46, 135, 137, 138, 140, 141, 151, 178, 194, 239, 250, 293, 306, 316, 360n44, 378n5
Colonial Realty Company, 247, 311
colonial secretary, 110, 135, 136, 137, 149, 178, 250, 252, 258
Columbia (riding), 130
Columbia Valley, 237

Columbia and Western Railway (C&W), 72-73, 81, 91, 99, 101, 109, 119, 126, 334n19, 340n19
Columbian College, 127, 350n20
Colwood Land Company, 249
Comix-Atlin, 192
Community Regulation Act, 243
Comox, BC, 169, 199
Confederation, 181, 251; compact theory of, 138, 249, 251
Connaught, Duke and Duchess, 235, 246, 258, 259, 310, 378n119
conservation, 103, 145, 172-73, 221, 222, 368n20
Conservative Party (federal), 179-80, 183; campaign funds, 343n47. *See also* Borden, Robert
Conservative Party (provincial): campaign funds, 79, 82, 124, 198, 203, 235, 309, 365n93, 367n9, 373n70; conventions, 27, 43, 67-68, 92, 108, 170, 173, 183, 198, 199, 208, 209, 213, 231, 237, 245, 280; discontent, general, 92; discontent in caucus, 94-95, 96, 98, 99, 100-1, 103, 218, 232, 233, 278-81, 320, 382n45; organization, 78-79, 124, 126, 233-35, 278, 290. *See also* Bowser-McBride
Cook, Fred, 375n96, 376n100
Cooke, Rev. A.E., 226, 271, 286, 287
Cooper, Chief Michael, 176
Copper Mountain, 42
Coquihalla Pass, 21
Coquitlam, BC, 34, 59, 106, 237
Corbould, Gordon, 21, 24, 27
Cornwall, C.F., 14
coronations: Edward VII, 66; George V, 174, 178, 184, 187, 188
Cotsworth, Moses B., 222, 286, 288, 321, 384n71
Cottonwood Canyon, 182
Coulson, W.L., 370n48
Courtenay, BC, 199
Cowan, G.H., 111, 112, 142, 152, 153, 193, 346n91, 348n7
Cowper, J.S., 268
Cox, Captain, 307

Index

Cranbrook, BC, 52, 80, 108, 109, 124, 130, 155, 156, 206
Creston, BC, 155
Croft, Mrs. Henry, 323
Crothers, T.W., 229
Crow's Nest Pass, 72, 73, 109, 126
Cumberland, 225, 226, 228, 370n48
Cunningham, Thomas, 80, 88, 271
Currie, A.W., 252
Curtis, David S., 27
Curtis, Smith, 51, 59, 60, 61, 63, 71, 72, 75, 88

Dalhousie University, 22-24, 36, 378n115
Daly, Harold Mayne, 379n10
Dan, Keatney, 26
D'Arcy, Edward F. (uncle), 19, 85, 171, 331n12
Davidson Royal Commission, 293, 385n79
Davie, C.E., 326
Davie, Theodore, 21, 27, 34
Dawson, Michael (historian), 5
Dawson City, Yukon, 213
Deadman's Island, 334n19
Deane, F.J., 341n25
DeBeck, Mrs. Clarence, 21
defence, coastal. *See* naval matters
Delta, BC, 106, 207, 311
Dewdney, Edgar, 136
Dewdney constituency, 33-35, 38, 44, 48, 55, 59, 78, 82, 90-91, 105-6, 107, 120, 121, 125, 130, 348n3
Dewdney Trunk Road, 35, 39, 48, 55, 59, 234-35
Dickie, C.H., 79
Dilke, Charles, 137
direct legislation, 290-91
Doherty, C.J., 313
Dominion Trust Company, 214, 262, 267-69, 278, 281, 308, 319
dominion-provincial relations, 4-5, 39, 45, 46, 61, 65, 71, 72, 81, 110-14, 142-44, 148, 149-50, 153, 155, 181, 182, 219-20, 274-75, 277, 346n85, 359n36, 372n59, 375n95. *See also* Better Terms

Douglas Lake, BC, 178
Doukhobors, 5, 241-43, 374n81; Royal Commission on, 224, 232, 241-42
Doull, Bishop A.J., 290
Drake, Mr. Justice, 16, 32
dry belt, 126, 148
Duncan, BC, 112, 155
Dunmore, Lord, 182
Dunsmuir, Dola, 323
Dunsmuir, James, 6, 37, 47, 49, 50, 53, 56, 57, 59, 61, 62, 63, 64, 65, 66, 68, 84, 93, 99, 101, 110, 118, 126, 136, 149, 150, 151, 249, 335n28, 337n69, 342n41, 342n44, 354n66, 357n11
Dyking, 106, 122, 348n3

Eberts, D.M., 50, 55, 65, 66, 67, 68, 73, 77, 310
economic depression, 147, 215, 248-49, 262, 269, 283
Edmonds, H.L., 281
Edmonton, Alberta, 161, 198
Edmonton, Yukon & Pacific Railway, 64, 337n62
eight-hour day, 45, 50-51, 97, 120, 130, 207
elections
  by-elections, federal (Burrard, 1900), 335n38
  by-elections, provincial: Alberni (1905), 97; Gulf Islands (1913), 370n39; Kamloops (1904), 84; Lillooet (1904), 86, 108, 165; New Westminster (1902), 59; Rossland, Vancouver, and Victoria (1916), 308; Vancouver (1904), 84, 86; Victoria (1902), 62; Yale (1900), 335n38; Yale (1910), 171-72, 183
  general, federal: (1896) 27-31; (1900) 52-53; (1904) 91-92; (1908) 111-12, 142, 143-44, 152-53, 157, 159, 349n7, 355n81; (1911) 5, 190-93; (1940) 324
  general, provincial: (1894) 27; (1898) 33-35, 38; (1900) 47-49; (1903) 77-78, 81-82; (1907) 109, 117, 118-26, 348n12, 349n10; (1909) 7, 159, 163-71, 349n9, 356n7; (1912) 7, 172, 174, 175, 196, 197-208; (proposed 1915)

279-81; (1916) 306-7, 309; (1924) 324-25; (1941) 324, 326
Elgin, Lord, 136, 137, 138, 140, 141
Ellison, Price, 52, 64, 79, 93, 98, 99, 164, 171, 172, 206, 214, 248, 278-79, 298, 378n2, 382n43, 382n44
Emerald Lake, 156
enemy aliens, 282, 295, 296
Esquimalt, BC, 142, 151, 176, 193, 208, 225, 263-64, 265, 347n93, 366n113, 378n2; naval base, 2, 112, 142, 193, 263(i), 264, 265, 292
Esquimalt and Nanaimo Railway (E&N), 50, 63, 65, 93, 199
Extension, BC, 225, 226

Fairview, BC, 108
Farrington, Frank, 229
Fernie, BC, 52, 97, 109, 122, 130, 155, 156-57, 166, 192, 205
Fernow, Bernard, 369n33
Field, BC, 139, 155, 203
Fielding, W.S., 136, 141, 182, 184
Findlay, James, 224-25
Firlands, BC, 156
First Nations. *See* Indians
First World War, 252, 261, 262, 265, 282-83, 293-95, 296, 304
fisheries, 20, 39, 54, 55, 56, 71-72, 113, 126, 142-43, 193, 195, 239, 271, 283, 383n58
Fitzsimmons, James, 14, 16
Flumerfelt, A.C., 146, 307, 308
Foley, Welch and Stewart (FWS), 192, 196, 211, 364n91, 367n9
Forbes, G. Bruce, 323
Forest Act, 1912, 221, 318
forest industry, 3, 102-4, 105(i), 145-46, 173, 221-22; policy, 89, 102-4, 105(i), 120, 145-46, 172-73, 318, 369n33; regulations and fees, 89, 103, 127, 145-46, 173, 217, 221-22, 222, 273, 348n1, 368n20, 382n29; US investment in, 5, 102, 104, 145, 173, 191(i), 202, 273, 316-17. *See also* lumber industry; Timber and Forestry, Royal Commission on

Forster, Harold, 203, 232, 233, 278, 365n103
Fort Fraser Land Company, 174
Fort George, BC, 131, 169, 182-83, 203, 211, 212, 213, 221, 233, 238, 266. *See also* Prince George
Fort Steele, BC, 10
Foster, George, 273, 307, 361n46
Foster, W.W., 370n39
Fouquet, Father L., 88
Fraser, Fred, 123, 349n10
Fraser, George, 95
Fraser, John, 234, 271
Fraser Mills, BC, 240
Fraser, Rev. W.W., 226
Fraser, Simon, 360n45
Fraser Canyon, 220, 235, 275
Fraser River, 11, 13, 20, 22, 31, 33, 34, 44, 48, 54, 107, 113, 120, 124, 143, 182, 199, 217, 360n45
Fraser Valley, 11, 20, 22, 27, 28, 46, 55, 80, 81, 105, 117, 120, 196, 197, 311, 319
free speech, 224-25, 371n53
freight rates, 57, 106, 110, 165, 199, 220, 273
French Canadians, 123, 192, 240
Friendly Help Society, 246, 297, 324
Friends of the B.C. Indians, 177
fruit industry, 88, 121, 148, 154, 155, 156, 173, 184, 205, 223, 258, 271, 304, 325, 342n40
Fulton, F.J., 7, 60, 68, 71, 83-84, 146, 156, 160-61, 164, 169, 171, 173, 197, 357n13, 369n33
Fushimi, Prince, 140

Gamble, F.C., 212, 221, 277, 279, 367n9
Garden, J.F., 60, 149
Garvin, J.L., 187
Gaston, E.P., 311
Germany, 254, 257, 259, 263, 282, 294, 295-96, 386n86; investment, 286, 295-96; navy, 4, 179, 264, 292-93, 294
Gifford, Thomas, 59, 60, 67, 68, 82, 85, 233, 281
Gilmour, H.B., 61
Ging Gong Ming, 26

Glover, F.R., 179
Golden, BC, 109, 129, 155, 156, 166, 203
Goldie, George, 137,
Goodeve, A.S., 77, 146, 355n81
Gosnell, R.E., 112, 136, 195, 249, 250, 252, 306, 375n96, 376n100
Gotfriedson, Henry, 25
Gothard, S.J., 10
Gotoh, Saori, 153
Gouin, Lomer, 113, 115, 347n95
Graham, Hugh, 187
Granby (Anyox), BC, 237
Granby Consolidated Mining, Smelting and Power Company, 144
Grand Forks, BC, 52, 88, 125, 163, 214, 241, 242
Grand Trunk Pacific Railway (GTP), 79, 81, 92, 93, 95, 97, 99-101, 109, 112, 114, 122, 136, 160, 161, 183, 198, 199, 236, 237, 271, 277, 286, 325, 340n18, 344n56, 349n9, 364n91
Granite Creek, 69
Grant, Robert, 95
Gray, A.W., 380n27
Great Northern Railway (GNR), 56, 93-94, 97, 154, 167, 205, 206, 209-10, 211, 276, 364n87
Green, Robert F., 40, 58, 60, 68, 75, 81, 83, 91, 92, 99, 101, 102(i), 108, 109, 110, 111, 118, 121, 124, 165, 175, 205, 247, 248, 269, 272, 280, 283, 323, 344n67, 348n7
Green and Burdick Brothers, 247
Greenshields, J.N., 62, 63-64
Greenwood, BC, 52, 78, 108, 124, 154, 163, 167, 206
Greenwood, Hamar, 4, 138, 140-41, 190, 310, 352n39
Grenfell, Wilfred, 240
Gretchen, Fred, 374n81
Grey, Edward, 239
Groundhog Mountain, 237
Gulf Islands, BC, 69, 90, 153
Guthrie, Samuel, 228

Hagel, N.F., 44
"half-breeds," 123

Hammond, BC, 124
Haney, BC, 107
Hardy Bay, BC, 214
Harmsworth, Harold, 311
Harrison Hot Springs, BC, 106
Harrison Lake, 33
Harrison Mills, BC, 167
Hart, F.J., 88, 247, 311
Harvey, J.A., 379n8
Hastings Townsite and D.L., 197, 320-31
Haszard, F.L., 181
Hatzic Prairie, BC, 107
Hawthornthwaite, J.H., 60, 63, 66, 96, 97, 125, 130, 148, 151, 169, 312
Hays, Charles M., 95, 194
Hayward, W.H., 60, 66, 232, 281, 285, 388n17, 394
Hazelton, BC, 108, 109, 175, 234, 236, 248, 266
Hazen, J.D., 185, 252, 253, 292
Heaps, A.M., 370n47
Heaps, E.H., 233, 304
Hedley, BC, 69, 167
Helmcken, H.D., 60, 66
Helmcken, J.S., 12
Henderson, Alex, 40, 122
Henderson, Stuart, 354n69
Hendry, John, 173, 364n92
Herring, Mrs. A.M., 20-21
Higgins, D.W., 46, 312
Hill, J.J., 94, 97
Hilliers, BC, 237
Hinchliffe, Joshua, 324
Hindus. *See* immigrants and immigration, from India
Hood, Francis Basil, 323
Hood, Francis Wheeler, 323
Hope, BC, 69, 199
Hope Mountains, 163, 199, 210, 211
Hopwood, Francis J., 137, 255, 377n109,
Horne-Payne, R.M., 196, 213, 214, 230-31, 364n87
Hose, Cmdr. Walter, 264
Houston, John, 77, 80, 83, 108, 125, 169, 336n52, 340n24, 341n26, 345n75
Howay, Frederic W., 22, 23, 27, 44, 121-22, 226, 359n45, 371n50

Howe Sound and Northern Railway, 211
Hudson's Bay Company, 269
Hughes, Charles Evan, 134
Hughes, Sam, 195, 294
Hunter, Gordon, 151
Hunter, Joseph, 66
Hutcherson, E., 20

immigrants and immigration, 147-48, 194(i)
  from Asia: 4, 5, 29, 31, 34, 45, 46, 49, 55, 62-64, 65, 81, 110, 119, 122, 148-52, 153, 154, 162, 163, 167, 192, 193, 194(i), 205, 207, 239, 254, 255, 256, 326, 340n18, 366n3. *See also* China; Japan
  from Britain, 2, 105, 120, 126, 147-48, 240, 306, 352n40. *See also* Salvation Army
  from Canada, 240-41. *See also* French Canadians
  from China, 20, 26, 30, 31, 71, 84, 122, 150, 239, 240, 243
  from Germany, 254, 263, 282, 294, 295-96
  from India, 122, 149, 151, 240, 294-95, 354n70, 378n5
  from Italy, 123, 366n3
  from Japan, 30, 34, 45-46, 49, 55, 56, 61, 65, 72, 82, 84, 122, 149-50, 151, 152, 153, 163, 207, 239-40, 254, 258, 265, 326, 349n9, 354n66, 354n69, 354n73
  from Malta, 240
  from Newfoundland, 240
Imperial federation, 4, 24, 61, 184, 185, 256, 312, 362n63, 362n64, 377n110
Indian Affairs, Royal Commission on, 244, 318, 326. *See also* McKenna-McBride Commission
Indian Rights Association, 244
Indian Tribes of British Columbia, 178
Indians, 5, 15, 20, 26, 157, 304, 330n8; enfranchisement of, 243; land questions, 157, 175-78, 236, 243-44, 318, 360n39, 360n44; Native title, 176-77, 243, 244, 326, 360n44; reserves, 111, 112, 121, 126, 160, 167, 193,
194(i). *See also* reversionary interests; Songhees Reserve
Industrial Disputes Investigation Act, 229
Industrial Workers of the World, 210, 224, 366n3, 367n9
Inkster, Rev. J.G., 290
Inter-Provincial Conferences: 1902, 113; 1906, 109, 114-17, 135, 141, 181; 1913, 257
Irish Home Rule, 184
Irrigation, Royal Commission on, 148
Irving, John, 47, 55, 329n3
Irving, Mr. Justice, 41, 45
island vs. Mainland, 37, 48, 61, 62, 65, 66, 68, 80, 82, 127, 130, 131(i), 171(i), 196, 210, 276, 284, 337n68

James Island, 248
Japan, 65, 122, 140, 149-50, 151, 152, 153, 239, 253, 255, 265, 293, 294, 354n66, 354n69, 354n70, 354n73
Jardine, John, 169, 356n11, 365n98, 370n47
Johnson, John A., 134
Joly de Lotbinière, Henri, 6, 68, 74, 75, 82, 83, 88, 91, 100, 104, 141, 319, 345n75, 346n88
Jones, Bertram, 263-64
Jones, Frederick William, 275-76
Jones, Harry, 319

Kaien Island, 95, 99-102, 109, 116, 119, 121, 160, 348n7
Kamloops, BC, 52, 83-84, 98, 112, 122, 124, 139, 150, 155, 156, 162, 164, 170, 199, 203, 210, 366n4
Kaslo, BC, 52, 124, 155, 166, 205
Kaslo & Slocan Railway, 199, 205
Keary, W.H., 81
Kelly, Chief R.P., 178
Kelowna, BC, 90, 122, 124, 153, 206
Kemp, A.E., 274-75
Kennedy, J.B., 27, 134
Kennedy, J.D., 56, 134, 321
Keremeos, BC, 108, 167
Kettle Valley Railway (KVR), 95, 163, 166, 170, 199, 200, 202, 205, 206-7, 210, 211, 356n8, 366n108, 366n109

Kidd, Thomas, 60, 68
King, Michael, 103
King, William Lyon Mackenzie, 354n66,
Kingsmill, Admiral, 295, 386n82
Kitchener, Lord, 264
Kitimat, BC, 65, 95, 314n19, 348n1
Kitselas, BC, 177
Kitsilano Indian Reserve, 234
Kootenays, 109, 130, 153, 154, 156, 157, 166, 173, 199, 205, 206, 209, 210, 237, 269

labour legislation, 71, 207. *See also* eight-hour day; mining; workmen's compensation
labour organizations, 226; B.C. Federation of Labour, 225, 240; British Columbia Miners' Liberation League, 226, 228; United Mine Workers of America, 226, 228, 229, 270, 371n49; Vancouver Trades and Labour Council, 149, 224-25, 270; Victoria Trades and Labour Council, 270
Labour, Royal Commission on, 203, 206, 224, 225-26, 228-29, 370n47
Ladner, BC, 28, 167, 207, 247
Ladysmith, BC, 69, 225, 226, 228
Lakelse, BC, 109
land: policies and resources, 38, 39, 63, 64, 84, 89, 90, 93, 95, 97, 98, 101, 103, 118, 119, 121, 126, 127, 144, 156, 163, 165, 173-75, 178, 181, 191(i), 195, 200, 202, 213, 217, 221, 222-24, 236, 249, 270-71, 285-86, 287, 305(i), 309, 318, 326, 344n67; settlement, 104-6, 120, 148, 173-75, 222-24, 236, 238, 249, 270-71, 285; speculation, 100, 105, 148, 156, 174, 175, 178, 179, 211, 213, 214, 220, 221, 222, 266, 268, 285, 286, 318. *See also* "Back to the land"; Columbia and Western Railway (C&W); forest industry; Indians, land questions; Kaien Island; Peace River lands
Lane, Franklin, 212, 277
Langevin, Hector, 13

Lash, Zebulon A., 250, 375n90, n96
Laurier, Wilfrid, 6, 29, 50, 92, 95, 110, 111-12, 113, 114, 123, 135, 136, 150, 155, 175, 177, 178, 179, 180, 181, 182, 183, 184, 187, 192, 241, 252, 254, 291, 317, 362n64
Laymen's Missionary Association, 15
Layton, Richard, 14
Lee, Martha, 31
Lee Sing, 31
legislative debates, record, 393-94
Liberal-Labour MLAs, 60
Liberalism, 6, 329n16
Lillooet, BC, 90, 108
Lillooet River, 59, 107
liquor matters, 25, 27, 44, 79, 84, 92, 123, 124, 168, 233, 339n12. *See also* local option; Peoples Prohibition Movement
Livingston, Stuart, 78
Lloyd George, David, 258
Local Council of Women, 246
local option, 167-68, 202
Logan, H.J., 23
Logie, Mrs., 101
Lougheed, J.A., 275
Lower Nicola, 69
Lucas, Alexander (Alex), 40, 171-72, 223, 280, 288-89
Lugrin, C.H., 182
lumber industry, 6, 34, 90, 103, 104, 108, 111, 127, 145-46, 184, 185, 192, 222, 264, 269, 271, 273, 282, 283-84, 304-5, 381n30. *See also* forest industry
Lumby, BC, 199
Lytton, BC, 69, 171, 276

MacBeth, R.G., 244
Macdonald, A., 341n33
Macdonald, Archie, 86
Macdonald, Hugh John, 179
Macdonald, J.A. (provincial Liberal leader), 96, 99-100, 109, 112, 121, 122, 123, 135, 145, 348n7, 356n10
Macdonald, John A. (prime minister), 15, 30

MacDonald, K.C., 122
MacDonald, M.A., 278, 308
Macdonald, Rt. Rev. D.A., 290
Macgowan, A.H.B., 95, 123, 367n9
Macintosh, MacGregor, 323
MacKay, Ian (historian), 6
MacKay, Neil, 348n7
Mackenzie, Alexander, 13
Mackenzie, Francis, 233
Mackenzie, William, 6, 61, 171, 188, 194, 197, 198, 218, 276, 383n52
Mackenzie & Mann, 62, 64, 160, 161, 163, 170, 206, 216(i), 219-20, 225-26, 276, 337n62, 357n13, 369n28
MacLean, W.R., 242
MacMillan, H.R., 273, 283, 381n30
Macrae, Lawrence, 7, 113, 136, 153, 154(i), 182, 296, 386n88
Maitland, Royal L., 325, 341n31
Maitland, R.R., 85
Malkin, W.H., 290, 379n8
Manitoba, 38, 40, 56, 114, 115, 166, 179, 182, 185, 190, 232, 250, 272, 288, 332n45, 354n65, 384n68
Manitoba School Question, 28, 29
Mann, Donald, 6, 61, 161, 165, 217, 161, 165, 218, 237, 256, 275, 281
Manson, A.M., 326
Manson, William, 97, 125, 130
Manufacturers' Association, 274
Maple Ridge, BC, 59, 106
Maritime provinces, 114, 181, 250, 251
Martin, Joseph, 37, 38, 39, 40, 41, 42, 43, 45, 47, 48, 54-55, 56, 59, 60-61, 64, 67, 68, 69, 70, 71, 84, 333n55, 334n19, 342n41
Matson, J.H.S., 176, 208, 216(i), 220, 360n40, 378n119
McBride, Arthur H., 2, 12-15, 16, 17, 58, 171, 330n3, 330n7, 331n14
McBride, BC, 271
McBride, Catherine Anna (Anna), 132, 133(i), 321, 323, 390n13
McBride, Christine Margaret (née McGillivray) (wife), 30, 32(i), 33, 41, 55, 59, 87, 131, 132, 134, 137, 139, 171, 183, 187, 188, 189(i), 194, 246, 254, 297, 302, 309-10, 313, 314, 321, 323, 324, 374n89, 394
McBride, Donalda Mary (Mary) (daughter), 40, 55, 133(i), 134, 194, 247, 259, 309, 323, 386n86
McBride, Dorothea (Dolly) (daughter), 55, 133(i), 134, 297, 321, 323,
McBride, Edward German (brother), 17, 19, 20, 247, 291, 314, 331n25, 385n75, 390n17
McBride, Gertrude (Mrs. Allison) (sister), 17, 18, 19, 21, 108, 215, 314, 331n15, 331n25, 332n29
McBride, Margaret Sydney (Peggy) (daughter), 40, 55, 133(i), 134, 194, 247, 297, 309
McBride, Mary (née D'Arcy) (mother), 16, 17, 20, 107, 134, 247, 331n13, 331n14, 331n15, 375n90, 390n17
McBride, Mary Dorothea (Dodo), sister, 17, 18, 134, 171, 314, 324, 375n90
McBride, Richard
  activities in New Westminster, 26-28, 31, 40, 59, 77, 107;
  birth, 1, 17
  cannery worker, 120
  childhood, 18-20
  death and funeral, 314
  education, 18-19, 21-24, 332n30
  finances, 86-87, 246-48, 258, 272, 295, 309, 310-12, 313, 321-22, 342n37, 342n40, 375n90, 375n91, 375n92, 378n115, 388n20, 389n1, 389n4, 389n5
  health, 29, 66, 82, 83, 107-8, 125, 140, 235, 259, 260, 262, 281, 283, 298, 302, 312-14, 361n52
  legacy, 319-20, 324-27
  legal practice, 24-26, 31, 41, 42, 44, 56, 134, 333n55
  liberalism of, 6
  loyalty to British Columbia, 5, 36, 142, 255, 316
  marriage and domestic life, 55, 59, 32-33, 132(i), 310, 336n46, 351n30
  optimism of, 1, 7, 10, 11, 30, 34, 75, 77, 156, 208, 209, 213, 214, 215, 220,

249, 262, 265-66, 269, 270, 271-72, 273, 280, 283, 298, 309, 311, 314-15, 366n1
- on the imperial stage: British patriotism and imperial sentiments, 1-2, 4, 18, 45-46, 138, 142, 175-76, 183-84, 185, 187, 190-91, 192, 193, 213, 249, 252-57, 262-63, 264-65, 283, 290, 296, 316-17; possibility of entering British Parliament, 187, 259-60, 378n119; knighthood, 4, 209, 246, 254. *See also* British investment; immigrants and immigration
- on the national stage: Canadianism, 4, 316, 317; ideas about eastern Canada, 46; re-entering federal politics, 5, 152, 178-79, 183, 184, 185, 186(i), 187, 190, 192-93, 259, 281, 361n48, 361n50, 362n67, 383n42; rumours re high commissionership, 259, 260(i), 282; Senate appointment offered, 298. *See also* Better Terms
- outdoor activities, 20, 52, 59, 107, 109, 124, 150, 192, 236-37, 248
- personal attributes, 7-10, 38, 47, 50, 76, 106, 107, 115, 158, 187, 199, 314-15, 318-20, 352n39
- political career in BC: agent-general, 261, 282, 298, 300-7, 301(i), 310, 312; chief commissioner of lands and works, 80; leader of the opposition, 60-74, 63(i); formation of government, 75-77, 82, 83; member for Dewdney; minister of mines, 50-58, 108, 335n33, 335n35, 336n39, 336n52; resignation from cabinet (1902), 58-59, 61; resigns as premier, 278, 297-99. *See also* elections
- relations with the United States, 194-95, 283, 295, 316-17
- religion, 16-17, 19, 20, 137
- travels: general, 351n36; in BC, 7, 41-42, 51-53, 69-70, 80-81, 106-7, 108, 109, 117, 124-25, 130, 139, 153-57, 166-67, 182, 203, 210, 235-38, 280; in Canada, 92-93, 117, 136, 139, 141, 194, 258, 264, 265; in Europe, 188-89, 258-59, 282, 295, 386n86; in the United Kingdom, 136-39, 187, 188(i), 189-90, 214, 215, 253, 256, 257-59, 264-65, 277, 282-83, 297, 310; in the United States, 33, 44, 54, 117, 134, 182, 187, 194-95, 257, 258, 259, 277, 282, 295, 362n58; to Montreal, 114, 117, 139, 160, 187, 190, 194, 258; to Ottawa, 113, 114, 136, 139, 253-54, 256, 258, 281, 282, 283, 293

McBride, Richard Jr. (son), 164, 165-66, 171, 246
McBride, Robert, 80
McBride, Ruth (daughter), 87, 133, 297, 321, 323
McBride, Sheila (daughter), 133, 246, 321, 323, 388n28
McBride, Thomas Darcy (brother), 17
McBride, William Leonard (brother), 17, 19, 20, 21, 67, 107, 331n25
McBride-Bowser "machine," 168, 307
McColl, A.J., 21, 24
McColl, J.W., 27
McColl, Mrs. A.J., 85
McDonald, Robert A.J. (historian), 6
McGill University College, 127
McGillivray, Christina (mother-in-law), 333n57
McGillivray, Christine Margaret. *See* McBride, Margaret Sydney (Peggy)
McGillivray, Donald, 33
McGillivray, Jean, 133
McGillivray, Neil (father-in-law), 32
McGillivray brothers, 367n9
McGuire, George A., 144, 218, 230
McInnes, T.R.E., 357n13
McInnes, Thomas R., 38, 42, 47, 49, 109, 333n4
McInnes, W.W.B., 18, 54, 61, 69, 73, 97, 103, 122, 349n7
McInnis, John, 125
McKane, John, 124
McKelvie, J.A., 370n47
McKenna-McBride Commission, 244, 302, 326
McLaren, John (historian), 243
McLean brothers, 95

McLennan, R.P., 266, 267, 379n8
McPhillips, A.E., 60, 76, 77, 80, 82, 85, 107, 108, 153, 334n8, 370n39
McWhinnie, A., 44
Merchants Protective Association, 291
Merritt, BC, 171, 207
Methodist Church, 16, 18, 31, 79, 127, 184, 287, 299, 356n7, 371n49
Mezladin Lake, BC, 237
Midway, BC, 72, 154, 163
Midway & Vernon Railway (M&V), 65, 98-99, 109, 163, 166
militia, 39, 226, 228, 229, 344n60
milk supply, royal commission on, 224
Miller, Ernest, 206, 242, 243
mining industry, 50-54, 72, 144-45, 154-55, 221, 237, 238, 269; legislation, 45, 53-54, 89, 336n39. *See also* coal industry
Ministerial Union of the Lower Mainland, 286, 287, 288, 289(i), 290
Mission City, BC, 34, 49, 59, 82, 106, 119
Mission Junction, BC, 124
Monk, F.D., 254
Moore, J.H., 323
moratorium, 272-73, 278
Moresby, A., 330n3
Morrison, Aulay, 23, 24, 28, 31, 56, 59
Morse, F.W., 160
Mottishaw, Oscar, 225, 370n48
Mowat, Oliver, 111, 346n89
Mowbray, Annie, 170, 358n30
Mowbray, Tina, 132, 134
Moyie, BC, 42, 147, 166
Moylan, J.G., 14, 16
Municipal government, Royal Commission on, 224, 231-32
municipal loans, 215
municipal reform, 202
Munro, C.W., 60, 80, 122
Murphy, Denis, 52, 60, 68-69, 308, 337n56
Murton, James (historian), 173

Nakusp, BC, 155, 166, 203, 204(i), 205
Nakusp & Slocan Railway, 205
Namu, BC, 81
Nanaimo, BC, 80, 125, 130, 147-48, 169, 207, 208, 226, 237, 268, 270, 282
Naramata, BC, 88, 342n40
Nass Valley, 175, 176, 177
Natal Act, 72, 122, 150-51, 239, 354n70
National Parks, 181
National Policy, 28, 29, 36
naval matters, 2, 4, 112, 179-80, 183-84, 192, 193, 207, 252-56, 263(i), 293-94, 317, 376n107, 377n109
Navy League, 179, 183, 377n109
Nechako, BC, 105, 156
Neill, A.W., 60, 334n10
Nelson, BC, 52, 80, 83, 108, 144, 154-55, 166, 172, 183, 205, 235, 341n25
New Denver, BC, 52, 155, 205
"New British Columbia," 108
New Westminster, 11-13, 29, 30, 81, 82, 87, 88, 90, 117, 125, 134, 139, 142, 143, 170, 171, 195, 207, 235, 239, 249-50, 272, 281, 324, 380n27; bridge, 57-58, 77, 82, 89, 90, 92, 111, 112, 120, 143, 235, 276, 342n41, 369n25; exhibition, 81, 107, 233, 237; fire, 40, 334n8; jail, 13(i); penitentiary, 13(i), 330n9; schools, 17-19, 21
New Zealand, 5, 46, 71, 72, 223, 264, 273
Newcastle, BC, 125, 169, 208
newspapers, biases, 7-9, 48, 70, 235, 338n81, 342n37, 350n26, 377n11, 387n69, 393-94
Nichol, W.C., 164, 169
Nicola, Kamloops, and Similkameen Railway, 163
Nicola Valley, BC, 52, 69, 98, 155
Normal School, 130
Norris, L., 129
Norris, T.C., 384n68
North Bend, BC, 69
North Thompson River Valley, 162, 210
North Vancouver, BC, 235
Northrup, W.B., 361n51
Norton-Grifiths, John, 182, 188, 190, 198
Nova Scotia, 110

O'Connor, T.P., 16, 138, 184, 189, 247, 258, 310, 311, 352n39, 362n64, 375n91
Odlum, Victor W., 104, 125, 312, 314
Offensive Weapons Act, 232-33
oil exploration, 311
Okanagan Valley, 105, 108, 109, 124, 153, 154, 156, 157, 166, 173, 205, 210, 218, 271
Old Men's Home, 156,
Oliver, John, 69, 70, 71, 72, 75, 78, 97, 106, 126, 127, 148, 163-64, 192, 278, 324, 325, 326, 348n1, 356n10, 356n11, 387n7
Ontario, 104, 111, 114, 161, 173, 179, 181, 197, 223, 232, 250, 257, 288, 354
Ootsa Valley, 174
Orange Order, 16, 80, 152, 165, 340n14, 357n14
Oroville, Washington, 154

Pacific, Northern and Omineca Railway, 95, 344n56
Pacific Great Eastern Railway (PGE), 198, 199, 200, 201, 203, 210, 211-12, 213, 217-18, 220-21, 222, 237, 262, 264, 280, 275, 276-78, 281, 283, 308, 309, 325-26, 327, 364n91, 365n93, 368n11, 369n23, 369n31
Pacific Highway, 234
Page, Jimmy, 26
Panama Canal, 203, 208, 213, 215, 258, 273
Parksville, BC, 237
Parliament Buildings (Victoria), 34, 37, 181, 195
Parson, Henry, 203, 365n103, 370n47
party lines, 7, 27, 33, 37-38, 43, 47-48, 49, 50, 56, 62, 67, 68, 70-71, 75-76, 249-50, 319, 326, 334n26, 335n27
Paterson, J.V., 292, 293
Paterson, T.W., 69, 75
patronage, 8, 78, 85, 91, 108, 122, 129-30, 152, 172, 233-34, 235, 241, 290, 318, 339n7, 341n32, 341n33, 350n25, 350n26
Patterson, Dr. E.P., 233
Pattullo, Mrs. T.D., 324

Pattullo, T.D., 326, 387n7
Peace River district, 175, 177, 199, 200, 202, 212, 213, 243, 271, 277, 283, 327, 365n100
Peace River lands, 114, 121, 142, 193, 194(i), 249, 277, 306
Peck, Cy, 314
Pendray, W.J., 101
Pennock, Charles G., 379n10
Penticton, BC, 72, 88, 96, 108, 124, 154, 163, 166, 167, 206
Peoples Prohibition Movement, 291
Perley, George, 180, 183, 250, 310, 314
Perrin, W.W., 177
Peters, Frederick, 101
Phillipps-Wolley, Clive, 92, 100
Phoenix, BC, 52, 154, 167, 346n82
Pilcher, H.B., 378n2
Pinchot, Gifford, 146
Pineo, A.V., 243, 374n83
Pinkerton's Detective Agency, 126, 225, 319, 344n65, 371n48
Pitt Lake, 20, 107, 134
Pitt River, 39, 59, 105, 235, 311
Planta, A.E., 309
Point Grey, 223, 224
Political Equality League, 245
Pooley, C.E., 61, 337n69
Pooley, Mrs. C.E., 323
Pooley, R.H., 208, 232, 325, 365n93, 366n113
Pope, S.D., 21, 133
Port Alberni, BC, 196, 237, 270
Port Hammond, BC, 59
Port Haney, BC, 34
Port Moody, BC, 34, 59, 88, 107
Port Simpson, BC, 157
Portland Canal, 237
Powell River, BC, 237
Powell River Company, 221
prairie provinces, 6, 71, 104, 127, 147, 161, 184, 185, 206, 222, 240-41, 270, 271, 274. *See also* Alberta; Saskatchewan; Manitoba
Prentice, J.D., 39, 50
Presbyterian Church, 16, 244, 297

Price, William, 361n51
Prince Edward Island, 117, 174, 250
Prince George, 277. *See also* Fort George, BC
Prince Rupert, BC, 95, 109, 157, 160, 175, 183, 200, 203, 223, 236(i), 247, 282
Princess Louise, 15
Princeton, BC, 52, 69, 108, 206
Prior, Edward G., 37, 62, 67, 68, 69, 70, 71, 72, 73-74, 77, 92, 323, 337n68
Prior, Mrs. E.G., 323
prohibition, 30, 167, 202, 244, 290-91, 307, 319, 356n7
prostitution, 244
provincial mental hospital, 46, 279, 334n24
Provincial Party, 47-48, 79-80
provincial police, 172, 234, 264
provincial rights, 29, 39, 45, 65, 71, 111, 196
Prudential Investment Company, 248
public accounts, 200, 215, 293
Public Service Commission (aka Public Utilities Commission), 232
public works, 90-91, 106, 109, 127, 157, 170, 172, 193, 207, 270, 282
Pugsley, William, 291-92
pulp and paper, 271, 273

Qualicum, BC, 237
Quatsino, BC, 148, 169
Quebec, 112, 113, 114, 123, 161, 173, 179, 180, 183, 250, 253-54, 257, 354n65
Queen Charlotte City, BC, 157
Queen Charlotte Islands, 63, 235
Quesnel, BC, 156, 182, 183

Radium, 221, 369n32
railway belt, 40, 181, 195, 251, 306, 359n36
railways, 5-6, 7, 30, 39, 48, 56-57, 61, 64-65, 81, 84, 94-95, 97-98, 98(i), 108, 120, 126, 159-64, 162(i), 194(i), 197-201, 201(i), 209, 211, 217-21, 264. *See also names of individual railways*
Rattenbury, Francis M., 37
Rattenbury, Mrs. F.M., 323
Raymur, H.W., 79
Reciprocity, 5, 184-85, 190, 191, 192

Red Cross Society, 246, 283, 297
Redcliff Mine, 237
redistribution, 33, 34, 46, 47, 55, 61, 62, 65, 72, 231, 278
Reed, Frank, 25-26
Reid, J.D., 180, 361n51
Reid, Robie L., 22, 23, 49
religion and religious organizations, 123, 226. *See also individual faiths*
retrenchment, 84, 93, 106, 120, 215, 269, 270. *See also* British Columbia, finances
Revelstoke, BC, 52, 108, 130, 155, 165, 166, 202, 203, 237, 245, 342n36
reversionary interests, 126, 167, 176, 177. *See also* Indians, land questions
Richmond, BC, 80
roads, 7, 52, 59, 78, 82, 90, 106, 108, 121, 129, 156, 167, 172, 173, 174, 207, 234-35, 236, 237, 238, 283, 345n78, 366n111, 373n68, 375n95
Robinson, J.M., 154
Roblin, Rodmond, 115, 179, 182, 190, 288, 384n68
Robson, David, 85
Robson, John, 38
Robson, Rev. Ebenezer, 18
Rogers, Robert, 166, 185, 253, 382n45
Rogers, S.A., 60
Roman Catholics, 16, 17, 29, 88, 123, 169, 240, 331n14, 359n31
Roosevelt, Theodore, 295
Roper, Bishop J.C., 290
Rosebery, BC, 205
Ross, W.R., 171, 192, 193, 237, 286, 359n31
Rossland, 51-52, 54, 80, 120, 123, 155, 166, 169
Royal Agricultural and Industrial Society, 31
Royal Bank of Canada, 87
Royal Colonial Institute, 188, 190, 312
Royal Colwood Golf Course, 249
Royal Theatre, 246
Runciman, Walter, 304

Saanich, BC, 196, 217, 248, 364n87
salmon canning, 20

Salvation Army, 147, 240, 353n60, 353n61
Sandon, BC, 217
Sanson, George, 69, 70
Saskatchewan, 113, 114, 123, 166, 181, 241, 274, 347n94
Savoy hotel, 188(i)
Sayward, J.A., 249
Scholefield, E.O.S., 360n45
Scholefield, J.H., 242-43
schools
    private: Dana Hall Seminary, 247; Lorne College, 19, 331n24; Queen's Academy for Girls, 133-34; St. Ann's Academy (New Westminster), 19, (Victoria), 321
    provincial, 2, 18-19, 21-22, 96, 106, 119, 127, 130, 270, 330n24, 350n20
    separate, 29, 123, 213, 347n94; St. George's School, 321; St. Margaret's School, 247, 321, 375n90; Whetham College, 35
Scotland, 188
Scott, R.W., 149
Scoular, Rev. Thomas, 3, 33, 331n25
sealing, 111
sectionalism in BC, 40, 48, 55-57, 65, 68, 70, 120, 131, 156-57, 199, 211, 238, 284, 319. *See also* island vs. Mainland
Semlin, Charles, 37, 38, 39, 40, 43, 45, 47, 67, 69, 70, 76
settlement and colonization. *See* land, settlement and colonization
Seymour, Frederick, 12
Seymour Narrows, 166, 196, 200, 202-3, 210
Shatford, L.W., 95, 206, 266, 267, 379n10
Shaughnessy, T.G., 90, 94, 114, 163, 187, 194
shipbuilding, 193, 304-5, 325
Sidney, BC, 208
Sifton, Clifford, 52
Silverdale, BC, 34
Silverton, BC, 52, 155
Similkameen, 78, 121, 123, 124
Skagway, Alaska, 157
Skeena Valley, 108, 176, 177, 236

Slocan, BC, 50, 52, 205, 242
Slocan and Sandon Railway, 205
Smith, E.C., 60
Smith, Frank O., 382n37
Smith, Mary E., 388n3
Smith, Ralph, 174
Smithers, BC, 236
Social Gospel, 244
Socialist MLAs, 6, 38, 69, 82, 89, 96, 109, 125, 130, 169, 170, 319, 344n60. *See also* Hawthornthwaite, J.H.; Williams, Parker
Socialists, 38, 68, 69, 96, 109, 126, 203, 205, 206, 208, 226, 326, 344n60, 359n31, 365n106
Soda Creek, BC, 182
Soldiers' Vote, 306-7, 313
Song Moon, 31
Songhees Reserve, 176, 216(i), 223, 233, 234, 360n40
Sooke, BC, 155, 170, 171, 276
South African War, 2, 51, 53, 329n3
South Fort George, BC, 182, 238
South Slocan, 242
South Vancouver, Royal Commission on, 224
South Wellington, BC, 226
speculation, 145, 156, 214, 215, 247, 290. *See also* land, speculation
Spencer, Dr. D., 168
Spences Bridge, BC, 69, 155, 166
Sperling, R.H., 197, 364n87
Spillimacheen, BC, 155, 156
Spokane, Washington, 155, 156, 183
Spuzzum, BC, 210
Squamish, BC, 277, 327
St. Andrew's Presbyterian Church, 314, 323
St. James Club, 248
Stevens, H.H., 168, 239
Steveston, BC, 28, 217
Stewart, BC, 175, 183, 202, 236, 237
Stewart, J.W., 199, 212, 277, 279
Stoney, R.A., 225, 370n47
Stramberg, H.M., 18, 21
Strathcona, Lord, 187, 259
Strathcona Park, 187, 284
Stuart, J. Duff, 84

submarines, 262, 263(i), 264, 275, 291-94, 378n2, 385n79, 385n80
Summerland, 153-54
Sun Life Insurance Company, 106
Sunday observance, 168, 372n6573, 372n68
Sutherland, Duke and Duchess, 188
Swanson Bay, BC, 157, 273
Sweeney, Campbell, 272
Sword, C.B., 34-35

tariffs, 110, 221, 271. *See also* reciprocity
Tate, D'Arcy, 198, 220, 279, 309, 378n116
Tatlow, Robert G., 7, 49, 60, 67, 68, 69, 70, 71, 76, 77, 79, 81, 82, 83, 84, 86, 92, 93, 101, 102, 113, 126, 127, 136, 137, 139, 144, 152, 158, 160, 164, 165, 171, 197, 246, 281, 318, 340n14, 342n35, 353n61, 357n13
taxation, 89-90, 96, 109, 120, 213-14, 217, 249, 353n53, 368n14, 386n92
Taxation, Royal Commission on, 203
Taylor, J.D., 48, 92, 143, 192, 272, 335n28
Taylor, Thomas, 60, 166, 212, 248, 365n93
Telegraph Creek, BC, 85, 124
Temiskaming and Northern Ontario Railway, 250
Templeman, William, 110, 136, 142, 150, 192
Terms of Union, 13, 39, 109, 112
Terrace, BC, 236
The Crisis in B.C., 286-90, 289(i), 384n71
Théroux, Théodore, 88
Thompson, A., 368n12
Timber and Forestry, Royal Commission on, 146-47, 169, 172, 173
Tisdall, C.E., 152, 169, 232, 307, 308, 334n8
Tolmie, S.F., 321, 325, 388n3
tourism, 284
Townshend, Mr. Justice C.J., 23
Trail, BC, 72, 205
Tramways Inspection Act, 231
Transcontinental Exploration Company, 121, 348n7
Treaty of Ghent, 295
Trembath, Jno, 26
Troup, Mrs. J.W., 310

Trutch, Joseph, 14
Tupper, Charles, 30, 43, 76
Tupper, Charles Hibbert, 76, 91, 92, 99-101, 112, 152, 165, 205, 211, 343n46, 344n68, 348n7, 357n14, 367n8
Turnbull, Miss, 85
Turner, J.H., 33, 34, 37, 38, 39, 40, 45, 47, 49, 50, 58, 62, 80, 105, 187, 188, 247, 272-73, 282, 298, 300, 301, 302-3, 313, 314, 333n3, 334n10, 363n70, 388n20

unemployment, 147, 221, 224, 237, 240, 262, 265, 269-70, 271-72, 278, 282, 285, 294, 296
Union Bank, 277
Unionist Party, 50
United States, 5, 46, 71, 111, 184, 185, 190-91, 212, 213, 223, 228, 263-64, 271, 295
United Suffrage Societies, 246
University of British Columbia, 7, 127-28, 155, 156, 178, 193, 195, 284, 326, 350n22
University of California, 128, 213, 284, 368n13

Vancouver, BC, 28, 32, 79, 117, 122, 125, 131(i), 139-40, 150, 161, 166, 193, 200, 203, 207, 210, 211, 212, 213, 219-20, 224, 231, 235, 244, 270, 276, 302, 367n7; anti-Asian riot, 150
Vancouver Board of Trade, 54, 221, 222, 346n92
Vancouver Gas Co., 231
Vancouver Island, 162, 170, 177, 203, 207-8, 209, 210, 218, 237, 243, 276
Vancouver Ministerial Association, 244, 270
Vancouver Power Co., 99
Vancouver, Victoria and Eastern Railway (VV&E), 56, 98, 160, 211
Vancouver, Westminster & Yukon Railway, 198, 276, 364n92
Veregin, Peter, 241, 242, 243
Vernon, BC, 52, 109, 129, 166, 199, 206-7

Index

Vernon, Forbes G., 95
Victoria, BC, 11, 80, 82, 101, 108, 117, 122, 125, 130, 131(i), 140, 147, 155, 161, 162, 166, 167, 168, 169, 170, 192, 196, 203, 208, 210, 214, 237, 266, 269, 276, 284
Victoria Industrial and Development Association, 270, 285
Von Alvensleben, Alvo, 266-67, 294, 295, 296, 379n10, 386n88
voters' lists: federal, 148, 354n65; provincial, 77, 78, 81, 169, 235, 280, 357n11

Wade, F.C., 165, 167, 312
Walkem, George A., 62-63, 65, 115, 347n101
Walker, Byron Edmund, 86, 188
war contracts and orders, 274-75, 282, 381n30
Warren, J.J., 163, 211, 366n108,
Wedildahid, Chief A., 177
Welch, Patrick, 211, 212, 279, 308, 367n9
Welch, Rev. G.R., 384n71
Weldon, R.C., 22, 29, 178
Wells, W.C., 50, 73
Welsh, F.W., 307, 309
Wesbrook, Frank F., 284
West Kootenay, 108, 167, 241
Western Fuel Company, 270
Westminster, Duke of, 137
Westminster Junction, BC, 107
Whetham, Charles, 34-35, 48
White, W.T., 277
White Pass and Yukon Railway, 37
Whitehorse, Yukon, 109
Whiteside, David, 313
Whiteside, W.J., 25, 27

Whitney, James P., 179, 181, 190, 250, 252
Whonnock, BC, 34, 35, 143
Willett, William, 311
Williams, Parker, 69, 107, 125, 169, 225, 227, 228, 273, 279, 282, 286, 388n17
Willow River, BC, 182
Wilmer, BC, 155, 156
Wilson, Charles, 38, 45, 48, 67-68, 71, 77, 82, 83, 84, 91, 99, 101, 102, 106, 110, 111, 123-24, 338n76, 340n14, 340n22, 344n65
Wilson, Woodrow, 212
Windermere, 155, 156
Winnipeg, Manitoba, 274
Wirth, John, 25-26
Wo Lang, 26
women, 225, 226(i)
women's suffrage, 202, 203, 206, 237, 244, 245(i), 246, 307, 324, 365n107
Wood, R.H., 263
Woods, Archdeacon, 19
Woods, Montie, 41-42, 44(i)
Woodworth, C.M., 218, 281
workmen's compensation, 130, 202, 206, 207, 229, 371n56

Yale, BC, 69
Yale constituency, 166, 169, 171
Yale West, 69, 70
Yellowhead Pass, 162, 166, 202
Ymir, BC, 52, 125, 242
Young, Henry Esson, 124, 125, 128, 153, 155, 215, 248, 251, 279, 298, 383n46
Young, Rosalind, 350n22
Yukon, 41, 212, 213, 326, 368n12

Printed and bound in Canada by Friesens

Set in Garamond and New Century Schoolbook
by Artegraphica Design Co. Ltd.

Copy Editor: Deborah Kerr

Proofreader: Dianne Tiefensee

Cartographer: Eric Leinberger